MARLENE
DIETRICH

Marlene before *The Blue Angel* in *The Woman One Longs For,* 1929.

MARLENE
DIETRICH

LIFE AND LEGEND

STEVEN BACH

UNIVERSITY OF MINNESOTA PRESS

Minneapolis

London

The author gratefully acknowledges permission to reprint photographs in this book from the following sources. The four galleries of eight pages each in the book are not numbered but are numbered here, left to right, top to bottom.

Frontispiece. Danish Film Museum, Copenhagen (Den).

First gallery. 1–2: Deutsche Institute für Film-kunde, Frankfurt (DIF). 3: Ullstein Bilderdienst, Berlin (Ullstein). 4: author's collection. 5: Süddeutsche Verlag Bilderdienst, Munich (SV). 6–8: Stiftung Deutsche Kinemathek, Berlin (SDK). 9: author's collection, courtesy Hasso Felsing. 10–11: SDK. 12: author's collection. 13: Österreichische Nationalbibliothek, Vienna (AUS). 14: Den. 15: AUS. 16: author's collection, courtesy Hasso Felsing. 17: author's collection. 18: DIF. 19–20: SDK. 21: SV. 22: DIF. 23–24: SV. 25: Alfred Eisenstaedt, *Life* magazine, copyright Time Warner, Inc.

Second gallery. 26: DIF. 27–30 (scene sketches by Fritz Maurischaat) and 31: SDK. 32: SV. 33–34: DIF. 35: SDK. 36: author's collection, copyright *Die Dame.* 37: Alfred Eisenstaedt, *Life* magazine, copyright Time Warner, Inc. 38: SDK. 39: Magnum, Manuel Moses Collection (MM). 40–41: The Kobal Collection (Kobal). 42: author's collection. 43–47: SV. 48: courtesy John Pommer. 49–50: SV. 51: George Eastman House, Rochester, New York (GEH). 52: SDK. 53: AUS. 54–55: DIF. 56–58: author's collection, frame blowups courtesy Stadtmuseum, Munich.

Third gallery. 59–60: Archive Photos Stock Photo Library (Archive). 61: courtesy Barry Paris. 62: GEH. 63–67: Kobal. 68: David O. Selznick Archives, University of Texas at Austin. 69: GEH. 70: Bayerische Staatabibliothek, Munich. 71: AUS. 72: DIF. 73: SV. 74: MM. 75–78: SV. 79: Kobal. 80–81: DIF. 82: Kobal. 83: SV. 84: MM. 85–86: DIF.

Fourth gallery. 87: SDK. 88: Kobal. 89: photograph by Earl Theisen, copyright *Look.* 90–91: Kobal. 92: Archive. 93–94: Kobal. 95: Archive. 96: courtesy Bernard Hall. 97: Archive. 98–99: Kobal. 100: Archive. 101–3: SV. 104: copyright Eve Arnold/Magnum. 105–8: MM. 109: copyright Anthony Armstrong-Jones/ Camera Press.

Song credits appear on page 626.

Originally published as *Marlene Dietrich: Life and Legend* (New York: William Morrow and Company, Inc., 1992).

First University of Minnesota Press edition, 2011

Published by the University of Minnesota Press
111 Third Avenue South, Suite 290
Minneapolis, MN 55401-2520
http://www.upress.umn.edu

Library of Congress Cataloging-in-Publication Data

Bach, Steven.
  Marlene Dietrich : life and legend / Steven Bach.
    p. cm.

ISBN 978-0-8166-7584-5 (pbk.)

1. Dietrich, Marlene. 2. Entertainers—Germany—Biography. I. Title.
PN2658.D5B3 2011
791.43'028'092--dc22
[B]   2010054347

Printed in the United States of America on acid-free paper

The University of Minnesota is an equal-opportunity educator and employer.

18 17 16 15 14 13 12 11   10 9 8 7 6 5 4 3 2 1

For Else and Werner Röhr

CONTENTS

III   LEGEND

IV   EXIT MUSIC

A NOTE
FROM THE AUTHOR

I spoke intermittently but at length with Marlene Dietrich while research-ing and writing this book. She did not "cooperate" with it (and at one point tried legally to stop it), though because I had known and been a student of her great director, Josef von Sternberg, she gave me the oppor-tunity to experience her as a generous, intelligent, sympathetic, shrewd, and witty woman, sometimes difficult, often very funny, unfailingly out-spoken, if not always candid.

She deplored "biographers," and always spoke the word in indignant quotation marks. Partly she felt vivid resentment that they were some-how appropriating what had been, after all, *her* life. More importantly, she understood Legend and wanted the world to remain unconfused by facts.

Those "facts," as presented in any number of Dietrich biographies (including the most recent) caused me often to sympathize with her, but to sympathize as well with those who attempted to pin the blue angel's wings to paper.

A biographer who wrote about her in the 1950s (of whose pen she did not approve) claimed he was ordered to cease and desist by none other than Dietrich's friend and admirer, Kenneth Tynan (of whose pen she *did* approve, as she approved of most big pens which did her tribute: Hemingway, Remarque, Cocteau, Malraux, Coward, and all the rest). Attempts at biography routinely roused litigious flurries, keeping lawyers on both sides of the Atlantic out of more important mischief.

Still, Miss Dietrich had a case, as even a cursory review of the biographical material to date makes clear. Her father, of whom she claimed no memory, is usually remembered by biographers for heroism in the Franco-Prussian war of 1870–1871, when he was, we discover, still in diapers. Her mother (called Josephine, not Wilhemina, as a recent scribe assures us) was either born (we are told) in 1883 or married in that year. She was, in fact, born in 1876 and was a bride in 1898 at twenty-two, not at age seven in 1883. Nor at age seventeen, as her daughter claimed.

These and similar errors have left inky footsteps for decades, rarely accompanied by so much as a modest blush of attribution or trace of evidence. We may blame this on the nature of publicity in show business. Or on the hurried state of research required to hit print before today's fifteen-minute celebrity is yesterday's news.

But now that Marlene Dietrich's life is fully rounded and complete after an astonishing seventy years of professional activity and public scrutiny, she remains—like Everest—tantalizingly *there*, and considerably more of a mystery than we might have supposed. Alexander Walker, the critic and biographer, wrote about Dietrich and registered his dismay more honestly than most. "It comes as a shock," he conceded, "to realize that we actually know far less *for certain* about Dietrich than we do about her far more reclusive contemporary, Greta Garbo."

A principal culprit in the inaccuracies and gaps in our knowledge of even routine fact about Miss Dietrich was, of course, Miss Dietrich. She rarely deigned to challenge her "biographers" in detail, because to do so might erect signposts leading to correction of their errors, and because the errors were often good for the legend.

Her father's military background, for instance, was real enough, though not quite what we were led to believe. Similarly, Miss Dietrich actively encouraged the notion that she sprang fully top-hatted and silk-stockinged from the inscrutable brow of Josef von Sternberg in *The Blue Angel* in 1930.

Marlene Dietrich cannot be held responsible, of course, for the fantasies of the Paramount publicity department. On the other hand she was the source, wittingly or not, of certain persistent misimpressions. The 1883 date for her mother's birth or marriage (wrong either way) can be traced back to her own faulty arithmetic. She reported that both her maternal grandmother and her mother bore children at the age of seventeen. This would have surprised them: her grandmother did so at twenty, her mother at twenty-three. It is entirely possible Miss Dietrich did not *know* this, or forgot it, or did not, as she liked to insist, *care*. It is equally possible that she cared very much, that she always cared very much, and that the quality and intensity of her caring made Marlene Dietrich what and who she was. And as we should see her now.

Contrary to a recent assertion that she was called Marie until she entered the theater, she named herself Marlene while still a child (as family memory and documents prove). She imagined very early what she might become and *became* it. There was nothing easy or careless about it, for all the appearance of effortless ease. It was grounded, as all art works are, in hard work and experience, with the occasional blessing of happy accident, and the perpetuation of "Marlene Dietrich"—the legend and artifact—was one of the most disciplined and sustained creative acts of the twentieth century.

Her control of her legend did not extend merely to casting shadows over her past, but to shaping (or delaying) what the future might bring to light. She persuaded copyright holders of certain films she "never made" before *The Blue Angel* to withhold many miles of celluloid from public view during her lifetime. The unedited tapes of her conversations with Maximilian Schell, from which the soundtrack for his 1983 documentary about her was fashioned, are now in vaults, safe from curious ears until the year 2022, thirty years after her death. (Biographers have their ways.)

It will be well known to those even casually aware of the legend that she was *not* an only child, she *did* have a sister, she was *not* a theater student when Josef von Sternberg plucked her from genteel obscurity (it wasn't so obscure and it wasn't so genteel). And so on.

It is less well known that she had powerful personal reasons to deny the existence of her sister, and powerful professional ones for denying her early career. Both denials—in very different ways—may ironically have diminished the larger dimensions of the woman, those beyond the legend, the ones I felt in conversation with her and hope I have conveyed here.

Time, distance, and language make the facts of her early career hard to come by, but, viewed in full perspective, that career was a nearly unique paradigm of twentieth-century show business. It embraced with greater or lesser zeal and impact the orchestra pit, bus-and-truck vaudeville, cabaret, classical theater, modern theater, musical comedy, revue, silent film, sound film, radio, recordings, television, nightclubs, the concert hall, Broadway, army camp shows in the rockets' red glare, even circus and the ballet. Her personal life—for decades the subject of rumor and fantasy her image encouraged—was richer and less conventional than we knew or than she wanted us to know.

Other corrections of myth and memory in what follows may be less obvious, but it would seem ungallant and pedantic to point them out as they march by. Neither the legend nor the woman is reducible to chronology or a parade of facts in which Miss Dietrich once confided to an editor she had no interest anyway. Which does not mean we must share her disdain for them: Notes are provided at the end of the text for what follows, as well as acknowledgments to all those who helped me get there.

The legend is firm; so are the facts. To investigate and describe how a legend *got that way* is neither worship at the shrine nor autopsy: It is celebration, and—very often—an act of wonder.

That sense of wonder was first transmitted to us in indelible, unforgettable fashion by Josef von Sternberg. I was privileged to know and study with him, to spend the better part of two years in his not always easy presence, to view with him all seven of the films he made with Marlene Dietrich, usually overlaid by the living "sound track" of his acerbic or cryptic comment. That time was spent in writing an academic dissertation on his life and work, echoes of which will be heard here.

He did not invent Marlene Dietrich, or even "discover" her: He *revealed* her. He was a great creative force whose genius was largely unacknowledged by his "peers," often thwarted by his "betters," finally undone by his private demons. What follows is in part tribute to him, and because this book began with a then-student's uneasy awe of him, so should it start with him.

OVERTURE

A VISIT
TO THE THEATER
1929

In September 1929, in the Hotel Esplanade in Berlin, a Hollywood film director and self-styled genius dressed for the theater. He was thirty-five years old and his name was Josef von Sternberg.

He was small, dark, and intense rather than handsome in his black tie and dress clothes. To the casual observer he might have appeared insignificant and ordinary without the turban, high-laced boots, and jodhpurs he wore to direct movies (which is why he wore them), except for the drooping oriental mustache that bracketed his small, tight mouth and gave him a look he liked to think "horrible." Looking horrible, he thought, inspired fear, and fear, he thought, inspired respect. He was (as noted) from Hollywood.

He affected a walking stick (a riding crop when cameras were rolling at his imperious command). The cane was a prop he had wielded all the way from Paramount Pictures here to Berlin, capital of the Weimar Republic, where riding crops and imperious commands were not unknown. He now fastidiously installed cuff links and shirt studs, studying in the mirror the face he would soon have cast in solid brass by Berlin sculptor Rudolf Belling, horrible mustache and all. (Art was immortality, whether one was genius creator or genius subject.)

Behind his reflection in the glass he could make out damask walls, paintings framed in gold leaf, gilded moldings on the doors and ceilings of his hotel suite. And a woman. She watched with her attentive—sometimes too attentive—eyes as he preened for the theater. She was a former English actress called Riza Royce, now called Mrs. Josef von Sternberg, and not for the first time. She was in Berlin with her diminutive, "horrible"-looking genius for a second honeymoon following repairs to a first tempestuous marriage which may or may not have been legally dissolved by a hasty Mexican divorce entered into at some earlier moment of high marital stress.

For Mrs. Josef von Sternberg this second honeymoon was a respite from Hollywood, a vacation in which to be fitted for couturier gowns, to eat in fine restaurants, to wander through galleries hung with the kind of modern art her husband collected. For him their second honeymoon was work, and had been for several weeks. So was this evening's visit to the theater, where he would not be accompanied by his wife. This was his work—his Art—not hers. And she spoke no German. Whatever he might see or hear on stage that night would be—they agreed—of no interest, no consequence to her.

Josef von Sternberg turned away from his mirror reflection and retrieved his walking stick and silk scarf from a brass-inlaid wardrobe. He was satisfied that his wavy hair fell at the right angle across his brow. His eye caught such things; his eye caught such things as made for beauty on film, and might do so tonight at the theater.

He was going to the Berliner Theater not because the evening's attraction (a musical comedy called *Two Bow Ties*) was of any particular interest to him, though it was Berlin's hit musical of the season on which no expenditure of cash or creativity had been spared. He was going because he was casting a film, a sound film, a "talker," to be made in both German and English—if he could cast it properly.

The leading man of *Two Bow Ties* was Hans Albers (a blond, cock-of-the-walk heartbreaker) and the featured character actress Rosa Valetti (a middle-aged cabaret artist who resembled a red-headed bulldog). Both were local stars, great favorites in Berlin, and both had been proposed for minor roles in Sternberg's film by producer Erich Pommer, whom he would join at the theater. Pommer was the most distinguished film producer in the world. He had caused great films like *The Cabinet of Dr. Caligari, Me-*

tropolis, and *Faust* to be made. This did not alter the fact that he was a producer. Nor did it soothe Josef von Sternberg's prickly awareness that he had been Pommer's second choice to direct the picture he was now preparing.

Josef von Sternberg would not have been in Berlin at all if the great Ernst Lubitsch (already famous for his "touch") had said yes. Or more precisely, if Lubitsch had been willing to leave Paramount Pictures in Hollywood, California, for the fee for which Sternberg was willing to work. Lubitsch, a Berliner by birth and background, had agreed to direct the great Emil Jannings in *Rasputin* for a fee of $60,000, which Pommer was unwilling to pay and which Emil Jannings was unwilling to have him pay. Jannings (then acknowledged as the greatest dramatic actor in the world) was receiving only $50,000 himself and wanted no doubts as to who was the star of this *Rasputin:* the monk, not some Hollywood "czar."

Sternberg would work for $40,000. He had already directed Emil Jannings in Hollywood. They had loathed each other, but the silent film they made together, *The Last Command*, won Jannings the very first Best Actor Academy Award. Sternberg could speak some German remembered from his boyhood in Vienna, when he was Jonas Sternberg (no "von" about it). And because genius is not always in high demand by those who count dollars and cents, he had no picture at the moment in Hollywood. (Lubitsch did.) For all these reasons Josef von Sternberg was now in Berlin, leaving his wife behind in damask'd solitude at the Hotel Esplanade. He nodded good-bye to her brunette sulk and made his way through hotel corridors of bronze and crystal and rococo cherubs caught in plaster freeze-frames on his way to the theater.

Not to select a cast for *Rasputin* at all, he congratulated himself as his walking stick touched soundlessly on the Esplanade's velvet carpets. True, he had allowed Pommer and Berlin's giant UFA Studios to think he was coming to Berlin for *Rasputin*. He had announced only when already there, already at a press conference in this very hotel, just steps from the Brandenburg Gate and the tree-lined sweep of elegant Unter den Linden, that he had no intention of directing *Rasputin*. The mad monk of Russia had already been the subject of two silent films in the past year, and such familiar material did not require genius. Or vice versa.

Producer Pommer had heaved a sigh of secret relief, well concealed from Emil Jannings and the bewildered press, for Pommer didn't want to make *Rasputin* either. He knew the subject was beset with legal problems from Romanoffs in exile just looking for invasion-of-privacy or libel suits to replace the rubles and jewels they had left behind when fleeing revolution and their palaces on the banks of the now-Red Volga. Which is why Pommer accepted Josef von Sternberg's haughty public rejection of the

5

already announced *Rasputin* with such equanimity. Pommer gracefully suggested instead a film based on a somewhat obscure novel by Heinrich Mann. It was called *Professor Unrat* and told of an aging professor of blameless reputation brought low by a common cabaret singer. Jannings had talked about filming the novel for years, and Pommer was already quietly negotiating for the film rights, though he didn't allow Josef von Sternberg to know that—he was to think the idea had been his alone. The story and cabaret setting would allow the director to use music as well as dialogue in his Berlin "talker." The lurid tale of the mad Russian monk allowed few opportunities for song.

Or cabaret singers to bring Emil Jannings low. But now, after weeks in Berlin, Josef von Sternberg had no cabaret singer for his film, though he had a keen eye for the sort of woman who might bring a man low (when Riza Royce von Sternberg was not being too attentive).

Sternberg crossed the marble lobby of the Hotel Esplanade on his way to the revolving glass doors and the waiting limousine. Crystal chandeliers shuddered with the syncopated rhythms pouring from the ballroom, where Ette's Jazz-Symphonie-Orchester ("30 Soloists!" promised the lobby card) blared out American and three-penny jazz tunes—harsh, potent, penetrating. The kind of music he already heard in the film he had begun to make in his head, fully cast or not.

And, he mused to himself, if the cabaret singer he found was mostly unknown but had potential to become a great star back in Hollywood, back at Paramount (as Greta Garbo had been at MGM for Sternberg's friend and colleague Mauritz Stiller), there would be little harm in that, for her or him. And might give his nemesis, the higher-priced, more powerful Ernst Lubitsch, pause.

The problematic truth was that no such creature seemed to exist, not in all of Berlin, not in the hundreds of photographs of actresses Sternberg had looked at after rejecting his own fleeting notion of Gloria Swanson—not well known for her cabaret singing or for her German. Nor was Swanson likely to agree to second billing to the great Emil Jannings, Academy Award–winning actor or not, since she probably viewed him (as did most of Hollywood) as a non-English-speaking, sausage-gorging, egomaniacal ham and bully.

Casting the cabaret singer was so consuming an obsession that Josef von Sternberg's concentration on Hans Albers and Rosa Valetti on stage this evening was likely to be scattered as he contemplated some interior vision of—what? He had already decided to call the film not *Professor Unrat* but *The Blue Angel*. He liked this title, for it conveyed a kind of romantic melancholy in English and another mood altogether in German, in which *blue* is slang for *drunk*. A heavenly creature drunk with love, or with self-love, or with love-making, who could act and sing and speak English and captivate the camera and bring Emil Jannings low with a song. Not easy to find. Not even in wide-open Berlin, where everything was available, and what was not did not exist. Certainly not in the Hotel Esplanade, through whose revolving bronze and glass doors he spun, out to the glinting Daimler-Benz and chauffeur waiting to drive him to the theater through the electric night of "the fastest city in the world."

Waiting with the driver were Sternberg's Hollywood aides, brothers Sam and Carl Winston, with whom he had attended public school in Queens. They had come to Berlin with him. Sam was a gifted editor who would cut the film to order, and Carl had script and casting skills and could liaise with Pommer, whom they all knew from Hollywood, where Pommer had produced for Pola Negri before returning from Babylon to Berlin.

The limousine crossed the city past the high-priced shops and high-priced hookers for every taste, past the great hotels and operas and cabarets and banks and monuments, along the tree-lined streets of Berlin's West End into the Charlotten-Strasse. There, the lobby of the Berliner Theater was noisy with the chatter of smart Berliners in white tie, furs, jewels, and up-to-the-1929-minute Berliner swank. Monocles glinted and winked and young breasts pushed against diaphanous silks and chiffons or peeked through cloth-of-gold at merchant bankers with big cigars and pockets full of promises.

Josef von Sternberg ignored them all and nodded to Erich Pommer and his wife. Gertrud Pommer had been pestering Sternberg about a young actress she knew and liked and thought a candidate for the cabaret singer in his film. Frau Pommer knew the actress from a certain popular salon that catered to the bright young things of Berlin. But Sternberg had already seen the actress's photograph in a casting directory. She had worked onstage and screen for most of the decade and was just a smudged portrait under the heading "Ingenue: Naive." Hardly what his cabaret singer—his Blue Angel—needed to be, and her photograph had suggested little more to him than the retoucher's clumsy art. Besides, who—*what*—was she? Gertrud Pommer described her as "a wife and mother," but Erich Pommer was said to have muttered, "Not that whore!" at the mention of her name. Producers' wives, like directors' wives, should stay at home, Josef von Sternberg thought.

Entering the lobby from the Charlotten-Strasse was Dr. Karl Vollmoeller, the immensely shrewd and successful playwright of *The Miracle*. This spectacle about nuns, produced by the great Max Reinhardt, had spun gold and stunned audiences all over the world. It had stunned London and America, too, touring the United States for a full five years. Josef von

Sternberg had met Dr. Vollmoeller there and had strolled Pacific beaches with him. They had talked of things erudite and sensual and formed bonds that caused Sternberg to refer to him as "my best friend" and "my father confessor," though he had not seen the man in half a decade. Now Vollmoeller was adapting Heinrich Mann's novel for him for the screen. Sternberg revered the bonds of friendship. He was from Hollywood.

With Vollmoeller was his current mistress, a striking actress-turning-journalist called Ruth Landshoff. She, too, had a candidate for the cabaret singer in *The Blue Angel*. Oddly enough, she was recommending the same young woman Gertrud Pommer was urging, the "Ingenue: Naive" that Erich Pommer may or may not have called a whore. Landshoff had worked on stage in Vienna with the actress and thought she had that extra "something" Sternberg was looking for. Landshoff's recommendation (quietly blessed by father-confessor Vollmoeller) suggested not wife and mother, but girl-about-town, for Sternberg knew Vollmoeller's tastes. He knew his duplex apartment in the Pariser Platz, and its all-night orgies of the best and most beautiful. He knew of the midnight Josephine Baker had arrived wearing a pink organza jacket, high heels, and nothing else. He knew (who did not?) of the girls who appeared wearing men's tuxedos and monocles, as Ruth Landshoff did now. Playwrights' mistresses, he thought, like producers' and directors' spouses, should stay at home.

The final member of the party was Pommer's Berlin assistant, Eberhardt Klagemann, who knew better than to recommend anyone at all, because he lived with an actress and wished to avoid competitive cross fire. The group was unctuously greeted and shown to their seats by the theater's impresario, Dr. Robert Klein, who extolled to the Hollywood visitor the exceptional charms of the evening's leading lady, delights he implied he knew at first hand. Sternberg withered him with a glance as the party took their seats in the sold-out 1,450-seat auditorium and waited for the curtain to rise.

Sternberg leafed through his program to note the surprising presence of a brief essay about Mrs. O'Leary's cow. *Two Bow Ties*, it seemed, took place partly in Chicago, that toddlin' town Mrs. O'Leary's livestock is said to have burned to the ground, making it even hotter than 1929's bootleggers, who seemed to figure in the musical's plot. As did an ocean liner. And Palm Beach.

He glanced at the program caricatures of the leading players. Albers . . . Valetti . . . He stopped at the sketch of the leading lady, she of the Dr. Klein–extolled charms. It was the same actress being pushed at him by Frau Pommer and Ruth Landshoff, but here she looked insolent and worldly— neither "Ingenue: Naive," nor wife and mother, nor whore, nor girl-about-town. She had an ironic, heavy-lidded, almost arrogant look, suggesting that none of those who had described her had been talking about the same woman. She starred, the program noted, as a Chicago jazz-baby "dollar-princess" called Mabel. She was in virtually every scene, had several songs, and would be impossible not to notice even among fifty singers and dancers Charlestoning across the high seas to Chicago and Palm Beach. In the unlikely event this woman had anything but the recommendations of busy-bodies, he would know it. He needed no producer's wife or playwright's mistress for his genius to see—if there was, indeed, anything to see. Or hear.

The overture began. It was as jazzy, sharp-edged, and syncopated as the audience, as racy as the wail of saxophones. This was not the classical German theater of Goethe and Schiller and Kleist, but that of Kurt Weill and Bertolt Brecht by way of George Gershwin and Jerome Kern and Paul Whiteman and others who were all the rage in Berlin. Josef von Sternberg sat back to focus his jaundiced eyes above his horrible mustache on the stage as the curtain rose. When it did—on an elegantly louche, vaguely bored young woman with heavy-lidded eyes that took in everything above her insolent smile—when that curtain rose he may for a moment have forgotten that he had left his wife back at the Hotel Esplanade, alone.

When the young woman on stage spoke, his memory may have faltered altogether. She had a musical, throaty voice, and called out the number of the winning lottery ticket that set the evening's plot in motion:

"Three . . . three . . . and three!! Three cheers for the gentlemen who has drawn the first prize!"

And she said it in perfect English.

Everything after was elegance and impudence. Chicago and gangsters; the gold-dust shores of Miami and Palm Beach; luxury-liner Atlantic cross-ings (ship's walls lined entirely in mirror to reflect the audience back to itself); lavish costumes, including puppetlike dummies as minstrel-servants serving up chorus girls on trays like mint juleps; three hours of music lampooning musicals, a pastiche score with operatic duets, sentimental Lieder, Heidelberg hymns to Love Eternal, and raucous, witty sound effects that made fun of film "noise" in the new "talkers."

Had Mrs. Josef von Sternberg been there, she might have distracted her husband from the stage, for she was a demanding woman, and if she had, he might not have seen and heard what he did, and everything that fol-lowed might have been different. But she was not there, and as Josef von Sternberg watched and listened that night (he would forever dismiss the evening's performance as "a skit"), what he experienced ended his search for a "blue" angel and changed film history and his life forever.

What Josef von Sternberg said when Frau Pommer and Ruth Landshoff turned expectantly to him to gauge his reaction to the leading lady with the heavy-lidded eyes and the throaty, musical voice was: "What? That untalented cow?!"

But what Josef von Sternberg saw that night, and heard, and dreamed was Marlene Dietrich.

I

BERLIN

ONE

BEGINNINGS
1901 - 1918

She was born Marie Magdalene Dietrich on December 27, 1901, at nine fifteen in the evening, and not in Berlin. Her birthplace was a modest flat in a modest building in the Sedanstrasse, a treeless street named after a famous battle, in a place called Schöneberg.

Schöneberg was a separate city then, with ninety thousand people burning Christmas candles and breathing icy air scented with holiday chocolate, gingerbread, and hot, spiced wine. It would not become part of Berlin until 1920, and in 1901 it was still an outskirt, made an official suburb three years earlier only because the kaiser's railroad troops were barracked and boarded there. They were bored, too, knowing that the ribbons of silver track led away from potato farms and petit bourgeois virtue over the bridge and across the canal to "the fastest city in the world."

Berlin was nearing three million people then, and slaughtered yearly two million cows (and ten thousand horses) to feed them. Half a billion hands each year clung to streetcar straps, rattling off to factories or foundries or dance halls that "closed" at two, but never cleared before the milk truck rattled by at dawn. The Berlin address book had six thousand pages and weighed twenty-five pounds, and there was a slender telephone book, too. Berlin was not just a city; it was the center of Empire.

Those were glory days, when an excitable man with an upturned mustache and withered arm could trumpet to his mother, "I am the one true emperor in the world!" His mother, daughter of England's Queen Victoria, knew something of empire, and if her son Kaiser Wilhelm II's bold assertion gave her any pause, she did too little too late, and by 1901 all remedy was in the grave and change was in the air.

Grandmother Victoria died in that year and Wilhelm's mother, too. His uncle Edward VII took the British throne. "He is Satan," Wilhelm raved. "You cannot imagine what a Satan he is!" and wondered why *he* didn't have a navy if his uncle did.

That same year an anarchist in America shot President McKinley, and his successor (who knew Wilhelm and found him "bully") charged over the slopes of San Juan Hill and up the bluffs of Mount Rushmore. Two gunslingers called Butch Cassidy and the Sundance Kid thought 1901 and the twentieth century the high sign to move on, and did—to Bolivia. And in far-off *Kalifornien* the local fathers of a sleepy mission town called Los Angeles mounted a light bulb on top of a flagpole, but took it down because it frightened the cows.

Nothing frightened Berlin, not even Wilhelm. They cheered him on. His operetta rhetoric went so well with the monuments and statues, the pompous architecture, the showy stretch of Unter den Linden, and the racier reaches of the Kurfürstendamm that led to lush gardens where willows trailed in lakes as blue as Aryan eyes.

The glory would turn to smithereens and dust, swirling with ghosts: the Hotel Adlon, the Café Bauer, the Hotel Eden, the Café König; the culture cauldron of theater and opera; the cabarets with their barbed-wire wit; the dance halls with their *Tingeltangel* girls in sweaty spangles; the back-street pubs where balls wobbled down beer-splashed alleys toward waiting skittles pins, rumbling like thrilling thunder, like the new underground railway, like echoes of once and future guns.

Nobody paid much attention to Schöneberg then. Years and wars later they did, when a shock-haired man with a Boston accent stood on the balcony of the red-brick Rathaus (from which something then called West Berlin was administered) and read some words he didn't know from a phonetically prepared text that went: "Ish bin ine bear-LEAN-air." Hardly anyone remembered that what they hastily renamed John-F.-Kennedy-Platz had once been the sleepy village square of just plain Schöneberg.

When Marie Magdalene Dietrich was born there, the land on which the Rathaus would stand (and stands today) was the site of Schöneberg's last remaining mill farm, and the poorhouse and public delousing station were just across the way. Streetcars were still drawn by horses already marked for the glue factory. The dirt paths of Schöneberg were turning to mosaics of cobblestone and the farms were yielding to tides of concrete. Landlords sowed tenements (*Mietskaserne* they were called: rent barracks) like the one in which Marie Magdalene was born: cheap, clean housing which yielded quicker harvest and harder cash than the old potato fields and tenant farms ever could.

Still, it was a pleasant enough place in 1901. There were beer gardens where steins got raised and songs got sung, and if the Kaiser's railroad regiments came and went, it was home and hearth to ordinary folk, with churches (two), shops (many), open-air markets (three a week, including one on Fridays for hay, straw, and wood), seven schools, two cemeteries (the Brothers Grimm were buried in one), a charity home for gentlewomen with nowhere else to go, and six local newspapers, none of which noted the arrival in 1898 of newlyweds Louis Erich Otto Dietrich and Wilhelmine Elisabeth Josephine, born Felsing.

Police Lieutenant Dietrich was thirty then (he was born in 1868) and a good-looking man by fin de siècle standards, with the full chest and stout bearing that suggested strength of character. He was not tall or wasp-waisted in the dashing imperial fashion, but sturdy, with a handsome broad face and deep-set eyes a daughter would inherit one day, a straight nose, a Kaiser Wilhelm mustache winging above an oddly melancholy mouth, and an erect military bearing that kept his tunic taut and the spike of his *Pickel-haube* pointing upright and true.

He was assigned to Police Precinct No. 4, whose station house occupied the same address in the Sedanstrasse where Marie Magdalene would be born, and where a courtyard sheltered police vehicles and the horses that pulled them. His post with the Imperial Police was not grand, but it had consequence in a time and place where authority was more than ordinarily respected, where even tightly laced ladies moved their parasols aside to make sidewalk space for a good-looking uniform.

Lieutenant Dietrich may have had an eye for them, and they for him, for he had the glamour and distinction of the five years' military duty that were requisite for any police officer. (Even an ordinary patrolman, like his father, Erich, before him, needed two years' military service to qualify for pavement duty.) Louis Erich Otto Dietrich had served in the lancer corps, the Uhlanen light cavalry, during the 1890s. His military career was marked by no recorded distinction, but he earned a corsage of medals to decorate his plum-colored policeman's tunic: an Iron Cross (second class), a life-saving award from his cavalry unit, and a medal from the Japanese Red Cross (also second class). He probably won the latter as part of Kaiser Wilhelm's ill-fated saber-rattling in the Far East between 1895 and 1897 and there, or near there, the young cavalryman may have heard some gunfire and saved some lives. He came back to Berlin with duty, discipline, and dignity pinned proudly to his chest. The transition to civil servant in a tight brocade collar may have clipped his wings, but left a saber on his hip. Sheathed.

The Imperial Police welcomed officers with medals and favored wives with connections. The service was so obsessed by status, in fact, that every officer's superior evaluated his prospective bride's dowry as a matter of policy, and Josephine Felsing had one.

Her dowry was acceptable enough to the Imperial Police Force, but not sufficiently grand to produce a marriage of social distinction. None the Felsing family could discern, anyway. The Felsings didn't even like the lieutenant's rather common name, for they were merchants, and "skeleton key" or "passkey" (which is what *Dietrich* means in German) may have made them nervous. That, and a certain military swagger.

Josephine, like the daughter she would bear, had a mind and will of her own and cared more about character and breeding than social position. One of her favorite words was *stable*, an allusion to pedigree, and she viewed it as the source from which all blessings flowed, from godliness to good teeth. This had little to do with Darwin and the exciting (or appalling) ideas going around then, and nothing to do with the nobility listings in the *Almanack de Gotha*. It was just a conventional, middle-class notion that breeding *was* character: Discipline and dignity both confirmed and culti-vated it. Happiness might come, but diligence and duty were more to the Prussian point.

All that emphasis on virtue may have dampened suitors' ardor until Police Lieutenant Dietrich came along with his handsome face and uni-form and medals. It must have been a love match for, though Josephine was pretty in a pleasant way, she was no great beauty and getting no younger at twenty-two. She liked the lieutenant's bearing and the cut of his genes and he liked her air of moral superiority and her gracious sharing of it with inferiors. They married in 1898 and moved to the Sedanstrasse to be near the precinct station. Josephine quoted Goethe's dictum that duty was the fulfillment of the day's demands, and settled down to satisfy them: *Kinder, Küche, Kirche*, children, cooking, church. So they called it; so it was.

Her family could be forgiven, perhaps, for feeling her marriage was something of a comedown. The Felsings had been prosperous clockmakers in Berlin since the early nineteenth century, when they changed their name from Völtzing to Felsing because it looked smarter on a clock face or shop window without that umlaut, vaguely French, perhaps.

They came to Berlin from Giessen in Hessen, and from Freiburg before that. Giessen is close to the Black Forest, where witchy woods frighten Hansels and Gretels still or get cut down to size and carved into cuckoo clocks, the local craft for generations.

The Völtzings had been clockmakers there since at least 1733, but by 1820 Johann Conrad Völtzing became Felsing and discovered himself in Berlin. He fathered three sons in the Prussian capital, but two of them went back to more bucolic Hessen to pursue engraving. The third stayed on to work in the shop his father founded and named for himself, Conrad Felsing.

The clockmaker patriarch died in 1870—just before the Franco-Prussian war and Bismarck made Germany a nation and King Wilhelm I crowned himself kaiser at Versailles (which the French thought arrogant and would not forget). The Felsing son and heir (Albert Karl Julius) changed his name to Conrad to match the name on the windows and the watches. Ambition and industry led to more clocks, more shops, and by 1877 there was one on Unter den Linden, where a royal patent, or appointment, from His Majesty the King of Prussia (now kaiser), and another from Her Majesty the Queen (now kaiserin) lent an aristocratic aura to all the ticks and tocks and were good for business, too. Black Forest artisans had become Berliner merchants, as kings had become kaisers.

The second Conrad, son of the founder, died in January of 1901 at the age of seventy-three, but married three times before he did. His third marriage, to a woman less than half his age named Elisabeth Hering, finally produced children, the first of whom was Josephine in November 1876, and two years later a son, Willibald Albert Conrad.

Though younger than his sister, Willibald took over the family concern when their father died in 1901, for German law passed property to sons, not daughters. He was called Uncle Willi within the family, but only there, due to a joke in which his name figured in an obvious anatomical pun, and he was—like the name on the windows, the name on the clocks—Conrad Felsing to the trade. He expanded the stock from watches (antimagnetic and not) to alarm clocks, to pedestal and mantel clocks of marble, bronze, and gilt in the popular Renaissance style, and finally to jewelry. The firm offered guarantees of exchange and advertised gift-wrapping "gratis" in local playbills, for Uncle Willi was a fan of the theater. And theater people.

And of that reprehensible thing, the *Kinematograf* (called *Kino*). It happened that the Felsing firm owned its building on Unter den Linden and rented out space, including the roof. This curious rental was to a one-time optical instrument maker called Oskar Messter, who had opened Berlin's first permanent movie theater in the street-level passageway just next door in 1896. He called it Messters Biophon and turned his back room and Uncle Willi's rented roof into Berlin's first working movie studio. He made actual sound films there (singing, really: little musicals) as early as 1903. Because the Felsings' building had a flat and level roof, with clear sightlines to pomp and circumstance under the Linden leaves all the way from the Brandenburg Gate right up to the royal palace, cameras could be set up there—and were—to make newsreels. History flickering on film.

The roof rent Uncle Willi collected was modest. Josephine frowned on her younger brother's frivolous passions, but such things went on in Berlin, and she was safely off in Schöneberg, with her policeman and her babies.

The Dietrichs delivered their first child, Ottilie Josephine Elisabeth, on February 5, 1900, the final year of the old century (assuming centuries end in zeros). She was called Elisabeth, or Liesel, after her grandmother on her mother's side. When Marie Magdalene arrived in the nick of time to enter the first year of the new century (assuming they begin with ones), she was at first called Leni or Lene (pronounced *Lay-na*), a common nickname for Magdalene. If she was named for some distant relative, no matter: She named herself, *casting* herself from the very beginning. She elided *Marie* and *Magdalene* (with their curious combination of the Virgin and the not-very) into something shorter and more romantic that alluded only to herself. No one else was called Marlene then (which was surely the point), and so she called and signed herself from childhood on.

She remembered herself as "thin and pale as a child, with reddish-blond hair and the translucent pallor that goes with ginger coloring, giving me a sickly look," but she had a habit of undervaluing herself, which did not help others to evaluate her later. The truth is she was born beautiful, pretty as a picture, and we have the picture to prove it.

In what is probably her first baby photo, at age two or three, she looks not delicate, not sickly. She looks like a vanilla pudding nestled in the doily-lace of her skirt, and around her plump waist (it would always be short) a creamy sash looks twice as long as she is tall. She stands easily on a chair seat, leaning against the back rest, chubby hands grasping the uprights. Her feet are firmly planted, neatly buttoned into white high-topped shoes, and her stockings wrinkle (as they rarely would again).

This delectable confection is no Dresden doll. She is too robust for that and seems to have a camera presence even here, though she is merely a Prussian child doing her duty. She would learn to love posing for pictures; it would become in family lore her childhood passion, a love affair the camera would reciprocate forever after.

There is something else, seldom remarked about this face: It is symmetrical, a surprisingly rare thing among faces. Such faces have no good or bad "side"; they can be molded and sculpted by light—or go flat if they lack bones and structure. This child would complain eight decades later that she had "been photographed to death," but it is easy to see why she attracted cameras for the better part of a century, and why they attracted *her* is easy enough to guess. Cameras were audience and reflected her back so prettily.

The Dietrichs' life in the Sedanstrasse was modest and fleeting, for Lieutenant Dietrich seemed ill-suited to a policeman's life after all. Perhaps it cramped him. He had taken a departmental examination when Marlene was born and received a mark of *recht gut* (quite good), a mark short of the *sehr gut* that would have put a star at the top of the Christmas tree, and less than two years later he slipped a rank to *ausreichend*, or merely adequate, the third and lowest grade, and at the bottom of a twelve-man list.

This was downward mobility, and the Dietrich family moved with it. By the time Marlene was six she was in her fourth home, and then suddenly a fifth, at which Josephine listed herself in the growing Berlin telephone book as "Dietrich, Josephine, *Ww.*," or *Witwe*—widow.

The police department closed its records on Lieutenant Dietrich after his merely "adequate" performance, and there is no extant official record of his death. The most often reported cause is a fall from a horse, but his absence seems more important than his presence. The year before his death he and Josephine had separate telephones at separate addresses, suggesting the love match (if it was that) was over. Whenever the family reins were placed in Josephine's hands, she took them firmly.

Marlene later said she had known her father only as a "shadowy silhouette," which is not surprising if her parents had separated before she reached school age. There was little to miss from an already absent father in an already matriarchal family headed by Grandmother Felsing, and Marlene accepted her mother as protector and—until duty conflicted with desire and independence—guide and authority. If she felt no wistful longings for the father she had hardly known, she identified with the romantic idea of his military background. She thought (correctly) that she looked like him, called herself Paul (pronounced *à la française*) in moments of intimacy with her mother, a habit Josephine indulged. The young girl wanted something more than approval, something more daring and suggestive: She wanted to take, as she later put it, "my father's place—against my mother's will."

Marlene's identification with male roles would run throughout her life and began in childhood. Her resemblance to her father persuaded her "Paul" was more Dietrich than Felsing, but caused her distress in a family she thought full of female beauties. She believed her mother "strikingly beautiful," and found her Grandmother Felsing "not only the most beautiful of women, [but] also the most elegant, the most charming, the most perfectly complete lady anyone knew." There were aunts and lady cousins from both sides of the family to provide feminine example and grace, to instruct in the pretty pleasures of boxes from Fabergé, hand-made French shoes, and necklaces of pink pearl. Josephine leavened Marlene's romantic imagination with calls to duty and self-control, but cherished the consolation of "Paul's" adoration.

Marlene did not need a police lieutenant father to remain an officer's daughter. She thought of her mother as "a good General," both stern and reliable, and resembled her more than she knew. Hemingway would one day apply exactly the same words—"a good General"—to Marlene herself. The rest of the family called Josephine—behind her back—the Dragon, and the back that now supported a family stiffened even more. Marlene admitted, "My mother was not kind, not compassionate, [but] unforgiving and inexorable. . . . The rules were . . . ironclad, immovable, unalterable."

Josephine's insistence on loyalty would become a theme of her daughter's life in worlds where loyalty is lightly valued, when at all. Duty, discipline, and a rigid rein on emotions accompanied her, too. They might have been inhibiting, but balanced childish passions and taught *restraint*, which was something very like acting. And bred in her a certain distance, a sense of quiet self-sufficiency, suggesting more than met the eye.

Marlene and Elisabeth were in school by the time their father died, in the Auguste-Viktoria Schule, a villa turned girls' school in Charlottenburg named for the kaiserin, whose portrait hung at the front of the classroom.

Marlene began in the spring of 1907 (the German school year started after Easter holidays), but Josephine's home tutoring had prepared her well. She had learned her letters at home: German in the old-fashioned Gothic script; some elementary French, the stylish language; and a smattering of English, the difficult tongue of the kaiser's difficult mother and his grandmother, Queen Victoria.

Josephine taught Marlene and Liesel to read from a brightly colored copy of a sentimental poem framed and hung on a succession of living room walls:

O lieb, solang du lieben kannst!
O lieb, solang du lieben magst!
Die Stunde kommt, die Stunde kommt,
Wo du an Gräbern stehst und klagst!

O love, while still 'tis yours to love!
O love, while love you still may keep!
The hour will come, the hour will come,
When you shall stand by graves and weep!

The sentiments were more than maudlin to a child who already knew about graves, and these lines could reduce her to tears for the rest of her life. She learned *Weltschmerz* and the impermanence of love along with her ABCs.

A police widow's pension did not go far, even with help from Uncle Willi and Grandmother Felsing. Josephine turned domestic skills to practical account, becoming what a classmate of Marlene's called "a glorified housekeeper" for the scion of a well-to-do Dessau family named von Losch. Eduard von Losch, who made his home in Berlin, was a first lieutenant in the grenadiers (he may have been a one-time military comrade of Marlene's father) and was frequently on maneuvers out of Berlin in imperial outposts like Königsberg and Danzig. Josephine looked after his house, and after his comforts on the rare occasions he was home.

Josephine's wages paid for "governesses," who were mostly country girls, rosy-cheeked peasants sent by nervous parents less to instruct than be instructed in the ways of the big city. What they learned was not always what provincial parents hoped, but they could perform *au pair* chores or provide lessons for the Dietrich girls while Josephine attended to the Grenadier.

Marlene roller-skated and played with marbles ("joy," she called them: brown clay for boys, swirly glass spheres for girls). She learned to play the lute, which she decorated with brightly colored ribbons; to sing sentimental folk tunes; to play the piano and violin. She took dancing lessons (Isadora Duncan was the rage in Berlin then); went to the pictures and the theater (Italian actress Eleonora Duse's hands were endlessly photographed, every schoolgirl's swoony attraction); and ate too many cream cakes.

In the summer she went to Uncle Willi's country house on the lake at Wandlitz for bathing or collecting starfish and in the winter visited his grand apartment in the Liechtensteiner Allee in Berlin, which was often filled with theater folk (of whom Josephine did not approve) and the aroma of the one hundred and twenty Russian cigarettes Uncle Willi smoked each day until, one day, they killed him.

But the real joy of her youth was music. She loved her lute and folk tunes, but the violin revealed a true musical gift. Her aptitude was so striking that Josephine bought Marlene a first violin for 2,500 Reichsmark, serious money for a serious avocation. Accompanied by Josephine at the piano, she exerted infinite pains perfecting fingering and finesse on beginners' pieces like Torelli's "Serenade" and was eventually rewarded with Chopin and Haydn as relief from the exacting demands of Handel and Bach. ("Bach, Bach, Bach, always Bach!" she complained.)

She exhibited patience in pursuit of the purity the violin requires. Rhythm, modulation, elegance of expression and tone—especially tone, that most elusive of expressive skills—would become touchstones for life. She poured Josephine's insistence on discipline into the strings and bow and found beauty there as well. And an early glimmering urge for what she called "public fame on the podium."

But first there was school. A classmate remembered her as a shy little girl who shrank into the last seat of the last row like "a little gray mouse." This was more restraint than reality, for the mouse soon developed a romantic attachment to a native-born French teacher called Mademoiselle Breguand. School was no longer the "prison" it seemed at first, and Mademoiselle Breguand became "my secret true love . . . desire and fulfillment," encouraging a lifelong devotion to France and providing a gentler model than her mother, however reliable the "good general" may have been with all her rules.

She developed another passionate crush that, with hindsight, seems more decisive. Like all German schoolgirls, Marlene was ecstatically devoted to Henny Porten, Germany's first great movie star and everybody's idol. Porten was not classically beautiful, but had warmth and a romantic, maternal simplicity that audiences found endearing, that schoolgirls worshipped, and that Josephine seldom conveyed.

She was known as "the Mary Pickford of Germany" mainly because, like Pickford, she had been a child star. She had, in fact, made some of those "little musicals" for Oskar Messter right next door to Uncle Willi's shop in Unter den Linden: a baby Aïda pantomiming to Mr. Edison's "playback."

Marlene and her classmates trooped devoutly to grown-up Porten movies like *Mother and Child, Captive Souls,* and *The Prince's Kiss* (Porten made a dozen films a year in the teens and rejected Hollywood when it called). They plucked their eyebrows to resemble hers and collected postcards picturing her famous roles. Marlene painstakingly hand-colored hers and sent them to the star as birthday or premiere greetings. Forgetting that she was "a little gray mouse," she stalked Porten through the streets of Berlin.

The great star was used to being followed by fans in days when no one was unlisted, but they usually just said *"Guten Tag"* and toddled off. Marlene, however, lay in wait. She hid behind kiosks near Porten's house hoping for a glimpse of her idol, and having determined the correct front door, arrived one day with violin in hand to stand in Porten's foyer serenading her with a sentimental tune called *"Engelslied"* ("Angel's Song"). "What's this?" thought Porten, with the noblesse oblige of a film star.

"Who is bringing me a serenade?" It was none other than "the same sweet little girl with the blond curls" who had been following her through the streets, hiding behind lampposts and kiosks.

Hero-worship is often irresistible to heroes, but Marlene's blond pursuit took on a certain aggressive zeal when it persisted beyond Berlin. Marlene was on a school excursion to the Mittenwald (a violin-making center in Bavaria) at a time Porten was on holiday with her psychiatrist husband, recovering in nearby Garmisch from contract negotiations.

"One morning as I awoke," Porten recalled, "my ear detected again a violin playing. I went to the window, looked out into the street, and down below stood this young girl once again, bringing me a second serenade." This was flattering, but it strained noblesse. "[Marlene] had . . . discovered my name on a resort guest list, and because the rules of her boarding house were rather strict, had secretly in the early morning—violin under her arm—climbed out the window and down the ladder she had placed there the previous night, and had ridden to Garmisch on the first train. So there she was again, and touched with joy as I was, I had no idea at all what I should say."

At a loss for words, Porten slammed the windows shut and remained "touched with joy" in privacy. Marlene tucked her violin back under her arm, having achieved her goal: a first audience. Shutters had been slammed in her face, but by a *star*.

Porten was a hint of an as yet unglimpsed future, but Mademoiselle Breguand represented the here and now and relieved the tedium of German and history and gymnastics and household crafts and numbers and geography and science. And then Mademoiselle Breguand wasn't here or now or anything anymore. She was gone, and in her place was war.

August 1914 changed the world and Marlene with it. The kaiser promised it would be over "before the leaves turn," a judgment no better than many others he had made in a parade of miscalculations that led to painful, protracted catastrophe.

In London and Paris as well as Berlin, the idea of a skirmish or two to clear the air excited not just patriotism, but a kind of spiritual ecstasy that had been steadily building—a new beginning for an old world, "as though fate were mixing the cards afresh in a game that had grown monotonous," said one historian. In Berlin, where the kaiser's flamboyant star turns gave everything a theatrical air, they "had a cast party," as another scholar put it, "an enormous celebration after a successful first-night performance by a cast of hundreds of thousands."

In England an aesthete and poet wrote a sonnet to war, thanking the God who had "wakened us from sleeping," and in southern Germany an Austrian volunteer to the Bavarian army wrote to friends of an "immense joy," marred only by his fear that in the inevitable march of German victories he "might come to the front too late." The poet Rupert Brooke would find unending sleep, and Adolf Hitler would be gassed, win an Iron Cross, and live to pronounce a treaty written at Versailles (which repaid a kaiser's arrogance) the "villainy of the century," for which he would make the century pay.

The "General's daughter" was just a twelve-year-old then, feeling herself "the first bereaved" in the loss of her Mademoiselle. But everything was lost, then or soon after, no matter what the kaiser had promised.

Josephine's employer, Lieutenant von Losch, was on maneuvers outside Berlin in August 1914 and was quickly promoted to captain for the victories ahead. A soldier's instinct caused him to order the removal of his household from the capital to his family's home in Dessau, and Josephine and her daughters went with it. Marlene left Berlin with a last childhood memory, the sight of "soldiers marching through the streets, flowers on top of their rifles, laughing, singing, kissing the women, flags hanging from windows. . . . Barbarians celebrating the outbreak of war."

Marlene arrived with her mother in Dessau and enrolled in the Antonetten Lyzeum, another "prison," full of schoolgirls and rules and no Mademoiselle Breguand to focus adolescent longings. It seemed a good time to study her catechism ("God had to come back. . . . He had to reward those who had suffered in this war that He allowed to take place," she thought), and she was confirmed at fifteen, the usual age for a Lutheran girl, which seemed shockingly tardy to the von Losches' Catholic cook. But maintaining routine away from Berlin paradoxically undermined faith in everything: "The fact that our education proceeded as in peacetime made us doubt the sanity of our elders."

It is no less sobering for its familiarity to recall how thoroughly German society was consecrated to its military identity. Marlene was a child of the military, as every German child was then. Every school was a garrison for little soldiers of the empire. Children were not shielded from war; they were enlisted in it and subsumed by it. It was an insidiously seductive part of their everyday lives.

Victories in battle were celebrated with school holidays (what child could resist?), classes for the day suspended if news arrived before the final bell, or, if not, then the following day was free. Death, too, was deliverance from drudgery, and when neither triumph nor defeat interrupted routine, the ritual of prayer for God's punishment of Germany's enemies did. Cries of "Gott strafe England!" filled what should have been playing fields.

Marlene and her classmates found studies deferred as they assembled in school gymnasiums to knit stockings and gloves for soldiers not much older

than they. Classes in domestic arts turned to ever more inventive preparation of potatoes, until there weren't any more to prepare (they established
an Imperial Potato Office in 1915), and then it was turnips: turnip soups,
turnip stews, even turnip marmalades and cakes.

There had been runs on shops even as the brass bands blared in 1914, but
neither nation, home, nor factory was prepared for the duration or the
shortages of this war. The giant industrialists refused to fill orders for can-
non because too many workers were being enlisted as fodder, leaving the
steelworks and munitions factories unmanned. Milk, cheese, meat, bread
(sawdust-filled), everything edible was rationed.

Instead of mooning over Henny Porten, Marlene and her schoolmates
were ordered into *Kinos* to view propaganda films made by a new company
called UFA (an acronym for Universum Film Actiengesellschaft, pronounced *oo-fah*), secretly financed by the War Office and General Ludendorff. There was the occasional Henny Porten film for diversion, but even
Henny paled in the light from the screen revealing Allied atrocities, so
craven compared to the glorious victories and noble deaths of Wilhelm's
loyal troops.

Girls conducted potato and charcoal drives, spent their evenings at railroad stations singing ever younger soldiers off to war or at military hospitals
singing them to a final peace. Boys trudged door to door soliciting war loans
(minimum two marks) for which they gave receipts that would never be
redeemed. Or they became streetcleaners, boypower replacing manpower
dying for the Fatherland.

Home was a war front like any other, and more so in the dislocation of
Dessau, where there were no more marbles with Berlin playmates or starfish collected at Uncle Willi's lakeshore summer house.

The home front was "a woman's world," "a world without men," and she
was growing older. She had learned about love and death from a poem
framed on her mother's wall, and now it was impossible not to feel the
connection.

She told the story generically and called the boy Jean or Hans or John,
depending on the version. Whoever he was, he kissed her—nothing more—
but his youth and vitality turned the glories of war celebrated by the UFA
newsreels into fearfully expendable flesh and blood. She was experiencing
herself as a young woman for the first time and weighing the maleness of
Jean or Hans or John, that species shielded from her at school and in that
"world without men."

"This war, the one that I was living, had not made itself quite clear to me
until [then]," she remembered. "The soldier [visiting] in our house, the air
he brought with him and then left with us, his steps echoing slowly through
the hallways, the bigness of him, the danger he had left behind and the

danger he went towards on leaving us, the kiss I had felt, his field gray shirts, the knowledge that he would never come back . . . made me see this war clearly for the first time."

She would see war again, and next time she would not be too young to show courage as a warrior or too inexperienced to show a woman's full tenderness to John or Hans or Jean.

If children were enlisted in the war their fathers were dying in, so were their mothers. Some took over their men's jobs in industry or exchanged their mourning bands for Red Cross uniforms and bandages. Some traveled to the front, east or west.

Josephine Felsing Dietrich did when Eduard von Losch was wounded on the eastern front, and there she married him sometime in late 1916 or early 1917. She was a forty-year-old bride in a Red Cross uniform, reciting vows over a field-hospital bed. The grenadier gave her his name in exchange for her promise to care for his mother in Dessau until he returned from the war.

He never did. He succumbed to his wounds within a week somewhere near the Russian front, and Josephine's last—perhaps only—wifely duty was to return to claim his body and bring it back to Dessau for his mother to bury in the family plot.

Widowed for a second time, Josephine was released from any obligations but her own and returned with nothing but a new name, the death-benefit pension that went with it, and her daughters to Berlin. The Felsings knew the von Losch union was what they called a "white marriage," but consoled themselves with, "At least it's a 'von' and not a 'Dietrich.' "

Josephine took an apartment in the Kaiserallee, and Marlene enrolled in the nearby Viktoria-Luisen-Schule in April 1917 for her last year of public schooling.

"The little gray mouse" had been metamorphosed by Dessau and the war into a young lady of startling self-possession. If before she had taken the last seat in the last row, she now took the front seat in the first. She used what the other girls gossiped about as her "bedroom eyes" on the few male teachers who had escaped the front. One young faculty advisor (*Studienrat*) responded openly enough to her provocative glances to be dismissed, exciting her classmates' disapprobation—and thrilling them, too. They avidly watched her "try out her effects," as one classmate termed her experimental vamping seven decades later, still clucking over the school-year scandal. Marlene the faculty wrecker was barely sixteen.

Mainly she turned her eyes to her lessons in German, French, English, history, geology, religion, mathematics, physics, chemistry, music, gymnastics, and homecraft. She earned acceptable marks in industry, attentiveness, and conduct, watched over by censorious sister Elisabeth, now in the upper form preparing for her teaching certificate.

The Dietrich girls continued to knit, to stand in line for rations, to share their allotted one thousand calories a day with their failing grandmother Felsing when they visited her. Marlene continued her violin lessons and played in a Red Cross pageant in June 1917 that coincided with the fiftieth anniversary of the execution of Emperor Maximilian of Mexico and so had a Mexican theme. It was her first public violin performance and she played "La Paloma" as accompaniment to girls her own age who rattled tambourines and twirled in flouncy Mexican skirts as dancers. Marlene (or was this Paul?) was dressed as a boy, violin tucked beneath her chin, sombrero covering her curls. Uncle Willi saw her perform and remembered being amused by her male attire, never suspecting that similarly androgynous costuming would later startle the world, sending messages about both fashion and sexuality.

Pageants, theatricals at school, knitting, and practicing the violin brought a semblance of order to a world that was engaged in an endless war that was to have lasted a season. The Americans were in it now, and Paris was cheering a general named Pershing and shooting a spy called Mata Hari.

Marlene's classmates both trembled and thrilled to such news. One, named Mary Bayczinsky, *was* American, and another was the sister of the German poet Gottfried Benn, who would write of the war, "Life is the building of bridges / over rivers that seep away." Most of the girls would build their bridges with diplomas, joining Elisabeth in the upper school and earning degrees, but Marlene's violin would be her bridge—to "public fame on the podium."

Marlene would not graduate at all, would never earn her *Abitur*, or degree, would never even take her final examinations. She would pursue not academics, but her music. She would be leaving behind her special friend Hilde Sperling, who worshipped her, emulating her in manner and appearance, hairdo and clothes.

Just before the end of Marlene's last term, at Easter 1918, one of her classmates persuaded an itinerant photographer to take a souvenir photograph of the class. They gathered in the courtyard of the fire station next door, some of them still in their middies from gymnastics classes Marlene claimed she hated, some in their regulation uniforms, and there they posed for a last memento of girlhood.

Marlene sits soberly in the front row, looking straight at the camera, her arm entwined in Hilde Sperling's, who clings to her with an air of possession. Some of the girls laugh or turn to each other, relaxed in a moment apart from everyday reality. Marlene alone stares down the camera directly—almost defiantly. These are not the bedroom eyes the other girls gossiped about, and far less those of a little gray mouse. They are somber eyes, searching a path through the debris of a collapsing order.

Marlene's sister, Elisabeth, two years ahead of these girls in their middies and uniforms, is not in the photograph, and would not have fit in with her sister if she were. She was not only older, but different. She was obedient and (perhaps because she had never been pretty as a vanilla pudding) accepted discipline like a dutiful daughter. A classmate remembered that she still curtsied at eighteen to teachers barely older than she, and to her cousin she seemed physically stooped, bent by the burden of being the Dragon's daughter, not—like Marlene—the resilient offspring of a good general. The only podium Elisabeth would ever seek would be in a classroom, where she would dutifully pass on the conventional wisdom she would cling to through an even greater catastrophe to come. Her only near-brush with public fame would occur then and would become a shock and threat to her younger sister. Marlene, when she learned the truth, would manage to extinguish it for almost half a century—by denying that Elisabeth had ever existed.

At the end of the school year it was the custom for the girls to sign one another's memory books. Marlene and Elisabeth both signed that of Gertrud Seiler, the girl who had organized Marlene's class photo. Elisabeth wrote a conventional homily, while Marlene wrote on the facing page a buoyant but earnest message: "In the long run, happiness comes to the diligent."

If we had no other indication how different they were, no more hint how dissimilar their futures would be, it is there to see in the yellowed pages of a schoolgirl's souvenir album. Elisabeth's hand, in its old-fashioned copperplate script, looks like this:

Elisabeth Dietrich.

Marlene's looks like this:

Marlene Dietrich

She wrote in the new modern script (it would be banned by Hitler), in the bold hand of a self-naming girl for whom the violin (and fame) had sung sweeter and truer than anthems that had turned to dirges of war. She just didn't know how much diligence happiness would take.

TWO

WEIMAR
AND BACK

1919 - 1921

The armistice was signed on November 11, 1918, in a railroad car in the misty forests of Compiègne. German signatories were civilian cabinet members—to spare the military the ignominy and the blame. The Allies' terms were simple and harsh, unconditional and without negotiation. The war was over. The bloodletting was not.

Six months earlier, as Marlene posed somberly for her class photo, the novelist Stefan Zweig had already noted (and later described) that "a bitter distrust gradually began to grip the population—distrust of money, which was losing more and more of its value, distrust of the Generals, the officers, the diplomats, distrust of every public statement by the government and General Staff, distrust of the newspapers and their news, distrust of the very war itself and its necessity."

Chaos had already begun with strikes over shortages of food and clothing. The reality of deprivation finally penetrated the imperial palace itself. The suddenly perceptive kaiser called—four years too late—for a truce. General Ludendorff urged yet another exhortation on an exhausted nation: "We must fight on. We must and we can!"

But pursuing ruin until the last man fell was resisted not only at the front, where they were falling, but in the homeland, where wives and children were starving. Mutiny, strike, and revolution began on the ships of the kaiser's ambitious, useless navy, and spread to the shipyards where the navy lay idle and to the cities and countryside beyond. "The one true emperor in the world" saw no reason to abdicate and never did. The newspapers (with a little help from Prince Max of Baden, the wartime chancellor) did it for him in a headline no one was more astonished to read than he: "THE KAISER ABDICATES!"

"Treason," the kaiser cried. "Bare-faced, outrageous treason!" but his hysteria was drowned out for once by the sound of the train wheels carrying him to exile in Holland. There he would live out his days concocting crackpot schemes to return to the throne, styling himself "the woodcutter of Doorn," chopping down trees and behaving eccentrically enough to be viewed by too many as a Grand Old Man. Harmless. But he kept track of things in Germany and meddled. His withered arm and addled brain embraced a spiritual heir: that Austrian corporal who had served in the Bavarian army. The ex-kaiser sent him congratulatory cables for exploits at which monarchy had failed because of "a stab in the back." Kaisers became cranks as corporals became Führers. Adolf Hitler had just such a telegram in his pocket as he strolled one day under the Eiffel Tower, from which fluttered neither tricolor nor imperial eagle, but a swastika.

Marlene turned seventeen shortly after the armistice was signed, and only weeks after that, on January 29, 1919, Grandmother Felsing died. Her share of the Felsing firm (the twenty percent not already Uncle Willi's) went to Josephine, who might now enjoy a financial security she had not known since before her newlywed days in Schöneberg. If all went well.

Nothing did. Berliners who were not starving by war's end were dying of influenza, a thousand of them a day, and there was no center anywhere. Wilhelm had been forced to leave the throne, but to whom? Communists, socialists, republicans, anarchists, speculators, and profiteers of every stripe and scruple—or none—rushed to seize the day. At the same time a postwar blockade imposed by vengeful Allies plunged what was left into deprivation unknown even in wartime.

No eyewitness has described those days of revolution, counterrevolution, and misery as vividly as Count Harry Kessler, a "protean figure" as Otto Friedrich justly calls him. Kessler breakfasted with Albert Einstein, lunched with the new German president, Friedrich Ebert, posed in the afternoon for his portrait by Edvard Munch, dined with the crown prince (still a social lion in Berlin: Uncle Willi knew him), supped at midnight with Max Reinhardt. He sipped champagne and frolicked (and took notes) at playwright Dr. Karl Vollmoeller's private orgies on the Pariser Platz in the very shadow of the Brandenburg Gate's goddess of victory, stunned by defeat but still on her perch.

Kessler was no apologist for imperial politics and knew the world's sympathies would not be aroused by the self-inflicted plight of the world's enemy. Vengeance was tasty to the victors.

"France," he wrote, "gave open vent to her desire for our extermination, expressing it monumentally in her prime minister's words: 'There are twenty million Germans too many.' The continuation of the blockade after the armistice was rapidly fulfilling this wish: within six months from the armistice it had achieved a casualty list of 700,000 children, old people and women. . . . The German people, starved and dying by the hundred thousand, were reeling deliriously between blank despair, frenzied revelry, and revolution. Berlin had become a nightmare, a carnival of jazz bands and rattling machine guns. . . . On the very day [of yet another bloody battle in the city center] the streets were placarded with a poster reading 'Who has the prettiest legs in Berlin?' . . . Profiteers and their girls, the scum and riffraff of half Europe—types preserved like flies in amber in the caricatures of George Grosz—could be seen growing fat and sleek and flaunting their new cars and ostentatious jewelry in the faces of the pale children and starving women shivering in their rags before the empty bakers' and butchers' shops."

They photographed children foraging in garbage and called it Art: "the new reality"—"die neue Sachlichkeit." It was new; it was reality. And—incredibly, indelibly—it was art. It stimulated one of the great creative outpourings of the century. Out of the debris (and building on it) came artists like Grosz, John Heartfield, Otto Dix, Max Beckmann; theatermakers Erwin Piscator, Max Reinhardt; novelists Thomas Mann with The Magic Mountain, Erich Maria Remarque with All Quiet on the Western Front; films like The Cabinet of Dr. Caligari and Metropolis; musicals like Weill and Brecht's Threepenny Opera and Mahagonny or operas like Alban Berg's Lulu and Wozzeck. The Bauhaus streamlined everything from knives and forks to (eventually) Park Avenue, all of it, only cultural moments later, to be banned or burned as "degenerate." Berlin in the postwar decade became what it always thought it was—"the fastest city in the world." It would become frenzied with velocity, and old Berliners still call that brief outpouring of creativity, bookended by horrors, "the Golden Twenties."

*　　*　　*

They were not golden for Josephine. Her inheritance and pensions dwindled to worthlessness in the raging inflation that followed the war for five full years. The mark would fall and fall to an incomprehensible low of 4.2 *trillion* to the dollar. Before it did, Elisabeth could teach and Marlene could study her violin for a while, but Berlin was a dangerous place for a girl "trying out her effects" on a populace alternately inflicting violence upon itself or fleeing it in search of "the prettiest legs in Berlin."

Weimar, Josephine decided, was the place for Marlene and her violin. Weimar: columned home of Schiller and Liszt. But especially of classical Germany's greatest figure: Goethe—poet, painter, playwright, statesman, scientist, philosopher, and the violin's only real competition for Marlene's aesthetic affections.

Her music studies might be safely conducted in Weimar, Josephine thought, far from the urban violence of a capital in turmoil. The newly formed government had a similar inspiration, and chose Weimar as the spiritually resonant place to frame a new Republic just a week after Marlene's grandmother died. Like Josephine, they hoped Weimar would lend an aura of classical *Humanität,* safely removed from the frenzied corruption of Berlin, so they wrote their constitution there. In a theater.

"The [Weimar] Republic was born in defeat, lived in turmoil, and died in disaster," the historian Peter Gay has noted, but Josephine's pious hopes would be even shorter-lived. Not all was classical in Weimar, anyway (or worse, maybe it was). It was a pastoral but narrow-minded provincial city. The German Shakespeare Society was (and is) located there. So is Buchenwald, just over the hill.

Marlene arrived in Weimar in October of 1919. She moved into a boarding house that in the eighteenth century had been the home of Charlotte von Stein, Goethe's "soul-friend" and his model for heroines. There Marlene shared a spartan room with five other girls, but was set apart from her classmates at once. Only she took private violin lessons to supplement classes at the *Musikhochschule.* She was going on eighteen and demonstrated at once that her provocative boldness would not be checked merely by checking into Frau Stein's hallowed halls.

"As 'the new girl' Marlene . . . stood there in the doorway in a pose that remains unforgettable to me," one of her roommates, a girl called Gerde Noack, recalled. "She fascinated us immediately as something special. It wasn't something made up, nothing 'put on'—it was *in* her."

She was fascinating partly because the unforgettable poses were allied to diligence. "She practiced five hours every day," her roommate recalled. "When the headmistress had a birthday, Marlene played Torelli's 'Serenade' for her [something of a Marlene calling card, it seems], and I accompanied her on the piano."

When there was something else to celebrate, Marlene composed poetry. If there was nothing to rhyme or serenade, she entertained her roommates with her impression of a Chinese pagoda, wearing only a bedsheet, a talent she is not known to have pursued. "When we wanted cheer and laughter, we'd say, 'Marlene, do your pagoda!' " And she did. "She was a great comrade," the girls agreed, and one of them wrote a poem to celebrate her in the not-so-stately atmosphere of postwar Weimar. It went something like this:

Marlen' comes from Berlin,
For us she fits right in.
Fun and cheer are her plaisir,
And that's the main thing here.

"Marlen' " led the girls in the *verboten* pleasure of buying sweets in town and gorging on them, protected from the nightly prowls of housemother Frau Arnoldi by a heavy armoire shoved against the door. She had always liked her cream cakes, but sweets were great luxuries following the war, and in strictly run boarding houses at any time. She did not escape the consequences. Wolfing down cakes and barley soup the other girls rejected at communal meals, she became (this was envied then) "full-figured, even voluptuous," Gerde Noack thought.

Her celebrity in Weimar grew voluptuous, too, as she went off to her private lessons dressed in chiffon that was sheer to the point of transparency: "sheerly obscene!" roommate Gerde punned later *("geradezu obszön!")*. She was quickly perceived as a girl who was " 'cooperative'—as one would dryly say today." So says her roommate, dryly, today.

All the girls knew about her private teacher, Professor Reitz (married with children), and couldn't help gasping and gossiping when Marlene sailed off to violin lessons in her filmy chiffons. They composed an unrenderable pun *("Marlene reizt Reitz!"*—roughly "Marlene gets a rise out of Reitz!") which was too good not to repeat and had consequences when it got around. Which it did.

But until then, the diligent daughter of the "good general" who could also be a "Dragon" knew when to tone down the allure, though those suggestive bedroom eyes were working, and Weimar had an alert new crowd to notice them.

At the same time that Marlene arrived in Weimar, so did the Bauhaus, the avant-garde group newly founded there by Walter Gropius, with a faculty of painters, designers, and architects including Paul Klee, Wassily Kandinsky, Lionel Feininger, Oskar Schlemmer, László Moholy-Nagy, and (later) Josef Albers, Marcel Breuer, and Mies van der Rohe, figures whose design revolution is still a powerful influence on the visual arts.

Marlene knew many of them, for they also favored Frau von Stein's house, for residence, studio space, and meals. With that instinct for star-shine that served her so well when pursuing Henny Porten, she contrived to meet the biggest *Bauhaus* star of them all: Alma Mahler-Gropius, the founder's wife.

Marlene had become friendly with the group's graphic and stage designer, Lothar Schreyer, and his wife. The couple found her "a kindly, quiet young girl . . . very musical and always friendly." When Schreyer's young son visited from Dresden, Marlene baby-sat. The boy found her as enchanting as her roommates did, though his father later admitted (apparently unfamiliar with her Chinese pagoda act) that "neither we nor anyone else in Weimar had an inkling that in a few years she would be world famous."

Marlene learned at lunch one day that Frau Gropius was due from Vienna for a visit, and she demurely asked the Schreyers for an introduction. Alma Mahler-Gropius was one of the most fascinating and intimidating women of her time, and in her regal prime in 1920. She had been the mistress of painters Gustav Klimt and Oskar Kokoschka and was the widow of the great Gustav Mahler, whose name she insisted precede that of her present husband. She would shortly leave him anyway to marry Franz Werfel, by whom she already had a child. Gropius affected not to know this, though everybody else from Weimar to Vienna to Prague did. Alma was obviously a woman not to be overlooked by an eighteen-year-old who was herself eager not to be overlooked.

The Schreyers advised Marlene to make herself casually, discreetly visible during the great Alma's visit, and Marlene chose the most casually discreet spot she could find: the stairway leading to the Schreyer's front door, where she would be impossible to miss.

"The stairway was well lit," Schreyer recalled. "Marlene Dietrich leaned there on the white-painted landing, violin in hand, gazing up with wide eyes. My wife introduced her. I should have done it, but I was too taken by the scene that now began.

"Marlene kept her violin in her left hand and sank almost to her knees. It seemed like the kind of a court curtsey cultivated long ago in Vienna when there was still an Emperor Franz Josef. It was flawlessly executed, enhanced by the quite simple, *calculatedly* simple frock she wore.

"Frau Gropius performed wonderfully in turn: There stood a duchess in the Viennese Palace receiving a young lady-in-waiting. And in that instant the duchess became as young as the girl before her. Radiantly restrained, she raised her hand with measured but imperious graciousness, and accepted on it the maiden's kiss."

Marlene could not have done better had she been studying direction. The scene had everything: the ingenue and the grande dame; the good lighting and carefully chosen setting; the simple but effective costume; the aesthetic prop; the maidenly obeisance—the sense of homage and of moment. That none of the Bauhaus photographers was present must be mourned as a major loss.

Alma Mahler-Gropius turned away from the girl who had just kissed her duchess's hand and whispered to her host, "What eyes this one has! *What eyes!*"

Josephine would doubtless have frowned at Marlene's obvious bid for attention. Alma Great-Artists'-Muse (an anti-Semitic tyrant in reality) was not unlike Mademoiselle Breguand and Henny Porten to Marlene. They were all female figures from whom attention and approval were thrilling, but also (in feminist professor and author Carolyn G. Heilbrun's phrase) women "living beyond conventional expectations," certainly any harbored by Josephine. They attracted a girl "not only talented but with a sense of great possibilities, great desires beyond the apparent possibility of fulfillment [who had no] girl companions with like desires."

She was looking for what we now call role models, with no very clear sense of where to look. Or for what. Neither Henny Porten's sentimentality nor Alma Mahler-Gropius's grandeurs had much to do with the teenage Marlene. They were studies in opposites, really; but the maternal quality of Porten and the seductiveness of Alma might not have seemed mutually exclusive to Marlene (who would later uniquely combine them). Both women had set themselves apart, had found public fame on their own sort of podium that made them appealing exemplars for a young woman's quest. That one was a screen star expanded the notion of podium; that the other was an erotic inspiration to great men of artistic renown suggested all kinds of things. They were unconventional figures in whom an unconventional girl might find confirmation in a world in which convention seemed, because of the war, to have proven its meaninglessness.

And they were important to her. Years later, when Marlene was world famous and had romantic credentials to challenge Alma Mahler-Gropius-Werfel's own, Lothar Schreyer bumped into her on one of her visitations from Hollywood to Berlin. After some nostalgic reminiscence about Weimar and *la vie bohème* at Frau von Stein's, Marlene breathlessly blurted out her query about the visitor from Vienna:

"What did she say about me?"

What others said about her in Weimar was various, widespread, and worrisome. Among those with whom she studied was Wolfgang Rosé, Mahler's nephew and a piano student at the *Musikhochschule*. He thought Marlene shy and unlikely to have succeeded as a concert violinist and thought her unaware of her beauty. She was either showing exceptional restraint or undervaluing herself, for her beauty caused a "sensation" according to Rosé, and "astonished us all. Young men were lining up to take her out," he said, but Marlene's sights were not then set on young men, who could not advance her musical ambitions, but on Professor Reitz, who could. Rosé didn't know that, though her roommates did. The young man allowed that in spite of his reservations about her musical abilities, her "passionate diligence" might have carried her further than he could guess.

It carried her right back to Berlin.

Marlene's later memory (which was not infallible) recalled that Josephine took the train from Berlin to Weimar every three weeks to make sure she was healthy, practicing hard, and to give her a proper shampoo. It is unlikely Marlene did her Chinese pagoda or Viennese lady-in-waiting impersonations for her, but the shampoos were administered amidst praise from teachers for what Marlene called her violin "triumphs," and at leave-taking, both mother and daughter were sodden with tears, perhaps of relief.

Josephine may have been too impressed by the sanctity of Frau von Stein's residence to notice all the free thinking going on in it. "I could play as long as I wished or had to," Marlene admitted, "and could divide my time as I saw fit."

Her division of time was diligent and precociously shrewd. Whatever Professor Reitz's charms as Marlene's first lover, he was something of a roué (he would soon leave his wife and children for another woman) and was a musician in a position to be helpful to her. Marlene was to reveal a lifelong predilection for friends and lovers who meshed neatly, sometimes crucially, with her ambitions, whether by intuition or design. The adolescent instinct that forced an introduction to Alma Mahler-Gropius, that had earlier stalked Henny Porten all the way to Bavaria, would serve her well for a lifetime.

Josephine might have wondered about Marlene's freedom in Weimar, and not too surprisingly, "disaster" (Marlene's word) struck. She was whisked all baffled and bewildered back to Berlin. It was quite inexplicable, she maintained forever after, but it is hard to imagine Josephine not spelling it out, as housemother Frau Arnoldi had apparently spelled out *her* concerns to the shampooing general. All Weimar was spelling it out.

Weimar was that kind of place. The Bauhaus crowd was so notorious for bohemian behavior that Weimar parents were known to threaten naughty children, "We'll send you to the Bauhaus," where the devil resided. Walter Gropius did, anyway, with his newfangled, profane ideas like "form follows function" that got rid of cherubs and rococo flourishes, replacing them with the "less" that was supposed to be "more." He went around saying things like, "Artistic design is . . . simply an integral part of the stuff of life." As music was to Marlene.

The stuff of life to pastoral Weimar was the stuff of gossip, often unfounded. Alma Mahler-Gropius's visit there had been occasioned by a rumor that threatened the very existence of the Bauhaus before it really got going. It had to do with life painting classes, which were said to provide shocking views of nude models to anyone innocently passing the atelier windows. The atelier *had* no windows—no life classes or nude models, either—which helped the crisis to pass, but tongues wagged on, not always quoting Goethe when they did.

There had been rumors about Marlene from the start, from that moment she leaned unforgettably on the doorjamb with that unique something that was *in* her and caused roommates to make up cheerful poems about her. Her astonishing beauty and the filmy chiffon get-ups she wore to her private violin lessons added fuel to furor. Less, Marlene may have heard on the grapevine, was more, but less looked provocative as all get-out to the other girls, and to Frau *Hausmutter* Arnoldi, too—she who could prowl the halls in search of forbidden sweets.

Professor Reitz was susceptible enough to Marlene's chiffon'd charms to remain indifferent to (or unwary of) local gossip and remained her private violin teacher until the summer of 1921. Then, in early July, Josephine whisked her *"plaisir-*bent" daughter back to Berlin.

She had a four-week summer holiday, and on arrival immediately contacted a Dr. Julius Levin, a violin-maker friend of Professor Reitz. She asked if she might bring in her violin for tuning. Dr. Levin (often misidentified as one of her teachers) responded affirmatively. They met, and he gave her a book with the prophetic title *Die singende Dame (The Singing Lady)*.

Marlene liked the book and entered into correspondence with Levin after she took a brief holiday out of Berlin in late July, following which she was bedridden. She described her illness as angina, as tonsillitis was then called, and complained of high fever and headaches that would delay her return to Weimar by several weeks.

Dr. Levin sent get-well books, for which she was effusively grateful, writing from her sickbed where she said she felt too unwell even to *listen* to her violin.

Invitations were extended, accepted, then postponed as Marlene's return to Weimar was further delayed (by "fever," she said), which prompted paternal sympathy from this friend of Professor Reitz. Then, suddenly, she was back in Weimar in late August, still suffering from headaches, but not too ill to write Dr. Levin the minute she arrived.

Their increasingly familiar correspondence over the period of Marlene's convalescence alludes to their conversations (probably by telephone) and to a trip she was planning to Hannover with Professor Reitz, to whom she refers boldly as "my lord and master."

Marlene teased Dr. Levin about the thirty-year difference in their ages, but once back in Weimar clearly felt she had found in him a confidant. Immediately after her arrival she wrote him that "slanderous gossip" was circulating there that greatly angered her, but that she had no one with whom to discuss it until Dr. Levin's not too distant arrival there on a visit. Even with her confidant she felt a certain demure apprehension. "Will you, too," she wrote him, "have something unpleasant to say? If so, be gentle, yes?"

Two days later she poured out more of her anxieties, which suggest that the "slanderous gossip" revolved around questions of marriage for base motives. "It would be *unbearable* to me," she wrote protestingly to Levin, "to have luxury in a marriage with a man I didn't love, that I can tell you!" She was grateful for Levin's assertion that even should the painful gossip be *true*, she would not suffer in his esteem, but added that if he knew "how vicious people [are] being" he might not feel so generous toward her. Her concerns, she said, were less for herself than for others (presumably Dr. Reitz), whom she termed "*totally innocent.*" She suffered that with no proof with which she could defend herself, she could not, of course, defend others. "I am so alone here," she wrote, with nothing to look forward to but Dr. Levin's impending visit.

Years later, when Marlene was staying with Billy Wilder and making a movie for him in Hollywood, she would use her lonely anxieties in Weimar as amusing anecdotes told in the company of professionals on whose discretion she could then rely. Wilder enjoyed entertaining his dinner guests by inviting Marlene to detail her love life for them, and he recalled "a piano player, violinist, violin teacher. Then there was this affair and then this man and [my guests] all sat there open-mouthed." It was a performance designed to *épater le Hollywood bourgeoisie* concocted by two old Berliners who knew how to *épater* and was not confined to enumeration of Marlene's *male* conquests. It usually ended with Marlene's casual, "Are we boring you?" to an audience of sophisticates that might include blasé New Yorkers like Moss Hart and Kitty Carlisle, who thought—until they heard Marlene's tales of old Weimar—they had heard everything.

Marlene remained friendly with Dr. Levin for years, even after marriage and motherhood. She confided to him her disillusionment with the "faithless society" of Weimar and heaped scorn on her former "lord and master" when she learned he had finally left his wife and children for another woman. But by then he was no more to Marlene than an object of some-what lofty disdain.

Marlene was back in Berlin in late 1921, a fearful time in a fearful place. Revolution and murder in the streets were as common as prostitutes and beggars. Leftist leaders fell to police murder, like Karl Liebknecht "while trying to escape," or Rosa Luxemburg, whose body was found bloated and bobbing in a Berlin backwater. (Poets and composers wrote songs about her.) Rightists and monarchists clamored for renunciation of the Versailles Treaty, claiming Germany's new leaders had treacherously forced the kaiser into exile. Those who urged compliance with the humiliating and crushing treaty were traitors, so rightists or leftists murdered them when they could (including Foreign Minister Rathenau in 1922), and received feather-light sentences. (One of Rathenau's murderers went on to become a successful screenwriter under the Nazis.) The tree-lined streets of what many had called "the most beautiful city in the world" had become alleyways for the violent exercise of brute power. Iron crosses were rusting in gutters running with blood long before anyone had ever heard of *Mein Kampf.*

No mother, not even a good general, could sanely prefer the chaos of Berlin to the bohemian goings-on of Weimar, but Weimar was costly, and inflation was achieving heights no one ever dreamed of. It would soon cost thousands, then millions, then billions, then trillions of marks for a loaf of bread (if wheat could be found to bake one).

Pursuing the classical arts can hardly have seemed propitious then, but Marlene said she returned to Berlin to further her violin studies unaware of inflation, revolution, assassination, and economic and political collapse. She may have attended the *Hochschule für Musik* in Berlin, but the records remain mute and no known witness remembers her there. If she was enrolled, her stay was brief and her "passionate diligence" unrewarded. The violin was to become "the symbol of my broken dream," she would romantically say forever after.

There are two versions of how the dream broke. The first was that from overrepetition of solo sonatas she strained a ligament in her fourth left finger, necessitating a cast that forever weakened her fingering. The other version cites a painful ganglion on her wrist. Either or both may have been true at some time or other, but truer was that the economic crisis demanded she get a job.

She got one. Playing her violin. At the movies.

At the height of the inflation, it was rumored that Douglas Fairbanks, Sr., was going to buy Austria.

Things were never quite that bad (or good), but the grim joke was a sharp reminder of how much had changed. Territorial imperatives of Habsburgs and Hohenzollerns were on fewer tongues than those of Hollywood, which had not won the war, exactly, but had conquered the world.

By 1919 some eighty percent of the motion pictures seen around the globe were produced in southern California. The Great War had given the early producers and distributors among the orange groves (and their financiers in the canyons of Wall Street) an edge and hegemony over worldwide motion picture exhibition they were never to lose.

Some call this cultural imperialism, and debate it still. But it is hardly ever appreciated that in Berlin, which was to be Hollywood's only world-class competitor in the 1920s (and its greatest talent pool), the impact of American filmmaking was largely unfelt until about 1924. Then Berlin first saw D. W. Griffith's 1916 *Intolerance*, which had been blockaded by the war and was, like all Hollywood films, no more than rumor.

There simply *were* no Hollywood movies in Germany from late 1914 for the next decade. During hostilities, they were "enemy propaganda." Following the armistice and the inflation that ensued, exporting American movies to Germany was pointless as the mark fell and the dollar soared. When Rudolf Valentino, Gloria Swanson, Mary Pickford, Charlie Chaplin, Douglas Fairbanks, Lon Chaney, and Lillian Gish (not to forget Strongheart, the world's first dog star) were all at or near their peaks in the summer of 1922, a daily Berlin gross of four million marks represented a return for Hollywood of only ten thousand dollars at the then prevailing rate of four hundred marks to the dollar. In more prosaic terms: about one week's salary for Miss Swanson. By the time the day's box office closed in Berlin, the exchange rate might have plummeted so rapidly that the takings would pay only Miss Swanson's maid—or *her* maid.

A year later (at one *million* marks to the dollar) a ten-million-mark gross was worth ten dollars to Hollywood, a tip to a waiter at the Cocoanut Grove. Berlin ticket prices were subject to inflation, of course, but that didn't offset the disastrous spiral. Berlin's market was meaningless to Hollywood, but its *talent* wasn't, and as things got worse (no one dreamed they could, but they did) Hollywood moved in with talent raiders and investment muscle as well as "Made in Hollywood, U.S.A." celluloid, with historic results.

Ironically, during this same five-year postwar period in which no Berliner saw *Intolerance* or swooned over Gloria Swanson or Rudolf Valentino, the German film industry would produce some of the most remarkable films ever made: *The Cabinet of Dr. Caligari* (1919), *The Golem* (1920), Asta Nielsen's drag *Hamlet* (1921), *Nosferatu* and *Dr. Mabuse* (1922), the two-part *Nibelungen Saga* (1924)—all were made innocent of Hollywood influence. And in Hollywood, apart from "the big four" (Griffith, Chaplin, Pickford, and Fairbanks, who styled themselves United Artists), filmmakers were churning out mostly junk, or scandals for the tabloids.

German film's development paralleled postwar political insularity and the enormous creative explosion in other fields. Out of chaos, art. Seen today from the comfort of a film museum seat, these films seem to represent watershed years. In reality, they were produced in cultural isolation resembling a crucible more than a vacuum, and were, for all their stunning accomplishment, a creative cul de sac, even within Germany.

Nor were they widely seen outside German-speaking territories. The influence they might have had on filmmakers elsewhere was slow to be felt and often irrelevant to foreign audience tastes when it got there. (Or just baffling: *Caligari*'s Expressionism was a sensation, but never a threat to little Mary's ringlets.) Most often, it was through the filmmakers themselves in their migration to Hollywood that such influences (and their silent but great debt to German theater, from which almost all German filmmaking talent came) were realized.

The first postwar German picture to be distributed in America was *Passion* in late 1920. It had been made in Germany in 1919 as *Madame Dubarry* by Ernst Lubitsch, and starred Pola Negri and Emil Jannings. Germans thought it was a satire on French decadence, but Americans pegged it for history in the bedroom, and promptly summoned star and director to Hollywood. Lubitsch would famously stay; Negri reigned supreme (she was as big as Swanson) until her Polish vowels and consonants did her in with the microphone; and Emil Jannings packed his bag with sausages and sauerkraut and headed west, too, to win the first Academy Award.

General Ludendorff's UFA was to rise above its original propagandistic raison d'être and, by merging with smaller German firms, emerge as the single most powerful film company outside Hollywood. It did so partly with the financial backing of companies with such interesting German names as Krupp and I. G. Farben. These firms would shortly lend their vast resources to a political party, which would result in UFA's becoming Dr. Joseph Goebbels's personal playground (his casting couch was infamous) from 1933 to 1945, making him easily the most powerful production head who ever lived. UFA's films could—and still *can* wherever cinéastes collide—claim a worldwide audience and a notoriously ambiguous place in history.

Silent film, as all buffs and historians know, was never truly silent. From the meanest sheet-hung backroom, where viewer comment supplied the "sound track," to early exhibitions in which lectors read titles for illiterate audiences; from the tinny upright piano of beloved legend to the Mighty Wurlitzer, and on to small or full-sized orchestras of quality playing original scores (Eugene Ormandy began his American career conducting for silents), silent film had a voice—or voices—and it was here that Marlene Dietrich found her first employment and an indirect first step toward that public fame she yearned for.

Her first real job was playing violin in an orchestra accompanying silent films of which she was the only female member, a measure of her self-confidence and the enlightened attitude of the Berlin music world. UFA had its own roster of musicians who traveled from one UFA theater to another, playing whatever score had been patched together from existing music or composed especially for the hoped-for hit of the moment.

Marlene was engaged by Dr. Giuseppe Becce, dean of Berlin's film-orchestra conductors and a noted composer, then and later. There was nothing nonchalant about her employment. Becce found her "highly gifted" and hired her as concert mistress. This did not make the twenty-year-old an overnight sensation, though being concert mistress for an orchestra of experienced men was hardly trivial. But instead of fame on the podium, it was anonymity in the pit.

She didn't earn much, according to Becce, but it was enough to keep her briefly afloat in perilous times, and a job was a job. She also continued private lessons with Professor Carl Flesch, the great Hungarian musician who wrote a book about violin technique that was a standard on the subject. He had his own string quartet, too, in addition to teaching at the Berlin *Konservatorium*.

Marlene remained faithful to old idols and pestered Becce for jobs accompanying Henny Porten films so she could study the star on screen as she played. Accompanying silent films sharpened her musical skills of tempo, tone, and mood, particularly if she watched the pictures as she matched music to moment, and Becce tells us she did. The limitation—or discipline—was that unlike the stage or concert hall, any variation in timing could prove fatal to what was happening on the screen, where images were metronomically frozen into their permanent rhythms of cutting and performance. Exactitude became second nature to Marlene and a lifelong habit.

Watching is learning, as any film student knows (and Marlene was becoming one, intentionally or not). Repeated viewings of almost any film can reveal hidden rhythms and rules and at least a superficial grasp of some of the grammar of film. Her later celebrated knowledge of the mechanics of film was born in front of a dimly lit musician's stand.

German films were at an artistic apex then, and if she fiddled as ambition burned (or at least smoldered), what was merely simmering in Weimar came to a boil in Berlin. Prophetically enough, it was not a damaged wrist or nerve ganglion that put an end to her violin dreams, but rather better known parts of her anatomy.

Maestro Becce was highly satisfied with her work, but was forced to fire her after only four weeks because her legs proved too much of a distraction to the other members of the UFA orchestra. Just as well, perhaps, for what had previously been flickering in her peripheral vision at twenty-four frames per second now came sharply into focus twenty-four hours a day.

Certainly Marlene's legs were not the hands of Duse she had so fervently admired as a girl, but they could carry her into a new world, and did.

The later oft-told tale that she also idly selected the theater as an avenue of expression is belied by her other post-Weimar training in Berlin. She continued with the violin, but she also took voice lessons with Dr. Oskar Daniel, who had studied in Italy with the teacher of Caruso. Dr. Daniel's operatic aspirations were limited by his being short, stout, and bald, but he quickly gained renown as one of Berlin's premier vocal coaches.

Marlene had no operatic ambitions, but she wasn't taking expensive voice lessons just for fun. Still, her initial approach smacked of the bohemian habits of Weimar. Unlike the Dietrich of later years (whose punctuality would become legend), she was chronically tardy for Dr. Daniel's lessons and was told that if she could not be on time she need not return.

Daniel's nephew, Hans Feld, later editor of *Film-Kurier* (the very influential German *Variety*), was assigned the task of warning Marlene about her tardiness. He remembered her as exceedingly pretty, free and easy of manner, following fashion on a budget with simple cloche hats and coats with *faux* ermine collars. Though his uncle thought her voice weak, he was impressed enough by her musicality to allow her to continue on a pay-when-you-can basis as inflation spiraled out of control, and especially when Marlene entered the theater professionally.

Her theatrical debut, according to a man named Georg Will, was in cabaret, in the basement club of the still famous and still operating *Theater des Westens*. Will was never an unimpeachable reporter, but deserves mention as the first on record to claim he "discovered" Marlene, who was about to become the most discovered girl in Berlin in the 1920s. No other major star in history was so often discovered by so many to so little immediate avail.

Will's reliability is debatable. He became Marlene's brother-in-law—married to sister Elisabeth—about the time of his boasted discovery. The marriage was an occasion of some relief to the Felsings (and to Elisabeth), who had thought they might never see the day. It was a relief to Marlene, too, for she was expected to marry traditionally, in sequence of age. What Josephine thought of a cabaret manager as son-in-law is unrecorded, but it left her little room to object when Marlene's legs promenaded before cabaret footlights, and they soon did.

Shortly after being fired by Professor Becce, Marlene was doing high kicks in a chorus line, touring cities like Hamburg and others more provincial with Guido Thielscher's Girl-Kabarett: vaudeville on the hoof.

Such jobs were not hard to come by for a pretty girl with pretty legs, nor did they demand intimate acquaintance with the arts of Terpsichore. Guido Thielscher was a much-loved *Schlager*-singer, a purveyor of pop songs that were mostly sentimental, sometimes naughty, always hummable. In his best days he had worked on Berlin stages with the great operetta star Fritzi Massary, who was so popular and famous they named a cigarette after her. The girls of the Kabarett neither needed nor earned fame. They were mainly required to wear feathers without looking like birds and to move to the beat of Guido Thielscher's belting. What the assignment lacked in style or glamour it made up for in elemental stage experience for a girl without training (Chinese pagodas didn't count) who could keep time with the legs that had providentially gotten her out of the orchestra pit.

Back in Berlin she extended her theatrical steps by filling in as an extra girl in the slicker, sleeker Rudolf Nelson revues, where she danced and sang with other neophytes like Camilla Horn, who would later play Gretchen opposite Emil Jannings in *Faust* and be leading lady (twice) to John Barrymore in America. The Nelson revues were intimate, impudent, and stylish, not unlike the Scandals and Gaieties of New York or London, except that Nelson was not only impresario, but owned his own theater on the Kurfürstendamm and mostly wrote and composed his own shows. He wrote a song called "Peter," which Marlene may have danced to on his own stage (where it became an instant standard) and would later make famous far beyond Berlin when she recorded it.

These were makeshift, catch-as-catch-can jobs, supplemented by attempts at modeling by a twenty-year-old who knew she was pretty enough and leggy enough to make her mark, and her showgirl period lasted little more than a year. There was, however, nothing makeshift about Marlene's energetic approach to her work. She showed her familiar "passionate diligence," but it undoubtedly took on a merrier tone on stage in feathers and spangles than in the darkness of the pit. Her enthusiasm for the locale and the life would earn her the catchy appellation "the girl from the Kurfürstendamm," which stuck to her for the rest of the decade. Still, these were vaudeville stages on which less was *less*, and they did little more than ignite ambition that hitherto had been a spark.

The later Dietrich would deny ever having set her sights on becoming a star—on stage or screen. She thought she wasn't the accepted theatrical type—neither Pola Negri nor Henny Porten—though not being the type would one day be part of the point, when her stunning originality would make her world famous overnight. If she couldn't play beautiful music because her legs got in the way, perhaps she could speak or sing beautiful words, like those of Goethe or her newer poetic idol, Rainer Maria Rilke, whom she admired passionately and whose work she committed to memory for the rest of her life.

Maestro Becce's reluctant farewell may have been the pivotal moment in Marlene's casting her career in the theater. Or perhaps the idea occurred in a noisy, beery cabaret basement, as her brother-in-law claimed. Or on a one-night stand with Guido Thielscher's touring ostrich feathers and spangles in some provincial music hall. Or even earlier.

Most likely it had always been there, inherent in the passion to perform. She had been performing since childhood, one way or another, since that first baby photo, since Josephine at the piano accompanied her daughter on the violin. The girl with the desire to perform was drawn not merely to the podium but to anywhere there was a spotlight.

Marlene was beautiful and desirable and knew it and liked it. The trick was to get everyone else to know it and like it. She also knew she was entering "a dangerous profession" and, without looking back (she never would), plunged saber-deep to the heart of her chosen métier. With the bravado of the born lancer's daughter, she decided to start at the top.

THREE

THE SORCERER'S APPRENTICE

1922 - 1923

Max Reinhardt was the top. Not just in Berlin or Vienna or Salzburg, but wherever he chose to display his theatrical wonders: from Moscow to San Francisco or anyplace between that had a stage or something that could be turned into a stage, and that had an audience he could astound.

He transformed beer halls, circuses, empress' ballrooms, auto-supply factories, cathedral squares into theaters and magicked them back into forests, palaces, blasted heaths, and moonlight.

He claimed to "approach the stage . . . not as a literary man [but] as an actor," which he had been, but that description minimized his gifts for any theatrical art. Almost everyone who ever worked with him (beginning with

Lulu's creator, Frank Wedekind) called him magician or sorcerer, but what he was was a genius of versatility.

His theater was "a house of light and dedication" in the words of theater historian John Willett, and was at its zenith when Marlene was twenty and marking time with her tap shoes in provincial music halls or the louche and lively cabarets in and around Berlin. Life on the road and Girl-Kabarett only underscored that there must be something more elevated and edifying, something more *enchanted*, than two a day or more in the chorus.

Max Reinhardt began as an actor in the theater of the 1890s, but broke with the prevailing naturalism in favor of a more romantic symbolist theater at the turn of the century. In Berlin he founded a famous cabaret (Schall und Rauch—loosely Sound and Fury) and discovered his true métier as *regisseur*, which can mean producer, director, or impresario. In his case it meant visionary.

His reputation is dimmed today, for his legacy was to actors and audiences, not to academics or theorists. The living experience of Reinhardt's monumental productions—*Oedipus Rex, Lysistrata, A Midsummer Night's Dream*—cannot be recaptured, though their influence reverberates still. His astonishing worldwide success has distorted our impressions of him, turning him into a kind of Barnum of world theater (Percy Hammond of the New York *Herald Tribune* actually called him that, shortly after—perhaps *because*—*Time* put Max Reinhardt on its cover in 1927).

He was a protean figure who could conjure forty-eight productions in a single year and over five hundred in his lifetime. There were the daring spectacles, but also the intimacy of his chamber theater, the detail and nuance he achieved with actors, the delicacy and wit that balanced the colossal productions. *The Miracle*—a religious spectacle performed in an actual cathedral or something that could be turned into one—may have been the "masterpiece of high *Kitsch*" many called it, but it played all over the world. Lady Diana Cooper acted the nun in it, and it toured America in the 1920s for five staggering years after three hundred performances in New York.

If Reinhardt's theater was not literary, it was never careless or contemptuous of the page. Aeschylus, Goethe, Molière, Shakespeare, Strindberg, and Shaw were his collaborators; they were the accomplices of his scenic designers, composers, lighting, costume and dance designers, and of spectators, too, the collaborators he revered above all. With them and for them he wrested a living theater from the academy and library of a tired naturalism, poured light onto it, dedication into it, and practiced his sorcery wherever they would let him, until they wouldn't anymore.

Until that happened he was one of those men—rare in any field—who inspire subordinates to seek not merely his approval, but his level. And that level was high: "Only that art is living," he said, "in whose inmost chamber the human heart beats."

It beat passionately in the ten theaters Reinhardt ran in Berlin, Salzburg, and Vienna until the Nazis demanded and got the keys. It beat, too, in the most important theater school in Europe, the Reinhardt Drama School in Berlin, where young Marlene Dietrich went to be auditioned and discovered and rejected.

Many years later Josef von Sternberg slyly told of being with Max Reinhardt and Marlene Dietrich at a Hollywood party in the thirties when Marlene mentioned to the then exiled Reinhardt that she had been his student in Berlin. "[Reinhardt's] eyebrows did not resume their normal position for almost twenty minutes," Sternberg reported, in a line with more wit than truth and more malice than wit. But Sternberg needed his own version of things and he wasn't there in 1922. Marlene was.

What she brought with her to that audition at the Reinhardt drama school in the Deutsches Theater was hope and *chutzpah*. She may not have marched on the audition stage trailing ostrich feathers from her Girl-Kabarett tour, but apart from her passion and memory for poetry, she had no training, no preparation, not a scintilla of evidence that she belonged there. Except a passionate conviction that she did.

Her audition probably looked less passionate than overeager that day. We know she looked less good to her Berliner examiners than a Swedish girl called Greta Gustafsson did—at almost the same moment—to *her* examiners at the Royal Dramatic Academy in Stockholm. But the Swede was four years younger and perhaps had less at stake.

Marlene had chosen her audition piece carefully, for she was one of scores of hopefuls, many of whom had training and background she lacked. She had prepared a passage from Hoffmannsthal's lyrical verse play *Der Tor und der Tod* (*Death and the Fool*), which Reinhardt had produced and which might therefore demonstrate discernment and taste. Hofmannsthal's romantic lyricism appealed to the twenty-year-old, and the tone of her reading (as she recalls to "the fool" his faithlessness in love) is easy to hear:

Es war doch schön. . . . Denkst du nie mehr daran?
Freilich, du hast mir weh getan, so weh.

It was so lovely. . . . Do you never think of it?
Of course you hurt me, hurt me so.

The melancholy *Weltschmertz* is built in, always one of her best modes, and they called her back the next day. In the final round of auditions, passages were assigned, not chosen, and Marlene must at first have thought the theater gods had smiled. It was a speech from her beloved Goethe, "Gretchen's Prayer" from *Faust*.

"Gretchen's Prayer" is a complicated text that demands simplicity, and nothing is more difficult to achieve. In addition, *Faust* was a standard in the Reinhardt repertoire, and Gretchen a revered role, played not long before with much-praised reserve by Helene Thimig, a hugely admired star-actress about to become the second Frau Reinhardt.

Marlene as a beginning actress was notably *un*reserved (Girl-Kabarett called for something else), and nerves instead of legs got in her way. Repeatedly crashing to her knees on the stage floor to pray the holy passage, she was startled to have a cushion fly at her from the auditorium. Disconcerted by what may have been a kindly gesture (or, then again, may not), she fell again to her knees, distracted by the notion that, as far as she could remember, Gretchen hadn't brought along a pillow to the church when *she* prayed. She began to recite to an imaginary statue of the Virgin:

Ah, look down,
Thou rich in sorrow's crown,
With the grace
Of thy dear face,
Upon the woe in which I drown.
*   With piercèd heart*
And cruel smart
Thou seest the death of Him, Thine own.

This is no easier than it looks, and the instinct for less-is-more that served Marlene well in Weimar failed her in Berlin. She was overwhelmed, perhaps, by the romantic combination of Goethe, Reinhardt's actual theater, and a living, breathing, *judging* audience. Her eagerness betrayed her lack of control or training and her uneasy intuition about the flying cushion proved correct. She had flung herself—or Gretchen—too far, too hard, too often.

She was not rejected by Reinhardt himself. He was in Vienna at the time and never auditioned prospective students anyway. Marlene forgot that later, when she told the story that he called out from the auditorium that her having shed real tears on stage was irrelevant—she had not made *him* do so.

The story was fictitious, but the logic faultless, and suggests the force the Reinhardt ethos had on her in imagination or in memory. It is tempting to wonder what Reinhardt might have thought had he been there, for he once famously noted that "the highest boon of mankind is personality," a quality in which Marlene was seldom deficient. Even her flinging herself repeatedly to her knees might have revealed to him some vital spark.

When she *did* come to his personal attention several years later, she was not flinging herself, but sidling elegantly through a chic, intimate musical revue at one of the Reinhardt theaters. There (no Gretchen, this) she sang songs that seemed to celebrate the joys of girl-girl love and the sexual frisson to be derived from kleptomania. Reinhardt had been taken to see her by *The Miracle*'s Dr. Vollmoeller, who had a famous eye for miracles of feminine beauty. Reinhardt was so impressed by this one that he was fleetingly infatuated. Vollmoeller took pleasure in deflating the sorcerer's ardor by informing him that this "discovery" had, in fact, been working for him off and on for five years. Reinhardt hadn't known. Vollmoeller kept track and would keep on keeping track. Marlene liked being someone people kept track of.

Her rejection in 1922 meant only temporary exclusion from the Reinhardt circle; she went looking for a sponsor.

Rosa Valetti was a short fireplug of a woman with a tough, pug-dog face, frizzy red hair, and one of the most avid cabaret followings in Berlin. Valetti remembered later that just after Marlene's failed audition the young woman appeared backstage in the Valetti dressing room at the Grössenwahn (Megalomania) cabaret with an introduction from a mutual friend. Valetti looked up from her makeup table and sniffed. The rankest of newcomers. "A natural talent," she thought acidly. "It'll take a lot of patience to develop *this* one. But the voice. *That voice!*"

Alma Mahler-Gropius had reacted to "those eyes!" and the gentlemen of Dr. Becce's ensemble to "those legs." Now it was "that voice." Valetti knew it wasn't Gretchen's voice and never would be (which had maybe been the problem), but it teased the ear like feathers on flesh, even the toughened hide of a hardened pro. She sent the newcomer back to the Reinhardt school to Felix Holländer, one of the Reinhardt administrators and uncle of Valetti's wunderkind cabaret composer, Friedrich Holländer.

Uncle Felix had a reputation for being absentminded and distracted (he was a novelist and playwright, too), but when Marlene arrived from Valetti with that voice, those eyes, and those legs, he turned her over for tutoring with Dr. Berthold Held, who actually administered the Reinhardt school. Marlene thus became not an official Reinhardt pupil, but something considerably more privileged: a private student with direct access to the Reinhardt management, as much on the landing of the inner circles responsible for scheduling and casting as she had been for the great Alma in Weimar.

Marlene was tutored with another girl, Grete Mosheim, who would become an important actress in German theater and films. She continued her voice lessons with Dr. Daniel and added to them informal tutorials in tricks of the cabaret trade from Valetti and her peers, performers who knew the facts of life—or were thinking up new ones.

Marlene and Grete Mosheim both regarded their tutor, Dr. Held, as "rather a fool, really," an ineffective teacher, but accepted his pomposity as a price easy enough to pay to be inside. They took outside lessons in English and in Swedish gymnastics while undergoing the routine Reinhardt disciplines of rhythmic movement, fencing, and elocution. Then there was voice projection: mouthing vowel sounds into the vastness of an empty auditorium while tugging on ropes without gasping.

The important ropes were those Marlene was learning of her "dangerous profession." She was spending hours in the classical Deutsches Theater itself, the thousand-seat main theater above which the school was located, or next door in the intimate Kammerspiele, which seated two hundred spectators, every one a connoisseur sitting inside a Stradivarius. There were noisy, convivial hours in the main theater's basement *Kantine*, called the D.T., with its low, vaulted ceilings and enormous wooden booths and tables set with baskets of black bread, where apprentices mingled with stars. They wolfed down German meatballs, herring, and beer, along with gossip and trade secrets, techniques, and tricks. Around them hung photographs and caricatures of great stars in great roles, of playwrights whose work was new when Reinhardt was an actor in this theater. It was hard work, but its own reward, which is the great and simple secret of the theater. It was surprisingly close to Weimar's Bauhaus principle: life-as-art and art-as-life and who could tell the difference? Or want one? Though just a twenty-year-old apprentice, she was discovering daily what the Sorcerer meant when he explained what keeps actors actors: "It is to the actor and to no one else that the theatre belongs."

Marlene quickly took possession of that prize on September 7, 1922, in the small and elegant Kammerspiele. The work was Wedekind's notorious play about Lulu, *Pandora's Box*. She played the small role of Ludmilla Steinherz in a cast that included her chum Grete Mosheim.

Ludmilla Steinherz (Stoneheart in English) is a coarse and common character drifting with vulgar élan through Lulu's Paris salon *cum* gambling casino in Act Two. She appears (as Wedekind wrote her) in a "garish red-and-white-striped frock" and comes and goes vivaciously hell-bent on being depraved. When asked if she ever sleeps, she replies, "Of course; but not at night."

The Reinhardt repertory called for different roles in different plays at different theaters in rotation. Two weeks later Marlene added a new role and a new theater with *The Taming of the Shrew* in the Grosses Schauspielhaus, the one-time circus seating three thousand spectators which

Reinhardt had turned into a theater. It was a huge house for a tiny role (the wealthy widow who wins Bianca's suitor Hortensio) and the part was cut to the bone to avoid Elizabethan wordplay that didn't translate. Still the production preserved the no-nonsense widow-woman's comic bits. Even if it hadn't, Marlene was heartened that she was fulfilling Reinhardt's dictum that "nobody is an actor till he's proved that he can play Shakespeare." The proof was perhaps slight and didn't keep her from comparing her role to that of Kate, played with grace and fire by Elisabeth Bergner, the Viennese darling of Berlin audiences and critics. Competing actors count lines and Marlene kept score of how few she had in this production for the rest of her life: three. But all three were by Shakespeare.

By January of 1923, just turned twenty-one, she had added two more Reinhardt credits to her work: a French farce called *Timotheus in Flagranti* at the Deutsches Theater (the main house) in which she alternated three small parts; and Somerset Maugham's mostly sparkling *The Circle*, back at the connoisseurs' Kammerspiele. Marlene played Mrs. Shenstone, who delivers some exposition from the bridge table but not much else, though the part gave her another chance to study Elisabeth Bergner at close range in another starring role. (This time Marlene tells us she had no lines at all; she had many. By Maugham.)

Marlene was, in truth, star-struck. When she appeared in February as an Amazon captain in Kleist's *Penthesilea*, it was not the words of the great poet nor the action of his classic tragedy that thrilled her, nor even the costumes of abbreviated armor that left Troy in little doubt about how Amazons differed from Trojans. It was not her occasional battle reports in high German verse or her spear that thrilled her, but being on stage with the Amazon general of the title, played by Agnes Straub, a great stage star with the stature of, say, Katharine Cornell or Judith Anderson. Berlin would soon name a theater for Straub. She was short-sighted to the point of blindness without glasses and Marlene's thrill came in being her seeing-eye Amazon, leading the general by the hand from one part of the revolving turntable stage to another during blackouts. Speaking tragic poetry was agreeable, but the rapture was the hand of a Star clutching hers as everything revolved in the dark. She had felt the thrill of star quality since childhood and Henny Porten; now she was holding hands with it, hoping it might rub off.

Marlene's résumé contained seven roles (counting all three in *Timotheus*) in five plays in just six months. They were played in rotation for a total of ninety-two performances from September of 1922 until April of 1923. By any theatrical standard this was solid journeyman work, giving her a grounding in stagecraft honed by productions of widely varying scales and styles, mounted in different theaters by different directors, all within the embrace of Max Reinhardt's immense prestige.

If that wasn't enough, there were the occasional fill-in or stand-in jobs she picked up here and there by chance or as favors. On nights off from Reinhardt, she stood in for friends like Anni Mewes (who had been in *Timotheus* with her) while Mewes pursued her rollicking social life—or possibly wrote thoughtful letters to Rilke—who wrote *back*—guaranteeing Marlene's awe.

Such appearances were fleeting and unrecorded, but one was in a popular American comedy called *The Great Baritone* (*The Great Lover* in America: MGM made it as a movie starring Adolphe Menjou). The play about an aging opera star (he is an ancient forty-six) had been refashioned for the great German actor Albert Bassermann, who made it into a personal annuity in both Berlin and Vienna between his more celebrated (but less lucrative) Shakespearean performances. Agnes Straub and now Bassermann. This was equivalent to winning walk-ons or even bit parts with any of the Sirs or Dames in England or any of the Barrymores on the other side of the Atlantic.

It would be a shock to find a beginning actress today so steadily and variously employed in any modern theatrical arena or with the energy to sustain the pace. Most important was the sense of community she was building with Reinhardt actors and others, with technicians (never unimportant to her), with The Life.

She was forming professional habits for which maternal discipline had prepared her well, and the diligence she wrote about in a schoolgirl's memory book was proving itself more than just words. It wasn't happiness yet, and she had far to go, but she had come a long way, too. The policeman's daughter was hobnobbing with Shakespeare and Kleist and Wedekind and Maugham, and (thrillingly) with Bergner and Straub and Bassermann. The sound that reached her ears was not reproach from Josephine von Losch, but the roar of the greasepaint. And more than an echo of the jazzy clamor of the Kurfürstendamm, out there glittering with a sorcery all its own.

Josephine may have sniffed at Girl-Kabarett, but Reinhardt was a culture hero. Marlene was moving too fast, anyway, for any clucking from Josephine to be heard over the din of the adventure. Marlene also had an ally in the family, for Uncle Willi loved the theater now more than ever. He had loved the pomp of imperial operetta; he now loved the impudence of republican revue. He loved the music, the modernity, the people. He still advertised to attract them, partied with them, and the other half of his villa in the Liechtensteiner Allee was occupied by one of them—Conrad Veidt, newly famous worldwide as César the somnambulist in *The Cabinet of Dr. Caligari.* And he had a new and exotic link to—of all places—Hollywood. Uncle Willi had gotten married.

His bride was a beautiful Polish woman named Marthe Hélène but called Jolly, as in *jolie.* He met her at a reception for the former crown prince, whose social allure was dimmed not at all by the absence of any crown but that embossed on swank invitations. Jolly had received one with a Mr. McConnell of Hollywood, California, who had the interesting job of selling rides to amusement parks and happened to be her husband. He was in Berlin promoting something racy called "The Devil's Wheel," and though Uncle Willi had no interest in the contraption, he thought the wife worth acquiring for himself. He puffed on a Russian cigarette, proposed, and the beautiful Hollywood visitor became Frau Felsing with a speed that made the Devil's Wheel seem sluggish compared to what made the world go round.

They married while Marlene was still in Weimar, and in 1922 had a son, Hasso, whose middle name was, of course, Conrad, the Felsing family's own hereditary title.

Jolly Felsing was nothing if not emancipated, and as she was only a year older than Marlene, became chum rather than aunt. She spoke her native Polish, excellent German, an amusing sort of Hollywood English, no French whatever, but was fluent, even eloquent, in the language of allure. Marlene found her fascinating, and Josephine Felsing Dietrich von Losch predictably found her alarming. The exotic young Jolly could afford to ignore Josephine's disapproval, for the beautiful interloper was now, by virtue of marriage, the senior Felsing female.

Every Junker value the Dragon stood for was challenged by Jolly's emancipated chic. She was a new type of woman, a bejeweled Phoenix emerging from the smithereens of the Great War; not a jazz baby, but a jazz *woman.* It was in her manner, her clothes, her style, her nonchalant life. Marlene may not have noticed the revolutions and turbulence of the postwar period, but she noticed Jolly and her *jolie joie de vivre,* with its enormous theatrical appeal, so very like star quality.

Josephine had her twenty percent of the Felsing firm (eroded daily by inflation), but Jolly had Uncle Willi and the jewels. The ones she didn't wear she gave to friends to hock against their debts during the financial crisis, a careless prodigality Marlene would emulate during a crisis yet to come. Jolly wore sables and foxes and jeweled turbans and loaned furs to Marlene when a night on the town or an extra call or interview required dazzle. Jolly was new as neon, old as Eve.

Marlene was feeling emancipated herself by her new career in the theater. She had moved away from home to a residence hotel where her nightly comings and goings (and the borrowed wardrobe in which she came and went) were the envy of other young actresses who wondered about the sources of her finery. Greta Keller (later the well-known chanteuse) lived in a simpler rooming house just across the alley and used to see Marlene climb in and out of limousines in chic that came from no Reinhardt wardrobe hangers. Grete Mosheim marveled at her "exquisite hose and the finest high-heeled shoes," noting that Marlene "could knock your eye out at seven o'clock in the morning," and wondered not only how she afforded them, but why she was still wearing them at dawn. Marlene had already a dynamic sense of self-presentation through apparel and would never *not* be identified with fashion—outré, outrageous, or high. She would define it on screen and inspire it on the street. No other female of the era so exploited or enjoyed it as part of her persona, and her nearly infinite variety was enriched by dipping into Jolly's trunks and rummaging through the furs and turbans.

And jewels. Jeweled everything. Jolly wasn't just chic, she was practical. She ordered up necklaces and bracelets from Uncle Willi's firm in which every third diamond was paste (which never showed), securing an economy of glamour with no sacrifice in glitter. She wore fingernails long, which Marlene copied to make her short fingers look slender. Jolly was the prototype for the allure and style Marlene's legs would shortly parade on the Kurfürstendamm. Marlene called her "the most beautiful woman I've ever seen in my life," and that she had lived in Hollywood and moved in the aura of Hollywood's gaudy glamour did nothing to diminish her appeal to an impressionable young actress.

Berlin—like London and Paris, but unlike Hollywood—was a center of both theater and filmmaking. It was also remarkably free of the prejudice that films were déclassé or to be disdained. Hollywood developed as it did (for good *and* ill) partly because of its spiritual and physical distance from the theater. But German film from the beginning suffered hardly at all from any such schism. Hollywood's D. W. Griffith had been a failed actor and playwright who, like many others, *gave up* the theater when he entered films. In Berlin the theater and its denizens took to the new medium as they had taken to electric footlights when they replaced gas, and the reciprocal benefits were apparent almost from the start.

Reinhardt himself directed films before the Great War, and there was hardly an actor, director, designer, or writer who did not move freely between both worlds. They couldn't afford to ignore movies during the inflation, but they never really had. Cross-breeding was inescapable not only because Berlin was the center of both, but because German theater was less struck by what separated them (words) than attracted by what they had in common (imagery). Reinhardt, Piscator, Brecht all used film effects (or actual *film*) on stage, and almost all the great filmmakers of Berlin's golden age—Murnau, Pabst, Lubitsch—had been theater figures, too.

Marlene Dietrich's entrance into films wasn't destiny—it was inevitable. It made sense economically; everybody did it. She had been movie crazy since adolescence. She may well have tried to get into movies before she tried theater and almost certainly auditioned for the camera before she did for Reinhardt. Uncle Willi and Jolly rubbed elbows with film people, and elbows that rubbed could also nudge.

Marlene had been pestering Uncle Willi for years for introductions to his film friends. She invited them (through him) to her appearances in Red Cross pageants during the war, as when she played "La Paloma" on her violin. She was, he said, "quite mad about movies" and maddeningly convinced her future was on the silver screen. Uncle Willi finally gave in to her pleas (to silence her, he said) and phoned a movie executive he knew named Horstmann at a company called Decla, imploring him to arrange a screen test for his niece.

Horstmann pressed the test on a cameraman then working for the studio, an immigrant Hungarian (later a journalist in England and America) named Stefan Lorant. Horstmann's favor to "a friend of the family" was greeted grudgingly by Lorant, for it meant overtime after a full day's shooting on a glass-enclosed film stage that focused light and heat like the greenhouse it resembled.

Lorant was accosted after a grueling hot day's shooting by a girl "lively as quicksilver, a very whirlwind of vivacity." Sour with heat and fatigue, he tried with no success to discourage the vivacious tornado.

"You promised to make a test of me," Marlene pleaded, and Lorant realized she was "prepared to wait till midnight, if necessary." He demanded to know *why*, and her answer rang with bravado: "Because . . . that's what I was born to do."

Rather than return to the glassed-in hotbox of the studio, Lorant set up his camera outside. He decided a nearby fence was sufficient prop for this sort of thing and told her to climb up and down, jump around and over and under. The good general's daughter eagerly followed the drill.

"Marlene must have been made to get up on the fence some fifteen times, and jump down again, and while doing this, she had to laugh, cry, grimace, scream, sob," Lorant recalled. "She didn't mind at all. She jumped down from the fence, she jumped into the ditch, she hopped and skipped and shouted for joy. . . . She turned her head from right to left, like a mannequin at a fashion parade. When her eyes met the lens of the camera, she had to laugh. She screwed up her mouth, then she turned her head further round into profile."

If all this seemed enchanting to the novice, it was because she had what quickens any actress: an audience. Lorant's colleagues on the film he was shooting were witnesses to her uninhibited performance.

Later Lorant chortled over the "good laugh" they all had when viewing the developed test. "In the close-up, the girl, who was quite pretty in real life, looked distinctly ugly. Broad face, expressionless eyes, uncouth movements. The opinion was unanimous: no talent whatever."

The opinion was not all that unanimous. The film Lorant was then shooting was called *Struggle for Myself (Der Kampf um's Ich)*. It featured Olga Tschechowa, a star of the day, and a young leading man called Wilhelm Dieterle, who was a well-known Reinhardt actor. He had just the year before played in Reinhardt's personal production of *Julius Caesar*, in which Emil Jannings got to ask him *"Et tu, Brute?"*

Dieterle had watched Marlene make her first test that scorching day and saw it later. He was fascinated by films and largely dissatisfied with what he saw in them (including himself) and was planning to do better by writing and directing his own. At the very moment Marlene made her running-jumping-standing-still test for Lorant's camera, Dieterle was trying to raise money for his first film as writer, director, and star, and in Marlene he saw not the awkward and comical figure Lorant found so amusing, but the ideal ingenue for his debut film.

Perhaps it took another actor to know what he had seen. "Many people have their dreams behind them, many before them," Dieterle remembered. "Marlene . . . carried hers with her, and wore them like a halo." It was that halo he would not forget, the one Lorant's lens had failed to record.

Until Dieterle could scrape his financing together, Uncle Willi had more than one friend in the movies. Marlene was determined to find the one who would agree she was born to be a film star. While still giggling behind Dr. Held's back with Grete Mosheim and tugging on ropes at the Reinhardt school, she prevailed on Uncle Willi to introduce her to a film director called Georg Jacoby, then preparing a comedy about Napoleon's younger brother, who had been king of Westphalia. It was to be shot outside Berlin for a new company called Efa (European Film Alliance), formed specifically to make films for the American market and high-flying dollar. Judging from the American reception of Lubitsch's *Passion* (the Stateside *nom de boudoir* of *Madame Dubarry*), Napoleon's younger brother seemed a promising subject. Uncle Willi asked Jacoby to give Marlene a role—*any* role to discourage her passion for movies.

Georg Jacoby had an eye for actresses anyway (he tended to marry them) and offered her the tiny role of a maid to the leading lady, Antonia Dietrich, who was no relation and no great star. The real star of the film was the popular Harry Liedtke, who had played Don José to Pola Negri's *Carmen* for Lubitsch.

The film was variously called *That's How Men Are* or *Napoleon's Little Brother* or *The Little Napoleon*. Though undistinguished under any title, a Berlin reviewer found it "very amusing" and thought it had "technical refinement." It never made it to America, and Efa itself was dissolved in November 1922 just after *The Little Napoleon* was finished, delaying the picture's release—and Marlene's first view of herself on screen—for a full year. A wag of the day dismissed the whole thing as "the bastard offspring of the mating of Madame Dubarry with the exchange rate."

Marlene would later deny she ever made films like *The Little Napoleon*, or if she did, she had played only bits with serving trays and brought news that "The horses are saddled" or "Coffee is served." Her reluctance to acknowledge her early films is easy to understand when watching some (not all) of them, but especially *The Little Napoleon*, which is just what she liked to claim they all were.

She is supposed to have remarked in horror on seeing herself on screen, "I look like a potato with hair!" which speaks well of her critical acumen. She actually looks more like an energetic turtle, her head emerging from a shell of starched linen to bob about in a sort of dither of gratitude to be on camera. She didn't yet know how light could flatten out a face whose cheekbones were still obscured by puppy fat, reflecting back a dumpling, or how the camera could overanimate her joy at standing in front of it, making her look giggly and gauche. She would learn all this, and soon, too, but one giveaway of the novice is remarkable for its absence: fear. She is bursting with confidence, bubbling over with it, however badly it photographs. The worst (and best) that can be said of her film debut is that she tries too hard—and that films are seldom lit to benefit the walk-on maid. Even if the director has an eye for her, or an eye her beauty or manner might attract. A co-worker on the picture remembered clearly that the pretty potato-with-hair "conducted a rather charming flirtation with [her director]. I think Jacoby was in love with her, but I'm not sure. At all events, his interest was obvious for everyone to see."

It is altogether possible he indulged her overexuberance. This was very early in her Reinhardt apprenticeship, and Jacoby was no Reinhardt. His career lasted until the sixties, but he was never more than competent or commercial. His artistic distinction peaked in 1923 when he directed Emil Jannings as Nero in the Italian version of *Quo Vadis?* with co-director Gabriele d'Annunzio.

If Uncle Willi's purpose had been to discourage Marlene, it backfired smartly. She was getting somewhere, and if she was getting there by using connections and "charming flirtations," that didn't matter. Nobody gets anywhere in show business without help from somewhere. Who you know is always important, but once you know everybody you are alone again, dependent on yourself. She would learn that, too.

Marlene went back from *The Little Napoleon* to Reinhardt and there Wilhelm Dieterle saw her again in her succession of small roles in big plays. She had stayed in his memory, not for her expertise but because of that cardinal Reinhardt virtue, the one she had exhibited since adolescence: that "halo" of personality.

"I picked one of those wonderful folktales by Tolstoy," Dieterle said, "and we got together. We had no money. We were just four [or] five very young, enthusiastic and revolutionary [Reinhardt] people who wanted to do something different. We brought it out; it didn't make any money, but was shown, and it was a very interesting experiment."

The Tolstoy folktale was a Good Samaritan fable called *Man by the Wayside (Der Mensch am Wege)*. Marlene played the ingenue in braids that pulled her hair back—peeling the potato, as it were—revealing the pretty symmetry of her features. She liked playing ingenues and imagined she was one for rather too long, but for Tolstoy and Dieterle braids and dirndls were appropriate.

The film was Dieterle's reaction to the studio-bound films in which he had been appearing and which would shortly stun the world with their virtuosity. But Dieterle didn't want sets. He wanted fresh air (which is easier to finance) and was strongly influenced by the outdoor realism of the new Scandinavian and postrevolution Russian films. *Man by the Wayside* was therefore shot mostly on location in sunlight and Schleswig for hardly the end of a shoestring. It won Marlene her first paid advertising (tenth billing) and her first critical notices anywhere.

She was "sympathetic" in one review, "superficial" in another, but they *noticed* her. Most encouraging to Marlene was that Dieterle, a respected and well-known actor, had recognized her aspirations and judged her fit to join his fledgling effort as director, an enterprise otherwise composed entirely of seasoned Reinhardt professionals. It was an inauspicious debut for Dieterle, but a first step in his second career that would take him to America, where he became William and directed films like *The Life of Emil Zola, Juarez, The Hunchback of Notre Dame,* and *Portrait of Jenny.*

As the first film director really to *cast* Marlene, Dieterle might later in Hollywood have felt justified in claiming credit for her discovery, but never did. Perhaps both of them viewed *Man by the Wayside* as better-off-forgotten juvenilia. Twenty years later, when he directed her again at

MGM in *Kismet*, there was no whisper that it was a reunion. The past was past, fitting enough for an actress whose dreams were always present tense.

That the world failed to discover *Man by the Wayside* did not daunt Marlene, for by the time it was released, she had made a discovery of her own.

His name was Rudolf Sieber.

Marlene knew when she met him that he had a reputation. It may have been hard for him not to have acquired one—along with the Rudi by which he was known to everyone who knew him, which was most of the workaday film world of Berlin.

He was young, handsome, blond with brown eyes, charming, bright, and ambitious. Rumors of his Lothario exploits excited women's interest and gave him a romantic aura even in days of increasingly casual and exotic liaisons.

He was born not far from Prague in Aussig on February 20, 1897, in the Sudetenland. Aussig was a good theater town and sparked ambitions beyond the production managing and assistant directing he was doing in Berlin, for he also identified himself on documents as "actor."

He was well placed for almost any advancement in 1922, working as assistant to director Joe May, a man Hollywood's *Variety* mentioned in those days in the same breath as Lubitsch. Rudi had the attractive power of assigning small roles in May's mostly big and important productions, which did nothing to tarnish his romantic reputation, even though he was engaged to May's daughter, the blond and beautiful Eva May, who was becoming a film star herself.

No one ever suggested Rudi's success with women was the result of his movie connections (though no one ever suggested they hurt, either), and when he or Joe May decided to hire some new faces for May's mammoth *Tragedy of Love (Tragödie der Liebe)*, new faces all over town (including Reinhardt ingenues') prepared to renounce obscurity.

Tragedy of Love was to be an expensive, four-hour prestige picture, starring Emil Jannings and Mia May, the producer-director's wife, whose presence in this and other pictures helped him secure his financing. The cast would include Rudi's best friend, Rudolf Forster, and other well-known Berlin stage and film personalities. Sets would be designed by the great Paul Leni, and the picture would be released in two full-length parts with numerous crowd scenes—high society to lower depths—all demanding extras.

Putting Rudi Sieber in charge of casting the girls was turning the hen house over to the fox, and Marlene and Grete Mosheim began preening their feathers and clucking to be discovered. Marlene was worried about appearing (as Mosheim did) "too innocent" and went to inventive lengths to disguise her unworldliness.

The Reinhardt (and other) girls lined up at Joe May's studios in Weissensee near Berlin for review. The initial selections were not made by Rudi Sieber, as it happened, but by the very co-worker on *The Little Napoleon* who had noted Marlene's "flirtation" with her director on that earlier picture. His name was Fritz Maurischat and he related that for *Tragedy of Love* "a line formed which went all the way down the corridor and down the stairs. In this line was a tiny, fragile creature, dressed in a loose wrap almost as intimate as a negligee. Despite this revealing garment, she could easily have been overlooked, since most of the girls were doing their best to attract attention by throwing their breasts or legs at me . . . but she had with her a puppy on a leash, and none of the other girls did. . . . Marlene picked it up and . . . came to my desk. As she did so, there was something about her movements that made me say to myself, under my breath, 'My *God!* How attractive she is!'"

The "negligee" handily masked innocence and the puppy suggested . . . well, the wide-eyed maiden in Weimar who curtsied for a Viennese "duchess." When Rudi Sieber's attention was called to this unlikely but striking visual contradiction, he got struck.

So did Mia May, the star of *Tragedy of Love,* who remembered the newcomer well, and rather favorably, too, considering Rudi was slated to be her future son-in-law.

"[Marlene] was very amusing and diverting and attractive and original," May remembered. "She was irresistible to men [and] used to go everywhere with a monocle and a boa, or sometimes five red fox furs. On other occasions, she wore wolf skins, the kind you spread on beds. People used to follow her through the streets of Berlin; they would laugh at her, but she fascinated them; she made them talk."

She made Rudi Sieber talk. To Joe May. She was cast as an extra, a party girl in the gambling casino sequences, a slightly tarnished morsel of *jeunesse dorée,* but Sieber helped her get an actual role, too. It was insignificant on a four-hour canvas stretching from Paris to the Riviera to the snowy North, but Sieber had seen something in her. What he saw, Mia May thought, was a girl whose eyes ("those eyes") said, "You're going to be the father of my child."

Marlene tumbled at twenty-one into the love of her life. She rationalized Rudi's not speaking to her beyond perfunctory instructions by reminding herself that she was hardly more than an extra and he was Somebody—and already engaged, a detail she permitted herself to forgive. He had, after all, gotten her a part.

The shooting—Marlene's portion of it—took place in late 1922 when she was working nights in the theater, hurtling from one role to another. With the energy that characterized her entire career, she managed daytime shooting, nighttime performance, and full-time pursuit of "the man I want to marry," as she described him to Josephine.

She was "hopelessly in love [and] anxiety ridden," she said. She worked at the film's casino tables and brought a certain vicious edge to her portrayal of Lucie, the mistress of a lawyer whom she badgers on the telephone for a seat at the murder trial of the Emil Jannings character, one of the big set pieces of the film (though not the climax, as is usually reported). Lucie was a tiny role, a pouty vixen, but what is called a "talk-about" in the trade. She adds brazen sex appeal to the courtroom scenes by flirting with a second lawyer to torment the one who is her lover, flashing the monocle Sieber suggested she use to highlight herself in the crowd, just as she did on the streets of Berlin.

Tragedy of Love was eventually released in America in 1926 in a one-part version called *The Apache's Revenge* to capitalize on the popularity of Emil Jannings, by then in Hollywood and an international star. This version, shortened by two-thirds, completely eliminated the Mia May story, which had been the major thread, climax, and "tragedy" of the title. The American version concentrated on Jannings, the "Apache" of Paris (where all the action was), and is notably short on tragedy *or* revenge, but artificially long on Marlene.

She was the lucky recipient of distribution and narrative fate; her role survived the cutting room floor because she was in the casino scenes leading to the murder committed by Jannings and in his trial scenes that followed. Less fortunately for the Marlene legend to come, an even later version was prepared in which her first appearance on screen is captioned "Marlene Dietrich," for the good reason that in no other way would the viewer recognize her.

She looks less like a potato than a floozy. In some courtroom shots there are hints of the later Dietrich face, but here it is peppy and plump. She is desperately mannered, busy as a B-girl. She still has no notion of how her movements or face photograph, because she had not yet *seen* herself on screen. *The Little Napoleon* was still unreleased, and *Man by the Wayside* was several months away.

Marlene finished her work on *Tragedy of Love* and continued at the theaters and at Rudi. Her memoirs record a chaste and innocent courtship, followed by a year's engagement and a church wedding in which she wears a myrtle wreath and everybody throws rice.

Reality is less like a movie. Marlene and Rudi met in late 1922 and were married on May 17, 1923, in the registry office of the Berlin suburb of Friedenau just after she finished making *Man by the Wayside* for Dieterle.

The civil ceremony was witnessed by Marlene's mother, who gave her age as forty-one (she was forty-six), and a salesman called Richard Neuhauser (forty-five), who may have been Josephine's beau. Marlene signed her name as "Marie Magdalene Dietrich." She was twenty-one years old and it may well have been the happiest day of her life.

That Rudi was employed in the film business piqued Marlene's ambitions, and he encouraged them. He was the sort of masculine model she had missed since childhood—no father figure, but an ardent and amorous man whose equilibrium and reliability (greatly like Josephine's) she was to depend on as long as he lived. No one who ever saw them together—even half a century later—doubted that she revered and trusted him, that he was mentor, advisor, friend, and soulmate, if no longer—for decades in fact—her lover.

If there is some measure of his romantic appeal to Marlene and the vibrant young things who flocked around him, it may be read in the footnote to their courtship, marriage, and *Tragedy of Love*. Eva May, Rudi's former fiancée, threw no rice at the Sieber wedding. She opened her wrists instead, and finished the job properly the following year with a shot to the heart that broke when Rudi left her.

Marlene, when her turn came, would prove to be made of sterner stuff.

FOUR

THE PERFECT
COUPLE

1923 - 1927

They were golden. Young, beautiful, and ambitious: toughened enough by the war and its waste to have few illusions about the future, romantic enough to have many about themselves.

The honeymoon lasted just long enough to get Marlene from the registry office where they were married to the casting office where she signed a theater contract with Carl Meinhard and Rudolf Bernauer. The producers could not equal Reinhardt in prestige or quality but had theaters to fill. Marlene filled one modestly by going on in June as the daughter in a "backstairs tragicomedy" called *Between Nine and Nine*.

The Siebers survived separation when Marlene went to the shore in July to be filmed as a bathing beauty for the first and last time in *Leap into Life*. Though merely "a girl at the beach" on the call sheets, she got to be "a girl at the circus" too. A minor sand-and-sawdust tale for producer Erich Pommer was bread and butter for Marlene and Rudi.

In September she was back on stage in a farce called *My Cousin, Edward*, a trifle that pleased Berlin for almost a year. Marlene left long before that to re-don her armor as Hippolyta ("the bouncing Amazon" Shakespeare calls her) in *A Midsummer Night's Dream*. This *Dream* wasn't Reinhardt's, but Marlene won her first theater review. It was from Berlin's most fearsome drama critic, Alfred Kerr, who headed his paragraphs with Roman numerals as if writing on tablets. Marlene brought him down from Olympus for earthly musings about "the flesh of Hippolyta."

Hippolyta's flesh was widely, if intermittently, on view that first year of marriage. In *Spring's Awakening*, Wedekind's long-banned play about adolescent sexuality, she was a slutty schoolgirl; in Björnson's *When the New Vine Blooms*, a merely eager schoolgirl; in Molière's *The Imaginary Invalid*, a maid—but *French*, and Berliners knew what *that* meant.

There is notable range from schoolgirl to queen of the Amazons, from Shakespeare to Molière. Her roles required stamina and style, kept her busy, in view, and paid.

Work was imperative. Marlene and Rudi had married just as inflation seemed to have peaked, but by November the exchange rate soared to 4.2 trillion marks to the dollar and paper money started selling by the pound. Economists projected an astronomical 12 trillion, which was too stratospheric even for vengeful or dollar-rich Allies. Mercifully, the five-year inflation fever broke when the American Dawes Plan simply lopped off all the zeroes (a dozen of them), bringing the exchange rate down to 4.2 marks to the dollar. The era of the Golden Twenties could begin.

So could Marlene. Less than two years after crashing to her knees and defeat as Gretchen, her résumé included a dozen stage productions and four films. It was time for a production of her own.

Maria Elisabeth Sieber was born December 13, 1924, two weeks before Marlene turned twenty-three. The baby was called Heidede within the family and "a wonder" by her mother.

It was not an easy birth, and Marlene convalesced and breast-fed the baby in new quarters in the Kaiserallee, just down the street from Josephine von Losch. With a working mother and father, Heidede would need a baby-sitter.

The child was a stabilizing axis around which a merry-go-round might revolve. Marlene poured love into Heidede and gloried in her role as mother; she was proud, possessive, and sentimental. Pragmatic, too. "Small children, small sorrows; big children, big sorrows," she would say, quoting the old German proverb. The big sorrows were yet to come, and motherhood awakened feelings that would become an integral part of her public image. The only film role she ever created for herself was a self-sacrificing mother (*Blonde Venus*), and her musical repertoire would counterpoint love song with lullaby. Only Marlene ever so adroitly blended the maternal and the erotic, the Marie with the Magdalene.

Public fame was not to be achieved at the bassinet. Especially not with news racing around Berlin about a young Swedish actress who made a picture there while Marlene was in labor with Heidede. The film was called *Joyless Street* and director G. W. Pabst had made Greta Garbo the new girl in town, only to see her whisked away to Hollywood by somebody called Louis B. Mayer. This sort of news could stir ambition even in the breast that nursed a wonder, and by March, when Heidede was three months old, Marlene was back in trim and looking for work.

She had been out of sight for almost a year (though Rudi had not), and to night-owl eyes the Siebers seemed to be making up for lost time, not always—or even especially—with each other. They still seemed the perfect couple, but less like mother and father or husband and wife than brother and sister. They were blond, beautiful, and ambitious as ever, but now wined and dined and danced all over jazz-mad Berlin with an independence suited to new times, new values, new partners. The Golden Twenties had dawned with nearly half the decade already gone, but the half that remained was defiantly free of drab, discredited conventions of the past.

"It was a splendid time," recalled an unemployed actor who would shortly make his fortune producing a novelty called *The Threepenny Opera*. "The long, bloody war was over and had become a ghost. Its victims hadn't died or suffered their sorrows in vain. . . . There would be no more wars; we had survived The Last."

Survival called for celebration—in life, art, and life *as* art. The Crash would come, but when brilliant young social observer Luigi Barzini came to Berlin it was "the artistic capital of Europe, full of brilliant theaters, cabarets, avant-garde art shows, trail-blazing films, experiments of all kinds." Some of the innovators seemed "characters dreamed up by de Sade, Havelock Ellis, Sacher-Masoch, Krafft-Ebing, and Sigmund Freud. [On the Kurfürstendamm] there were men dressed as women, women dressed as men or little schoolgirls, women in boots with whips . . . legless veterans on crutches, *culs-de-jatte*, armless or blind veterans wearing iron crosses, and the hungry unshaven unemployed, all of them begging. I saw pimps offering anything to anybody, little boys, little girls, robust young men, libidinous women, or (I suppose) animals."

This was the "new reality" they wrote manifestos about, and gallows humor laughed away the shadows. Barzini related the local jest "that a male goose of which one cut the neck at the ecstatic moment would give you the most delicious, economical, and time-saving frisson of all, as it allowed you to enjoy sodomy, bestiality, homosexuality, necrophilia, and sadism at one stroke. Gastronomy, too, as one could eat the goose afterward."

Anita Loos bounced through Berlin and noted that if gentlemen preferred blondes, well, "the prettiest girl on the street was Conrad Veidt." Stefan Zweig was less amused: "Along the entire Kurfürstendamm powdered and rouged young men sauntered and they were not all professionals; every high school boy wanted to earn some money and in the dimly lit bars one might see government officials and men of the world of finance tenderly courting drunken sailors without any shame . . . hundreds of men costumed as women and hundreds of women as men danced under the benevolent eyes of the police. In the collapse of all values a kind of madness gained hold particularly in the bourgeois circles which until then had been unshakable in their probity."

In such "divine decadence" (as *Cabaret*'s Sally Bowles called it), Marlene and Rudi's tours of ambisexual clubs like Le Silhouette or The White Rose or El Dorado (at whose entrance were floodlit posters of dancing couples: man/woman, man/man, woman/woman, man/poodle—something for everyone) were just keeping up with the times. They *were* the times, too attractive—together or separately—not to be noticed.

Marlene got noticed at once. She was night-clubbing in March with Rudi when film director E. A. Dupont's assistant was dazzled by "her legs, her divine legs!" Dupont was then preparing a film called *Varieté* for Emil Jannings and Lya de Putti, set mostly in the Wintergarten, Berlin's nightclub/theater/circus. The assistant "discovered" Marlene and her legs; perfect, perhaps, wrapped around a trapeze.

Dupont sneered. He knew Marlene's work and said the only place he would dream of using her was already occupied by Rudi. She might be talented, but "has had no occasion to prove it." He condescendingly told his assistant, "Maybe someday *you* can give her a chance, if you ever have a bit part that needs a mini-vamp with beautiful legs."

Dupont's disdain epitomized the problem to plague Marlene through the twenties. She was too beautiful, too vivacious, too much "the girl from the Kurfürstendamm" to be taken seriously as an actress or inspire much more than envy of Rudi, who didn't seem to mind. Nor did she.

Rumor swirled about her. Those charming flirtations and her self-presentation invited it. Those eyes, those legs, that voice—those *clothes* (and jewels borrowed from Jolly)—ensured her being talked about. The editor of the widely read *Berliner Zeitung* saw her one evening at a cabaret and was so overwhelmed he wrote a profile about her, masquerading behind a pseudonym he was never overwhelmed enough to use again. The great *Sezessionist* painter Max Liebermann, then in his seventies, saw her strolling by the Romanisches Café like something out of Otto Dix. He turned to his companions and sighed, "Oh, to be fifty years younger . . ."

Such reactions seldom prompted questions about her art. Not long after Marlene placed Heidede in Josephine's lap, Messrs. Meinhard and Bernauer placed their theaters in that of producer Viktor Barnowsky, who voiced the prevailing attitude. Marlene was "very young, dazzlingly fresh, elegant, exceptionally pretty [and] slightly mysterious, [but] unconscious of her many charms—except, perhaps, for her legs." She was, he said, "too beautiful." Elisabeth Bergner was working for Barnowsky then and purred, "If I were as beautiful as Dietrich, I wouldn't know where to begin with my talent."

Three months after Dupont's cavalier rejection of her, *Manon Lescaut* was a prize. Shooting began in June on the highest-quality film Marlene had been near since *Tragedy of Love*. It was an Erich Pommer Production for UFA, but no B-movie programmer like *Leap into Life*. The star was Lya de Putti (fresh from *Varieté*); the designer of sumptuous sets and costumes was Paul Leni; the director was a major Berlin film figure (today unjustly neglected), Chicago-born Arthur Robison.

Manon Lescaut is usually cited as another of Marlene's "bits," but she played the second female lead. Micheline was a Parisian courtesan who was flippant, flirty, and scornful of everything but her own allure. Marlene had lost weight after her pregnancy and was beginning to resemble the Dietrich to come. Her performance flits, but she has moments of striking prettiness, coarsened by her playing to the balcony, not the camera. She heaves the riffraff aside with contemptuous shoulders when an eyebrow would do.

Prettiness attracted attention from reviewers. One singled out "the exceptionally pretty Marlene Dietrich, whom one would like to see again," while another thought "Marlene Dietrich [is] certainly ready for bigger things." The bigger things happened instead for already big Lya de Putti, who left for Hollywood and Paramount (flying high on *Varieté*'s trapeze) just as *Manon Lescaut* premiered at UFA's Palast am Zoo, the largest cinema in Europe. Producer Pommer and designer Leni went to Hollywood, too, joining a German colony there lorded over by Emil Jannings, already complaining about the shortage of good sausages in California.

Manon followed its makers to America. *Variety* found Lya de Putti less impressive than Wladimir Gaidarow as her lover, Des Grieux. *Variety* seemed not to know the story. After a synopsis of its tragic events the reviewer reassured the reader, "It's not as sad . . . as it may sound. Everyone seemed to have had a lot of fun while it lasted. . . . While the two lovers were often troubled[,] the [Grieux] kid could kiss! And how! And where!"

Variety spelled Marlene's name right.

*　*　*

She might have gone to Hollywood, too, if anyone had asked her. Or anyplace else there was meaningful work, in spite of Rudi and the attractions of Berlin. The familiar notion of Marlene during this period as a heedless jazz baby and nothing more ignores the depth of her ambition and aspiration. It is belied by a letter she wrote to the same Dr. Levin to whom she had confided her woes in Weimar back when gossip still hurt. Her apprenticeship with Reinhardt had not made her a star, but it had made her a professional with standards beyond the nightlife and her reputation as a beautiful but frivolous creature, which she was all too conscious of having acquired. The startling fact is that she still longed to be a serious actress and was not alone in feeling such a goal was within her range. Shortly before Heidede was born she was invited to join the respected and innovative Schauspiel company in Frankfurt under the direction of Richard Weichert, and complained bitterly to Dr. Levin at being bound to Berlin and the mostly boulevard fare she was cast in by the contract she had signed with Meinhard and Bernauer just after her marriage.

Not only did she have to refuse a challenging opportunity to develop herself as an actress, but Meinhard and Bernauer's surprise abandoning of their theaters to Barnowsky left the "too beautiful" Marlene at liberty. Barnowsky wanted to be Reinhardt, and while no one thought he had Reinhardt's gifts, he had Reinhardt's *stars*. With the Sorcerer in Vienna, Barnowsky scooped up Elisabeth Bergner, Wilhelm Dieterle, Fritz Kortner, and Rudi's best friend (Heidede's godfather), Rudolf Forster.

Marlene may have attempted another charming flirtation, but it was leaning on Forster that worked. Barnowsky conceded Marlene "threw herself body and soul into her work," but was perplexed by her conviction that she was a tragedienne when not viewing herself as an ingenue. Neither fit very well with her bold habit of cutting in on dancing couples at parties and going around looking "like a portrait by Toulouse-Lautrec." Nevertheless, he gave her a job, and Lautrec would have applauded.

George Bernard Shaw's *Back to Methuselah* opened in September complete with *Musik und Tanz*. Part One of Shaw's History of History played at one theater at the same time that Part Two was being rehearsed and opened in a second in November. Marlene was in both. Shaw's romp featured Wilhelm Dieterle as Cain, Fritz Kortner as Confucius and Napoleon, the great Tilla Durieux as Lilith and the Delphic Oracle, and Marlene as Eve in a body stocking. She got reviews and a chill.

Barnowsky kept her on, ignoring her pleas for roles that were either tragic or virginal. In February 1926 he sent her from Eden to Venice in *Duel on the Lido*, a satire starring Rudolf Forster, Fritz Kortner, and a young actress called Lucie Mannheim, a serious future rival.

Also in the cast was an actor called Veit Harlan, whose claim to fame should not go unremarked. As the pet director of Dr. Joseph Goebbels, Harlan's film of Lion Feuchtwanger's *Jew Süss* was the most infamous (and successful) anti-Semitic film the Nazis ever made. Harlan later claimed he was forced to make it, but documents reveal that he courted the job with Master Race fervor. Klaus Mann's novel *Mephisto* (and the 1981 movie) was based on the actor Gustav Gründgens, but Mephistos were many in the Berlin theater world Marlene knew. Her later anti-Nazi stance was shaped by intimate acquaintance with the cast of Third Reich characters—and victims. *(Duel on the Lido* was a little paradigm of the future: Author Hans Rehfisch became an exile and teacher at New York's New School; greatly admired director Leopold Jessner wound up a script reader for Walter Wanger in Hollywood; both Fritz Kortner and Lucie Mannheim were driven into exile; Rudolf Forster, best friend and godfather to Heidede, found Hollywood and Broadway insufficiently awed by himself and went back to gather awe from the new masters of Berlin; Viet Harlan became the preeminent Mephisto director.)

Duel on the Lido was very modern stuff, even for 1926. Marlene swerved about alarmingly in silk pantsuit, slippers, and monocle as a French man-trap vacationing on the Lido. The type was called a *garçonne*, a fast young woman who dresses and behaves like an androgynous young man. They were so common around Berlin that the leading weekly had pleaded in headlines "Enough Already!" to girls in wolf's clothing. It would not be Marlene's last appearance in pants.

Critics thought her costume failed to disguise her "agreeable femininity," and her "saucy, quick-tongued impertinence" embodied the "carefree morality of the modern girl." One singled her out for playing "not 'demonic-ecstatic,' but icily." Mini-vamp was giving way to mini-cool.

She went directly into a drawing-room comedy, *The Rubicon*, for Barnowsky and star-director Ralph Arthur Roberts, with whom she had worked in *From Nine to Nine* right after her marriage. Her best *Rubicon* review came from Uncle Willi; it was his favorite. It was also the eighth time she had been cast as French. There was something exotic about her, not virginal, not tragic, and more on the way.

Rudi was now working in Berlin for the one-time Hungarian journalist turned producer-director Alexander Korda, Joe May having withdrawn from production (and from Rudi) following his daughter's suicide. Rudi had something of Korda's high-living style and Marlene helped supplement it by going from featured roles in the theater to bits or even extra work on films Rudi oversaw with his famously roving eye. She got a small role in Korda's

A Modern Dubarry, starring Maria Corda (from whom her husband borrowed his name). The picture was so overproduced it sank like a stone in a soufflé. Marlene (billed as Marlaine, perhaps because it looked French), played a Parisian playgirl. She was spoiled and petulant and got to cry and tear a handkerchief to tatters. Reviews noted "the decor [was] worth more than the film."

"Marlaine" had four quick scenes, and though she is overanimated, she is more modern than the star and far prettier, which is *never* the job of a bit player. Especially not when an article supposed to be about the star in the *Berliner Zeitung* begins: "The beautiful Marlene Dietrich runs between the tables wearing an ermine cape. . . ."

The writer of the piece was the one-time screen-test cameraman Stefan Lorant, now writing for Berlin's leading daily. When Maria Corda read about "the beautiful Marlene Dietrich" she slapped the smile from his face. It was all typos and gremlins, he protested, which may have been true, because, prescient as ever, he still could see no future for Marlene in films.

"Why don't you do something else?" tact inquired.

"I'll get there yet," ambition explained.

Alexander Korda, the weary Hungarian, advised Rudi's wife to go home and bake cakes like a good little *Hausfrau*. He would live to rue (and pay for) the suggestion.

Any cakes Marlene baked were for Heidede. She and Rudi dined out. They continued to raise temperatures and eyebrows on their elegant prowls through Berlin nightlife, helpfully financed by more extra work in films like *Madame Wants No Children*, another Korda (and Corda) French society comedy in which Marlene was reduced to a dance extra. She filled the same minuscule function in Korda's *My Wife's Dancing Partner* (*Dance Mad* in England). Working with her on the latter picture was the future Paris celebrity photographer Alexander Choura, friendly then with both Marlene and Rudi. Choura never forgot the picture. It ended his friendship with Marlene because during shooting he introduced production manager Rudi to a Russian dancer he knew who called herself Tamara Matul.

Marlene knew Tamara Matul, too. Her real name was Nikolaeyevna, she was several years younger than Marlene, and the two may have danced together on cabaret and revue stages before Marlene graduated from the chorus. They would work together again shortly, when Marlene had a leading role in a hit musical and Tamara was still just a showgirl, leaving her time to chat backstage with Rudi while Marlene was on stage becoming a star.

Rudi was bound to meet *a* Tamara one way or another at one time or another. But open marriage is not the same as *no* marriage. It is commonly assumed that Marlene's extra roles for Korda were desperation jobs secured by Rudi to finance champagne evenings in black tie. Perhaps so, but keeping an eye on Heidede's father may have been motivation enough, as Marlene was being better paid, better noticed, and better challenged in the theater. *And* in movies Rudi had nothing to do with. Marlene was working night and day while Rudi cheered her on with advice from the nightclub trenches.

Simultaneous with her bits for Korda, she was making two other films, and not as an extra. In one she was a co-star. Both films were for a minor star and producer called Ellen Richter, whose pictures were directed by her husband, Dr. Willi Wolff. The first picture, *Chin Up, Charly*, was a comedy about the double standard. It was not quite a feminist brief, but a look at jazz-age sexual politics, when sexual mores were changing as fast as Zelda and Scott Fitzgerald changed dance steps. Marlene played another chic young flapper (French), complete with monocle, and reviewers found it all "mediocre" and "not for the overly sophisticated."

The second picture was a Richter Production *sans* Richter. Wolff was impressed enough by Marlene in *Chin Up, Charly* to cast her in the co-starring role opposite Reinhold Schünzel in *The Bogus Baron*, based on a popular operetta.

Marlene got second billing to Schünzel, who would go on to direct the original *Viktor/Viktoria* and a delicious *Amphitryon* (before the Lunts *or* Cole Porter discovered it) and play Germans in Hollywood exile in pictures like *Notorious* and *Golden Earrings*, "together again" with Marlene.

The Bogus Baron is a farce revolving around an attempt to marry Sophie (Marlene) to the rich but bad-mannered Baron von Kimmel ("A man with ten million can afford bad manners!"). He skips out just as Sophie is ready to land his millions, and a wandering hobo (Schünzel) is hired to impersonate him. Operetta stuff, indeed.

Marlene wears her monocle again, and despite hair that photographs dark and a figure that photographs full, she comes to life on screen as a beautiful young woman on the make. She's good-natured and shallow, drives like a demon, smokes cigarettes, flashes her legs like semaphores, makes a charming fool of herself trying to impress the "baron" by singing and playing the piano (the scene cries for sound).

The whole *picture* cries for sound. This was an operetta, after all, dramaturgically no sillier than *No, No, Nanette* or *Lady, Be Good!* and equally impoverished without the songs. This was Marlene's best screen work to date, shrugged off by critics. One can only wonder how the picture worked with melodies wafting up from the pit, for her performance suggests the very idea of music filled her with vitality and assurance.

*　　*　　*

Music accompanied Marlene everywhere *except* on the silent screen. She was hardly ever without her portable phonograph, which played (incessantly) everything from Ravel and Debussy to Irving Berlin and Whisperin' Jack Smith. There was music in the theater, to be sure, and even as Marlene was bouncing from one film to another by day, she was working by night onstage, back in the one-time circus in which she had played in *The Taming of the Shrew:* the Grosses Schauspielhaus.

Reinhardt had never succeeded in making the huge house pay and turned it over to dancer-choreographer Erik Charell, whose hugely popular musicals would soon include the durable *White Horse Inn.* Charell rivaled Ziegfeld or Cochran in showmanship. His revues flowed along on melody reminiscent of Gershwin or Youmans or Kern when it wasn't actually *their* music that was playing. His shows were lavish, leggy, and the rage, so popular that an industrial psychologist wrote a ponderous tome about the phenomenon titled *Girlkultur.*

Erik Charell's shows weren't nude (many shows were); they didn't have to be. He took over the former circus from Reinhardt in 1923–1924, presenting Paul Whiteman and His Orchestra, a breakthrough blast of American jazz. Rudolf Nelson retaliated by importing Josephine Baker and La Revue Nègre from Paris, from which Charell stole Baker's partner, Louis Douglas, so café au lait he had to wear blackface when performing, and made him his live-in assistant, too.

Charell's 1926–1927 extravaganza was *From Mouth to Mouth* with dialogue by humorist Hans Reimann and music by almost everybody. The score included Jerome Kern's "Who?," Irving Caesar's "I'm a Little Bit Fonder of You," the Charleston hit "Go South," and as antidote to the acidic modernity of Friedrich Holländer, there was syrup from Rudolf Friml.

The show was two lavish acts of four extravagant scenes each: five children fantasize in the Garden of Eden about Things to Come. After intermission they met in Marienbad to relate what happened After the Fall.

The five "children" were stars of cabaret and theater. Curt Bois had been a famous performer since 1906 at the age of five and would turn up in American exile in *Casablanca.* Claire Waldoff was a cabaret favorite, a cross between a calliope and a hurdygurdy in need of oil; Erika Glässner (who had driven Emil Jannings to murder in *Tragedy of Love)* was mistress of ceremonies.

Glässner fell ill, not on opening night, but not long after, and left the show. Maybe it was appendicitis but no one really remembers. What they remember is Marlene—anticipating Ruby Keeler and *42nd Street* by half a decade—going on in her place.

Boy-about-town Hubert "Hubsie" von Meyerinck (he had been in

Manon with Marlene) was eyewitness to what happened: "You wore a yellow dress. It was long, with a train and a rose-red ruffle at the neck. You casually leaned your head . . . toward your shoulder and sang some song by some modern tunesmith. You were mistress of ceremonies . . . and your sensuous, exciting legs moved you along the runway in a slow, bored calm.

"It wasn't actually anything you played or *did*; it was exactly the 'nothing' [of it] that later made you famous. Out of this 'nothing' born of indifference (or so it seemed) you created a style . . . and not just a style, but your Art. With a glance, with a breathy word you said more than a knockabout comedienne with an entire scene."

It is seldom possible to say exactly when, why, and how a performer finds a style, but this sounded like the when. Many in Berlin believed the why and how came from co-star Claire Waldoff, as much a symbol of her sort of Berlin as boy-about-town Hubsie was of his.

Waldoff at forty-two was an institution, a comic provincial who was also a frank and cheerful lesbian. Her mannishness raised no eyebrows in Berlin. She had worked for the impresario Charles Cochran in England, made recordings (which still sell), and her life would be made into a movie called *Claire Berolina*, which elevated her to a symbol of Berlin and victim of the Third Reich. (Her comedy routine about a certain Hermann gave offense to a certain Göring.)

Rumors were so open about Marlene's debt and attraction to Waldoff that Janet Flanner, *The New Yorker*'s Genêt, heard them on her Paris *Girlkultur* grapevine and put the offbeat couple in print not long after. Waldoff's hefty wing settled around the long-legged newcomer, and Berlin buzzed with imitations of Waldoff's beer-barrel coo: "How bee-oo-tee-ful the child is!"

It is now a commonplace among survivors of the Golden Twenties that Waldoff formed Marlene's style, teaching her the art of putting over a song without a legitimate voice. Curt Bois, on stage then, thought this was euphemistic nonsense.

"Marlene's style was *Marlene*," said Bois, who found her "exceptionally sexy and beautiful. What Claire taught Marlene was *back*stage, and it made her *more* sexy and beautiful." Marlene confirmed the lesbian initiation in those stories she told on herself to shock Billy Wilder's dinner guests in Hollywood. Claire Waldoff had taught her about a kind of love that not only dared speak its name in Berlin of the twenties, but actually *sang* it. Marlene would shortly do the singing and it would make her famous.

What she learned backstage was that her appeal to women was as great as her appeal to men. Kenneth Tynan would call it sex without gender: What it was was sex with whatever gender one wanted to see or Marlene wanted to project—something for everyone.

*   *   *

Except Rudi. Rudi needed a job after Korda went to Hollywood, and got one as assistant to Harry Piel, a crowd-pleaser who styled himself "the Douglas Fairbanks of Germany" because of his daredevil stunts and plots. Piel was popular and served as his own director. He had already made over fifty films and would go on to create over one hundred, almost all unwatchable today.

His Biggest Bluff was another Piel potboiler, doubling chuckles and thrills as he played twins in a jewel thief caper with (surprise!) mix-ups in identity. Marlene played the part of a Parisian lady of little virtue with a passion for jewels.

It was low farce, low pay, low billing, and low is how she played it. None of that easy indifference, none of that head-on-the-shoulder ennui or breathy allure transferred from stage to screen. She lost it at the movies. This was her worst film work since her potato-in-a-pinafore debut four and a half years earlier. It provided only a paycheck and reviews in which Marlene was "quite impossible" and the picture "a Harry Piel film—that says it all."

That said it all for tandem careers in the Sieber family. Marlene would never work on another Rudi film again. There had been almost a dozen films, more than a dozen stage productions, but no apparent cumulative or reciprocal effect. It was still catch-as-catch-can, always starting over and getting nowhere. She had missed out on the Frankfurt job, which had offered a serious acting opportunity; instead she was playing second banana to third-rate Harry Piel.

If that was all the career help Rudi could be, it was lucky indeed she had Betty Stern.

Betty Stern was a friend of the famous or the famous-to-be. She was the wife of a buyer for a Berlin textile firm, and the Sterns lived with their young daughter, Nora, in an unpretentious two-room apartment in the Barbarossa Strasse, not far from the lively something-for-everyone El Dorado.

The apartment was small, but Betty Stern's heart large, and her appetite for show people insatiable. She was "incomparably carefree," someone remembered, and kept a costume of Elisabeth Bergner's under glass. She was star-stuck. She loved knowing stars or stars-to-be, knowing their hopes, their fears, their loves, their secrets, and loved bringing them together. In her modest surroundings she created a *salon*, a halfway house for those climbing ladders of the theater, movies, journalism, and publishing.

The more established salons of Berlin were like Rudolf Nelson's: elegant Sunday afternoons or evenings "at home" attended by Heinrich Mann or Arnold Schoenberg or Max Reinhardt, with a scattering of artistes like

Josephine Baker, or Paris's Mistinguett, or operetta star Fritzi Massary. Nelson's son Herbert (later a revue producer and songwriter himself) was young enough to appreciate the prominence of his father's fogies while casting an eager eye at the vibrant promise of Betty Stern's: "If you had already made it, you got invited to my father's. But if you didn't get invited to Betty Stern's, you weren't *going* to make it in Berlin. It was as simple as that."

The ticket of admission was talent or beauty or charm, plus a little "offering": liquor, sweets, cheese, cocaine (it was everywhere in Berlin), anything to stock the larder and load the buffet.

Stern made sure there were plenty of free-loading journalists around to notice her favorites, and no one was more favorite than Marlene. She was Betty Stern's "bosom friend," as film historian Lotte Eisner put it. Eisner didn't like either of them much (she boasted improbably that her legs were better than Marlene's), but admitted that "every famous actor and director strolled through [Stern's] petit bourgeois apartment" and because of "her comic, uninhibited manner, [she] knew how to introduce the important people to each other, so that many films and projects began there."

Stern's enthusiasms took on an aura of prophecy. If she had Bergner's dress in a glass case, she had Bergner's challengers on the sofa. Her sense of discovery was uninhibited, infectious, and shrewd.

"Marlene, may I introduce Herr So-and-so? Marlene, do you already know Fräulein Whatshername? Marlene . . . Marlene," prattled Betty Stern for all to hear. One who heard was Erich Pommer's wife, Gertrud, who would remember.

Willi Forst heard, too, and didn't *have* to remember. Marlene tagged her luggage "Vienna" and tagged along.

Willi Forst *was* Vienna, with a dash of bitters instead of *Schlag*. He was then on the verge of a great career that would make him first a matinee idol, then a director who brought witty gallantry to films that were mostly musical and mostly about the waltz capital.

He had become popular in Berlin in Rudolf Nelson revues and was lured back to Vienna by Sascha-Film, Austria's only important film company, to star in *Café Electric*, to be directed by Gustav Ucicky, the illegitimate son (it was said) of Gustav Klimt.

Sascha-Film was headed by "Sascha"—Count Alexander Joseph Kolowrat-Krakowsky, or Count Kilowatt, as admirers called him. He owned grandiose palaces in Vienna and Prague and smaller castles in between. He was grandiose himself, weighing in at over three hundred and fifty pounds, and he could gobble down an entire goose at a single sitting. He was dedicated to creating an Austrian film entity to rival Berlin's and had earlier produced a spectacular *Sodom and Gomorrah* directed by the Hungarian Mihály Kértèsz, who would become pronounceable and famous in Hollywood as Michael Curtiz, making films like *Casablanca*. Kolowrat was convinced that *Café Electric* could be something entirely new that would put Vienna on the filmmaking map.

So could "a young actress with magnificent legs" who was trying to change her luck by changing her address. She was already in Vienna appearing in an intimate revue called *Three's Company* with popular comedian Max Brod before going into rehearsal for the sensational American stage hit *Broadway*. Kolowrat looked at her the way he would have eyed a state banquet; Forst, to no one's surprise, demanded her; director Ucicky (a Mephisto to come) demanded a test.

Karl Hartl, later a director and head of Sascha-Film, was an assistant then and remembered that "Dietrich appeared for the screen test in a red suit with a cloche hat. . . . She had the feeling she was not photogenic and it might be better to devote herself to the stage. Her solo tests weren't very helpful, so we made more with Willi Forst in a love scene. In view of their romance, it wasn't especially hard."

Marlene played a magnate's daughter who goes bad for the love of a petty thief and pimp (Forst) who hangs out in the lively but low Café Electric. The film generously featured Marlene's legs doing the Charleston or Black Bottom or just stretching after a night in Forst's bed. She plays jazz records and goes from bed to worse, rifling Daddy's safe to provide proof of her passion. She shakes her bare, broad shoulders with will-o'-the-whip impatience, and otherwise makes no advance over her earlier film work.

Critics thought her either "a spirited and very gifted actress," or "unmistakably full of talent, but miscast," victim of a role that was "too one-sided."

The subplot to *Café Electric* was two-sided. There was Forst and an actor called Igo Sym. In *Café Electric* his love for a bad girl gone good counterpointed Marlene's good girl gone bad. Sym had looks and Bavarian charm and liked boys and music and Marlene. During the making of *Café Electric*, he taught her to play the musical saw, an instrument of limited challenge from which she would extract limitless mileage in the future.

Café Electric failed to provide anything Count Kolowrat had hungered for. The count felt poorly during shooting and went to Carlsbad for a cure. Surgery and a rapid wasting followed. Shrunken to a fraction of his normal girth, he screened *Café Electric* in his hospital room and expressed a dying wish: to gaze upon the legs of Marlene in the flesh. He got his wish, the legend goes, though Willi Forst said the story wasn't true, that the count saw no one, and wished no one to see *him* in his emaciated state, but Marlene may not have told Forst everything, either. "Count Kilowatt" dimmed permanently in December 1927 just after the picture opened in

Vienna, but he would become an odd footnote in movie history. When Marlene played a Viennese streetwalker turned spy in *Dishonored* for Josef von Sternberg she was called X-27, but her civilian name was Widow Kolowrat.

Willi Forst, not *Three's Company* or *Café Electric*, had drawn Marlene to Vienna, but ambition and professional opportunity kept her there. They clearly overrode whatever homesickness she felt for her husband and child.

Rudi could fend for himself and headwaiters were there to help when he couldn't. Heidede at two and a half had her grandmother Josephine, her cousin Hasso, Uncle Willi and Aunt Jolly, and other relatives as well, but she didn't have a mother. She was not, strictly speaking, an abandoned child, but it is hard to imagine she didn't notice and feel her mother's absence at a crucial moment of childhood. Perhaps the best that can be said of Marlene's professional and emotional mobility is that it prepared the child for more of the same at even more crucial moments of her development.

Marlene may well have relied on Josephine to supply the sort of reliable good-general discipline she had valued so highly herself, but this was surrogate nurturing, however expert or efficient. Marlene may also have felt that her working—wherever and with whomever—compensated for Rudi's lackluster professional progress, particularly as his career seemed more and more to consist mainly in promoting or admiring Marlene's own. Wherever and with whomever.

Motherhood (and grandmotherhood) would become major and lasting components of the legend to come, and there is no particular reason to doubt Marlene's claims of deep, genuine maternal feelings. Nor is there any reason to ignore the fact that while her child was little more than an infant, Marlene was working, far from home, and hoofing.

Broadway was a backstage story, a Manhattan melodrama by Philip Dunning and director George Abbott. It had been a sensation in New York and London and opened at Vienna's Kammerspiele in September.

The play was jazz, snappy dialogue, hard-boiled characters and bootleg gin, tap dancing to the rhythm of bullets. Guns are "gats," gangsters "rats," and girls are "girlies" no better than they should be. The cast includes speakeasy sharpies and a ham-footed (and hare-brained) hoofer called Roy, who says things like, "Every night is opening night!" and wants to know when the Sullivan Act goes on. Six chorus girls flesh out the Paradise Club wearing as little as *Girlkultur* and the law will allow. The waiter, serving gin in teacups, was played by a baby-faced actor named Peter Lorre.

Marlene was Ruby, the smart-mouthed, hard-drinking one. It wasn't the best of the chorus girl roles, or even second best. Best, or most prominent, was Billie, the innocent of the troupe, but Marlene's Ruby was loud and brash, giving her a hard-edged contemporary role and a chance to exhibit her legs nonstop along with some of the musical comedy technique she had picked up in *From Mouth to Mouth.*

Broadway was a hit and Marlene stayed on in Vienna. She was cast in Carl Sternheim's *The School of Uznach or: New Objectivity.* The satire opened in late November at the jewel-box Theater in der Josefstadt, where a giant chandelier hung over the orchestra and had (and has today) to be hoisted at curtain time to let the audience see the stage.

The play was set in a progressive school and Marlene was progressive, too, a modern maiden who announces her wedding night will "make world history!" She didn't make world history, but she was convincing. "Among the girls," wrote a critic, "Marlene Dietrich expressed most honestly what the type should be: a beautiful, impulsive, unthinking young chatterbox." The critic was Felix Salten, author of *Bambi.*

While the play alternated in repertory with *Abie's Irish Rose,* Marlene spent time with a young director called Otto Preminger, who tried persuading her to stay in Vienna by taking her home to meet the family.

That didn't work, so he tried to get her a contract. Preminger's producers thought she had no talent or future, but he knew that if she played hard, she worked hard. She may have spent the year-end holidays with Forst, Sym, or Preminger—or all three. What is certain is, she was working. Diligent ambition came before anything.

She spent Heidede's third birthday, Christmas, and her own twenty-sixth birthday on stage. The day after her birthday, December 28, 1927, as the chandelier was rising in the Theater in der Josefstadt, something curious happened on a screen in Los Angeles: Al Jolson sank on one knee. He stretched out his arms, opened his mouth, and—changing everything—started to sing.

FIVE

BREAKTHROUGH

1928 - 1929

Vienna, for all its Old World charm, was still Old World. No place to be during a revolution, and sound in movies was nothing less. Except, of course, for Berlin's box-office champion, the one film star in the world with no sound worries at all: Rin Tin Tin. Nor was Marlene worried, not with "that voice." She never expressed anxiety about the demands of sound, but its demands—and benefits—would come slowly, resisted mightily by the moguls who had to pay for all the new technology. Talk—in movies—would not come cheap.

The primitive disk process inspired the joke that a parrot was "a canary that's taken up Vitaphone," but movie sound would not long remain on disks that broke, skipped, or went out of sync. Nor would it remain only in Hollywood.

Nowhere in the world was there a studio, movie house, or laboratory; a set, costume, camera, or electrical shop; a distribution or advertising or publicity or casting department not altered by sound. First it paralyzed the industry, then the camera. It created technical havoc, commercial chaos, and artistic regression. There was every reason to block, thwart, or forget it, except one: Audiences loved it.

They loved their new radios and gramophones, too, still infant novelties, but that competition helped prepare audience ears for tinny sound leaking through screens perforated with little pinholes to let the squawking through. The big American radio networks were only just forming (NBC in 1926) and breakable disks, far more than personal appearances, introduced American jazz to European ears, to composers and to performers like Marlene, who swung her portable phonograph from Berlin to Vienna and back again. She would soon appear in a musical in which Whisperin' Jack Smith (not known ever to have visited Berlin) would "star" on a Berlin stage—on a gramophone. Kurt Weill had already composed a "tango for Victrola" for an opera, and Weill and Brecht would soon write full-length works for radio, including a cantata for orchestra and chorus celebrating Charles Lindbergh's solo flight across the Atlantic.

Movie sound was crossing the Atlantic, too, though the sound-on-film process that would become standard originated in Berlin in the first place. Three physicists developed what they first called "the singing flame," then Tri-Ergon (three worked on it). It was demonstrated in Berlin in 1922 to great public excitement. William Fox (whose name survives in 20th Century-Fox) bought it, but was too overextended to use it, and rival Hollywood czars didn't much want him to. He renamed it Movietone, and it was absorbed by a cartel composed of RCA, American Telephone and Telegraph, and many lawyers. (Fox walked away with eighteen million dollars, rich reward for a finely tuned ear.) Sound on film became the standard by 1929, replacing Vitaphone's unreliable disks. Berlin had had it since 1922 and had shrugged.

They shuddered now, along with Hollywood's Mayers and Thalbergs and Zukors and Schulbergs, for whom silence had been golden. The box office would make the decision for them, but Hollywood's dominance meant that sound film from the very beginning spoke loudest when speaking English—or American.

Marlene spoke American. Ruby in *Broadway* did, anyway, and when *The School of Uznach* closed in Vienna in January, Marlene was already plumping for a role in Barnowsky's Berlin production of *Broadway*. She turned again to Rudolf Forster to help her get what she had wanted all along, the role of innocent ingenue Billie.

Barnowsky was "indecisive," but came to his senses and cast the "portrait by Toulouse-Lautrec" as the same Ruby she had played in Vienna. Berlin's *Broadway* was wholly new except for Marlene and Harald Paulsen, who again played Roy, the dimwitted hoofer. The new production would lead both to the biggest shows of the year: Paulsen to Mack the Knife in *The Threepenny Opera* and Marlene to her breakthrough as a star.

The Berlin casting reunited her with her one-time cabaret coach Rosa Valetti as Lil, a piano-pounding chanteuse who has seen better days. The girls in the chorus were all new competition for Marlene, and she rushed off to tone things up after the whipped cream of Vienna.

She took boxing lessons from Berlin's "terrible Turk," Sabri Mahir, boxing instructor to bankers, magnates, and *Grand Hotel* novelist Vicki Baum. The lady writer called Mahir "a roaring tiger, a slave driver, a man of steel and stone," but he was just a German from Cologne named Sally Mayer. Another *Broadway* chorus girl, Elisabeth Lennartz, remembered "what he was able to do to a body! [Marlene and I] were his most faithful followers. He was insane and took no care of our nerves, but [he] knew what a body *was*." He knew so much that Marlene brought Heidede along so he could straighten little legs that had begun to bow during Marlene's long Vienna absence. They straightened.

Marlene recovered from the "roaring tiger" with massage, and Mahir's masseuse indiscreetly gave an interview confiding the intimate secrets of Marlene's corpus delectable: "Long legs . . . short waist."

Athletics and frustration at not playing Billie inspired scene stealing. Käthe Haack, a Reinhardt actress, witnessed the theft: "[Marlene] acted very close to the audience, right at the front of the stage. She was very, very sexy. She was lying on the floor and sort of bicycled with her breathtakingly beautiful legs. . . . we all talked . . . *every*body talked. . . . Marlene's name had already become a byword for sexiness, for beauty."

Calisthenics helped her steal the show and break her arm. It was a first fracture in a career plagued by bone breaks, an inheritance from milk shortages in childhood. Elisabeth Lennartz discovered only later that the break had occurred. Marlene draped her arm "very elegantly in a chiffon shawl. This looked fantastic, and only later did she mention her extreme pain. We hadn't known anything. She always used these chiffon things, or furs, [and] was able to hide it all."

Hiding pain was an inheritance from Josephine and earned respect. So did hard work and a reputation among co-workers for being always punctual, always professional. "Daring," too, said Lennartz. Marlene didn't wear panties or a bra on stage or off, which many considered "advanced."

* * *

"She was very beautiful, very young," remembered Barnowsky's then-assistant, a young playwright named Felix Joachimssohn. "We sat next to each other [as] I was supervising the rehearsal. She showed me a picture of her little daughter, and said, 'You know, I'm going to be a big star one of these days.' I smiled."

Joachimssohn would savor the irony of disbelief. In Hollywood exile he married Deanna Durbin, changed his name to Felix Jackson, and changed his *mind* when he wrote a script for Marlene called *Destry Rides Again*. But in 1928 he saw only the determination of a young woman whose talent seemed all in her legs, whose emotional gifts seemed limited to fondness for a baby photo she showed around, as if a snapshot compensated for not being at home tending to *Kinder, Küche, Kirche*.

Marlene had returned to Berlin not entirely without career capital, which may have heightened her boldness on stage. She had the promise of a Reinhardt contract in her pocket from the new artistic director of the Reinhardt theaters. Robert Klein had gone to Vienna to see an actress in *Broadway* (the one playing the Billie part Marlene coveted).

He bought a ticket, saw Billie, and decided to leave. Then one of the chorus girls caught his eye. "Fascinating," he recalled. "I decided to stay. After the performance I offered her a contract for Berlin."

It guaranteed three years in Berlin's most prestigious theaters, but Marlene didn't sign right away. She may have thought Klein was using his Reinhardt calling card to get a closer look at her legs. He soon did.

As she was bicycling on stage in Berlin, Klein was preparing an intimate musical revue. "There wasn't sufficient sex appeal on the stage and I remembered Marlene. We called her and I asked her whether she had any special talents which might be used in a revue. She said she could play the violin and the saw. I had never heard anyone play the saw and I asked her to display this art for us [the] next day. . . . She took her legs apart, put the saw in between and played."

And got the job.

New York was then optimistic and exclamatory with shows like *Hit the Deck!* and *Good News!*, but musical theater in Berlin had a keener edge, with harsher harmonies. There had been attempts to marry jazz and opera long before Gershwin, and in just a few months Weill and Brecht would premiere their *Threepenny Opera*, which would have startled *Nanette* and alarmed *Rosalie*.

The Great War and its long shadows were never quite driven away by the footlights' glow. The twenties were golden, but they were also the calm before the storm troopers. Premonitions are easy to read into lyrics that bite, to hear in melodies discordant with echoes of the recent past. Broadway celebrated showgirls and "the American century"; Berlin celebrated show-girls and survival. In America they argued about Darwin; in Berlin they danced nude and bantered lyrics informed by Freud. Marlene's new revue signaled the "new reality" in its title: *It's in the Air*.

The show was basically five actors and an onstage jazz band, but it became the big hit of mid-1928. It would have been the biggest hit of the year had it not been for Brecht and Weill and Mack the Knife, who opened in August, relegating *It's in the Air* to second place.

The locale was postinflation paradise: a department store. Children get lost, grow up happy in consumer heaven. Music was by Mischa Spoliansky, with lyrics and book by Marcellus Schiffer, an Aubrey Beardsley character who wore dead-white makeup, was addicted to cocaine, and would soon be a suicide.

It's in the Air was designed for Schiffer's wife, the highly stylized Margo Lion. Skeleton-slender but supple as a question mark, she was French, exotic, and otherworldly, spoke and sang perfect German, and was rumored to care as little for men as her husband did for women.

Former cabaret performer Robert Forster-Larrinaga directed a cast in-cluding Lion, Oskar Karlweis, Hubsie von Meyerinck, Josephine Baker's ex-dance partner Louis Douglas, Marlene, a chorus of ten dancing girls, and phonograph records by Whisperin' Jack Smith.

The show opened in June, an instant sensation. Marlene had nine major scenes and with Margo Lion sang Berlin's biggest hit until "Mack the Knife" took over in August. "My Best Girlfriend" was a breezy lesbian duet. Margo Lion and Marlene played it for chic as young matrons shopping for lingerie, exciting each other with undies. The nonchalance made it a scandal, and to add a third dimension to the ménage, Oskar Karlweis joined in a final chorus about the surprising things to be discovered at the peek-aboo counter.

Marlene later claimed (rather charmingly) that the girl-girl part was all an innocent misunderstanding, but no one misunderstood it then. Mar-lene packed them in. The musical saw remained in the show (there was a "music department," too). Klein said, "The box office informed me that elderly gentlemen had come to see the show twenty-five times, in-sisting on front row seats and making sure that Miss Dietrich was playing that night."

"My Best Girlfriend" was recorded (Marlene's first recording) and be-came a hit along with an eight-minute potpourri of the score by the original cast. Typically impudent was "Kleptomaniacs," in which Marlene and her good pal Hubsie revealed the therapeutic value of shoplifting:

Perhaps it sounds pathetic,
But we find it quite magnetic;
Though our palms and pants get wettish,
It is nothing but a fetish.

We're not in a financial fix,
It's not to do with wealth.
We do it for the sexual kicks,
And now —
We feel in perfect health!
Oh, yes!
We feel in perfect health!

This was the breakthrough. Herbert Ihering, the leading drama critic in Berlin who did *not* write in Roman numerals or on tablets, singled out her "ravishing, splendid" songs, "delicate carriage and weary elegance." He summed it up neatly: "This was perfection: an event."

Herbert Nelson remembered that "with *It's in the Air* Marlene became *the* girl in Berlin. No one in Berlin was unaware of her from that moment forward."

Including *Girlkultur* connoisseur Dr. Karl Vollmoeller, who brought along Max Reinhardt. It was then Reinhardt experienced "discovery" and was astonished to learn that the scandalous creature with the legs, the saw, and the fetishes had been and was—of all things—a Reinhardt actress!

The elegance of Lion's style influenced Marlene as greatly on stage as Jolly Felsing's chic had in life. Marlene's and Lion's voices were similar (almost indistinguishable on recordings) in timbre, phrasing, and that throwaway weariness that struck Hubsie and the critics. One hears Marlene playing her voice as she must have played her violin, with subtle tonal variation and insinuating humor Stradivarius would have envied. Marlene was never as stylized as Lion; she had sex appeal, and Lion—like Claire Waldoff—did not.

Now she was a star on stage, and as she sang to her "best girlfriend" before the footlights, Rudi sang to *his* offstage. Tamara Matul was one of the dancing girls in *It's in the Air*. Marlene kept on singing.

She and her legs were suddenly everywhere. The Etam "artificial silk" stocking company used them to publicize their product in playbills; local arbiters ended a perennial search, deciding they were "the most beautiful" in town; it was said they were insured for a million marks with Lloyd's of London (they weren't, but nobody cared). An American magazine printed Marlene's first photograph to appear in the New World, the caption introducing "Fräulein Marceline [sic] Dietrich, the pretty young German actress and film star who is at present fulfilling an engagement in Berlin."

Several. Robert Land, an UFA director, saw *It's in the Air* and cast her in the title role of *Princess O-la-la*, another operetta-based film. The stars were Walter Rilla and Carmen Boni as prince and princess of an arranged marriage. They don't know about "love," but Chichotte (Marlene) does. As "love instructress" she lends the title her *nom de lit* and the film her naughty allure.

Princess O-la-la was her thirteenth picture. Only now that she was a talked-about stage star did the movie world waken to a "new Garbo." *Film-Kurier*, Berlin's *Variety*, devoted its entire review to her, noting her Garbo-like qualities and her suitability for G. W. Pabst's film of *Pandora's Box*, subject of a well-publicized Lulu search. "They've already spun [Dietrich] into a new film [the *Kurier* wrote]. Is Pabst going to pass right by this Lulu? What will film make of this charming kitten? What *can* film make of her? Dietrich plays a coquette . . . and turns it into a Garbo experience . . . in which an artistic director can find endless expressiveness. He need only guard against coarsening her qualities. And then the eyes . . . ! O-la-la."

Another announced, "Marlene Dietrich achieve[s] her first film success. There are the Garbo eyes, the Swanson nose, the movements of clear erotic tension and fulfillment we have until now resigned ourselves to admiring in American actresses. An entire generation of hollow temptresses can be dethroned by this actress." Another noted "the glance and persuasive eroticism of a Garbo." Berlin's leading weekly published a Garbo vs. Dietrich cover.

G. W. Pabst read *Film-Kurier* (everyone did), but he wanted Louise Brooks for Lulu in *Pandora's Box*, though Brooks (or Paramount, to whom she was under contract) hadn't responded to his offer. Reluctantly, Pabst decided to cast Marlene, perhaps knowing she had made her stage debut in the play. At the last moment Brooks accepted the role, snatching away what looked like a once-in-a-lifetime coup.

Brooks later said Marlene was actually in Pabst's office to sign the contract when he received word Brooks was available after all. Pabst remarked (said Brooks) that "Dietrich was too old and too obvious—one sexy look and the picture would become a burlesque."

Marlene was twenty-six and Brooks twenty-one. *Pandora's Box* confirms Brooks's freedom from the obvious; Pabst may have been right. Marlene was never unconscious of her effects, and innocence never her mode. It was her self-awareness that suggested so much, was so provocative on screen. With Brooks what one saw was what one got, an uninflicted sexual clarity Pabst wanted. *Pandora* was a disaster when released (critics rejected the non-German star) and did nothing for Brooks until it became a cult film many years too late.

Marlene didn't waste time with regrets. By September she was back on stage in George Bernard Shaw's *Misalliance* as Hypatia, daughter of underwear magnate Lord Tarleton. The cast included Reinhardt's first wife, Else Heims, as her mother, and as the emancipated aviatrix, the beautiful Lili Darvas, wife of Ferenc Molnár, author of *Liliom*.

Marlene was now a focal point in Berlin. She was working with a confidence onstage that recaptured that trademark "weary elegance." Hypatia in *Misalliance* thinks herself "such a ripping girl," and Shaw prescribed "movements that flash out of a waiting stillness, boundless energy and audacity held in leash." For once she was cast correctly, with a subtext to play: vitality *and* restraint. She had a speech with ironic personal relevance: "I can imagine all sorts of men I could fall in love with," she tells her mother, "but I never seem to meet them. Of course one can get into a state about any man . . . but who would risk marrying a man for love? *I* shouldn't."

Critics paid attention to Marlene now, but found it hard to raise their sights above her skirts. Alfred Kerr wrote a Roman numeral over "legs under the jurisdiction of Marlene Dietrich [that] went way beyond middle class." Another said she had "a way of sitting that one certainly cannot characterize as discreet. If she showed less, it would still be enough." The critical whoop of delight was probably closest to what the audience felt and liked: "Marlene Dietrich nabs her man more with her charms (Legs! Legs!) than with her money."

It was Lili Darvas who sensed what reviewers didn't and defined Marlene's appeal and star quality at the same time. "[Marlene] had a quite rare ability [she said], the ability to stand completely motionless on stage and still draw the audience's expectant attention to her. . . . Marlene simply placed herself on the platform and smoked a cigarette—very slow and sexy—and the audience forgot there were other actors there. Her pose was so natural, there was so much melody in her voice, her gestures were so sparing, that she fascinated the audience as if she were a painting by Modigliani. . . . She possessed the most important quality for a Star: She could be great without doing anything at all."

At the same time she was doing nothing at all in *Misalliance*, director Robert Land cast her again in a film called *I Kiss Your Hand, Madame*. Sound had arrived in Berlin, but not what Darvas called the "melody in her voice."

The movie starred Harry Liedtke, the star of Marlene's first picture, *The Little Napoleon*. Both Marlene and Liedtke would be drowned out now by someone who wasn't even *in* the picture. The great tenor Richard Tauber sang the title song, making it world famous, but it was mimed on screen by Liedtke in the film's only sound sequence, which qualified it to boast of being Germany's first *Tonfilm* in the new sound hysteria.

Harry Liedtke was probably the most likable leading man in German film history. *I Kiss Your Hand, Madame* wasn't vintage Liedtke; it wasn't fresh apart from the song; Marlene wasn't original in it. It was another of her spoiled French girl parts, in which she flounced about with big shoulders and displayed high dudgeon that wasn't even very worldly.

The plot is a Russian-count-working-as-a-waiter concoction, in which divorcée-about-Paris Marlene falls for the count (Liedtke), then finds he is a waiter and pouts until discovering he really *is* a count. No independent woman here, and not much Marlene.

She has one or two nice romantic scenes, but mostly she is busy and shallow, powdering her nose often and with conviction. It is only after she realizes her error about "the waiter" that she softens, and there are sudden hints of the later Marlene. She becomes more expressive the less she does; the camera reads things *into* her.

The picture was a very big hit. It had some sound, a hit song, two box office names in Liedtke and Tauber, and the new girl in town. Louise Brooks saw it in Berlin and said what Marlene "couldn't wear she carried." Brooks described her as "caparisoned variously in beads, brocade, ostrich feathers, chiffon ruffles, and white rabbit fur, [galloping] from one lascivious stare to another." It's a good quote, but doesn't fit the picture. Critics of the day saw a very different Marlene, wasted in a film that was "banal."

"Marlene Dietrich has filmed in Vienna and Paris [sic]; isn't someone soon going to take this gifted actress—viewed with equal pleasure on the stage—off to America?" asked one. Another thought "Marlene Dietrich, whose aptitude for film has finally been recognized, plays charmingly the well-bred 'Madame' with the oft-serenaded hand." The Garbo comparison now turned to complaint: "Why must they give her the hairdo of the Swede, why stick her in Garbo's clothes? . . . Why not look for the personality of [Marlene Dietrich] herself, instead of forcing on her that of a stranger?"

Today it is hard to see what seemed so Garbo-like, but if the comparisons were inapt, they were good for Marlene's career and self-image. Berlin was the town that had let Garbo go to Hollywood without a murmur back when Marlene was delivering Heidede. Still, the Marlene of *I Kiss Your Hand, Madame* was far from the Garbo-like recluse offscreen, and everybody knew it. Fred Zinnemann was assistant cameraman on the picture and remembered her as "a good-time girl, especially with the crew. She had a good sense of humor, earthy, sometimes almost, well, smutty. She was *very* well-liked."

The real attraction was the voice of Richard Tauber anyway. Marlene was photographed with him for the front cover of *Film und Ton* (*Film and Sound*), and stories went around about them. One was that during *It's in the Air* Marlene so overplayed her then paramour Max Hansen's recording of the tongue-twister *"In Ulm und um Ulm und um Ulm herum"* (it means "In and Around Ulm") in her dressing room that Hubsie shouted at her, "Why don't you fall in love with Tauber, instead?!" and so, (Hubsie said), "she *did*." The other was that at a Tauber recital Marlene took a box seat, the better to extend madame's hand for kissing, and almost fell into the orchestra pit, neatly upstaging the great tenor with her homage.

She was a celebrity compared to Swanson and Garbo rather than *being* Swanson or Garbo. Perhaps this nettled her, compelling her to rush events. *It's in the Air* and *Misalliance* had advanced her greatly, but Robert Klein, who had produced both, was leaving the Reinhardt theaters and Marlene wanted to go with him.

"Marlene sent me a letter that she would prefer to work under my management to staying with Reinhardt," Klein remembered. "That same evening she came to see me at the famous Restaurant Horcher and there—in a *chambre séparée*—she signed a three-year contract with me."

That *chambre-séparée* contract would lead to Marlene's final Berlin stage appearance and the man and part to change her life. That contract would come close to costing her everything.

I Kiss Your Hand, Madame had opened tardily, more than a year after *The Jazz Singer*. Even with one song sequence it made it clear that sound was the future. Nothing anybody did from this time forward (except Chaplin) would count very much unless it could be heard as well as seen. The fissure between sound and silence into which films and careers would fall was widening and, as that breach widened, Marlene's career—at last in high gear—tumbled into it.

Hundreds of films became suddenly obsolete and unsalable, including some of the most accomplished silent films ever made. Some tried on their merits, like Josef von Sternberg's exquisite *Docks of New York*; others added sound bits to placate the patrons, like Garbo's *Woman of Affairs*; still others were "talkers" so bad they were *re*converted to silents, like Emil Jannings's *Betrayal* at Paramount, which would have been Jannings's (and Gary Cooper's) sound debut, except that not even Adolph Zukor could understand the sound track.

Eventually the means for silent exhibition would virtually disappear. The now standard twenty-four frames per second wasn't standard then; it was a speed for synchronization, an average of the varying running speeds of silent films, which had never been fixed. Silent film stock itself would be sent to the chemical baths to extract silver from the silver nitrate bases, and no museum or curator existed yet with vaults to save them.

It thus became possible for an actress like Marlene to downplay or deny her silent past with little danger that anyone would produce evidence to contradict her. Sound wiped the slate and memory clean, erasing whole careers with it.

A good case can be made that *without* sound Dietrich would never have become the great international star she became. All the comparisons to the biggest female stars in the world were based on her screen image, but mostly by critics *who knew her on stage*, where the "melody in her voice" was always there. Her film roles came very seldom from her previous film work; they resulted almost always from her constant rediscovery on stage. The sound of her was as important as the look of her, and she would become the first international star actually *created* by sound.

Ironically, her strongest bid for silent film stardom came at precisely the end of the era. It was the best picture of her early career, and though outmoded, obsolete, irrelevant—a cinematic buggy whip—it proved there was more to Marlene than legs.

The Woman One Longs For was a popular novel by Max Brod (not the actor of the same name with whom Marlene worked in Vienna) a writer who was part of the German-speaking Prague literary circle dominated by Franz Werfel and dwarfed by Franz Kafka, whose literary executor and editor this Brod was. The novel had been a bestseller in Germany and was published in England and America under the title *Three Loves* (the American film title). It typified Brod's obsession with the eternally elusive Female. The narrator fails to find Stascha at the Folies Bergère, in Berlin, Rome, Vienna, Serbia, or any of the other colorful locales in which he searches and despairs. He ends jaded and melancholy in Paris to tell his tale.

Brod was a journalist, too, and his personal literary ambitions would be satisfied only second-hand through Kafka, who begged Brod on his death-bed to burn his manuscripts. Brod did not. A malicious friend is said to have advised, "Max, why don't you burn *your* works instead?"

Brod threw *The Woman One Longs For* onto the reading public rather than the bonfire, and Marlene was cast as the title figure in the Terra Film production with first billing opposite Fritz Kortner, with whom she had worked several times on stage. The film greatly altered the novel to tell of Stascha and her lover, Dr. Karoff (Kortner) escaping to a luxurious Alpine resort after Karoff murders Stascha's husband. The dead husband and Karoff are two of Stascha's *Three Loves*. The third was Danish actor Uno Henning, who bore a marked resemblance to America's Gary Cooper.

Henning, as Henri, embarks on his wedding trip with the monied bride he has wed to save his family's smelting factory. He falls abruptly in love with Stascha, abandons his bride, pursues Stascha and Dr. Karoff to their Alpine resort (big New Year's Eve party), thwarts the criminal Karoff, and gets "the woman one longs for" killed. It was the closest Marlene would ever come to the tragic roles she longed for, and in it she gives the kind of performance that makes a star. At any other time it would have made one.

Director Kurt Bernhardt was not quite thirty in 1929 and wanted credit for discovering Marlene in the theater. "She was ravishingly beautiful," he said, "but I had a hell of a time selling her to the directors of this company, Terra Film. They said, 'Who is Marlene Dietrich? Nobody knows her.' I fought for her and finally got her through."

Giving first billing to an unknown was odd (she was unknown only to Bernhardt and Terra), but Bernhardt's claim had another, less arguable merit. He was the first to bring to the screen the Dietrich image the world would later know. Josef von Sternberg would usurp the claim, and Marlene's denial that she made such earlier films may account for Bernhardt's assertion that she had gone from being "a great pal" or "a good-time girl" to being "a real bitch."

"Marlene waged intrigues," he remembered, "one man against the other," pitting Kortner against himself in some divide-and-conquer plot of her own. This was exactly, he might have noted, the character she played in the film. It would not be the last time Marlene would adopt a screen role in life. The legend to come would, in fact, derive from a perceived merging of private personality with her screen image.

If Marlene was "an *intrigante*, pure and simple," as Bernhardt said, Josef von Sternberg was later neither pure nor simple. He not only poached Bernhardt's credit for the first real "Dietrich" performance, but did not hesitate to appropriate credit for UFA's first sound film, too, which was *also* directed by Bernhardt *(The Last Company)*. Sternberg seemed intent on erasing Bernhardt from history or barring him from the American industry, where Bernhardt might tell tales. When Sternberg was one of a handful of star directors with real power and Bernhardt was an escaping refugee trying to save his own life, he wrote to Sternberg in Hollywood asking for help. Sternberg loftily replied, "You want to come to Hollywood, Mr. Bernhardt? My only question is, as *what?*"

He got there and, as *Curtis* Bernhardt, forged a solid commercial career directing Bette Davis, Joan Crawford, Rita Hayworth, and others. No tension between director and star showed on screen in *The Woman One Longs For*. The picture is stylistically uneven and seems slow today, but is easily the best Marlene made before Sternberg, the first to capture her sympathetic eroticism and aura of ambiguity and mystery.

The most memorable sequence in *The Woman One Longs For* is one rare in films in that it *must* work for the rest to be credible. It is early in the film on the train platform, just as Henri is departing for his honeymoon. A window shade rises on the train, revealing behind an icy pane the face of Stascha (Marlene), gazing onto the midnight platform as if looking for a reason to go on living. She sees one in Henri. He also falls instantly, helplessly in love. He looks at her. She looks at him. They regard each other in a moment of suspended narration that tells all the story we need.

It is textbook-perfect filmmaking. Just at the end of the shots, when glances have set Fate wheeling with the train they will share, Fritz Kortner as Dr. Karoff rises in the frame behind Marlene, revealing himself as Nemesis. These few moments are masterful in their simplicity, and the rest of the picture works because they are. Marlene looking from her window is the key image in the film and in her career thus far. This is the film in which Marlene found "Dietrich," though she may not have known she had.

Significantly, Bernhardt complained that she ignored his direction. He said she was always seeking the light, and the film shows it. She had long been dissatisfied with the way she photographed. Part of her dissatisfaction was technical: film emulsions and lamp filaments were changing and rendered color values differently from film to film and lamp to lamp. Red-sensitive film darkened her hair because of its red highlights and often made her makeup look garish. Fred Zinnemann remembered that the lamps used on *I Kiss Your Hand, Madame* were outmoded because of the film's restricted budget, and that their effect had been to make harsh on film what was fresh in nature.

In addition, her nose had a slight uptilt at the end (the "Swanson nose" the critics cited), which earned her the irritating nickname Ducknose on film sets. From this minor flaw a whole mythology has grown, ranging from refusals to be photographed in profile to facial surgery, all of the stories false. The tilt of her nose had been apparent from the beginning, and she made no particular effort to avoid profile shots then or later (the evidence is ample), but concern about how she photographed was as vital to the actress as tone had been to the aspiring violinist.

The technician in Marlene had experimented. In Hollywood cameramen would claim they "invented the Dietrich face," as if it were something developed in a darkroom. It was Marlene who discovered the lighting that gave her face clarity and drama.

She found it in an automatic photo booth in Berlin, the kind that prints out cheap photographs on strips. She stepped into one to pose, actively searching for a look, and discovered that with a single overhead lamp, her hair went light, she had cheekbones, her pale blue eyes went dark, the upturned nose became straight. There would be sophisticated refinements of makeup and technique, but now the difficulty was getting cameramen to light her *her* way. Bernhardt tells us as much in his complaint: "She never moved her head from the spotlight. She stayed stiff and would talk to her partner indirectly *if the light guided her to.*"

Marlene's playing to the lights also gave her an oblique air, a hint of mystery. Without distance there is no glamour, and this is the first time she seems enigmatic rather than merely haughty or aloof.

When *The Woman One Longs For* was released, Terra Films (now allied with Hollywood's Universal) made the dire mistake of asking novelist Max Brod for a press endorsement. Brod replied with a broadside, firing off an article saying he had written both Terra *and* Bernhardt offering his aid and had not received so much as a reply. Bernhardt admitted it (also in print), wondering cavalierly "what use an answer could have been?" The noisy contretemps encouraged violently partisan reviews of the film, all about artistic integrity, all predictably on the side of the friend and editor of Kafka.

Marlene had begun a next picture (another silent) by the time the press furor broke and must have despaired when reading her reviews. "We see the lips, they say something, they move, [but] we hear nothing." All they heard was the score for the film, composed and conducted by none other than Dr. Giuseppe Becce, who had hired Marlene for the orchestra pit almost a decade before. His "Stascha" and "Are You the Happiness I Longed For?" became popular in Berlin and seemed more expressive to reviewers than the movie or Marlene.

Bernhardt was "overrated," Marlene a disappointment after the promise reviewers had seen in *I Kiss Your Hand, Madame.* The Garbo comparisons were now déjà vu. One critic deplored "vain efforts concerning Marlene Dietrich, who after this lifeless, passionless performance must be given up as any kind of hope." She was a "slavish imitation" of Garbo, "expressionless malice in every look, every movement studied, and all of it without personality, where every shred of personality was needed."

But even negative reviewers could not avoid noting female fans standing before Marlene's photographs murmuring moonily, "Isn't she *swee-eet!*" or gentlemen gliding silently into the theater to catch her Garbo imitation, of which "even small doses," one critic admitted, "can beguile." If Marlene imitated, "she simultaneously banishes any doubt that the similarity is absent from her own original essence."

What critics of 1929 objected to were the very qualities of cool, passive eroticism that in 1930 would overwhelm them, exactly what Hubsie and Lili Darvas had called her riveting "Nothing" on stage. It is the restraint of her Stascha that foreshadows her later screen persona. *The Woman One Longs For* isn't any kind of classic (Bernhardt didn't make classics), but its appeal lies precisely in those areas critics derided at the time. Marlene had found "Dietrich" as an *image*, too soon. C. H. Rand would shortly rhapsodize about "temptation without temperament," but critics couldn't see that yet. It lacked what Kenneth Tynan would call her "third dimension"— "that voice."

Marlene privately suffered severe depression over bad reviews. After losing the once-in-a-lifetime Lulu, and doing a series of popular but trivial films, it must have been crushing to give a subtly modulated performance and be dismissed for it. Small wonder she threw herself carelessly into her next two films and longed to get back to the theater, where eyes, legs, voice, and personality all worked together.

She was back on stage in March, just as *The Woman One Longs For* was readied for release. It was a one-night-only midnight production of Wedekind's *The Marquis von Keith* mounted by Leopold Jessner as tribute to a recently departed Grand Old Man of the theater, Albert Steinrück.

It was the single most star-studded event of the Weimar Republic. The cast included so many personalities of note that it was the occasion on which, had the proverbial bomb gone off, Berlin theater would have ceased to exist. Decades later, it is still remembered simply as "the Steinrück evening."

The event certified Weimar Germany's theatrical elite, and its like would never, *could* never be seen again. The proverbial bomb was waiting to go off. Within half a decade the *majority* of that glittering elite would have fled into exile, been banned or imprisoned, never to appear on any stage— except history's—again. There were "Mephistos," too (Veit Harlan was on stage that night), who would become bystanders or worse to the fate of the others.

The Steinrück evening was thrilling and Marlene had "arrived" just by being there. Only days before, the Berlin trade papers had carried full-page ads announcing a picture being prepared *for* her.

"Maurice Tourneur," the ads trumpeted, was making a "World Film" in Germany called *The Ship of Lost Souls*. The title echoed Tourneur's *Isle of Lost Ships*, which had been the first big American hit in Germany after the war. *Lost Souls* was being fashioned for the international market, a last gasp of pictorialism defying sound.

The story concerned an outlaw ship that sailed from port to port, adrift from society and awash with dread. An American heiress crashes into the sea on her solo trans-Atlantic flight (American heiresses did that then). She is saved by the evil ship and from the depraved ship's captain (Fritz Kortner again) by a young English doctor (Robin Irvine), who has been shanghaied. Marlene predictably inflames the randy crew once they discover that *aviatrix* means *she*.

It cannot have seemed terrible to be the only woman in a cast of males rampant with desire. Tourneur prepared meticulous storyboard sketches of her as the aviatrix, symptomatic of what became a ruinous exercise in directorial perfectionism and authenticity.

Tourneur had had a long and distinguished career in America, but was now defiantly lavishing pictorial gifts on an unnuanced melodrama, hoping what he called "Hollywood principles" and an "international" cast would overcome story and silence.

He insisted on props that had to be shipped or flown in. Marlene's flying costume was a real, *used* leather overall found in London; beer mugs for the waterfront bar were flown in from Hamburg dives. The ship could *only* be one built in 1856 for the Brazilian run to Chile around Cape Horn, but it proved unusable and was rebuilt to "hair-splitting exactness" in the studio, requiring eight-hundred-thousand nails. Authenticity and a four-month shooting schedule cost six-hundred-thousand marks, a very high budget then and staggering for a *silent* film in 1929.

It would be good to look at, which was why one hired a visual artist like Tourneur. But audiences like story, too, and one hundred miscreants chasing one woman around the poopdeck excited less suspense than a World Film should.

Film historian William K. Everson rather liked the "rich melodrama" of it all and pointed out that Tourneur handled Marlene "as though she had already established a screen mystique." Perfectly true, and perfectly curious. Marlene had not yet established any screen mystique except in *The Woman One Longs For,* which Tourneur had undoubtedly seen, but failed to recapture here in any sustained way because of the story.

Nor was it captured in her next film, which never promised more than to reunite her with her old Vienna lover Willi Forst, the reason she made it. The picture had already gone through a number of titles (never a good sign), all centering on Forst as a Mister Casanova. The final choice was the dreadful *Dangers of the Engagement Period* (just as bad in German) to emphasize the central episode in which Marlene is wooed and seduced by Forst, who is unaware he is bedding the fiancée of his weekend host, toward whose home they are both *en route.*

Forst learns the truth, an altercation ensues, he is shot by his host, and (being a good guest) makes his own murder appear a suicide. Marlene faints and the movie abruptly ends.

The mishmash of titles makes it clear: No one involved had any idea what the movie was about. It has a high-comedy plot (Lubitsch would use it in *Angel*) with a low-rent denouement and a lot of Art Deco furniture that doesn't talk: *Any* actress would deny having made it.

Lotte Eisner, despite her personal antipathy toward Marlene (and her conviction that she had better legs), recognized in *Dangers of the Engagement Period* something flickering through all Marlene's late silent films: "a woman who materializes mysteriously and sadly in a railway compartment [she wrote], charming and alluring in her blend of mysterious behavior and strange passivity, her lovely face shadowed by a presentiment of tragedy." Eisner thought it was all the cameraman, not realizing the passivity was the performance. She might well have been describing Stascha. Or Shanghai Lily.

Marlene finished this last silent potboiler and went to the seashore with Heidede. Rudi stayed home in the apartment he still shared with Marlene, though he appeared to be more faithfully devoted to Tamara than he had ever been to his wife. Mother and four-and-half-year-old daughter enjoyed the island of Sylt in the North Sea. It provided a brief respite for both—one from work, the other from childhood loneliness. The holiday would be their last before Marlene left the family circle altogether.

She returned to Berlin for the opening of *Ship of Lost Souls*. She and Fritz Kortner were booed off the stage of the UFA Pavillon by the outrage that greeted this World Film, eight hundred thousand nails and all. Critics called it "a film of lost content" and thought neither Kortner nor Marlene bothered "getting around to acting." She was lucky to have the theater to fall back on.

She went into rehearsal for *Two Bow Ties*. It was her first production under the three-year contract she had signed with Robert Klein in that *chambre séparée* at Horcher's. It was also her last.

Producer Viktor Barnowsky had watched Marlene work her way from George Abbott to George Bernard Shaw. He was not a great intellect, but neither was he undiscerning. As Marlene came to the end of her theatrical career he noted, "In Marlene the theater lost a jewel. . . . Entirely a child of her time, Marlene Dietrich has become the model and symbol of the seductive woman. . . . Garbo on the other hand is the symbol of suffering Womanhood. . . . Bergner, the ideal modern Girl. . . . Marlene is perhaps the Woman of Tomorrow."

Dietrich's memoirs tell us that in *Two Bow Ties* she "had only one line." Josef von Sternberg told us in *his* memoirs "I remember only one line."

It must have been the story line, for Marlene was the leading lady.

Tomorrow had arrived.

SIX

THE BLUE
ANGEL

1929

September 5, 1929. Marlene Dietrich stepped on the stage of the Berliner Theater and read a winning lottery number:

"Three . . . three . . . and three!! Three cheers for the gentleman who has drawn the first prize!"

Two Bow Ties was the first big musical success of the season. Its credentials glittered. Director Forster-Larrinaga and composer Mischa Spoliansky were reunited after *It's in the Air,* and debuting as musical comedy librettist was Georg Kaiser, the most versatile, most successful, most performed German playwright of the 1920s. The cast boasted fifty actors, singers, dancers, and featured Berlin's top pop group, the Comedian-Harmonists (not unlike having the Beatles in the chorus). The leading performers were matinee heartthrob Hans Albers, cabaret favorite Rosa Valetti, and Marlene.

The show was a romp about a waiter (Albers) who trades his workaday black bow tie for the white bow tie of a gentleman-gangster eager to go on the lam. Changing ties and accepting the bribe of lottery ticket *"Three . . . three . . . and three,"* the Cinderella waiter is whisked off to Chicago and Florida and off his feet by the leading lady.

The critics cheered and cheered Marlene. One said, "The effect on the public is fabulous." Another called Marlene "beautiful and *exactly* what one means by 'something else,' " with "the veiled voice and the heavy-lidded eyes."

None of that mattered. What mattered was the visitor from Hollywood in the audience, who would ever after call this production "a skit" and tell his hosts the beautiful " 'something else' " looked to him like an "untalented cow."

Josef von Sternberg was not immune to star-spangled evenings. He was born Jonas Sternberg on May 29, 1894, within sight of the Prater, imperial Vienna's vast amusement park. His first light had been carnival glitter, the glow of a tawdry world. The flash of tinsel made the poverty almost bearable.

His mother, Serafin (née Singer), had been a child circus performer. His father, Moses ("a lion," his son called him), was a physically brutal and headstrong Orthodox Jew who had defied his family to marry Serafin and father her five children, of whom Jonas was the first. The family subsisted in a small apartment clattering with carpenters below and washerwomen above, whose din may have drowned out the beatings Jonas's father administered to discipline his son, or simply to express his rage at life's injustices. The boy never forgot that he had "howled like a dog."

Jonas spent his early youth in the streets or roamed the ragtag grounds of the amusement park, burning its imagery into memory. The giant Ferris wheel loomed like an image of Fate, to return in his films as a dredging machine, a carousel, a clock, an executioner's rack.

Moses Sternberg left his family in Vienna to seek his fortune in America when the boy was only three. Prospects in the promised land seemed large (or lonely) enough that Moses sent for wife and son in 1901 when Jonas was seven. The summons came with no money, no steamship tickets, but somehow Serafin (who had once been a tightrope walker in the circus) got them to Ellis Island. Three years later, after epidemics of scarlet fever and chicken pox, the family was driven by their New World poverty from Manhattan's German-speaking Yorkville back to Vienna, with no souvenirs but humiliation, the clothes on their backs, and the lice in them.

The boy who felt himself already an outsider resisted Hebrew school in fiercely anti-Semitic Vienna. The language of the *Torah* was thrashed into him, but there was again the Prater to escape to, where he mingled with the fraternity of the tanbark. He fed circus horses for pocket money and filled his head with images of shimmer and squalor. He became an injustice collector, hoarding resentment against the Hebrew schoolmaster, a figure no less tyrannical than his father. Both patriarchs would be immortalized on film. Or *mortalized*. Sternberg, in a plot innovation of his own, would kill off the bearded master(s) in the last reel of a film about a professor. Art would be the best revenge.

At fourteen the boy escaped ghetto and Old World to reembark for the New, leaving mother and siblings behind. There were relatives in America to take him in. He called himself Jo and attended high school in Queens for a year, struggling to learn English, but ended his formal education at fifteen, convinced he could educate himself better than any school or any schoolmaster. The autodidact would learn much, retain much, but there would be grievous gaps in his practical knowledge of ordinary human behavior, including his own.

He eked out a vagabond life in America with the oddest of jobs, the meanest of menial tasks. He improved his English, lost much of his German, visited galleries, museums, and libraries, reading whatever came to hand. He fancied himself an artist (and would all of his life), painting and drawing when he had paper and pencil. He soaked up images, shielded from his own feelings by his prodigious visual hunger and memory: "I can reproduce in my mind every street I have walked," he remembered, "each room or shop I have entered, and no face has lost its shape, but of the tapestry of my emotions not a single shred remains." He had hidden them too well behind the armor he needed to survive.

The scholar-wanderer returned to New York to apprentice in a milliner's back room, then to a lace house on Fifth Avenue, full of the nets and veils through which he would later filter his objects of desire. He wandered into a job cleaning film, then patching it, then delivering it to theaters by hand or wagon, then projecting it, and eventually writing titles or reediting it for William A. Brady's World Film Corporation in the early movie center of Fort Lee, New Jersey.

World War I snatched him from the back rooms and set him to making training films for the army signal corps. He filled them with images of battlefield horrors until the army (his first front office) saw them and hastily shunted him off to the medical corps. The war destroyed the world he knew, but in film he had found another and returned to it after the armistice.

William A. Brady made fifty pictures a year then in Fort Lee and gave Jo

Sternberg not only a job but two vital insights into the film world he had now determined to conquer. First, Brady was a producer *and* a distributor. Secondly, his wife and daughter, Grace George and Alice Brady, were stars. (His daughter would originate the role of Lavinia in *Mourning Becomes Electra* on stage and on film would and one day win an Oscar.) Stars in the family helped Brady secure financing and playing time. The would-be director thus began his career with glimpses into two crucial areas: distribution and exhibition (without a grasp of which no director survives), and an appreciation of the uses of the star system. He would learn to exploit both with notable success until the autodidact's arrogance sabotaged his artistry and the artistry and arrogance began to look like the same thing to men of lesser gifts but greater power.

Working for Brady in Fort Lee in 1919, Sternberg became assistant to director Émile Chautard, who had acted with Sarah Bernhardt before turning to film. Chautard taught him to see with the lens, to focus there the lights and shadows that had followed him from the Prater. Jo Sternberg was twenty-five and still a beginner.

After two years of no advancement, he wandered again, back to Vienna, where bravado or desperation or hope against hope led him to announce himself as a film director. Vienna was no quicker to recognize his gifts than Fort Lee, New Jersey, had been, and to establish credentials as an artist he translated an obscure Austrian novel into English. His version was privately printed in 1922 to frank self-acclaim for its sordidness. *Daughters of Vienna* was "freely adapted by Jo Sternberg from the Viennese of Karl Adolph," who may have been a friend from childhood. Sternberg claimed credit for type style, format, and cover; they were not his. There would never be enough credit to claim.

He moved on from Vienna to England to work again as an assistant for directors who convinced him only that he could do better. By 1923 he had wandered on to Hollywood, where he assisted on a film called *By Divine Right*. There he "discovered" a pretty young extra named Georgia Hale, who might become a star.

The credits of *By Divine Right* listed him as Josef von Sternberg. He claimed the von was his producer's pretension, but kept it. It rang so euphoniously with echoes of another one-time resident of Vienna, the imperious director and actor ("the man you love to hate") Erich von Stroheim, whom Sternberg revered, and whose von was equally Hollywood-invented, but as distinctive as the Stroheim monocle. Besides, "Josef von Sternberg" suited the assistant's view of himself as Art's Aristocrat.

Sternberg was never a *Wunderkind*. He was thirty before he made his first picture in 1925. It was called *The Salvation Hunters*, and he made it on his own and his leading actor's shoestring savings, both of them financing celluloid calling-cards. It was squalid realism shot in and around San Pedro Harbor in Los Angeles, in the Stroheim manner, beautifully photographed derelicts, and "The Girl" (as she was identified in the titles) was the one-time extra Georgia Hale. A dredging machine was the central and recurring image of the film, scooping up a river bottom and causing its banks to collapse for eternal redredging. This image of futility was "an attempt to photograph a thought," the titles of *The Salvation Hunters* proclaimed, and it was squalid enough, stark enough, and (above all) cheap enough on Sternberg's minuscule budget to look like art to Hollywood in 1925. It looks mannered and static today, but its "poetic" depiction of flotsam, jetsam, and human degradation suggested high purpose on a low budget in the land of the lotus, *Ben Hur*, and Cecil B. DeMille.

When Douglas Fairbanks and Charles Chaplin bought the roughly $5000 film for United Artists for $20,000, the film and Josef von Sternberg became famous overnight. The one they called art, the other a "genius."

He believed them and felt he had found a home at last. It was a mistake he would never make again.

"Oh Hollywood, my beloved Hollywood," he exulted on a hilltop, arms outstretched to embrace the lemon groves below, posturing in newly found celebrity for a journalist. The reporter printed his effusion and his "beloved Hollywood" laughed. The community driven by basest cupidity ridiculed him for having passion. It was one thing for them to call him genuis; quite another for him to decide they meant it or that it was true.

Armor became pose, the genius poseur. He put on jodhpurs and a turban and carried a swagger stick. If he could not win Hollywood's respect, its scorn would do; outrage was preferable to neglect.

He was small and vain. Fascination with his own image led him to design the "horrible" oriental mustache he wore and adopt the reptilian stare with which he regarded the world. "The only way to succeed is to make people hate you," he told an actor, perhaps thinking of Stroheim. "That way they remember you." They remembered him and would not shrink from the harm they could do when they hated him.

A famous and cruel remark about Sternberg served as epitaph to his career: "When a director dies, he becomes a cameraman." It was made not at the end of his career, as one might suppose, but at the very beginning. After buying *The Salvation Hunters* for distribution, Charles Chaplin in-vited Sternberg to make a second film starring the comedian's one-time leading lady, Edna Purviance. The film was meant as a final gesture to a former lover and co-star who was at the end of a career and lost to alcohol. It was called *A Woman of the Sea*, and Chaplin financed it, screened it, and destroyed it. He may have been performing a merciful kindness for Purvi-ance, but it was nothing of the sort for "genius." Only a handful of professionals ever saw it and one who did (the same who wrote Sternberg's epitaph) called it "the most beautiful picture ever produced in Hollywood, and the least human."

Embarrassed, perhaps, Chaplin added to injury by explaining his acquisition of Sternberg's first film as a joke. "Well, you know, I was only kidding," the funnyman told the press, as if he had put one over on Hollywood with all the talk about Art and genius in a film that was, after all, static and "poetic" only because its director said it was. Chaplin then announced that *The Salvation Hunter*'s leading lady, Georgia Hale, would become *his* leading lady in *The Gold Rush*, which may have been his motive all along.

Chaplin sent the director whose work he had destroyed to his partner in United Artists, Mary Pickford, with a project about the world as imagined by a blind girl, in which The Little Tramp promised to play a bit part. Sternberg wanted to set the picture in Pittsburgh and call it *Backwash*, which Miss Pickford thought not quite "normal." He needed a job now, and found one in a dream factory.

In no time at all he was famous again. MGM had given him a picture to direct, but rather than subordinate his genius to the antics of *Merry Widow* star Mae Murray in a picture called *The Masked Bride* (it was that kind of picture), Sternberg turned his cameras to the rafters in a gesture of contempt for one of the day's great box-office stars. Not even Stroheim could get away with this sort of thing at MGM (and didn't: see *Greed*). "I don't think [Sternberg's] working anywhere," Walter Winchell chortled in print. "I think he's a genuine genius again." Sternberg wandered on to Paramount, an assistant once more.

Paramount in 1926, like other studios, was rife with boardroom and bedroom politics, and production head B. P. Schulberg was famously "politicking" Clara Bow. As a favor to the head of the studio, Sternberg reshot portions of *Children of Divorce* (with Bow and young Gary Cooper) and didn't ask for credit. He did the same for *It*, the picture that defined the "It" Girl and defined the era, too. He was shrewdly building credit with the front office, not credits on the screen.

He had demanded a puppet's obedience, not star temperament, when he turned the camera to the ceiling rather than photograph Mae Murray at MGM, but Sternberg proved neither too respectful nor too averse to reworking another genius, not even the one he admired most, Erich von Stroheim. He recut Stroheim's *The Wedding March* for Schulberg and Paramount, earning more studio credit and eternal contempt from his fellow Austrian.

The studio threw Sternberg a bone. He was assigned to newspaperman

Ben Hecht's *Underworld*, and made it—to everyone's surprise but his own—a worldwide box-office sensation.

Sternberg called it the "first gangster picture," which it was not, but it established a glamorous gangster vogue that is with us still. Hecht wired Sternberg, "You poor ham, take my name off the film," but kept the Academy Award he won for his story. The picture made a star of the dull and brutish George Bancroft and—once again—of Sternberg. And of a girl named Evelyn Brent.

Ernst Lubitsch came to Paramount then to make a Czarist epic with Emil Jannings called *The Patriot*. Jannings followed that with *The Last Command*, Sternberg's first masterwork (co-starring Evelyn Brent). It was about a former imperial Russian general working as a Hollywood extra, who goes pitiably mad playing himself in a film about the Bolshevik Revolution. The story was based on an anecdote by Lubitsch about a Hollywood extra who really *was* an imperial Russian general. Jannings won the first Best Actor Academy Award for impersonating him (and for his role in *The Way of All Flesh*). Sternberg observed Jannings's triumph by claiming that "under no circumstances, were he the last remaining actor on earth, would I ever again court the doubtful pleasure of directing him."

Sternberg claimed many things. He claimed *The Last Command* was the first film about Hollywood (it wasn't), but he was famous again. He made more Paramount pictures (more Evelyn Brent). None was indifferent, and one was a masterpiece, the silent *Docks of New York* (*no* Evelyn Brent), which suffered the bad timing of previewing the same week as *The Jazz Singer*.

So he made a "talker." It was called *Thunderbolt*, another gangster drama with dull and brutish George Bancroft. This time the girl was Fay Wray, whom he knew from *not* cutting her out of Stroheim's *Wedding March*, in which she was the bride. Sternberg now had a bride of his own, a former actress called Riza Royce who spent time on her husband's set, which may have delayed Fay Wray's stardom until she was taken in hand by a gorilla.

Thunderbolt was a success because every sound film was, but it was just a gangster talkie with a pretty girl. The marriage was a success in the same way: It sounded good. There was a quick trip to Mexico and a quickie divorce that seemed, on second thought, ill-considered, and slow days waiting for a next picture. He was typed again: "gangster director." Hollywood *liked* typing him. It made his "genius" easier to take, especially when he wasn't working, which is how he found himself in Berlin.

*　　*　　*

The traffic between Berlin and Hollywood had always been two-way, in both talent and money. Emil Jannings and Lya de Putti went to Hollywood; Louise Brooks and Lionel Barrymore went to Berlin. There had been something called Parufamet, a combine of *Paramount*, *UFA*, and *Metro-Goldwyn-Mayer* that guaranteed distribution of Paramount and MGM films in Europe in return for dollar loans to and reciprocal distribution of UFA's films in America. Plan and practice diverged. The American distribution that was to bring UFA the dollars to pay back the loans somehow never happened, but American films did. They overwhelmed the German market in UFA's own theaters.

UFA needed saving from Parufamet and predatory Americans. German press lord Alfred Hugenberg saved it. He was a "hopelessly reactionary and politically ambitious magnate," historian Peter Gay reminds us, "animated by insatiable political passions and hatreds masquerading as convictions."

Hugenberg bought out Paramount's and MGM's shares of UFA with industrial and banking partners, and their political passions at once influenced UFA's production, especially of newsreels. Politics would soon prompt them to turn production over entirely to Dr. Joseph Goebbels, restoring UFA to the propaganda organ it had been when General Ludendorff founded it in 1917.

Two-way traffic slowed. Lions roared now and jazz singers sang and UFA needed the American market as never before. UFA's ties to elite Paramount had always been closer than to MGM (still a challenger, not yet champ). Paramount was more "European," more congenial to the likes of Lubitsch, Pola Negri, Mauritz Stiller (Garbo's mentor, discarded by MGM). It had been home and host to "the Greatest Actor in the World."

Emil Jannings made his sound debut at Paramount in *Betrayal*, the picture Adolph Zukor had to silence in order to release, though few in Berlin were aware of the fiasco or cared. Jannings had never liked Hollywood anyway and was happy to come back to Berlin, back to UFA, back to all those sausages, back (as it soon turned out) to Goebbels, Göring, and their crowd.

He would now make what UFA called his "sound debut" with Germany's greatest producer, who needed the American market to break even. Erich Pommer had worked at Paramount, too, and knew the chances of selling a Jannings talkie there (after *Betrayal*) would be greater if it were made by a Paramount director who not only spoke German, but could guide Jannings through an English version as only a bilingual director could. Lubitsch, of course, the undisputed star director at Paramount. And to explain Jannings's accent in English—well, he had won his Oscar playing a Russian . . . *Rasputin!*

Lubitsch was willing. For a price. He wanted $60,000 for directing, almost a fifth of the $325,000 (1,250,000-mark) budget, and more than Pommer wanted to pay. Jannings suddenly decided that *he* was being un-derpaid at $50,000, and demanded $75,000. Pommer shrewdly reworked the contract. Jannings would get his normal fee (in dollars: Jannings knew currencies), and a bonus of $25,000 for an English version, to be paid if the picture *opened* in America, powerful incentive to enunciate.

Negotiations continued until late July, when Lubitsch refused to budge from his price and Pommer refused to budge from his refusal. He knew there was another German-speaking director at Paramount who had worked with Jannings, who had made a sound film, and who might work cheaper. Pommer offered Josef von Sternberg $30,000. Sternberg wanted $40,000. Pommer agreed. Sternberg and Riza Royce undid their quickie Mexican divorce and hastily remarried to get passports back in order and set sail for Berlin, where the press recorded their arrival at the Zoo Bahnhof on August 16, 1929.

Sternberg waxed eloquent: "I have freed myself from America, because my heart drew me back to work with Emil and because I long to make an artistic film. Sound . . . has brought me back to German film [with] one and a half years of sound film experience. . . . What the talkie must achieve today, above and beyond the technical, is the human. . . . We [must] pay less attention to how it sounds, and more to what it has to say."

This is the sort of thing directors say even when they mean it. It may have surprised some that the one sound film Sternberg had made amounted to one and a half year's experience. More may have wondered about a return to German film as he had never worked in Germany a day in his life. Everyone, however, was gratified by news that his heart belonged to Emil after their famous mutual loathing on *The Last Command*. The big surprise was yet to come.

The welcoming party adjourned to the Hotel Esplanade where Sternberg resumed waxing: "It's as if I died in Hollywood and woke up in Heaven!" he said, and even had something nice to say about Erich Pommer, for whom he was going to make "a world-class film," hinting that Pommer could use one. A strolling gypsy band serenaded the guest of honor with Al Jolson's "Sonny Boy."

Sternberg chose that effulgent moment to drop his bombshell. He had no *idea* he had been hired for *Rasputin*, he said; no intention of making it, either. Unless something else was found he would return from Heaven to Hollywood forthwith. It was a modest enough power play, a flaunting of contractual amnesia, but shifted attention from the strolling guitars.

At the moment he didn't know what he might condescend to direct, but his heart belonged to Emil, who had been so effective in *Varieté*. Some-thing like that trapeze picture set in the Wintergarten might do, with the tanbark-and-tights flavor Sternberg knew and liked. With a lady in the tights.

Pommer was stunned, but saw welcome relief from legal problems surrounding *Rasputin*. (They were real: MGM made the picture with the Barrymores, losing money *and* lawsuits.) Even Jannings seemd unperturbed. The portly star who had been saying ever since 1927 that he *must* play Rasputin had even earlier declared (to the great F. W. Murnau, now directing Janet Gaynor in Hollywood) that he *had* to play a character from a not very well known novel by Heinrich Mann that had no trapezes or tights, but had a cabaret. It was called *Professor Unrat, End of a Tyrant*.

Jannings and Pommer had discussed the novel earlier that summer. Pommer had been intrigued by the idea of a proper *Gymnasium* professor falling in love with a cheap cabaret singer and being destroyed by her. He also knew Heinrich Mann needed money. Pommer's assistant lived with the dancer La Jana, then working in an Erik Charell extravaganza with Mann's mistress, Trude Hesterberg. Pommer nudged his assistant to nudge La Jana to nudge Hesterberg to nudge Mann, and got nudged back that *Professor Unrat*, kicking around for years, was for sale.

Pommer's indirect route to information hinted inadvertently that Mann's mistress might be right for the role of the cabaret singer because she was one. Sternberg, however, was thinking thoughts of America's Gloria Swanson or Phyllis Haver until he realized their German might be rusty. The cabaret background was the attraction anyway. He had included a song sequence in *Thunderbolt* and musicals were all the rage in America. Even Maurice Chevalier sang American. For Lubitsch.

A week to the day after his arrival in Berlin, Sternberg was presented with *Professor Unrat* signed and sealed. The same day Pommer hired the playwright Dr. Karl Vollmoeller to work with screenwriter Robert Liebmann. The following day a third writer was engaged, playwright Carl Zuckmayer.

The day after *that*, press lord Alfred Hugenberg, master of UFA, looked at the contracts and thunder pealed.

Hugenberg had misunderstood the whole project. He thought the author of *Professor Unrat* was *Thomas* Mann, who had just won the Nobel Prize for Literature, not his brother Heinrich. Hugenberg threatened to cancel everything on grounds of fraud. He was outraged by the story of a symbol of German rectitude sinking to a sordid end. Hugenberg and his cohorts demanded that Pommer "completely rework" the story. The professor represented, if not their class, then their *outlook* and "should be . . . humanly understandable, so that no occasion for [critical] attack might come to pass."

This was a clear sign of worse to come. More immediately bothersome was the revelation that Heinrich Mann and Trude Hesterberg thought *she* was going to play cabaret singer Rosa Fröhlich. Sternberg had a courtesy meeting with them, assuming the author's mistress was the model for the character (she wasn't). He rejected her "maturity" out of hand. Now Heinrich Mann was angry, too.

Sternberg rose above it. Hugenberg and Hesterberg somehow focused everything. This picture was not about a professor's fall (Jannings could play *that* in his sleep), but the woman who caused it. "Without the electricity of a new and exciting female," he realized, "[my] film would have been no more than an essay reflecting on the stupidity of a school tyrant."

To "completely rework" and refocus he decided to change the title from *Professor Unrat* (with its untranslatable pun on a German word for excrement) to the name of the cabaret in which the professor meets and becomes obsessed with singer Rosa Fröhlich: a waterfront dive called The Blue Angel.

Pommer and Jannings agreed. What was clear to no one but Sternberg was that the title change shifted weight to the cabaret singer (she, not the dive, would become the angel), and he didn't have one.

Art's aristocrat didn't know Berlin actors (he had not been there since a brief visit in 1925) and *The Blue Angel* demanded actors who could *speak*—though not English for the most part, even in the English version. The professor, some of his students, the actress playing Rosa, and a few others would speak English, the professor because he taught it; Rosa because she was being written as an American or Cockney whose lack of German would require others around her to speak English if they wanted her attention. And they would. In the German version, everybody would be German, including Rosa, whom Sternberg decided to rename with a nod to Wedekind's Lulu—Lola Lola.

No casting contest like this had been seen since Lulu or would be seen again until Scarlett. Virtually every German actress remotely suitable was rumored to be in the running or have been offered a contract. Except Marlene Dietrich. Names flew like confetti at a parade, which is what the female flesh trooping in and out of the *Blue Angel* offices resembled, most of them German stars then or later. One candidate who did not claim to have the part was privately convinced she did: Leni Riefenstahl. The future director of *Triumph of the Will* and *Olympia*, two of the greatest documentaries ever made—Nazi showpieces—was an ex-dancer and actress looking for work. She admired Sternberg and said so.

Riefenstahl did not audition—she dined. And was taken aback to hear Sternberg mention an actress's name over roast beef at the Hotel Bristol. Riefenstahl answered carefully:

"Marlene Dietrich, you say? I've seen her only once, and was struck by her," she said. "She was sitting [in a café] with some young actresses, and my attention was drawn by her deep, coarse voice. Maybe she was a little tipsy. I heard her say in a loud voice, 'Why must we always have beautiful bosoms? Why can't they hang a little?' With which she lifted up her left breast and amused herself with it, startling the young girls sitting around her. She might be a good type for you."

Riefenstahl must not have known how much this sounded like Lola Lola or how much more it told Sternberg than he already knew. He had passed over a photograph of the almost twenty-eight-year-old Marlene, still advertising herself as "Ingenue: Naive." An assistant had remarked, *"Der Popo ist nicht schlecht, aber brauchen wir nicht auch ein Gesicht?"* ("The bottom isn't bad, but don't we need a face, too?")

Others had mentioned the woman with the not bad *Popo* and the free-floating bosoms. Gertrud Pommer had—she knew her from Betty Stern's salon; Dr. Karl Vollmoeller's mistress, Ruth Landshoff had—she had acted with her in Vienna in *The School of Uznach*. Vollmoeller himself had. But Sternberg made his *own* discoveries and kept his own counsel and kept looking, though he knew something the others did not.

As he and his wife had passed through New York en route to Berlin, a film opened there at the 55th Street Playhouse. Sternberg may or may not have seen it then, but knew what *The New York Times* said about it because Paramount knew; so did Universal. The *Times* had noted that *Three Loves* (the American title for *The Woman One Longs For*) featured "a rare Garboesque beauty in Marlene Dietrich." The movie was held over on 55th Street. And held over again.

It was still playing when a jazz-baby "dollar princess" with jewels from here to there stepped onto the stage of the Berliner Theater to announce in English who had won the lottery.

She did. That night.

"Toulouse-Lautrec would have turned a couple of handsprings," Sternberg later crowed, but until he saw the "untalented cow" for himself he had all but settled on Lucie Mannheim as Lola Lola. Mannheim had made a sound film, was younger than most other candidates (Jannings admired her *Popo*), and Sternberg had already scheduled a singing test.

That was all pointless now, but it was too late to cancel and Sternberg simply extended the crew time to make a test of Marlene, before he had even met her.

He had not gone backstage at *Two Bow Ties* (he did not court actors), but his interest in nothing but Marlene had been so obvious from the stage that Hans Albers later said he would gladly have pissed on Sternberg's head had the director been sitting nearer the footlights.

Marlene presented herself at Sternberg's office sullen and disinterested. She was "a study in apathy," he said, "attempting to blot herself out [and making] not the slightest effort to intensify my interest." Her heliotrope suit, hat, gloves, and furs seemed likely to blot out nothing but everything *else*, and her apathy was likely resentment at being ignored in the highly publicized talent search or—*worse*—now being offered some minor role.

Sternberg, the son of "a lion" and the one-time tightrope walker Serafin, believed it was "the nature of a woman to be passive, receptive, dependent on male aggression, and capable of enduring pain," and inflicted some. Why, he asked, had he heard such dismal reports about Marlene's career?

Marlene told him she photographed badly, got poor press, and had made three films and was no good in any of them.

This was reckless or daring or both. She knew he had seen her in Berlin's biggest hit the night before. Her answers challenged his reputation as a cameraman; blamed whatever he might have heard about her on the press; and flat-out lied about her experience.

Sternberg wasn't entirely taken in. He thought she had made nine pictures (it was seventeen). The show he had seen her in the previous evening was her twenty-sixth theatrical production, and he had heard about some of them from Vollmoeller and Landshoff. When he said he wanted to test her, she can hardly have thought it was for a minor role, but she agreed on condition he see all three films she admitted to (*I Kiss Your Hand, Madame, Ship of Lost Souls,* and *The Women One Longs For:* star parts all). She added gratuitously that she had seen his films and didn't think he knew how to direct women anyway.

This wasn't apathetic—it was breathtaking; no "charming flirtation," this was insolent challenge. It ran the risk he would dismiss her; it was also as provocative as a snapped garter. And shrewd. He would see her in three starring roles and would undoubtedly attribute her failings to the lesser talents of lesser directors. The only thing more astonishing than an actress who would make such demands was a director who would agree to them. He agreed. Her insolence was inspired intuition; it was the essence of Lola Lola, Eros on a high wire.

"The theater was in her blood, and she was familiar with every parasite in it," he decided. "Her energy to survive and to rise above her environment must have been fantastic," he said, and felt its powerful erotic charge. "Never before," he said, "had I met so beautiful a woman who had been so thoroughly discounted and undervalued."

He saw her films and knew why. "She was an awkward, unattractive woman, left to her own devices, and presented in an embarrassing exhibition of drivel. Ice cold water was poured on me," he said. But *not* left to her own devices, he thought, or those of hacks, she could be anything, for he saw a face that "promised everything."

The Lucie Mannheim test was painless and fruitful, for Mannheim brought along Friedrich Holländer as accompanist. This was not unlike bringing George Gershwin to an audition in Manhattan, and Sternberg knew at once he had found his composer for the *Blue Angel* songs.

He still had to make a test with the indifferent Marlene. He had already decided on her and needed no test for himself. Nor was he making the test for UFA (for whom he had contempt), or for Pommer (who already wanted Marlene), or for Jannings (who did not). He was making it for Jesse Lasky, Jr., in Paramount's home office. Paramount production chief B. P. Schulberg would see it in Berlin, as he was even then on board the *Île de France*. Neither executive would be disinterested in a "rare Garboesque beauty" whose face "promised everything"—or in the man who discovered her.

Marlene arrived showily unprepared, with neither material nor pianist, and her passivity was as provocative as her insolence had been. Sternberg called for a piano player, pinned her into a spangled costume, frizzed her hair with a curling iron ("the air was filled with smoke," she said). She sang a German song called *"Wer wird denn weinen?"* ("Why cry? There's another on the corner!"). When Sternberg asked for an American song, she nudged the pianist from atop the piano on which she sat and ordered, "So *play* something!" The pianist paused, and she jumped down to fiddle at the keys while singing along, then hopped back on her perch. The song may have been "You're the Cream in My Coffee," as she later said; it may have been "My Blue Heaven," a hit in Berlin just then and not inappropriate for a "blue angel's" audition.

"She came to life and responded to my instructions with an ease that I had never before encountered," Sternberg marveled, half congratulating himself. "Her remarkable vitality had been channeled."

Marlene never even asked to see the test. She *knew*.

"You will rue the day," Jannings predicted, echoing the UFA brass, though later he would claim Marlene had been his idea all along. Pommer was glad the decision had finally been made and didn't care *who* got the credit. "Everyone connected with the film claims to be the discoverer of Marlene," he said privately, "and they all really believe it. Let them be happy and think so; it is not important."

It was important to Berlin and word flew out. Hans Feld, editor of *Film-Kurier*, heard it from Leni Riefenstahl because he was there when she heard it on the telephone. She was so distraught she cancelled him *and* the goulash she had been warming up for dinner. Lucie Mannheim heard it from UFA. Friedrich Holländer heard when he was told to compose songs for Marlene's voice, not Mannheim's.

Marlene heard it from Holländer. She had been on stage all evening and was relaxing at the transvestite hot spot, Le Silhouette, where Holländer saw "two question marks in two worried, wide-open eyes" whose appeal he could not resist.

"She ordered so much champagne you could have bathed in it," he reported.

Songs were vital to *The Blue Angel*, and Holländer began composing even before the script to contain them was written. Sternberg ever after maintained "no comprehensive scenario was ever made," but one was. It was shaped in September and October in Berlin and in St. Moritz, where Jannings had gone to lose weight (no more sausages). Sternberg, Pommer, and the three writers trekked to the Alps to work with the star on his characterization, which was based on Heinrich Mann himself. And Sternberg's hated Hebrew teacher.

The major alterations from the novel were the addition of the professor's degradation as a clown and his madness and death at the end instead of imprisonment (for running a gambling house corrupting the bourgeoisie). The tone became romantic pathos instead of Mann's bitter attack on a hypocritical society which had so alarmed UFA's Alfred Hugenberg. The script narrowed—or deepened—the end of a tyrant into a story of fatal sexual obsession.

That Sternberg was experiencing obsession of his own charged the development of Lola Lola, who became younger, and the child she had in the novel was deleted. She became a coarse but inviting honky-tonk girl who turns tricks on the side while protesting she is an "artiste." What was revolutionary about her screen character was her utter amorality. She is neither vamp nor flapper. She is provocative, seductive, and unsentimental. Though not without sympathy (she has some), she is ruthlessly lacking in remorse for inspiring the reactions it is her pleasure and trade to elicit. As the professor goes off to die, she sings what she knows is true: If wings burn, she is not to blame.

We know her almost exclusively through her songs and Sternberg's camera treatment of her, which violently signals her carnality as the professor first sees her on a crowded, chaotic stage, and ends in the cool, steady camera that adores and caresses the self-adoring, self-caressing Circe at the end. It is four years and a lifetime later. She straddles her chair and her siren song assures us she will go on falling in love again forever, catalyst and survivor. It's her nature; what is she to do?

*   *   *

Shooting began at the UFA studios on November 4, 1929. The stock market crash at the end of September exacerbated pressures from Hugenberg & Co., and were not relieved by the poker face of Buster Keaton visiting the set the first day of shooting. He didn't see much. Sternberg shot in sequence and began with models to establish town and milieu. There was no sound to record but foghorns suggesting a melancholy sea.

Sternberg patterned sound as he patterned light and shadow. *The Blue Angel* was perhaps the first sound picture to convey something quite new to filmgoers: the expressive power of silence. Character is revealed through sound in ways impossible without the microphone: the professor's unanswered whistle to his dead canary; his thunderous nose-blowing in the classroom; the drifting voices of an unseen choir, abruptly silenced by the shutting of a window; the German boys' hopeless attempts at the English *th*; the "cock-a-doodle-doo" of the clown-professor's madness; a glockenspiel chiming time and Fate. Nowhere is sound more striking or effective than backstage at the cabaret. Sternberg creates a jagged, jumpy weave of silence and sound with the opening and closing of doors. It seems naturalistic, but is pieced together with jigsaw exactness, difficult to control with primitive sound technique that had not yet discovered mixing and separate tracks.

Jannings was less difficult to handle than on *The Last Command* because he was terrified of the microphone. Speaking dialogue on a film set seemed like acting to an empty theater. He compensated by being language-pompous back in Berlin, and Sternberg fought with him to speak German like a person, not a proclamation or a poem.

Scenes were shot first in German, then in English, and the effort for Jannings sometimes showed. His English is tight and overcorrect, while Marlene's English (or American) seems nonchalantly free, with her slangy dialogue ("Sugar Daddy," she calls the professor), though it is never quite clear if she is from Battersea or Battery Park.

Marlene had fewer problems of technical adjustment than Jannings because she had made recordings and had grown up in a newer, more intimate theatrical style. Most of her scenes are played to on-screen audiences; Rosa Valetti was there to instruct her once again in the finer (or coarser) points of cabaret performance; the composer was in the pit to provide rhythm and rapport. She takes possession of the screen with an assurance that is breathtaking; for the first time on screen she can use her voice to insinuate what she could earlier only mime.

Not that she was averse to conveying Lola Lola physically. She was creating what critics would call "a new incarnation of sex," and the incarnation sometimes got graphic when visitors were present, which was most of the time. Sternberg welcomed homage.

Keaton's visit had signaled that Stage Five was the place to be, to learn and listen. Guests streamed through, not only film people like Russian director Sergei Eisenstein and Sternberg's George Bancroft, still dull and brutish (he was a big star in Berlin), but nonfilm people, too, like artist George Grosz and even Max Reinhardt.

Leni Riefenstahl dropped by the day Lola Lola sang to the professor seated on her barrel in silk stockings and top hat. Sternberg was setting lights for "Falling in Love Again" as Marlene showed off her legs to visitors: her *Woman One Longs For* director Kurt Bernhardt, Uncle Willi's neighbor Conrad Veidt (they were shooting on the adjoining stage), Riefenstahl and her Alpine-films director, Dr. Arnold Fanck.

Riefenstahl had never seen Marlene be daring in the theater and thought it was *her* presence that caused Marlene to flaunt more than legs. Dr. Fanck, who mostly shot Alps and glaciers, found Sternberg's set agreeably animated. He did not forget Sternberg's outraged, "You sow! Pull down your pants! everyone can see your pubic hair!" Leni Riefenstahl recalled a gentler, "Marlene! Don't behave like a swine!" She may have remembered it that way because it was the sort of thing she had warned Sternberg to expect.

Marlene's playfulness relieved tension as Sternberg's fury reflected it. Nothing in *The Blue Angel* was as technically demanding as the songs, all of which were shot live. They projected, far more than any scripted scene, the ripe and irresistible presence of Lola Lola. Their impact remains undiminished after six decades. Marlene on her barrel singing to the professor is allure itself: face, body, voice, personality working together. What captivated theater audiences in Berlin is up there crooning and crossing her legs on that barrel. Sternberg's direction of the song is (for him) surprisingly simple and shrewd. We have seen Lola Lola's electricity and charm from the start, but it is only now that he allows Marlene to use the lower registers of her voice, the full wattage of her personality. His filming of her song sequences now and later was mostly turning on the cameras and letting her perform. She knew what she was doing and needed only a setting, no camera embellishment or cutting for cover. Her songs are always photographed in long, uninterrupted takes, among the simplest sequences Sternberg ever shot. Genius can sometimes leave well enough alone.

All her song numbers crackle with sex, and it was through them that Jannings realized he was no longer the star of the movie. Sternberg lavished time and attention on the shooting of the cabaret numbers, and more and more of the preparation for Marlene's scenes seemed to be taking place not on the stage but privately. Erich Pommer had noted from the beginning an obsessiveness Sternberg could only partially conceal behind his artist's "horrible" mask, but perception of their affair widened through the company as Marlene began bringing lunches she prepared at home to share with him in her dressing room.

Jannings was self-important and self-involved enough to have missed this or to dismiss it as flirtation, but the sheer weight of the musical numbers was inescapable on screen. It was Holländer who heard Jannings's oath during rushes. "I'll strangle her," he muttered, and almost tried to in his mad scene. His jealousy of her became legend. She was singing—and walking—away with the picture. That he caused her to be hospitalized was just publicity, but his full fury in the strangulation scene was sufficient to interrupt shooting so the make-up department could cover the bruises his fingerprints made on Marlene's neck.

Shooting was over budget and two weeks over schedule almost from the beginning. Sound recording and multiple cameras caused production costs to explode, creating crisis among UFA brass already panicked by the Wall Street crash. They frantically badgered Pommer to rein in costs and time, and one way to do that was to get rid of Sternberg. Sternberg's hiatus from Paramount had a time limit: After January 14, 1930, UFA had to make weekly penalty payments to Paramount for his continued presence in Berlin. The budget soared to two million marks, making it the most expensive picture Pommer had ever made and the costliest sound film yet made anywhere.

Sternberg and editor Sam Winston had been cutting as they shot, and when shooting finished two weeks late at the end of January, they had an almost completed film. From arrival in Berlin and rejection of *Rasputin* to the nearly final cut of *The Blue Angel* had taken five months and one week.

Sternberg was ordered by UFA to return to America and bring an end to their penalty payments to Paramount. He booked himself to leave just after the Press Ball, a lavish annual affair at the end of January. He asked Leni Riefenstahl to be his guest, but at the last minute withdrew his invitation. Marlene, he told Riefenstahl, had hysterically threatened suicide if he attended with anyone but herself. Sternberg prevented the untimely end of Marlene's career by yielding to her demand. Riefenstahl went anyway, and she and Marlene were photographed together with Anna May Wong, then filming in Berlin. Marlene never looked less suicidal in her life.

Still, she had reason to be anxious. Sternberg had only two days left before turning *The Blue Angel* over to Pommer and Sam Winston (who would stay behind) for finishing touches he would not see until the picture was in release. (The English version was cut and finished even later by Pommer and Sam Winston's brother Carl.) Sternberg had allowed Marlene to watch the editing of the film and she had learned more from November to January about film and *herself* on film than in her entire career to date. She knew enough to be grateful and to want more.

Sternberg was now sailing away, leaving her alone to handle what was literally the turning point of her life. She could share some of her anxieties with Rudi (who knew Sternberg and didn't mind at all that he was obsessed with his wife), but her future balanced on the whims of people over whom she had no control, sexual or otherwise, and who—with any luck—would hate her.

Of all the many visitors to Stage Five during shooting, by far the most important had been Paramount's B. P. Schulberg. Sternberg had very early wired his enthusiasm for Marlene to Jesse Lasky in America, who dispatched Paramount sales manager Sidney Kent to see for himself if Sternberg was on to something or just sexually obsessed. Kent wired Lasky, "SHE'S SENSATIONAL—SIGN HER UP!"

Schulberg saw Marlene's test in Berlin and approved a contract. There was urgency, as Universal's man in Berlin, Hungarian Joe Pasternak, was also pursuing Marlene for America. He had been ever since production of *The Woman One Longs For* for Terra Film, which was allied with Universal. Pasternak had even met with Marlene to discuss it. She received him in her dressing room "wreathed coolly in a sheer peignoir and nothing else," he said, and she thanked him graciously for his interest. Sternberg knew of the meeting (Pasternak had had to ask his permission), which intensified his own sense of urgency.

Marlene did not accept the Paramount contract when it was offered because she *could* not. Her *Blue Angel* contract with UFA contained an option for her services that could be exercised—or not—only after UFA's executives had screened the film, only after Sternberg had sailed for America.

Sternberg later spun an anecdote in which he gave Marlene five minutes to say yes or no to Paramount and himself, but that was fiction. He left Berlin consumed by Marlene personally and professionally, and there was nothing whatever he could do except hope UFA would be blind to what he and she had created for them on screen.

There was later much talk of Marlene's tortured uncertainty about going to America and Paramount at all, and Marlene undoubtedly worried about Heidede, now five years old. Nor was America a sure thing, no matter how confident or passionate Sternberg seemed. A contract was only a contract. She might turn out to be another Georgia Hale or Evelyn Brent, decorative for a few films and never heard from again. *The Blue Angel* was only an unseen, unreleased German picture with (as yet) no American distributor. All Marlene needed to do was let word of the Paramount offer leak in Berlin and the news would undoubtedly have stirred UFA to exercise its option on her, perhaps even tying Rudi to it in some production capacity. Or *Rudi* could have leaked it. To UFA or Terra or Universal or anybody else. Neither did. Both remained silent in a business in which silence is rare, enduring no indecision about her going to America, only the suspended animation of waiting for UFA to see the picture and cast the dice of her future as they would.

On January 30, four days after the Press Ball, Sternberg left on the *Bremen* for New York. His leave-taking must have been excruciating for one so dedicated to control. He sailed without seeing the final version of his film or knowing his future with Marlene. His only consolation was the bon voyage bouquet of mimosa she brought him and a cheap popular novel to read on shipboard, to which she may have been attracted because the title reminded her of Uncle Willi's chic and beautiful wife: *Amy Jolly: Woman of Marrakesh*.

A week or more after Sternberg's departure. *The Blue Angel* was screened for Hugenberg and his executives. Perhaps their alarm at what they saw on screen should have been expected from men who didn't know the difference between Heinrich and Thomas Mann. They canceled the premiere of the picture. The February opening was aborted to force Pommer to make changes they insisted on if they were to release the picture at all.

Movie history is full of moments that seem apocryphal, and many are, but this one was real and nonnegotiable. The UFA insistence on the professor's humanity had not been satisfied because he did not do the truly "human" thing for them and die at the end.

Their reaction was not only psychologically revealing, but suggested they didn't know what they were looking at even as they looked at it. Sternberg had used a moving camera only twice in the picture, in identical shots closing off the first half and then at the end of the film. Both were long, slow camera retreats from the professor at his classroom desk. The first time he slumps over it mourning the career he is sacrificing for Lola Lola. At the end, the shot is repeated exactly. He returns to the same desk in the middle of the night and slumps over it to die. Pull back: FADE OUT.

Hugenberg and company didn't get it. They didn't know if he had died or *what*. The professor's humanity was insufficiently clear and they refused to release the picture until it was. Pommer was left with an inflexible management and no director to shoot any other, clearer ending. He fought and lost. Beethoven won.

Beethoven on the sound track—not the silence Sternberg wanted, or even Friedrich Holländer (as in the later reedit of the film)—but Beethoven would convey the wages of sin and their message of humanity.

In their consternation over moral clarity the UFA overlords ignored the woman on the screen and dropped the option of this minor player in what looked like sure catastrophe. Within hours Marlene was in the office of Paramount's Berlin representative, Ike Blumenthal, signing a two-picture contract guaranteeing her $1,750 per week, with Paramount sales manager Sidney Kent to countersign the paper guaranteeing Josef von Sternberg would be her sole director.

The Berlin press (in understandable confusion) simultaneously announced the cancellation of *The Blue Angel* premiere and the signing of Marlene's Paramount contract. Conflicting signals led to open speculation about director and star. A Bavarian newspaper reported it was *not* true that Marlene and Sternberg were "engaged," and added that their nonexistent affair (an issue gossip forced them to raise in order to deny) had nothing to do with her going to Hollywood. Marlene carelessly allowed a journalist from Vienna to quote her that Riza Royce von Sternberg's hasty and premature return to America during shooting had nothing to do with her, as Sternberg wanted to be rid of his wife anyway, a remark that would circulate quickly in far-off Hollywood.

Paramount made no comment at all regarding *The Blue Angel*, which they hadn't seen. It was UFA's picture, not theirs, though the Paramount publicity department was already at work on "Adolph Zukor's" new star, sending press releases to the world (without photographs, which Sternberg forbade for the moment). On February 26 the *Los Angeles Times* announced that "Malena" Dietrich had arrived in Hollywood.

She had arrived noplace but in hot water, for in all the anxiety over the UFA option and the Paramount contract, Marlene forgot—or forgot to mention—that she was no more free to sign with Paramount than ever. In a *chambre séparée* the year before, she had signed a three-year contract with Robert Klein, producer of *Two Bow Ties*, who had no intention of letting her forget it now.

Marlene's instinct for friendship sent her to the man of the world Sternberg called his father-confessor, Dr. Karl Vollmoeller, who had so quietly helped her to obtain Lola Lola in the first place. She told him how depressed she was and asked him to use his influence with Klein to get her out of the contract, while Paramount lawyers were simultaneously negotiating a settlement with Klein and wondering what on earth Sternberg had gotten himself and them into. Vollmoeller did as he was asked and Marlene wrote him a thank-you note, inviting him to dinner.

Paramount settled with Klein for twenty-thousand marks, or exactly the salary Marlene had received for *The Blue Angel*. She received a bonus of five-thousand marks for the English version (*not* dependent on American release), which she used to buy a fur coat. Klein accepted his payoff and berated himself for the rest of his life for settling for too little and not even getting credit for that.

The Blue Angel premiere was rescheduled for April 1, allowing time for Beethoven and some unknown censorship changes demanded in Berlin and made by Pommer. Right up to opening night, perhaps the only other Berliner aware of the sensation Marlene was about to create was, curiously, Heinrich Mann. Pommer had screened the picture for Mann in Nice, hoping for an endorsement. Mann gave him a pointed one: Posterity was now likely to remember him only because of "the naked thighs of Miss Dietrich."

The picture's gala April 1 opening at the Gloria-Palast on the Kurfürsten-damm began as Jannings's evening. Every Berlin newspaper wrote exten-sively about the film before the premiere, discussing the novel-to-film process, with articles by Vollmoeller, Zuckmayer, and Heinrich Mann. As Jannings's "first" sound film and UFA's most expensive film to date, the gala attracted captains of industry and finance, artists, writers, all of theat-rical Berlin not working elsewhere that night, plus squadrons of police to direct traffic outside the theater.

In the audience, young actress Dolly Haas sat next to Trude Hesterberg and remembered sixty years later hearing Mann's mistress confidently pre-dict that the evening "belonged to Emil." Everyone knew Marlene was untalented, Hesterberg said. Why, she had recently complained all over Berlin that "Nothing's ever going to happen to me. No one wants to know about me, not in Vienna and not now in Berlin. I'm going to give it up and find a new career!" Perhaps Heinrich hadn't telegraphed from Nice about those thighs.

The picture had been screened for critics that afternoon. Jannings had been there and saw in the finished film how prescient he had been in watching dailies, and now he rued the day. A few evenings before, he had had dinner with Count Harry Kessler and had loudly proclaimed that talking pictures made theater obsolete. What he saw on screen that after-noon suggested the obsolescence of something else. He was a bully and an egomaniac and often a ham, but he was a professional and knew a star when he saw and heard one.

From the first shot of Lola Lola on the cabaret stage, she electrified. It wasn't just her image, so erotic and aggressive; it was the *sound* of her, too. Her first song—"Tonight, kids, I'm gonna get a man!"—is an alley cat's aria, and her shrill voice cuts through the cabaret smoke like a beacon through fog.

It is the only moment in the film in which she is so nakedly, lustfully the incarnation of sex critics would comment on for decades. So stunning is that first moment, so shocking the professor's reaction to it, that the image almost overwhelms the more romantic and seductive ones to follow. She crooned Berlin to helpless capitulation, and her image still does wherever eyes look and ears listen.

All through the evening Hugenberg and his associates sat in shock that the vulgar tramp they had so casually dismissed was becoming a star before their eyes. Emil Jannings stood alone at the coffee bar. He drank cup after cup, drowning rue in caffeine, hearing Marlene's songs pour out of the theater, to go, he knew, around the world. He had not been wrong about the woman he wanted to strangle and perhaps now regretted his restraint. For those dressed up fit to kill with *Schadenfreude*, like Trude Hesterberg, that night was a revelation never to be forgotten. Or forgiven.

The Berlin theater world knew Marlene basically as a musical performer. They knew she had never come alive on screen as she had in *It's in the Air* or *Two Bow Ties* or even *Misalliance*. They knew she was beautiful and suggested Garbo somehow but they thought she didn't—maybe never would—quite *connect*.

Sound film was too new for them to anticipate how that look and that voice, joined and amplified and more than life-size, would not merely connect, but overwhelm.

Few reflected in the tumult of the night's enthusiasm that Lola Lola was the first character Marlene played on screen who was what she was, a stage performer who sang, who knew how to use voice and body to insinuate, provoke, charm, and excite. The microphone merged the sound of her to the look of her. That voice, those eyes, those legs, that *allure* captured in the fervent, fervid intimacy of Sternberg's camera formed a whole greater than the sum of parts they thought they knew.

Lola Lola is one of the most vivid characters in all film history, endlessly present, never repeatable, not even by her makers. One looks back through the shifting imagery of the Dietrich persona Josef von Sternberg would now pursue, and wonders.

Sternberg did not. He serenely donned the Svengali cape the press threw around his frame. "Her behavior on my stage was a marvel to behold," he explained. "Her attention was riveted on me. No property master could have been more alert. She behaved as if she were there as my servant, first to notice that I was looking about for a pencil, first to rush for a chair when I wanted to sit down. Not the slightest resistance was offered to my domination of her performance. Rarely did I have to take a scene with her more than once."

He "put her into the crucible of my conception, blended her image to correspond with mine, and pour[ed] lights on her until the alchemy was complete," allowing her "to externalize an idea of mine, not an idea of [hers]."

Thus spake Svengali of Trilby.

But when we watch Marlene Dietrich in Lola Lola's silk stockings we wonder what *she* brought to that female archetype, so persuasive, so effort-less in its immediacy. She tells us only that "I, the well brought up, the reserved, still entirely unspoiled girl from a good family, unwittingly had accomplished a unique feat that I was never again to repeat successfully."

Thus spake Trilby.

Lola Lola speaks for herself. When we watch and listen to her sovereign, mocking sexuality we do not see and hear Svengali *or* Trilby. We see an ostrich-plumed chorus girl of *Girl-Kabarett*; we see Ruby from *Broadway*; we see "such a ripping girl" from Shaw; we see Shakespeare's "bouncing Amazon"; we see "the girl from the Kurfürstendamm"; we see Rosa Va-letti's pupil; the Sorcerer's apprentice; Eve, catching a cold in a body-stocking on a drafty stage. We see ambition finding fame on a podium after surviving every humiliation of casting and rejection or, as Sternberg re-minded us, "every parasite" in the world to which she had devoted herself with diligence for a decade.

We also see the birth of a great star and seldom note that it is also the end of something. Lola Lola was the last role Marlene Dietrich would ever play in her life that was not created *for* her, or tailored to her measure. There was challenge and aspiration to Lola Lola that would never be there again, the stretch she had to make *as an actress* to fit a role. The roles would now have to fit *her*, and something got left behind in the Blue Angel cabaret.

In the Gloria-Palast that night nothing was missing. Curtain call followed curtain call. Marlene, in a long white gown and furs, bowed from the stage to cheers. She accepted a bouquet of roses nearly as large as co-star Jan-nings, who looked on quietly dazed as photographers lit up her triumph with flashbulbs. The curtain calls reached such a crescendo they disrupted traffic on the Kurfürstendamm.

Marlene had begun to lose weight on Sternberg's order, and looked far more elegant than the blowsy Lola Lola for whom the audience stamped and roared. She was, it turned out, dressed for travel. She left the theater with ovations still ringing and took her roses with her to Uncle Willi and Jolly's villa in the Liechtensteiner Allee. A going-away party was in full riot, but she spent most of it hunting for the steamship tickets she had forgotten in the premiere excitement. Her driver ate the ice cream cone of a small boy—Marlene's cousin Hasso—who hated him for it while Marlene said good-bye to Berlin.

She left for the boat train and the *Bremen*, the same ship that had carried Josef von Sternberg to America two months before. After nearly a decade, after more than forty parts in films and plays, she had become a cliché that, unlike most clichés, almost never happens: an overnight sensation. With less than overnight to savor it.

She was leaving much behind, but there were few backward glances in the fever of fame that night. In none of the legion of accounts that commemorate that evening, with all the detailed memories of police and press and chagrined industrialists and astonished celebrities and adoring public does anyone mention Rudi Sieber or Heidede. Not one. Not even Marlene.

The boat train left at midnight.

HOLLYWOOD

SEVEN

FAME

1930 - 1931

The decks of the *Bremen* shuddered as the ship hoisted anchor at dawn on April 2, 1930. The spring morning was raw and blustery. Marlene's traveling companion, Resi (her Berlin dresser, sent along by Rudi), lost her breakfast with the ship's first lurch, and her dentures went with it. Banished to the cabins below, thick with the scent of roses from last night's premiere at the Gloria-Palast, she left Marlene alone on deck to turn her face to the west.

Stormy seas would delay docking in New York by a full twenty-four hours, but the swells of the Atlantic were no fuller than the expectations of the woman who viewed them now, no greater than the ambition driving her or the diligence needed to realize, or survive, it. But the "overnight sensation" had been around the theater long enough to land on her feet—

with or without roses—no matter how the ground or sea shifted beneath them.

She had no guarantees for what lay on that far horizon, but she could smell Fame on the sea breeze. She had wanted it fiercely since childhood and was willing to cross an ocean to get it now, not unmindful of what she was leaving behind or that distances cannot always be measured in miles.

She was sailing partly *for* Rudi and Heidede, she believed. Rudi had urged and encouraged her, and he was happier on his own anyway, or with Tamara. Heidede had been alone before without damage anyone could see or had attempted to assess. Marlene's fame could build a future for them all—here or there—somewhere—though its features were not much clearer than the cloud-banked horizon ahead.

The biggest star in Berlin, after all, still barked rather than talked; the world's greatest comedian was still mute; the world's most admired love goddess wanted to be silent and alone. But that couldn't last. Pictures were being made now in bi- or trilingual versions. Stars like Lilian Harvey could make films in Berlin and act and sing in German, English, and French as she had just done in Pommer's *Liebeswalzer* or *Love Waltz* or *Valse d'amour*. So could Marlene if it came to that.

Hollywood perched higher and richer on the new Tower of Babel, and maybe the view was clearer from up there. "Made in Hollywood" German-speaking movies were already on Berlin screens. Marlene's long-ago director Wilhelm Dieterle was even now making a Warner Brothers' German version of the old Arabian nights fantasy *Kismet*. And when American marquees finally boasted that "Garbo Talks!" they would boast in Berlin that *"Garbo spricht Deutsch!"* because she would.

The power, the money, the dream were all across the sea. It wasn't just that Josef von Sternberg was there and staying there, but Lubitsch and Murnau and Eisenstein were too. She was only going for two pictures, whatever happened. She had a round-trip ticket. There would always be Berlin. . . .

A cabin steward called out (he had been calling out for some time) for a "Frau Sieber." He bowed with a little heel-click when she recognized her name and smiled to the page. He held a little silver tray on which lay a neat pile of cablegrams. He would know her next time. They would all know who "Frau Sieber" was (though not by that name), for the cables were the first of scores that would clatter over ship-to-shore, shore-to-ship airwaves from Rudi and Berlin.

She opened one to read that the *Berliner-Zeitung* said *The Blue Angel* was "the first work of art in sound film" and she was "the Experience." There was another ("Extraordinary!") and another ("Fascinating as no woman has ever been before in film") and another ("You feel the heat from the screen"). There would be an unending stream from Berlin, then Vienna, then London, Fame chasing her as she sailed. Even as the ship built steam she tore one open to read "Marlene Dietrich has already gone to America; German film is one artist poorer."

But German film—UFA, anyway—had rejected the artist, even *after* seeing her artistry as Lola Lola. As she watched the shore dissolve in fog she knew that coastline had been cold, rocky, stingy with opportunity. She folded the cables carefully so Resi could paste them in scrapbooks, put them in the pocket of the fur coat she had bought with her bonus for the English version of *The Blue Angel*, and turned her back on the receding shore that no longer turned its back on her. There would be an endless procession of little silver trays full of typeset echoes of the cheers of the night before, ovations that would never truly recede; tardy but lasting vindication for the years of being ignored or miscast or not cast at all.

She set her face again to the horizon, to the future, to the man who made these cables possible, this Fame. With him there might be more, big as any podium she had ever dreamed of. Big as the Atlantic. *Bigger*.

There would be a sea change, *had* to be, and even as the *Bremen* sailed, Josef von Sternberg was trying to dictate what it would be. To a roomful of ink-stained wretches behind high, fake-Moorish gates on Marathon Street in Hollywood, he began to orchestrate the sea change of Paramount employee #P-1167.

P-1167, he told them, was pronounced Mar-*lay*-na. She was twenty-five or twenty-three. She was born in Berlin or Weimar or Dresden. She had a baby who was four or two or new and a husband who was a producer or a director or an executive. Her real name was von Losch and Maria or Marie and Magadalena or Magdalene, and her father had been a Franco-Prussian War hero or major in the imperial cavalry—or both—who had fallen during the Great War fighting Russians. She had taken Dietrich (*Dee*-trick) as a *nom d'artiste* to spare the sensibilities of the aristocratic court jewelers to whom her mother was heiress, and of the von Losch family, so noble they might not notice her at Max Reinhardt's theater school without her von. She had been a concert violinist before something happened to her wrist, whereupon she married, had a baby, appeared as a student in "a skit," and was discovered by Josef von Sternberg.

P-1167 was, like the *Bremen*, launched.

As her ship crossed, Marlene read and reread her reviews, played Ping-Pong, and reveled in celebrity. She met a young American couple called Stroock, known to New York show folk as Jimmy and Bianca Brooks as in Jimmy's Brooks Costume Company. Marlene tried to seduce Bianca with some illustrated lesbian literature she had tucked away in her luggage. This relieved Bianca, who had feared the beautiful German actress receiving all the cables had her eyes on *Jimmy*. When Marlene explained her telegrams and European folk ways the Americans relaxed, nicknamed her Dutchy, and decided she was a greater card than that other famous kidder, New York mayor Jimmy Walker.

They landed in New York on April 9, a day late because of weather. Marlene was photographed sitting on twelve pieces of luggage, including her portable phonograph and two violin cases (one with a musical saw), by photographers who had not the slightest idea who P-1167 was, and P-1167 knew it.

She was hustled to a breakfast press conference at the Ritz, where Paramount co-founder Jesse Lasky introduced her to the press and (not too sure who she was himself) did all the talking. Lasky said *The Blue Angel* would open at the Criterion in May (pure invention) and that P-1167 might appear on Broadway for producer Gilbert Miller (more invention, but Miller was financed by Paramount and was on the board). At least this suggested "the Potsdam peacherino" (as the press dubbed her) could speak English.

She did. And told them she was homesick for her "baby."

This created a mild sensation in the days before peacherinos had babies or admitted it in any language at all.

She assuaged homesickness right away by sitting for the camera of New York photographer Irving Chidnoff and creating another sensation, less mild. Sternberg had exacted from Paramount a contractual guarantee that she would not be photographed without his supervision. He had no intention of letting any Marlene Dietrich be revealed to the world but his, not even hers. His rage melted telegraph wires as he ordered photographs and negatives destroyed. Marlene scooped up an armload, scrawled them with green-ink autographs, and flung them back across the Atlantic, where they landed on magazine covers in Berlin and Vienna.

Marlene was restless in New York. She left Resi trying out her new teeth on room service at the Algonquin and went dining and dancing with Walter Wanger, Paramount's East Coast head of production and Lothario-about-town. Wanger introduced her to bootleg hooch (right out of *Broadway*), and troubadour Harry Richman lisped his famous hit, "On the Sunny Side of the Street," to her. When Marlene called long distance to explain her whereabouts, Sternberg (who knew Wanger's side of the street) ordered her, "Leave New York immediately." She got on the Twentieth-Century-Limited.

Sternberg boarded a train, too. He had stayed discreetly away from the New York reception, but photography sessions and speakeasy crawls forced him to abandon discretion—and Riza Royce von Sternberg. His train met Marlene's in New Mexico and they arrived together in Pasadena on April 13. "Script conferences," he explained to the press—and Riza Royce von Sternberg. He had taken with him a screenplay based on the novel Marlene had given him when he left Berlin two months before. Marlene said she thought *Amy Jolly: Woman of Marrakesh* "weak lemonade," but Sternberg thought it stronger as *Morocco*.

Paramount didn't want to wait for *Morocco*; they wanted $1,750-per-week P-1167 to go to work *now*. *Paramount on Parade* was already shot, one of those all-star, all-talking, all-everything extravaganzas studios felt obliged to produce then, including every face under contract, some of them in Technicolor, guided by Paramount directors. There was still time to shoot an introductory segment for the German market, with Marlene singing a new song by Friedrich Holländer. She would wear top hat and tails and be directed by—Lubitsch.

Another sensation, not remotely mild. Sternberg was Marlene's sole director by contract (hers, not his) and claimed breach, while Lubitsch shot publicity stills with Marlene in top hat and tails. Friedrich Holländer's song got lost in the cross fire, leaving the idea songless and, therefore, pointless. Sternberg commandeered the production paraphernalia already in place, kept the top hat and white tie, and made an unprecedented trailer for Paramount's worldwide sales staff called "Introducing Marlene Dietrich." Marlene in men's clothes shocked the salesmen, but they knew who P-1167 was and who was in control.

Marlene meanwhile scooped up the *Paramount on Parade* stills and sent *those* to Berlin. One she autographed in her trademark green ink "*Vati* Marlene"—"Daddy Marlene"—just the sort of lively self-promotion that would amuse lesbian friends in Berlin, but that Sternberg was eager to quash. He would unveil his female archetype in *his* fashion—not hers— when he was good and ready.

B. P. Schulberg, as head of the studio, was good and ready. He had power and occasion. Schulberg's assistant, David O. Selznick, was newly engaged to Irene Mayer, daughter of Louis B., a union that socially joined blue-chip Paramount to rival MGM. Schulberg produced a lavish engagement party at the Beverly Wilshire Hotel, inviting A-list Hollywood. No one declined. There was dining and dancing, which suddenly, in the swank of the evening, stopped.

"There was suddenly a silence, a suspended silence," Irene Selznick remembered, "not the clarion call of bugles, but its equivalent in soundlessness. Then these high double doors at the end of the ballroom opened and in walked Marlene. No one had ever laid eyes on her before. She entered several hundred feet into the room in this slow, riveting walk and took possession of that dance floor like it was a *stage*. I can't think of any greater impact she ever made. It was something out of a dream, and she looked absolutely sensational."

Schulberg trumpeted, *"Ladies and Gentlemen, Paramount's New Star, Marlene Dietrich,"* from his seat on the dais next to his assistant's fiancée. "B. P. could sure write off *that* party!" Irene Selznick recalled. Notice had been served on Hollywood and on the lords of Garbo.

And on Riza Royce von Sternberg. Her husband's need to control his new star had led him to install her in an apartment opposite the one he shared with his wife. Marlene, stranger in a strange land, invited him at all hours to confer about script or commiserate with her about homesickness. Riza Royce von Sternberg glowered at all the traipsing back and forth across the hall and asked, "Why don't you just marry her? Maybe that will make her happy." Sternberg replied, "I'd as soon share a telephone booth with a frightened cobra."

He kept the cobra and kicked out the wife. On May 11 he ejected her "with force." Two days later she secured the legal separation being thrown out can lead to and on June 2 filed suit for divorce on grounds of cruelty.

Sternberg went back across the hall. He put Marlene with a voice coach to remove Teutonic traces that made her English sound harsh. He subjected her to the dietary and physical training of groomers, including Sylvia of Hollywood, who claimed to massage away not only fat, but cartilage, too. He supervised a makeup makeover from Paramount's Dotty Ponedel, who elevated and winged Marlene's eyebrows, lengthened and darkened her upper lashes, and drew a white line along her lower eyelids to "open" her eyes. This made them seem larger, drawing attention away from the "Swanson" or "duck" nose that had always bothered her, on which Ponedel drew a fine silver line that caught the light and "straightened" it.

Marlene's cheekbones got higher as she grew thinner, sculpted by lighting Sternberg used that was very like that of a photo booth in Berlin. Key light came from above, highlighting the cheekbones, hollowing the cheeks, shadowing the heavy-lidded eyes, and creating a halo effect that lightened the red-gold hair.

Sternberg's light and makeup melted away Lola Lola's coarseness, bathed the symmetry of that face that "promised everything" to suggest everything: mystery, yearning, temptation, warmth, vulnerability, irony, invitation, weariness—a whole gallery of looks. He enlisted the skills of Paramount still photographers Eugene Robert Richee and Don English, and Marlene took to their cameras as diligently as she had as a baby in Schöneberg. She looked at the face in the Sternberg photographs and later told a friend she thought it "the most beautiful thing I've ever seen in my life." She got thinner, blonder, more beautiful, less homesick.

*   *   *

The "weak lemonade" Marlene saw in *Morocco* needed, in fact, considerable dilution from page to screen. The novel told of a cabaret singer, prostitute, and cocaine and ether addict who calls herself Amy Jolly (pretty friend) after having been known under Paris streetlamps as Dorine d'Anjou. North Africa awakens a weakness for Legionnaires, unsatisfied by cocaine, ether, or turning tricks in a brothel for a lesbian pimp. In the end she loses her Legionnaire *and* the tolerant white-haired millionaire-artist who finds her *piquante*. She sails off to what she gamely hopes will be a triumphant cabaret engagement in a dive in Buenos Aires, wreathed in brave dreams and clouds of chemical substances. It was the tragic ingenue Marlene always thought she should play, an innocent whore.

Sternberg saw other virtues, including the Foreign Legion background (*Beau Geste* had been a huge success in 1926), a landscape easy to recreate in California and Mexico, and a story that could be peeled to the bone. Sternberg and screenwriter Jules Furthman could invent a world-weary, stateless heroine ("There's a foreign legion of women, too," she says in the film), a woman of beauty and mystery who emerges from fog and disappears into wind. Such a creature might make the parts of the world that already knew Lola Lola forget about her. Or about Greta Garbo.

Sternberg and Furthman stripped away everything that did not contribute to an image "of extreme sophistication and of an almost childish simplicity," which was the way Sternberg viewed his star. Amy Jolly had been around, but could take care of herself; beneath the beautiful, world-weary mask, the heart of a great romantic beat like the Arab tom-toms on the soundtrack. The script asked her to choose between a *vie de luxe* with a rich aesthete or hot desert sands in which to pursue hot passions and a Legionnaire. The call of the desert won.

Sternberg is usually considered an ornate, even florid director, but everything here is stripped and spare. Amy Jolly has a Past, but no past. All we know is she speaks (and maybe *is*) French, has lost her faith in men, and used to wear sables ("If I still had that coat, I wouldn't be here," she says to explain an old photograph). Morocco is reduced to light and shadow, a few palm trees, some dunes, and the odd burnoose. The millionaire-aesthete ("He'd be a great painter if he were not so rich") is a Sternberg-like *homme du monde*, the Legionnaire a rough-hewn American who never looks back.

The script concocted an ending that is one of the great romantic finales of film history or the most absurd. Or both. Amy Jolly abandons her rich fiancé (and his Rolls-Royce) to kick off her high heels and trudge barefoot through the desert after her Legionnaire.

Sternberg wanted John Gilbert to play Legionnaire Tom Brown, but

Gilbert was living out a disastrous contract at MGM that would effectively end his career. Fredric March was second choice, but David Selznick wanted him for the thinly disguised John Barrymore role in *The Royal Family of Broadway*. Gary Cooper, under contract to Paramount anyway, lobbied Selznick for the job, reminding him he had already played a Legionnaire in *Beau Sabreur*, the sequel to *Beau Geste*, and had briefly worked with Sternberg on those Clara Bow pictures Sternberg reshot for Schulberg in the late twenties. Sternberg thought Cooper "harmless enough not to injure the film" (he had just become a star with, "If you wanna call me that . . . *smile!*" in *The Virginian*), but the director actively fought for Adolphe Menjou as millionaire-aesthete La Bessière. Menjou was a star then (especially in Europe) and looked enough like Sternberg to *be* Sternberg. "I appear by proxy," the director said, and the proxy voices in one scene what sounds like a rationale for the entire film to his dinner guests (including Sternberg's one-time mentor, Émile Chautard, the director who acted with Sarah Bernhardt): "You see . . . I love her," he says. "I'd do anything to make her happy."

Sternberg knew what would make her happy and knew that sexually and romantically, he wasn't it. But by giving her the stardom she wanted, to which she was willing to devote every ounce of diligence she possessed, he might receive her occasional favors and find more than sexual satisfaction with her. He might find artistic glory.

Morocco seems a high (or low) romantic hoot today, but its structure was then as daring as that ending. The entire first third of the picture is devoted to nothing but the creation of a Star. Milieu, mood, and other characters are established, but, in a ninety-seven-minute movie, nothing happens for the first half hour that is not dedicated to creating star mystique. Sternberg's unveiling of Marlene Dietrich may be the most memorable star introduction in movie history.

We meet her on a foggy shipboard as she arrives in Morocco from nowhere. The "vaudeville actress" rejects a gallant offer of help from La Bessière ("I won't need any help"). The ship's captain calls her one of the "suicide passengers—one-way tickets. They never return."

This one does. Backstage. We see her getting ready to perform in her top hat and tails. The surprise of her dress is made more enigmatic by snatches of the French song she sings to herself in the hand mirror. Sternberg then brings her out before a hostile crowd (they, like film audiences, don't know what to make of her cross-dressing). Gary Cooper, alerted to something utterly new and beyond his or their ken, silences their booing. She waits on stage, coolly passive, cigarette smoldering.

Sternberg had already learned to leave Marlene alone when she sang, and he shoots the number in two basic shots: full and medium close, intercut with cabaret reaction, mainly Cooper's. She sings entirely against the lyric of the song about the death of love ("*Quand l'amour meurt*"), punctuating it with jaunty accents of defiant energy on syllables with the beat. To demonstrate her nonchalance she flicks her top hat back with a finger, then flips it forward in an ironic gesture of self-coronation. It is an exhibition of astonishing self-possession and authority; she takes the stage as if it were the ballroom of the Beverly Wilshire Hotel. Film critic Richard Schickel calls this "star narrative." *Morocco* is not about Amy Jolly at all, but about Marlene Dietrich. She is its content, style, and raison d'être.

The song is followed by the most memorable enunciation of sexual ambiguity in any picture. Amy Jolly takes a flower from a female patron, kisses her full on the mouth, then tosses the flower to Legionnaire Cooper. Sternberg called it "a lesbian accent," but it is more than that, more than just a private reference to Marlene and Berlin. It is one of the great defining moments in film history, and contemporary reviewers understood it not as a message about "*Vati* Marlene" (of whom they knew little or nothing) but as a signal that the woman who "won't need any help" is prepared to take on a man's world in a man's uniform with a man's daring. The top hat and tails are her armor and warning, the flower her invitation and challenge. Dietrich looks like indifference, but she's just leveling the field. It's not *her* gender she's bending, it's Cooper's. To prove it he puts the flower behind his ear.

Sternberg heightens the daring (and the dare) by at once serving up another song, this one with bare legs: Eve in a feather boa. "What Am I Bid for My Apple?" was written to culminate in a public auction for Amy Jolly's room key, but censorship watchdogs at the Hays Office got *that* (the "lesbian accent" went right by them). Amy Jolly now just passes her key to the Legionnaire, taunting him with, "You are pretty brave . . . with *women*." This—after two songs, one armored, one stripped for action—is clearly no ordinary woman.

Andrew Sarris, writing in his Museum of Modern Art monograph about Sternberg, noted that if *The Blue Angel* is about a man brought low by love, then *Morocco* is in some sense its reversal. But Professor Unrat is destroyed by love; it defines and redeems Amy Jolly. She doesn't need the pearls or French table talk of La Bessière or the sables of her past; she needs to love her man without condition, qualification, or complaint. She sacrifices the World to her heart. This is not subjugation (as more militant feminists might conclude) but loyalty to her passions. As she disappears over a sand dune at the end of the film accompanied by nothing but a goat and the sound of the wind (it continues over the Paramount logo), Tom Brown doesn't even know she's coming. It doesn't matter: The consummation is her union with her romantic self. A modern critic notes that even today the final scene "elevates Dietrich's stature as a passion artist." It's the passion that saves it, and what made her seem so Garbo-like in a role impossible to imagine Garbo attempting.

Morocco started shooting in July, and by August Paramount had seen the stills, been stunned by Amy Jolly in rushes, and read the box-office figures out of Europe on *The Blue Angel*. Schulberg began negotiations for U.S. distribution of the German picture, on which he had been dragging his feet in a Depression economy. He wanted not to promote it, but to withhold it until after *Morocco* had been released.

"SHE'S SENSATIONAL—SIGN HER UP" became "SELL HER." Sternberg picked the most inviting of the Eugene Robert Richee still photographs he had supervised and had it blown up to billboard size and plastered on walls all over the world with the caption PARAMOUNT'S NEW STAR—MARLENE DIETRICH and not another word. When it didn't fill a wall or billboard, it filled full-page ads from Santiago to Stockholm. Film magazines encouraged fan clubs based on nothing but stills (the ones in top hat and tails were earmarked only for Berlin). The world outside of Europe that would not see *The Blue Angel* for almost a year "knew" a softer, more romantic Marlene before they had seen her in *anything*. Even Louella Parsons, no stranger to Hollywood hype, wrote headlines about the "Famous Actress" nobody had seen except on billboards. Marlene Dietrich may have been the first woman in the world to be famous for being famous.

There was something to be famous about. The casting of Gary Cooper was not merely "harmless"—it had chemistry. It was the first pitting of Marlene's exoticism against the rough-hewn, down-to-earth maleness of an American type who cut her down to size and kept her ambiguity in line. Sexual tension leaped from Dietrich to Cooper with their first glances at each other and then right off the screen.

Cooper was then involved in a famous, tempestuous love affair with Lupe Velez. The "Mexican Spitfire" began doing a wicked Marlene impersonation around Hollywood (she would repeat it on Broadway after the affair with Cooper was over). Sternberg wasn't any happier than Velez about chemistry combusting on and off the set and took it out on Cooper by ignoring him.

Sternberg directed Marlene mostly in German, as much to exclude onlookers as to aid her. Cooper was annoyed anyway by Sternberg's "compelling the whole cast to stand around him in hushed silence while he was thinking," and "just grabbed him around the neck by the coat and lifted him," reported screenwriter Jules Furthman, working on the sidelines.

"You goddamned Kraut [Cooper said], if you expect to work in this country you'd better get on to the language we use here."

Cooper knew perfectly well that Sternberg was almost as American as he, but he made his point. Sternberg stalked off the stage for the day. P-1167 watched him go with "a kind of Mona Lisa smile," as Sternberg veteran Furthman noted with malicious satisfaction.

Cooper's gallantry was aroused by Sternberg's displays of what looked like cruelty toward the very Marlene he seemed to be making love to with the camera. Filming the barefooted walk into the desert that ends the picture, Marlene fainted from heat prostration and when revived asked Sternberg from her stretcher if he needed another "cloze-up." He corrected her pronunciation. Marlene told the story all over Hollywood, winning sympathy while seeming to praise him. "Isn't he wonderful?" he parodied her as saying. "He even corrects my English when I don't come out of a fainting spell properly."

Sternberg's concern over Marlene's English was necessary but overstated. Her first line in the picture was French ("*Merci, Monsieur*"), followed by "I won't need any help." According to Sternberg (Dietrich later repeated the same story) "help" came out as "hellubh," requiring hours of retakes until inspiration struck. He told her to pronounce the letters h-e-l-p as if they made a German word; it came out perfectly. He might have saved a great deal of time and lost a colorful anecdote if he had told her to pronounce the word just as she had in *The Blue Angel*, when she repeatedly sang "can't help it" with no difficulty whatever.

Sternberg boasted that his direction consisted of "Turn your shoulders away from me and straighten out. . . . Drop your voice an octave and don't lisp. . . . Count to six and look at the lamp as if you could no longer live without it." The puppeteer at work. Marlene infuriated him by being a good and obedient puppet. "She was the modest little German *Hausfrau* and I was the villain who would not allow her to speak or to appear in public," he grumbled. Marlene was kept away from publicity people, and when they complained, *he* complained—about his own coverage. "His symphony of ego," they called it, but ego was—and always had been—his only anchor in a world in which it was better to be reviled than ignored. So they sympathized with her, even as she sympathized with him, which created more sympathy for her.

What seemed clear to everyone was that Sternberg was in love and Marlene wasn't. She obeyed him, praised him, worshiped him, but worship is not love, and being "the man [she] wanted to please most" did not put him in her bed. It kept him behind the camera, making her beautiful for Gary Cooper and that greater rival, the world.

✳ ✳ ✳

Morocco finished shooting in August and was in final cut by late September. A story has grown up that *Morocco* was a surprise success, taking Paramount unawares and "saving" it in the process, but Paramount had invested fortunes in making "Paramount's New Star" famous all over the world and Schulberg knew exactly what he had because Sid Grauman told him. Paramount had never before secured Grauman's Chinese Theater in Hollywood for any showcase. One look at *Morocco* persuaded Grauman to change a long-standing anti-Paramount policy. He was willing to open the picture on Hollywood Boulevard after it had premiered in November at New York's Rivoli.

Even before *Morocco* opened there *The New York Times* had run a long article headlined "MARLENE DIETRICH EXPECTED TO BECOME SCREEN STAR OVERNIGHT." The *Times* (which, ironically, ran the icy train window still from *The Woman One Longs For* to illustrate the article) noted "if Miss Dietrich does the expected it will be the first time in the history of the talking screen that any foreign actress has won her way to stardom 'overnight.'"

Morocco broke every box-office record at the Rivoli and reaped reviews the worldwide billboards and full-page ads might have poisoned by overkill. *Photoplay*, a respected journal then, noted concisely that "[Josef von Sternberg] not only gave the picture to Marlene; she took it."

The *Los Angeles Times* flashed news of huge Depression box-office in New York and advance word that "Miss Dietrich is distinguished by . . . provocative poise and beautiful economy of expression." Her songs "echo nothing of Broadway babies, hot mamas, sweeties or honeys. The ballad about the apple is a gem of polite innuendo, far bolder in its implications than . . . anything sung to the accompaniment of swinging hip and shouting voice."

The Chinese Theater opening ten days later (complete with stage show) was as spectacular as any Hollywood opening had ever been. Gary Cooper came with Lupe Velez. The Schulbergs came; so did Adolph Zukor himself, Mr. and Mrs. Irving Thalberg themselves (Norma Shearer's chinchilla got raves), Douglas Fairbanks and Mary Pickford, newcomer Joseph L. Mankiewicz with Mary Brian, Lily Damita (an old friend of Marlene from Berlin), Joan and Constance Bennett, not to mention Prince Gabeshi Lall of India, whose maharajah regalia lacked only the elephant on which to ride through the lobby.

Marlene arrived with Sternberg in a party that included Chaplin, escorting none other than Sternberg's one-time discovery, Georgia Hale. Marlene wore black chiffon, green evening slippers, a rope of green beads, all surrounded by a black velvet wrap trimmed in silver fox.

Reviewers reviewed Stardom. Louella Parsons headlined her notice "FAMOUS ACTRESS WINS ACCLAIM AT CHINESE OPENING." Parsons noted the "waiting to pass judgment, to see if she were worthy of the amazing publicity campaign waged on her behalf." She was. "We have to admit Paramount's superlatives are not misplaced in the case of Miss Dietrich. She has a poise, a calmness and a subtlety that are fascinating." After lecturing Sternberg for his sins (and wishing Menjou's part were more "sane"), Parsons forgave all, as "[it] is mostly Dietrich."

Louella did not overlook the inevitable. "There is a definite likeness to Greta Garbo," she reported, "although Miss Dietrich is prettier." The National Board of Review said "the newly risen star shines forth, a personage indeed, something different on the screen, an actress to wit, a symbol of glamour, like whom there is but one other in motion pictures—and when you see *Morocco*, you will be reminded who that is."

Everyone was consumed with the comparison but Garbo herself. When asked her opinion, she is said to have asked, "Who is Marlene Dietrich?" perhaps the wittiest public statement of her life.

Marlene professed to be "heartbroken" by such talk. "If they had only shown *The Blue Angel* first, then people would not say these things. [In that picture] I was," she confided, "not a very nice girl, a little tough. I was not like Garbo," she asserted, "I was myself. In *Morocco* it is different. Maybe I do look a little like her, but I don't try to. If I do, I can't help it . . . it [is] cruel of people to say such things," she moaned as the Chinese and the Rivoli broke box-office records night and day.

Fame feeds on and inspires speculation. Conjecture about Marlene was orchestrated into a blend of contradictory images reinforced by the contradictions of character in *Morocco*. On the one hand there was Amy Jolly, the "passion artist," and Marlene, the continental who might be a Hollywood homewrecker. On the other there was the Amy Jolly who gives up riches for love, and Marlene, who stayed home, worshipped her absent child, read Goethe and Kant, and baked cakes. ("When you think about the amount of bakery goods she supposedly made," Irene Selznick recalled, "she must have had a *factory* someplace").

The only factory she had was Paramount, which made certain that "*Mutti* Marlene" was photographed telephoning Baby Heidede in the middle of the night, or planted items that the temptress gave so few interviews not in imitation of Garbo, but because she carried her baby's tooth around in her mouth. The contradictions got entered into the public logbook to temper the screen image and defend against scandal, still simmering along with Riza Royce von Sternberg's dark rage.

The factory was aware it had only a two-picture deal with P-1167. Even before *Morocco* was finished they realized with alarm that P-1167 had a return ticket to Europe. They offered her another contract almost tripling her guarantee at $125,000 per picture, two a year. Making her second picture under the old contract became imperative.

Sternberg wanted to call it X-27. *Dishonored*, it got called. It was hastily conceived and went into production in early October, just weeks after *Morocco* finished shooting. It has a hurried air about it that makes it the least of the Dietrich-Sternberg pictures, but in some ways the easiest to take. It tells the story of a prostitute on the streets of Vienna recruited by the head of the Austrian Secret Service as a sort of love-spy (X-27) to avenge her soldier husband's death (this is the Widow Kolowrat). It was familiar stuff to begin with, reprising Garbo's *Mysterious Lady* and anticipating her *Mata Hari* a year later, when MGM realized how vigorously Marlene had shaken the Garbo throne.

X-27 falls in love with Russian H-14, helping him to escape her masters. She gets executed for it. After the electricity of Marlene and Cooper in *Morocco*, Sternberg tried to pair them again, but Cooper refused to work with him. Sternberg (perhaps with relief) cast burly Victor McLaglen as her lover, an actor who belonged in a poolroom, not a bedroom, which put all the weight on Marlene's sequined shoulders.

For once Sternberg's claim to story was real (Daniel N. Rubin wrote the screenplay). When shooting began the director removed most of the pesky dialogue (to the annoyance of actors eager to talk), but what he left shows what happened without an Erich Pommer or Jules Furthman around to edit him.

The picture begins with a close-up of Marlene's legs in the rain. A suicide has been discovered in the streets of wartime Vienna. In a continuation of the cadenced dialogue Sternberg had forced on her in *Morocco*, she remarks: "I've had an inglorious life / it may be / my good fortune / to have / a glorious / death." Love is again the key to redemption.

To get it, X-27 wears a lot of clothes, including a sequined cape that looks like chain mail and the same aviatrix uniform she wore in *The Ship of Lost Souls*. (The "ice-water" poured on Sternberg by Marlene's Berlin "drivel" did not inhibit his borrowing from it.) She loves her cat (which betrays her), but it doesn't matter: "I suppose / I'm not / much good / that's all." Being executed is just "another exciting adventure / the perfect end / to an imperfect / life."

Dishonored is now and then lightened by humor that may be intentional. The exchange between X-27 and a general she exposes is classic: "What a charming evening we might have had," General von Hindau (Warner Oland) tells her, "if you had not been a spy and I a traitor." "Then," she points out, "we might never have met." "How true!" he says, admiring her logic before going into the next room to blow his brains out.

The pièce de résistance was again a subversive ending. X-27 is to be executed for not betraying love and requests that she be dressed in "any uniform / when I served my countrymen / instead of / my country." She puts on her hooker garb, applies her lipstick using a guard's saber as a mirror (Sternberg tried but failed to shoot the reflection), and refuses to wear a blindfold before the firing squad. A veil will do. The young officer in charge goes hysterical because "*I will not kill a woman!*" While gallantry is subdued, X-27 refreshes her makeup and adjusts her stockings. They shoot her. The head of the Secret Service salutes her body in the snow. Dishonored, maybe, but what *style!*

It is easy to imagine any actress having fun with the audacity of it all as antidote to the stale formula. *Dishonored* mainly presents Marlene as a dramatic actress without songs (though she decodes spy messages at the piano!) and furthers Sternberg's increasingly ceremonial presentation of his female archetype, insolent but gallant. The cadenced dialogue, the photographic effects of Marlene, now in this lighting, now in that, the all too sardonic glances all contribute to the feeling of a museum in which Marlene is the only exhibit for the curator-camera's contemplation. You forget Victor McLaglen is in it even as you *watch* him (he complained about "feminine camera angles"). After the vitality of Lola Lola and the smoldering passion of Amy Jolly, X-27 offers nothing but insolence and irony, which were new enough. And more beautiful than ever.

Shooting ended in late November just after Thanksgiving, a day on which Marlene, cast, and crew feasted on work for eighteen hours. *Morocco* was now packing theaters all across America and Resi was packing bags for Berlin. Two days later Marlene appeared in person at a midnight screening of *Morocco* at Grauman's Chinese Theater. The reception was as jubilant as that at the Gloria-Palast less than a year before. This was rapture, the aphrodisiac of applause and public adulation after the private tortures of dieting, exercise, drudgery, diligence, and perfectionism. All for a lens—a piece of glass that filtered light and shadow—and for a man who loved her but could satisfy her only when looking through a viewfinder. The roar from the audience was the fame she had longed for, rows and rows of it, a crescendo of what performers like to call love. She embraced it as it embraced her. It warmed and consoled her and confirmed that she was more than just shadows on celluloid, more than a puppet, more than P-1167.

She left the next day for New York, dropped in on Jimmy and Bianca Brooks, and got on a ship.

Six days later she was greeted in Berlin by fanatical press, by Josephine and Rudi. She was just in time for Heidede's sixth birthday party, and two weeks later she herself turned twenty-nine. She enjoyed for a few weeks the first and last public jubilation she would ever experience in the city of her beginnings. She was toasted, fêted, photographed, mobbed, and celebrated wherever she went. She visited old haunts, causing riots; went to see the latest Friedrich Holländer revue, where the audience demanded she sing "Falling in Love Again" from the stage before allowing the performance to continue. *Morocco* opened and was as big a hit in Berlin as in Hollywood and New York, as big as it would be all over the world.

She visited Betty Stern's, hoping to be a friend among friends. It was impossible. Her notoriety among opportunists who had previously ignored her was not sweet revenge, but claustrophobic. Fame crowds and isolates at once. She sought refuge on the stairway in the hall, where she was joined by a journalist friend from the old days of careless work and play.

He asked her how she liked it, the fame, the jubilation. After a moment she said, "I had it hard as a young actress in Berlin. Maybe you know that. I could have been spared a lot. Maybe you *don't* know that. . . . Well, fame doesn't make me truly happy anymore. Funny, isn't it? Naturally, its very nice and I'm not ungrateful. . . ."

She paused, then added, "It came too late."

But it had only just begun.

EIGHT

EMPRESS OF
DESIRE

1931 - 1932

Fame unfurled in a black-and-white ribbon that wound around the
world. In little more than four months Marlene Dietrich had become
one of the most famous women in the world, admired, desired, and envied.
Morocco was still breaking house records when Paramount opened the
English-language *Blue Angel* in December, quickly following with *Dishonored* in March.

The newly minted goddess was in Berlin when it happened, preparing
Heidede for her first day of school just after Easter. Then Marlene—or
Dietrich, as the world began to call her—would return to Paramount and
Sternberg, leaving Heidede in a German school where (she told the Ger-
man press) a German child belonged.

Whether Marlene believed what she told reporters or not, she knew how to play to local prejudices. At least for a time. More had changed in the eight months since Marlene left than Marlene. Berlin was changing, and so were the people who had once made it home.

She discovered after her arrival that just as she had embarked from New York, a political party called the National Socialists had met in Bayreuth and declared *The Blue Angel* "mediocre and corrupting *Kitsch*," demanding its total ban on German screens.

She discovered that after audiences had clamored for her to sing "Falling in Love Again" to them from a stage, the star of Friedrich Holländer's revue (his ex-wife) had excoriated her as a Hollywood Movie Star slumming at the Theater.

She discovered that Berlin critics were enchanted by her, but sneered at *Morocco* as the "weak lemonade" she always thought it was; that resentment roiled at press reports that she would be making a quarter of a million dollars a year (worth roughly four million early 1990s dollars) in America while unemployment and misery mounted at home. And why was she playing first French, then Austrian in those American films? How *German* was that?

She discovered that Jolly Felsing, the chic and beautiful exemplar of her youth, had left Berlin and Uncle Willi to fly over Africa with World War I air ace Ernst Udet (then the most famous stunt flyer in the world). A resigned Uncle Willi tended clocks and jewelry that sold more slowly now, still smoking the one hundred and twenty Russian cigarettes a day that would kill him. His young son Hasso spent time with Heidede and the nursemaid Rudi had hired to look after her and played games with sister Elisabeth's son, Hans-Georg. Hasso would soon, on Uncle Willi's death, become Josephine's ward in that dragon-strict household in the Kaiserallee, heir to all the Conrads, all the slower and slower-selling ticks and tocks, winding down with the worldwide Depression.

Then there was Rudi. Marlene had a contract, a career, and (rented for her by Sternberg) a house in Beverly Hills with a pool. Tamara had Rudi, though they still lived apart in deference to a curious press, while Rudi played attentive father to Heidede in the apartment they shared with the child's nursemaid. It was unexpectedly durable, this dalliance with Tamara, but nothing to mourn. In his mid-thirties, Rudi needed to settle down from the nightlife, dwindling anyway as the Depression grew more depressing. Jobs were scarce and Marlene's fame made it harder, not easier, for a man of Rudi's pride and dash to be "at liberty." Millions less proud, less dashing, less conveniently well married were also out of work.

Marlene had always relied on Rudi for advice, guidance, and approval. When she looked at him she saw the blond, brown-eyed charmer of *Tragedy of Love* and knew she always would. She was willing to pay more than bills to keep the perfect couple—*that* Rudi and *that* Marlene—young and alive. The drives of passion had faded long ago, but bonds of parenthood and loving friendship were resilient as ever, no matter how many nightclub tables or lovers or oceans intervened. Additionally, the marriage was the perfect excuse to cut off or control Marlene's other relationships, particularly with Sternberg.

She put Rudi and Tamara out of mind long enough to go to Paris, then to the London opening of *Morocco*, where she was serenaded by pages in braid-covered uniforms blowing trumpets, and her name was spelled out in arrangements of massed gardenias. On to Prague, in Rudi's homeland, where crowds and more fame kept her company.

Back in Berlin she posed for sculptor Ernesto de Fiori, who did a bust to be exhibited at New York's Museum of Modern Art. She saw Willi Forst and went to the Press Ball with him. They dressed identically in what was now—and would be to the end of her life—Marlene's signature look: top hat, white tie, and tails, with chrysanthemums in their lapels. She was photographed in the same costume by Alfred Eisenstaedt, who had photographed her exactly one year before with Leni Riefenstahl and Anna May Wong. This time she looked not ebullient, but assured, cooler, wiser.

She recorded her songs from *Morocco* to follow her hit *Blue Angel* records and played them endlessly for Rudi, who both negotiated the contracts and applauded. She welcomed Chaplin to Berlin on his triumphant world tour. He seemed (perhaps having his own little "Who is Marlene Dietrich?" Garbo joke), not quite certain who his hostess was. The Berlin press took spiteful glee in what looked like a slight from the great Charlie. "The fastest city in the world" felt slow and sour in economic distress, hardly *gemütlich* at all. But no place did.

"Over there" Josef von Sternberg was working (or practicing puppetry, as he always called directing actors) without her. Paramount (and B. P. Schulberg) had acquired another new star, an exotic-faced actress from New York called Sylvia Sidney. Sternberg agreed during Marlene's absence to direct Sidney in material long on the Paramount shelf resisting adaptation, first by D. W. Griffith, then by Sergei Eisenstein: Theodore Dreiser's *An American Tragedy*.

Sternberg was an odd choice for social realism, but got a script he claimed was his own (it wasn't) and proved that Svengali Jo could still direct an efficient picture without his Trilby. Dreiser found the result hokum, not social critique but romantic melodrama, and sued. The film helped establish Sylvia Sidney but failed at a failing box office. When Dreiser went to court, Sternberg went to Berlin to be puppeteer of a romantic melodrama offscreen.

*   *   *

Sternberg later claimed he had intended only to make two films with Marlene, hurl her into orbit, and admire his creation from afar. But when he had helped negotiate her new contract the previous October he was already making *Dishonored*, a third picture, and did not challenge the fine print that specified Josef von Sternberg as Marlene's exclusive director. Now with the unprecedented triple play of *Morocco, The Blue Angel,* and *Dishonored*, his prestige was hardly bruised by *An American Tragedy*, which he had done as an old-boy favor to Schulberg anyway. But no failure ever helps, and Sternberg was loner enough to know that being a household name and an Artist were not enough to guarantee autonomy. If the studio thought him indispensable to Marlene, he knew Marlene was vital to *him*.

After the deepening economic doldrums following the stock market crash, Paramount power coalesced in New York, closer to the Wall Street that had crashed. Corporate reluctance to turn Sternberg loose became clear when they refused him *A Farewell to Arms* for Marlene. Paramount may have suspected Ernest Hemingway's hugely successful love story didn't need—or couldn't *survive*—Svengali Jo's cynicism. Instead, they gave it to Frank Borzage, who directed Gary Cooper and Helen Hayes in a film so sentimental it made *An American Tragedy* look as grimly realistic as bread-lines. But it was a hit and helped Paramount hold off the creditors. For the moment.

Apart from Paramount's wariness of "genius," they knew *The Blue Angel* (still a foreign film, still very German even in English) had not been the American box-office sensation that *Morocco* was. Critics praised *The Blue Angel*, but it gave them cause to reevaluate *Morocco* and genius. Sternberg had made Marlene overnight one of the two most important female stars in the world, but he seemed to be stifling her, too. Marlene in *The Blue Angel* seemed a revelation of freshness, energy, and dramatic gifts subdued by Sternberg in Hollywood, no matter how stellar he made her.

Even *Dishonored* earned praise for its star, while critics denigrated Stern-berg, perversely accusing him of dimming the very star power he was re-vealing on screen. Louella Parsons, silly but shrewd, thought Marlene "seductive, charming, and the type that any man would find dangerous . . . a superb actress." *The New York Times* found her in *The Blue Angel* "much more the actress than she is in *Morocco*" and as X-27 she was "intelligent and beguiling." In *Dishonored*, according to *Variety*, "Miss Dietrich rises above her director [,who] smother[ed] her while making *Morocco*. Dietrich is dom-inant [with] high command of herself. . . . She knows what it is all about all of the time. The girl should be given a big picture for big results, as it must now be accepted that she is a creative actress."

Sternberg was, appearances to the contrary, only human, and resented press denunciation even as he clipped and saved every column for his injustice file. They wanted a "big picture for big results"? He had one in his luggage as he sailed for Germany. In his head, anyway. And he had more. He had perspective: personal for Frau Sieber; professional for "Dietrich"; little for himself.

Sternberg knew Marlene clung to Rudi with some loyalty he didn't understand and it caused him pain even as he admired it. She was using Rudi partly to deflect his own obsession with her, but Rudi was not the enemy; he and Sternberg understood each other only too well. Marlene's marriage was both too open and too secure to be manipulated. What wasn't was Heidede, essential to Marlene's emotional life and to her somewhat romanticized vision of herself as mother.

That vision was publicly vulnerable, not because she was *not* a loving mother but because Heidede's absence and Marlene's enigmatic lifestyle invited skepticism. All the mother talk in Hollywood raised eyebrows as well as sympathy. At least one cynic wrote that it revealed "a mother complex which would interest our most astute psychoanalysts." American women's groups (mothers, most of them) had tried to boycott Marlene from her very arrival in America, because she was: (a) a Teuton who (b) had left her child among "the Huns" with whom America had so recently been at war, and (c) seemed to play nothing but prostitutes.

Marlene dismissed puritanical criticism from women she thought cared only about jewelry, cocktails, and who prepared dinner from tin cans anyway. Not only could she play roles other than prostitutes, but she had a mother-love project of her own invention that she wanted to make later in the year. Sternberg promised to consider it, but the crucial mother role was the real-life one. Heidede's well-being did not, Paramount and Sternberg and Rudi agreed, conflict with Marlene's career, which was the Dietrich-Sternberg-Sieber best economic hope as the Depression deepened.

If Rudi and Tamara wanted to live together (they did), Heidede should be with Marlene in America, not in school in Berlin, cared for by a hired nursemaid. Marlene would be happier and the press would no longer have to wonder why she missed her child if her child was *there*. Her reputation as love goddess and mother would not be enhanced, however, by her husband's living openly with another woman in high-profile Berlin. Rudi and Tamara ought not to remain where jobs were scarce and reporters plentiful. How about Paris? Where the living was good and Rudi could take charge of dubbing Paramount's American films for the European market and supervise the occasional European production at the studio in Join-ville. He would be employed, he and Tamara could stop the pretense involved in living apart and "overnighting," and curiosity about a curious marriage would be stilled.

Marlene saw the sense of it. It would save Rudi's pride, give him Tamara, give *her* Heidede. Nobody would suffer: not her career, not her growing legend as irresistible seductress. And there would always be Berlin.

Sternberg returned to America to prepare "the big picture for big results" (something about "a woman on a train"), while Marlene canceled Heidede's Berlin school plans and told the press it had nothing to do with Germany and everything to do with maternal loneliness. She left Berlin on the boat train shortly after midnight on April 16, seen off by mobs of fans and the press. Friends supplied high jinks. Willi Forst came with Rudi for a fond "*Auf Wiedersehen*." Songwriter Peter Kreuder, who had conducted Marlene's recording sessions, brought along a brass band to serenade her as she embarked in a movie-star leopard coat, child in hand.

More press and Sternberg greeted Marlene and Heidede (to be called Maria now) when they arrived in California on April 24. Marlene, now reducing three years from her own age, said six-and-a-half-year-old Maria was four, and Paramount released a photograph of them that had been published in Berlin when Maria really *was* four. It made the front page of the *Los Angeles Times*.

Sternberg installed Marlene and Maria in the Spanish-style Beverly Hills house with pool that he had rented for them at 822 North Roxbury. In the drive stood the Rolls that La Bessière drove in *Morocco*, a welcome-home gift from the proxy's original. Marlene hired an ex-boxer as chauffeur to drive her and, as tutor for Maria, a female journalist called Gerda Huber with whom she had roomed in her "girl from the Kurfürstendamm" days in Berlin.

She went back to work as "a woman on a train." Another prostitute. *Plus ça change* . . . as Maurice Chevalier might have observed from the dressing room next door.

Paramount had been "saved" by *Morocco* (It had returned a then-phenomenal $2 million profit and was nominated for four Academy Awards, including one for Marlene), but the company was real-estate-poor, audience-poor, and too revenue-poor to be grateful. The Depression pinch had incited power struggles in New York's home office, where Jesse Lasky's assistant, Emanuel Cohen, was ascendant. Lasky liked being co-founder and taking credit, but Cohen liked taking charge (more than anyone suspected, it would turn out). Schulberg reported on various projects for Marlene to both Lasky and Cohen, but Cohen did the answering.

"IT IS THE COLD UNDISPUTED FACT," he cabled Schulberg, that "ALL OF THIS MYSTERY AND GLAMOUR WERE NOT SUFFICIENT TO GIVE THE PUBLIC

COMPLETE SATISFACTION STOP IT IS TRUE THAT MOROCCO WENT OVER BUT WITH THE MYSTERY OF THIS PERSONALITY IN HER FIRST PICTURE IT HAD AN OPPORTUNITY OF MAKING A MUCH MORE TREMENDOUS SUCCESS THAN IT ENJOYED AND ESTABLISH HER ON A MUCH LARGER SCALE THAN SHE ENJOYS EVEN NOW." As for *Dishonored*, it had been "A FAIRLY COMPLETE FLOP."

Any kind of "INGENUEISH SCHOOL OF ACTRESSES" mother-love story was out of the question. All that mystery and glamour had to do what mystery and glamour were supposed to do. Cohen wanted "DIETRICH TO GET HER MAN" as she had not in *Morocco* or *Dishonored*, which might lead to "A BETTER BOX OFFICE RESULT THAN BE SOLELY AN ARTISTIC TRIUMPH."

Implicit in the almost hourly cables from New York to Marathon Street were warnings about Sternberg and Art, and the director heard them. He began laying tracks for his "woman on a train" picture, which would result in both box office *and* art. Wags would call it "Grand Hotel on Wheels." Sternberg described the source material over which his inspiration played as "a single page" by Harry Hervey (it was twenty-two) about the hijacking of a train between Peking and Shanghai during the Chinese revolution: *Shanghai Express*.

Jules Furthman turned the twenty-two pages into a script as Sternberg baptized his latest female archetype Magdalen (Marlene's own name). Riza Royce von Sternberg read all about the news, about Marlene's return to Hollywood, and Maria, and Rolls-Royces, and houses in Beverly Hills, and nursed dark vengeance in Long Beach.

The press had long since styled her ex-husband a "fool for femmes," couching innuendo in jokes about Marlene's legs. "I didn't know whether I was looking at a spy drama or a hosiery show," wrote one reviewer of *Dishonored*. "We can't see the genius for the legs."

Leg jokes could be ignored, but revived threats of a Marlene boycott in a morally straitened Depression atmosphere could not. Such threats seemed mysteriously to emanate from Long Beach, where Riza Royce was not just fulminating. She was waiting for alimony checks Sternberg wasn't bothering to send on the near-lunatic grounds that his ex-wife had caused him enough trouble already. She hadn't even begun.

Paramount had long feared *something* from Royce, and as an eleventh-hour precaution Marlene invited Paris-Paramount employee Rudi Sieber to a happy-family reunion in late July. Paramount invited the press. The conjugal visit began at the Pasadena train station where Rudi was met by Marlene, Maria, and a regiment of photographers. *And* Josef von Sternberg. They smiled for the cameras, demonstrating Three Musketeers' solidarity, while Maria clung to her father's neck and the Hollywood wags clucked "Von for all and all for von!"

Riza Royce didn't cluck—she detonated. The press greeted her "major earthquake" and "bombshell" as if she had announced the end of the Depression *and* Prohibition. Royce slapped Marlene with two lawsuits on August 6, one demanding $500,000 for "alienation of affections" and the other asking $100,000 for libel, the result of Marlene's long-ago Vienna interview in which she said (or didn't) that Sternberg had wanted to get rid of Royce even before they arrived in Berlin for their "second honeymoon."

Riza Royce exploded at assertions of a purely professional relationship: "He is madly, heart and soul, in love with her!" Rudi's savoir-faire demonstrated how friendly *he* was with Jo. Hadn't Jo met him at the train with all those photographers providing proof? Paramount's lawyers lit the midnight oil; Rudi quietly took his savoir-faire back to Paris; front-page headlines bannered "MARLENE DIETRICH DENIES LOVE THEFT"; fan magazines asked *"Is Marlene a Love Pirate?"* In an attempt at dignified rebuttal, Marlene announced she had been misquoted by that Viennese writer, which didn't for a minute mean that what she said hadn't been *true.*

Public reaction was not wholly negative (it rarely is to scandal). Paramount's awareness of sensation's value was obvious in those cables from Cohen to Schulberg, their bite louder than the barking of the moral watchdogs. The demand for "DIETRICH TO GET HER MAN" and forget the "INGENUEISH" was cabled by Cohen the day *after* Riza Royce's "major earthquake" in the press. What hardly anybody noticed—except Sternberg—was that Dietrich already *had* her man. Someone else noticed, but Madame Maurice Chevalier was in Paris. Like Rudi.

Shanghai Express began shooting in late September, its "love pirate" star more defiantly, sleekly erotic than ever. The whole moviegoing world would soon chant along with her on screen, "It took more than one man to change my name to Shanghai Lily." The line is the epitome of camp excess, but it is self-mockery, too, in a picture that looks and plays like a melodrama but is also an ironic essay on deception, hypocrisy, and redemption through love, Sternberg's standard theme.

The picture opens in a virtuoso display of atmospherics at the Peking station. The frame is jammed with exotica created on the back lot (and in nearby Bakersfield and Chatsworth: they had railroad tracks). The evocation of an imaginary China is dense with detail, elaborately layered, festooned with flags, cages, calligraphy, and blank-faced livestock suggesting inscrutability much as Sternberg's mandarin manner did. Through warrens of detail we board the Shanghai Express with its passengers, experts of deception all, except—oh, irony!—Shanghai Lily and her prostitute traveling companion Hui Fei (old Berlin pal Anna May Wong).

Chief among travelers is Shanghai Lily's ex-lover, a starched Englishman

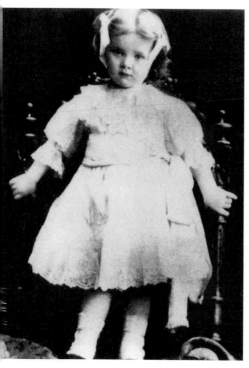

Marlene at five with her father and mother.
Sister Elisabeth has been cropped from the left.

Marie Magdalene Dietrich, aged three.

Not her graduation photo, because she didn't graduate. Marlene is second from the right
in the first row. The girl clinging to her is best friend Hilde Sperling.

Teenage Marlene's idol, Henny Porten,
"the Mary Pickford of Germany." Marlene
chased her from Berlin to Bavaria,
collecting wardrobe tips for the future.

Marlene (*left*) in the chorus line of
Guido Thielscher's Girl-Kabarett.

"A potato with hair!" The first film —
The Little Napoleon, 1922

A humiliating screen test got her this
role in *Man by the Wayside* opposite
Wilhelm (William in Hollywood)
Dieterle in 1923.

Marlene in one of several tiny scenes in *Tragedy of Love* (1922–1923), the picture on which she met Rudi.

"The most beautiful woman I ever saw in my life," Marlene called Uncle Willi's wife, Jolly Felsing, who taught her about style . . . and jewels.

Marlene as a French bad girl in *Manon Lescaut*, 1925.

Marlene in the theater. She stands at left wearing a monocle with the cast of *Duel on the Lido*. Seated left is Rudolf Forster, Heidede's godfather and Rudi's best friend. Seated middle is Fritz Kortner. Seated far right, Lucie Mannheim, the girl everbody thought would play Lola Lola. 1926.

Far right: Marlene the showgirl in the 1926 musical revue *From Mouth to Mouth*, which featured Jerome Kern's "Who?" The answer to "who?" was . . .

. . .Claire Waldoff, star of the show. She thought Marlene had potential. Here she advertises her latest hit record.

When Rudi worked for Korda, so did Marlene (*left*), as a dance extra in *Madame Doesn't Want Children*.

Marlene and Heidede about the time
Marlene left for Vienna and for . . .

. . . Willi Forst, here with Marlene in
Vienna and *Café Electric*, 1927.

Heidede was a big baby.
Here she is with cousin
Hasso about 1924.

Back in the chorus. Marlene (*left*) in *Broadway*. She and Harald Paulsen (*left*), the original Mack the Knife later that same year, were the only holdovers from Vienna. Marlene *still* played the bad girl. 1928.

Marlene (*right*) with "best girlfriend" Margo Lion and Oskar Karlweis in the scandalous musical that made her famous, *It's in the Air*, 1928.

Left: Marlene "swung" as *Princess O-la-la*, another French bad-girl movie part in 1928. The director had seen her in *Broadway*.

Gazing from the icy train window in *The Woman One Longs For*, the key shot of Marlene's silent career. 1929.

Left: Marlene and hugely popular Harry Liedtke in *I Kiss Your Hand, Madame*, a part "singie." The world-famous title song was sung by Richard Tauber. 1929.

Marlene (*center*) showed her legs even in George Bernard Shaw's *Misalliance* in 1928. Standing at left is Lili Darvas, Molnar's wife, who said Marlene could be "great without doing anything at all."

Ingenue trying to find a "look."
Princess O-la-la.

The perfect couple:
Marlene and Rudi at the
Berlin Press Ball, 1928.

called Doc Harvey, played by Clive Brook, whose recent face-lift froze his already inexpressive features. Brook was a favorite Sternberg actor; it was he on whom the one-time assistant had long ago tested his "horrible"-looking mustache. Brook's stone face, it turns out, is the perfect foil for Lily's silky toying with truth and deception.

The former lovers meet by chance on the train and Harvey politely asks, "Let's see, exactly how long has it been?" as if looking at her medical chart. Lily *knows*: "Five years and four weeks." He answers petulantly, "Well, for five years and four weeks I've thought of nothing else." There's the plot before the train is out of the station, and Harvey is derailed within seconds by the famous line about how Magdalen got to be known as Shanghai Lily, "the notorious white flower of China."

"You always believed what you heard," she taunts him. "I still do," he replies, and we know past, present, and—one look at her sculpted-ivory face beneath the black feathers—the future, too. Dietrich will get her man.

It was a commonplace by now to note that Marlene was more beautiful than ever each time out, and each time it was true. Harvey notes it, too. "You're more beautiful than ever," he says, adding absurdly, "It was nice to see you again, Magdalen." She answers, "Oh, I don't know," and puts on a jazz record to silence his single-entendre, stiff-upper-lip dialogue. Everything about *her* is double-entendre—name, veils, and those eyes that go up and down like a spider sizing up a fly.

This is the perfection of the streamlined, dangerous Dietrich, the exquisitely beautiful temptress half hidden behind veils that give away nothing but her mocking smile. She is decked out by designer Travis Banton in costumes of no period that became as notorious as her dialogue: trunks of black egret feathers, black veils, black chiffon, black marabou. She looks like the Angel of Death, and all this wardrobe fits into a tiny compartment that still has room for Anna May Wong and Lily's gramophone, too.

We meet the other passengers, the "Grand Hotel" assembly, none of them what they seem to be and most of them engaging, thanks to Jules Furthman's dialogue. If Shanghai Lily and Hui Fei are the "cargos of sin" they seem, they are still more honest than the rest, and self-sacrificing to boot. They turn stuffy Doc Harvey's blind moral universe on its head, saving his life from Chinese warlords and revolutionaries as they do, paving the way for Dietrich's redemption and "getting her man." The confinement of the train tests and exposes identity. In the corridors of deception that Sternberg's camera roams, faith is risky, but all there is.

Shanghai Lily charges Harvey with too little faith. When he confesses he should never have disbelieved or left her, she tells him she would have done things differently, too: "I wouldn't have bobbed my hair!" At once she taunts him with a telegram. "From one of your lovers?" he asks.

"No," she answers.

"I wish I could believe you."

"Don't you?"

"No."

"Will you ever learn to believe without proof?"

"I *believe* you, Magdalen." The fly surrenders, eagerly wrapping himself in her web.

The telegram is, of course, from her new Shanghai lover. "When I needed your faith, you withheld it," she says. "Now, when I don't need it and don't deserve it, you give it to me!" It is a startling moment, dangerous and dizzying, revealing Sternberg's long, never-realized flirtation with Pirandello. It is also humiliation for Harvey, whose "scientific" mind can penetrate a brain, but not a heart. It is bitter triumph for unrepentant Shanghai Lily, who has brains *and* heart.

The passengers get kidnapped en route by Warner Oland as Chang, revolutionary warlord, and their masks fall one by one. Doc Harvey is hostage for the return of a captured rebel, and Shanghai Lily is given a choice: Become Chang's mistress ("I'm weary of you *now*," she tells him) or he will blind Harvey. She agrees, but prays behind Chang's back. We see only her white hands in the dark, pale suggestions of something spiritual beating beneath Shanghai Lily's black feathers.

"I wouldn't trust you from here to the door," Chang tells her (he's shrewd), but Harvey has no choice. Love must be an unconditional yielding to faith in love, as Lily unconditionally yields to Chang to save Harvey's faithless eyes, already blind to the truth of love.

The prostitute Hui Fei kills Chang in the nick of time, allowing the train to arrive safely in Shanghai, all its passengers' secrets revealed. Among them: Shanghai Lily loved Doc Harvey all along, even if she *has* "wrecked a dozen men up and down the China coast."

Shanghai Express is a masterpiece of visualization. The train is as much a character as the actors (Sternberg later said it *was* about a train). The variety of travelers allows air to stream through the corridors in spite of Sternberg's insistence that they speak in the click-clack rhythms of a train, an effect even more stilted than the cadences of *Morocco* and *Dishonored* except for Clive Brook, who was stilted anyway.

Still, this is the most entertaining of the Dietrich-Sternberg pictures, the one in which formal experiments with sound and visuals least get in the way of narrative. It can be taken as adventure story, love story, or perverse pilgrims' tale. Andrew Sarris has commented that if "*Shanghai Express* was successful at all, it was because it was completely misunderstood as a mindless adventure," but it was hugely successful because it *is* a mindless adventure. Warner Oland as the leader of the revolution is just a routine villain, a half-breed Chinese ashamed of his white blood but not above raping oriental Hui Fei and taking Caucasian Shanghai Lily as his mistress (what kind of revolution was this?). The China atmosphere is persuasive but patronizing and, indeed, the picture was banned in China. What holds it together is Dietrich, whose mystery is dramatically strategic, not a static series of lighting experiments. "There's a scheme of things," she says. She's it.

Sternberg always used props for symbolic gestures and, sure enough, as Lily is seducing Harvey she removes his military cap and dons it herself. After safe arrival in Shanghai, she buys him a watch at the station (this is a man who *needs* to know the time). They reconcile in an embrace. If one wonders at the apparent absence of a mustachioed director's proxy, one is revealed in that embrace. Shanghai Lily wraps herself around the lover whose faithlessness almost cost him his vision and benevolently takes his riding crop from him. Hands that pray also hold the whip.

Marlene's ascension to "Dietrich," the merciful temptress taking charge of Fate and her man, was ravishing and complete. No one on screen could touch her for erotic power, for irony and humor. She was what Sarris says this picture made her—the screen's undisputed "Empress of Desire."

Shanghai Express was nominated by the Academy for Best Photography, Best Picture, and Best Director. It won for photography (its actress had been nominated for *Morocco* and would never again receive a flicker of Academy recognition), but the real victory was at the box office. It was the most successful of the seven Dietrich-Sternberg collaborations and, as always, controversial.

The New York Times thought it Sternberg's "best picture" but *Variety's* commercial judgment erred in finding it nothing "to command real attention . . . [just] a trashy story." *Variety* thought "Miss Dietrich's assignment is so void of movement as to force her to mild but consistent eye rolling, a trick [that] never develops the punch audiences may expect, but neither does the story."

In London the *Times* knew more about punch, observing that Marlene's "acting finds its strength and impulse in her careful elimination of all emphasis, and the more seemingly careless and inconsequent her gestures, the more surely do they reveal the particular shades and movements of her mind."

John Grierson, who wrote that premature obituary about what happens to a director when he dies, noted with sour ambivalence that "the scenes of Chinese life are massive, painstaking to the point of genius in their sense of detail . . . the rest is Dietrich. She is shown in seven thousand and one poses, each of them photographed magnificently. For me, seven thousand poses of Dietrich (or seventy) are Dietrich *ad nauseam*. Her pose of mystery I find too studied, her make-up too artificial, her every gesture and word too deliberate for any issue in drama save the very gravest."

America's *Vanity Fair* traded chic for hostility: "In the early days of his career, Sternberg presented . . . the honest American idiom of the open attack. But soon he was cultivated by cult. . . . He traded his open style for fancy play, chiefly upon the legs in silk, and buttocks in lace, of Dietrich, of whom he has made a paramount slut. Sternberg is, by his own tokens, a man of meditation as well as action; but instead of contemplating the navel of Buddha his umbilical perseverance is fixed on the navel of Venus."

Venus turned thirty and Maria seven in December 1931 during their first Christmas away from the land that invented it. Marlene was denied one present, the previous year's Oscar for *Morocco*, which went to Marie Dressler for *Min and Bill* as Sternberg had predicted. There were more things than Oscars on the horizon.

January brought unpleasant news from Berlin, where the National Socialists, increasingly noisy, announced their party ban of *Dishonored* for its criticism of imperial war politics; the empire in the picture was Austrian, not German, but so was Nazi leader Adolf Hitler. They called *Dishonored* "second-rate Remarque," alluding to the film version of Erich Maria Remarque's antiwar novel *All Quiet on the Western Front*. Storm troopers had disrupted the American production's Berlin opening by releasing hundreds of white mice in the theater. Dr. Joseph Goebbels himself was there, and so was Leni Riefenstahl—as an old friend of Remarque's, she said.

Banning *Dishonored* made a political point, but was just the latest volley in a campaign of criticism against Marlene's making her career in Hollywood (which had asked her) instead of in Berlin (which hadn't) and taking Maria with her. Her "Germanness" was in question, not only to the Nazis, who still seemed a fringe group to most sensible Germans, but to Josephine, too, who missed her daughter and granddaughter. The still pending lawsuits from Riza Royce and the unwelcome public attention they brought forcefully demonstrated the negatives of fame, making Marlene fanatically wary of her privacy for the rest of her life, even as she gloried in her fame. Puritan disapproval made her wonder if she weren't too European for spacious skies and amber waves of grain after all.

Maurice Chevalier wondered, too. As Paramount's biggest male star with one Lubitsch hit after another, his dressing room conveniently adjoined that of Paramount's biggest female star, both of them Continental as all get out. Chevalier was making *Love Me Tonight* for Rouben Mamoulian as Marlene was making *Shanghai Express* for Sternberg. As he rehearsed

Rodgers and Hart's great score, strains of "Isn't It Romantic" and "Lover" wafted through the air ducts.

The great French star had seen Marlene on the Marathon Street lot for almost two years and found her "ravishing" but so under Svengali's influence she seemed "almost like a sleepwalker . . . simply not there at all." They didn't meet or speak then, but when they finally did, he knew "this time we would speak long and earnestly."

Chevalier was not only glamourous and European and musical and an accomplished lover: He understood her feelings of estrangement in America. He gave her someone to spend time with on the lot who was romantic rather than obsessive. He found her "an extraordinary comrade, a woman of great intelligence and sensitivity, spiritual, kind, amusingly and charmingly unpredictable," not to mention that "bewitching face with its delicate yet sensuous sculpture." Chevalier was going back to Europe himself soon; perhaps she should consider relocating, too. He knew a producer in London called Clifford Whitley who would be only too happy to present her in the theater there. Clifford Whitley announced he would, indeed, be only too happy, until Madame Chevalier pointed out to her lawyers how close London was to Paris. It put an end, Chevalier said, to an "amity [that] was surely not over, it was simply to be packed away for moments of remembering." He packed it away, but lightly.

Talk about theater worried Paramount, and there was more. Marlene had never completely abandoned the stage in her own mind, and Chevalier's favorite director, Lubitsch, might work with her on Broadway. Perhaps a production of *The Merry Widow* or a Lubitsch-directed musical by Dmitri Tiomkin with dances by Florenz Ziegfeld's Albertina Rasch (formerly of the Vienna Opera Ballet School) in the fall of 1932.

Nothing ever came of these plans (except a remake of *The Merry Widow* by Lubitsch and Chevalier at MGM, which owned it). This was a relief to Paramount, to whom Marlene still owed pictures. The next movie was undecided and debated, referred to only as "a New York picture," but what it was was Marlene's mother-love project, and she was determined to make it.

Paramount had never been strong on mother love (that was Louis B. Mayer territory). Shanghai Lily affirmed Marlene's box-office appeal when she got her man, as New York had said all along. "WE FAIL TO SEE THIS TYPE OF MYSTERIOUS AND GLAMOROUS PERSONALITY OBTAINING THE SYMPATHY OF THE AUDIENCE AS THE MOTHER OF A CHILD RATHER THAN AS A SENSUAL LOVER" they kept on saying; oddly, considering their star's private life.

Marlene demanded mother love. She had actually written a story (credit would be withheld by agreement) and got $12,000 for her literary efforts (deeply resented by Paramount). If renewed threats of returning to Europe had any force in bringing her story to the screen she would make them. She did.

She had been happy working in Hollywood, she said, but "the urge to be among my own people is stronger than the desire to remain here. . . . Germany is not satisfied with me. It wants to hear me in German. . . . So, I am returning to appear in German-speaking roles."

This was news to Riza Royce, who wanted to hear Marlene in English. Or better yet, *read* her in the *Daily Star-Spangled Banner* in black and white. Paramount got a retraction from the Viennese journalist who helpfully agreed that he had misquoted Marlene and the studio relaxed with what seemed a fait accompli: The lawsuits would be dropped, they announced. Royce announced that nothing was *accompli*, that nothing would be dropped until the retraction was published, as well as a letter of apology from Marlene to her, as well as a letter from her to Marlene in which she would say whatever was on her mind, which seemed to be plentiful: *for all the world to read*. The Paramount legal department relit the oil lamps, and Paramount's Rudi Sieber once again got on a ship to America.

Rudi's visit had more than publicity value this time. The mother-love story was to have started production in February, but it was now April. Marlene made her return-to-the-theater and return-to-Germany speeches while Sternberg battled an administration that simply didn't want to make the picture. Rudi's arrival intensified pressure in ways Paramount didn't suspect. The studio hoped he would play peacemaker with his wife, not realizing Rudi might have an agenda of his own.

UFA was making overtures—to *him*, but designed to entice Marlene to return to Berlin. Marlene's unhappiness seemed mere star antics to Paramount, but Rudi knew her dissatisfaction was real. With Riza Royce suing her, Madame Chevalier threatening (and finally taking) divorce action, and the studio refusing to go forward with the story she had written and wanted to make, Marlene was vulnerable to offers. UFA's sounded attractive. Josef von Sternberg thought so, too. He had made his greatest film there, and Paramount was clearly nearing bankruptcy in spite of the enormous $3 million in profits he had returned to them with *Shanghai Express*.

All Paramount knew was that Marlene's mother-love story presented so many censorship problems to the Hays Office that the industry's moral guardians flatly said they hoped the studio would "forget the story altogether." Even Schulberg wanted to, in spite of what the Hays Office called his tendency to promote "sex stuff on a heavy scale."

Mixing mother love with the "sex stuff" was the central problem: oil and water; fire and ice. Title changes usually reflect lack of focus and did so here: *Deep Nights* became *East River* became *Song of Manhattan* became

Velvet and finally became *Blonde Venus*, lifted from Schulberg's old favorite project, *Nana* (on its way to Goldwyn and Anna Sten), in which Zola's heroine appears in a play of that name.

Mother-love sobber-weepers were potent at the Depression box office and usually sordid (there had to be something to sob and weep *about*), but *Blonde Venus* was not sordid; it was lurid. Paramount assigned Jules Furthman and a young playwright from New York called S. K. Lauren to salvage the script, but its first version was resistant to anything like improvement.

Blonde Venus (wife and mother Helen Faraday) finds her scientist husband suffers from "radium disease." She secretly goes back to her old profession as cabaret singer to pay for his cure and support their child, Johnny. While her husband recovers in Europe, Helen moves in with a politico moneybags she falls in love with. When her husband finds out who's been paying the bills and how, she kidnaps her own child and becomes a prostitute. Her husband recaptures the child, causing Helen to think about suicide. She decides instead to become the Toast of Paris. Mr. Moneybags turns up, she marries him, and returns to New York, where she is reunited with home, hearth, ex-husband, baby, and her *new* husband, who is understanding about her loving two men at the same time.

Small wonder hair stood on end at the Hays Office. By the most liberal interpretation the picture seemed to tolerate, if not condone, adultery, prostitution, and kidnapping; the wages of sin turned out to be everything Helen ever wanted—*and* show business stardom.

Rudi's mysterious failure to talk sense to his wife and her director caused Paramount to deliver an ultimatum that Sternberg shoot a script so heavily bowdlerized it made no sense at all. Sternberg refused and got on a train to New York. The studio suspended him, suing for damages of $100,000, which he found so insultingly low he threatened to countersue. Paramount assigned the script to director Richard Wallace. Marlene's contract stipulated Sternberg; she refused to work with Wallace, so Paramount suspended her, too.

This show of strength with the studio's biggest star looked like executive "can-do," and Schulberg, himself in serious trouble, received a temporary vote of confidence from Cohen and the New York board. He threatened Sternberg with legal action that would prevent his (or Marlene's) working anywhere for anybody, including Berlin, about which Schulberg had no idea. Rudi decided to play peacemaker after all; Sternberg capitulated to legal necessity; Marlene became more exquisitely beautiful than ever; and a still unfinished version of a script *nobody* now wanted to make went into production at the end of May.

*   *   *

Franklin Delano Roosevelt was in the White House by then, but it had been Herbert Hoover when the picture was in development. Ten million people were walking American streets unemployed, not a few of them former employees of Paramount, whose profits had fallen by two thirds from the previous year, even with blockbuster *Shanghai Express*. Paramount stock was plummeting from a 1930 high of 77¼ to a 1932 low of 1½, ample reason for panic.

Blonde Venus had attempted in early drafts to render the Depression and social conditions as meaningful background to the story. All of that fell away in the attempts to make the mother-prostitute-singer sympathetic. Making her make *sense* fell away in attempts to satisfy the Hays Office.

Because the picture was contemporary and American, it seemed to present not a female archetype, but a real woman in a real world. the Dietrich legend was built partly from audience identification of Marlene with abstract aspects of Amy Jolly, X-27, and Shanghai Lily. *Blonde Venus* was a nightmare of implication for those drawing parallels between a real player and a role seemingly rooted in everyday reality. Helen Faraday was German; she was a performer who sang; she left her homeland for America; she abandoned her husband; she took their child with her; she moved in with another man who offered her fame and luxury. Finally, she expected to be (and *was*) welcomed back, suffering only stunning Travis Banton costumes and stardom for her sins. This heroine signaled her duality with another of Sternberg's "lesbian accents" (in the Paris club where she headlines), and her moral justification was simply that she loved two men at the same time. Not to mention her child.

Maria later claimed that she was, indeed, the model for the child in the picture and that the movie frankly mirrored a life situation in which mother love and child were obstacles to the man-woman relationships in and out of marriage. It was not "von for all and all for von" after all. It was Rudi and Sternberg and Chevalier and whoever else for *Marlene*, and Marlene for *Maria*. Everybody's rival is the child. Maria was not yet eight when the film was made, and her interpretation of it may be fantasy or projection, but it is what Maria believed when she made the assertion at age fifty. Whether the film reflected the lives of its makers or not, its overtones surely did.

This was delicate for a star who was a regular focus of growing concern about morality in the movies, but there was an additional *Blonde Venus* theme that seemed cynical at best and callous at worst. The heart of the film was Helen's flight with her child, which looked like kidnapping. Kidnapping was the most riveting of public issues, as the tragic Lindbergh kidnapping had taken place in March, exactly when Paramount was refusing to go ahead with the project at all. The Lindbergh case did not prompt moral misgivings on Marathon Street (it was too topical not to be useful), but it seemed perverse on screen when it was revealed the picture had yet another linkage to offscreen life.

Marlene began work on *Blonde Venus* as near hysteria as she ever got. Few besides Rudi, Sternberg, Chevalier, and Schulberg knew it. On June 2, a few days after the picture started shooting, it was revealed that since mid-May Marlene had been receiving kidnap letters threatening Maria. Without publicity and in spite of warnings, Rudi had notified authorities, and police units were despatched to supplement private bodyguards on Roxbury Drive and at Marion Davies's Santa Monica beach house, which Marlene also rented.

A police trap was set with Marlene, Rudi, Sternberg, and Chevalier inside the house with rifles, and the Beverly Hills police force outside. Money was placed, per instructions, on the running board of a car, but no one arrived to claim it, and suddenly the threats were in the papers.

A letter composed of newspaper and magazine cuttings had been mis-delivered to another Los Angeles woman who was similarly threatened, and she unaccountably made it public. The wording seemed oddly informed: "You, Marlene Dietrich, if you want to save Maria to be a screen star, your own girl, pay and if you don't she'll be but a loving memory to you." The demand for $10,000 became $20,000 with repeated warnings not to involve the police.

The worldwide headlines were not unsympathetic publicity for a "love pirate." Threats evaporated with public exposure. Police announced extortion, not kidnapping, was behind the plot. Marlene was the victim of an ex-Paramount employee angry at having been fired in the studio bloodletting earlier that spring. Rudi took it all with remarkable calm and left it to police, Sternberg, and Chevalier to sort out, leaving California the day the kidnap threats made headlines around the world.

His leaving may have seemed careless, but he returned to Europe with a sense of mission intensified by the incident: Work something out with UFA. Marlene and Sternberg went back to work on a picture they both now hated. Maria spent the balance of the summer sitting on a stepladder overlooking sets where *Blonde Venus* was shot, watching Dickie Moore impersonate her for the cameras. In a fragile atmosphere of life as usual, Paramount quietly settled with Riza Royce for a sum undisclosed, but rumored at $100,000, which removed the last trace of scandal threatening a woman whose child was now the object of worldwide sympathy. The dropping of the Royce lawsuits was announced with the release of *Blonde Venus* in late summer, absolving Marlene of love-piracy in a timely fashion.

Blonde Venus as a screen story had only one distinction, the theme of a woman simultaneously in love with two men. In the final version she was not allowed to love or marry her rich protector, which removed even the flimsy justification of a fickle heart and reduced the narrative to that of a woman who sleeps around for affection, diversion, or money. That her motivation was money for her husband's cure was so transparently a sop to blue-stockings it neither fooled nor moved anyone. *Blonde Venus* remained a story of kidnapping, adultery, and prostitution on the run, and both script and studio were in such disarray that it never rose above the spurious logic of soap opera, soured by a feeling that everybody involved was slumming. You can *feel* their boredom.

Kidnapping threats, suspensions, threats of lawsuits corporate and private did not help. The picture was Schulberg's last gasp as head of a studio sliding into bankruptcy, and in such an atmosphere it is surprising only that the picture got made at all. Panic, not reason, ruled the day.

Production lasted longer than on any previous Sternberg picture. Song lyrics were still being submitted to the Hays Office for approval in the last week of shooting. Major sequences (including the "Hot Voodoo" number) were completely recostumed and reshot.

Casting underscored the appalling weaknesses of the enterprise. British actor Herbert Marshall, new to American films and best known for his marriage to actress Edna Best, was cast as Helen's husband. As Helen's rich lover, Paramount insisted on young Cary Grant, who had looks and voice but not yet the persona that would make him one of the great stars. Sternberg changed the part in his hair, making him look better, but not to Marlene, who seemed not to care for him on or off the screen. A German woman was thus cast against two Englishmen in what was meant to be a specifically American film. Both actors were too gentlemanly—or too inhibited—to offer her the kind of resistance against which she played best, as with Gary Cooper. There weren't enough sparks to ignite one love affair, let alone two. More surprisingly, there was little maternal warmth in the scenes with her child, played by Dickie Moore, who was finally the most convincing actor in the picture. Perhaps he was too young to understand the nonsense in which he was appearing, though years later he remembered the uneven mood on the set between star and director. "I still remember every detail. Marlene and Sternberg—how they screamed and laughed, fought and fell all over each other."

Tension extended beyond the set because of Marlene's continuing relationship with Chevalier. The falling over was left to the Paramount management. Studio production manager Sam Jaffe (not the actor) left the company following violent altercations with Sternberg. Jaffe could not be protected by his brother-in-law, B. P. Schulberg, now also gone, having been given Hollywood's equivalent of the exploding cigar: an independent contract. At least Schulberg didn't have to hang around and try to justify the plot.

The only reason to see *Blonde Venus* turned out to be Dietrich's musical numbers, in such high relief they substitute for character. They are charged with sex and insolence, the only satisfying moments in the picture, and far more convincing than Marlene's portrayal of mother love.

They have a perverse fascination that remains amusing and compelling. The notorious "Hot Voodoo" number (even Shirley Temple parodied it) is simply unforgettable, despite or because of its absurdity. Marlene emerges from a gorilla suit to don her silver-blond Afro (suggesting Harpo Marx) against a Cotton Club background of African "native" girls. There are tom-toms, palms, the black bartender with a stutter (Sternberg borrows here from his first sound picture, *Thunderbolt*, which has a trial run of this sequence; it's even the same stuttering bartender-actor). Helen's—*Dietrich's*—astonishing confidence in her allure is near-dictatorial with star presence. She shifts her weight from one hip to another as she sings. She need not do more; her voice insinuates the rest. The absurd lyric—"Hot Voodoo gets me wild / Oh, Fireman, save this child!"—goes on for five minutes in two long takes intercut with shots of Cary Grant paying stunned attention. This is a witch casting her spell; that hip-to-hip sway is the mesmerizing come-on of a blond cobra.

Marlene's song numbers are all but seamless. The next is a throwaway (Sternberg's song selections are seldom memorable) called "You Little So and So," delivered in one take (there is a single cutaway), as Marlene sidles through a nightclub. No actress ever made boredom so erotically riveting.

In Paris, we meet Dietrich Triumphant in her androgynous mode, top hat, white tie, and tails (all white, this time), complete with insouciant lesbian gesture to a chorus girl before she goes on. The mediocre song, "I Couldn't Be Annoyed," is rendered in French (translation by Marlene) and English as a declaration of self-sufficiency, of independence from anyone, man, woman, or child. (On her dressing room mirror is scrawled, "Down to Gehenna or up to the throne—He travels fastest who travels alone.") She has fun with the song and permits the audience to adore her. This Helen achieves greater intimacy with a crowd than with her child. Dietrich makes love to multitudes; she comes alive when singing; her personality and humor find release when on display, not on duty.

Helen Faraday is finally all performance. Her child is audience for her, whether she bathes him in her *Hausfrau* apron or later tells him bedtime stories in Travis Banton cloth-of-gold and black satin. She is motherly in much the same way that Lola Lola could be perfunctorily soothing to Professor Unrat. One might excuse the performance by noting that Maria was present on the set, which may have caused Marlene to downplay the affection she showed the child actor. But Dietrich and Helen Faraday's self-awareness is too overwhelming and carefully beautiful to persuade us of self-sacrifice; her narcissism, particularly in the Paris scenes (with their lesbian accents) is what fascinates and what one remembers, not the mother with a washrag.

Because there are moments of beauty in the film (no one ever made squalor more decorative than Sternberg), one wants *Blonde Venus* to be coherent. Helen's transition from flophouse drunk to stage star in Paris defeats critical inquiry. Much has been made of the dissolves of posters and neon lights to chart her progress and "explain" the ascent to Toast of Paris, but the central image is the Atlantic Ocean, heaving and swelling, pathway to a life change Marlene and Sternberg had both experienced. That ocean may simply be personal code, a sardonic wink. In that dissolve, so seemingly empty of content, may lie the key to the whole picture, too "inside" to bear or require explication. Otherwise we accept Helen's stardom only because we know she is really Marlene Dietrich.

Blonde Venus finished shooting at the end of August and was rushed into theaters. Paramount was in no financial position to let an expensive negative with its biggest star languish on the shelves. It opened without premiere at the Paramount Times Square Theater in New York and was derided by critics. *The New York Times* called it "a muddled, unimaginative and generally hapless piece of work, relieved somewhat by the talent and charm of the German actress." The *Herald Tribune* was only a little kinder, finding "Marlene Dietrich is still Marlene Dietrich, whatever the plot, whatever the dialogue, whatever the intention of her sponsors," but the picture was "long and slow . . . conventional and banal."

Dwight Macdonald attacked. *"The Blonde Venus* is perhaps the worst [Sternberg picture] ever made. In it all Sternberg's gifts have turned sour. The photography is definitely 'arty'—a nauseating blend of hazy light, soft focus, over-blacks and over-whites, with each shot so obviously 'composed' as to be painful. Sternberg's rhythm has declined to a senseless seesaw pattern. . . . The film is all pace and nothing else."

Reviewers knew Sternberg had gone on suspension rather than make the picture Paramount's way and assumed this was *his* way. The most vociferous critics went after the *auteur* and did not spare his star. This, too, was predictable. Marlene's rise had been too meteoric, too *directed* by a man presumed to be in thrall to her, to exempt her from the condemnation heaped on him. Had they known the story was hers, the reviews would likely have been even more derisive.

Documentary filmmaker Pare Lorentz, then writing for smart *Vanity*

Fair, went in for the kill. "There is no possible excuse for *Blonde Venus*, except that it supports the incredibly accurate prediction made in this department some months ago that Marlene Dietrich was due to explode with a loud hollow pop. . . . Miss Dietrich, as usual, smiles serenely, crosses her legs, lights cigarettes, and waits for Sternberg to make her exciting. . . . He starts with her in the raw, then puts his star in all the old clothes he could find around the lot, makes her first wife, then mother, then mistress, then tramp, and asks her to do everything but skin a cat to amuse the customers. For all these antics she remains unexciting. The explanation is near at hand. Mr. Sternberg's employers, despite repeated warnings, allowed their erratic cameraman to write his own scenario [*sic*]; and not all the directors in the world could have taken such a dramatic curiosity and made Miss Dietrich, or anyone else, exciting. [She gives] as complete an exhibition of somnambulance as any actress ever gave an enthusiastic, if misled, public."

There is glee in these attacks from the ivory tower. *Blonde Venus* looked like a high-handed exercise of directorial power over wounded-dinosaur Paramount, and the blow Sternberg had struck for creative freedom resulted in something trivial and "unhealthy," as *The New York Times* called it.

The audience rejected it utterly. They could not be blamed. Paramount was not at fault. If *Dishonored* had been "a fairly complete flop," *Blonde Venus* was a definitive disaster. Sternberg's and Marlene's.

After five pictures in less than three years, it was time for a change.

NINE

APOTHEOSIS
1933 - 1934

Marlene did not think the change that should be made was at Paramount, which had seen too many changes as a consequence of bankruptcy. The very management that had spent and reaped millions by bringing her there was either in purgatory awaiting contract settlement, like Schulberg, or fired, like Sidney Kent (who had countersigned her first contract in Berlin). Even company co-founder Jesse Lasky had been ousted. Control of the company was going, too, reeled in by receivers as the 1932 deficit reached $16,000,000.

Reduced box-office revenues were a factor, as everywhere in the Depression, but Paramount's vast Publix Theater Chain was the greater cause. Once pride of the company and key to its economic power, it was now just a money drain. Casual investments (including one in a fledgling radio network called CBS) were now liabilities and, as always, the major assets were the ones who "went home at night."

Paramount's primary asset, P-1167, had a contract that ran only until February of 1933. There was still time in late 1932 to make another picture that might balance spreadsheets and salvage her box-office appeal after the red ink (and bad blood) from *Blonde Venus* had been washed from the walls. Sternberg's contract, however, would end three months earlier, in December. In early October the studio urged him to the West Indies to film hurricane footage (with cameraman Paul Ivano) for a South Seas adventure being scripted by Jules Furthman. Time was tight, but corporate panic demanded immediate action.

Schulberg's fall from power fueled speculation that without him as protector, Sternberg would soon crash to earth, a prospect viewed with alarm by some and with cheer by many. Marlene broke the press silence she had held since Riza Royce's lawsuits the previous March: "I will never make pictures in America with anyone but Mr. von Sternberg.

West Indies weather remained maddeningly calm, and Sternberg returned to the storms of Hollywood without *Hurricane* footage (the project would later be revamped for a sultry Chicago elevator operator dubbed Dorothy Lamour). After some conversations with Paramount's new chief executive, Emanuel Cohen ("a pony's ass" Dorothy Parker called him because he was so tiny), Sternberg announced he was sick and tired of the whole business and would retire at age thirty-eight to paint and read and build a stainless-steel house, complete with moat, designed by Viennese architect Richard Neutra.

Marlene announced that in that case she would go back to Europe to do stage work in Paris and Berlin. "This is not because of any Svengali and Trilby influence," she declared, "but because he is the best friend I ever had in the world. People have said he casts a spell over me. That is ridiculous. . . . Can you think of anyone casting a spell over me?"

Paramount could. Marlene's contract did not permit her to walk out just because he did—even if he got pushed. Especially not when he wasn't too sick and tired of the whole business to avoid talks with Jesse Lasky, now at Fox, or with Chaplin at United Artists, both of them eager to finance Svengali, especially if Trilby should be up his sleeve.

Sternberg was a veteran of the Hollywood wars and knew he might be charged with inducing Marlene to breach her contract, for which he could be sued. He went on talking to Fox and United Artists about a big Spanish picture he called a "capriccio."

Rudi Sieber arrived in California for show and for the 1932 Christmas and birthdays (Maria's eighth, Marlene's thirty-first), leaving Tamara behind, alone but in Parisian *luxe* financed by Marlene. Tucked in Rudi's gift satchel was a script from UFA based on a novella by Carl Zuckmayer called *Liebesgeschichte (Love Story)*, a generic sort of title that Paramount would return to forty years later. Now the Zuckmayer script was good enough reason for Sternberg to pack his bags for a holiday in Berlin.

Paramount, desperate to maximize asset P-1167 before her contract expired, agreed to pay her $4,000 a week even when she sat by the pool reading they knew not what. They rummaged through the piles of properties they already owned and dusted off a project proposed the year before for Tallulah Bankhead, whom they had hoped would be a Dietrich threat to keep Marlene in line until Bankhead's behavior raised more hackles than hopes. It was Hermann Sudermann's 1908 novel *The Song of Songs*, and could be readied for shooting before Marlene's contract ended in February. But not by Josef von Sternberg.

Marlene resisted. She remembered this dated material. It had already been filmed twice by Paramount, with Elsie Ferguson in 1918 and again with Pola Negri in 1924. Sternberg surprisingly supported the notion, thereby stilling any charges of undue influence from him and giving him time and space in which to reconsider his life. Should he continue with Marlene, he knew he had nothing to lose by her working with another director: *Song of Songs* could fail, proving he had been puppet master all along, or succeed, making the puppet an even more attractive negotiating chip for him—at Fox, UA, or UFA.

Paramount, wary of forcing a director on Marlene after the Richard Wallace-*Blonde Venus* fiasco, went to its elite list and plucked out Rouben Mamoulian, confident Sternberg would advise Marlene to accept him. Clearly Sternberg would fight any suggestion of Lubitsch, who might have been perfect for the assignment as he was, like the material, German, and his style could update almost anything. Sternberg's touchy rivalry with Lubitsch precluded that and would soon lead to calamity in any case.

Thirty-five-year-old Mamoulian was a Russian-Armenian stage director who had mounted the original *Porgy* and would soon repeat with the Gershwins' *Porgy and Bess*. He had made the early talkie *Applause* with Helen Morgan, guided Fredric March to an Oscar in *Dr. Jekyll and Mr. Hyde*, and had just put Maurice Chevalier and Jeanette MacDonald through their stylish Rodgers and Hart rhythms in *Love Me Tonight*. Mamoulian had everything: versatility, style, experience, and the confidence of the Paramount board.

He also had "taste," which might take the curse off the material's decidedly prurient interest. When *Song of Songs* was reworked for Bankhead the Hays Office had gone out of its way to warn that the original play had been successful partly because of the censorship problems it raised. Its story of a girl "wrecked upon the rocks of her ignorance" was really the story of "a harlot at heart." The Code was under increasing attack from moral guardians, awakened from hibernation by hard times and the tom-toms of "Hot Voodoo," not to mention Mae West's earthquake hips. West was the old new-girl-in-town at—where else?—Paramount, delivering that "heavy sex stuff" with a wink and a wisecrack. Schulberg's firing had changed nothing in the area of heavy breathing.

Critics in the past had denounced *Song of Songs* as "worthless for moral instruction" and for its outrageous suggestion that young ladies who indulge in "lewdness and drinking" could keep their looks. This sounded made for Marlene. The executives were not troubled that in her first four American pictures she had played a prostitute and would now play another. This "harlot at heart" had literary prestige and Mamoulian planned to use lots of Bach, Beethoven, Brahms, and Tchaikovsky on the sound track to edify the goings-on. Moreover, the entire picture was *about* Art.

The story had been simplified to that of an innocent country girl, Lily (she to be gilded; there is a perverse Pygmalion or Svengali theme here), who comes to Berlin as an orphan, sells books for her rum-sodden aunt ("Jamaica—that's somewhere in Asia Minor, isn't it?"), and is lured by a good-looking sculptor into posing for his statue representing Solomon's Song of Songs. Nude. Lily falls in love with Solomon and the sculptor, but the latter passes her on to a rich sadistic baron with a taste for nudes (a career move: the baron buys art). She marries the baron, but after being tutored by him in the ways of the Old Aristocracy (the Pygmalion or Svengali part), she searches for Love from her riding master. Doing so, she manages to burn down the castle and is banished from her gilded cage. She becomes a prostitute who has a way with a song and is rediscovered by the sculptor. Seeing her not nude, but in Travis Banton's ravishing black egret plumes, he realizes what a wow she is, feels bad about the wrong he has done her, and begs forgiveness. In a fit of reawakened virtue, Lily removes the cigarette dangling from her lips and destroys the nude statue that started it all, as strains of the *Pathétique* soar. Model and sculptor are reunited for a tearful but joyous recital of the Song of Solomon.

Art was written all over this one: sculpture, poetry, music. Marlene would get to sing lyrics by Goethe (music by Schubert) while entertaining the sadistic baron's aristocratic guests and, in her prostitute's plumes, Friedrich Holländer's old (1920) "Jonny," with English lyrics by Edward Heyman, who had just written the hit song "Body and Soul."

Paramount called a production meeting for the film in December, just as Josef von Sternberg announced he was "retiring," and Marlene didn't show up. They asked her again and she stayed home to wrap Christmas presents with visiting Rudi and offer *Joyeux Noël* when Chevalier dropped by. (The ever-obliging Rudi photographed his wife and her lover for the family photo album.) Paramount decided to stop sending her the $4,000 per week she was receiving as pocket money in the depths of the Depression (with buying power of something like $60,000 in the 1990s), and Marlene decided Paramount had breached her contract and she, like Sternberg, was now a free agent.

Paramount slapped her with a lawsuit in the federal court in Los Angeles, suing for accumulated costs on *Song of Songs* of $182,850.06. The studio was granted a temporary injunction preventing her working elsewhere. The federal judge who heard the case declined to grant the order for her arrest that Paramount requested to prevent her fleeing the country, but did so "without prejudice," leaving an arrest warrant as Marlene's alternative to posing for a statue.

Paramount executives may have been greedy, tasteless, and desperate, but they were not idiots. They knew Rudi was in town and that Josef von Sternberg was on his way to Berlin and they could guess why. If they couldn't, Sternberg's secretary, Eleanor McGeary, was ready to testify about hearing Marlene and Sternberg—right there on Marathon Street!—discuss plans to fly the Paramount coop for Berlin anyway. Paramount decided the $4,000 per week they had sent to Marlene was a retainer guaranteeing her services and were not about to let it gurgle down the Depression drain.

Marlene telephoned Sternberg, now in Berlin dining with press lord and Nazi financier Alfred Hugenberg of UFA. Svengali Jo advised her to make the picture, as did a legion of lawyers. Two days later, just after New Year's Day 1933, she was back at Paramount, back at work under what she viewed as house arrest. She would do as she was told; Lily would sing the *Song of Songs*.

It is possible the Hays Office saved a few pictures by insisting on denunciations of immorality, but *Song of Songs* wasn't one of them. What one saw on film (and in the ads) was not Marlene/Lily's moral regeneration and Bible readings, but a statue of her. Nude. Almost as anatomically correct as . . . well, Marlene herself.

Mamoulian could be trusted with nudity, for his "taste" was a much-admired quality that had made him acceptable to "pony's ass" Cohen in the first place. "Taste" is also what makes his films seem so dull and lifeless today. They are impeccably mounted and produced, often innovative without causing trouble (his uses of sound and color were historically important), but there is a stately, premeditated quality to them that leaves every scene polished but bloodless. There are impressive moments, and one immortal one a year later as Garbo memorized a room with her fingertips in *Queen Christina*, but mostly they're so tasteful they're dull. It is therefore surprising that *Song of Songs* should have turned out to be so vulgar, so tasteless, so prurient it makes Marlene's Sternberg essays look merely eccentric or naughty. If Sternberg sometimes turned smut into art, Mamoulian turned what looked like art into what looked like trash. His taste made discretion seem sly, even dirty.

Solomon would not have objected: Marlene standing on her tip-toes, shoulders thrust back, breasts thrust forward, nipples at attention, pudenda smooth as a baby's bottom at a time when even a baby's bottom was a no-no at the Hays Office. It is not merely nude; it is *naked*. All Marlene's peasant braids and Mamoulian's Tchaikovsky cannot direct attention to the Art of It All when the statue is on screen, which is most of the time. When it isn't, the sculptor's sketch for it *is*, usually with the baron drooling over it or applying a lit cigar to its body parts. Or, before there *is* a statue, we see Marlene disrobing behind a curtain, each movement intercut with a nude statue in the atelier so we will know just what private part she is baring at the cutaway moment. The sculptor, played by Brian Aherne, kneads and kneads and kneads the clay to get the breasts *just right*, and it is an absurd concession to the Code that Lily's redemption is symbolized by her smashing the thing to bits while Tchaikovsky oozes over the plaster fragments, here a nipple, there a nipple.

The picture doesn't appeal to prurient interest; it flogs it. Paramount had thousands of replica statues manufactured for display in theater lobbies, arousing the same women's groups who had earlier picketed displays of ankle and calf. A theater in Claremont, New Hampshire, bowed to local outrage by clothing its promotional lobby statue in overalls, a witty allusion to Miss Dietrich's style-setting penchant for slacks, which had created a worldwide sensation and more scandal when she first wore them on the streets the year before.

The Hays Office had neatly sidestepped whether Marlene's Lily really knew about the birds and the bees (or the whips and cigars) while allowing her exposure in the altogether for most of the picture. They were shocked and appalled at what Art turned out to look like.

Mamoulian wrote the Hays men a hilariously disingenuous letter about how artistic it all was and what connoisseurs of art he knew them to be. It didn't work. Before the picture could be released in the summer of 1933, Will Hays ordered Paramount to cut a reel and a half (about fifteen minutes) before issuing a seal. Even so, the New York State censors were so flushed with moral fervor they rushed to judgment and multiple screenings, viewing and reviewing the picture on their own and threatening a collapse of the Hays Office censorship system, which few Americans realized the studios paid for anyway, making Will Hays their *de facto* employee. All the artistic goings-on in the name of Solomon were a revelation, and not only of Marlene. The half of the cast that isn't trying to get Lily into bed is pimping for the half that *is*. Her aunt and the sculptor she loves both work at maximizing Lily's assets (was this a sly Depression allegory?), while the baron, the riding master, and the demimonde of Berlin try to return her to the natural state in which she posed as Solomon's muse.

Marlene rather liked nudity but didn't much care for all the hypocrisy. If Paramount was secretly encouraging her loyalty to Sternberg and his franker brand of exotica, they could hardly have done better. Marlene, at the end of each take, would state for the microphone (and thus for executives watching rushes the next day), "Jo, Jo, why hast thou forsaken me?" She said it in German when a visitor to the set, like the young ballerina Vera Zorina, understood that language; she said it in English when a caller like the aviatrix Amelia Earhart did not.

Marlene alleviated despair by commiserating with Maurice Chevalier, who had been pushed by management into something called *The Way to Love*, which was so bad it would be his last Paramount Picture and almost his last in America for decades. She cajoled in pillow talk with Mamoulian himself (but tastefully). She also found solace in her *Song of Songs* leading man Brian Aherne, new to American pictures and fresh from Katharine Cornell and *The Barretts of Wimpole Street*. Aherne accepted the role of the sculptor, he said, after seeing *Shanghai Express* and being "moon-struck" by Marlene's beauty. He finally read the script and figured out why Fredric March had turned it down. He was plunged into gloom, brightened only by the moon goddess.

"Why have you come to do this silly picture?" she asked him. "I have to do it because of my contract, and because Mr. von Sternberg has walked out and I am left without any protection, but you are the great actor from New York and can do what you like. Are you crazy?"

She baked him a cake, inspiring him with the notion that the picture might be endurable if he could find opportunities enough "to bake Miss Dietrich," as he put it in his memoirs. Not even the 1933 Long Beach earthquake could shake this devotion to cookery. Everybody else at Paramount went home for the day; Marlene and Aherne remained in their dressing rooms on Marathon Street, basking in self-generated moonlight.

When not whipping up *Küchen*, Marlene got away from it all by riding in the Rolls-Royce Sternberg had given her to Santa Barbara in pursuit of *le ballet* and Vera Zorina. The teenage ballerina, who had worked in Berlin, was young enough to find Marlene "beautiful," "languid," and "a sensation," but old enough to resist her bedtime advances with good humor.

In Santa Barbara she introduced Marlene to conductor Leopold

Stokowski, who seemed somewhat detached when he asked, "And you, my dear—are you in the ballet, too?"

"Of course," Marlene answered, thinking he must be a real wit or seriously out of touch.

"And in what ballet do you dance?" he asked with a straight face as the boys and girls of the ballet looked on.

"*Union Pacific!*" the chorus chorused, creating mischief. Marlene, in a reawakened surge of Berlin humor, agreed to be smuggled on stage that evening, swathed in black as part of the laying of the Union Pacific Railway. Vera Zorina, Léonide Massine, and the Ballet Russe de Monte Carlo did *tours jetés* around her as she impersonated a railroad track.

Sternberg, far from Marlene's ballet debut, was receiving a belated lesson in the sort of political dance he prided himself on caring little about. He was in Berlin at the precise moment a young Dutch housepainter called Marinus van der Lubbe achieved tragic notoriety. The Dutchman was legally blind from lead in the paint he had applied in days when he could get work. He was now in Berlin, unemployed, and unhappy enough about it to spout a lot of Communist ideas he dimly understood. The unfortunate housepainter managed somehow to strike a match (it was said) and set fire to the Reichstag building, home of the German parliament. Some Nazi officers were conveniently nearby to ensure his being arrested and brought to justice for the "Communist plot" he had enacted—penniless, sightless, powerless, and alone. This was on February 27, 1933, just as Sternberg was taxiing to the airport to leave Berlin and magnate Alfred Hugenberg of UFA, with whom he had been negotiating for creative freedom in Berlin. Sternberg's taxi driver calmly pointed out the smoldering Reichstag building, voicing the rampant supposition that the torching had been done by the Nazis to provide a scapegoat. It had worked. The next day Chancellor Hitler suspended the constitution and assumed powers never dreamed of on Marathon Street.

Sternberg did not quite comprehend the significance of the glowing embers before him, for he had spent most of his time in Berlin dining with Leni Riefenstahl when not with Hugenberg. He had noticed not a single Brownshirt or tremor of the cataclysm into which he was negotiating to deliver Marlene and his genius. He deluded himself that Hugenberg had second thoughts about Adolf Hitler, although Hugenberg was even then Nazi economic minister and remained in that post many months after Hitler's seizure of power and Sternberg's return to Hollywood. To be fair, Sternberg wasn't the only one slow on the uptake. Thomas Mann, with that touching but fatal faith in German *Kultur* that would permit the condemnation of millions to the ovens, remarked to a friend at this time, "Yes, things look bad in Germany, but, once again, they are surely not so bad as they look."

They were. Marlene understood instantly, if Sternberg didn't, that any notion of her making pictures in Germany with a Vienna-born Jew was folly.

Confirmation was brutally quick. By April 1933 the Nazis began revoking citizenship of some of Germany's greatest names and artists. Some were Jewish, like Max Reinhardt, Kurt Weill, Lion Feuchtwanger, Fritz Lang, Billy Wilder; some were not, like Franz Werfel, Heinrich and Thomas Mann, and half the Bauhaus. Some had already left, like Bertolt Brecht, Arthur Koestler, and Albert Einstein, and others were packing. Composer Arnold Schoenberg, raised a Catholic, learned in Paris that he had been dismissed from homeland and job and promptly converted to Judaism. Others, like Nobel Prize–winning playwright Gerhardt Hauptmann, stayed home to be near Aryan loved ones and their royalties.

The writing on the wall was easier to read by May 10, when it was branded there by flames from the burning works of Marx, Freud, Heine, Remarque, both Mann brothers, Stefan Zweig, Franz Werfel, and hundreds of others, including André Gide, who wasn't even German, but was "degenerate" enough (in Nazi-speak) to add to the glow illuminating the walls of Berlin's once-great Humboldt University, where scorch marks remain to this day.

This was a signal hard to miss (though tragically, many did), and it created *the* great culture gap of the twentieth century. Painter-manqué Hitler and his criminal cohorts set critical standards for everything in German life and forced out or murdered those who didn't measure up—or down. This permitted an incalculable enrichment of American culture as the flood of refugees arrived on U.S. shores, many of them treated like flotsam and jetsam.

Hollywood provided occasional employment and not always comfortable refuge. There was a German base already there willing to open doors and checkbooks. People like Lubitsch, Salka Viertel, and, soon, the Feuchtwangers saved many lives, and so—with an open and nearly ruinous generosity—did Marlene.

It was now more important than ever for her to fix her status as breadwinner for those old friends and colleagues who might need her help, most crucially her mother, sister, brother-in-law, their son, and her young cousin Hasso, still living in Berlin. Marlene and Sternberg's fantasies of establishing themselves at UFA were forever out of the question and practicality dictated renewing negotiations with Paramount. Marlene's second contract had ended and Sternberg had none at all.

Hollywood paid less attention to the awful portents from Berlin than to *The Song of Songs*. It was released in July to surprising critical approval. Much of the praise followed a single tack: The *Hollywood Reporter* thought the picture "confirms the wisdom of emancipating La Dietrich from the Svengali-like domination of von Sternberg." The *Los Angeles Examiner* thought "no Trilby sans Svengali ever gave so fine a portrayal." There were more oblique allusions to Sternberg: "The way of the world, the sneer of the sophist, the leer of the lewd, these are of the dead past," intoned the London *Times*.

Newsweek thought that "so vibrant and compelling is Marlene Dietrich . . . she turns [the] material into an individual triumph," and *The New York Times* went giddy and rapturous: "Marlene Dietrich floats through [*Song of Songs*] with the lyric grace of that apparition which was sent by Heaven to be a moment's ornament."

Powerful Berlin critic Alfred Kerr wrote one of his Roman-numeraled reviews, thirteen polyglot paragraphs in which he managed to work in German, French, English, and Italian. Paragraph VI was a succinct "*Hm.*"

Kerr wondered why she was "playing the innocent maiden," when "no other world screen artist, so admired . . . remains always, when sleeping with a man, something of the instructress." He focused largely on her scenes as the baroness turned prostitute, cigarette hanging from a mocking lip, who turns down five hundred marks a night and sings to "Jonny" about what he'll get for his birthday. He saw there "a somehow boisterous melancholy, a tragedienne with wit, full of disdain, but with verve to her despair, the last word in beauty in her grief." His "*Hm*" meant that Marlene was "a rare creation," that when all was said and done, "one remains shaken by beauty. That is it: *shaken by beauty.*"

The great Berlin critic's multilingual showing off was purposeful. He had had to see *Song of Songs* in Paris, for it had been banned by the Nazis. From this time forward, news of Germany's greatest star would come filtered and secondhand from abroad. At home it would come from Dr. Goebbels's propaganda machine, first spiteful, then vicious, and its effects would never be entirely erased. Already the fruitless talks between UFA and Sternberg had resulted in the malicious editorial comment that "it remains doubtful if the German public in the future will receive more Marlene Dietrich films, as long as she opts for the dollar."

Marlene had been deemed effective by critics in *Song of Songs* largely because Sternberg had nothing to do with it, and of those who liked the picture, most liked the conventionality of her performance. She is credible as Lily and her beauty seems to focus even sunshine. She underplays with charm and delicacy. Lily is one of the least mannered performances of her career. But Lily is dull. It was the innocuous safety of her performance that

MARLENE DIETRICH

looked like "lyric grace" to critics long since surfeited by Sternberg's visual extravagance. For those few who realized that the only really interesting moments in Song of Songs are those near the end, when she sings "Jonny" with a take-no-prisoners frontal attack, it was clear that Marlene Dietrich— the woman she was in public imagination and almost always was when singing—was more interesting than any character she ever had capacity or opportunity to impersonate as an actress. For all the "taste" of Mamoulian's production, the picture—except for the audacity and abandon of "Jonny"—is old-fashioned, even for 1933. This Lily is gelded, not gilded, and audiences gave it a merely lukewarm reception at a box office that should have responded ecstatically to all that lyric grace at last unshackled from Sternberg. If it truly was.

Marlene had been eager to finish Song of Songs and return to Europe to see for herself the changes wrought by the Nazis. The news of friends and former colleagues scattering for refuge to Paris, London, New York, Vienna, Budapest, or Prague had reached California, and with no Rudi or Sternberg there to share her anxiety, she had nodded one night to Cecil Beaton, sitting behind her at a dance concert by Berlin's Harald Kreutzberg. Marlene turned from Beaton to his "date," writer Mercedes de Acosta, then in Hollywood working on the script for MGM's Barrymore-family festival, Rasputin and the Empress. Marlene smiled shyly, literary interests quickening.

The next day she showed up in slacks at de Acosta's house, laden with white roses. Mercedes de Acosta was a lady large on Buddha, spiritual kinship, and vegetables, whose liaison with Garbo was known or suspected by everyone in Hollywood who knew or suspected such things. She declared herself baffled by Marlene's spontaneous homage to her pen and person.

"As [Marlene] entered," she later wrote, "she hesitated at the doorway and looked at me in the same shy way [as the evening before]. I asked her to come into the room and put out my hand. She took it in an almost military manner, bent over it and [explained], 'I hope you will forgive me. I noticed you last night in the theater and wanted to meet you. I know very few people in Hollywood and no one who could introduce us, so I just found out where you live and I came myself.' " The lady writer found this "charming and informal," and wanted to talk about movies. *

* Why not? She was a screenwriter. She was also well known in Girlkultur circles. Alice B. Toklas is said to have remarked, "Say what you will about Mercedes, she's had the three most important women of the twentieth century." A wag wondered who the third conquest might have been: Gertrude Stein? Eleanor Roosevelt? Shirley Temple?

172

" 'Oh, let's not talk about pictures,' " Marlene said. " 'I would like to tell you something if you won't think I am mad. . . . You seem too thin and your face so white that it seems to me you are not well. Last evening when I looked at you I felt you were very sad. [Garbo was out of town.] I am sad, too. I am sad and lonely. . . . You are the first person here to whom I have felt drawn. Unconventional as it may seem, I came to see you because I just could not help myself.' "

This is de Acosta's account. The breathlessness that made Marlene forget that she had all Hollywood at her lonely feet and such well-known friends as Josef von Sternberg, Gary Cooper, Maurice Chevalier, Rouben Mamoulian, and Brian Aherne to share barren hours (not to mention Maria) may smack of forgetfulness on Marlene's part or poetic license from Mercedes. As de Acosta told it, she said she thought Marlene wasn't pale *enough*, and Marlene rushed into the bathroom to remove her makeup. The day lengthened into evening, when de Acosta (apparently as ignorant of fashion as Stokowski was of movie stars) suggested Marlene wear slacks in public and later took credit for a style trend that had long since swept Main Street and whole continents.

Marlene didn't feel so lonely anymore. She cooked for de Acosta, "swamped [her] house with flowers . . . sometimes twice a day, ten dozen roses or twelve dozen carnations. . . . We never had enough vases and when I told Marlene this, as a hint not to send me any more flowers, instead I received a great many Lalique vases and even *more* flowers. The house became a sort of madhouse of flowers." Marlene switched to bibelots and *objets*. "Bullock's Wilshire had moved into my house," despaired Mercedes, apparently too tactful to say no.

They repaired to the Santa Monica beach house Marlene rented from Marion Davies, where Maria romped on the sand with hired help while Marlene and Mercedes gossiped with actor Martin Kosleck and his new friend (Marlene's *old* friend), Hans Heinrich von Twardowski, one of the first refugees from Nazi Berlin to wash up on Pacific shores. Kosleck, who would have a minor career playing Nazis on screen, painted Marlene (not very well), while Twardowski landed a job in Marlene's next picture, for there would be one. And at Paramount. Directed by the man from whom critics had rejoiced she was "free at last": Josef von Sternberg.

Less than a month after Sternberg's ill-fated UFA expedition he had signed again with Paramount. He had tried and failed to return *without* Marlene to MGM (from which he had been fired ten years before) and, telling himself he had been forced to return to her, exacted a Paramount contract that united him to her as never before. The new contract provided near absolute autonomy and front office resentment to go with it. Sternberg went to work on what he called "the private diaries of Catherine the Great," a discovery he failed to share with anyone else.

Marlene took Maria to Europe and to Rudi on the German ship *Europa* and, after a fond New York reunion with Maurice Chevalier (out of Paramount for good), she wrote Mercedes de Acosta from the ship "how much she longed for Hollywood."

She arrived in Paris at the Gare St. Lazare on May 19 to be met by Rudi and a battalion of photographers. She wore a man's polo coat, pearl gray man's suit, tie, beret, and Hollywood-sized sunglasses color-coordinated to her costume. Crowds "besieged the platform," the papers said, and . . . "jeered."

This was not the reception Marlene had expected, and Rudi whisked her through the noisy mob to the quieter precincts of the Hotel Trianon at Versailles. There they moved into a Louis *Quelquechose* suite with pianos and Josephine von Losch, in from Berlin. They admired the front-page photographs of Marlene in drag and read official warnings from the indignant Préfecture de Police that her wardrobe made her "liable to arrest." Travesty was illegal even in Paris, and the police weren't kidding. They frowned not only at the implications of her costume, but also the crowds such getups might and did attract.

In Paris Marlene visited with old best girlfriend Margo Lion, now in exile from Berlin. Lion had just made a French picture for G. W. Pabst (only temporarily fleeing the Nazis; he would find them easier to handle than the Warner Brothers), which featured Marlene's old stage colleague Peter Lorre, also in exile, and a young French actor named Jean Gabin.

Marlene's Paris visit was noted by Janet Flanner, who reported to *The New Yorker* that though under police surveillance in pants, Marlene was "asked everywhere in skirts. She is the sweet pepper that brings crowds to the modest Hungarian restaurant on the Rue de Surène where she customarily dines; she is the bitters at fashionable cocktail parties only when she fails to appear. She was the belle of the Baron de Rothschild's ball—or would have been had she consented to dance with any husband but her own. At Cécile Sorel's farewell to the *Comédie-Française*, when the Comte de Ségur made his debut as an actor, she was more observed as her old self in a box than he was on the stage. . . . At Richard Tauber's chic *auf Wiedersehen* concert, her silent silhouette was the most effective part of the program."

Marlene's mission in Paris was to find song material for recordings. Rudi negotiated a deal and Marlene spent days with Berlin exile Kurt Weill, who composed two songs for her that she never sang. They were *Lieder* of great tonal beauty, but as gloomy as Weill felt as a refugee and not particularly suitable for Marlene's voice or persona. Weill's music would remain on her mind and her voice in his ear for years to come, and there would be encores.

Rudi, meanwhile, tried to track down a song Marlene had been sent in Hollywood by a Berlin journalist friend. She had misplaced the song, but remembered the songwriters' names. Rudi finally located the lyricist, a Berlin refugee called Max Colpet, through the émigré grapevine. He was living in the Hotel Ansonia, sharing digs and laundry chores with Billy Wilder, Peter Lorre, and composer Franz Wachsmann (later Waxman). The hotel, which had a casual attitude about identity papers, was well known to German exiles in Paris, including novelist Erich Maria Remarque, who would later use it as a major setting for *Arch of Triumph.*

Rudi reached Colpet by telephone, telling him Marlene Dietrich wished to see him at Versailles. Colpet hung up, thinking it a joke. After repeated calls and hang-ups, Marlene's sixteen-cylinder Cadillac, which she had brought with her from Hollywood (she had traded in the Rolls) berthed in the rue de Saigon before the clandestine hostelry. The chauffeur drove Colpet (and a friend) to the Trianon in Versailles, where Colpet saw "on the imposing stairway leading to the hotel entrance . . . a 'blue angel,' in a fantastic chiffon dress, the summer wind playing through its folds."

This vision explained that she wanted to record a song Colpet had written lyrics for, but she had left the music in Hollywood. Colpet, desperate for work in Paris, moaned that he no longer remembered the lyrics, which didn't matter, because Marlene did, but what about the music . . . ? Marlene's conductor, Peter Kreuder, needed it for the July 19 recording date. No one had been able to locate the song's composer, Franz Wachsmann, thought to be hiding out in Paris, too.

It might have been a "meet-cute" from a Paramount picture. The friend accompanying Colpet in the block-long Cadillac was Wachsmann, who went directly to the piano and played *"Allein in einer grossen Stadt"* ("Alone in a Big City") as Marlene sang it, letter perfect.

Marlene recorded it that July of 1933 with other songs, some with jazzy, wailing saxophone backgrounds, but it was *"Allein"* that definitively captured the *Weltschmerz* of Berlin, the urban loneliness of twentieth-century life. The recording was issued with "José d'Alba" as composer and "Kurt Gerhardt" as lyricist. As Jews, neither Wachsmann nor Colpet could sell records in Nazi Germany (and this was only 1933). By any names at all, *"Allein"* is world class, the most beautiful, most *Dietrich* song Marlene ever sang, and she would keep on singing it for the rest of her life.

Marlene finished her Paris recordings, with Brian Aherne just across the Channel in London pining and giving discreet interviews about working with a "moon-goddess." London was not far, but Marlene bundled Maria and Rudi to Vienna instead. Rudi took Maria to the Prater and bought her balloons while Marlene visited Willi Forst. Her former lover was then directing his first film, *Leise flehen meine Lieder* (*The Unfinished Symphony* in its English release), a Franz Schubert biography that would establish Forst's second career as a director. Rumors flew in Vienna that Marlene was financing the picture (the rumors persist: She denied them forever) out of old amitié for Forst, but it was the film's Franz Schubert who attracted her attention.

Hans Jaray was then twenty-eight, had startled Vienna with his *Hamlet* not long before, and became a matinee idol as the young emperor in Fritz Kreisler's *Cissy*. Marlene and Jaray became lovers, inseparable in Vienna, though they contrived to be seen in public with tolerant Rudi or understanding Willi Forst or both. Vienna had always been Marlene's favorite European city, and the old Sascha-Film Company was now reorganized under Karl Hartl, who had been an assistant when she and Forst made *Café Electric* there in 1927. The Josefstadt (where Hans Jaray was becoming a major star) seemed an eventual alternative to Paramount now that the Nazis had made Berlin and UFA out of the question.

Marlene was idolized in Vienna as she was not in Berlin. Just before leaving to return to Paris she spent two straight nights from 11:00 P.M. to 2:00 A.M. signing autographs at her hotel as mobs outside chanted "*Mar - le - ne! Mar - le- ne!*" She said good-bye to Hans Jaray and dropped in on *Faust* at the Salzburg Festival en route to Cape d'Antibes with Rudi and Maria. (More letters to Mercedes.)

In a brief pause at the Plaza Athénée in Paris, she wrote Maria's godfather, Rudolf Forster, in Berlin, describing her life of glamour and adulation as meaningless. She admitted to homesickness and nostalgia, not for Berlin so much as for the theater, an interest resurgent since the affair with Hans Jaray. She felt she had organized things all wrong even before Hollywood, which had become home only by default, and said she felt a longing to *act* again, to be a real Actress, not just someone standing passively before a microphone or camera or impersonating railroad tracks or signing autographs. Producing her own records, selecting material, and, in essence, directing herself for the first time had awakened old ambitions and a longing for new challenges.

Not that she was rejecting fame. Marlene loved fame and reveled in it more radiantly than any other star ever did, but she was now thoroughly familiar with its intrusions and the isolation it could bring. Nothing she did was truly private. Fans and photographers followed her everywhere, and if they didn't, the wire services did. If she saw Chevalier in New York or Hans

Jaray in Vienna, Brian Aherne read about it in London. If Aherne came to
Paris, Mercedes de Acosta knew about it in Los Angeles.

She would many years later describe fame as "hell on earth," but the
tristesse of its absence was sharply emphasized when she and Maria returned to New York on a ship flying the French flag, which the American
press thought "significant." She declined comment on "her reported refusal
to return to Germany," *The New York Times* noted. More personally significant was that the once-great, once-famous Pola Negri was on board, her
career finished at not quite forty. Negri, like Marlene, had abandoned the
stage—Max Reinhardt, in fact—to become a great star who was now no
more than a footnote to press reports of Marlene's travel itinerary. The only
thing worse than fame was its slow, lonely fade-out.

Maybe all the power plays at Paramount had suggested Catherine the Great
of Russia to Sternberg, or maybe it was just that Elisabeth Bergner was
filming the same story opposite young Douglas Fairbanks, Jr., in England
at the same time, and Sternberg knew he and Marlene could do better. It
was an oddity of the time that at the height of the Depression all the great
stars suddenly went royal. Garbo was playing Queen Christina; Norma
Shearer was preparing to be stately as Marie Antoinette; Katharine Hepburn
was announced as Queen Elizabeth I of England, but typically contrary,
chose to play her rival, Mary Queen of Scots, instead. Some Depression
notion that even royalty has bad days may have been at work, but most of
these queens went into exile or onto the chopping block. Sternberg chose
one who sent everybody else there.

Paramount was forced under Sternberg's new contract to allow him to
proceed with those "private diaries" he had found and their tale of Prussian
Princess Sophia Augusta Frederica's rise to the throne as Czarina Catherine
the Great. The script would take Marlene from porcelain innocence to
jaded licentiousness, her absolute power achieved through assassination
and bedding what seemed to be the entire Russian army. It would become
Sternberg's most physically ambitious picture, suggesting mad profligacy at
a time that Paramount was virtually bankrupt. The vindictive power of
creativity has seldom been more nakedly announced. Sternberg boasted to
Marlene, "If this film is a flop, it will be a grandiose flop."

He wanted to call it *Her Regiment of Lovers*, but the Hays Office predictably paled, and the title briefly became just *Catherine the Great*. Under
its final title, *The Scarlet Empress*, it truly became what Sternberg termed
"a relentless excursion in style." It also became one of the great curiosities
of Hollywood studio filmmaking.

Sternberg was at heart a silent-film director, for all his musical pretensions and experiments with sound. He thought of this picture as prelude, rondo, scherzo, etc., and personally took up the baton for recording the Tchaikovsky, Mendelssohn, and Wagner that made up the score. He tried in *The Scarlet Empress* to move the story with images (and silent-film titles), which he could do (the reason some people love this picture), but he couldn't move the emotions or intellect (the reason others loathe it). It is a picture that defies neutral reaction, the most *intentionally* delirious big-studio picture ever made and one of the coldest—less remote only than the next Dietrich-Sternberg collaboration.

It is unlikely Sternberg cared much about Catherine the Great, but he cared and knew about Marlene and sexual politics, which is the subject of the picture. No transition occurs that is not motivated by sex or sexual jealousy, liberally laced with sadism. The structure is episodic and not so much musical as just nondramatic. It is Catherine's perverse Stations of the Cross (her husband, the mad duke, is strangled behind one). External historical forces play no role whatever: There is a war going on in—Finland? Doesn't matter. Back to the real battlefield—the bedroom. Or the stable.

Our first view of Catherine—Princess Sophia—is of a child, played by nine-year-old Maria Sieber. Maria was a pretty child but self-conscious, and it shows. She is stiff and unnatural, perhaps because, as she told Shirley Temple, "I can't have still photos taken of me. One side of me is no good." Sternberg planned more than one short scene for Maria, but could not do more because the child was already overweight. It cannot have been easy for any girl born and raised by a beautiful mother who pointed out her "sides," and Maria was painfully conscious of her shortcomings. Photographs of mother and daughter together almost always show an unsmiling, anxious child, and she had already taken to eating as a weapon against the very notion of beauty, perhaps against Marlene's aspirations for her as an actress. Her mother's work and relationship with Sternberg may not have been a young girl's dream.

Maria grows up in a screen dissolve to become Marlene. In no other picture does Sternberg so daringly use light to define personality, and here he pours it on Marlene as the young princess, who was fourteen when betrothed to the Grand Duke Peter of Russia. Marlene doesn't try to play fourteen, but she attempts a virginal innocence that clearly owes something to her early orphan scenes in *Song of Songs*. We know too much about Marlene Dietrich to truly believe in the Princess Sophia. Marlene at this age was already using her bedroom eyes on the faculty; Sophia thinks a bedroom is someplace to sleep and keep her dolls. Still, the performance is technically adroit, an actress's work.

Sternberg details the stages in Sophia/Catherine's corruption with increasing shadow and modeling of her face, collapsing the notion of any simplistic "Dietrich lighting." She—and light—play the widest range yet, progressing from dew-dropped innocence to hopeful virgin eager to be deflowered to speechless horror as her fate with the creepy grand duke becomes clear. She moves on to provocation and seduction and lust for power, to which sex is the means, and love, if present at all, an incidental. Marlene plays extreme youth as a baroque doll, all white blond, full of curiosity about that world beyond her rococo cage. Her first words on screen focus her erotic curiosity and potential: "I wonder what he looks like," she says when told she is to be married.

She finds out soon enough, but not before she has fallen in crush with dark, lion-maned Alexei, played by John Lodge, who has come to take her to Russia. Lodge was never an actor (he was one of the Boston Lodges and later governor of Connecticut and ambassador to Spain), but he *looked* good all in black, and Marlene stares at him as if at an obsidian phallic symbol. He gives her sables to keep her warm.

She wants to be warmed up by *him*. Her shock is palpable when she discovers that her husband, described to her as "godlike . . . *and* he can read and write," turns out to be Sam Jaffe, leering, mad, hunched over, with an unsavory drool and a white spiderweb wig no one failed to compare to Harpo Marx. The young princess has just arrived in St. Petersburg when a court doctor climbs under her skirts to perform a gynecological examination in full view of the empress and her courtiers, one of whom is Marlene's old friend, Hans von Twardowski, wearing a beauty mark and carrying a white fur muff and lorgnette.

Sternberg's Russia is a barbaric world expressed in decor with a vengeance. The picture is notorious for sumptuousness, though it is mostly logs for walls, grotesque plaster statuary, and studio-painted icons. No Hollywood director ever achieved such pictorial effects at such little expense.

Sternberg photographed most of the picture himself, riding a boom and issuing orders over a public address system like a general or a pope. He kept referring to the dialogue as "titles," a clear betrayal of his silent-movie heart, and the most impressive sequence in the picture (one of the most beautiful ever shot) is the no-dialogue five-minute-twenty-second wedding sequence with only music over. Sternberg remains mostly on Marlene's face and manages through her eyes to capture the oppressive power of the Russian Orthodox Church, the tyranny of the court and the old empress, the madness of Catherine's groom, the spiteful jealousy of his mistress, the bride's terror of it all as she is (literally) bound to her lunatic and struggles with the sexual attraction she feels for Alexei. Eisenstein borrowed from this scene, as did many others, and no wonder. It remains unequaled in claustrophobic beauty and its sense of the corrupting sensuality of power.

As the scene progresses, Marlene holds a candle before her face, the flame measuring her breath, quicker and quicker as she looks at Alexei, almost flickering out, then blazing back to life. She was never more beautiful on screen, never so *iconic*, and is sometimes reduced to close-ups so extreme they frame only her eyes and nose behind marriage veils so perfectly photographed we can count the fibers in their weave. No camera was ever more in love with any woman than in this extraordinary sequence, and no woman ever yielded more serenely to its worship. The sequence ends on a triumphant close-up of the old empress, her plans for Russia's fate now secure.

TITLE: "And thus Catherine took the first innocent step to become Russia's most powerful and most sinister empress, while the machine of the marriage went on."

It's all machinery. Later Catherine tells the archbishop, "I have far more powerful weapons of my own than any machine," rejecting him *and* his church. She has everything she needs, and if she doesn't, she knows how to get it.

The machine of Sternberg went on delivering one stunning sequence after another. Catherine hurls a locket from a window and we trace its delicate fall through tree branches to a guardsman below to whom she gives herself. He impregnates her with the child who ensures the succession, a child we never see. This is no drama of mother love.

There is a banquet scene, with a literal skeleton at the table, at which Catherine duels with her husband and his mistress; another in a stable, in which she draws a straw back and forth between her lips so suggestively you expect it to combust.

As she becomes the "Messalina of the North" (as a title calls her) she is ripe, *rife* with carnality. This empress wears black; her eyes miss nothing from under their soaring, penciled eyebrows; she is mocking, insolent, imperial, amused at the power of her weaponry, her sex. This is superb stuff, and one can think of no other actress who could bring off the ruthlessness without becoming repellent. Dietrich becomes only more desirable, more casually, transcendently beautiful.

Finally, she has seduced the army (one by one, from the looks of it) and with their aid ascends the throne. They murder Peter for her and invade the palace on horseback, galloping through wooden corridors, up wooden stairways to the imperial eagle throne itself, where Marlene stands dressed as a Hussar all in white, delirious with victory, and in her wild-eyed power and triumph, quite mad.

This was apotheosis: Marlene's, Venus *become* Mother Russia, all-conquering, all-voracious, beautiful beyond humanity, ecstatic with self-love. But Marlene's apotheosis as Star was Sternberg's as Star-Maker. "Miss Dietrich is me," he would say in a kind of madness of his own. "I am Miss Dietrich."

But Sternberg wasn't Marlene, and she wasn't Sternberg, apart from viewers' identifying *him* as the reason they avoided *her* by staying away from *The Scarlet Empress* by the millions. This was the year of *It Happened One Night*, not skeletons at the banquet, and every Sternberg scholar repeats the story that Paramount so hated the picture they kept it on the shelf for eight months to avoid competition with Elisabeth Bergner's *Catherine*. The truth is, they couldn't wait to get rid of it.

Bergner's *Catherine* was released in February 1934, just as Marlene's began filming, and Marlene's *Scarlet Empress* had an immediate, disastrous premiere in London in May, only three months later. The London *Times* seized upon "scenery and decor. People move endlessly between statues far livelier than they; no actor can compete with the violence and passion of the decadent Byzantine art, which degenerates into some sort of German expressionism."

The film's catastrophic reception in England (Bergner's film was a London Films production for Alexander Korda, its dullness much admired) prompted Paramount paralysis in America. Critics there in August were no less appalled; audiences fled from screens on which Marlene rode her horse to ecstasy. Paramount had put Trilby together again with Svengali, and this was the result? Sternberg realized bitterly that the picture was viewed mainly as "an attempt to assassinate a superb actress." His enthusiasts pointed out vainly (weirdly) that the film was "primarily a comedy," but audiences suspected that if there was a joke, it was on them.

The film divided partisans like a cleaver. Critic Aeneas Mackenzie worshipped the "Leonardo of the Lenses" while *The New York Times* bemoaned "so many obvious talents, inextricably confused with so many obvious faults." Richard Watts, Jr., thought *"The Scarlet Empress* displays so emphatically all [Sternberg's] weaknesses . . . that the film repeatedly works as a particularly cruel satire on the much celebrated style of the director and his countless failings."

Andrew Sarris notes that *The Scarlet Empress* violated the "repressive reasonableness" of Hollywood and Depression audiences, that it flew in the face of prevailing moral concerns ("land reform would seem to be the last thing on [Catherine's] mind," he noted.) Sternberg had tried to flee censorship and contemporary society in his "relentless excursion" into eighteenth-century Russia. The picture was obsessional and ecstatic and "let 'em eat cake," while Frank Capra was dishing up popcorn and daily bread.

Marlene's obliging insistence that she was merely Sternberg's puppet spared her much of the abuse heaped on the picture. *Variety* noted, "Dietrich has never been as beautiful as she is here. . . . But never is she allowed to become really alive and vital. She is as though enchanted by the immense sets through which she stalks. . . . That [Sternberg] succeeded as well as he did is a tribute to his artistic genius and his amazingly vital sense of photogenic values."

It was as relentless as he had said it would be and just as relentlessly rejected.

"The roles I have played in films have absolutely nothing to do with what I really am," Marlene kept insisting in oblique praise of her mentor. "I'm not entitled to the least recognition. . . . I was nothing but pliable material on the infinitely rich palette of his ideas and imaginative faculties."

The statements were becomingly modest and took her off Catherine's Byzantine hook, but the relationship between Marlene and Sternberg had worsened as his autonomy—and her power—at Paramount had grown.

Sam Jaffe, who played Grand Duke Peter, dined out for the next forty years on his Sternberg horror stories, a peculiar genre enjoyed by few other Hollywood directors. He delighted in stories of Sternberg's disdain for any human dignity but his own, and thought he "wanted to play all the parts. He would tell you [how to do it], you see," Jaffe said, "not the function of a director at all." Jaffe's final day of work was at the bier of the dead Empress Elisabeth. "I was to inherit," Jaffe explained. "And I had a speech to make in which I poured forth my venom against her. He didn't like it. I did it about thirty-seven times. . . . He wanted to get something else out of it. So he said, 'If you can't do it right, I'll just have you spit and go out.' I said, 'If I spit, it'll be right in your face.'

"I took off my wig and said, 'I'm through.' . . . He walked [off] with me and said, 'You know, I have seventy million followers in Japan alone.' I said, 'Christ only had *twelve!*'

"But I wasn't the only one. Miss Dietrich—very lovely, very charming, everybody liked her—had the same kind of thing. Not that she would spit in his face, but she refused to come back and work, because he made her blow candles and keep on blowing candles. . . . So she quit. She said, 'I quit,' and they had the hardest time getting her back. . . . He said he could do everything with her . . . *except stop her from loving him.*"

Mercedes de Acosta interrupted her work on Garbo to visit Marlene during shooting and described Sternberg as "a friend . . . but he was often very difficult and explosive on the set. One day they had a violent quarrel and Jo refused to speak to her except when directing her in front of the camera. After three days of this Marlene hit on a solution." She had fallen from a horse in *Song of Songs,* and she arranged to take a fake fall, with de Acosta's doctor present to pronounce her badly hurt.

"The moment came," de Acosta related, "and I saw her, every inch an empress, high up on the horse before the camera. . . . She quietly tumbled off the horse, slipping to the ground as though it were a feat she often performed. The camera stopped grinding and everyone, stagehands, grips, assistant directors, and Jo, rushed in wild confusion to her side. Marlene lay as though she were dead. Jo picked her up in his arms and screamed for a doctor, who appeared in an unnaturally short time. Luckily, Jo was too beside himself to notice this. He kissed Marlene's hands and begged her to forgive him, as if she were dying and they were parting forever."

Fatally, they were not.

Not all of the magnificence of *The Scarlet Empress* was Sternberg's. In an effort to keep the budget within some sort of bounds, Sternberg had simply cut into the picture several crowd scenes from Lubitsch's 1928 *The Patriot,* the Emil Jannings picture about mad Czar Paul. Sternberg later allowed it might have been "ten feet" of film, but it was much more and jarringly obvious.

Under the new corporate structure at Paramount, Emanuel "Manny" Cohen was out of his depth as any kind of creative arbiter and began consulting more and more with Paramount's leading director, who might advise him about creative problems: Ernst Lubitsch.

Lubitsch bit down on his cigar as he saw *The Scarlet Empress* unreel in a screening room, knowing such "artistry" had the potential to unreel the entire company. He cited his own mammoth crowd scenes cut in from *The Patriot* as proof of what he characterized as Sternberg's profligate extravagance, failing (Sternberg said) to recognize that they were his own. Whether Lubitsch knew that or not didn't matter. Nor did it matter if it was ten feet or ten thousand.

Lubitsch had never liked Sternberg or his pretensions and was poised to become the first director elevated to head of production at any major studio. He was painfully aware that Sternberg and Marlene had one more picture to make under their unrestricted contracts. Lubitsch had things of his own in mind and began quietly talking to Marlene (and her new agent, Harry Edington, who also represented Garbo) about a Paramount contract beyond her present one, beyond Sternberg's.

If Marlene was longing to be an actress again, as she had written Rudolf Forster, fine. Lubitsch knew Sternberg had his own discontents. Even as megalomania pushed him to abuse every advantage for his art, Sternberg knew his obsession with Marlene could not continue without crippling him creatively. He had once been typed a gangster-film director; he was now almost solely identified with Marlene. He had become a household word uttered with contempt by competitors, with a sneer by those who couldn't touch him. He needed no enemies, but could not help making them. His amorous frustrations with the star he had created drove him to rivalry with her, to demonstrate once and for all who was the artist, who the artifact.

"Miss Dietrich is me—I am Miss Dietrich."

Lubitsch reeled out the rope with which Sternberg could hang himself and Sternberg took it. With typical self-scorn, or self-delusion, or both, Sternberg wrapped the noose of celluloid about his neck and called his impending self-immolation—he may have believed it when he said it—"a final tribute to the lady I had seen lean against the wings of a Berlin stage."

TEN

TRIBUTE AND
FAREWELL

1934 - 1935

"I never talk politics," said Marlene with the shrewd reticence of a resident foreigner. She still had family in Berlin, where a statement with the force of an edict had been issued at the end of 1933:

> "It is proposed to make further work in Germany impossible for such Aryan film workers who remain abroad beyond their present contractual obligations or who go abroad now, thereby showing they are not interested in the great cultural upbuilding of Germany or are even sabotaging it. . . . The new Germany will turn with all the means at its disposal against such economic and ideological traitors."

The words were strong; their impact was felt. Marlene had returned to Berlin quietly in early spring of 1934, immediately after finishing *The*

Scarlet Empress. It was a last attempt to mend bridges or assess how thoroughly they had been burned. She had no assets in Berlin but the most valuable, family and reputation, the latter increasingly under assault. On March 14, the head of the Nazi National *Filmkammer* announced Marlene's contribution of "a considerable sum" to the film organization's welfare fund. The gift was publicized as a "reconciliation" and reeked, to those with a nose for Dr. Goebbels's tactics, of blackmail. Two days later, the Nazis banned *Song of Songs* to demonstrate they could not be bought. Marlene, they announced, was "a German actress who has shown a preference for prostitute roles in America, who is known worldwide as a German . . . and thus [gives] the world a thoroughly false and unrealistic picture of Germany."

A news report soon surfaced that she wasn't German, after all, but *Russian*, the daughter of an army officer from St. Petersburg. She had arrived in Berlin, the story went, after having exhibited herself in the chorus line at the Folies-Bergère in Paris. Or maybe she was a Pole . . .

This did not alter the fact that Marlene, her child, and her husband were all German citizens, her mother and sister still residents. Goebbels refrained from revoking her citizenship because she was not Jewish and he secretly hoped she would return to Berlin. Her propaganda value was immense. That old friends and colleagues were not only emigrating, but disappearing, some of them forever, was a political "sanitation" action and should be irrelevant to an actress. Marlene saw it differently and urgently wanted Rudi to leave Europe altogether. Her contribution to the film welfare fund was *quid pro quo* for Rudi's exit visa to America as well as a "goodwill" gesture to keep her own identity and travel papers valid.

As compensation, perhaps, for the unpleasantness of what she could not guess would be her last trip to Berlin for more than a decade, Marlene formed one of the enduring relationships of her life on the return journey to America on the *Île de France.*

"I was crossing cabin on the *Ile,*" Ernest Hemingway told A. E. Hotchner, "but a pal of mine who was traveling first loaned me his reserve tux and smuggled me in for meals. One night we're having dinner in the salon, my pal and I, when there appears at the top of the staircase this unbelievable spectacle in white. The Kraut, of course. A long, tight white-beaded gown over *that* body; in the area of what is known as the Dramatic Pause, she can give lessons to anybody. So she gives it that Dramatic Pause on the staircase, then slowly slithers down the stairs and across the floor to where Jock Whitney was having a fawncy dinner party. Of course, nobody in that dining room has touched food to lips since her entrance. The Kraut gets to the table and all the men hop up and her chair is held at the ready; but she's counting. Twelve. Of course, she apologizes and backs off and says she's sorry, but she is very superstitious about being thirteen at anything and with that she turns to go, but I have naturally risen to the occasion and grandly offer to save the party by being the fourteenth. That was how we met. Pretty romantic, eh?"

Marlene—"The Kraut"—and Hemingway were instant soulmates, not lovers. Hemingway claimed they were "victims of unsynchronized passion," while Marlene maintained that "Hemingway never *asked* me to go to bed with him." Besides, Hemingway had heard the stories; he used to kid her about "your girls." Androgyny was part of the attraction and he proved it in writing. Marlene never played a Hemingway heroine on screen (though she had wanted to play Catherine Barkley in A *Farewell to Arms*), but he wrote her into both *Islands in the Stream* (as Thomas Hudson's wife, the "good general") and (probably) *Garden of Eden*. He would write at essay length about her in the 1950s, when comradeship had mellowed to a mutual, sometimes fierce protectiveness.

Marlene was reaching out for new friendships as the relationship with Sternberg deteriorated. Not long after she returned to California she saw Paramount's Ben Hecht and Charles MacArthur picture *The Scoundrel* and telephoned its star, Noël Coward, at his home in the English countryside to introduce herself and to lavish praise. It became an *"amitié amoureuse"* (the term is Cole Lesley's) "only really understood by themselves, not always by their friends." This loyalty, too, would last until death: Marlene, Coward, and Hemingway all knew about "grace under pressure," and only Hemingway, who coined the phrase, would fail to maintain it until the end.

Hemingway and Coward found a Marlene-for-life, but Hollywood, seismographically acute to box-office tremors, registered more transient affections. The press, following *The Scarlet Empress* and Marlene's indecisive "I'm going/I'm staying" announcements—not to mention her mostly baffling loyalty to Sternberg—began to display that hostility reserved for those they feel have been made by the power of their pens. Even here she could not escape comparisons with MGM's Swede, also target of a cranky press.

"Garbo is in love!" shouted a fan magazine. "Dietrich is in love! . . . They are in love with—themselves! Garbo's Great Love is—*Garbo*. Dietrich's Great Love is—*Dietrich!*" Another writer, a Paramount publicist at the time of Marlene's arrival in Hollywood, wrote scathingly of her " 'yes' and 'no' " interviews:

"The subservient writer pounds out a story which dresses up the Dietrich rudeness in glamour, her lack of opinions in mystery, her ruthless disregard for the men and women who have pushed her to the heights [as] picturesque eccentricity."

The brush of Sternberg's arrogance was tarring Marlene, and Marlene was getting careless. She had walked out on Ethel Merman in mid-song in *Take a Chance* on Broadway, a serious breach of performer etiquette that may have signaled nothing more sinister than a visit to the ladies room, but like everything Marlene did, it got written about.

Fan magazine writers were not Hemingway, and though they were (are) a necessary evil for film stars (or their studios), none of them understood her anxieties about Berlin or the increasingly complicated development of Maria, now ten years old—unhappy, overweight, largely friendless. Nor was any privy to Rudi's quiet removal from Paris to America shortly after Marlene's final visit to Berlin. It was impolitic with an overcurious press to publicize her husband's reality rather than the *idea* of him, which might lead journalists to conclude "DIETRICH GETS HER MEN BUT NOT HER MAN." Especially when the Nazis were waging a public relations war to bring her back to Germany or, failing that, defame her so thoroughly in her home-land that her reputation could never recover. But Rudi's move to America was too tempting for Goebbels to resist retaliation, however indirect:

The New Year's cover for the *Berliner Illustrirte*, Germany's leading weekly, featured a faked photograph of Marlene being drooled over by a lascivious John D. Rockefeller, then in his nineties. Marlene smiles her secret smile as the ancient old man pleads:

"When will you finally say 'yes,' Marlene?"

"Save up another billion, Mr. Rockefeller!" she says.

Marlene moved into the secluded Bel-Air home of Colleen Moore, another rental (she would never own her own home). The disastrous critical and box-office response to *The Scarlet Empress* had resulted in an announcement that Trilby and Svengali's next picture, over which they still had free, full rein, would be their last. "My being with her," Sternberg told the press, "will not help her or me. If we continued, we would get into a pattern that would be harmful to both of us."

She read it in the papers. He dared not confront her personally, a sign of both weakness and resolve. She understood, if she didn't quite believe. He had made her "Marlene Dietrich," the world's foremost erotic symbol, but there was torment there for him because of its offscreen truth and her serial love affairs with both men and women. She knew that if he had told her directly she would have used every wile at her disposal to penetrate his vulnerability and prevent his leaving, which might be no kindness. And she believed, as few did, in his genius. The greater loyalty could be to let him go. His tribute to her could be hers to him.

Berlin treachery was one thing, but there was rascality going on at Para-mount. Emanuel "Manny" Cohen had succeeded in toppling his mentor, company co-founder Jesse Lasky, but had not the slightest ability or interest in running the spoils he had grasped in the days of bankruptcy. His only virtue, Herman Mankiewicz's wisecrack went, was that he was so short that "having a story conference . . . you don't have to see the little sonofabitch—unless you look under the desk."

Someone should have looked. Cohen's sole contribution to the running of the studio was his delegation of creative matters to Ernst Lubitsch, while Cohen turned his own attention to stars' contracts and their expiration dates. As Mae West, or newcomer Bing Crosby, or even long-time asset Gary Cooper came up for contract renewal, Cohen renewed them. To himself. In personal management contracts which he intended to sell back to the company.

Front-office malfeasance is rarely secret in Hollywood and has been used more than once by artists to justify their own flouting of schedules, budgets, or other obligations. In the land of filthy lucre, lily-white hands are few, and Sternberg, knowing his days were numbered under a regime now ruled creatively by Lubitsch, decided to go for broke. He had talked before about "a big Spanish picture," a "capriccio," when negotiating with Fox and UA, and after rejecting something called *Red Pawn* (of which nothing is known), he announced he would make his "final tribute" to Marlene with Pierre Louÿs's novel *La Femme et le Pantin* (*The Woman and the Puppet*).

It was the story of the heartless Concha (the name means shell) Perez and her destruction not of one man, as in the novel, but of most of Seville in Sternberg's version. For a man who spoke publicly of actors as puppets, the invitation to view the picture as somehow confessional was irresistible, sharply underscored by his casting *Song of Songs'* evil baron, Lionel Atwill, who looked almost exactly like Sternberg, as Concha's exquisitely refined and masochistic protector. And (maybe) puppet.

The novel had been filmed before with Geraldine Farrar in 1920 and Conchita Montenegro in 1929 (and would be made twice again, once with Brigitte Bardot, and then by Luis Buñuel as *That Obscure Object of Desire*, requiring two actresses to portray Concha's heartlessness). Sternberg's interest was less the story than the sadomasochistic flavor of Louys's novel. It brought into highest relief aspects of the Marlene character he had been developing on screen ever since *The Blue Angel* and aspects of their personal relationship as well. Tension resulting from the impossibility of possession had become the very fabric of their work. It had always been, perhaps (it lay at the heart of *The Blue Angel*), and *The Scarlet Empress* is easily readable as an essay on sexual politics and power as Sternberg experienced them.

The creation of Marlene as a world-famous love object had been largely his doing, and the image was not one from which he could detach himself. It had contributed to the end of a bad marriage and had given him autonomy and power at Paramount, in spite of the resentment with which they were extended. He had clung to the afterburn of Marlene's comet with the fatalism of one of his heroes—or proxies—maintaining less and less convincingly that she was the puppet who danced to his strings. The image would be literally reversed in *The Woman and the Puppet*, which he wanted to call with surprising bravado *Caprice Espagnol*, the title borrowed from Rimsky-Korsakoff, as would be the music.

The film story is capricious only to those who find matadors, dancers, or bullfights witty. The story of Concha ("the most dangerous woman you'll ever meet") is told in flashback narrative by Don Pasqual (Sternberg-double Lionel Atwill), a grandee forced to resign his commission—and all social position—because of his degradation by "the most beautiful creature I've ever seen, a goddess." He tells his story in measured, ironic tones to young revolutionary Antonio, played by Cesar Romero, then an unknown contract player from Universal. Antonio is in Seville incognito during carnival, wearing a festival mask, helping establish masks as a decorative and thematic motif of the picture.

Pasqual's story inflames Antonio, who has already seen the beautiful Concha through several hundred thousand balloons and carnival streamers in the picture's opening sequence. Pasqual, after a recital of his humiliations by this woman who "has ice where others have a heart," extracts a pledge from Antonio never to see the mysterious carnival beauty again. Antonio, of course, cannot wait to pursue her.

Antonio is Concha's new toy in town. Pasqualito (as Concha calls her quarry) doesn't really love her. "If you had loved me enough you would have killed yourself," she complains with a pout. Pasqual, consumed with sexual jealousy and dark thoughts, asks, "Aren't you afraid of anything, Concha? Have you no fear of death?" (This is Spain; death is ritual.) "No," she answers. "Not today. I feel too happy. Why do you ask? Are you going to kill me?" She flashes another taunting smile.

"I told myself there were only two ways out: either to leave her or kill her," Pasqual tells Antonio. "I chose a third . . . I submitted." Concha knew he would: "You've always mistaken your vanity for love," she tells him, and—most devastatingly—"Are you my father? No. Are you my husband? No. Are you my lover? No. Well, I must say, you're content with very little." It may be the most cruelly withering line in any movie.

Death—or its ritual—inevitably intrudes. Pasqual, just as we suspected, has warned Antonio about Concha because he fears the younger man's competition. A duel in the woods must follow. Concha shows up, rain slashing through the night onto a hundred umbrellas. Only one of them twirls merrily: Concha's.

Pasqual uses the duel as a suicide attempt, not even shooting, but he isn't killed, merely half blinded. Concha admires this ("Only Pasqual can do such things") and visits him in the hospital to admit petulantly, "I suppose I deserve this. [What? *He's* the one who's shot.] I know I've always done everything wrong. Will you forgive me, Pasqualito, and then I'll go."

She receives no blessing of forgiveness, but goes anyway, with Antonio, to catch the train to Paris. They toast "to the future," and just as it is too late for Antonio to do anything but be amazed, she saunters casually back in the direction of Seville.

"I'm going back to Pasqual. Don't forget me, Antonio," she orders as the train pulls out. She strolls back past the border guard. ("I've changed my mind," she says, echoing Tom Brown's message in *Morocco* to Amy Jolly), and asks her coachman for a cigarette. She contemplates it ironically, twirling it in her fingers, then stunningly, unexpectedly, shoots out a non-sequitur like an arrow that laces Seville to Berlin: "You know, I used to work in a cigarette factory."

A coach takes her back to Seville.

Sternberg and Marlene experimented with the look of a Spanish Dietrich, and the surviving stills reveal a gradual streamlining of the face, a Deco-izing of the makeup treatment, until the final version is a mask, hard-edged, beautiful, brilliant as a diamond. And scarcely less cold.

Marlene knew her function in the Sternberg pictures was to represent an image of desire, longing, erotic attraction, and frustration; "both command and invitation," as film critic-historian Richard Schickel called it. But this was to be, as even Sternberg's admirer John Baxter admitted, "his most vicious [portrait], a symbolic act of revenge on the woman who had dom-inated his life."

The conventional view of Marlene as Sternberg's puppet is sometimes used to dismiss her, sometimes to dismiss *him*, but either way it oversim-plifies everything: their personal drama, Marlene's contribution to her screen image, and Sternberg's mandarin but relentless obsession. Even Marjorie Rosen, in *Popcorn Venus*, her analysis of the feminine mystique in movies, retails the notion that Sternberg "rehearsed [Marlene's] every glance and inflection," but this is naive, as any actor or director knows. The puppet's properties are always in play, dancing or dancing resistance, and while actors often play *against* roles they find unsympathetic to their self-images, Marlene *realizes* Concha in every sense. She is nowhere so clearly Sternberg's partner or accomplice than as Concha Perez.

Her fondness for the picture suggests to many that she but dimly understood her uses to Sternberg, that her vanity and narcissism were so enormous, so necessary to her that even this act of sabotage could be accepted as an homage. But it *is* homage—however perverse—*and she knew it.*

The picture began shooting on October 10, 1934, and finished in mid-January 1935. New émigré Rudi Sieber worked as unbilled assistant to Sternberg. The script had been assigned to John Dos Passos (because his name sounded Spanish?), but little of his style or concerns, apart from allusions to some labor troubles in a *Carmen*esque cigarette factory, can be detected in what is mainly Sternberg. (He claimed Dos Passos had undulant fever, but it was brought on by whiskey in a Los Angeles hotel. Sternberg's boyhood friend and longtime assistant Sam Winston received credit for the adaptation.)

Production problems were many, beginning with Sternberg's firing of his first Antonio, Joel McCrea, for insubordination (McCrea's wife, Frances Dee, had been indiscreetly courted by Marlene and had been in *An American Tragedy*; she may have forewarned him). Hence the casual importation of the unknown Romero from Universal.

Romero hated Sternberg. "He was a mean man, a little Napoleon," he said, but found Marlene "marvelous, just marvelous, just great, wonderful to work with." Romero recounted Sternberg's fury with Marlene, his browbeating of her in German, his reduction of her to tears, his endless takes for all the actors, who found finally that the first or second take of twenty, thirty, forty, or fifty got used.

Sternberg photographed the picture (with Lucien Ballard) and for the first time took official credit for it. He inundated the screen with rhythmic waves of balloons, streamers, and confetti for the carnival scenes and made tight, eerie close-ups (they seem to be taken underwater) of his proxy, Pasqual.

He painted the sets white, the better to reflect light, and when that wasn't enough, spray-painted them with aluminum in the rainy forest duel scene. He indulged in camera jokes: a jack-in-the box that goes detumescent; the literal puppet Don Pasqual plays with so idly (Antonio?); the grotesque masks with phallic noses; Marlene's costumes themselves, Travis Banton gone *loco* with lace in Iberia.

In spite of what Sternberg considered humor (a painfully dithery performance by Edward Everett Horton as the unlikely mayor of Seville), the picture seems drugged, overdosed on itself. Its extravagance is admired by many, and Dietrich's beauty is ravishing, startlingly unreal and always breathtaking. But the picture is airless; there is no relief—it is the most unrelenting picture Sternberg ever made. The only deliverance is when

Concha sings "Three Sweethearts Have I" in the Spanish cabaret which so studiedly resembles that of *The Blue Angel*. She is wild-eyed, reckless with self-assurance, as she was in her first song as Lola Lola; she knows she has become the most beautiful woman on earth, but there's no invitation to it now: it's *all* command.

Marlene works on the audience quite as heartlessly as she does on Pasqual and Antonio. Death doesn't bother her; nothing bothers her. She is totally amoral, in love with her own whimsical cruelty and so beautiful she expects others to let her get away with it. They do. One sympathizes with Pasqual's self-destructive obsession (if one does) only because Concha's beauty is so extraordinary it justifies his desperate passion, his suicidally masochistic torment. Or game.

And it *is* a game. Never is Pasqual unambiguous; the first half of the picture is *his* version of Concha, as he craftily paints her and himself in flashback for Antonio while he plays with his puppet. Pierre Louÿs thought Pasqual the puppet; Sternberg thought it more ambiguous. He refuses to forgive Concha from his hospital bed (why forgive her for the pain he begs for?), but she goes back to him, or says she does, in the end. Sternberg, in one of his ritually inscrutable interviews, told Peter Bogdanovich, "I don't know if she goes back. Maybe she doesn't." Maybe not, but her *coach* does.

The one moment of relief in the entire picture comes at the end in Concha's reflective, almost fatalistic line about having once worked in a cigarette factory. It sounds meaningless, out of nowhere, leading nowhere, but it is a glimpse into some aspect of Concha hidden from us by the rest of the film which is, mostly, Pasqual's version of her. If it is a glancing allusion to the past over which Dietrich triumphed with Sternberg's help— and over Sternberg, too—the voice recalls, "It came too late," uttered from a stairway outside a crowded apartment in Berlin when fame was at last assured, its rewards arrayed at her feet and not nearly as fulfilling as anticipation had promised. There is something like forgiveness in that line.

For the rest of her life Dietrich regarded this as her favorite film "because I was most beautiful in it," but she is more. Concha is a highly stylized farce performance, the best this actress ever gave. She never stops moving in her "caprice"—she flits from whim to wile with the speed of castanets, and her vocal tone and physical animation (pouts, shrugs, sudden turns, the stamp of a foot, the tilt of a head) are perfectly modulated, flawlessly executed.

Concha is diabolical, but intelligent, too. The giant close-ups of Pasqual (she never has one so tight) suggest she is a creature of his invention (this is Sternberg's proxy, after all) but there are a couple of quiet, entirely enigmatic shots just as she leaves Pasqual's hospital room to escort Antonio to the border, in which her face suggests calculation beyond and deeper than her monumental narcissism. This Concha has as many layers as she has clothes. Part of her fascination is how many remain concealed from us. The cryptic ending isn't the enigma of this picture—Concha is.

Paramount had let itself in for as much trouble as Pasqual and Antonio. There was a general feeling on the lot that the disgraced, double-dealing Cohen could take the rap for this one (he was still around as an "indie prod" [independent producer]: Such people know where too many bodies are buried to be loosed on a suspecting world), but no one anticipated the alarms rung by the picture itself.

The Hays Office had been leery from the beginning: Here was Dietrich, plying her trade on another Sternberg mattress. Lubitsch's retitling the picture *The Devil Is a Woman* over Sternberg's objections rang all kinds of bells. (Antonio somewhere mutters, "What a devil of a woman!"; it was still called *Caprice Espagnol* in some foreign territories.) The Hay Office didn't know what it meant, but objected anyway. Once they saw the picture, alarm was so great that Will Hays "personally and officially" took up the matter with chairman of the board Adolph Zukor. One of Hays's minions atypically turned critic with, "Dietrich is laughable . . . she has attempted a role she does not come within ten miles of getting over . . . terrible, childish, amateurish effort." What really troubled them was that it came over all too well.

Code suggestions for "improving" the film included Concha's seeing herself as "a scrawny, impoverished hag" in a mirror at the end (they didn't want her to keep cash *or* looks), or Pasqual leaping (blind?) from his bed to "choke her to death." This was anger, not judgment.

The issue was not the movie, but independent censorship groups like the recently formed Legion of Decency: These Hays people could lose their jobs with pictures like this! By October the new Legion would condemn not only Marlene in *The Devil Is a Woman*, but *The Scoundrel* with Noël Coward, *Catherine the Great* with Elisabeth Bergner, *The Private Life of Henry VIII* with Charles Laughton, *Anna Karenina* with Garbo, *The Informer* with Victor McLaglen, and more. Hays's second-in-command, Joe Breen, told his superior that the picture raised an "extra-code question," that of "classification of films, which the industry apparently is not ready to meet at this time," nor would it be for decades.

The picture was screened for the Hays Office and the trade papers in February. It was then ninety-three minutes long and still contained Concha's second song, the lushly masochistic "If It Isn't Pain (Then It Isn't Love)," which was finally cut and sung later by Carole Lombard in *Swing High, Swing Low*, where it got no merrier. Subsequent screenings of the picture were at lengths of eighty-five minutes, then eighty, and finally, when it was released in May, seventy-six minutes, a net loss of seventeen minutes including the second song, or almost two full reels of material now permanently lost or disintegrating in some Paramount vault. Whatever rights of final cut Sternberg thought he had were suspended following Paramount's stricken assessment of the film, and Lubitsch (head of production since February 4) took scissors to negative as Sternberg had once taken shears to Stroheim.

The worst was yet to come.

On March 3 (Lubitsch didn't dally) *The New York Times* reported, "The future of Josef von Sternberg seems to have been settled. Following the preview the other evening of *The Devil Is a Woman* . . . the studio indicated that no attempt would be made to hold Mr. von Sternberg and that, in spite of *certain financial loss* [italics added], the film would be released in its present form, without retakes. The temper of the [Lubitsch] production regime was described as favoring the immediate departure of the director, with the whole thing charged off to experience."

The worst was yet to come.

Reviews were hardly better than the Hays Office critique. The *New York Sun* found it "the dullest picture of the season"; the *Herald Tribune* thought it "almost entirely devoid of dramatic substance"; the *American* reported "the delightful Dietrich pouts and poses through dreary, repetitious reels of dull story clumsily told, and the boresome botch makes even the magnificent Marlene appear amateurish and almost ridiculous."

Only *The New York Times* found merit, but not very helpfully. "The uninformed will be bored by *The Devil Is a Woman*. The cultivated filmgoer will be delighted by the sly urbanity which is implicit in Mr. von Sternberg's direction, as well as excited by the striking beauty of his settings and photography." But cultivated filmgoers weren't looking for sly urbanity then, they were looking for jobs, and *Variety's* ritual "[Dietrich] has never looked better in pictures" was only what one expected and, as the trade paper noted, "the picture needs more than good photography."

It was as nearly complete a disaster as when Chaplin shelved and burned Sternberg's *Woman of the Sea*.

The worst was yet to come.

The picture offended not just censors, reviewers, and audiences, but whole countries. Spain, whose ambassador had been invited to a courtesy screening in Washington in July (months after release), responded three months after that with a demand that sounded like a Paramount publicity stunt, but was not. On or about October 24, the Madrid office of Paramount received an order from the minister of interior affairs. It read: "You are hereby advised that if within three (3) days you do not withdraw from circulation the Paramount picture titled *The Devil Is a Woman* the government will prohibit absolutely in the entire territory of the Spanish Republic and indefinitely all pictures of said concern."

Zukor hastily issued an unintentional side-splitter to *The New York Times* that "we do not make pictures with any idea of depicting real life," but Spain thought they did. It felt defamed by Sternberg's depiction of a Guardia Civil that drank and frequented low dives, and they weren't just being spoilsports: This was a country headed for civil war and dictatorship.

By November 27, Spain threatened to shut Paramount down entirely. Joe Breen of the Hays Office circulated a confidential memo to David Selznick, Walter Wanger, Sam Goldwyn, Jesse Lasky, Harry Cohn, and to officers of Warner Brothers, 20th Century-Fox, RKO, and MGM. He included the text of a letter from Paramount's man in Madrid, who wrote: "a hell of a fight here on the . . . picture. . . . The Spanish government has given orders that Paramount will have to close up here on Monday if they don't withdraw this picture from circulation all over the world and burn the original negative. . . .

"They take their civil guard here more seriously than the French take their foreign legion, and that is going some. . . . They have gone ahead through all revolutions just the same, being the most powerful body here, not just as they were under the monarchy. . . . They are not only the police but the military force as well."

Print-burning was announced, but by November, when the demands from Madrid were absolute and nonnegotiable, it was clear the picture had no audience anyway, and it was withdrawn, a "lost film," a *film maudit*.

The worst was yet to come.

It came in ashes, cruelly prolonged. Josef von Sternberg never made another significant or even very good picture for the rest of his life. The few he made were slow to come and quick to die. Ten years later he was just an object lesson in hubris, an unbilled assistant director on *Duel in the Sun*, a film that was the epitome of hubris for producer David O. Selznick, Schulberg's assistant when Sternberg brought Marlene to America. Selznick was now in love with *his* star, Jennifer Jones.

Sternberg was finished with and by *The Devil Is a Woman* at only forty-one, "liquidated by Lubitsch" as he chose to view it, but it was never that simple and he knew it. Amazingly, *shockingly*, his great career, one of the handful of great film careers, was already half over that day he arrived in Berlin in August of 1929. No other major director had the freedom of his art for so brief, so controversial a span. There would be a last defiant spark, in Japan of all places, no less arrogant or provocative than his first blaze of ego to scorch Hollywood. Nobody cared about provocation from a relic by the 1950s, and that final work, *The Saga of Anatahan*, guttered out on

Japanese screens, a freak film from a forgotten man with nothing left but defiance. "My best film" he anointed it, "because . . . the least successful."

Then, Fate turned once more, cruelly late and laconic, but better fickle than never. The "lost" *Devil Is a Woman* turned out not to have been burned after all, and Sternberg's personal copy was screened at the Venice Film Festival in 1959. A critic called it "without question . . . one of the crowning masterpieces of the American Cinema," and others were awed by its blighted beauty. Sternberg was back—or his ghost was—to haunt the retrospectives and lecture halls. It was tardy recognition and vindication came too late. Lubitsch was long dead, and applause meant little to a man who had never really cared about the audience. The savory revenge had been in the picture itself, now a bitter aftertaste on a cryptic tongue. He was honored and praised and fed and fêted and unemployable. Elevation to cult classic couldn't compensate for the end of a career. And he remained as arrogant as ever, as aloof, as unapproachable.

The worst had come: He scorned *and* embraced his fate. The scorn was for his enemies, and its vigor belied his indifference; the embrace was for his role as doomed poet. Better damnation than oblivion.

For Marlene, the failure of *The Devil Is a Woman* was less important than the end of her association with her mentor. His public humiliation by Paramount and Lubitsch in March dashed whatever hopes she had that they might continue, and out of deference to him she signed no new contract with Paramount until Sternberg was well and truly banished. Director and star could have gone together to Fox, to UA, to Vienna, but Sternberg meant what he said and left with that other wounded veteran of the Paramount wars, B. P. Schulberg. They went to Columbia to make bad pictures together that Sternberg later tried to disown, and he finally walked away from Schulberg, too, who could no longer point to Sternberg's art as a defense.

Marlene issued a statement that had grace, if scant truth: "Mr. von Sternberg wants to make no more films for a while. He has a number of interests outside the cinema, especially painting. He wants to rest, and his opinion is that this is for me the best moment to begin to follow my own road."

Which he had paved for her, wherever it might lead.

"He taught me," she later said, "that the image of a screen character is built not alone from her acting and appearance but out of everything that is cumulatively visible in a film. He taught me about camera angles, lighting, costumes, makeup, timing, matching scenes, cutting, and editing. He gave me the opportunity for the most creative experience I have ever had."

He rejected her praise, presumptuous from a puppet. Her gratitude and admiration of him as creator were insufficient compensation for that deeper vein of feeling he could never elicit from her. He would not elaborate and made his standard speech: "Everything I have to say about Miss Dietrich I have said with a camera." Which was not the same as everything he knew or felt.

The Devil Is a Woman was not just the picture in which Dietrich was most beautiful (if it is), but the one that summed up whatever each had to say to, about, and for the other. Just as they had fought, sometimes violently—the cobra and the mandarin—the tugs and tensions of sexual attraction had shaped their relationship, and there remains an enigma, a complexity in what they created together that defies generalization.

David Thomson has argued that Dietrich—or her image—never advanced beyond the one in Sternberg's lens, that "more than any other great star, she was a cinematic invention—a message understood by viewers but not by herself." Great images need not "understand" to have power. Beauty, personality, presence, aura, these are *givens*, too deeply embedded in unknowable things to yield to analysis, self- or otherwise. We yield to them, not they to us.

It was, as John Russell Taylor has noted, "some kind of artistic *folie à deux*" completely apart from the art industry that was its podium and that it decorates with such unique, enduring beauty. Perhaps it is as simple (and profound) as it was for Berlin's great critic Alfred Kerr. Perhaps Sternberg, too, was simply "shaken by beauty. That is it: *shaken by beauty*." This is no small thing in the life of a man. Perhaps that—as for Don Pasqual— justified it all. Almost all.

Sternberg lived to read not only his own obituaries, but the autopsies as well, the critic-coroners' reports, and defiantly bookmarked them in the garage he turned into a den in a small house on a quiet street in suburban Westwood, not far from UCLA, where he lectured, mostly on his past. He outlived many of his enemies and critics and would turn to them at the end of his life in bitter silence, relishing their condemnation. It confirmed his survival in art's memory.

A French theorist wrote, "He was the first victim of the myth he had created, chained to Marlene, polishing her from film to film to transform her into a diaphanous idol with a lacquered face who soon would no longer need her Pygmalion." An American saw "high seriousness and misdirected purpose. Made up of ravishing pictorial effects, peppered with lewdness and suggestive symbols, set in a macabre, unreal world created solely for the senses, [his films with Marlene] trace the gradual withering of a talent who has withdrawn into a cinematic ivory tower." And, of course, there was the Englishman's cruelly dismissive "when a director dies, he becomes a cameraman." But that, one is startled to recall, had been at the beginning, before Marlene ever stepped out on that fateful stage in Berlin.

David Thomson thought that "Sternberg's world is pessimistic because it mocks the idea of meaning." It had meaning for *him*: those images, those seven pictures, those six years he spent with her. Legions would have been content with as many minutes.

"I failed him," his puppet said when she was alone. "I was never the ideal he sought. I tried to do what he wanted, but I didn't succeed. He was never quite satisfied. . . . He expected . . . something we never achieved."

For the rest of her life she called him "the man I wanted to please most," but he was not kind to her in his memoirs. There was no camera with which to say anything anymore; there lingered only the echo of his assertion to Sam Jaffe that he could do anything with Marlene but make her stop loving him. He may even have believed it. If he did, his leaving her was the closest he could come to saving himself from what was and always would be unrequited. Except on screen.

She had pleased him—or not—for six years. Those years destroyed him and made his reputation forever.

ELEVEN

SAVING
DIETRICH

1935 - 1936

She was "Dietrich" now. The ads for *The Devil Is a Woman* announced just "Dietrich," twice as big as the title. Garbo got similar billing at MGM, and the one name only—regal, monumental, remote— was Hollywood's salaam not to box-office or awards, but sheer mystique.

"Dietrich" was both "the most glamorous woman in the world" (Garbo was "divine," not really *of* this world) and something of an amusement. Cecil Beaton and Edward Steichen photographed her; Lorenz Hart and Cole Porter in New York wrote lyrics about her; Charles Koechlin in Paris wrote a symphony about her, but Groucho Marx, Lupe Velez—even Shirley Temple—impersonated her wickedly. After the Sternberg pictures, her prestige as a star was so notoriously tenuous that the running gag in the

Broadway comedy *Boy Meets Girl* was that its screenwriter heroes were being offered "two thousand dollars a week to save Dietrich!"

Screenwriters couldn't "save Dietrich" except indirectly. A giant of one sort had made her and maybe a giant of another sort *might* save her, if his name was Lubitsch.

Lubitsch didn't think she needed saving so much as she needed humanizing after her apotheosis. There was too much "Dietrich" and too little "Marlene." He talked of a Josephine-Napoleon epic, but that reminded everyone of Catherine the Great (and "little Napoleon"), and Josephine isn't the star of Napoleon pictures anyway. Marlene toyed with the notion of doing an act at the Casino de Paris, but that was an idle threat that helped no one at Paramount.

Just before *The Devil Is a Woman* was released, Paramount had tried to find something in the picture to promote, and Marlene made some silent footage modeling her Travis Banton wardrobe. It was released as a short subject called "The Fashion Side of Hollywood." Designer Banton was on camera, sounding like he had gargled with mint juleps, and it was narrated by "fashion authority" Katherine Howard, lately of *Harper's Bazaar*. The short included clips from Paramount pictures, with Paramount stars like Mae West, Claudette Colbert, and Carole Lombard dressed by Banton, but it began and ended with Marlene, the whole thing designed to promote *Devil*.

It was just "Dietrich"—wearing Concha's clothes but unmistakably "Marlene's" personality. She walked to the camera as if toward a lover, turned, smiled as she pulled at a glove, smiled from under a hat brim, smiled as she twirled to show off a Travis Banton fantasy, smiled again, and *there it was*—what Paramount had been missing all along. Marlene! Dietrich! Together again! Friendly, unthreatening, incredibly beautiful (it may be the most beautiful footage ever made of her), approachable and *approaching*. And with *humor*, savoring the joke of herself as fashion model, thinking back perhaps to modeling days in Berlin before her apotheosis.

Lubitsch didn't need "The Fashion Side of Hollywood" to learn Marlene had wit and humor: They had been there since the Kurfürstendamm; they had been there under the lace and feathers and veils and *decor* with which Sternberg had smothered her. All Lubitsch had to do was give them free play, translate the humor into something less racy than Berlin, something closer to Main Street. Like—the Champs-Élysées.

Lubitsch had already pulled the property from his vast grab bag of obscure European properties. It was a recent German movie with Brigitte Helm (she made it in French, too, opposite young Jean Gabin) about a lady swindler reformed by love called *The Beautiful Days of Aranjuez* (*Die schönen Tage von Aranjuez*). The title came from Schiller's *Don Carlos*, but it was just romantic comedy, sparkling enough to be remade beyond the Reich, and a luscious subject for the first Paramount Picture in the new, expensive, three-strip Technicolor.

Lubitsch planned to direct *The Pearl Necklace* (as it was to be called) himself, but his duties as head of Paramount production made so many demands he could not. He would produce, instead, turning direction over to Frank Borzage, who was romantic (*Seventh Heaven* and *A Farewell to Arms*), and down-to-earth enough to "save Dietrich." Borzage would smother her in nothing but Gary Cooper. Frank Capra wanted Cooper then for something about someone called Mr. Deeds on Poverty Row, but Capra had to wait while Cooper reunited with Marlene in—where else?—Paris.

The Pearl Necklace quickly became *Desire*, a hotter title to go with a story that was sexy and swank but still took place in the real world. Or some real world that had a Marlene Dietrich and a Gary Cooper in it.

A beautiful jewel thief heists a pearl necklace in Paris and speeds to her confederates and their hideout in Spain. She encounters a vacationing Detroit auto engineer on the road, slips the stolen pearls into his pocket at customs, and spends the rest of the picture retrieving the pearls, falling in love, and becoming an honest woman in the process.

While Lubitsch, Borzage, and their writers added bubbles to the champagne, Marlene looked after Maria or saw to it that maids and cooks did (rather too many cooks baking too many cakes that settled solidly on young hips). Marlene accompanied Rudi to New York to wish him bon voyage on a ship back to Paris and Tamara, leaving her free to give interviews in Waldorf Towers luxury, or go the theater with Elsa Maxwell, or write intimate little notes to Katharine Cornell, or dazzle hoi polloi (and *Vogue*) at the races, at nightclubs, at premieres. She wore emeralds and rubies to outflash the flashbulbs. Back in Hollywood she went to a famous "come-as-the-person-you-most-admire" costume party dressed as Leda *and* the Swan, perhaps the ultimate bisexual statement for those who got it. If that wasn't startling or blatant enough, her "escort" was. Young English actress Elizabeth Allan, recently in Selznick's *David Copperfield* at MGM, clung to Marlene dressed *as* Marlene in her *Morocco* top hat and tails.

When not at parties or entertaining at the Benedict Canyon house she rented from Countess Dorothy di Frasso, Marlene turned her *Hausfrau* touch, her Florence Nightingale compulsion, to someone she thought needed it, someone who was, like Mercedes de Acosta, a former lover of Garbo: John Gilbert.

*   *   *

No star in Hollywood history was as synonymous with the great divide between silence and sound that destroyed careers as John Gilbert. He had been the quintessential romantic film star in the late silent period, dashing, impetuous, passionate in *The Big Parade*, *La Bohème*, and *The Merry Widow*. He had starred opposite Garbo in *Flesh and the Devil*, *Love* (née *Anna Karenina*), and *A Woman of Affairs*, and almost married her twice in the silent screen's most famous doomed romance.

Gilbert is remembered today as a shadow cast by Garbo's radiance, and as a victim: of Garbo, of Louis B. Mayer, of sound, and of alcohol. He was all of these, but when Marlene met him through Dolores del Rio and her art director husband, Cedric Gibbons, Gilbert was still a vivid presence for filmgoers and as nearly a tragic figure as matinee idols ever get.

He was viewed as the microphone's casualty, the epitome of the once-great star laid low by sound. There was truth to the story. His voice—perfectly acceptable in life—did not record well, or not as audiences had imagined it. "Jack" Gilbert talking prose violated fantasies of John Gilbert urging hot poetry on Garbo in a voice fans dreamed up for him.

But it wasn't all true. Recording techniques improved, capturing his light baritone well, and he made ten talking pictures after his "ruin." He was broken not by his voice, but by what it said to Louis B. Mayer, who had signed Gilbert to a ruinously rich MGM contract just before sound blared out a future in which Mayer decided Gilbert would have no role.

Garbo and Gilbert were to marry in a double ceremony with director King Vidor and actress Eleanor Boardman. Garbo decided she wanted to be alone and didn't even send Western Union. Gilbert stood alone at the altar, devastated and humiliated with a drink in his hand. Mayer said to him, with a callousness astonishing even among moguls, "What do you have to marry her for? Why don't you just fuck her and forget about it?" Gilbert physically attacked Mayer in front of the mostly MGM wedding party and Mayer cried, "You're finished, Gilbert. I'll destroy you if it costs me a million dollars."

It cost easily that, but it cost Gilbert more. Finally, in 1933, Mayer relented when Garbo insisted on Gilbert as her lover in *Queen Cristina* (after rejecting Laurence Olivier *and* John Barrymore), a supporting role in a picture that was famous but a commercial failure. Gilbert never regained the public he had charmed before sound, not because of his voice, but because public imagination had turned away from princes of romance to the democratic virility of Gary Cooper and Clark Gable. So Gilbert drank. And drank. He was the classic alcoholic whose only hope lay in lifetime abstinence. There just wasn't any lifetime to be abstinent for.

When Marlene met Gilbert she understood at once he must have a *reason* to stop killing himself, and she wanted to be it. She took him in hand, brought him what his daughter called "the full sunlight of Marlene," and the Jack Gilbert who had been a failure at everything—four marriages, a great career, fatherhood, and love—was given promise of a new life.

He was a project with a passion. Marlene took him dining and dancing, got him into analysis, sunned with him by his pool or hers, did his Christmas shopping and trimmed the tree with little German candles. She wrapped the presents for his daughter, Leatrice (named for her mother, actress Leatrice Joy). She quenched his thirst with sunlight and beauty and grace, and love that perhaps remained platonic because of what was rumored to be Gilbert's alcoholic impotence. She kept him dry and got him a job. There had been an inquiry from a producer for a picture in England: Maybe they would co-star in a remake of *The Garden of Allah*, but it came to nothing, for the rights were confused and, anyway, there was *Desire* at Paramount, ready to shoot in September of 1935. There was a part in it for Gilbert, a strong supporting role as a crook and ersatz nobleman, the third side of a romantic triangle with Marlene and Gary Cooper. It was still to be filmed in color then, and Gilbert could show that after being ignored in *Queen Christina* in his hat with a plume, he could do romantic comedy and *talk* and show off a clean-and-sober Technicolor tan. And Marlene could show *him* off.

The screenplay had been polished to a sheen for the better part of a year by Edwin Justus Mayer, Waldemar Young, and Samuel Hoffenstein; every page glittered with what had long been known as "the Lubitsch touch." Lubitsch was such a star director that *he* got first billing on the picture. "Produced by the Great Ernst Lubitsch" the ads proclaimed, before announcing "the screen's most beautiful woman in love with the dashing 'Bengal Lancer.'" Still, Marlene was the paramount Paramount star and got billed over Cooper, though each received an obligatory introductory star turn.

Cooper's came first, to delay Marlene's entrance and set the picture up on long American-in-Paris legs. His first scene takes place in an office on the Rue de la Paix, but is pure Peoria (Cooper's character is actually *from* Peoria). Detroit automobile engineer Tom Bradley (Cooper) struggles with his American boss to determine the relative virtues of being "happy," "elated," or "glad" to drive a Bronson 8, the car Cooper will drive to Spain with an advertising slogan on it. He's "happy," they agree. He will get happier.

Marlene's entrance is the most stylish of any 1930s romantic comedy, maybe the most elegant ever. Tom Bradley, "happy" in his Bronson 8, backs into a white, chauffeur-driven limousine as he is leaving Paris, but a velvet voice from within the not-from-Detroit chariot urges him to drive on.

Madeleine de Beaupré (Marlene) alights from the white limousine dressed in white. She enters swank Duvall et Cie, jewelry store extraordinaire, to select a pearl necklace of staggering price to be delivered by Monsieur Duvall to the office of her "husband," the famous psychiatrist Dr. Pauquet.

We next see Madeleine descending elegantly all in black from a black limousine. She enters the offices of Dr. Pauquet and makes an appointment for her "husband," Monsieur Duvall. He has, she explains, an embarrassing habit of presenting bills to perfect strangers and, well . . . wearing ladies' nightgowns to bed.

> DR. PAUQUET: "That's bad. I don't like that."
> MADELEINE (sweeping up the floor with her eyelashes): "Neither do *I*."

Dr. Pauquet will, of course, see him, after hours.

Madeleine greets Duvall in Pauquet's anteroom, takes delivery of the necklace, introduces the men, and slips away as they circle around bills and nightgowns, finally getting to, "She's *your* wife." "No, no, I assure you, she's *your* wife. . . ."

Nobody's-wife-at-all is discovered racing across France to the Spanish border in a sleek convertible (jewel thieves require many cars) and soon overtakes a "happy" Bronson 8.

The opening is so flawless we are willing to accept almost anything that follows. Madeleine stops briefly on the Spanish Riviera, to be joined by confederate Carlos Margoli (the Gilbert part), with whom she plots to retrieve the necklace she has slipped in the American's pocket to elude border guards. With the police in pursuit, the two crooks invite the American to their hideout villa, where Madeleine vamps Bradley at the piano (no plum ever so eager to be plucked), but—surprise—he's on to them and hot to reform Madeleine.

Will Madeleine remain a crook with Carlos and their partner, the tough, tippling Aunt Olga, or go off to Detroit with Hunk Finn? Carlos, urbanely threatening, discusses European politics at dinner, allowing the new world a nod:

> CARLOS: "You can't underestimate America. . . . It's a big country."
> BRADLEY (friendly persuasion): "*Six foot three.*"

Europe doesn't stand any more chance than Madeleine. If it were up to Bradley, he would just spank the Continent back to its senses. He turns to her: "Still hurt, darling?"

MADELEINE (radiant): "Just a little."

She swoons.

The Hays Office didn't. Lady criminals, even with character witnesses like Gary Cooper, needed more than an offscreen spanking. Reshooting was ordered and Lubitsch himself did it. Madeleine returned the pearls to M. Duvall, who could not, *bien sûr*, simply ignore *la justice*.

Cut to a courtroom: Madeleine, Bradley, Duvall, and Pauquet. The document Madeleine inadvertently hands the judge is her parole paper, not the marriage license he expects. It is romantic comedy's neatest resolution and wittiest wedding.

The role of Carlos Margoli was a good third part, and Gilbert tested for it with Marlene and Cooper in color. Costume stills were made of all three, Gilbert looking older and less debonair than once upon a time, but healthy and sober and happy. It was a part to bring him new prominence as a character actor, still suave, still dashing. But there was a cruel sort of parallel to changing Hollywood. Gilbert, symbol of an earlier, more passionate school of romance, didn't get the girl; the new screen type, strong, often silent, not a bit less romantic, did. Cooper and Gilbert were separated not by their mere two years' age difference, but by generations.

Still, Gilbert's regeneration might have worked. Legend has it that Marlene left Gilbert when Garbo dropped by his house on Tower Road and Marlene witnessed the reunion, but the story is apocryphal. Gilbert's daughter repeated it in *Dark Star*, the book she wrote about her father, but it was a romantic fabrication. Gilbert and Garbo never saw each other after *Queen Christina*, and Marlene didn't see Garbo in the driveway; she saw Cooper on the backlot.

Marlene's reunion with her *Morocco* co-star, now freed from Lupe Velez (he was married, but there were rumors), dazzled her. Her attention turned from one passionate project to another, and Cooper may have reminded his socialite wife, Rocky, that she had first fallen for him when she saw the steam rising from the sands of *Morocco*.

Gilbert had been in good health thanks to Marlene, good enough to test for *Desire* and schedule a personal appearance tour in July and August of 1935. Louella Parsons reported, "Jack Gilbert, whose devastating sense of humor and his absolute disregard of the powers of the studio [read Mayer] have all but wrecked his career, has completely reformed."

Reformation without Marlene seemed pointless. Gilbert had a drink, then another, then a series of small heart attacks, which were medical grounds to replace him in *Desire* with John Halliday, a kind of Adolphe Menjou without charm. Halliday hurt the picture because there could never be, as there might have been with Gilbert, any real choice for Marlene as Madeleine. Halliday was sleekly repellent, not anybody's match for "six foot three" or for Marlene, either.

Marlene was shocked by news of Gilbert's health into a return to him after *Desire* was finished, but Gilbert was finished too. The heart attacks kept coming like the drinks: bigger and more frequent, including one terrifying seizure in Marlene's pool. At Christmas there were the tree, the candles, the bright and shiny wrappings, the discreet withdrawal when little Leatrice arrived, but it was all too late.

On January 9, not yet thirty-seven but weary and wasted, Gilbert swallowed his courage and—horrifyingly—his tongue and was discovered dead early the next morning. Marlene's own doctor was summoned to administer adrenaline, but whatever was broken could not be mended.

John Gilbert's tragedy was not his death but his life, and it was over. A private funeral was arranged to avoid a Valentino-like riot, and Marlene attended with Dolores del Rio and her husband, Cedric Gibbons, but Cooper was there, too. So were photographers. Marlene collapsed in the aisle of the church, the most uncontrolled public performance of her life. Camera records of Marlene in mourning made "private" grief not poignant, but unseemly, overdramatic, almost a star turn.

Irene Mayer Selznick, whose father had done as much as anyone to destroy John Gilbert, remembered Marlene's collapse at Gilbert's funeral with dry eyes. "She didn't put a gun in his hand, or even a bottle, and her remorse was genuine. She was desolate that she might have caused Jack's heart attacks. She had dried Jack out, but she wrung him out, too. Chicken soup doesn't cure everything; neither does apple strudel." It was a not entirely disinterested observation, and she repeated it to Gilbert's child when Leatrice Joy Gilbert began as an adult to sift other people's memories in search of the father she had never really known.

Except, perhaps, through Marlene. After Gilbert's death, no one in Leatrice Gilbert's memory was kinder, more mothering and fathering than Marlene. She hurled herself at lawyers on the child's behalf over a never-found last will she swore she had seen, which left everything to the child and not to Gilbert's last wife, Virginia Bruce. She took Leatrice to movies, to the theater, bought her charm bracelets and a miniature of her father, and sent fond notes addressed "Tinker," Gilbert's nickname for his only child.

Tinker, as it happened, knew Marlene's child. Maria was sometimes included in the trips to movies and the theater. She was a head taller and a foot wider than the other girls, who thought "she must be at least two years older than she says." She wasn't (she was eleven, to Tinker's ten, but her age would always slip and slide), and to the others "she was much more mature in outlook and rather looked down on [our] childish ways. She made me very nervous the few times we were together," Gilbert's daughter remembered, "but I imagine being Marlene's daughter was a learning experience, and not always an easy one."

Leatrice Gilbert was given solace by Marlene's generosity and sent her a gift, a ring inscribed with a child's misspelling, "Marlane, from Tinker." She never heard back, ever. Later, she learned that when Gilbert's estate was auctioned, Marlene's agent (who had been Gilbert's—and Garbo's, too) bought for her "all the bedroom furniture, rugs, wall hangings, and draperies." The bed itself went to the Summit Hotel, to cradle honeymooners in romantic Uniontown, Pennsylvania.

Desire wasn't finally made in Technicolor and didn't need it. Black and white was sexy enough, everyone agreed. Marlene got spanked and went off to Detroit in her most entertaining American picture yet, deliciously full of humor and silky scenes about what the title announced.

Marlene had help; Cooper was not just her first American leading man, but her best. Richard Schickel reminds us of his "perfect masculine grace," that he was "the only truly beautiful actor who did not spoil the effect of his handsomeness by seeming vain or self-absorbed."

He couldn't be; he was too absorbed in her. When she plays and sings "Awake in a Dream" (by new Hollywood émigré Friedrich Holländer), the camera cuts back and forth; Marlene croons and Cooper rolls his eyes and tries to conceal arousal. He blushes in black and white, and his hands are in his pockets for a reason *Time* then noted was so "sensationally explicit . . . the Hays organization [was] not sophisticated enough to understand it." More likely they enjoyed it too much; it was all-American Gary Cooper up against what Pauline Kael calls "the most elegantly amusing international jewel thief ever." Kael notes that when Marlene leans in a doorway in clinging white satin and furs looking "simply peerlessly sexy . . . she's so captivating you almost feel sorry for him," but you don't. You want to *be* him and you want her to *stay* her. This kind of chemistry appears only rarely in a decade, and makes sense of the whole star system.

Critics liked *Desire* and most agreed with Louella Parsons that Marlene seemed "an entirely different person." Frank S. Nugent at *The New York Times* thought it was Lubitsch who had "freed Marlene Dietrich from Josef von Sternberg's artistic bondage, and has brought her vibrantly alive." *Newsweek* announced the end of her "ninny films" with Sternberg and *Time* found it "a romantic comedy of grace, dexterity and charm in which Marlene Dietrich's performance is the best she has given since she became too dignified to exhibit the legs which brought her her first U.S. fame."

Variety thought "the combination of Dietrich and Cooper is one that will open the safe vaults," for "sexy it is," and *Film Daily* confidently predicted "big box-office." It was, but not big enough fully to counteract the poison beauty of Concha Perez. *San Francisco* and *Swing Time* and *Poor Little Rich Girl* with Shirley Temple were the big hits of the season. Those, and Gary Cooper's delayed Poverty Row project for Capra, *Mr. Deeds Goes to Town.*

No matter how liberated in her private life, Marlene had stumbled across too many stages and screens in Berlin to allow "Dietrich" to free-fall at Paramount. She had a powerful parachute in Lubitsch, but he was free-falling himself as production head. Box office had been good in 1935 and would be better in 1936, but Lubitsch had little time to "personally super-vise" Marlene (as her contract decreed) while fighting front-office and sound-stage battles over "audience" pictures like *The Big Broadcast of 1936.* Such stuff precluded his polishing the sort of prestige product he had been hired to do in the first place. It quickly became apparent that all Lubitsch's art, wit, and sense of studio politics did not necessarily imply administrative savvy. It looked as if there had been no reason to suppose a director could run a studio better than anybody else, if anybody *could.*

Lubitsch had decided Marlene's second picture under his aegis should be another humanizer, and he reopened the creaky *Hotel Imperial,* which Pola Negri had occupied back in 1927. Lewis Milestone, who directed *All Quiet on the Western Front,* was replaced at the last moment by Henry Hathaway and the title of the picture became *Invitation to Happiness,* then again *Hotel Imperial,* and then *I Loved a Soldier.* The revolving-door title proved as ill an omen as usual.

Hotel Imperial told of a simple chambermaid in the war whose love for army officer Charles Boyer causes her to flower into someone who looks just like Marlene Dietrich in the last reel. This was a return to the same bottom of the same trunk Paramount floundered in while singing *The Song of Songs,* also an old Negri vehicle. Lubitsch decreed; Marlene agreed.

Marlene knew Henry Hathaway because he had worked as Sternberg's assistant on *Morocco, Dishonored,* and *Shanghai Express.* He had recently broken into the ranks of commercial directors with Gary Cooper and *Lives of a Bengal Lancer,* and was a rare and outspoken champion of Sternberg, which didn't make him *Sternberg.*

Shooting began on January 3 (six days before John Gilbert died) in yet another mood of corporate crisis. Lubitsch was struggling with New York as *The Big Broadcast* became *The Big Budgetbuster.* He assigned writer-producer Benjamin Glazer to oversee the picture, and Marlene, reading her contract and the John van Druten script at the same time, balked. This caused Glazer, whom Lubitsch had weirdly shifted from the out-of-control *Big Broadcast* to the in-control Marlene, to resign in a huff. Glazer announced he "would not supervise a story over which the star was given so much authority."

Lubitsch took over the picture while Marlene went into mourning for Gilbert and the script went into emergency surgery, with the costly production meter running.

Henry Hathaway, a practiced master of Old Hollywood anecdote, contributed colorful detail decades later. "My idea for *Hotel Imperial* [*I Loved a Soldier*]," he remembered, "was to start with a shot of a long, wide hallway, and a woman scrubbing and mopping the floor. She has dirty hair and dirty clothes; she is wearing old carpet slippers. She's a slob. As she gets [Boyer] and . . . falls in love with him, she gets progressively prettier. Then you see Dietrich in all her beauty coming out of the cathedral married, with the Uhlan swordsmen framing her on either side. She has become completely transformed."

Marlene thought her transformation should not be too delayed. She knew as much about beauty from within as Hathaway and had her own schedule.

"You're not supposed to be beautiful until next Thursday," Hathaway would tell her when she came to the set looking like Marlene instead of an unkempt slob. Marlene would search for sanity and her key light, asking, "Please—can't it at least be *Wednesday?*"

The facts were considerably more serious and shed light on the dream-factory procedures of the day. Paramount had begun production to satisfy distribution promises of "two Dietrichs" for 1936 (*Desire* was the first) without a budget, without a schedule, and without a script. All those writers under contract meant scripts under pressure, not under control.

Marlene had approval of everything and had approved nothing but Lubitsch's assurances that all would somehow work. Charles Boyer had been on salary since mid-November and had worked only three days by the end of January. Marlene had been willing to work day to day as long as Lubitsch was there to approve what Hathaway could do without a script. On February 7 Lubitsch complicated matters further by removing Marlene from the picture for two days of *Desire* retakes (he did them himself), leaving Hathaway nothing to do but shoot "scatter scenes" with Boyer.

An assistant director recorded script revisions on the set with Lubitsch dictating to flying pencils, but it was all too late and too confused with too many people on too much salary doing too little. Suddenly Paramount saw that twenty-eight days of production had been clocked to February 11 at a cost of $900,000 and decided if "the great Ernst Lubitsch" were to take the rap for *The Big Broadcast*, he might as well take it for *I Loved a Soldier*, too. They fired him.

With Lubitsch fired, Marlene walked off the picture. She wasn't saved. She had lost Sternberg *and* Lubitsch inside of a year, as well as John Gilbert, for whom she felt grief and remorse. Paramount decided to blame on her what they couldn't blame on Lubitsch. Lawyers pointed out that they had, indeed, breached her contract by firing Lubitsch, and they now had no Queen of the Lot at all. Except for Mae West, under "personal contract" to Manny "Conflict-of-Interest" Cohen, who was busily ruining *her* career by collecting commissions and ignoring the newly censorious Code.

Marlene had no reason to suppose that a Paramount that would fire Sternberg and Lubitsch while keeping Manny Cohen and Benjamin Glazer would be any more salubrious a place to be than ever, and she walked.

To Culver City, to another industry giant. Back to the desert, too, but a long way from *Morocco*, and she would keep her shoes on this time.

David O. Selznick had not owned *The Garden of Allah* when Marlene and John Gilbert were asked about it the previous year by someone else. Nor had he owned it when he suggested it to Garbo, who turned it down as "antiquated." Nor had he owned it when he proposed it as a vehicle for Joan Crawford. MGM owned it—*picture* rights, at least but, in a curious legal defect inherited from the silent days, no *dialogue* rights. Not owning it did not diminish zeal to make it. Selznick, now becoming the one great independent in the days of major studio supremacy, needed something as vast as his talents. Something as big, say, as the Sahara.

The Garden of Allah had been successful as a shocking novel by Robert Hichens in 1904, then later as a play, and had been made by MGM in 1927 by Rex Ingram with Alice Terry (Mrs. Ingram). *Variety* found the story dated even then. Selznick knew that. The tale of a Trappist monk who flees the monastery (with the secret for the house brandy) and marries a beautiful, unsuspecting girl in the desert was as aged in the wood as the monastery Schnapps. It was clap-trap, but *colorful* clap-trap, and Selznick's partner in Selznick-International was John Hay Whitney, who had major holdings in Technicolor.

Allah had been in preparation for months before *I Loved a Soldier* collapsed. Selznick had signed Alexander Korda's discovery, Merle Oberon, to star as Domini Enfilden, the young woman so romantically naive she marries a renegade monk without knowing it. The monk, Boris Androvsky, was to be played by some exotic type like Gilbert Roland, but as the costs of a major Technicolor feature loomed, Selznick thought more and more about looming names. With Lubitsch axed by Paramount, he knew Marlene and Charles Boyer would both be "at liberty" and could fill the Sahara (which Bedouins call "the garden of Allah") with starshine. His intelligence services had been providing him daily secret reports on *I Loved a Soldier*'s production in anticipation of just such a turn of events.

Selznick's astute story editor, Kay Brown (who in just three months would urge on him a manuscript called *Gone With the Wind*) had come up with the notion of *The Garden of Allah* as a "dream subject" for Oberon or Marlene. Selznick had been mostly appalled at Marlene's films with Sternberg but remained convinced she was "one of the most magnificent personalities that the screen has had in many years and I think it a crying shame that she has been dragged down as she has been."

Marlene had quietly expressed interest in Selznick's ending this crying shame when Sternberg "retired," and in his jotting notebook Selznick had scribbled roles her personality might make as magnificent as she was: *Jezebel, Madame Sans Gêne, Camille*.

Magnificent or not, Marlene was, Selznick grimly put on record, "hurt to such a terrible extent that she is no longer even a fairly important box-office star. There is no personality so important that he or she can survive the perfectly dreadful line-up of pictures that Marlene has had. . . . She is in no position to command any fabulous salary," he stated, and in any case, he would not be interested in her for just *one* picture, to "save" her and then pass the benefits and profits on to others. Selznick negotiated even when saying no.

He had gone about his business trying to cast a leading monk before Boyer, considering (among others) Gilbert Roland, Robert Taylor, Vincent Price, Basil Rathbone, George Brent, Laurence Olivier, Fredric March, Brian Aherne, Noël Coward, Maurice Evans, Robert Donat, Ivor Novello, and John Gielgud. Tests were made, with results discouraging to Selznick, who thought one of those tested, though "a superb actor, would frighten not merely Domini but the audiences—especially the male half." There was one other candidate for the role, a French actor called Jean Gabin. Kay Brown looked at some film on him and decided he was "a refined edition of Victor MacLaglen, heavy set . . . around forty [he was not quite thirty-two] . . . totally unfitted for the monk."

The second male role of sophisticated Count Anteoni went to Basil Rathbone, who had been campaigning with futile vigor to play the monk, and a young actor called Alan Marshall was cast in a smaller role as a French officer after failed tests by David Niven, Cesar Romero, and Ray Milland. Selznick's star-making instincts were not infallible.

He was casting his net in a wide arc, as usual, but indecision lasted only until he collected enough information to sway himself—and until he saw *Desire*, with its revitalized Marlene. He agreed to Marlene's demands for the thoroughly "fabulous salary" he had gone on record he would never pay, $200,000. At $20,000 a week (for ten weeks), she became "the most highly salaried woman in the world," *Time* reported, but Selznick may have thought he was getting a bargain. He knew her next picture was already contracted for more than twice that amount, and he knew this because it was for the same Alexander Korda whose mistress was Merle Oberon, the actress Selznick would have to buy out of *Allah* to make way for Marlene.

Selznick took no chances. Before telling Oberon she was out of a job, he made top-secret color tests at night with Marlene and her occasional tennis partner Gilbert Roland.

Secrecy was hard to maintain with scores of technicians looking on and eager to describe the results all over Hollywood. Marlene's makeup (dead white with scarlet fingernails) was done by the faithful Dotty Ponedel from Paramount (where people also talked), and following the tests her skin color was darkened slightly, her nails stripped of lacquer, her hair sprayed with real gold dust (using a baby enema), and word got around. Oberon sued for $125,333.33, which Selznick settled for $25,000 and a soothing promise to star her in a color version of *Dark Victory*, conveniently owned by Jock Whitney.

The *Allah* script was in continuous search of "desert poetry." Selznick talked with everyone from Vicki Baum to Sidney Howard and S. N. Behrman about it, and even considered *Blue Angel* script co-author Dr. Karl Vollmoeller, who had written about nuns in *The Miracle* and at least knew something about the Church. Marlene's agent pushed Mercedes de Acosta (who knew something about Buddhism), which Selznick sensibly ignored. The producer finally secured dialogue rights to the Hichens novel for $62,000 (more than *Gone With the Wind* cost three months later, perhaps the greatest movie bargain of all time at $50,000). A Selznick assistant called Val Lewton campaigned to add dialogue to an *Allah* script already in hand from another assistant named Willis Goldbeck, who had worked on the silent *Garden of Allah*. Script credit eventually went to W. P. Lipscomb and Lynn Riggs, author of *Green Grow the Lilacs* (the basis for *Oklahoma!*). He, at least, knew about sand. And poetry.

Marlene left Hollywood on April 14 for Yuma, Arizona, and the Buttercup Valley locations in which "desert poetry" had to make rhyme or reason. She took Maria with her, as Maria would play a bit part as a convent girl, her first time on camera since *The Scarlet Empress* and the onset of avoir-dupois.

The cast assembled in Yuma and in the scorpion-infested tent enclave Selznick built in the desert, where daytime temperatures routinely reached

130 degrees, forcing work to begin at a cool three o'clock in the morning and end in exhaustion before high sun at high noon.

Selznick-International meant just that. The players made up the most international cast of any American movie of the 1930s. There were German Marlene, French Boyer, English C. Aubrey Smith as a priest, American John Carradine as a sand diviner, and two Austrians, Joseph Schildkraut as a comic-relief Algerian and Tilly Losch as a burn-down-the-oasis dancer in a nightclub located at a heavily trafficked camel stop in the middle of the Sahara.

To orchestrate the accents, including that of director Richard Boleslawski, Polish-born veteran of the White Russian cavalry and the Moscow Art Theater, Selznick imported twenty-six-year-old Joshua Logan from New York as dialogue director. Logan knew Boleslawski and had earlier made a wide-eyed tour of wide-open Berlin, including places like the notorious El Dorado, giving him something (he thought) to gossip about with Marlene. He got, instead, a baptism of desert fire and anecdotes to decorate several autobiographies and enliven Hollywood lore.

Logan was alarmed by Hichens's novel when he read it on the plane. He thought it "a rather pretentious piece of junk . . . written in a very fancy, sort of embroidered prose, with little roses and cherubs and things in the middle of all the sentences . . . [but] absolutely full of atmosphere." The script, meanwhile, was shifting like the desert sands and seemed less vital than getting people to pronounce it correctly. Logan was under orders from Selznick to sell the script to Marlene, who—as Paramount had learned too late with *I Loved a Soldier*—could read something more than a contract.

Logan met Marlene in Selznick's Culver City offices and found her "very strange" but "the most beautiful thing I had ever seen." She gave him the up-and-down Dietrich treatment and said (*he* said, imitating her difficulty with the American *r*), "Oh, you're the one fwom New York. I love people fwom New York. They're so bwight, so tasteful. Tell me, have you wead the scwipt? . . . It's twash, isn't it?"

Logan tried to answer, but "she spoke so quietly I had difficulty hearing her, and her eyes disturbed me deeply."

Marlene's eyelashes kept upping-and-downing. "It's twash . . . Garbo wouldn't play this part. They offered it to Garbo and she said she didn't believe the girl would send the boy back to the monastawy. She is a *vewy clever* woman, Garbo! She has the pwimitive instincts—dose peasants have, you know."

But script conferences for Marlene were subterfuge for a more important mission. Not having been saved by Lubitsch, she didn't want Boleslawski. She was "furious that she had to take [him]," Logan finally realized. "She wanted to have von Sternberg direct it, and [Selznick] wouldn't allow that."

Marlene persevered, carrying her Sternberg campaign to her desert tent in the Buttercup Valley, where "there were pictures of [John Gilbert] all over the room." Logan gasped. "Each picture, unbelievable as it may seem, had a votive candle burning before it. She explained the candles were there because she worshiped him."

She didn't worship Boleslawski. "He's a tewwible man," she cooed to Logan, as she stretched him out on her desert bed like a human prayer rug. "He's Wussian. No sensitivity. He can't diwect women." (He had already directed Garbo in *The Painted Veil*; Marlene may have been right.) Logan stared at the votive candles flickering before the portraits of Gilbert and, hypnotized by Marlene's eyes and gold-dusted hair, equivocated by passing out. She revived him and advised, "Think ovah what I said; only think fast."

When not working on Logan, Marlene was pillow-talking things over with Willis Goldbeck. The scriptwriter-cum-Selznick-assistant entered and left Marlene's bed and her desert shrine to Gilbert with more-than-religious devotion. He banked Marlene's spiritual fires and acted as a sort of two-way love spy, carrying messages back and forth from Marlene to Selznick's indefatigable memo machine in Culver City.

Meanwhile, wandering across the sand dunes in a kind of heat trance was scriptwriter Lynn Riggs. He thought Marlene "ravishing" and wrote dialogue for her like, "No one but God and I knows what is in my heart," which caused Marlene's eyes to stop upping-and-downing and roll Heavenward in disbelief.

Logan thought what was in Marlene's heart was Marlene. "Dietrich was probably the most self-centered woman I ever met in my life," he recalled. "She was absolutely fascinated by herself and by her photographs." He recalled "some amusing sides," though she "could get her tongue on anybody and sharpen it." A costume test of dancer Tilly Losch was run and "it really was quite a stunning costume. Tilly was sitting next to me, and suddenly Dietrich said, 'Oh, Tilly, what a shame.' And [Tilly] said, 'Why?' And [Marlene] said, 'They used blue, and you know blue disappears in Technicolor.' " Except, it turned out, on Marlene, who wore it for half the picture.

Selznick was too busy to bother with petty feuds. He had yielded to Marlene's salary demands and the penalty payment to Oberon besides, but would not give in on Sternberg. With the attention to detail for which he is justly famous, he would remain master of the shoot. The day before production began he met with Marlene and (he told Boleslawski) "gave her a last-minute pep talk. I pointed out to her that our budget was fantastically high [$1.2 million] and put it more or less on a personal basis [that] it was up to her to keep it from going higher. I told her once more, frankly, about the tales around town about what she goes through between takes with her makeup, costumes, etc. . . . curiously, I believe in her sincerity—she told me this was all nonsense and that she NEVER indulged in such carryings on. . . . I honestly and sincerely believe her spirit is most helpful and what we all want it to be, and until we are proven wrong, I don't think we should look for any trouble in her direction."

Shooting brought a response from Boleslawski that was weak on English but generous to his star: "Marlena [sic] is no trouble," he wrote Selznick. "She is a good disciplined trouper. She did today many things which she did not wanted to do and did them nicely. One little scene we tried to teach her by intonations of the readings—it did not worked so well—but finally we got it the best way she could do it." Plain-spoken cameraman Hal Rosson had turned to Logan the same day, listening to Boleslawski, Boyer, Schildkraut, and Marlene in their symphony of accents, and muttered, "I don't understand a fucking word they say."

Boleslawski was as worried about Boyer as Selznick was about Marlene. Boyer had been in movies since 1920, but was only now, at almost thirty-nine, becoming a major star after *Mayerling* and Fritz Lang's *Liliom*. He was, Boley told Selznick, "apt to push and punch to [sic] much (French school of acting) but I am trying to hold him down. I hope you'll like him. He is a good influence on Marlena [sic]."

Boyer's major problem, apart from language, was his toupee, which caused trouble from the second day of production. Logan told Selznick, "The best take of the day . . . was spoiled by a large drop of perspiration which rolled down Mr. Boyer's forehead and dropped into Miss Dietrich's eye."

It was easier, somehow, to focus on such trivialities than on the troublesome script. Boley had reminded Selznick in a cable that "YOU REALIZE I START WITHOUT SCRIPT AND I PROMISED MYSELF ID NEVER DO THAT FOR ANYBODY IN WORLD AND HERE YOU ARE YOU CHARMER."

It is questionable if anyone in the world had enough charm to make the story work after 1904, including Selznick. The central problem, which no one seems to have noticed, was that the story belonged to the monk in a production being built around his bride who—even surrounded by roses and cherubs—had never in her life been remotely credible as a woman who was naive or unsuspecting about much of anything.

In an early draft Domini had been conceived as a former convent girl who had supped rather too frequently at the banquet of life and went to the desert to clear her palate and find spiritual peace. That might have made some sense, but got lost in all the rewriting. She became a former convent girl who has just lost the father she has nursed since graduation and is now . . . drifting. "I travel," she tells the convent Mother Superior (Lucile

Watson). "Paris, Vienna, the Riviera. But in the midst of people I was always lonely . . . desperately lonely." The Mother Superior, meaning well, tells her to forget the Riviera and head for the sands. "There in the solitude," she counsels, "you may find yourself. In the face of the infinite your grief will vanish. . . ." Unluckily for Domini, she boards *the very train* to vanishing grief that carries guilt-ridden Boris (and the secret brandy recipe) far, far from the monastery.

Selznick had objected to the Sternberg Dietrich, but threw out every saving grace of irony and humor in sending her to desert poetry. He was showman enough to allow her a costume designer, Ernst Dryden (né Deutsch, out of Vienna: one more accent), who would drape her in enough chiffon and silver lamé and blue madonna robes to tent the Middle East. Marlene had decided the whole picture was "a poker game" without Sternberg anyway and resigned herself to Willis Goldbeck.

At least he distracted her from the script, Boyer's toupee, and her own hair, left mostly to ex-Paramount hairdresser-companion Nellie Manley, who wielded the baby enema and kept the votive candles burning. No matter. Marlene's coiffures, too, became the basis for one of Selznick's famous memos, addressed to Boley and titled with more drama than the picture: "MISS DIETRICH'S HAIR."

"Would you *please* speak to Marlene about the fact that her hair is getting so much attention, and is being coiffed to such a degree that all reality is lost? Her hair is so well placed that at all times . . . it remains perfectly smooth and unruffled: in fact, is so well placed that it could be nothing but a wig.

"The extreme in ridiculousness is the scene in bed. No woman in the world has ever had her hair appear as Marlene's does in this scene, and the entire scene becomes practically unusable because everything is so exactly in place that the whole effect of a harassed and troubled woman is lost. . . . Surely a *little* reality can't do a great beauty any harm."

A little script reality would have been more to the point. Marlene, having lost the Sternberg battle and getting nowhere with dreamy Lynn Riggs (who now referred to her as "the bitch"), found script allies in Boyer and Rathbone, "who for some strange reason agrees with everything Marlene says," Boley complained. "They are just like a couple of cooing doves." Selznick heard mutiny, not cooing, and fired off a return cable to Boley.

"I AM GETTING TO THE END OF THE ROPE OF PATIENCE WITH CRITICISM BASED ON ASSUMPTION THAT ACTORS KNOW MORE ABOUT SCRIPTS THAN I DO. . . . WOULD APPRECIATE YOUR HAVING A FRANK HEART-TO-HEART TALK WITH MARLENE AND WITH BOYER. . . . MARLENE'S PICTURES HAVE BEEN NOTORIOUS FOR

THEIR GHASTLY WRITING. . . . CHARLES IS YET TO HAVE AN OUT-
STANDING AMERICAN PICTURE, AND NEITHER OF THEM HAS EVER
HAD A SINGLE PICTURE COMPARABLE WITH ANY ONE OF FIFTEEN
THAT I HAVE MADE IN THE LAST FEW YEARS. . . .

"IT IS HIGH TIME FOR A SHOWDOWN, AND I AM PERFECTLY PRE-
PARED FOR IT. . . . I WILL HAVE A LOT MORE RESPECT FOR YOU IF
YOU TURN INTO A VON STERNBERG WHO TOLERATES NO INTERFER-
ENCE. . . . MAKE CLEAR TO THE ACTORS THAT IF THEY CHOOSE TO
SULK THROUGH SCENES AND GIVE BAD PERFORMANCES I AM PER-
FECTLY PREPARED FOR THIS TOO AND . . . WILL RELEASE THE PIC-
TURE WITH THOSE PERFORMANCES. . . .

"RIDICULOUS ASSUMPTION THAT THEY KNOW ANYTHING ABOUT
SCRIPT. IF THEY WILL ONLY DO THEIR JOB AND GIVE PERFORMANCE,
THAT WILL BE ENOUGH. THAT IS ALL THAT THEY ARE BEING OVER-
PAID FOR."

Boleslawski made the mistake of transmitting Selznick's remarks to Marlene almost verbatim, which "made a mess of things," as Willis Goldbeck
had already conveyed them. Marlene countered that "she always told everybody that her scripts . . . were badly written and she was always right [but]
no one ever listened to her." Like *now*.

She "changed her tactics with Goldbeck," she confided to Boley, "by not
talking to him at all about the picture" the following night, as if script
conferences were uppermost on Goldbeck's mind. "Just a woman's vengeance for being asked not to interfere," said Boley, who still judged her
"very much interested and concerned and works very fine."

Costs on the picture mounted steadily above the already enormous budget. A Selznick emissary reported "they were so far out in the desert that
they were all eating, drinking, and breathing sand. There were about sixty
people and . . . all these internal feuds; people were getting sick from
sunstroke." Including Marlene, who fainted from heat on at least four
occasions. Sandstorms destroyed desert sets or turned artificial lagoons to
silt. Boley came down with desert-water dysentery that, in Hollywood
apocrypha, killed him (it didn't; he died of a heart attack on a golf course
after making *Theodora Goes Wild* the following year). But mostly there
were problems with color.

Technicolor could be infinitely adjusted in final processing, which was
one of its greatest virtues, but nobody knew what they shot day to day, as
rushes were printed in black and white in Hollywood, and the Technicolor
team exercised a tyranny of expertise over the entire production. Selznick
finally had enough and brought everybody back to Hollywood in early
June. Sand from Chatsworth and Malibu failed to match that of Buttercup

Valley, and Arizona sand was imported grain by grain by truckload to Culver City.

Marlene, meanwhile, went to the theater with Goldbeck to see her friend Katharine Cornell in *Saint Joan* and accompanied old Berliner Fritz Lang to the premiere of *Fury*, his first Hollywood picture since he boarded the midnight train from Berlin to Paris the very day Goebbels offered to "Aryanize" him if he would take over UFA.

Selznick's control of the production, even without a settled script, was exemplary if scattered, perhaps because his second son Daniel's birth during shooting provided diversion from call sheets. Nevertheless, he asked the production department to prepare a memo detailing how many *minutes*— not days or weeks or even months, as might be common (or necessary) today—of production time had been lost to star temperament. Delays by Boyer amounted to a scant sixty. Marlene's totaled seven hours and ten minutes. To anyone even remotely familiar with star antics, this is an astonishing record of discipline by a "difficult" woman who hated the script she was shooting, disliked her director, found her producer "repulsive— especially his hands," was lighting votive candles for one man while entertaining another, and had a daughter entering puberty and courting obesity, not to mention the problems of heat prostration, wayward hair, and a baby enema full of gold dust.

Marlene's discipline was bred in the bone, but she had real reason to get Boris back to the "monastawy." She was committed to be in England by late July for her fourth start date since October. *The Garden of Allah* finished shooting without further mishap on July 7 and Marlene and Maria left immediately for New York and Europe while Selznick and Technicolor adjusted desert poetry.

Alexander Korda was waiting for her in London with the biggest paycheck of her life. She needed it, not so much for her own lavish lifestyle and Maria, or to help out Rudi and Tamara in Paris or her mother and sister and *her* husband and their child in Berlin. She needed it as well for that swelling tide of friends and former co-workers and sometimes even complete strangers who were, like Fritz Lang, nowhere at home. Any more than she was.

Alexander Korda was a wanderer, too. He had gone moviemaking from his native Budapest to Vienna to Berlin to Hollywood, back to Berlin, on to Paris, and finally to London, where he almost single-handedly gave international presence to British film with pictures like *The Private Life of Don Juan* with Douglas Fairbanks, Sr., *Catherine the Great* with Bergner and Fairbanks, Jr., and *The Private Life of Henry VIII* with Charles Laughton and Merle Oberon.

He had known about sheen and star value as long ago as *A Modern Dubarry*, in which Marlene had played her bit part in ermine and tears. He had since left Maria Corda for Merle Oberon and had mostly given up directing for producing. His pictures were so polished and Important that United Artists, desperate for product, wanted to share in their distribution profits more than they wanted to exclude their competition.

Korda, like Selznick and Erich Pommer, was a producer on the grand scale (inevitably, he joined forces with both of them at one time or another) and was frequently just as overextended. Korda's financing came from the immensely rich Prudential Insurance Company, now willing to back his most expensive picture ever because of Marlene. Her willingness to work in England was a reversal of the usual Europe-to-Hollywood migration and legitimized Korda's international ambitions.

To get her, he offered a fee of $450,000, then the highest single picture price paid to any woman in film history (roughly equivalent to between six and seven million dollars in the 1990s), and more than double the "fabulous salary" Selznick had complained about. That Marlene had once been a Korda dance extra and bit player whom he had advised to go home and bake cakes gave a certain piquancy to the phenomenal fee.

She would now star for him in a sweeping romantic adventure based on James Hilton's novel *Knight Without Armour*. Hilton had also written the hugely successful *Lost Horizon* and (still to come as a movie) *Goodbye, Mr. Chips*. The script for *Knight Without Armour* was being fashioned for Marlene by Hollywood veteran Frances Marion (who had known Sternberg before his "von") and Korda's house writer, Lajos Biro, the one-time Hungarian diplomat who had written *A Modern Dubarry* as well as *The Last Command* for Sternberg and Jannings and the original *Hotel Imperial*, perhaps with the ballpoint pen he invented in his spare time.

Knight Without Armour, like *The Garden of Allah*, was the male star's story, though both pictures' success depended on Marlene and they would be judged as "Dietrich vehicles." Robert Donat was the *Knight Without Armour*, a star on both sides of the Atlantic since *The Count of Monte Cristo* and *The 39 Steps* for Hitchcock. Here he would play a Russian-speaking English journalist, imprisoned in Siberia during World War I, who is freed during the October Revolution. Making his way back to England (pretending to be a Bolshevik), he helps the beautiful Countess Alexandra (Marlene) evade both Reds and Whites in a trek across most of Mother Russia.

The production was conceived on Korda's typically grand scale, opening at Ascot in 1913 in order to introduce Countess Alexandra as part of international aristocracy at home anywhere there are races. It is a nice touch that removes in an instant all suspense; audiences wise to the ways of photoplays know she's going to wind up in England at the end, too. The title announces it; the marquee announces it; and the trade ads—"Dietrich Plus Donat Equals Dough"—boasted it.

Marlene and Maria set sail on the *Normandie* for England in mid-July. Marlene was so much the epitome of stardom that "all the rules of astronomy stopped [and] the earth—and the ship—turned around Marlene instead of the sun," as *Vogue* reported. She was photographed with most of her sixty pieces of monogrammed luggage; seated at the grand piano in her four-room Deauville suite with its blue satin upholstery; raptly watching herself in the ship's screening of *Desire*. She made eighty-one transatlantic telephone calls and received twenty telegrams. Her hairdresser and confidante, Nellie Manley, was along in her old-lady tennis shoes to dust gold where it was needed, and Marlene paraded daily on her private terrace in lounging pajamas. Mere mortals were permitted to gape, and they did. There was no Hemingway on board, but two-fisted Ham Fisher, creator of the funny papers' two-fisted Joe Palooka, won five months' free drinks at "21" from friends who bet him he couldn't wangle a private invitation for cocktails from a blue angel. "Even the waves succumbed" to Marlene's charms, according to *Vogue*. "The second day out, when the seas were misbehaving, the captain said to Miss Dietrich. 'A thousand pardons. I'll see that it never happens again.' " It didn't.

Marlene disembarked in Le Havre and went directly to Paris to turn Maria over to Rudi, who would enroll her in a private girls' school in Lausanne. The pace of Marlene's career was an unnecessary burden on Maria's already difficult adolescence. She may have been oversophisticated for her age, as her friends thought, or just overwhelmed by her mother's relationships and professional life. The girl's experience on *The Garden of Allah* had been "purgatory," she said later. Marlene had announced to the location crew that they should ignore Maria's moods as "my daughter is eleven and has menstruation." This announcement might have raised no eyebrows in Berlin, but in Buttercup Valley it was mortifying. Maria withdrew into a shell of adolescent humiliation that Bonita Granville, also playing a convent girl, interpreted as acting "Dietrich's daughter," high-hat and aloof, when she was just lonely—and eating.

Marlene was as alert to Maria's appearance as to her own. When she saw Maria's *Garden of Allah* rushes, she viewed them with a professional eye and saw a red-headed, plump-faced girl sullenly doing needlepoint. She insisted Maria's scene be cut and spent hours personally excising her stills from the contact sheets so thoroughly that only one survived. Maria got lonelier and ate more.

Marlene left her with Rudi and Tamara and crossed the Channel on the

Maid of Kent on her first visit to London since the premiere of *Morocco* in 1931, five years earlier. She was mobbed on arrival at Victoria Station, draped in mink and red velvet, and looked "more like her glamorous screen self than any star I ever met," thought a reporter fighting his way through the police-controlled crowd.

Marlene announced she had "no love of cooking and no desire to play Camille," and flattered local pride by insisting untruthfully and with curious logic that she would enroll Maria in an English school when she went back to Hollywood, because Maria was "used to being left."

Marlene's stay in London was taken up mainly by story conferences with Korda and Belgian director Jacques Feyder, fresh from the triumph of *La Kermesse Héroïque* (*Carnival in Flanders*). Marlene met Robert Donat and liked him, but told screenwriter Frances Marion that Donat was romantically off limits because happily married. Donat quickened in her the Florence Nightingale instincts John Gilbert had awakened, for he was subject to debilitating asthma attacks that might prevent his working with Marlene at all.

Korda wanted to replace him or reduce his role (in which case there would have been no story). Marlene was adamantly opposed and rehearsed with Donat to perfect a dialogue technique to get him through the film. He learned to inhale deeply, speak his dialogue in single, controlled exhalations of breath without a sign he was suffering anything more than the occasional pause in which he thought about England.

It was excruciating for him, made little easier by an overliterary script. Marlene's calm made duets of their scenes, most notably in an abandoned train station where he recites Browning to her, and she recites something Russian and pessimistic back, while Bolsheviks stealthily surround them.

Their pairing was without erotic sparks and never really works because Marlene is the least helpless of actresses and the story depends on *his* chivalry, not hers. She has such self-assurance one feels the Revolution would come to a dead halt if she could only confront Lenin directly. When the two escape into a forest, he asks her if she is familiar with it. "It *belongs* to me," she says, and so does the picture. Donat is too tactful for her exotic beauty, and her star power is so much greater than his that it makes the excessive mechanics of the escape plot seem intrusions on her glamour rather than anything to do with life and death.

Still, Donat got through it with her help. She called him "Knight Without Asthma," and her nurturing was an open secret in London theatrical circles, easing resentment aroused by her spectacular Hollywood glamour in an industry sensitive about inferiority to Hollywood. It was also a side of Marlene's character that could not be publicized or photographed, just as her loyalty to Sternberg with Selznick could not be.

Among Donat's friends who admired Marlene's compassion was young Douglas Fairbanks, Jr. She got to know him as part of Korda's glittering London prizes, and said good-bye to him only briefly when she left London to visit Vienna with Rudi and Maria while Donat's health improved and costumes and sets were prepared. In Vienna she discovered that Austrian anti-Semitism was on the rise and left after only a few days.

She rented a half-timbered chalet outside Salzburg, not far from Max Reinhardt's magnificent *Schloss* Leopoldskron, and invited Fairbanks to join her there after Maria was enrolled at Brillamont girls' school in Lausanne. The two shared the country house with Rudi and Tamara, though when Marlene went into photographer-infested Salzburg, she did so with Rudi. There she had reunions with old friend-in-exile Betty Stern, now turning the hostess skills that had made her *salon* a focus of Berlin's Golden Twenties to more practical use as an actors' agent in Paris.

Twenty-six-year-old Fairbanks (who spoke no German) found himself "flustered" by the urbane and cheerful way in which Marlene and Rudi behaved not like husband and wife, but "like old friends, or siblings." He told himself he was lucky not to be in love with Marlene, but was increasingly drawn into a relationship of "sophisticated intensity."

Marlene and Fairbanks had met casually in Hollywood when he was still married to Joan Crawford and living in the shadows of Pickfair. Now they became lovers, continuing their relationship at Claridge's Hotel in London, where Korda occupied an entire floor and where Marlene's suite was lit by the still-flickering votive candles in memory of John Gilbert.

The Claridge's staff saw nothing untoward when Fairbanks left the hotel at five or six in the morning, collar turned up to hide his white tie, with coat tails tied behind him in what must have looked an odd disguise. He clattered down fire escapes in acrobatic exercises of romantic discretion, only to be greeted by bobbies on the beat, "Morning, Mr. Fairbanks!"

Fairbanks had known, worked with, and liked John Gilbert and was troubled by the votive candles and his own "growing infatuation." But he had a more lively rival than Gilbert at Claridge's. Marlene was being courted fervently by CBS's young mogul, William S. Paley, then on a London stopover following a high society hunt in Scotland. Paley and Fairbanks knew each other, too, and Fairbanks enjoyed the competitive derring-do of fire escapes and dodging Paley, whom he ran into in the corridors of Claridge's at dawn-patrol hours.

"I know where *you've* been!" accused the frustrated Paley. Fairbanks raised a discreet finger to his lips in gamesmanship and gallantry and whispered, "Yes . . . *but don't tell Marlene!*"

Joshua Logan had just months before perceived Marlene as "the most self-centered woman I ever met in my life," but he had observed "Dietrich," trying for the first time to bring her own sort of expertise to a production under less than perfect control. Fairbanks saw "Marlene" off-duty, and the view was strikingly different.

"She was not quite a *Hausfrau*," he said years later, "but a good, hearty German girl who liked to swim, exercise, lie in the shade, and had some pretty Bohemian ideas." Fairbanks defended his use of the term *girl* as his way of differentiating "the two faces of Eve. She knew what the mask should be for the public, and liked to play the maddeningly aloof and untouchable Venus, [but then] there was maternal Marlene, who *swamped* Maria with love, the poor child who could rarely appreciate who or where she was. Then there was the regular girl who liked to cook and play games. A terribly sweet, nice *gal*," he stressed, "very gifted, very gallant, very intelligent, and a glamour girl only because Jo had told her to be."

Hotel and Salzburg visits became trips to the English countryside with Fairbanks's friends, like novelist-playwright Winifred Ashton (Clemence Dane), who was "intellectually enchanted" by Marlene, or the Kents—Prince George and his Greek-born wife, Princess Marina—who might have tidbits about other royals. There were weekends with Constantine and Lady Morvyth Benson "in their big English house. Marlene would just put on an apron and cook for a whole weekend houseparty. She was a great favorite, the *un*-glamour girl, wearing her apron off-stage, so to speak." The Bensons loved Marlene's informality, her scrambled eggs, and hardly minded her penchant for nude swimming, which troubled Fairbanks until Fritz Lang explained later, in Hollywood, that nude bathing was a common German custom.

Fairbanks withheld any "inner endorsement" of "the Dietrich-Sieber lifestyle," but it stimulated an outward manifestation. German casualness about nudity seemed suited to sculpture, and he modeled a full-figure nude of Marlene, giving her the original and retaining a plaster copy for himself. He thought it "possibly idealized," but Marlene's body at thirty-five looked as enticing in bronze as it had in marble a couple of years earlier in *Song of Songs*.

The London press reported extensively on Marlene and Fairbanks's "romantic attachment," perhaps because of what they could not print about another local romance concerning a certain Mrs. Simpson. As *Knight Without Armour* began filming, the couple found more privacy in Fairbanks's penthouse flat on Grosvenor Square. An apartment became available in the building and Marlene took it for her sixty pieces of luggage and wardrobe, put her name on the bell-plate for the curious press, and moved in upstairs with Fairbanks.

She proved "a wonderfully unconventional lover, philosopher, and friend," Fairbanks recalled, and "rather naughty," too. The persistent Paley continued his pursuit by telephone, calling to tell her what an error she was making in seeing Fairbanks instead of himself. Marlene sometimes took his calls in bed, sharing the receiver and his romantic fervor with Fairbanks's mischievous ear on the adjoining pillow.

Production on *Knight Without Armour* was uneventful except for Marlene's slipping on a bar of soap during a bathtub scene and falling spread-eagle naked before cast and crew. Laughing, she picked herself up and resumed shooting. The pratfall made the predictable headline: "Countess Without Armour."

She coaxed long, beautiful sentences out of Donat, wore wardrobe ranging from high Russian court to Bolshevik military dress, brought occasional fire and noblesse oblige to her role, but in the end it seemed there was too much Countess Alexandra and too little Marlene. The role was less interesting than the actress and the performance was ignored.

Marlene's playing is delicately modulated rather than a star turn. The picture is sumptuous but subdued, overcomposed and underacted. Nuanced, rather than sweeping. It has action (trains are a visual motif, criss-crossing the story and screen like elegant phantoms of orders old and new) and it is better than *The Garden of Allah*, but it is cool and distant. Feyder polished surfaces and stirred no depths. Dietrich Plus Donat didn't spell Dough, it spelled yawns. *Knight Without Armour* was a picture with everything Korda could buy but passion.

The riveting emotional upheaval was happening not on the Russian sets at Denham, but in and around London. The unfolding of Edward VIII's abdication drama was a much bigger story than even Korda could produce. Marlene's monarchist sympathies and sense of historical trauma propelled her to action.

She ordered Briggs, the chauffeur, to drive her in the sixteen-cylinder Cadillac to the king's country residence at Fort Belvedere so she could plead with him to sacrifice romance to the honor of the crown. Fairbanks waited edgily in Grosvenor Square, fearing the crown somehow depended on the king's succumbing to Marlene's seductive powers, and his sacrificing romance meant sacrificing only Mrs. Simpson, whom Marlene thought "frightful, terrifyingly vulgar."

Marlene's leap into the sheets of history ended at Fort Belvedere's gates, thwarted by guards of the very crown she was there to save. Briggs drove her back to Grosvenor Square where she and Fairbanks listened to Edward's abdication speech on the radio in penthouse privacy. Marlene wept.

As the Windsors' love story was unfurling, so were Selznick and *The Garden of Allah*. The picture opened at the Radio City Music Hall in New

York just as Marlene was blocked from saving a crown. The prestigious New York showcase had become available at the last moment because James Hilton's (and Frank Capra's) *Lost Horizon* was delayed and the Music Hall had no Thanksgiving picture.

Marlene's grief for the fate of monarchs was assuaged by the cable Selznick sent about her own: "I CAN NOW TELL YOU WITH COMPLETE SAFETY THAT PICTURE IS OBVIOUSLY A GREAT SUCCESS AND . . . EVERYONE UNANIMOUS THAT IN HISTORY OF SCREEN NO ONE HAS LOOKED MORE BEAUTIFUL THAN YOU DO IN THIS PICTURE AND THAT IT IS YOUR BEST PERFORMANCE TO DATE."

This good omen was confirmed by the richest Thanksgiving weekend in the Music Hall's history. Marlene graced the covers of both *Time* and *Newsweek* (infuriating *Time*'s Henry Luce, who thought he had an exclusive, but Selznick's partner Jock Whitney owned part of *Newsweek*). Marlene's cover biography in *Time* was written by Niven Busch and paid ample obeisance to *Allah*'s and Marlene's Technicolor glories, though no one thought the picture anything but dated. Archer Winsten in the *New York Post* admired "the Sahara, the Algerian costumes, the natives, and the cold, sharp beauty of Marlene Dietrich [which has] never been more beautifully photographed," though he thought her so "impassive" she became "a beautiful, animated wax figure." *Variety* found it "the last word in coloring" and noted that "Miss Dietrich and Charles Boyer are more than adequately competent . . . although sometimes slurring their lines." The *World Telegram*'s William Boehnel found Marlene "effective and beautiful" in a plot that was "hollow and unconvincing." *The New York Times* thought it "a distinguished motion picture rich in pictorial splendor . . . engrossingly acted," and Whitney's *Newsweek* (no surprise) claimed "Dietrich and Boyer achieve the finest performances of their careers."

Time's cover story noted that "if *The Garden of Allah*'s weak point is its story, its strong point is its female star . . . if there is any actress in Hollywood whom cinemaddicts have always yearned to see in the flesh—to which color film is the closest practical approach—Marlene Dietrich is the one." She provided the flesh when *Allah* opened in London at a charity premiere in mid-December. Selznick was cabled: "MOST BRILLIANT FIRST NIGHT AUDIENCE FOR MANY YEARS AT TEN DOLLARS TOP STOP HUGE CROWDS BLOCKED THEATER STOP DIETRICH . . . RECEIVED GREAT OVATION STOP"

No ovation could stay Graham Greene's pen right there in London where Marlene and Korda could read it, their own new picture barely finished. "The great abstractions," Greene wrote acidly, "come whistling hoarsely out in Miss Dietrich's stylized, weary, and monotonous whisper, among the hideous Technicolor flowers, the yellow cratered desert like Gruyère cheese, the beige faces." Even sending Boris back to the Trappists rated a sneer from Catholic Greene. "Alas! my poor Church, so picturesque, so noble, so superhumanly pious, so intensely dramatic."

If such reviews caused Korda anxious moments, he had more urgent worries. With *Knight Without Armour* finished and Marlene's final $100,000 payment due, Korda didn't have it.

The Prudential's indulgence was already stretched beyond the chronically lavish Korda style, which didn't slow his preparations for another picture to cost even more than unpaid Marlene's. Korda's relationship with Merle Oberon was dependent partly on his making her a star, the timing of which had been delayed by Selznick, Marlene, and *Allah*. Korda's other star, Charles Laughton, also needed a picture, and Korda found brilliant and demanding material for them in Robert Graves's *I, Claudius*. Laughton as the crippled Roman emperor Claudius and Oberon as the beautiful, evil Messalina were international and classy enough for any ambitious producer, and Korda planned to turn ancient Rome's decadence and decadents over to scenic designer William Cameron Menzies to direct. With $100,000 of Marlene's salary unpaid on *Knight Without Armour*, Korda found himself on the kind of economic precipice that plagued his whole career. This time he was rescued not by the "Pru," but by Marlene. She offered to forfeit her money if he would use it to replace Menzies on *Claudius* with Josef von Sternberg.

Sternberg had made two pictures since leaving her: a pedestrian version of *Crime and Punishment* with Peter Lorre and a disastrous Emperor Franz Josef musical, *The King Steps Out* with Grace Moore and Franchot Tone, which he ever after tried to pretend didn't exist. He was thoroughly played out in Hollywood and, after building his Richard Neutra all-steel house complete with moat (he sold it to Ayn Rand: it may have inspired *The Fountainhead*), had embarked on travels to the Far East, somehow ending up in a London hospital with what may have been appendicitis. He received the offer to direct *I, Claudius* in his recovery bed, and being virtually unemployable in Hollywood, deigned to think it over.

He was intrigued, he said, "to show how a nobody can become a god, and become a nobody and nothing again." He was talking about Claudius, but it was an ominous self-sketch if ever there was one. Korda was more concerned about Messalina. Sternberg was likely, if anyone was, to turn Merle Oberon into the star she was determined to become. Korda accepted Marlene's offer; Sternberg accepted Korda's.

Douglas Fairbanks, Jr., knew everybody concerned and held his breath. He had known Sternberg since his father and Chaplin bought *The Salvation Hunters* back in 1925, and saw Marlene's $100,000 gesture as "overdramatic." He both admired and deplored it, but knew enough to keep quiet. "In many ways Marlene was superior to Jo," he reflected later, "and had this 'thing' of gratitude towards him. She went to such exaggerated lengths of defense and promotion, helping him and talking people into helping him—getting *jobs* for him. She would never hear the slightest criticism, even when he was terrible to her. He was always bitchy about her and she took it; she'd just smile sort of ironically, and the money would flow out. She was certainly his most loyal friend."

Marlene's proof of loyalty may be the most tangible in Hollywood history, to tragic avail. Sternberg was as autocratic and tyrannical on *I, Claudius* as he had ever been with Marlene, but Charles Laughton lacked her resilience or steel. He was fodder for Sternberg's abuse machine and was having difficulty with a role that would not prove castable for another forty years until Derek Jacobi played it for the BBC. Sternberg, wearing his turban and high-laced boots and carrying his menacing swagger stick, was never the director to provide guidance or motivation in characterization. Laughton floundered in search of his character. Expense and time mounted ruinously. Finally, Merle Oberon suffered a curious automobile accident which allowed Korda to cancel the picture in mid-production and write the whole thing off to his insurers, who were also his backers.

The accident was staged, as everyone suspected and no one would state for fear the Pru might not pay off. Merle Oberon's "facial cuts," which the press reported as having nearly destroyed her exotic beauty, made headlines to rival Marlene's nude slip on the soap, though they amounted to no more than a slight facial bruise and a sprained ankle.

The episode effectively ended what career Sternberg had left after *The Devil Is a Woman* and the mediocrities he had directed at Columbia. Korda made some showy attempts to replace Oberon with Claudette Colbert, knowing she was not available. The production was shut down forever and Sternberg was admitted in secrecy to Charing Cross Hospital psychiatric unit, where visitors were not allowed.

Almost thirty years later, in 1965, Sternberg's footage was found and cut together to form the heart of a BBC documentary by Bill Duncalf called *The Epic That Never Was*. It dealt very gingerly with the "accident." Merle Oberon was interviewed on camera and repeated the official story. Only Emlyn Williams (who had played Caligula) had the malice or wit to suggest that Korda must have been Oberon's "chauffeur" the night that ended the picture and saved him from ruin.

Sternberg appeared on camera, too, ever his inscrutable self, content to allow the footage to speak for him. It revealed what surely would have been a creditable film, though perhaps not the crowning glory of his career many claim to see in the fragmentary evidence. He blamed Laughton for being a bad puppet and displayed a wounded dignity as a man more sinned against than sinning. Perhaps he was. Or maybe he was now beyond even the help of Marlene's loyalty. Neither then nor at any other time in his life did he acknowledge Marlene's role in his getting the job in the first place. Nor did she ever claim credit.

Douglas Fairbanks, Jr., was offered a role in Hollywood when Marlene finished *Knight Without Armour*, and she urged him to take it. It was the supporting role of Rupert of Hentzau in a remake of *The Prisoner of Zenda*. The part had once made a star of Ramon Novarro and might do the same for Fairbanks now in a Selznick production starring Ronald Colman.

Fairbanks, Sr., advised his son to take it and he did, partly because he knew Marlene was going back to America—to Paramount, in fact—and he was not ready to say good-bye. Nor was she prepared to let him.

She stayed in London over the holidays with Maria, celebrating their birthdays (Maria's twelfth, Marlene's thirty-fifth) and the arrival of 1937. If Fairbanks had qualms about leaving her behind as he sailed for Selznick and swordplay in Hollywood, he counted too little on Marlene's self-possession when it came to gentleman callers, and there was one.

The visitor was unwelcome, though Marlene realized that one way or another he was as inevitable as history. She refused to see him at all when he was announced, but was finally moved by Maria's entreaties that no one should have to sit alone day after day in a lobby at Christmastime.

Not even a Nazi.

TWELVE

EXILE

1937 - 1939

Marlene had had gentlemen callers before, but never one offering her "Tomorrow the World." She needed only return to Berlin as Queen of UFA, where she could name her price, her script, and her director (Gentile, please), and her protector would be powerful indeed: Dr. Joseph Goebbels.

Hitler liked to screen Marlene's films privately at Berchtesgaden, his mountain aerie (Leni Riefenstahl surprised him at it once), but *der Führer* had more in mind than private pleasures. The very prestige of the Reich was on his mind.

It has been said that her visitor that Christmas was Goebbels himself, whose title was Minister of Enlightenment and Propaganda, though Nobel Prize–winning journalist Carl von Ossietzky called him "that club-footed psychopath" and paid for the remark with his life. Goebbels's presence in London the Christmas of the abdication would have caused comment even in an atmosphere of appeasement, but his fervent desire for the world's enlightenment (and beautiful actresses) might have given his presence credibility.

Others have reported that the man kept waiting in the lobby until Maria's Yuletide sentiment overcame Marlene's resistance was Joachim von Ribbentrop, the vain and arrogant wine merchant, now Hitler's ambassador to Britain, who had sent a *Frohe Weihnachten* Christmas tree to Grosvenor Square. Ribbentrop was so offensive to so many that even unrepentant Nazis didn't much mind when later he swung from the end of a rope.

Still others have claimed the visitor was a woman, an actress friend of Marlene's (and Goebbels's) named Maedy Soyka, whose husband had once been Marlene's agent in Berlin. Marlene allowed rumor to identify her caller, but late in life confided to an interviewer that it had been Rudolf Hess, the fanatic true believer and deputy of the Führer who had taken down *Mein Kampf* in shorthand in a prison cell in 1923. Hess was scheduled to be Hitler's successor (after Göring) in spite of the code name "Black Bertha" by which he was known in the gay bars of Berlin, haunts disapproved of by his Führer, who was straitlaced about many things: He was vegetarian and neither smoked nor drank.

Whoever carried the message, it was clear: "The Führer wants you to come home."

Marlene's response was clearer: *"Never!"*

"Home"—by default, profession, or preference—now lay on the other side of the Atlantic, and on March 6, 1937, Marlene reinforced her response to Berlin by raising her right hand in allegiance to the stars and stripes and the rocks and rills for which they stood. She did it in the new Federal Building in downtown Los Angeles. She wore a severely tailored suit and floppy fedora and smoked throughout, giving her name as Marie Magdalene Sieber, and fudging her birth date as December 27, 1904. "My eyes, they are blue and my hair, it is blond," she told a sweaty clerk, adding, "I weigh one twenty-four and I am five feet and eight inches tall."

"I live here, I work here, and besides," she avowed to reporters, her elegant ankle poised on the running board of her sixteen-cylinder, chauffeur-driven Cadillac, "America has been good to me." The Hearst papers, not entirely disapproving of Hitler and his cronies, characterized her application (there would be a two-year wait) with the flat headline, "Deserts Her Native Land."

The Nazi press was less ambiguous, retaliating with vigor. Julius Streicher, most vicious Jew-baiter of them all, cranked out calumny in his notorious journal, *Der Stuermer:* "The German-born Dietrich has spent so many years among the film Jews of Hollywood [that] her frequent contacts with Jews render her wholly un-German." The photograph of Marlene taking her oath was captioned, "Shirt-sleeved judge administers oath to Dietrich so that she may betray the Fatherland."

Naturalization clerk George Ruperich, the "shirt-sleeved judge" in the picture, clarified his identity and rolled-up sleeves for the press. He wasn't a judge, he wasn't Jewish—he was just hot.

Marlene's *"Never!"*—and her contacts with Hollywood Jews—did not discourage Dr. Goebbels. He continued to track Marlene's movements in his diary and the UFA executive minutes, hoping for a change of heart or status even as she returned to Paramount with another traitor to the Reich, one of those Berlin-born Hollywood Jews, Ernst Lubitsch.

Their return to Marathon Street looked like sweet vindication for both. Lubitsch had been sacked the year before in the chaos of *I Loved a Soldier* and *The Big Broadcast,* but yet another new management team invited him back with virtual carte blanche. Marlene's new contract compromised between Selznick and Korda fees at a still-phenomenal $250,000 per picture (two a year, plus perks majestic enough for any Queen of the Lot). Paramount even bought her a play she and Douglas Fairbanks, Jr., had seen in London, *French Without Tears.* This first big hit from Terence Rattigan seemed a likely film vehicle for them now that they had discreetly relocated from Grosvenor Square to Marlene's latest Beverly Hills rental, complete with pool and greenery to shield her nude swims from any eyes but those of the renter next door (Fairbanks) or of guests she invited to lounge around the pool, like Fritz Lang. Marlene swam while Fairbanks blushed. Lang polished his monocle and explained European custom, to which Fairbanks was becoming accustomed without becoming inured.

Lubitsch had been preparing Marlene's return project, *Angel,* for almost a year, and they began shooting just as she applied for American citizenship and Fairbanks began swordplay in *Prisoner of Zenda.* Fritz Lang engaged in some swordplay of his own, European custom being what it is. It didn't last long: The fling ended when Marlene reached across the pillow and picked up Lang's own phone to make a date with another man. Besides, she was working.

Angel was based on a Hungarian play (Budapest was rumored in those days to have whole playwriting factories). This one was by Melchior Lengyel, the spirit behind *Ninotchka,* adapted for America by musical comedy librettist Guy (*Girl Crazy*) Bolton with Russell Medcraft, suggesting high spirits and verve. *Angel* as a play told of a philandering couple whose marathon bed-hopping is meant to add spice to matrimony, but is finally just enervating and the marriage bed proves, in the end, the ideal venue for rest and recreation.

Lubitsch and his favorite screenwriter, Samson Raphaelson (with some uncredited help from Frederick Lonsdale), used their carte blanche to overbake an *Angel*-cake many today hail as Lubitsch's most sophisticated and underrated concoction. Its admirers did not then include the holders of the Paramount purse strings, the Code, or the leading lady.

Lubitsch teamed Marlene again with Herbert Marshall (had he not seen *Blonde Venus?*). They played Lady Maria and Sir Frederick Barker, she the epitome of Continental elegance, he of English diplomacy and stiff upper lip. The adroit Melvyn Douglas was co-starred as Lady Maria's enraptured lover. Unbilled was Luigi Pirandello, whose spirit hovered over a theme Andrew Sarris has defined mysteriously as "appearances for appearances' sake," in which the enigma of Lady Maria (shimmering and slippery as silk) is the subject of the movie, her shifts of persona mirrored by swank, swankier, swankest wardrobe from Travis Banton.

In the Lubitsch-Raphaelson-Lonsdale-Pirandello version, Sir Frederick philanders only with Yugoslavia at the League of Nations in Geneva, and Lady Maria feels . . . *neglected*. In the stateliest home in all England. She puts on a Travis Banton traveling costume and flies off via private plane to Paris, checks into a hotel under an assumed name and visits what is called a salon, but looks very like a high-class brothel. There, it seems, she was once one of the girls. This establishment's character is revealed bit by bit, window by window as the camera glides along the exterior in a justly admired traveling shot crammed full of telling "Lubitsch touches." Here Lady Maria meets Tony Halton (Douglas), in search of . . . *adventure*. He buys her violets while she goes mysterious, giving her self (apparently), but not her name, and suffers more ennui from attention than she did from neglect. Tony calls her Angel, and she flies off into the night.

The infatuated Tony turns up—surprise—at the stately home in England of Sir Frederick. (The situation is exactly that of Marlene and Willi Forst's *Dangers of the Engagement Period* in 1929.) We wait for spicy delicacies when Tony discovers who the Angel really is that he rhapsodizes about to the politely bemused and unsuspecting Sir Frederick. Instead, we get leftovers: The servants tell us what's going on among their betters by discussing the veal remaining on the plates of the stars after their offscreen dinner. This is the film's most admired scene, and it sparkles. It is as sly and amusing as Lubitsch scholars claim, but there is surely something wrong with a movie that gives the best lines to the servants while the stars get dialogue so oblique it seems to glance right off the page. When Tony presses the subject of female identity (she won't admit that she is *she*), the talk turns to lampshades: Sometimes they look green, sometimes blue, depending on the bulb or the wattage or the time of day or the viewer or *appearances*. Sir Frederick, meanwhile, frets about Yugoslavia and Lady Maria plays the piano and drags eyelashes up and down as if scanning the script for a plot. She also hauls around a thirty-pound beaded gown that Diana Vreeland described as "a million grains of golden caviar," and liked so much she put it on display at the Metropolitan Museum of Art almost fifty years later.

Finally Sir Frederick gets suspicious of Lady Maria's slow-motion eyelashes and all the lampshade talk (there is also a theme song by Friedrich Holländer) and winds up confronting her back in the Paris "salon" (he has been tipped off to her Paris jaunts by his rent-a-plane purveyor), where she may or may not be running away with Tony. Gary Cooper would just have spanked her on her beaded gown, but Sir Frederick wonders in his cashmere voice, "Where *is* this?" and "What kind of woman are you?" and where is this Angel person Tony keeps swooning over?

Marlene's Lady Maria suffers another wave of ennui, but drips with black sable and shrewder diplomacy than her husband, who drips with indignation and hurt pride. Angel is in the next room, she says, and advises him to take her word for it: "If you go into that room, I'm afraid our marriage is over. If you find Angel in there, you will be happy that I'm not Angel, and you'll want to continue our old life. That would not be satisfactory to me."

Sir Frederic negotiates: "And if I don't find Angel?"

ANGEL: "In that case, I think you'll want to see your lawyer as soon as possible. On the other hand, if you don't go in at all, you will be a little uncertain. You won't be so sure of yourself—or of me. And that might be wonderful."

There it is—character, theme, confrontation—even if it is the end of the picture: a challenge to conventional notions of marriage and fidelity from a star who could believably carry off the unconventional if anybody could.

Sir Frederick's wounded pride drives him into the next room. He contemplates the Angel-free emptiness around him and comes back to flatten the only interesting point of the picture: He agrees to a long-delayed second honeymoon in old Vienna. And, incredibly, Lady Maria/Angel *buys it!* That's all she wanted after all; nothing unconventional, no private planes or stately homes or sophisticated one-night-stands with Tony or even respect as an independent wife or liberated woman—just a little attention in *alt Wien*. The most emancipated woman in 1930s cinema settles for a weekend. With Herbert Marshall.

Angel is all foreplay and no release. What makes it so tantalizing to scholar-critics is they don't know how to explain that so exquisitely subtle an artifact (it *is*) can also be so dull. Marlene plays enigmatic with a delicacy unique in her career (it may be her most controlled performance), but she, too, is dull. She fought Lubitsch every inch of the way over script, and later said she had no idea who any of the characters were supposed to be. Their arguments degenerated into wrangles over detail.

Lawrence Langner of New York's Theater Guild visited the set and came away with tales of rage over a hat. Lubitsch said wear it; Marlene said no. They stopped speaking to each other and the dispute led to reshooting at a cost of $95,000. Marlene sighed that she wanted to play parts where she could wear "just a little black shawl and working-women's clothes," presumably by Travis Banton. The cost of the hat contretemps may or may not have been accurate, but stills were made of Marlene in a hat she doesn't wear in the film. *Garbo* wears it—a near duplicate, anyway—a year later in *Ninotchka*, Lubitsch's little hat trick on Marlene.

What is clear is that star and director were working at cross purposes and the enervated quality of the picture shows it. Their conflict caused him to reevaluate the joys of directing her in *French Without Tears*. An additional wet blanket was thrown on that romantic comedy when Fairbanks came home from swashbuckling in *Zenda* to leaf inadvertently through some of Marlene's private correspondence. He found himself shocked by a batch of "intense love letters" from someone he'd never even *heard* of. In a rush of Sir Frederick-like indignation he compounded his indiscretion by flying into "a jealous rage" over what he still called "the Dietrich-Sieber lifestyle" and demanded an explanation. Marlene explained the location of the door. Rudi (once again visiting in California) did not bar Fairbanks's way.

Lubitsch's troubles with Marlene were minor compared to those presented by Paramount and the Code. Paramount had no idea how to handle what looked like blatant subtlety, and prepared full-page ads that pointed out Marlene's "simple gown, bedizened with gold beads, pearls, diamonds, rubies and sable." Bold-faced type asked "WHAT DOES ANGEL DO?" and answered the question with, "She dares to love two men at the same time!!!"

Offscreen this applied with a vengeance, but on-screen she does no such thing. She doesn't even seem to like them very much, and the Code office was out of love, too. The puritan gentlemen were aghast at the Parisian bordello, the affair with Tony, and the subversive notion of love among equals. The movie's marriage (so reminiscent of "the Dietrich-Sieber lifestyle") was the only thematic point the picture made, and the Code wanted to forbid it.

Lubitsch had been prepared for this, had even formally asked to shoot the picture two ways: once for provincial America and once for sophisticated Europe. The Code had refused and now insisted that the bordello/salon be introduced with a shot of a Russian coat-of-arms, which made the place seem an annex of the Russian embassy. The affair with Tony was reduced to supper chaperoned by a wandering violinist in a private dining room. No wonder Marlene looked bored. After issuing a seal, the Code people came to their senses and retracted it, demanding the picture be totally recut and rescored, even though prints (sixty-three of them) had already been shipped to theaters. The cost, Paramount howled, was "staggering."

As *Angel* was snipped and Paramount staggered, it became common knowledge in Hollywood that *Garden of Allah* hadn't a prayer of returning its cost of $1.4 million. Just after the Fourth of July, *Knight Without Armour* opened at the Radio City Music Hall, where Dietrich Plus Donat spelled Disaster.

Paramount, stricken by their Queen of the Lot's box office, bit their nails and the bullet and released the recut, rescored version of *Angel* in October, hoping that Marlene and Lubitsch's names on the marquee might supply the thrills that "appearances for appearances' sake" lacked.

Angel has acquired the reputation of being unappreciated in its time, but reviews were more admiring than not. *The Hollywood Reporter* called it "an extremely well bred continental comedy of manners" (a sure kiss of death for *The Great Ziegfeld* and *Lost Horizon* audiences of that year), while *Variety* thought it "one of the best films Lubitsch has made . . . exciting and engrossingly entertaining." Marlene, it was noted, "speaks clearly and distinctly." Weekly *Variety* reported, "She is wearing eyelashes you could hang your hat on and every now and then . . . flicks 'em as though a dust storm was getting in her way," adding astutely that it was all "sophisticated, smart and provocative, perhaps too much so."

Other reviewers noticed her eyelashes more than the plot. One remarked "when she blinks them, monstrous and sinister shadows flap bat-like across her curiously ascetic features," and C. A. Lejeune in England professed to have no idea what it was all about, "except possibly Miss Marlene Dietrich, the film star, practising acting."

The New York Times wondered if Lubitsch were not voicing "agree[ment] with the Schopenhauer notion that women are sphinxes without riddles," and the *Literary Digest* found it all "very sophisticated, very subtle, very chic . . . exactly the kind of film the producers out Los Angeles way shun in holy terror."

So did audiences. *Angel* was promoted as Paramount's big prestige package of 1937, but *Waikiki Wedding* with Bing Crosby, a ukulele, and "Sweet Leilani" brought home the bacon. The final humiliation came when the Independent Exhibitors of America (theater owners not controlled by the studios) felt abused enough to take out full-page ads in the Hollywood trade papers declaring Marlene "box-office poison." The ads remain notorious in

Hollywood history, not least because they exposed the exhibitors' true instincts for showmanship. Marlene was box-office poison, but so, too, were Garbo, Joan Crawford, Fred Astaire, and Katharine Hepburn. That these "poisonalities," as the columnists were quick to call them, had considerable mileage left at the world's ticket counters was not clear or didn't matter in the long run of the Depression. Paramount decided that *French Without Tears* might be even less dreary without Marlene. They added a staggering footnote to the history of workmen's compensation and created headlines in *Life* and *Look* by paying Marlene $250,000 *not* to make the picture and please get lost.

Lubitsch and Marlene, being flawlessly subtle at the height of the screwball comedy craze, had done in just one picture what all Josef von Sternberg's extravagance had failed to do in seven: They got her fired, made her virtually unemployable. "The most highly salaried woman in the world" was without a job.

Paramount may have thought her washed up, but others sensed opportunity. Frank Capra at Columbia decided her look in slacks would make her the perfect George Sand in a picture about Chopin (with Spencer Tracy as the composer!), and Warner Brothers offered her a remake of director Tay Garnett's old shipboard tearjerker *One Way Passage*. She signed with both, but then Harry Cohn and Jack Warner read the box-office poison ads and cancelled the projects.

Marlene fired her agent, Harry Edington, who was also Garbo's agent (or he fired her) and sailed for Europe. Now Fairbanks-less, with Maria in school in Switzerland, she turned where she always turned when in trouble or in doubt: to Rudi and Rilke. Rudi brought her consolation; Rilke brought her romance.

In the summer of 1937, the publicity agent for the Hotel des Bains on Venice's Lido was Elsa Maxwell, and "the exile table" in the dining room must have seemed her greatest coup. There sat Marlene, banished from Paramount and self-exiled from Germany; Rudi, momentarily absent from Tamara and soon to be sacked by Paramount-Paris, where his employment had been one of Marlene's perks; and, newly released from Charing Cross Psychiatric after the debacle of *I, Claudius* the year before, Josef von Sternberg, exile from Hollywood and almost everywhere else.

Sternberg was planning a return to directing with a version of Zola's *Germinal* to be made in Vienna; Rudi was drumming up projects for Marlene in France; Marlene was pretending not to brood about being box-office poison.

Then, another exile dining at the Hotel des Bains invited her to dance.

Rudi and Sternberg watched them glide across the dance floor, where violinists may well have played "Falling in Love Again" in her honor. The most unemployed woman in the world looked into the monocle of the best-selling novelist in the world, and his monocle looked back into the eyes of the sphinx, searching out that riddle.

Marlene had casually met Erich Maria Remarque in Berlin in the twenties when he was a frequent freeloader at the buffet of Betty Stern's salon and Marlene was the house favorite and still the girl from the Kurfürstendamm. Remarque then had a scattered résumé, reputation, and a wife. He wrote occasional fashion dispatches from Paris for Berlin's *Die Dame* (the German V*ogue*), composed jingles for tire manufacturers, and wrote about his racing-car passion for *Sport im Bild* (Berlin's *Tatler*). He had served briefly in World War I, taught school, and once played the organ in an insane asylum, an unnerving experience he gave up, claiming (an odd echo of Marlene's violin canard) an injury to a finger that prevented pursuing a musical career.

He was born Erich *Paul* Remarque, though the Nazis spread the rumor that Remarque was just Kramer spelled backward, and perhaps not quite Aryan. When his mother died he adopted her name, Maria, for his own, and gave Paul to the hero of a novel he was writing when not looking melancholy at Betty Stern's or suicidally testing racing cars. He finished the novel. His publishers advertised it untruthfully as his first, buying up and suppressing all copies of his two earlier self-admitted embarrassments, and when *All Quiet on the Western Front* was published it became the then best-selling novel of the twentieth century. It made his name and fortune and set a standard he spent the rest of his life trying to equal.

In 1933 the Nazis requested the pleasure of his absence (he was neither Jewish nor Communist, but a self-described "militant pacifist"), and he decamped from Germany (and his faithless wife) for a life of luxurious drifting through the pleasure domes of Europe, having left cash and art works behind as the mandatory price of an exit visa—"refugee tax," the Nazis called it. This had not caused undue hardship, as *All Quiet on the Western Front* sold a million copies in its first year of publication in every important language (and currency) of the world. He had already shipped most of the Cézannes and Utrillos to Switzerland, where banks were bulging with *All Quiet* movie money, for Universal had made it a world screen sensation in 1930. Gold was small compensation for the sacrifice of homeland, citizenship, and language. He was now a platinum-heeled wanderer, still writing, still moping (the monocle added an elegant Prussian note to his melancholy), still attracted to dangerously fast cars, excesses of alcohol, and spectacularly beautiful, independent women.

Berlin, old friends, and mutual exile were instant bonds for the movie star and the writer, but they needed something more. They found it in sunlight. Marlene strode along the boardwalk the next day, wearing beach pajamas and carrying under her arm a volume of her beloved Rilke. Remarque, arching the eyebrow above his monocle, observed caustically, "Of course, *all* film stars read poetry. . . ."

Marlene placed Rilke in his hands, challenging him to pick a page. He did. On it was Rilke's "The Panther," which she recited perfectly from the perfect memory for poetry that would not desert her for the rest of her life. "Another," she commanded, and "Leda" followed "The Gazelle," and that was followed by "The Good-bye." Page followed page as poem followed poem, and then Marlene followed Remarque to Paris, and he followed her to Hollywood.

Rudi accompanied them as far as Paris, where he resumed his lifestyle with Tamara, handsomely supported by Marlene's quarter-of-a-million-dollar severance pay from Paramount. Josef von Sternberg, displaying true genius for bad timing, went on to Vienna to roll cameras on Zola's *Germinal* just as Hitler and his tanks rolled to an ecstatic Viennese reception on the Heldenplatz. Austrians and Germans called it the *Anschluss*. The rest of the world called it a shame, but none of our business.

The failures of *Allah*, *Armour*, and *Angel* were trivial compared to the failures of courage and conscience plaguing most of Europe. England and France's betrayal of Czechoslovakia at Munich was less than a year away (in late 1938), but Hollywood and isolationist America increased their distance from foreign entanglements in the pages of *Gone With the Wind* or on the screens where *Snow White* and her seven dwarves celebrated an optimistic work ethic ("Heigh Ho, Heigh Ho"), confident that princes and prosperity were just around the corner.

Marlene had her prince of sorts in Remarque, but there was a hitch before they could set sail for Hollywood. Marlene needed to assert her rights with dwarves of a more sinister nature than Disney's at the Germany embassy in Paris. Until her American citizenship was final, she remained a German citizen and required a renewed passport to return to America.

Goebbels, "that grotesque dwarf" as she called him, had known this formality would be necessary and prepared for it. Marlene arrived at the embassy to be confronted by four German princes and the ambassador. They flourished her American citizenship application and un-German statements attributed to her by the press, which she counterpunched with "slanders" about her in the German press. To receive her passport extension she declared herself "thoroughly German" and threatened legal action against libelous suggestions to the contrary. It may have occurred to the princely assemblage that her idea of "thoroughly German" was not necessarily theirs, but her papers were renewed, as were those of Maria and Rudi, also citizens of the Reich.

Goebbels entered Marlene's embassy visit into his private diary and sent another emissary to her in Paris to tighten the bonds of *Heimat*, this time someone Marlene knew and respected. It was Heinz Hilpert, who had directed her in George Bernard Shaw's *Misalliance* in Berlin in 1928 and was entrusted with management of the Reinhardt theaters now that the Sorcerer was just another Hollywood Jew looking for work.

Hilpert met with Marlene and reported her readiness to return to Berlin and the Deutsches Theater when her commitments in Hollywood permitted (she had big-money contracts from Columbia and Warners, but no pictures), not more than a year away. Goebbels exultantly confided this news to his diary, adding, "Now I will take her under my personal protection." Within days the German press rotated 180 degrees with front-page announcements that rumors—from heaven knew where—of Miss Dietrich's "un-German-ness" were wholly untrue, as were reports—from Heaven knew where—that she had contributed heavily to the antifascist forces in the Spanish Civil War.

Marlene and Remarque reserved a bungalow at the Beverly Hills Hotel as soon as visas were stamped and steamships set sail. They traveled on separate ships, discreet but pointless, as the front pages carried photos of the lady and the writer wherever they went. Remarque's currency in Hollywood was greater at that moment than Marlene's. She was unemployed and everywhere regarded as the bane of the box office—though not a whit less the Epitome of Movie Star than ever—while MGM was following Universal's *All Quiet* success by filming Remarque's subsequent *Three Comrades* from a script mostly by F. Scott Fitzgerald (the only screen credit Fitzgerald ever received).

Marlene may have been persona non grata before movie cameras, but she had lost none of her allure for still photographers or the public, who respond lastingly to the *idea* of stardom, its almost mythic aspect, more than the banal (and short-term) realities of the box office. Her every appearance was captured on film, dining, dancing, attending premieres with Remarque. Or with Fairbanks. Or both. Or with Henry Fonda. Or with what the smart set called "Marlene's Sewing Circle," a just-girls assembly including Ann Warner (wife to J. L., "Jack" of the studio-owning brothers), Dolores del Rio, and old Berlin chum Lily Damita. She was never less than bejeweled and dazzling, her variety of partners never less than riveting to reporters and readers, even in the oblique, discreet journalism of the day.

Privately she had patched things up with Lubitsch after their quarreling on the disastrous *Angel*, which he followed with *Bluebeard's Eighth Wife* with Gary Cooper and Claudette Colbert, which got *him* fired from Paramount, too. (He went on to Garbo and *Ninotchka*, on which Garbo fought with him no less than Marlene had on *Angel*, but she wore that hat). Marlene quietly joined Lubitsch in giving aid, comfort, and cash to the swelling flow of exiles from Hitler's Europe through what would be called the European Film Fund, founded mainly by Lubitsch, agent Paul Kohner, and writer Salka Viertel.

Meanwhile, the Hollywood Jews with whom Marlene had such well-publicized contact—Mayer, Cohn, Warner, Goldwyn, Selznick—exercised what observer of the period Ian Hamilton calls "contemptible timidity" about what was going on in Europe, most of them more concerned about their film markets than with what they knew to be happening in them. Irving Thalberg, following a trip to Germany in 1934, had calmly remarked "a lot of Jews will lose their lives," but thought Hollywood should stay out of it. Marlene, Gentile and Aryan, could not.

Erich Maria Remarque was hardly among the needy or unknown, but felt no less an exile in the Land of the Lotus than in Paris, Venice, or Ascona. He was a refugee, he said, regarded as a traitor in his native land and alien everywhere else. He marveled at Marlene's self-sufficiency as she went about the business of seeming at home and supporting herself, Maria, Rudi, and Tamara, as well as total strangers washed up by the Brown Tide, and did it all on yesterday's income. He thought of her as "this steel orchid" and sought refuge in work.

He began to sketch out a novel in their bungalow at the Beverly Hills Hotel about his early exile days in the darkening City of Light and decided to call it *Arch of Triumph*. Much of it would be set in the Hotel Ansonia in the Rue de Saigon (renamed), the Parisian exile hideaway where Billy Wilder, Friedrich Holländer, Peter Lorre, Franz Wachsmann, and Marlene's lyricist Max Colpet once lived (Colpet still did). It would be a love story set against despair, with a singer-actress as heroine, whose name he toyed with, playing with Madonna and Madeleine (versions of Marie and Magdalene). The novel's hero was self-portraiture, a doctor in exile reduced to the ignominy of patching up botched abortions who meets his heroine—finally named Joan Madou—in the first paragraph:

"He saw a pale face, high cheek-bones and wide-set eyes. The face was rigid and masklike . . . a face whose openness was its secret. It neither hid nor revealed anything. It promised nothing and thereby everything."

It was a fatalistic sort of beginning (and might have been written by Josef von Sternberg). *Arch of Triumph* would take Remarque years to complete and he could not know how it would end until he ended with Marlene, or she with him, but intuition guided his pen darkly and his dedication read "To M. D."

In the meantime, MGM and *Three Comrades* did not need (or want) him, and no one in Hollywood needed (or wanted) Marlene. The two set sail for Europe as 1938 became 1939 and brought with it a series of falling curtains: Munich, Czechoslovakia, the Hitler-Stalin pact, Poland.

Marlene had been unemployed before, but not nearing forty. Before Marlene changed things almost single-handedly, forty was the signal for tresses to stop flowing and wind themselves into buns, for feet to lace themselves into sensible shoes, and a bosom was something to dream on, not about. "A woman of a certain age" was put on no pedestal, but out to pasture or in a rocking chair. Marlene would rock—and soon—but she would not do so sitting down.

Marlene's mother was getting no younger, either, and set an example for her daughter by not yielding to time. After Uncle Willi died in 1934, she had been effective head of the Felsing family firm, though young Hasso inherited most of it. Marlene returned to Europe in 1938 not merely to search for work on which many were dependent, but because she sensed a last opportunity to persuade her mother—and sister—to leave Berlin before it was too late.

Marlene had assiduously avoided Berlin since 1934 and gathered the clan near Maria's school in Switzerland. Tourist visas for Berliners to the neutral Swiss Alps were freely dispensed and Lausanne was easier terrain in which to evade the press than Paris. Even so, sister Elisabeth's husband, Georg Will, willingly paid a price to attend the family reunion. He ran a couple of small movie theaters in Berlin and was required on this visit to restate the Führer's desire for Marlene's return to home and *Heimat*. Marlene exploded in full fury that her brother-in-law would carry messages for Dr. Geobbels and viewed this as further proof of why her family should get out while the getting was, if not good, then possible.

There was nothing alarmist or prescient about Marlene's attitude. Hitler was already known worldwide for dispatching opposition with bayonets or bullets, and *Mein Kampf* had been there to read for fifteen years. The Night of the Long Knives in 1934, the Munich "Degenerate Art" exhibition of 1937, Düsseldorf's "Degenerate Music" counterpart of 1938 (complete with Marlene's voice crooning "Jewish music" like "Falling in Love Again" over loudspeakers), and the *Kristallnacht* of November 1938 were not shrouded events known only to the Gestapo. They were deliberated public orgies of power and policy. They made worldwide headlines, gratifying the

Minister of Enlightenment and Propaganda. The world sent regrets while windows and lives shattered by torchlight.

Marlene, as a sometime target, knew this better than most, and Remarque's constant exile-presence reinforced it. She pleaded with her family to leave Germany, if not for America, then at least for gentler France, where Rudi had succeeded in arranging picture deals for her. One was to co-star with the great French actor Raimu, another was a film noir titled *Dédé D'Anvers* in which she would co-star with Jean Gabin, and a third, called *L'Image*, to be directed by Julien Duvivier. Goebbels's intelligence services informed him of all this, and he was determined UFA should distribute Marlene's "Jew-free" French pictures in Germany.

In spite of Marlene's entreaties, Josephine von Losch stood the ground she was born on. She would not or could not leave Berlin or the firm she now controlled, or abandon her ward, Hasso. Marlene said her good-byes to them in Lausanne, not knowing she would not see her mother or sister again for the better part of a decade, not until catastrophe had run its course, with her family at its dreadful center.

She returned to Paris, where she fell into friendship with her future co-star, Jean Gabin, who had captured fame and great stardom in Jean Renoir's *La Grande Illusion*. He and Marlene discussed the script for *Dédé d'Anvers*, but her French projects were nervous, then delayed, then cancelled, leaving her just as unemployed as before.

Her soignée surface was ruffled momentarily when she became the innocent focus of an angry Parisian audience. Ex-lover Maurice Chevalier gave a concert at the Casino de Paris and, after ridiculing the Nazis with a song, blew Marlene a kiss from the stage, ignoring his discoverer and even earlier lover Mistinguett, also in the audience. The theater rafters rattled with boos, forcing Chevalier to acknowledge the great music-hall star, now in her sixties. Mistinguett, once famous for her beautiful legs, reminded Marlene of the power of the audience, of durability in the theater, and of memory, which seemed short only in America.

Another old intimate in Paris then was Mercedes de Acosta, and the two commiserated on the state of the world while Remarque continued thinking about *Arch of Triumph*. In November Marlene sailed back to America on the *Normandie* to trade her green card for U.S. citizenship. On the crossing she socialized with Cary Grant, the Jack Warners, the Baroness Eugénie de Rothschild (who had sheltered the Duke of Windsor near Vienna until his marriage to Mrs. Simpson), and listened as her closest shipmate pal (again), Ernest Hemingway, coolly laid out for her how "worthless" Remarque was. Hemingway was depressed about the end of the Spanish Civil War that

March (it gave him the idea for a novel), and it was hard for him in the best of times to find another (living) writer he liked. Remarque, generous and melancholy, said, "I'm only a small man in comparison with Hemingway."

Marlene received her Citizenship Certificate #4656928 in June in Los Angeles. Federal Judge Harry Hollzer told her and two hundred other new citizens, "We must be on our guard against propaganda, oral as well as written, which seeks to turn any class or race or religious group against any other. Events abroad have proved the tragic consequences of a propaganda of hatred."

Hollywood, meanwhile, practiced its propaganda of silence. The industry was only socially interested in Marlene's return: She was washed up, yesterday's news, history, except at parties, where few were more au courant. She chummed with Basil and Ouida Rathbone, socialite Countess Dorothy di Frasso and friends (including Bugsy Siegel), with pre-*Mr. Belvedere* song-and-dance man Clifton Webb and his mother Mabelle, and the durable star Paramount gossips referred to as "Uncle Claude."

Producer Walter Wanger (who had rung Sternberg alarm bells by speakeasy-hopping with Marlene in New York in 1930), listened uneasily to her notion of reviving the abandoned *I Loved a Soldier* with Sternberg directing and quashed the idea by proposing another. He thought a reteaming of Marlene and Gary Cooper might work in—of all things—a Western, but Wanger's director, John Ford, disagreed. He stuck to his casting guns, insisting on a virtually unknown B-picture cowboy called John Wayne in the part Wanger had seen for Cooper. The not-much-better-known Claire Trevor was cast in the Marlene role as the *Stagecoach* girl with a past.

Wanger's notion that Marlene might somehow be fetching in sunbonnet and gingham had been suggested to him by her new agent, Charles Feldman, who thought she needed a change of image. He would not forget the Old West as the place in which she might change it.

Marlene, now "thoroughly American" as a matter of principle if not affinity, sailed back to Paris, but not before a bon voyage party could be launched on the decks of the *Normandie*. In an odd display of what it meant to be an American, the Internal Revenue Service delayed the ship's sailing for almost an hour, presenting Marlene with a delinquent tax bill of $142,193 for the *Knight Without Armour* money she had not earned in America at all (and not earned *all* of, even in England, having sacrificed that large chunk of it to Sternberg and *I, Claudius*). James S. McNamara, the revenue agent in charge, had no desire to be confused by facts, and grandstanded to the press that he was there without an arrest warrant only because he couldn't find a judge to issue one.

Marlene was "surprisingly calm" now that she had her passport, "astonishing reporters who have seen her at her temperamental worst," those

Ethel, the American aviatrix in *The Ship of Lost Souls*, learns from director Maurice Tourneur that she is the only woman in the picture. 1929.

Marlene got "storyboarded" as Ethel, American heiress and aviatrix about to crash into *The Ship of Lost Souls*. So many American heiresses made solo trans-Atlantic flights in 1929.

Marlene took Maria on a last vacation on the North Sea before meeting Josef von Sternberg. Summer 1929.

Marlene in *Two Bow Ties*, in which Sternberg "discovered" her, with Hans Albers and Rosa Valetti, both already cast in *The Blue Angel*.

Josef von Sternberg found the look . . .

. . . in one of the most famous film stills ever made. Rosa Valetti, Marlene's cabaret tutor, gets a load of Marlene's talent. Jo cautioned Marlene when this shot was made, knowing she liked to expose more than her legs.

Marlene, Hans Albers, and Rosa Valetti witness Emil
Jannings's descent into madness in a never published
still from the climax of *The Blue Angel*.

Meanwhile, Mrs. Josef von Sternberg posed for
Berlin fashion magazines like *Die Dame* on her
second honeymoon, while her husband and
Marlene made a movie.

Marlene – with Anna May Wong and Leni Riefenstahl
at the Berlin Press Ball – doesn't *look* suicidal, but Leni
said she was. "Svengali Jo" left for Hollywood two days
later to prepare *Morocco* and her new life.

Right: Marlene and Emil Jannings on the opening night
of *The Blue Angel*. She went directly to the boat train
and America, taking the flowers and cheers with her.

Lubitsch wanted her to look like this in *Paramount on Parade*, but Sternberg put a stop to that. Marlene sent this still back to Berlin inscribed "Vati Marlene" in green ink (*lower right*): "Daddy Marlene."

But Sternberg wanted her to look seductive . . . or vulnerable . . . or just beautiful on billboards all over the world before they ever saw her on the screen. The one below appeared in Garbo-land – "Paramount's New Star."

PARAMOUNTS NYA STJÄRNA

MARLENE DIETRICH

In *Morocco*, Marlene gave all for love and got Foreign Legionnaire Gary Cooper.

The *Blonde Venus* in costume for "Hot Voodoo."

It took more than one man – and a lot of feathers – to change her name to Shanghai Lily in *Shanghai Express*, Marlene's most successful Sternberg picture – their fourth.

Marlene's mother and Rudi met the world sensation on her return to Berlin in December 1930.

Marlene taking Maria (as she was now called) back to Hollywood with her in 1931. Note the brass band.

Marlene's chief sponsor in Berlin of the twenties was Betty Stern (*left*), who fled the Nazis for Paris. They reunited in Salzburg in the summer of 1936.

Mother and child in Hollywood . . . one radiant, one not.

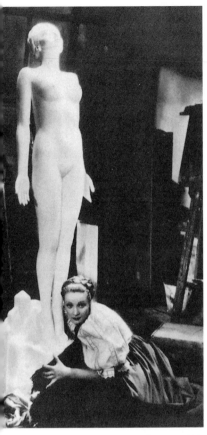

Marlene and Marlene in *Song of Songs*, 1933.

The perfect couple plus Marlene's latest
lover: actor Hans Jaray. Vienna, 1934.

When not trying to "bake"
Marlene, Brian Aherne helped her
study lines for *Song of Songs* . . .

. . . but Maurice Chevalier
dropped around during shooting.
His wife sued.

Catherine the Great in
her apotheosis in
The Scarlet Empress, 1934.

Marlene in *Fashions of Hollywood,* the
short she and Sternberg made to
promote their last film together, in
which she thought she was at her most
beautiful.

Concha with Lionel Atwill, uncannily
resembling Josef von Sternberg, in
The Devil Is a Woman, 1935.

same reporters reported. Marlene had been an American citizen for a whole week, and her calm was Mount Rushmore monumental. She posed for photographers as T-men rummaged through her thirty-four pieces of luggage. They scooped up a haul of diamonds, rubies, sapphires, and emeralds set in gold and platinum and estimated in value at anywhere from $100,000 to $400,000 by the I.R.S., who placed the jewels in escrow. Marlene and the shipful of gawking passengers at last set sail.

Back in Paris, Marlene collected an entourage including Rudi and Tamara, Maria, Erich Remarque, Josef von Sternberg, and Max Colpet, and led her troupe to the Riviera, where her presence was jewel enough for photographers and sightseers. That Jean Gabin had a home nearby was coincidental but convenient, should anyone want to discuss a script.

Days were sunnier at Cap d'Antibes than in Paris, growing tenser by the day as September of 1939 drew near. Maria found playmates among the vacationing Kennedy clan of Boston, and Marlene danced at the Eden Roc with both teenaged John F. and ambassador-aged (to Britain) Joseph P., whom she tried to dissuade from his notorious Nazi appeasement policy while interesting him in financing her French film with Raimu. Ambassador Kennedy had a well-known history with Gloria Swanson and contemplated a return to production.

Remarque wrote and drank Calvados (it became a leitmotif of his novel) and raced from the Hôtel du Cap each evening in a wire-wheeled two-seater, drunk and endangering his life while careening away from Marlene's admirers. Marlene dispatched Max Colpet to search for him in coves and inlets of the Côte d'Azur and bring him back to sleep it off at the hotel. Colpet usually found him too drunk to realize he was draining the Riviera of apple brandy in Cannes's merriest gay bars, where habitués mistook his drunken melancholy for an amusing parody of despair. Hopelessness was all too real and finding its way into his novel.

Summer lengthened in days of café society indolence and ruinous expense for Marlene, who was footing most of the bills. She was photographed in gowns by Schiaparelli, now with Rudi, now with Remarque, now with Sternberg, sometimes with all three, swizzling her champagne and looking bored, perhaps because she was never photographed with Jean Gabin.

A Canadian whiskey millionairess called Jo Carstairs lightened the mood by mooring her yacht near Villefranche-sur-Mer. Concerned by Marlene's world-weariness, Carstairs urged her to sail away to a private island she owned in the Bahamas, where she was prepared to build a palace in which Marlene could be princess of a court composed of nothing but ladies-in-waiting. Chief lady: Carstairs, in crew cut and slacks.

Marlene spent time on the yacht but stayed otherwise anchored at the

Hôtel du Cap. "Women are better," as her refrain went to friends at Billy Wilder's Hollywood parties, "but you can't *live* with a woman."

She was having a hard enough time living with the men who surrounded her: Rudi, Remarque, Jo, Max Colpet, and the ambassador with German sympathies whose son had such an unforeseeable and contrasting "*Ich bin ein Berliner*" future.

Marlene had not appeared before cameras for over two years, to no apparent outcry from film fans or producers. Only Charlie Feldman, still pursuing his odd notion of a Marlene in satin and sagebrush, seemed to care. It was that deepest darkness that precedes the dawn and the dwindling to nothing of the cash reserves when the telephone rang at the Hôtel du Cap and Marlene picked it up to talk to Hollywood. Joe Pasternak was on the line.

Pasternak had known Marlene *when*. He had never forgotten her in Berlin in *I Kiss Your Hand, Madame* or *The Woman One Longs For* (which he had supervised for Terra and Universal), or in her stage musicals, *It's in the Air* or *Two Bow Ties*, and certainly not that day she had received him in her *Blue Angel* dressing room, when she sat "shimmering like the moon on a cloudy night" in a peignoir that concealed nothing but ambition.

Now Pasternak was in Hollywood, at Universal himself, where he was the studio's top producer. He had made a series of successful pictures with young singing star Deanna Durbin, mostly written by old Berliner Felix Joachimssohn, now called Felix Jackson. Jackson, with whom Marlene had worked in the Berlin production of *Broadway* in 1928, was not only writing for Deanna Durbin but married to her and was sketching out for Pasternak—of all things—a Western. Pasternak, after listening to Feldman, told Marlene he thought she would be dandy as a saloon singer playing opposite young James Stewart, even though Paulette Goddard had already been announced for the role.

Marlene told Pasternak he must be out of his mind and hung up. She returned to her swizzle stick and champagne, where a surprisingly agreeable Josef von Sternberg looked up from *his* swizzle stick and said he thought it a good idea.

"I put you on a pedestal, the untouchable goddess," he told her. "[Pasternak] wants to drag you down into the mud, very touchable—a bona fide goddess with feet of clay—very good salesmanship."

Marlene was not persuaded.

Joe Pasternak was.

With nothing else to do but pay bills and wonder what the Internal Revenue Service was doing with her jewels, Marlene said yes. She was an American citizen, after all, and Maria needed now to attend school as far from Nazi Germany as possible. Rudi needed a job, too, and Universal and

Pasternak were willing to give him one in the Stateside foreign department, and maybe Remarque could write a script for Universal (he would) while working on his novel. It was mid-August of 1939, five minutes before midnight in Europe.

Marlene sailed to America on the *Normandie* ten days later. Rudi, Maria, and Remarque took the *Queen Mary*.

They were on the high seas when Hitler's tanks rolled into Poland. The world that had been limping along with a whimper looked prepared to end with a bang.

So—fortunately—did Marlene.

THIRTEEN

PHOENIX
1939 - 1941

Every apprehension Marlene Dietrich had had about her homeland's destiny was steel now, rolling in Panzers across Polish borders, over cavalry troops astonished by the brutality of evil and fate. Act One of the holocaust had begun.

She was down, not out. She had no hesitation in setting her course to her homeland-by-default and turning her back on the one she had known, as she had turned her back on its Führer. Which was not the same as having no regrets or fears.

She needed diligence to rise above them and luck to rise from the ashes of a career deemed over by those who deem such things. If catastrophe was the context of her times, courage was the best weapon for a steel orchid. And a sense of humor, no matter how gallows, no matter what. And if they wanted her in a Western (of all God-forsaken trivial things), at least they wanted her. She'd *give* them a Western.

Destry Rides Again had been Tom Mix's first talkie back in 1932, and thrifty, penny-pinching Universal wanted to recycle any old properties it could. Joe Pasternak had been looking for a vacation from Deanna Durbin when somebody mentioned *Destry* and then someone mentioned Jimmy Stewart.

Stewart was not a star then. He had kicked around MGM's casting department since 1935, fitting in well enough in *Thin Man* sequels or *The Ice Follies of 1939* (directed by Marlene's long ago *Bogus Baron* co-star Reinhold Schünzel, another Hollywood exile), and had even introduced Cole Porter's "Easy to Love" in *Born to Dance*, in spite of which the song became a standard. It took Frank Capra and Columbia to capitalize on Stewart's gawky sincerity and make it appealing in *You Can't Take It With You* and then stellar in *Mr. Smith Goes to Washington*, the latter not yet released when Marlene agreed to make *Destry*.

Marlene's getting first billing compensated little for the salary comedown to $50,000 plus a percentage of the gross. Still, it was $50,000 more than the nothing she had earned for the last two years, and the I.R.S. was still rattling her jewels in a threatening manner.

Everyone speaks of 1939's *Destry* as a remake, but it isn't really. Tom Mix's *Destry* was based on a pulp novel by Max Brand (still in print, still pulp). The title character ("a ridin', fightin' fool!") is framed for murder, goes to prison, and feigns illness on his return to the town of Wham (really) to disarm the villains before his six-guns start blazing the bad guys out of their saddles. The love interest was Tony the Wonder Horse, though there was a schoolmarm called Sally who seemed to have heard of the three R's, and Zasu Pitts did her Chicken-Little "The sky is falling" routine (here-a-cluck, there-a-cluck). That's *it*, and that Pasternak saw anything in it at all is testimony to vivid Hungarian imagination.

When Marlene agreed to play the completely new character of saloon singer Frenchy (originally called Angel, which may have suggested her to Pasternak even before Feldman did), there were plenty of scripts, but no *script*. Pasternak had inspiration instead.

The notion of Marlene as a dance-hall moll was to prove so durable it seems obvious today, but it wasn't then. Surrounding Amy Jolly, Shanghai Lily, Concha Perez, Madeleine de Beaupré, and Lady Maria Barker with cowpokes, teaching her to roll her own cigarettes, swindle at cards, slug it out (with Una Merkel) in the champion catfight of all film history, and not lose "Marlene" or "Dietrich" in the process was a box-office-defying gamble that resulted in the greatest single comeback in screen history.

An incalculable contribution to *Destry* and Marlene's comeback was made by another old Berliner, Friedrich Holländer. Marlene would sing again for the first time since she made Gary Cooper hot in *Desire*. Songs were a good idea, because *Destry*'s plot actually gave her little to do. Pasternak and Felix Jackson weren't hard to convince that Holländer was right for the job, for they had known his versatility from Berlin even before his *Blue Angel* songs became world famous. For Universal and good measure, Frank Loesser (before *Where's Charley?*, *Guys and Dolls*, and *The Most Happy Fella*) was hired to rhyme lyrics. Together they provided Marlene with a popular hit and a second trademark song she could sing for the rest of her life called "See What the Boys in the Back Room Will Have." She got two others almost as good.

Pasternak wanted Universal to pay for Technicolor, but that was expensive for what seemed at first a dubious venture. The real color came from Felix Jackson, who had smirked when Marlene told him back in 1928 that she would be a big star one day. Then she was stealing *Broadway* by bicycling on her back at the front of the stage, but Jackson now admitted his smirk had been premature. It was Jackson, too, who altered *Destry*'s feigned shyness at gunplay to a matter of Jimmy Stewart principle: This Destry doesn't believe in guns at all, not even in corrupt Bottleneck (as the town was renamed), where sheriffs rolled in and out of office like tumbleweeds, settling mostly in unmarked graves. Not until he *had* to. Tom Blake, as Jackson called him, was renamed Thomas *Jefferson* Destry (echoing *Jefferson* Smith, who went to Washington).

A bunch of ex-Berliners and a boy from Princeton rewrote Western film history and did it without a script. So much has been said about the factory system of studio heydays that it comes as a shock to realize how many of the pictures now regarded as classics were put together by people making things up as they went along. Smart and fast, because they knew what they were doing and the audience they were doing it for.

Nineteen thirty-nine was, we know, the most fabled year in Hollywood history, contributing not only *Gone With the Wind*, *Mr. Smith Goes to Washington*, and *Destry Rides Again*, but *Ninotchka*, *The Women*, *Beau Geste*, *The Wizard of Oz*, *Young Mr. Lincoln*, *Babes in Arms*, *Dark Victory*, *Midnight*, *Wuthering Heights*, *Golden Boy*, *The Hunchback of Notre Dame*, *Juarez*, and *Goodbye, Mr. Chips*. Why 1939 happened that way has been the subject of countless articles and even books, but it was less a watershed year (things would never be so good again) than a culmination of everything that had been learned since Al Jolson burst into song. All the elements of a popular art coalesced at a moment of maturity—sharp and fresh, without cynicism or contempt for the audience (which explains many things).

Certainly it was a new, more mature Marlene who kicked up her heels in Bottleneck. Gone were the fatalistic pauses, the fantabulous poses, the fantastic plunges into glamour that had drowned Paramount and Selznick and Korda in red ink. Those strong shoulders even shrugged off Travis Banton: her wardrobe in *Destry* is just feather boas and cowgirl drag. Gone, too, were any rumors of a Marlene who held up production or pulled rank or star antics.

Production on *Destry Rides Again* started—with only forty-five pages of script and no budget—on September 4. Hitler was taking Poland as Marlene was taking the San Fernando Valley. Shooting went rapidly, partly because director George Marshall was an unpretentious old hand who found Marlene, contrary to reports, "just delightful, did everything she was asked to do. . . . Great woman." Cameraman Hal Mohr found her "just wonderful" to work with, but he made sure to set her lights in advance where he knew she would insist on having them, and thus heard nary a discouraging word about how *Jo* would have done it.

Still there was no script, no budget. Pages came in line by line and day by day, furnishing Stewart with the tall tales with which he punctuated the movie, little moral fables that began, "had a friend once, who . . ."

Felix Jackson wrote one day or one hour ahead of cameras for the entire shooting period, impeded slightly by another old Berliner in the Old West. "Remarque was on the set all the time," Jackson complained, "and tried to rewrite things." Jackson's resentment was tempered by awareness that they both were refugees and out of respect for Marlene. "What this woman [was doing] for refugees and for former friends or even *foes* was unbelievable. . . . I know scores of people she saved without ever talking about it," he recalled with undiminished admiration fifty years later. "She is a wonderful woman. I never thought she was a great actress, but she certainly made the most of being a woman in *every* respect. She made the most of Frenchy, too. That's why *Destry* worked."

Production raced forward until the end of October, when a second unit was assigned to enable shooting to continue night and day. Marshall received the last script page on the last day of shooting and wrapped at 5:40 A.M., dawn of November 11, 1939, Armistice Day for an old war and two weeks before Josephine Felsing Dietrich von Losch's sixty-third birthday.

The rough cut was one hour forty-eight minutes long. The final cut, one week after shooting was completed, ran one hour thirty-four minutes, or just fourteen minutes less. The picture was fully scored and previewed within the seven days used to achieve final cut, and opened at the Rivoli Theater in New York eleven days after that, on November 29. From George Marshall's first call of "Action!" to final cut and premiere had taken less than three months and cost $768,000, including Universal's twenty-five percent overhead.

It was just a Western competing with some of the best-crafted entertainments Hollywood ever made, and a blockbuster from Marlene's very first banshee howl.

No one failed to remark on the "new Marlene," including the ads, which contradict a lingering notion that Universal (or Pasternak, anyway) had made a sleeper and weren't wide awake about what they had on film. Those who did not cite Marlene's newness cited her "oldness," her return to the energy and vitality of Lola Lola.

They were both right. Lola Lola had been a slattern, but Frenchy, even with too much makeup and too many yards of tatty feather boa, is the most elegant biped where the deer and the antelope play. Frenchy need not, like Lola Lola, protest that she is an artiste; she has merely to step onto a stage, hike her skirt an inch, wink at the audience, and croon to them that they have a look that leaves her weak. She knows well *she's* the one with the look, and the knees that buckle are in the audience.

She croons, she winks, she widens her eyes, she sings through a smile, she presses her tongue against her upper teeth to suggest how tasty she finds the fun; she kids the song, the audience, her own world-weariness and throwaway glamour, and turns the Last Chance Saloon into the last frontier of good-natured sex and elegant nonchalance.

To prove she's just a regular gal, the movie begins with her voice singing about "Little Joe, the Wrangler" (whose "likker" got him "quikker" than his "tikker"), hidden from sight at a crowded bar until she turns to the camera and, rolling a cigarette, belts her ballad clean across the Badlands, Queen of the Barroom.

In the movie's masterpiece moment she takes command of the camera, the saloon, Bottleneck, and the picture. "Marlene Dietrich in short skirts, singing 'See What the Boys in the Back Room Will Have' on top of a bar, is a greater work of art than the Venus de Milo" was the sober assessment of no critic, but of the editorial page of the *New York Post*. It is one of the great moments of musical performance in movie history. This is the "new" Marlene, but it's the "old" Marlene, too, the one who danced and sang in cabarets and musicals for ten years before anyone outside Berlin or Vienna had ever heard of her. She trots out the skills of the professional that no director or screenwriter or composer can supply if they aren't *there*. It is personality focused by technique. It is also joy of performing, narcissistic exhibitionism (all great performers have it) *in excelsis*. Almost every musical number she ever did was in one take or two because she didn't need direction; she needed room to sell herself and the song, and here she does it to a Glory Hallelujah.

The "new" Marlene is introduced in a memorable moment early in the film when Jimmy Stewart tells her to wipe off the "war paint" sometime and find what's probably "a real pretty face underneath," a face she might think about living up to. It's as if he is telling her to wipe away all those years of Paramount artificiality and climb down off the pedestal, not to the mud but to the world of decency he represents. At the end of the movie, she takes a bullet in the back meant for him, and he holds her while she dies. Just before she does, she wipes off the last of the "war paint" with the back of her hand, the last of the old Marlene before he kisses her into the Great Beyond. The movie ends as it began, with a chorus of "Little Joe," this time sung by schoolchildren. Destry launches into another of his moral fables about an old friend, but pauses for "the likker" that got him "quikker" and remembers the friend who counted when it counted—Frenchy.

Destry (with *Mr. Smith* and *The Philadelphia Story*) would solidify James Stewart's stardom, but he credited Marlene with the picture's enormous success. "I believe it was Marlene who made *Destry Rides Again* a hit," he said much later. "After a week's work on the picture, I fell in love with her. She was beautiful, friendly, enchanting and as expert at movie acting as anyone I'd ever known. The director, cameraman, cast and crew felt the same way. We all fell in love with her."

That's show-biz talk, of course, but there were those who didn't think it was only that. Erich Maria Remarque was so alarmed by the chemistry between Frenchy and Destry that he sought commiseration from playwright Clifford Odets, darkly warning him, "Never fall in love with an actress."

Odets had been married to two-time-in-a-row Oscar winner Luise Rainer and already knew. He knew, too, that Remarque was pegged at Universal as a member of Marlene's Alumni Association, but the German author was not the only one jealous of the spontaneous combustion on the set.

Maria Sieber was now back in Hollywood, fifteen wise years old and uncomfortably nowhere between her father with Tamara and her mother with her Alumni Association and Sewing Circle. Fifty years later Maria told people who would listen that Stewart had made Marlene pregnant during the making of *Destry*, that Marlene confronted him with the fact on a dance floor in Hollywood, that Stewart (unmarried) walked away without a word, and that Marlene (married) did what women do who don't want unexpected souvenirs of romance.

The story was true or it wasn't, but it rang with the authentic resentment of a heavy adolescent girl so uncertain about her mother's affections for her (and for everybody else) that her insecurity would resonate for decades.

Maria had seen too much through too-young eyes, and the fear of another child, another *rival* among so many, may have been a projection, but the telling of the story signaled conflict between mother and daughter that would get worse before it got better.

If Jimmy Stewart "fell in love with" Marlene, critics did no less. Erskine Johnson set the general tone with his opening line, "Yippee-e-e-e-e!" Johnson didn't stop there: "Marlene Dietrich returns to the screen after a two-year absence to be hailed once again as one of the great glamour film stars of all time." The same paper was so enthusiastic a second review was filed by a second critic: "Here it is folks, the rip-roaringest, dang busted Western to hit the screen in many a day. . . . Here is a Dietrich we have long suspected existed behind that eternal mask of beauty and who now breaks forth with all the fury of an exploding firecracker."

In New York, the *Daily News* gave the picture four stars and thought it had "everything . . . Marlene Dietrich come[s] back to the screen more beautiful and alluring than ever." *The New York Times*'s Frank S. Nugent reported that the picture "has taken Marlene Dietrich off her high horse and placed her in a horse opera. . . . She's hard and tough and painted to the margins of the palette." He added, "Mr. Stewart is all right, too."

Nugent unintentionally touched off a small classic of screwball comedy with the Code. He described Marlene's singing "with quite the proper whisky contralto effect," but "she cold-decks a poker player with complete nonchalance, tucks her earnings down her dress front and doesn't bat an eye when a cowhand murmurs, 'Thar's gold in them hills.' (And where the Hays office was when that line sneaked through we'll never know, not that we mind it)," he crowed.

Wherever they were when they issued the seal, the Hays men were reading *The New York Times* when Nugent nudged them and now demanded Universal cut the offending line, even if the picture was open and doing land-office business from East Hampton to West Covina. Universal complied. This gave Nugent a second, Sunday *Times* chance to rhapsodize about the "jaunty, jocular, and rowdy show which seems to have snapped Miss Dietrich out of her long von Sternberg trance" and to needle the gentlemen of the Code. "We should have known better," he wrote. "We should have known you can't congratulate a censor for letting an amusing, if naughty, line or scene slip through." No matter. "Dietrich's return to the land of the living is the occasion we celebrate most."

Of all reviews, none was more important than the one in the hometown Bible. *Variety* noted that *Destry* "does more than jack [Dietrich] back into primary Hollywood constellation. It sets her down as a trouper with a wealth of talent for comedy and character delineation. Her work as the hardened, ever-scrapping ginmill entertainer serves pretty much as the teeter-board from which this picture flips itself from the level of the ordinary western into a class item."

Marlene had found her way home in more ways than one. She had in several strokes of performing magic reestablished herself as one of the screen's great personalities. Now all she had to do was live up to her revitalized career and live down Frenchy, who would follow her as Lola Lola had done.

Show business is always starting over. Phoenixes don't nest; they fly.

The best known Hollywood maxim is, "You're only as good as your last picture"; truer is "as good as your next *deal*," and on both counts Marlene was good as gold.

She had gone from Jo Sternberg to Joe Pasternak, and while the art of *Destry Rides Again* might be arguable, its success as an entertainment was not. *Destry* delighted everybody, not least exhibitors, who suddenly found "poison" had turned to an aphrodisiac. Warner Brothers and Columbia, who had deals with her they had been regretting, began dusting off scripts, but Universal's resurrection of her career had a moral claim on her services, and a piece of paper, too, thanks to Pasternak and Charlie Feldman.

Marlene signed a contract for two more pictures with Pasternak and involved herself quietly with refugee work, just as if she had never been away or toxic to anything or anybody. She played the Hollywood game of publicity in a less aloof style than on her arrival at Paramount. Things were done differently at Universal.

This time she was willing to be photographed with her aching feet in a tub of ice water as she cast her first American vote on the set of *Destry* in the presence of an election-board notary. She was tickled red, white, and blue to be captain of a baseball team called The Leading Men, which opposed The Comedians in a charity game (their captain: Paulette Goddard). Marlene was photographed in baseball cap, holding a bat, and hitting a home run. It was all a little silly, but did good things for Mt. Sinai Hospital and for Marlene's image.

Even the Internal Revenue Service decided she was okay and they had been hasty: she got back all the jewels they had confiscated on the *Normandie*, plus $23,000 she had *over*paid. Democracy in action.

The only place Marlene remained poison was, *natürlich*, Hitler's Germany, where *Destry* would not be seen until 1960, long after catastrophe had run its course. The films Hitler was screening at Berchtesgaden then were of tanks rolling across Poland, then Belgium, Holland, and into France and Paris itself. The French "armistice" in June 1940 demolished hopes anyone had for a quick end to the fascist march across Europe. It also ended most

European markets for American films as the moguls had feared (they had been contemptible, but right) and ended the career of Greta Garbo, whose foreign box-office had been vital to her success. Garbo, unlike Marlene, had no "Frenchy" in her. And, perhaps, no need for one. She retired rich.

Maria and Rudi were both safely in America, Rudi employed by Universal as part of Marlene's new contract. Maria, now sixteen, lived with neither her mother nor her father, but with the former secretary of crew-cut Canadian yachting millionairess Jo Carstairs. Violla Rubber would be Marlene's secretary now, a startlingly worldly choice as housemother and chaperon for a teenage girl, but Maria never had been, never would be, an ordinary teenage girl.

Marlene, the working mother who had taken baby Heidede to her own boxing trainer in Berlin to straighten her legs, was not about to let adolescent Maria suffer the humiliations of professional Hollywood. Mother, more svelte and glamorous than ever, was criticized for hiding Maria by the same tabloids that tried to photograph and publish proof of the teenager's excess poundage. Marlene could kill footage and stills from a Selznick picture, but she was no match for freelance shutterbugs. She had always assumed Maria would become an actress, had even pushed it, and knew the value of discipline if anyone did.

The presence in Hollywood of Max Reinhardt was fortuitous for Maria, if not for him. The theatrical titan was a victim of cultural and language displacement (and of Jack Warner, too, who tore up a five-picture contract after the failure of A *Midsummer Night's Dream* even *with* James Cagney, Mickey Rooney, and Olivia de Havilland). Reinhardt was admired and praised and shunned. He had opened a Sunset Boulevard version of his once great drama school in Berlin, and as a Reinhardt drama student Maria might become a *real* Reinhardt actress, working with the Sorcerer himself, as Marlene had never done. Maria didn't have her mother's legs or glamour or admirers, but she had ambition. She might never escape being Dietrich's daughter, but Marlene did what she could to discourage comparisons and allowed Maria Sieber to try finding herself as "Maria Manton."

Marlene's first Phoenix flight after *Destry* was *Seven Sinners*, another Pasternak comedy in which she would not get her man. (She got him in fewer than half her pictures after *Morocco*.) *Seven Sinners* would repeat elements from *Destry*, including songs by Holländer and Loesser, with long, lean Mischa Auer and short, round Billy Gilbert back again for comedy. The big set piece would try to re-create the gleeful shambles of Marlene's catfight with Una Merkel in Bottleneck and her attempt to assassinate Jimmy Stewart ("Don't call *me* a lady!" which might have served as title for this one).

A bar brawl (in the Blue *Devil* Cafe) would open the picture before the credits rolled (an innovation in those days), with an even rowdier fracas for a finale.

Tay Garnett as director may have been suggested by Warner Brothers' old notion that Marlene should remake his 1932 weeper-on-a-ship, *One Way Passage*. But Marlene's new mood and mode were cheerful, not tearful, and Pasternak dug up more obscure Hungarian source material, transplanted it to the South Seas, and hired Garnett.

Garnett was known for pictures like *Trade Winds* and *China Seas* with Clark Cable and Jean Harlow, typing him for pictures on or near water (he had been a navy pilot). *Seven Sinners* wasn't a sea picture, exactly, but it featured boats and the boats featured the United States Navy, and the United States Navy was eager to feature Marlene, however it could.

Seven Sinners is set principally on the island of Boni-Komba ("Boni" was Marlene's pet name for Remarque) not distant from shores on which Miss Sadie Thompson frolicked before getting religion. On Boni-Komba, the Seven Sinners (like the Blue Angel) is a nightclub harboring the talents of a good-time chanteuse, this one an inciter of riots and a threat to the Pacific Fleet. ("The navy has enough destroyers," a killjoy remarks.) Bijou Blanche, this blond heat wave calls herself, and in a moment of reminiscence reveals that she was once a convent girl in Marseilles who had the misfortune to meet a dashing young officer from Saigon. Following this *crise de coeur* and armed by the nuns with good advice and that *nom d'artiste*, she has remained undaunted, cheerfully doing her bit for the boys and inciting mayhem ever since. Island governors deport her at the mere downbeat of a sultry song. She has almost run out of islands as the picture opens, but there is a new governor in Boni-Komba unfamiliar with her blowtorch legend, and plenty of sailors to sing to at the Seven Sinners.

Pasternak saw less Sadie Thompson in *Seven Sinners* than a reworking of a Puccini opera he kept calling "Poor Butterfly." Garnett was a salty sort not much given to erudition and thought "Poor Butterfly" a fine analogy. (His level of subtlety was revealed in an earlier picture featuring the immortal line, "There's an octoroon in the kindling!") But Pasternak knew the picture's Lieutenant Pinkerton required Marlene's approval and asked Garnett to find "a big, rugged he-guy type with competent fists, plus sex appeal. T'aint gonna be easy," warned Pasternak, but Garnett had, as he remembered in his memoirs, "an inspiration."

He arranged lunch with Marlene at the Universal commissary. John Wayne would be there, hanging about in the doorway, where his competent fists and sex appeal couldn't be missed.

"Dietrich," Garnett tells us, "with that wonderful floating walk, passed

Wayne as if he were invisible, then paused, made a half-turn and cased him from cowlick to cowboots. As she moved on, she said in her characteristic basso whisper, 'Daddy, buy me THAT.' "

It may have happened just that way. On the other hand, Marlene may have been demonstrating the merging of actress and career, as "Daddy, buy me THAT" is a line from Somerset Maugham's *The Circle*, in which she had appeared on stage with Elisabeth Bergner some twenty years before. Marlene had entrusted her new career not only to Pasternak, but to Charlie Feldman, who had discovered packaging. Feldman was inventing a new profession (or a twist on the oldest and merriest one) which would eventually take over the movie business. Feldman also represented Tyrone Power, who was supposed to be Marlene's leading man in *Seven Sinners*. Darryl Zanuck saw no reason for 20th Century-Fox's hottest male star to receive "with" billing under Marlene at Universal. Feldman's client grab bag also contained up-and-coming John Wayne (still under contract to dusty Republic), and suddenly there was a package labeled:

MARLENE DIETRICH in SEVEN SINNERS

and for those with the eyes for fine print:

with John Wayne.

Wayne played the naval lieutenant whom "Poor Butterfly" gives up to the governor's daughter rather than ruin his career. (He seems to descend from a long blue line of Texas admirals.) Before she does the Noble Thing, she sings "I Can't Give You Anything But Love, Baby" and two new songs by Holländer and Loesser. One she performs unforgettably in a white naval uniform ("The Man's in the Navy") and the second ("I've Been in Love Before") in a feathered headdress and a gown made of sequins scattered on not much of anything, the first of what she liked to call her "nude dresses." Another new song called "I Fall Overboard" fell overboard before release (but is still listed in the credits). The three remaining numbers were incendiary enough for any number of sinners, nicely complementing the music being made offscreen by Marlene and John Wayne, and it wasn't Puccini.

According to Wayne's biographers, "He was mesmerized by her." Not only was Marlene willing to go hunting and fishing and drinking with him, but accepted the challenge of teaching him the magic of books. This didn't much work, and Marlene later said, "Wayne was not a bright or exciting type, [not] exactly brilliant, but neither was he bad." He remained not brilliant and not bad for two more Marlene pictures.

Show-business chronicler Maurice Zolotow had the entertaining notion that Marlene found in Wayne "an actor who was an animal, an animal of honor and dignity." Whatever that may have meant *off* screen, she needed Wayne's leatherneck masculinity as foil to her glamour *on*. There, her depth-charge glances worked almost as well on him as they had on Stewart in *Destry* and Cooper in *Morocco* and *Desire*. Her giving him up at the end of *Seven Sinners* diminished him, not her; she could live without him.

Marlene's jaunty adventures in the South Seas had no higher ambition than amusement, and the picture is the most effortlessly entertaining movie-movie she ever made. Her glamour was never so accessible nor self-parody so cheerful. Bijou Blanche is worldly-wise: to herself, her past, her future. She is human enough to be sentimental and intelligent enough to ring her heart with irony. She and Wayne are ships that pause in the night, but it's over when it's over.

Bijou and Frenchy are tarts with hearts of gold, but with senses of honor, too. It takes some slapping around in both pictures for principles to develop or take over, but they do, and may be the reason *Destry* and *Seven Sinners* were among the most genial films Marlene ever made. The theme was hardly new. It was Sternberg's notion of redemption through love that worked every time he used it (*Morocco, Dishonored, Shanghai Express*) or when anybody else did (*Desire*). The *un*redeemed Marlene (Catherine the Great, Concha, even Angel) almost never worked, because her triumphs seemed heartless. There was awe there, and grudging admiration, but no affection. (Garbo's audiences, by contrast, were only really happy when she suffered. So too, one feels, was Garbo, for whom Bottleneck or Boni-Komba lay quite off limits. Garbo might laugh, as the ads said, but not at herself.)

Bijou is the character that defined Marlene for the decade to come: tough but touchable, seductive but funny. She was a realist with scruples and a sense of humor. Joe Pasternak didn't drag her down in the mud as the other Jo thought (and perhaps hoped) he would; he brought her down from extravagant, inhuman heights and put her feet firmly on common ground. The humbled but game movie star merged with the bruised but gallant characters she played. Myth emerged human, and *Seven Sinners* was advertised as "Dietrich Rides Again." She never gave a more *likable* performance in her life.

Critics liked it, too. Bosley Crowther in *The New York Times* found the movie "noisy, robust fun," and Marlene "a delightfully subtle spoof of all the Sadie Thompsons and Singapore Sals that have ever stirred the hot blood of cool customers." William Boehnel, an astute, often critical Dietrich watcher, thought her "both devastatingly stunning and amusing . . . a really talented actress who at long last seems to have come into her own." The *New York Daily News* inevitably found her "alluring and more beautiful-than-ever," and to the *Herald Tribune* she was simply "superb."

*　　*　　*

Joe Pasternak was nothing if not an opportunist, and a good one. The fall of France yielded what looked like pure gold. France's greatest film stylist, René Clair, was in full flight to Hollywood from the Nazi squatters in Paris, arriving with a huge reputation based on *The Ghost Goes West* and his earlier French pictures *Le Million* and *À Nous la Liberté*. He wanted, oddly, to do something with W. C. Fields and Deanna Durbin, but Pasternak proposed Marlene instead and a script by Norman Krasna called *The Flame of New Orleans*.

Clair was an elegant fantasist, an odd choice to follow pragmatic and efficient directors like George Marshall and Tay Garnett. But Marlene *wanted* Clair. She was a lifelong Francophile, shocked and moved by the Nazi occupation of the city containing what she liked to refer to (courtesy of Remarque) as "my arch." She had just been approached by the Comédie Française to star in their first-ever movie, now cancelled by the Nazis as her other French pictures had been.

Destry's Frenchy had arrived in Bottleneck via New Orleans, and that may have suggested *Flame* as some sort of prequel with lace instead of leather. It was set as a fable about a wedding dress found floating down the Mississippi in the mid-nineteenth century. Marlene plays Claire, a European adventuress eager to settle down in the New World in as much luxe as possible. She arrives in New Orleans, captivates a suitably rich, doddering fiancé (Roland Young), but gets sidetracked by a roughneck ship's captain (Bruce Cabot). Her campaign to conquer New Orleans society is compromised when she is recognized from her red-hot past in St. Petersburg by Mischa Auer, and Claire impersonates a bad girl "cousin" she invents in order to explain away the uncanny resemblance Auer keeps winking at. Hence Claire's last name: Ledeux— the two.

The picture is exquisitely photographed by Rudolph Maté and lushly costumed by René Hubert. It has charming set pieces, including one supremely stylish scene as Claire sings and plays at the spinet a ditty about "the blush of May" (it's "sweet") while whispers of her past (not so sweet) circulate unheard by us through the salon full of whale-boned relatives and friends of Claire's groom-to-be. She is helpless to do anything but continue singing (sweetly) as she watches her reputation sour before her horrified eyes and Auer continues maddeningly to wink at her in memory of hot nights in a cold clime. She faints.

She faints often in the picture, as at her wedding at picture's end. This causes a commotion, during which she escapes to sail away with her ship's captain, jettisoning her wedding gown into Ol' Man River, where its discovery inspires the fable the picture "explains." The Hays Office fainted, too, or nearly so, when they saw the finished picture. Not only was Marlene up to her old tricks, but this director was *French*.

René Clair and Norman Krasna, who had worked closely together on the script, took rather different lines in explaining what went wrong. Clair maintained that "nothing was forced on me. Norman and I were completely free."

Krasna, who thought Clair "absolutely brilliant" and their script "ideal" (he never mentioned the four other writers who worked on it), put the heavy blame on the Hays Office, which went into fits over "the sex stuff." They pronounced it "dirty," and refused to grant a seal at all. Universal, Krasna claimed, simply dropped the middle two reels in order to keep the picture off the shelf.

It is hard to guess how those two reels might have helped things, as casting never coalesced from the beginning. Most seriously miscast was René Clair as director. He had doubted Marlene was his kind of actress (he had wanted W. C. Fields and Deanna Durbin, after all), and Marlene found him cold and autocratic even though she ran all over Los Angeles to find French bread and French coffee so he'd feel welcome. She thought him "not exactly one of the friendliest of men" and resented his treatment of the crew, who "loathed" him. This was a curious complaint from one schooled by Josef von Sternberg, but Clair may have thought himself above directing a Dietrich vehicle, and Marlene was angry anyway at having to accept Bruce Cabot as her ship's captain.

Marlene found Cabot "stupid" (she was still trying to interest John Wayne in literature) and claimed she had to pay for acting lessons for him to remember his lines. Clair admitted that Cabot was a mistake ("he lacked subtlety") and graciously took the blame.

Krasna's version put away *every*body. "Marlene Dietrich wasn't right for the picture" (he had written it for her), and, "I said to Clair, 'since you've got one frozen face [in Marlene], try to get someone like Cary Grant for the other part. Otherwise it won't even be talking heads; it'll be *looking* heads.' They got Bruce Cabot—as far away from Cary Grant as you can get. . . . He stands still; she stands still. But there's only one person in the world who stands still more than both of them. For the third part I said, 'Get Menjou.' And they went and got Roland Young. You couldn't tell if his lips were moving. Between him, Cabot, and Dietrich—three people who didn't move!"

They *did* move, in three different styles, never made coherent by Clair's direction. Marlene plays her double role, one beguiling, one solid brass (double roles were all the rage then); Cabot does his wooden Clark Gable imitation; Roland Young blithers about amiably like Elmer Fudd in a jabot. Also on hand are a fluttery Laura Hope Crews with an ear trumpet (warning of the mysteries of the wedding night, she counsels the Toast of St. Petersburg, "Be brave!"); Theresa Harris as a "now I've heard every-thing" maid straight from Bourbon Street; and Andy Devine, popping eyes and vocal cords in his trademarked bottom-drawer buffoon wallow. This hodgepodge of ingredients hadn't a prayer of blending, and didn't.

Critics might have been expected to line up in support of Clair because he was Clair, or just because he was a refugee, but perhaps *because* of the gravity of events in France, they were dismayed by the triviality of it all.

The New York Times asked, "'What, pray, has happened to René Clair? . . . The master has become apprentice. . . . *The Flame of New Orleans* is a feeble effort from one of the finest comic directors of our time." This was churlish but apt, and every American critic expressed similar disappointment. They had expected more from the master of French wit and style, and more from Marlene, too, who had recently seemed so direct, so appealing, so forthright, so "superb." Suddenly she was again "an enigma as an actress," and the picture a flop.

The Flame of New Orleans was never as bad as the critics thought; it had charm and humor and seems today an inconceivably stylish picture to have come from Universal. But it was inconsequential. It just didn't *matter*, and expectations had been too high.

Charlie Feldman went into action at once, snatching Marlene away from Joe Pasternak and shuttling her over to Warner Brothers to fulfill her two-year-old Burbank contract in an entirely different piece of work from an entirely different sort of director with a co-star not discernibly less wooden than Bruce Cabot.

George Raft goes down in film history less for roles he played than for those he turned down, and one wishes *Manpower* had been one of them. Raft had rejected as unworthy of him both *The Maltese Falcon* and *High Sierra*, the pictures that finally made a star of Bogart, and Raft *would* have turned down *Manpower*, he said, had it not been for Marlene. He had been fascinated by her ever since he arrived at Paramount as part of Mae West's baggage. Mae was fun, he thought, but Marlene was "the most elegant woman that ever lived." He had followed her around the Marathon Street lot, lusting. He remembered telling Gary Cooper, "Oh, Jesus, isn't that wonderful? Oh, Jesus, just once! I'd give a year's salary for one night!"

Marlene thought Raft was all right (after Bruce Cabot), and according to Raft's biographer, he got more than one night, for she moved into Cold-water Canyon with him, leaving John Wayne plenty of pages to move his lips over and Erich Maria Remarque with plenty to write. The sylvan mood of Coldwater Canyon did not extend to Burbank or the set (the one Benjamin Siegel visits in *Bugsy*).

Manpower was about two high-tension linemen who battle nature and each other for the favors of a clip-joint singer called Fay Duval, who has "done time." Warner Brothers thought it needed more voltage than Marlene and Raft on the marquee, and gave her top salary ($100,000), while giving Edward G. Robinson top billing and less money ($85,000). It was the first time since *Morocco* that Marlene had failed to get first billing, but she seemed untroubled as long as she got the cash, and Raoul Walsh to direct, and Holländer and Loesser to write her songs. Raft, who got third billing, simmered, seethed, and boiled over.

Robinson had already made the picture when it was about fishermen and called *Tiger Shark*. Unlike his screen image, he was a gentleman with a famous art collection he not only hung, but liked, and Marlene not only knew the paintings, but some of the painters. He thought her an "intellectual" as well as "the quintessential sex goddess. . . . She is rough and tough—and absolutely and uniquely and gloriously herself," he said.

Robinson also thought "Dietrich and I . . . were a stunning combination, and our joint presence was tough box office. Add George Raft, and you had showmanship casting. Bad—but showmanship."

Raft, quite like his screen image, got tough-guy jealous, not only about Marlene's art talk with Robinson but about his billing. Director Walsh, something of a tough guy himself, couldn't control Raft, who abused Robinson so vigorously that Warner Brothers was forced to file formal charges against him with the Screen Actors Guild when time lost because of Raft's antics caused the picture to go $200,000 over budget.

"Instead of conducting himself as called for by the script," the complaint read, "Mr. Raft immediately undertook to and did violently rough-house and push . . . Edward G. Robinson around the set in an unusually vigorous and forceful manner, with the showing of a great deal of personal feeling and temper . . . causing Mr. Robinson to wheel around and say to Mr. Raft, 'What the hell is all this?' In reply to Mr. Robinson's question, [Mr. Raft answered] 'Shut up,' and, in the immediate presence of [actors and crew] directed toward him a volley of personal abuse and profanity, and threatened [Robinson] with bodily harm . . . in a loud and boisterous tone of voice, [including] numerous filthy, obscene and profane expressions."

This is the kind of publicity a producer prays for, and the altercation (one of several) made its way into the papers, but not into the picture (though it did provide some truth in advertising. The ads read: "ROBINSON—he's mad about Dietrich! DIETRICH—she's mad about Raft! RAFT—he's mad about the whole thing!").

Marlene plays the chippy married to Robinson after she gets out of jail. Raft thinks she stays with Robinson only for his Los Angeles lineman's salary, even though she bakes biscuits for breakfast and gives up her job "chirping" at the Midnight Club. Secretly, she *does* have the hots for someone else—Raft—but packs her bags for Chicago rather than cause short circuits on the power lines. Her tentative departure for State-Street-That-Great-Street precipitates a knockdown and drag-out between Raft and Robinson on the high-tension lines during the storm to end all storms. Robinson is hit by lightning *ex machina*, but with his last gasp blesses the union of misunderstood, rain-drenched Marlene and loyal buddy Raft, who (it turns out) has been suppressing more than scorn for this babe with a song and a slink and a nifty way with Bisquik.

Raoul Walsh directed all this in a pedestrian but muscular manner, and allowed in his memoirs that he did so to escape his reputation as a "man's director." It was a chance to work with Marlene. It is hard to know what he did with her, as her performance is one of the least likely of her career, the kind of thing an actor does when seized by ambition to prove versatility or pay bills. She tosses off dialogue Lola Lola would have found coarse. When another B-girl at the Midnight Club (Eve Arden) tells her, "Fay, there's a guy at the bar for ya and he isn't bad," Fay curls her lip around a cigarette and snarls, "He isn't good or he wouldn't *be* here." It's Raft, of course, whom she greets with, "You're so cheap, you're wholesale." When Raft slaps her around (de rigueur now in Dietrich pictures) she smirks, "Hit me again if it makes you feel any better. I've been hit before and *harder*."

Not by dialogue she hadn't (by Jerry Wald, the model for Budd Schulberg's *What Makes Sammy Run?*), and she had rarely been so implausible. Even her accent slips, but how could it not on lines like, "If I want to woll in the guttah, let me woll!" Her two songs are cut to one, and that is truncated to the last few bars of "He Lied and I Listened," which she growls as if announcing lights out at the women's penitentiary.

Staggeringly, *Manpower* got good reviews when it opened nationwide on the Fourth of July to big business. Perhaps the critics were just amused, as was *The New Yorker*, which viewed Marlene as "a tragic article . . . a type to upset any of the public utilities." *Variety* thought she played "to perfection" and liked all the "racy action and spicy dialogue." *Life* headlined "Dietrich Makes Trouble for Linemen" when it named *Manpower* "Movie of the Week." Bosley Crowther in *The New York Times* thought "the Warner Brothers, like Vulcan, know the pat way to forge a thunderbolt," which was favorable or not, but Howard Barnes in the *Herald Tribune* spoke as plainly as the movie. "The trouble is that *Manpower* has a really bad script . . . Robinson, Raft and Dietrich are no novices at handling conventional screen situations and infusing in them a bit of vitality, but they are stopped in their tracks by the inanities of *Manpower*."

*　　*　　*

There was nothing inane about Marlene's performance; it was as vulgar as it was meant to be and centers the picture, but it didn't need her. (It was a natural for Ann Sheridan, under contract then to Warners.) It was cynical to ask the Dietrich who had just dismounted from her high horse to "woll in the guttah" as well, and we sense that any woman who'd go off to Chicago to avoid the whole thing *knows* she's in the wrong picture.

Charlie Feldman acted briskly to provide her with a more suitable role. It was one, oddly, that she had never played before on screen, though the very essence of her image: A Star. He provided a new producer, as well: Charlie Feldman.

Columbia's old Frank Capra–Marlene/George Sand project metamorphosed into "A Charles K. Feldman Group Production" called *The Lady Is Willing,* co-starring Feldman-client Fred MacMurray, directed by Feldman-client Mitchell Leisen. Packager producers produce packages, not pictures, and *The Lady Is Willing* was just an assemblage of Feldman clients trying their hands at screwball comedy without the antic writing that was vital to a genre now dated anyway. It put Marlene back in swank (and hats by John-Frederics) and played into, rather than against, the glamour she could project in her sleep. There was no challenge in her being a little ditzy (all those hats), but neither was it degrading, as *Manpower* had been.

Marlene plays Broadway musical-comedy star Elizabeth ("call me Liza") Madden, who spends a lot of Mad-Hatter money on millinery and finds herself with an abandoned baby she decides, in a fit of maternal longing, to keep. (This lady is willful, too.) She needs a pediatrician (MacMurray) to tell her the child is a boy (the Code again), but she also needs MacMurray to marry her In Name Only so she can legally adopt the foundling. Mac-Murray would rather find a new cure for pneumonia by researching rabbits, but is intimidated, perhaps, by Marlene's hats. He also likes the baby (played by twins, David and James "X"), who gets sick, but MacMurray performs an emergency mastoidectomy and the baby recovers in time to prevent Marlene's show-stopper finale from flopping because she has the blues. The baby gets well, Miss Madden gets the doctor, and the doctor (nuttily) gets to take a curtain call at the end of Miss Madden's big show.

Marlene started shooting *The Lady Is Willing* in August 1941, wondering why Fred MacMurray wasn't falling in love with her. Leisen lectured, "Listen, Marlene, Fred's so much in love with his wife, Lilly, he couldn't care less about any other woman, so you lay off. Just make the picture." She turned her attentions to the baby and again made headlines. She broke her ankle in a fall in which she tripped over a toy fire engine while holding the baby and protected him by executing a neat twist which was followed by a neat snap. She wound up in a cast and in *Life,* to whom Columbia furnished the frame-by-frame proof of the mishap. Cameras rolled as Marlene reeled.

She did the rest of the picture with her plaster cast or ankle brace draped in white satin and fox fur when not knocking 'em dead in what film historian Charles Silver points out must be "the most ghastly musical comedy in the history of Broadway." Her big song was weirdly but aptly called "Strange Thing (and I Find Love)"—no "Boys in the Back Room." (Holländer and Loesser were not on hand; they were not Feldman clients and were sorely missed.) It is, in fact, the worst movie song ever written for her, and she does it twice (once in the finale), wearing something silvery and bat-winged, topped with headgear that appears to be the Woolworth Building draped in bugle beads. On stage with her, several hundred chorus boys and girls with violins and guitars fail to distract attention from her song or her hat.

Director Leisen was in his element. He thought Marlene "the most fascinating woman who ever lived," though he was not much interested in women. He had once been costume and set designer for Cecil B. DeMille before Lubitsch made him a director at Paramount (where he had refused to direct "the most fascinating woman who ever lived" in *French Without Tears* after Lubitsch bowed out). Leisen never quite lost his touch with decor and clothes, perhaps because he was part owner of a famous Hollywood tailor shop. He had made stylish pictures like *Midnight* with Claudette Colbert and *Hold Back the Dawn* with Charles Boyer, both of which had scripts by Charles Brackett and Billy Wilder. Wilder so hated the way Leisen directed his scripts (though they were hits) that Leisen was the immediate cause of Wilder's forcing his own auteur ambitions at Paramount, with famous results.

Leisen was competent and stylish at his best. He could always make a picture *look* better than it was, but never *play* better, for he had no sense of material. *The Lady Is Willing* was negligible, anyway, and the picture's gravest (and most risible) attempt at drama is during Marlene's finale reprise of "Strange Thing." She sings through tears until MacMurray, who should be at the hospital with the baby, signals her from the wings that the baby will live. It's good-bye blues! and a big finish, with a final chorus of That Song.

This sort of thing didn't hurt Marlene any more than *Manpower* had, though her roles were becoming less events than expedients. Critics found it easier to sneer at minked-up mother love and screwy hats than they had at the nation's power supply in wartime. Some found it "lively, inventive, sparkling fun" until it "drives down the side road of banality"; the *Hollywood Reporter* found Marlene "stunningly decorative" and thought she gave "warm depth of feeling to her scenes with the baby." *Variety* mysteriously found "Miss Dietrich reaches new heights as a dramatic actress," but Bosley Crowther pegged it for what it was: "a very stagy exhibition in rather revolting taste."

Reviewers of the picture did not know or care that Marlene had undertaken *The Lady Is Willing* to retire an old commitment so that Feldman, now her producer as well as agent, could make new deals to finance her future. That future was irrevocably altered by headlines six weeks before the picture's release announcing that the Japanese had bombed Pearl Harbor. Three days later Hitler declared war on America.

Marlene's future could not now be in Hollywood. She, like millions of others, was going to war.

FOURTEEN

HOME FRONT
1942-1943

Wheń the Japanese bombed Pearl Harbor and Germany declared war on the United States, it was far from certain what role, if any, Marlene could play in the Allied war effort. She had recently been a German national who had a mother and sister still living in the enemy capital, with two cousins fighting on the wrong side: Hasso Felsing, and Jolly Felsing's first son, Randolf, still an American citizen, who would die in the Battle of Stalingrad.

Her mother's safety alone might have been a powerful inducement to remain discreet and distant from the war effort, churning out diversion, and many in Hollywood (including a future president of the United States) did little more. Her passion for Germany and hatred of what the Third Reich had done to it compelled a less practical, more perilous course: to help end the war and the Reich as soon as possible, whatever the personal cost.

There was no USO (United Service Organization) on the "day of infamy" nor yet a Hollywood Canteen to provide entertainment and a home away from home and the battlefield for the armed services. Marlene's background in cabaret, musical comedy, her apprenticeship in Wedekind, Shakespeare, and Shaw—not to mention the violin and the singing saw—had been so neatly expunged from her past by publicity machinery that few thought of her as a live entertainer, not even Hollywood's old Berliners, who had forgotten or never really knew. As Niven Busch had noted in *Time*, she was "the distilled essence of a Movie Actress," not—in the public mind anyway—a trouper or a trooper.

But she was. She always had been. She had fought her way up from the orchestra pit and that energy and determination did not desert her now. On the day Hitler declared war on America, the Hollywood Victory Committee was formed "to enlist the movie industry's help in entertaining the armed forces and in supporting the war effort." Clark Gable was named head of the Screen Actors' Division of the hastily formed group, and its first meeting took place on December 22 in the same ballroom of the Beverly Wilshire Hotel in which Marlene had made her sensational Hollywood debut a dozen years before. She was there this time for organizing the selling of war bonds. The next day she, Judy Garland, and others appeared on radio's *Treasury Hour* to promote them, and within a month Gable's wife, Carole Lombard, became Hollywood's first casualty, dead in a plane crash returning from a bond rally in her home state of Indiana. Suddenly, the war seemed real.

Hollywood's signing up was swift when it came, but shamefully overdue. Hitler had goose-stepped across Europe, west to France and east to Russia, for two years during which Hollywood and Congress draped themselves in flags, playing to isolationists and the moguls' fear of offending markets and madmen.

Until only weeks before Pearl Harbor, the House Un-American Activities Committee (HUAC) had been in Hollywood doggedly investigating violations of the Neutrality Act, identifying persons (or studios) "inciting to war" or those it labeled "premature anti-fascists," a phrase that would turn poisonous in the mouth of Senator Joseph McCarthy when he later rode the same committee to vainglory and disgrace.

They had tried to block or defuse pictures like Alfred Hitchcock's *Foreign Correspondent* with Joel McCrea, which ended with McCrea's stirring blackout broadcast: "The lights have gone out in Europe! Hang on to your lights, America—they're the only lights still on in the world!"

Not in Hollywood, they weren't, where HUAC investigated Shirley Temple in 1938 as a possible Communist agent, where Bette Davis and Miriam Hopkins were denounced for belonging to "The League of Women Shoppers" (of which neither had ever heard), where Chaplin was almost prevented from making *The Great Dictator* at all. Even *That Hamilton Woman* aroused congressional hackles as Heathcliff and Scarlett O'Hara seemed to be goading America to aid an ally in some Alexander Korda kitsch about Lord Nelson, Lady Hamilton, and Trafalgar.

At the same time, every commissary in Hollywood (and coffee shop on Broadway) was full of refugees who had barely escaped with their lives, only to receive papers stamped "Enemy Alien." Without the tenacious efforts of the European Film Fund, few of the writer-refugees (most badly hurt because most dependent on language) would have been able to get jobs. The writers' bungalows of MGM and Warner Brothers now served as begrudged shelters for authors of world renown, surviving exile in Hollywood anonymity on $100-a-week charity or guilt contracts. Most such contracts were wheedled by Lubitsch and agent Paul Kohner, with the help of Salka Viertel, William Dieterle, Walter Reisch, Billy Wilder, Reinhardt's producer son Gottfried, and others. Among them was Curtis Bernhardt, Marlene's *The Woman One Longs For* director, who had once applied for refugee help himself from Josef von Sternberg and been imperiously rejected with "as *what?*"

When Marlene made *Manpower* at Warner Brothers, Heinrich Mann, the now seventy-year-old author of *The Blue Angel*, was on the same lot, eking out $125 a week while his refugee wife drank herself to death and brother Thomas avoided Hollywood altogether by writing *Dr. Faustus* in Santa Monica.

Marlene had been discreetly part of private refugee funding since Paris of 1933, since her first contact with the German exiles about whom Remarque was still writing in *Arch of Triumph*. Marlene had known most of the German and French refugees in Europe; many had arrived in America on tickets she provided, for which gratitude was not the inevitable result.

One of these was Rudi's friend and Maria's godfather, Rudolf Forster, who had emigrated to America with the help of Lubitsch and Marlene. Forster was cast as a Nazi diplomat by Otto Preminger (a refugee from Vienna) in the Broadway production of Clare Booth Luce's *Margin for Error*. Unhappy about his billing, Forster walked out, leaving a note for Preminger that read, "I'm going home to rejoin Adolf." Preminger took over Forster's role, beginning a famous secondary career playing Nazis. Back in Berlin Forster reclaimed his star billing: The mother of his godchild never forgave him.

In the *Vaterland*, even as Remarque wrote of darkness over Europe, his youngest sister, Elfriede, involved herself with a group of dissident students in Munich—"premature anti-fascists"—in the very "capital of the Movement," as Hitler liked to think of the city. She let it be known she believed a German victory neither inevitable nor desirable, causing a court to rule she was un-German. They beheaded her.

Marlene was selling war bonds, on the radio and in person, before America was mobilized. She made four nationwide tours, becoming Hollywood's champion bond salesperson, leaving runners-up Rosalind Russell and Linda Darnell in her glamorous dust. She received a Treasury Department citation presented by Governor Olson of California and accepted it on condition that the governor, too, buy a bond. He did as he was told.

She sold bonds at rallies, on street corners, and in bars from coast to coast, while Rudi and Remarque had an 8:00 P.M. nightly curfew imposed on them in California as enemy aliens. She sat on the laps of drunks in nightclubs to keep them in their seats while Treasury agents called a bank hot line to make sure their checks would clear. When these nocturnal excursions came to the attention of Franklin Delano Roosevelt, he summoned her to the White House in the middle of the night to lecture her on propriety. "I hear what you're doing to sell bonds, and we're grateful to you for it," the president said. "But I won't allow this sort of prostitution technique. You will henceforth no longer appear in nightclubs. That is an order." *She* did as *she* was told.

But she had bills to pay and back taxes (again), she was informed by the T-men who escorted her as she sold bonds for them. Charlie Feldman was less concerned than FDR with propriety and sent her back to the saloon.

The saloon was at Universal, where Feldman made another deal. The projects were as undistinguished as anything she had ever made in Vienna or Berlin. It didn't matter. Money mattered: The warrior in her needed it as much as the war needed warriors.

It was two more pictures, both with John Wayne and with Randolph Scott, another Feldman client. Feldman was producer on both films; Marlene liked and trusted him. She liked and trusted his wife, too, one-time Ziegfeld showgirl Jean Howard, for whom Louis B. Mayer considered ending it all when she rejected him in favor of marriage to an agent. Feldman, almost as much as Pasternak, had put Marlene back on top with *Destry* and had kept her going through four more pictures until war broke out. He made Marlene's deals and produced her pictures and paid her bills and taxes and handled the occasional lawsuit and saw to it that income had some fleeting acquaintance with outgo. "I never remember writing a check," Marlene recalled gratefully, if carelessly. Feldman wasn't an artist like Jo, or a showman like Joe, but "he was a wonderful agent." What he needed to be was a wonderful producer.

Before the smoke cleared at Pearl Harbor, Marlene lumbered with Wayne and Scott to California's resort-y Lake Arrowhead in January 1942. They slogged through the fourth remake of Rex Beach's *The Spoilers*, the old reliable about tough guys who jump claims (and tough gals) in Alaska, a story reduced in significance every time it got made (it would be made again in the fifties) to the ever-bigger brawl at the end. By the time Marlene made it there was hardly anything else, except her gold Gay Nineties wig. She announces to customers of her Nome gin mill, "We have no brawls here, gentlemen, unless they're over me," but she had been in better brawls and better pictures.

The Spoilers was only "worthy of the attention of those who like this stuff," sniffed the *Daily News*, but Marlene delivered "double entendres nearly as frankly cut as [her] gowns," *The New York Times* reported. *Time* thought it in "a great Hollywood tradition . . . the sturdiest of melodramas." It wasn't; it was just a programmer gussied up by Marlene as Mother Lode of the Klondike. It made money in the hinterlands and bought Marlene time to sell bonds and visit hospitals and military bases with comedians like Groucho Marx and the Ritz Brothers. The comics told jokes and Marlene sang "The Man's in the Navy" from *Seven Sinners* or changed it to "The Man's in the Army" or "The Man's a Marine" if he was.

She went in wartime secrecy to the desert village of Indio to work up an army camp show. She had not performed on a live stage since *Two Bow Ties* in Berlin, but desert sessions in relentless heat and merciless sun would evolve, she hoped, into something for the boys. The boys hoped so, too.

By August she was back before cameras, again with John Wayne and Randolph Scott, in *Pittsburgh*, a stars-and-stripes saga of men, mines, and a girl. Pittsburgh is not only the picture's locale, but the Wayne character's he-man nickname. Scott was called Cash, and Marlene Countess until she turns out to be Hunky. John Wayne kept telling everyone, "I love ya, baby, I love ya." His affections were not to be trusted, as he played the villain (and got third billing), but Hunky turns him red, white, and true blue by the end.

She wears a lot of soot in a story narrated by Frank Craven, who tells us about life in Pittsburgh as he had recently told Broadway about life in *Our Town* playing the stage manager. *Our Town* may have inspired the movie's narration (so may *Citizen Kane*), but not much else. Marlene pulls coal, steel, and titans of industry together, persuading them to put aside brawling over her hunky self so that Pittsburgh and Cash (Universal symbolism) can fight the enemy instead of each other. Marlene didn't sing, but the sound track was noisy enough without her, counting off the gritty decades (and reels) with yesterday's hits and (for some reason) endless choruses of "Garden in the Rain." Jukebox music for a jukebox movie: Yankee Doodle Dietrich.

Critics treated it with the dignity it deserved, *The New York Times* calling it "lusty and totally synthetic" and *The New Yorker* summing up its attractions with, "It's getting so you know that where Marlene Dietrich turns up . . . there's bound to be a brawl." The *Herald Tribune* chimed wickedly faint praise with "the acting is the best feature of the film," adding that Marlene appeared "fetchingly seductive whether garbed in evening clothes or covered with coal dust."

Pittsburgh was patriotic, but the kind of picture that anyone could have made and *did*. Once Marlene's disasters had been noteworthy; now her hits were just something to fill the bill. Once a Reich had offered her its treasure; now she was just resident glamour girl in the San Fernando Valley, where Abbott and Costello reigned as Kings of the Lot, attended by ghouls-turned-court-jesters Boris Karloff and Bela Lugosi.

She wasn't getting any younger, either.

She was forty. More. She had turned forty just after Pearl Harbor, and though Hollywood and those who kept track of time and its threat to big movie stardom thought she was five, or maybe three years younger than that, it still made her older than Bette Davis, Katharine Hepburn, Joan Crawford, Paulette Goddard, Joan or Constance Bennett, Ginger Rogers, and retired Garbo. There was a whole new generation of Lana Turners, Rita Hayworths, Hedy Lamarrs, Betty Grables, and Gene Tierneys ready to challenge her in freshness and allure. *Morocco* would have been laughed off the screen just a decade after it created a sensation, and *was*, in *Road to Morocco* with Bing Crosby, Bob Hope, and Dorothy Lamour.

"Of course, I'm going to quit working," she told a reporter before war broke out. "I want a chance really to see a bit of life before I die. . . . A film star's career . . . can last only as long as one's youth lasts, and one's youth fades far quicker on the screen than on the stage. The public can be fooled on the stage, but never on the screen—and I'm going to quit while I'm still at the top."

But she wasn't *at* the top anymore, and it was hard to miss that hint about the stage. It is surprising that, until *The Lady Is Willing*, no one had thought of Marlene on screen as a musical comedy performer. The idea had been on offscreen minds for years. There had been those rumors of a Broadway *Merry Widow*, and Cole Porter, Irving Berlin, Mike Todd, and the Shubert theatrical organization had all approached her at one time or another.

She was actually announced on Broadway as the blackmailing adventuress, Mrs. Cheveley, in Oscar Wilde's *An Ideal Husband* for the fall of 1942, but *Pittsburgh* and war bond sales happened instead. *Seven Sinners'* Bijou inspired producer Cheryl Crawford and composer Vernon Duke with the notion of Marlene as a musical *Sadie Thompson*, but she declined. Kurt Weill, who had written songs for her in Paris that she never sang, mentioned (out of school) something he was working on with Moss Hart for Marlene's good friend Katharine Cornell. It was turning out to have musical and glamour demands the Great Lady of the American Theater was too stately to deliver, but Marlene showed no interest and Gertrude Lawrence, instead, made Broadway history in *Lady in the Dark*.

Weill was haunted by the sound of Marlene's voice (and its echoes of Berlin), and his failure to write successfully to her measure goaded him. (She claimed his "Surabaya Jonny" was her favorite song, though she never recorded it.) He approached her with another musical idea, again with Cheryl Crawford as producer. This time Marlene said yes. It was based on a Victorian novella called *The Tinted Venus*, and Weill wanted to call the musical *Love in a Mist*. That sounded too romantic, so librettists Sam and Bella Spewack (who had written *Boy Meets Girl* about those screenwriters offered $2,000 a week to "save Dietrich") changed the title to *One Touch of Venus*, which sounded more Broadway and more Marlene, too.

Weill began writing his score (with lyrics by Ogden Nash), and Mainbocher designed filmy, floaty costumes for Marlene as a statue of Venus that comes to life in a Manhattan department store and falls in love with a barber. Pedestal to tonsorial parlor.

Meanwhile, for cash and country, Marlene made one more picture for Feldman and Universal, one of the all-star war-effort grab bags every studio made, this one called *Follow the Boys*. The picture had a plot starring George Raft, as a hoofer with an ego, married to Vera Zorina, who is too miffed by his conceit to tell him she's pregnant. Raft goes off to entertain the troops, learns humility, gets torpedoed in the Pacific, and Zorina becomes the symbol of motherhood for the USO, or that part of it under contract to Universal or Charlie Feldman.

Sophie Tucker, the Andrews Sisters, Donald O'Conner, and Slapsie Maxie Rosenbloom did turns. Jeanette MacDonald sang "Beyond the Blue Horizon," Dinah Shore introduced the unkillable "I'll Walk Alone," the Delta Rhythm Boys hymned "The House I Live In," Artur Rubinstein teased "Liebestraum" from the ivories, and W. C. Fields did his poolroom routine. But what wit the picture had came from Marlene and Hollywood's latest and noisiest boy wonder, Orson Welles, as the Magician. Welles proposes (with the help of GI volunteers) to saw Marlene in half, right across the midriff of her harem costume. Marlene agrees, but reconsiders once she's in the box:

MARLENE: "But, Orson, how does this trick *work?*"
WELLES: "Just wait, Marlene. This'll kill you."

The trick accomplished, Marlene's most famous attributes walk off the stage, unaccompanied by the rest of her. Her top half gets revenge by hypnotizing the wonder boy, who falls over like Charles Foster Kane thinking of Rosebud.

Bosley Crowther was not amused, calling it "cheap screen entertainment—and hardly a tribute to the players it presents," but that wasn't the point. It was a tribute to the *boys,* very low-rent, alternately mawkish and manic.

Welles had been performing his magic act for servicemen in a tent on Hollywood's Cahuenga Boulevard for some time. He originally planned to saw in half his spectacular new wife, Rita Hayworth, but Harry Cohn neither liked nor trusted Welles and wouldn't allow Hayworth to leave Columbia to aid Universal's (or Welles's) war effort. Marlene stepped into Hayworth's harem pants as she had stepped into Welles's life sometime earlier, diverting the press from his *real* relationship with Marlene's still married friend, Dolores Del Rio. It was a trio to inspire confused rumors.

Marlene and Welles were, like Marlene and Hemingway, buddies. She thought Welles "a genius" and he thought her "the good soldier of all time." Even if Welles had been partial to blondes (he wasn't, as Del Rio and Hayworth proved), his timing was off. So were the rhumba rhythms of George Raft and the lumbering lurch of John Wayne, though neither knew it. Marlene had left Raft with a photograph of herself bearing the injunction "Love Me!" (Goethe signed letters that way), which he kept over his bed for the rest of his life. John Wayne, having failed the Great Books test, was allowed to go on to Paulette Goddard.

Erich Maria Remarque would, too (he would marry her), but before he did he finally discovered the resolution for the love story in the Paris novel he had been writing all through Stewart, Wayne, and Raft. Remarque's refugee doctor and his actress-singer could not have a happy ending in a world "so dark that one could not even see the Arc de Triomphe," the novel's last line. Marlene was Remarque's Joan Madou in a literary sense, rather than an act of portraiture, but she was his model and obsession and suggests his mood and mind at the time.

"Never fall in love with an actress," he had cautioned Clifford Odets. "These actresses [are] so typical," Odets recalled his saying, "meaning Marlene Dietrich. He said such women fell in love with men with minds, loved and admired and built them up for that, but really the only sort of artists they really understood were actors." Remarque had laughed then and continued with gallows humor, "They hit you hard on the head and you fall, you are stunned—you don't know where you are. But next they are saying, 'Why do you have such a long face? That man over there, look how charming he is to me.' "

A "man over there" turned up in the novel, and Joan Madou rationalizes him and all her other lovers as "just restlessness." She believes (significantly) that one grows old only "when one no longer loves," but the author's surrogate tells her, "I don't share women I love with other men."

Remarque ended his novel with his heroine killed, shot to death by a violently jealous French actor, object of her "restlessness." In the novel Remarque scrupulously (or spitefully) avoids giving him any name at all, but the jealous French actor already dominating Marlene's life had a famous one Remarque knew well: Jean Gabin.

Jean Gabin had arrived after the fall of Paris with the other French refugees, among whom Marlene moved easily with her near-perfect French. She was disenchanted with René Clair, but that did not keep the *Hausfrau* in her from ladling up choucroute for the gentle and humane Jean Renoir, who was a close friend of Gabin and had directed him unforgettably in *La Grande Illusion*.

After that film, Gabin was so big a star in France that saying his name there was like saying Clark Gable *and* Spencer Tracy in America or, in England, Leslie *and* Trevor Howard. There had been no bigger French star since Chevalier; there has been none bigger since, not Delon, not Belmondo.

Marlene had known Gabin from Paris, and they had seen each other on the Riveria that fateful summer when Remarque got drunk and Marlene danced with Kennedys and yachted with Jo Carstairs. In spite of his enormous French stardom and reputation, Gabin was just a Frog out of water to Hollywood. Marlene had been seeing him there since *Manpower*, when George Raft thought (wrongly) his competition was Edward G. Robinson. Gabin's lost feeling in America, exacerbated by anger and guilt at not being in uniform to fight the Nazis, aroused Marlene's maternal as well as romantic instincts. He seemed to her both "an ideal being, the kind that appears in our dreams" and "helpless." She allowed the tough guy to "[cling] to me like an orphan to his foster mother, and I loved to mother him day and night." She entertained Gabin and the rest of the French exile community, shopped and cooked for him and them, drilled him on his English and became, she said, "his mother, his sister, his friend—and more still."

They moved into a house Marlene found in Brentwood. There Gabin hung the possessions he had been able to spirit out of Paris, which he cared about more passionately than anything except Marlene and France: three paintings that *were* France, a Vlaminck, a Sisley, and a Renoir (*père*).

Just after Marlene finished *The Spoilers*, Gabin went off to make a bad picture called *Moontide*, giving Marlene time to rest and recuperate from the rigors of their relationship. *The New York Times* carried the headline MARLENE DIETRICH ILL, adding she was "convalescing from an illness at the La Quinta Hotel, a spa in the desert southeast of Palm Springs." Gossips wondered if she was overworked, overwrought, or overloved, as the *Times* continued without specifics, "she has been there ten days already and expects to remain for two weeks more."

She recovered, and Gabin made another bad American movie (*The Imposter*) and no impression at all on professional Hollywood. He bicycled around Brentwood or stayed at home playing his accordion, staring at the Vlaminck, the Sisley, the Renoir. He dodged the nosy next-door neighbor, who appeared each afternoon at four in a floppy straw hat and sunglasses. The neighbor displayed fanatic devotion to the shrubbery separating the properties, creeping along and peering through for a glimpse of grass she suspected was greener than her own. Her lope was vaguely familiar, but horticulture was a previously unsuspected passion of the female Peeping Tom, whom he finally realized was Greta Garbo.

Marlene, never shy about nude swimming and sunbathing, seemed unperturbed by Garbo's spying, but Gabin was. He was jealous. He was jealous of Marlene's work, of her Alumni Association, of the USO. When Marlene did her mind-reading act in Orson Welles's Wonder Show in the tent on Cahuenga Boulevard (dressed in sequins scattered over fog), Gabin worked as stagehand, "backstage every night," Welles recalled, "loading rabbits and everything so he could keep an eye on Marlene."

One eyewitness account of her mind-reading act ("Oh, think of something else; I can't talk about *that*!") suggests Gabin had reason to stay alert. "When she came on the stage with that gown—she was really *no* chicken, you know—and with her *knowing* look, she just devastated everybody. The soldiers went insane."

Gabin went a little insane, too. He beat her. The "tough guy" persona was no pose; he used his fists when jealousy proved overwhelming. When she bought lingerie, he wanted to know for whom. When she went to the grocery for the makings of a pot-au-feu, he was certain it was an alibi for a stew of another sort. Her men friends were potential or past alumni, her women friends might belong to the Sewing Circle. Gabin was simply uncontrollably jealous. He was unhappy with his American films, with America, with himself. He wanted desperately to join the Free French

Forces and finally, in the spring of 1943 at the age of thirty-nine, just after Marlene made *Pittsburgh,* he got his orders.

Marlene took him to Norfolk, Virginia, where he was to report before embarkation from the port of Newport News. Marlene agreed as a token of fidelity and the future to keep the Vlaminck, the Sisley, the Renoir, as well as the bicycle and accordion. What she would do with them was uncertain, for she was pleading with the USO to go overseas herself. Her camp show had evolved into an act complete with musicians, a comic, and a girl singer (originally Kitty Carlisle, for the highbrow, serious stuff), and she was waiting for government permission to tour at the front.

Marlene and Gabin said their good-byes on a foggy dock at two in the morning, and he sailed for North Africa on a tanker. He hoped the paintings would hold Marlene hostage, that he would return to reclaim them both, for he wanted less to be Marlene's child than to marry and have one with her.

But Marlene already had a child, one who was now a young woman of independent, rebellious nature. As "Maria Manton," she had continued studying with Max Reinhardt's second wife, the actress Helene Thimig, and occasionally with Natasha Lytess, later drama coach to another M.M., Marilyn Monroe. Maria played demanding roles, though she was not notably slimmer as Manton than she had been as Sieber. She appeared as Lavinia in Eugene O'Neill's *Mourning Becomes Electra,* as Regina in Lillian Hellman's *The Little Foxes,* in works by Schnitzler and by Marlene's chum, Noël Coward.

Maria was building a small reputation as a serious young actress and was adamant about being more than Dietrich's daughter. She became legally independent on her eighteenth birthday in December of 1942, and immediately announced her engagement to British actor Richard Haydn.

Haydn had achieved celebrity in America in Noël Coward's revue *Set to Music* starring Beatrice Lillie, in which he had impersonated a fish. He was perhaps more suited to an aquarium than matrimony, certainly no likelier husband material than Coward. When Haydn and Maria announced their engagement he was thirty-seven, twice Maria's age and only four years younger than Marlene, who frostily informed the press that no marriage would take place "for the duration."

Haydn got (perhaps *wanted*) the message and went back to England, while Marlene prepared to move from Universal to MGM where Charlie Feldman had made a two-picture deal for her. It was short money, just $50,000 a picture, but that and the sale of her emeralds would finance the USO tour she hoped to make.

Touring for the army was complicated less by MGM than by her old commitment to *One Touch of Venus.* Kurt Weill had written most of the score and S. J. Perelman had been hired by producer Cheryl Crawford to rewrite the Spewacks, who got fired and went home to write *Kiss Me, Kate*. The composer and his producer went to Hollywood to play the score for Marlene, and Marlene listened, made helpful suggestions, and took out her musical saw. Cheryl Crawford was uneasy, even though Marlene had signed contracts. "I was accustomed to many varieties of eccentric behavior from stars," Crawford said, "but I must confess that when Marlene placed that huge saw securely between her elegant legs and began to play, I was more than a little startled . . . . We would talk about the show for a while, then Marlene would take up the musical saw and begin to play; that, we soon found out, was the cue that talk was finished for the evening."

Marlene had approval of songs, script, costumes, even the eventual movie deal. She cannot have disliked "Speak Low," the score's haunting hit song, but she hated the book by Perelman. She found it and the goddess costumes by Mainbocher "too sexy and profane." As the mother of an eighteen-year-old, she could not possibly degrade herself in such revealing garments. She walked out, opening the way for Mary Martin to become a star when Martin took *Venus* and *Venus* took Broadway.

Marlene's "ankling" of *Venus* was widely viewed as One Touch of Stage Fright. She had not been on a legitimate stage for almost fifteen years except for her military camp shows. To confirm the wisdom of a return to the theater, she had tested her voice for Weill from the stage of the 46th Street Theater in New York, and both singer and composer were satisfied with what they heard. Whatever her qualms about Broadway, her zeal to go overseas was greater, and she could not do both. She used the risible excuse of the costumes and the book to leave herself free for the more important work ahead, but she also had real anxieties about her eighteen-year-old daughter.

Maria bore watching. Only months after Marlene told the world that any wedding with Richard Haydn would have to wait for the war to end, Maria defiantly proposed to someone else and got married without waiting for anything.

She married a young actor she met while Marlene was watching Jean Gabin sail into Atlantic fog. The mother of Joan Fontaine and Olivia de Havilland had introduced Maria to Dean Goodman, a men's clothing store clerk and aspiring actor with whom Mrs. Fontaine had acted at the school run by Russian character actress Maria Ouspenskaya. The twenty-three-year-old Goodman studied there and worked as a secretary to the tiny, wizened "Madame." Maria had seen Goodman's work on stage and invited him to Marlene's house while the cat was still away.

Goodman was what used to be called a "congenital bachelor," but didn't know it then and found Maria "plump, lost, and beautiful in her way, which was not at all her mother's way." Maria was "very aggressive and very persuasive, for she wanted to get married very badly." The two took vows at the Hollywood Congregational Church on August 23, 1943, followed by a honeymoon night in a borrowed apartment which they spent looking at the lights of browned-out Los Angeles. Marlene's terse press announcement was "I wish them every happiness." Privately she exploded.

Maria had found a soul mate, not a lover, and Marlene's Hollywood informants told her he was homosexual or involved romantically with the ancient Madame Ouspenskaya. Either way, or both, Marlene was not going to be taken advantage of, as she feared Maria had been. Her Hollywood lawyer summoned the bridegroom to his chambers, where in acute discomfort he posed the questions as he had been instructed to by Marlene.

"Are you homosexual?" was followed by, "Are you the lover of Ouspenskaya?" The young groom later recalled feeling as much sympathy for the lawyer as for himself and denied both rumors, pointing out they might be mutually exclusive. He added he was in love with Maria and a more suitable soul mate than Jo Carstairs's ex-secretary, Violla Rubber. The lawyer apologized and suggested Goodman telephone his new mother-in-law.

Marlene was back living in the Brentwood house with the Vlaminck, the Sisley, the Renoir, and a woman Goodman calls Dorothea, the source (he believed) of the rumors about him. When he telephoned Marlene, she abruptly told him she would not support the couple and seemed taken aback by Goodman's asking if it had occurred to her that Maria might be worth loving for some reason other than her mother or her mother's money. Marlene paused, but Goodman was convinced "Marlene didn't want Maria to marry *any*one."

The couple moved into a $45-a-month apartment in Westwood, and Marlene had furniture moved into it from Brentwood. She surreptitiously showed up herself to scrub, scour, and paint. "Marlene enjoyed playing the matriarchal role," Goodman observed later. "She wanted to be the one everyone depended on." But *without* meeting her son-in-law, then or ever.

Maria continued her studies while Goodman went on the road with John Carradine's Shakespeare company. When he returned Maria had moved in with Marlene and the marriage was de facto defunct. He thought he detected signs his bride had ended a pregnancy and asked for a divorce. Maria refused. "My mother and father never divorced," she said, explaining rather plaintively, Goodman thought, "that way they'll have each other when they're old." Goodman doubted the Sieber marriage was a model he wanted to imitate and had discovered anyway that in spite of his feelings for Maria, he was not sexually attracted to her and both of them knew he never would be.

They finally divorced after the war. Goodman, who is still acting, thought Marlene's disapproval "may not have ruined me, but it certainly slowed me down as an actor." For Maria the marriage, however clumsy and rebellious, demonstrated her independence. And Marlene, whether she approved or didn't, was clearly the mother of a grown-up, and the marriage signaled, as few events could, that grown-up's need for autonomy. And the passage of time.

MGM had work to take her mind off Maria and finance the rest of "her" war. She was cast opposite Ronald Colman in a lavish, Technicolor version of the old (1911) Arabian Nights fantasy *Kismet*, and this, too, was a reminder of time's passage. Her director was William Dieterle, the one-time Reinhardt actor who (as Wilhelm) had witnessed Marlene's impromptu screen test on the UFA backlot twenty years before, the one Stefan Lorant so breezily ridiculed. As a result, Dieterle had cast her in her first film, the Tolstoy-on-a-shoestring parable, *Man by the Wayside*.

Dieterle always liked and admired Marlene. No one in Hollywood knew her from so far back or realized how long the path had been from UFA to Baghdad. He had seen the dream in the novice and saw it now in a middle-aged woman who still "carried her dream with her, and used it for a halo."

Her dream may have looked a little tarnished that summer to the dreamer. Marlene knew that expanding her harem bit with Orson Welles to a whole picture was a long way from Tolstoy. She wouldn't get first billing; she wouldn't even get star billing. Below-the-title billing was a low to which she had not sunk since *The Blue Angel*. Her *Kismet* function was to decorate the harem (though the Code wouldn't let them call it that), warble a few "oriental" tunes by Harold Arlen and E. Y. Harburg (woefully far from *Oz*), and provide legs.

With the instinct for survival and focusing attention on herself that she had displayed since adolescence, she accepted reality, hiked up her nerve and her skirts, and told Dieterle, "If it's legs they want, it's legs they'll get!"

"Colossal is the word for *Kismet*!" MGM crowed, but the word was *preposterous*. For Marlene; for Ronald Colman; for Dieterle's direction; for the art direction, sets, and cotton-candy color photography (all nominated for Academy Awards, along with sound recording). Most preposterous of all was the box office, which was . . . colossal.

Kismet is the old wheeze about Hafiz, the rascally beggar-poet whose "rosebud" daughter loves and weds Baghdad's handsome young caliph after a lot of similes and scimitars have dropped, all of it richly perfumed with that "desert poetry" to which Hollywood found Marlene indispensable ever since *Morocco*.

Hafiz, the Prince of Liars, had been a dream role for Otis Skinner, who parlayed it into an annuity on the stage and made it twice as a movie, once silent, once not. The "grotesque dream play" (ominous subtitle) had also been made into a movie in German in 1930 by the same William Dieterle who now dipped it in MGM's dye pots of glorious Technicolor. Dieterle, in the white hat and gloves he wore on set to signify The Director, set about conjuring up all the colossal trappings MGM needed to win the flying carpet contest of mid-war. *Kismet* outdid *The Thief of Baghdad* and *1001 Nights* in lavishing fantasy on audiences weary of reality.

Kismet means *fate*, and Marlene, like Dieterle and his wife, was an astrology devotee, loath to ignore omens. "How anyone can deny the influence [of the stars] is beyond me," Marlene said, an attitude stemming from her having denied them the day astrologist Carroll Righter told her to stay home and she broke her ankle on the set of *The Lady Is Willing* instead. Apparently the stars (and Carroll Righter) were positively aligned and fate, a.k.a. *Kismet*, would deliver. The stars MGM cared about aligning were those on the marquee.

Ronald Colman was brought over from Shangri-La and Savile Row to lend tone and distinction to the bazaar. It was hard to get much tone and distinction into, "Let no man make hash of fairy tales, my rosebud," which was MGM's idea of poetry, but Colman could give it sonority if anyone could, and it served as fair warning to the critics, too.

MGM and *Kismet* wanted their poetry to have oomph. That meant Marlene. That meant legs. Marlene gave them gold ones. *Life* reported in many picture pages how four coats of gold paint daily gilded her from hip to toe, taking hours to apply, inducing hypothermia (a kind of spaciness not medically understood at the time, but which may explain her going along with the gag), and removable at the end of each day's shooting only with wood alcohol, which turned the famous gams a ghastly shade of green.

The first idea had been gold chains, but they kept breaking when Marlene rehearsed her kootch dance as Queen of the Baghdad Dancers. (A euphemism: If MGM could not say *harem*, then *concubine* was out of the question.) Marlene's role—Lady of the Moonlight, Hafiz calls her when visiting the dancers' dormitory—had previously been a bit part in the romance between Rosebud and the caliph, a sort of Juliet's nurse in a burnoose. But Marlene turned her into a Baghdad sex bomb, wearing a lot of gold braid and nothing, topped not by a halo, but by hairdos that were twisted, braided, roped, swirled, and tortured around a six-inch cone set on top of her head by Sydney Guilaroff. These tokens of the hairdresser's art beggared not only the screwy hats of *The Lady Is Willing* but the minarets and plaster-of-Persia palaces of downtown Baghdad, too.

Marlene mainly lounged about in gold getups, snacking suggestively on grapes and looking at the star-strewn heavens (even indoors), perhaps checking out her horoscope. The grapes were only hors d'oeuvres to the daily diet of kitsch. For the first time since her silent days (the Dieterle influence, perhaps), Marlene went flirtatious, a mistake in a woman over forty wearing the heaviest, most unflattering makeup of her career. It wasn't just the legs and the hair; it was all that crimson obliterating her lip line and suggesting less a pucker than that she had just chowed down on a particularly succulent pomegranate.

Marlene's role was the big innovation in this *Kismet*, and one that "took." All *Kismet*s now feature what theater historians are forced to call "the—well, the Marlene Dietrich role." *The New York Times* described this role wryly as "an attaché, so to speak, in the household of the Grand Vizier," but she is a haughty and uncooperative one. The grand vizier (Edward Arnold, done up as a Baghdad Göring in black and gold) contemplates chopping off her head, coiffure and all, but reconsiders. "She's a gift from Macedonia, and we *can't* offend Macedonia"—which explains the presence in eighth-century Baghdad of a gold-dusted blonde with a European accent and a Harold Arlen tune to strum on her lyre. (The song was called "Tell Me, Tell Me, Evening Star," an astrological allusion—or plea.)

Marlene was supposed to be the kumquat in the Garden of Earthly Delights, and her dance was designed (by Jack Cole, who later choreographed it better on Broadway) to recall Isadora Duncan's stark artistry. Marlene slithers from one angular pose to the next, while the actual dancing is provided in cutaways by an obvious double in long-shot and veil. Marlene flings and rolls herself across a highly waxed palace floor in an attitude of predatory passion that suggests the Coney Island School of the Dance. This causes Ronald Colman to get hot in a tony and distinguished manner. Pulchritude, not terpsichore, is the point. The dance may be a classic of camp, but it is the only endurable thing in a movie that fifty years later is not merely incredible (grotesque dream plays often are), but as unwatchable as anything Marlene ever committed to or on film.

In spite of below-the-title billing, it was the Dietrich legs that sold the picture. They stretched from 44th Street to 45th Street, languorous and golden, on a Broadway billboard big as a B-52. Somehow they outdazzled the posing-for-a-postage-stamp portrait of Colman—tony, distinctive, tiny —above the title.

Probably the best thing that can be said of *Kismet* (besides its box office) is that it suggested to Wright and Forrest how much better it might be with Borodin melodies turned into "Stranger in Paradise" and "Baubles, Bangles, and Beads" ("Tin Pan Allah" someone called them) than it was with Harold Arlen's not-very-lyrical lyre. The blockbuster Broadway musical of 1953 suggests, as the picture did, that *Kismet* may be critic-proof.

The New York Times salaamed the film with a straighter face than most of the actors: "There's not much doubt but this latest production is far and away superior to the others both in lavishness of production and story treatment." *Variety* thought *Kismet* "a b.o. click. . . . Miss Dietrich's terp specialty and getup is out of the dream book but boffo" which, translated, is praise. *Film Daily* thought Marlene "definitely something for the boys," but *The Hollywood Reporter* lost its sense of humor: "The picture drags in only one spot, the overlong, slow-motion dance executed by Miss Dietrich, clad chiefly in gold paint." One unchivalrous but clear-eyed trade critic found Marlene "properly exotic, even though her age is beginning to show."

Time thought all the Academy-nominated sets "look suspiciously like the inside of a Hollywood nightclub"; *Newsweek* dismissed it as "Arabian nonsense"; and Howard Barnes in the *Herald Tribune* began, "Allah be praised," but ended in a huff, calling it "a rather lavish bore." Still, Marlene stretched out seductively between 44th Street and 45th Street and packed 'em in to see one of the worst Hollywood movies she ever made.

Most Dietrich chroniclers note some discernible embarrassment in this golden footnote to her career, but this is untrue. She is clearly enjoying herself and the only thing low about it was her billing. Dietrich actually *liked* the picture, and was known to arrange screenings of it for the unsuspecting. Her affection may have reflected pleasure at her reunion with Dieterle or pride in a hit picture. She may also have remembered agreeably that she was paid double: $50,000 for *Kismet* and $50,000 for the second MGM picture that never happened.

It's just as well. MGM's style of glamour was less sophisticated than Paramount's. At MGM it was mainly a case of heaping it on until there wasn't any more to heap. Certainly Marlene got heaped on: Never before and never again did she appear so hard on screen, so . . . *gamy*. The pomegranate lips, the condor-taking-flight eyebrows, the feverish filigree hairdos all served to suggest years numberless as the desert sands, so much trouble was expended in disguising them.

Marlene had long been notorious for fanatic devotion to her screen image (she was a Movie Star), and in addition to collecting dressing-room-door plates inscribed with her name (a habit spanning her entire professional life), had taken to collecting whole dressing rooms, or nearly so. It was as if she could invoke success by surrounding herself with talismans of past triumphs. Everything followed her from picture to picture. Her makeup table was a brass, light-bulbed, mirrored contraption from *Destry*; her writing desk a souvenir from Buttercup Valley, David O. Selznick, and *The*

Garden of Allah (she wrote letters for years to make sure she got it); the silver tea service an end-of-shooting crew gift from *Seven Sinners;* the cheval glass placed next to the camera, in which she mercilessly scrutinized the goods she was delivering to the lens, was from *The Flame of New Orleans.*

The professionalism was ritual, and *Kismet* hinted that ritual was becoming fetish. Ronald Colman thought it was and ever after told the story of their first MGM meeting:

"Do you have a side of your face?" Marlene asked.

"How do you mean?" he answered, startled.

"A left side or a right side that's better on camera?" she explained.

"Well . . . yes," he allowed. Marlene sighed, "Darling, you are so lucky. I have none! I have to face the camera."

"And you know," Colman said, "it was perfectly true, she played every single scene looking straight ahead!"

Perfectly *un*true, in fact, but Colman was the man who had agonized for months over whether to shave his mustache for *A Tale of Two Cities* and so knew something about vanity.

As did Marlene. The professional variety, at least. Since *Destry* she had been stretching and taping her skin back in a kind of temporary face-lift before the cameras, concealing the tape with wigs. Her makeup had grown increasingly formalized to replace the dew no longer on the rose and in *Kismet* achieved a masklike quality suggesting a face painted on a hat (or wig) stand. Partly this was because she didn't photograph very well in color. She was too pale and required a cosmetic palette to give her face the definition her bones could sculpt all by themselves in black and white. She was never one to leave such things to chance, on or off screen, and sometimes it looked like vanity and sometimes like she took no trouble at all. Many years later Mike Nichols observed that Marlene was the only woman he'd ever spent an evening with who never looked in a mirror once: "She didn't have to; she got it right in advance."

But now the hints that age was showing rang bells like knells. She was a hit in *Kismet,* but this was an end-of-the-line picture, a luscious freak show. Where could she possibly go from Baghdad? Only, perhaps, exactly where she went, without all the movie star trappings, with nothing but what she could carry with her: legs and personality, which turned out to be quite enough, under the heading "Government Issue."

For months she had been showing up night after night at the Hollywood Canteen to do something for the boys after a day doing something for MGM and Baghdad. The bilious green aftercolor left by her *Kismet* leg makeup caused Marlene to leave the gold on, hypothermia or no. The boys were eager for something to write home about, and Marlene was willing to provide it. Teenaged Roddy McDowall was then a busboy at the Canteen and remembered her gilded entrance as "nuclear, before there was a Bomb. She leveled the place and popped the eyes of every serviceman there, and not just theirs. I thought later that nobody in the history of show business had ever done so much with so little. I don't know if she was a real blonde, but she was real *gold*."

Many of the boys at the USO were no older than Maria, and perhaps none—in an age without television, video recorders, or even revival houses —had seen her in *The Blue Angel* or *Morocco* or *Shanghai Express*. Most of them had come in on *Destry* or *Seven Sinners* or later and knew her mainly from her hit record of "See What the Boys in the Back Room Will Have" or from the many pages in *Life* every extension of her legs seemed to inspire.

Her appearances at the Hollywood Canteen were not all the atomic visitations of a goddess. Often she appeared on the business end of a push-broom, made coffee or scrambled up eggs or washed dishes; or just danced with GIs young enough to be her sons and old enough to be glad they weren't. This was *doing* something, but not enough. Gabin was somewhere in North Africa. Remarque was in New York finishing his novel and worrying she might try to sell his love letters to finance her war work (she didn't: She saved them for later use). Josef von Sternberg had married his twenty-one-year-old secretary, his career reduced to making a twelve-minute documentary for the Office of War Information about the town of Madison, Indiana. Rudi had fled California's Enemy Alien Registration Act (which could have sent him to an internment camp) for New York, where rumors circulated he was working as a taxi driver, though he was doing dubbing for 20th Century-Fox. Maria was still overweight, still legally married, still in search of someone who wasn't Dietrich's daughter.

More disturbing than this diaspora was Marlene's sense of an American distance from events close to her. In spite of the Hollywood Canteen and Orson Welles's Wonder Show and patriotic or escapist moviemaking or even defense bond sales, she felt with a mixture of frustration and scorn that in America "one was hardly aware of the war."

On the last day of 1943, the day *Kismet* finished shooting, she packed up most of the life she had built for herself since Berlin and put it on the public block. Dishes, silverware, clothing, furniture, jewels, and a collection of 150 pieces of European porcelain went up for auction. "I needed money for my family to live on during my absence," she said, shrugging, and packed not dozens of monogrammed suitcases and hatboxes, but her old kit bag. She held back from the auctioneer's gavel a few baubles and beads (mostly rubies and diamonds she would manage to hide from creditors in a Geneva safety-deposit box to the end of her life) and the tokens of fidelity and future placed in her care by a member of the Free French Liberation Forces: a bicycle, an accordion, and paintings signed "Vlaminck," "Sisley," and "Renoir."

She left Hollywood for New York and what she would refer to for the rest of her life with astonishingly honest perspective as "the only important thing I've ever done."

FIFTEEN

LILI
MARLENE
1944 - 1945

If American plenty made the war seem remote to Marlene, it was contrast with the privations of a previous conflict she remembered all too well. Sunset Boulevard and Fifth Avenue bustled, but bombs were falling elsewhere. Her mother—if, indeed, her mother was still alive—and her sister, brother-in-law, nephew, cousins, and the friends and colleagues of the first three decades of her life were directly in the cross hairs of bombsights. *Hers*. It was a disagreeable irony: She could only save those she cared for by helping tear down the steel that sheltered them, the kind of dilemma— painful, principled—that defines conscience and the moral parameters of a life.

"I will not sit here working at my little job and let the war pass me by," she announced to anyone who would listen. The USO and the Office of

Strategic Services (forerunner of the CIA) seemed unaware that her father had been a soldier before he was a policeman or that her mother had married a second one and been a good general herself, or that Marlene could be too, if only they would let her.

She had a keen sense of history and her place in it and only rarely lost her sense of proportion. She had failed to prevent the abdication of Edward VIII, she believed, only because she had been denied opportunity and an audience. She would be denied neither now. Perhaps she had been wrong to turn down offers to return as Queen of UFA or even Queen of the Reich. Had she missed a rare historic opportunity? What if she had gone back? Not just to UFA, but to Berchtesgaden itself? "I sometimes wonder," she would muse, "if I just might have been the one person in the world who could have prevented the war and saved millions of lives." However exaggerated, the thought would trouble her for the rest of her life. "I'll never stop worrying about it," she said, and never did.

The USO gave her plenty of time to worry, plenty of hours, days, and weeks in the waiting room at 1 Park Avenue, where the William Morris Agency's Abe Lastfogel calmly vetted Stateside and overseas USO acts. A total of 7,334 entertainers would eventually be mustered in and out through 1 Park, but until they were prepared, vetted, censored, and approved it was mostly hurry up and wait, a formula of command and discipline not unlike that of a Hollywood set.

Marlene fumed at the delay, but used the time to pull her act together in a shabby rehearsal room just off Broadway above Lindy's Restaurant. It was twenty years and thousands of miles from the Kurfürstendamm, but the sweat, the cold coffee, the tin ashtrays, the air of raffishness and purpose made it just around the corner, up a short flight of stairs trod not so many years before.

Assigned to her unit as master of ceremonies was a young Chicago nightclub comic called Danny Thomas, unknown then but fresh and cocky from a four-week stand at the Roxy in New York. Thomas rehearsed with Marlene, teaching her his tricks of the comedy trade: how to get the laugh you want and kill the one you don't; how to keep cool before audiences wanting to get hot; how to handle hecklers; how to let silence do it for you. Rehearsals reawakened dormant skills she thought were forgotten while they tried to keep the act within bounds the army censors (and FDR) would find "proper" for the boys, nothing much spicier than the cinnamon in Mom's apple pie. Marlene had strudel in mind.

The act was a kind of American melting pot. It included Lin Mayberry, a hillbilly comedienne from Texas; Milton Frome, a Jewish crooner who could sing "Besame Mucho" and mean it *macho*; Jack Schneider (a.k.a. Snyder) a hard-drinking Oklahoman who did one-man jam sessions and played piano when there was one and accordion when there wasn't.

The act tried out at Stateside camps and bond rallies in late February, working out wrinkles in what were essentially auditions for the War Department. It was like going out of town with a show. On March 20 they premiered on the War Department's Broadway: Fort Meade, Maryland, where Marlene's "million-dollar legs . . . glided gracefully" across the stage of War Department Theater No. 4, accompanied by the 128th Army band.

Marlene wore "a long-sleeved gown of flesh-colored net peppered with dazzling golden sequins," a witness recorded, and played "Pagan Love Song" on her musical saw. She did the mental telepathy act Orson Welles had taught her, and twelve hundred GIs "whistled, howled, and stamped their feet," most of them threatening to appear the next day for Marlene's tour of the Station Hospital. The army had a hit.

Finally on April 4, 1 Park told her to report for overseas duty. She and the others boarded an aging army transport C-54 and rattled across the Atlantic in a raging hailstorm. Marlene had twice played aviatrixes on film, but this was her first real plane flight; air travel had been *verboten* by insurance policies on her films or legs. Only when they were shakily aloft were flight plan and destination revealed: via Greenland and the Azores to Casablanca, which (Warner Brothers notwithstanding) was never Nazi occupied, then on to Oran.

This wasn't the front, where GI audiences were grateful for anything they got; this was a tougher audience, jittery with nerves and frustration. North Africa was a holding station, a jumping-off place for the Italian invasion, stalled since January by bitter German resistance just across the Mediterranean. Here, on April 11, in the red and gold of the Algiers Opera House, Marlene launched her first offensive against the Third Reich.

The show began with Danny Thomas bouncing smartly on stage to master both ceremonies and audience, which began heckling with two thousand voices demanding to know why he was not in uniform carrying a gun. He calmed them down with a joke and a laugh. "Don't you guys know there's a war on? A fellow could get *hurt!*"

Thomas then made his dramatic announcement: "Marlene Dietrich *was* to have been with us"—news to the GI audience—but she would *not* appear after all. An American officer had pulled rank for her . . . *services.* Catcalls and boos peeled gilt from the proscenium. Then a voice called out from somewhere in the auditorium, "No, no, I'm here," and the rank-pulling American officer—Officer Dietrich—fought her way to the gilded stage in her army uniform, custom tailored in New York.

Once on stage, Officer Dietrich opened a small overnight case, withdrew evening slippers, a whisper of fabric covered with sequins (custom tailored by Irene), and began to change from one uniform to the other in riveted, ravenous view of four thousand eyes. Hormones sang Hosannas. "The guys *screamed,*" Danny Thomas remembered. He pulled Marlene behind a screen, from which she emerged seconds later looking like "every woman in the world they were hungry for rolled into one." Jack Snyder hit a downbeat on the piano and Marlene sailed into "See What the Boys in the Back Room Will Have," a rhetorical inquiry if ever there was one. In floods of testosterone and cheers, gilt cherubs blushed when Marlene unpacked her musical saw, sat down, hiked sequins-on-nothing up to her thighs, smiled, placed the saw between her perfect legs, and gave the boys a glimpse of what Thomas called "Paradise." Rafters rang. She came; she sawed; she conquered.

Later that night, after the dust had settled in the opera house, there were fireworks over Gibraltar. Marlene and the soldiers lined the Algiers water-front at midnight "peering at distant flashes which turned out to be the fire of Coastal Air Force Beaufighters shooting down three German Junker 88s and a Dornier 217." It was a final German attempt to repulse the Italian invasion, a vivid reminder after all the songs and jokes of why they were there.

Marlene sounded serenely soldierlike about it: "It was my first real air raid, although we had practices at home, but I didn't feel at all frightened. I watched from the balcony of a friend's house." She may have felt so calm because the friend was press titan Lord Beaverbrook (a fan, said to own prints of all her films) and she held hands on the balcony with a member of the Free French Forces: tank commander Jean Gabin. Their reunion resulted from Gabin's running into American army officer John Lodge, Marlene's dark-maned leading man in *The Scarlet Empress*, who told Gabin she was there. The impromptu meeting seemed a good omen for the future and was undeniably movie-romantic. Amy Jolly, lately of *Morocco*, and *Pépé-le-Moko*, lately of the Casbah, watched sea and stars and bombs bursting in midnight Mediterranean air.

The pattern of Marlene's shows never varied much and never had to. Another old colleague, Joshua Logan, happened unawares on one of her performances while searching out sites for jeep shows with which he was touring. "Someone said, you must see the performance tonight at this opera house," he remembered. "It was actually packed with GIs in full equip-ment . . . their guns, their canteens, their everything. And there was a sound from the orchestra and Dietrich walked onto the stage in what she calls her 'nude dress.' It had spangles, but there was sort of a pink space in between the spangles that looked as though the spangles were sewn on a nude body. And she held her arms out and there was an animal sound from these men that lasted five or six minutes. They just roared and *ahr-r-r-r-r-ed*, and it was a thrilling thing to see, because they really cared, you know. And she was just wrapped up in it. She just stood there and it held her up."

No performer is immune to this sort of thing. This is the incurable, essential performer addiction. No cure or vaccine exists and would be rejected if it did; the high is what they do it *for*. The roars and *ahr-r-r-r-rs* support and sustain, validate and vindicate. The hunger Marlene satisfied in audiences fed one in her that would, after a decade's indecision, determine the great final arc of her professional life. Now it buttressed the emotional commitment necessary to endure the hardships, fueled the energy to freshen the grind.

There was one change in her act almost immediately: the addition of a new song that was an old song. It had been written in 1915 during the First War, but got a new melody in the thirties from a dedicated Nazi composer called Norbert Schultze. "Lili Marlene" had been a favorite with German troops until its melancholy for things lost took on new meaning after Stalingrad, and Goebbels banned it. That alone might have recommended it to Marlene (if the title had not), but it was that rare thing, a song that crossed front lines as "Silent Night" had done at the end of World War I.

"Lili Marlene" was a man's song, a soldier's song about his whore "outside the barracks, by the corner light." (John Steinbeck called it "the most beautiful love song of all time.") It was a crossover song for a crossover soldier, and nothing more vividly demonstrated how Marlene's war transcended politics. She was an American, but she was German, too, and blood spilled was tragedy, no matter whose blood it was.

The complex depth of her commitment was revealed in North Africa in a dramatic moment quite without warning. She was making a radio broadcast for the Armed Forces Network to include "Lili Marlene." Suddenly, she burst into the microphone, *"Jungs! Opfert euch nicht! Der Krieg ist doch Scheisse, Hitler ist ein Idiot!"* ("Boys! Don't sacrifice yourselves! The war is shit! Hitler is an idiot!") A dazed army announcer heard her launch into "Lili Marlene" in German and pulled the microphone from her, reminding her sharply that this was an English language broadcast—for *American* troops. Perhaps so, but radio waves traveled far, and so did her convictions and sympathies. Music's reach was long, and "Lili Marlene" would follow her like a personal hymn to the end of her life.

It followed her into front-line hospitals. She described the experience for young Leo Lerman, then writing for *Vogue*. "I walk into a tent. It's rather dark in that tent, quite dark but with streaks of light coming in, cutting sharply into the darkness . . . . Terrific silence. . . . There's a nurse, but she's seated, waiting in case she's needed, motionless . . . absolutely no movement anywhere. There are those rows of beds. In them, boys are sleeping or unconscious. Next to each bed stands a pole, and on that pole hangs a jar—a jar of blood. The only movement in that whole place . . . the only sound in that whole place is the bubbling blood . . . the only color in that place is the color of blood. You stand there with actual life running from bottles into the boys. You see it running into them. You hear it. . . . The fact that you have to make propaganda to get it, that you've had to beg for it . . . that's amazing. . . . I remember all the big things and all sorts of little things—how those angel-hearted wounded boys in the hospitals would say, 'There are some Nazis over there. They're sick. Please go over and talk to them. You can speak German.' And I'd go over to those blank-faced, very young Nazis. They'd look me over and ask, 'Are you the real Marlene Dietrich?' "

She was.

The invasion of Italy pushed forward in late May. Marlene flew from Algiers to Naples, where she and her troupe performed twice a day for the Fifteenth and Twelfth air forces, flying in and out of service camps on the same day. On to Sardinia, on to Corsica, on to Anzio. There they experienced the adrenalin rush of entering in a jeep just heartbeats after the Fifth Army battered through the beachhead on May 25 to join defenders stalled since late January.

She was the first Allied entertainer in Anzio and sang on shell-littered beaches at two in the afternoon before hopping another jeep to follow the soldiers triumphantly into Rome. The liberation of the Eternal City, she said, was "like an Easter parade . . . the boys threw cigarettes and chocolate." She extended her Italian tour by two weeks, spending part of it in an Italian hospital in the seaport of Bari. She was not singing or visiting the wounded for once, but ordered there by army doctors. The persistent sore throat she had been carrying on stage two times a day, sometimes four, had progressed to pneumonia.

She received a special store of newly (in 1943) manufactured penicillin, and it probably saved her life. The drug's discoverer, Sir Alexander Fleming, earned her effusive and practical gratitude; she sent him baskets of eggs to supplement wartime rations whenever she could get them and included his horoscope, one scientist to another. Fleming in turn gave Marlene a sample of what he claimed to be the original culture from which he had made his then ignored discovery in 1928. She had it framed and later hung it on Park Avenue walls.

Her first tour of duty—North Africa, Sicily, Corsica, Italy—came to a stunning and dramatic end. Singing for twenty thousand Allied soldiers, she was handed a piece of paper. She broke off her song and read the announcement half the world had been waiting to hear: The armies of

liberation had landed in Normandy. It was June 6, 1944; D-Day had
dawned.

She wept.

Marlene and her troupe were ordered back to New York. Still recovering
from pneumonia, she decompressed by recording American pop songs in
German for broadcast across enemy lines. Such recordings were standard
propaganda weapons on both sides of the Siegfried line and put Marlene
head to head with Goebbels, who was broadcasting in the opposite direction. "Lili Marlene" sang of love and longing, while the Nazi Minister of
Enlightenment and Propaganda provided a more poisonous repertoire. Jazz
was forbidden to ordinary Germans as "degenerate," but Goebbels maintained his own private jazz band and it broadcast swing as far away as South
America until the very end of the war. Nazi lyrics revised American standards like Cole Porter's "You're the Top":

> You're the Top,
> You're a German flyer,
> You're the Top,
> You're machine gun fire . . .

"You're Driving Me Crazy" acquired a typically nasty touch in the bridge:

> Jews,
> Were the ones who were near me,
> To cheer me,
> When I needed Jews . . .

Listening to enemy shortwave in the Reich—even to music—was a capital crime calling for summary execution. Marlene's songs were meant for
broadcast and for loudspeaker transmission across nighttime battlefields.
Songs like "Taking a Chance on Love" and "Time on My Hands" conveyed messages of the heart rather than politics, and their power was all the
greater for absence of rhetoric and for the *Weltschmerz* in her voice: a
German making love to the Germans with German.

These recordings were classified until after the war, but in New York
Marlene took on other propaganda work, striking out at what she viewed as
the front lines of American indifference. The voice that crooned could
scold, even sting.

"The people over here must know that whatever we are doing will never
be enough," she insisted in a fifteen-hour interview she granted Leo Lerman for *Vogue*. She made a fashion statement by wearing her GI khakis
and Anzio suntan and lighting her cigarettes with a GI Zippo made from

airplane metal. Lerman found her "funny, with that baggy pants comedian funniness, that belly-laugh vigor which her friends adore," but Marlene's campaign against apathy was not comic. "There's something about an American soldier you can't explain," she said. "They're so grateful, so heartbreakingly grateful for anything, even a film actress coming to see them."

She felt gratitude of her own. The GIs had performed wonders for her, trimming camouflage tents with fresh roses twined through netting, painting road signs with arrows and "Dietrich Here Today" for passing jeeps and convoys, sometimes just an arrow with a sketch of gartered legs, eloquence enough. GI flashlights made the sequins sparkle when power failed, and one night an orchid—not a steel one—materialized exotically for a frontline show. "We were happier then," she would sigh half a century later, her voice tough and tender with old-soldier nostalgia.

"Of all the soldiers I met," she asserted, "the GIs were the bravest. Bravery is simple when you're defending your own country," but these were "lonely men fighting on foreign soil . . . [and] because they had been told to, had their eyes shot out and their brains, their bodies torn, their flesh burnt. They accepted pain and mutilation as if they fought and fell defending their own soil. That made them the bravest of all."

The second war was changing the woman in ways more profound than the first had changed the child. The goddess was becoming flesh and blood lover, mother, sister, schoolmarm, confidante, conscience: Woman in every sense. She called it *her* war and because she spent more time entertaining at the front than any other performer, male or female, she became a small part of its history as it became a large part of hers. It was a turning point, culmination and foreshadowing at once, allowing her to draw on the past while fashioning—quite alone—a persona for a future too distant to calculate, but one surely larger than Hollywood's compass could contain.

Paris. The City of Light was liberated by De Gaulle and Leclerc on August 25, 1944, while *Kismet*'s foolishness was drawing crowds in New York. Pausing long enough to replace Danny Thomas with Freddie Lightner, she and her troupe boarded a transport plane back across the Atlantic. They performed at stopovers in Labrador, Greenland, Iceland, and England, and arrived in Paris in mid-September to revisit "her arch" and an old friend. Generals had liberated Paris; a writer had liberated the Ritz.

Ernest Hemingway was covering the war for *Collier's*. He was still married to Martha Gellhorn, but Gellhorn wasn't in Paris or the Ritz and Mary Welsh was. He and the *Time* correspondent welcomed Marlene—the Kraut—in the rue Cambon bar of the Ritz. Georges the bartender made his legendary martinis and allowed cognac and champagne to flow, much of it into Papa—as Marlene called Hemingway—who had liberated the Ritz's wine cellars, too.

Hemingway called petite Mary Welsh his "pocket Venus," but the Blonde Venus was not impressed. Papa thought Remarque "worthless"; "the Kraut" thought the female scribbler with the chopped-off hair "stiff, formal, and not very desirable." Welsh more generously found Marlene "as sinuously beautiful in her khaki uniform and the knitted khaki helmet liner . . . as in the see-through sequin dresses." Welsh was perhaps relieved to find nothing in Marlene calculated "to glorify the air around her. . . . [She] was a business woman concerned with every detail of her program from transport to accommodations, to sizes of stages and halls, to lighting and microphones. Business seemed to be her religion."

But her religion was Hemingway. "He was the pope of my personal church," Marlene said, and the papal pursuit of his Venus was something she found "impossible to explain." Or to feel much reverence for, certain as she was that Welsh did not love Papa back. Still, Marlene allowed him to cast her as Cupid of the Ritz, carrying papal bulls to and fro after he got drunk and unpopelike and slugged Welsh, who walked out, calling him "You poor, fat, feather-headed coward."

Marlene carried not only Hemingway's apologies but a marriage proposal as well. "I didn't render him any special good service," she sniffed later, perhaps because her diplomatic mission was so persuasive. When the three dined together that evening at the Ritz, Welsh accepted.

Marlene went back to war, to newly liberated Belgium and Holland, but was prevented from entering Germany by the ferocity of German resistance called the Battle of the Bulge. The sweep across Europe to Berlin was stalled at terrible cost. Remarque once told Marlene "courage is the fleeing forward," but she could not flee forward to the bloody border of her homeland and felt, as the targeted enemy of her former countrymen, more acutely than ever in her life, fear.

The sweet solace of Calvados helped, but immediately vomiting it up in the gasoline fumes, the smoke and smells of war did not. There was more Calvados to keep down what was left of the first, to warm the head and hands, to lubricate whatever needed oiling just to keep going.

She was sent back from the violent stalemate of the front to Paris, where she reunited with the ink-stained lovebirds. Her disapproval of their romance softened with news that Hemingway's son Jack had been wounded and taken prisoner by the Germans that October 1944. She responded with gallows humor, lightening her fears and his by turning her funeral (not then far from her mind) into a production to rival MGM.

Mary Welsh recalled "the program" was "not lugubrious."

"Notre-Dame would be the setting and the time late afternoon, so that flickering candles would embellish the scene. One corner of the cathedral would be curtained off.

" 'For your girls?' Ernest asked. . . .

" 'For what would you think, Papa?' "

Rudi would be travel agent, major-domo, usher, maître d', and undertaker, welcoming friends, lovers, and admirers.

"Enough to fill the church?" Mary Welsh asked.

"Who knows, darling? It is quite a big cathedral, isn't it?" Marlene answered, counting the house.

The guests would include Douglas Fairbanks, Jr., in a full-dress naval uniform, carrying a wreath from the English monarch. Gary Cooper, James Stewart, and John Wayne would be admitted in cowboy boots, while Jean Gabin would lean sulkily against the cathedral doors, wearing a trench coat with a cigarette dangling from his mouth. Remarque, melancholy and vague, would be at the wrong church at the wrong time for the wrong funeral. The list went on.

"There'll never be such a show," said Hemingway. "You're immortal, my Kraut."

She wasn't, and she knew it. Jokes about death were an antidote to fear. So was her crooning to Hemingway as he shaved at the Ritz and she perched on the edge of the bathtub or the toilet seat for a chorus of "Lili Marlene" or one of the songs she had recorded for the OSS. He tried to sing along in a voice that was higher and lighter than hers.

Her humor brightened an early 1944 Christmas, celebrated before Hemingway and Marlene went off separately to the front. Her gift to the writers caroled with goodwill. Papa found it "useful as well as beautiful," for it was the double bed from her own room at the Ritz to replace Mary Welsh's twins.

Furniture was moved by a crew of two: a movie star and a female war correspondent. They heaved mattresses and springs beneath the quivering nostrils of protesting Ritz personnel. *Toujours l'amour* to you, too, the ladies hooted.

Hemingway went to the front and Mary Welsh had the bed to herself. Marlene's gift was thoughtful but had a life of its own. She had left behind a dividend: a full-scale case of war-front scabies which required treatment with benzyl benzoate, to which the "pocket Venus" was allergic—and she *wondered* . . .

Marlene cheerfully admitted her own insect invasion. She admitted it cheerfully for years, turning it into one of her bawdy set pieces, like the funeral story, or her famous deadpan response when asked if it was true she had slept with Eisenhower: "Darling, Ike wasn't *at* the front." She would elaborate and embellish the tales, as in the one with the young soldier invited back to her tent after a performance. Prepared to sample "Lili Marlene," he got instead a deflating third-degree on how to get rid of crabs.

Crabs were real; so were rats; so were the cold and K-rations and confrontations with the enemy, so recently her countrymen. She spent the Christmas of her forty-third birthday entertaining the Ninety-ninth Army near Bastogne at the center of the Battle of the Bulge. Hitler had diverted troops needed on the disastrous eastern front to hold back the Allies, now advancing into Germany itself. Allied casualties mounted to sixty thousand, close to seven thousand of whom would never come home.

These were the days and nights of brutal cold and frostbite that ever after turned her hands blue under spotlights; of sleeping bags in frozen fields or rat-infested ruins; of a month-long siege of "the GIs," necessitating the periodic dashes from performing on the back of a flatbed truck to attend to the call of the amoeba. She washed her face and hair and underclothes in snow melted inside her helmet; drank Calvados again and vomited it up again. She joked and sang and played her musical saw, wore sequins over nothing in subzero weather, provided visions of Paradise and then pretended to read minds ("It's not difficult to read a GI's mind overseas") through teeth chattering like hail on helmets.

As the Third Army advanced into Germany, her personal danger increased. "I'm not afraid of dying," she told the generals, "but I am afraid of being taken prisoner." In the Hürtgen Forest General Omar Bradley ordered her to remain behind. She vamped him into relenting and he did, on condition she accept two bodyguards for the entrance into Germany with the forward troops. In the night outside of Nancy, General George Patton gave her a pearl-handled revolver just like his own. "It's small, but it's effective," he said, leaving no doubt he meant as a suicide device. Were she to be captured, her propaganda value, her being an officer in the United States Army could subject her to a terrible ordeal. "They'll shave off my hair, stone me, and have horses drag me through the streets," she thought. Or worse, "force me to talk on the radio," say things she didn't want to say.

These were the days and nights of mud and squalor, of trying to flee forward, to maintain grace under pressure. She could accept personal danger, but every advance into Germany brought her closer to Berlin and her mother. She had been able to perform all along mainly by not thinking about the possible consequences in Berlin of her actions. Everybody knew now about the camps, about reprisals. Himmler, in an attempt to stem desertions from the German army, had announced in November that "ignominious behavior will entail the most severe consequences for [the] family. . . . They will be summarily shot." If there was anybody left to shoot.

She had no idea what had become of her mother and sister, but she knew what was happening to Berlin. In the winter of 1944–1945 the capital was under relentless bombardment, waiting for the end. Hitler ranted in his bunker beneath the Wilhelmstrasse, insanely searching astrological charts for signs that ruin might be avoided or, if not, how best to inflict it.

Marlene had moved in hops and jumps alongside the front lines, sometimes in Belgium, sometimes in France, often not sure of where she was as the lines advanced, retreated, splintered, regrouped, and moved forward again. Then she was in Germany. First in Stolberg, then in Aachen, just across the borders from France, Belgium, and Holland. She surveyed the ruin of the country she had not seen since 1934 and told a reporter with a steely resignation that would be held against her for the rest of her life, "I guess Germany deserves everything that's coming to her."

In Aachen she performed in the ruins of a movie theater for troops pouring through the town on their way to offensives at Remagen and points east and south. She made love to countless battle-weary GIs, got and got rid of body lice, and sang "Lili Marlene" and translated in debris-strewn streets, on food lines, in hospitals, and met the dazed German acquiescence to defeat and their admiration of her discipline with scorn. "If they had any character," she said, "they would hate me." But they took orders like good Germans, and stared, wondering if this warrior in field boots and helmet could really be the Lola Lola of garters and silk stockings.

In late winter she was ordered back to Paris to recover from frostbite and influenza contracted in the Ardennes. The American Theatre Wing opened its Paris edition of the Stage Door Canteen on a newly liberated Champs-Élysées with three gala opening nights in March, reminders of Paris-then, previews of Paris-soon. The glittering Parisian names were there: Molyneux, LeLong, Lanvin. There were international celebrities, generals and admirals, and French movie stars for that Gallic *quelque-chose*.

Hitler had sent mad cables a year before asking *"Brennt Paris?"* ("Is Paris burning?"), but only the swing was hot now as the multinational Swing Bands of Liberation burned the place down with "Tuxedo Junction" and "Stompin' at the Savoy."

Marlene and pals Maurice Chevalier and Noël Coward performed at all three galas, as did soprano Grace Moore. Chevalier sang "Mimi" in a French cap with a bandanna round his neck; Coward wore a Savile Row suit, sang of "Mad Dogs and Englishmen," and recommended not being beastly to the Germans. Marlene serenaded boys in the back room and Lili of the lamplight in an Eisenhower jacket and skirt made of silver lamé, and astonished even old friend Coward that she could hold her own on stage with, well . . . himself.

She accepted champagne and flowers from an audience that mostly ignored Grace Moore, who suffered glamour girls poorly and stuck her tongue out behind Marlene's back right there on stage. Marlene was too busy taking bows to take notice when Diva Moore went backstage and threw up.

Marlene was mobbed by servicemen on the dance floor and cried out, "But what do you want with me?" which, according to *Life*, "provoked many answers." Marlene calmed urges to merge by agreeing to one kiss for each of the Allied nations, "to demonstrate her international goodwill."

It was almost the end. She later made it part of the legend that she listened sobbing on May 8, 1945, as de Gaulle announced on Paris radio that it was over, Jean Gabin at her side. Gabin wasn't there. He was touring the ruins of Hitler's hideaway at Berchtesgaden on V-E Day, searching with French troops in vain for Field Marshall Göring, who had an appointment in Nuremberg he hoped to avoid.

Marlene wasn't there either. American occupation forces were mopping up southern and western Germany and she was with them in Bavaria. She had pestered American army officers who had met with Leclerc in Munich and learned a few days before V-E Day that Gabin was based there, too. She begged for and got permission to "fraternize" with French troops. The request was relayed to Gabin's superior officer, Daniel Gélinet, who was French, after all, and understood romance.

In the middle of a review of the 2nd French Tank Division in Landsberg-am-Lech, conducted by De Gaulle himself, Marlene materialized in her army uniform and penny loafers, running along the lines of tanks crying out, "Jean! . . . Jean!" A woman's voice calling a not uncommon French name turned many heads away from towering De Gaulle, but even he must have known who *this* Jean was. She raced to Gabin's *Souffleur II* tank, and her tough-guy "child" greeted her with, "Damn it to hell, what are *you* doing here?"

"I want to kiss you," she explained, and did. It was coincidence that when the kiss ended, so did the war.

Odd news filtered into U.S. army headquarters in Munich. The liberation of the Nazi concentration and extermination camps had taken place gradually as the Allies pushed eastward, baring the evils of the Holocaust, the horrors and atrocities. One of the first camps liberated in mid-April (by the British) was Bergen-Belsen, near Hannover. There was a woman there claiming to be Marlene's sister.

It had been seven years since Lausanne and the refusal of Marlene's family to leave Nazi Germany. In that time, Belsen had grown from an

SS-designated "recuperation camp" (*Erholungslager*) for prisoners from Holland and wealthy Jews who might barter for their lives to a death camp for prisoners transferred from Auschwitz. Nearly one hundred thousand men, women, and children were delivered into this valley of death, twenty-eight thousand of them so wasted they would die *after* the camp was liberated. Two months earlier, in March, a young Jewish girl named Anne Frank had died there.

The Nazis had cut off all food and water and simply abandoned Belsen to the British, who discovered signs of cannibalism in the midst of a raging typhus epidemic. Medical officers set up hospitals and found—somehow—thousands of beds for victims who continued to die, five hundred of them every day. An American signal corps officer was allowed to view the pit thirty feet wide, fifty feet long, and ten feet deep in which five thousand bodies lay rotting. He murmured, "Jesus Christ Jesus Christ Jesus Christ and I kept saying that to myself because I couldn't think of anything else."

News that Elisabeth might be at Belsen was terrifying—and mysterious. General Omar Bradley ordered his army plane to fly Marlene at once from Munich to a tiny airfield called Fassberg, from which an army jeep drove her through fifty miles of ruins to Belsen the day after V-E Day.

Assistant camp commandant Captain Arnold Horwell of the British army was then in his office in what had been Belsen's Wehrmacht headquarters. Horwell was a Berlin-born Jew now in the British army, able in spite of his personal history to cope with continuing horrors by clinging to a merciful sense of humor. When others noted his (still) strong Berlin accent he told them that when he escaped from Nazi Germany to England in 1938 he had changed his name from Hor*witz* to Hor*well*. "I went to England and lost my 'witz,' " he would say, "but 'all's well that ends well.' " The diminutive young doctor of theoretical economics could laugh, though he knew quite enough about tragedy. His own mother and father had died in the camp at Theresienstadt in Czechoslovakia.

He was worried now about survivors marked for return to their countries of origin, to homelands whose regimes had attempted to wipe them from the face of the earth they had been born on. He made it his mission to get the repatriation orders revoked—and did—so the victims might have more say about final destinations than they had had about final solutions.

Captain Horwell was interrupted at his work by an orderly who told him sourly that an American officer claiming to be General Omar Bradley's driver was asking to see him.

"Send him in," said Captain Horwell.

"It's a *she* officer," the orderly growled.

"Send *her* in," the captain ordered.

The Britisher from Berlin was stunned. He recognized "General Omar

Bradley's driver" from the screen, that "face in a million," he later called it, now crowned by a field helmet from beneath which blonde hair curled untidily. She wore army fatigues and reported smartly as Captain Dietrich.

Her sister and brother-in-law had been located at Bergen-Belsen, she explained, and wanted to know what she might do for them. Captain Horwell greeted her concern with compassion and unease, for he was well aware of Elisabeth and Georg Will. Herr Will had gone to unpleasantly aggressive lengths to identify himself as someone with an American army "connection" of (Will stressed) considerable propaganda value. No one had guessed the "connection" was a plane flight away.

The Will family were not prisoners or hostages at all, but members of the support group working hand in glove with the Nazis who ran the horror camp. Elisabeth and Georg Will and their son lived in a comfortable private flat with their own furniture and private stores of canned food. Georg Will was a Special Services Officer (*Truppenbetreuungsoffizier*) for the German army. He had, ironically, provided entertainment for the Third Reich much as Marlene was still doing for the Allies. He ran the Wehrmacht canteen and cinema at Belsen for the masters of the Holocaust camp and another small cinema at nearby Fallingbostel for German troops.

The camp's liberation by the British was a mixed blessing for the Wills. It meant the war was almost over, but as part of the German army support group, they were the enemy. They had been in custody and safe haven for a time before Belsen became a death camp, after Will's Berlin movie theaters and cabaret were closed on orders from Goebbels, as all civilian theaters were in September 1944. They had remained cooperative and industrious during the horrors that followed.

Georg Will was humanitarian enough to have helped a well-known Czech actor called Karel Stepanek hide from the Nazis in Berlin and escape to London in 1943. He later claimed air attacks made it too dangerous to stay in the capital and had simply resettled with his wife and son in a safer district to the north. But the Wills were part of the machinery of Belsen, part of the murderous juggernaut. Their plight as Germans captured by the British was "a trifle," Horwell knew, but his instincts were to alleviate or end hardship of any kind. The quality of mercy, he had learned when learning English, was not strained.

Horwell had the Wills brought to his office. Elisabeth was not well and would spend two months in a hospital in the nearby town of Celle with pleurisy. That day after V-E Day, Marlene's ever-obedient older sister arrived blushing with reunion excitement, wearing what the assistant commandant called "an impossible straw hat that kept slipping from her head." Horwell offered her a cigarette. She took it but refused a light; she didn't smoke. Marlene asked sharply why she had taken it. Elisabeth explained not that cigarettes were wartime currency (which they were), but that one never refuses a cigarette from an Englishman. "That would be considered impolite!"

"What a world this is," thought Horwell, in which politesse counted more than politics in a landscape of death and cannibalism. He promised Marlene to do what he could, though the Wills' fate, as part of the camp administrative population, was a matter for the Military Governor. Marlene was grateful and, having nothing to repay his kindness, offered an autograph. Horwell secreted a cigarette that bore her lipstick's traces as a souvenir of their meeting for his wife, Susie, also a Berliner, also Jewish.

Marlene understood the awful ironies that confronted her in Elisabeth's official role and presence at Belsen and did not flinch from worse. She asked to see Belsen's Camp Number One, the horror camp. Horwell spared her the sight, but wrote his wife that evening with gentle regret, "I gave her enough details to make her almost sick."

Marlene said good-bye. General Bradley needed his plane. She stayed in touch with Captain Horwell for months, hoping the press would be kept ignorant of Elisabeth and signing herself "Love, Marlene," even after the British took away Georg Will's movie theater and the flat and the furniture and the stores of preserves. Horwell wrote on their behalf to his commandant, yielding not to Will's absurd and vigorous complaints of "unjust treatment," but to the unflinching grace of the woman he called "the divine Marlene."

The truth remained unbroadcast. If it had been published it might only have read that the Wills had done their duty, like so many who later viewed themselves as "good Germans." Marlene, whose bitter hatred of the Third Reich would remain an obsession for the rest of her life, never spoke of the incident, though she referred to her brother-in-law bitterly and bluntly within her family as "a Nazi." As for Elisabeth, Marlene never referred publicly to her again—except to deny her existence.

Marlene learned from Elisabeth that their mother was last known to be in Berlin and might be still if she had survived both the Germans and the Russians, though the Kaiserallee flat she had lived in since the 1920s had been destroyed in Allied air attacks. Marlene's search for her would have to wait; she was still subject to army orders and was officially on duty in Bavaria. She continued to entertain troops in places that recalled her childhood, like Garmisch-Partenkirchen, where she had escaped from a girls' boardinghouse one winter dawn centuries ago to serenade her film idol

Henny Porten with her violin. Now in July, suffering from a jaw infection, she was returned to New York for treatment, her first furlough in almost a year.

She flew with Texas hillbilly comedienne Lin Mayberry by military transport to New York's La Guardia Airport. They traveled with GIs, many of whom survived V-E Day only to fight for V-J Day on another front. On July 13 it rained at La Guardia, and there was no reception committee but Rudi to greet his wife, who was still wearing her GI fatigues and battle boots. He stood by helplessly as U.S. Customs confiscated the pearl-handed revolver General Patton had given her.

They taxied to the St. Regis Hotel, where Rudi said good-bye. Marlene persuaded reception to pay for the taxi, including "a big tip," drew money on account from the cashier, and checked into a suite where she could be hostess to the GIs she had met on the plane. They bathed as she ordered food and drink from room service. Luxuriously sluiced and gorged, her guests finally left. Marlene nursed her impacted jaw and called Charlie Feldman in Los Angeles. Her agent and producer hailed the conquering heroine without mincing a word. There was no money to pay for the taxi, or for the cash advance she had received at the desk, or for the hotel suite, or for the room service. There was, in fact, no money at all, and no prospects of any. She had just spent a year in battle conditions being glamorous on a soldier's pay. She had suffered pneumonia, frostbite, the GIs, influenza, and now had a severe jaw infection. She was sick and she was broke.

She hung up on Hollywood. "I was utterly confused," she admitted later. "I had already accustomed myself to being a resident alien and then becoming an American citizen. Now I had to adjust and reintegrate myself all over again. . . . I came back to America, a country that had not suffered in the war, a country that really didn't know what its soldiers had gone through over there on foreign soil. My hatred of 'carefree' Americans dates from this time."

Her identification with the returning GIs was so great that she was capable of lifelong indignation that watering holes like El Morocco, where *she* was a celebrity prize, turned away GIs wearing no neckties. Purple Hearts didn't count. She became passionate about chroniclers of the war, like Irwin Shaw, who became a friend; or cartoonist Bill Mauldin, whom she admired because Hemingway did; or photographer Robert Capa, to whom she gave her fur-lined cap the night before he was killed in the Ardennes. When she said the war was "the only important thing I've ever done" she meant it and held the war in a proprietary embrace, defining unbridgeable barriers between those who had lived it and those who hadn't: "If you haven't been in it, don't talk about it."

She dutifully went through the motions of a returned heroine in New York, kissing servicemen for photographs that were sometimes spontaneous, sometimes staged, including one that made a full page in *Life* as soldiers boosted her by the legs to a porthole so she could kiss the boys hello on the troopship *Monticello*. She answered letters from women who wrote saying their sons or lovers had mentioned seeing her in Italy, the Ardennes, Germany though few (one supposes) admitted making love to her there. She gave interviews to *Yank* with Lin Mayberry in their rooms at the St. Regis and admitted she had "been so close to the Army for so damn long that [she] didn't feel normal talking to civilians." She was, she confirmed, hoping to go to the Pacific once her jaw was repaired in New York. Hollywood? "Not now," she said. "I'm not in the mood. I don't think I could concentrate now on keeping every eyelash right like you have to do there." The Pacific needed her and she had regained her sense of humor. "I have dates with so many divisions there," she teased.

Hollywood was prepared by habit to accept her absence, but she was on her way back to Europe anyway. She had not yet finished her tour of duty, and Gabin was there.

By V-J Day in August she was back in Paris at the Olympia Music Hall, doing a version of her front-line show, singing to troops who would rather have been at home. She checked into the Hotel Magellan near the Trocadero, commandeered and maintained for army women by the WACs, but spent little time there. Gabin had been mustered out of his tank corps in July, and she moved into Claridge's with him.

In Paris she was reunited with Margo Lion, who had spent the war out of the occupied zone in Marseilles, and with faithful friend and lyricist Max Colpet, who had been interned by the French. She moved Colpet secretly into her room at the Magellan, where he remained in hiding after curfew— and in agony. He was a man who appreciated women and passed his nights listening to siren voices through the walls, lashed to the mast of his stowaway status.

Marlene returned to Germany and made the rounds of the camps east and south of Munich, in Regensburg and Salzburg, where she learned her cousin Hasso had been a Russian prisoner of war, now transferred to the Western Allies. She crossed into Czechoslovakia at Pilsen, then was shipped back to Paris to await repatriation at Châtou, at last to be mustered out of the U.S. army she felt nobody cared about at "home."

It was hurry up and wait all over again, sweetened by visits to Claridge's and Gabin. Then, in mid-September word came from Berlin. Her mother had been located by the American army. She was living in a furnished room in the Fregestrasse in Friedenau, not far from where Marlene had been born. Marlene flew there in a military plane, wearing her army uniform for the photographers who appeared at Berlin's Tempelhof Airfield as she linked arms with a sparrowlike Josephine von Losch, dressed quite like her daughter in a skirted suit with a man's tie, clutching at her little black hat in the wind of the propellers.

Their reunion was widely reported in the world, though hardly at all in Berlin and there were no press leaks about Elisabeth and Belsen. Army intelligence finally understood what Marlene had known from the beginning: Her war work had made her persona non grata among her countrymen. They openly called her traitor and some of them, it was feared, might act against her in fulfillment of old Nazi threats. The ghosts of Hitler, Himmler, and Goebbels were fresh and restless.

Marlene moved into her mother's room and sent a note backstage to her old friend Hubsie von Meyerinck, who had known her since she took the stage with "that . . . *Nothing*" in a showgirl's costume in the twenties. He was now appearing as Mack the Knife in an Allied-approved revival of *The Threepenny Opera*, which had been banned by the Nazis since 1933. She gave him a list of old friends she hoped to see, inviting them to a little *Wiedersehen* in her mother's room: Alexa von Porembsky, who'd been a showgirl with her; Heinz Rühmann, with whom she'd appeared in Shaw's *Misalliance*; a few others who were all pre–*Blue Angel*, pre-Hitler, preeverything.

The guests arrived on their bicycles at Frau von Losch's furnished room to discover Marlene was no longer in Berlin. She had received word that Rudi's family was alive in Czechoslovakia and had gone to visit them for him. It had been Bohemia when he was born there, then Czechoslovakia, then the Sudetenland, then the Bohemian-Moravian Protectorate of the Third Reich, and was now to become Czechoslovakia again, if the Russians didn't swallow it whole.

Another date was scheduled in Berlin, and Marlene appeared. She inundated her guests with questions and opinions about colleagues who had stayed in Berlin or Vienna, too many of them too rich, too fat, too tardily antifascist. Some could be forgiven, some not. And there were many to whom nothing could ever be said. There was no way to honor or put flowers on the graves of, say, Kurt Gerron and Karl Huszar-Puffy, with whom she had acted in *The Blue Angel* and in pictures and plays before that. There are no private graves at Auschwitz.

She poured *Ersatz-Kaffee* and passed out American cigarettes and advice. She urged Heinz Rühmann to latch on quick to Mary Chase's *Harvey*, then a hit on Broadway (he did and made it a hit in Germany), and suddenly, irrationally, she saw herself back in Berlin, back on stage in a revival of *It's in the Air*, singing again with Margo Lion the lesbian duet that had titillated

Weimar, singing again with Hubsie their chic ditty about swank "Klepto-maniacs." They would *all* be in it; they would recreate the glamour and bite of Weimar Berlin there in the ruins!

Nobody said anything. What could they say to this woman in her Amer-ican army uniform who was singing nightly to Germany's conquerors from the stage of Berlin's Titania-Palast? Ten years and more of Nazi propaganda and German reaction to a "traitor" soured the coffee, turned the tobacco bitter. She looked suddenly, thought Hubsie, more beautiful than ever in her uniform, but weary and worn, too. There was too much ruin, not all of it stone.

Some of the rubble belonged to her, or soon would. The Felsing firm was just debris in the Russian sector, the boldly scripted "Conrad Felsing" flowing with absurd grace across the front wall of the gutted building on Unter den Linden.

Marlene's mother had hung on to the business under surveillance by the Gestapo as "politically suspicious." She was brought in for questioning from time to time and managed to unnerve even the elite of the Master Race. She was a dragon, after all, and the widow of not one, but two military men, and Hasso, her nephew and ward, was a German officer. More than once Hasso appeared to dampen her fire-breathing indignation, to point out that he and she, as joint owners of the Felsing firm, were the major source of engagement rings for Wehrmacht officers going off to the front and looking for a discount. Even Gestapo men had sweethearts and were not immune to bargains. Now the Russians would send a bill for repairs to the ruin they had inflicted: public safety, they said. There was no money to pay for repairs; no good reason, either.

Marlene said good-bye to her mother and reported back to France. The army sent her to lecture at Biarritz where, six weeks later, she received the news that would forever—she thought—put Berlin behind her. It was a telegram telling her that Josephine had died of a heart attack in the night of November 6, 1945, only days short of her sixty-ninth birthday.

The Wilmersdorf chapel was bombed out, so the service was held in the rain in the cemetery itself, where monuments and headstones were wet with ash. Hubsie stood with Marlene as Josephine Felsing Dietrich von Losch was lowered in a coffin constructed from old German school desks by GI hands.

This was, she later said, "the last bond that tied me to my homeland." Her mother had lived through the creation of the German state, the end of monarchy, the collapse of the Weimar Republic, the destruction of the Third Reich, spirited and independent to the end. But this *was* the end. Rain and earth closed over the last emblem of childhood, and Marlene

recalled in her memoirs that she wept, remembering the words her mother
had hung behind glass in a frame to teach her to read:

O love, while still 'tis yours to love!
O love, while love you still may keep!
The hour will come, the hour will come,
When you will stand by graves and weep.

Those were words to read by and to mourn by and they would stay with her
to the end of her life. But her mother had given her words to live by, too.
No nonsense, no self-pity, no wasted words.

"*Tu was,*" she had always said. "*Do something!*"

SIXTEEN

SURVIVOR
1946 - 1947

She was a survivor, that much was clear. A woman who could live through Hitler and Hollywood could cope with anything, and she sounded determined not to look back. "I am through with Hollywood," she had told a war correspondent at the height of the Battle of the Bulge, "It was a very difficult place to live in anyway."

She was in her mid-forties and meant it when she said it, but there were dependents to think of and the matter of making a living. She might have quit, might have packed up her silk stockings and sequined gowns, but she couldn't pack up responsibility or ambition or will. Or the lure, the thrill (she always conveyed it) of being "Dietrich."

Had she retired then, she would have earned her place in film history, even if she had made nothing but *The Blue Angel* and *Destry Rides Again*.

But there had been all those other pictures, and more estimable directors than any other actress had ever worked with: not just Josef von Sternberg and those who preceded him, but Rouben Mamoulian, Frank Borzage, Ernst Lubitsch, Richard Boleslawski, Jacques Feyder, George Marshall, Tay Garnett, René Clair, Raoul Walsh, Mitchell Leisen, and William Dieterle. As a glamour symbol she had but one peer (now withdrawn), and she had carved a notable niche as a live performer with her war work, acquitting herself not just as entertainer or erotic icon (though the two seemed increasingly indivisible), but as a Woman, which, ironically, deflected attention from the Actress.

What now seems startling to realize—it would have staggered her—is that in 1945, after a quarter century's work, after two dozen plays, three dozen movies, and three years of camp and tent and truck and jeep and hospital and Paris and Berlin and Salzburg "victory" shows, her career wasn't yet half over. She was everywhere a legend (though the legend was still evolving), and the satisfactions of those twenty-five years would have been enough for almost anyone, *should* have been enough, perhaps, for her. But neither "Marlene" nor "Dietrich" was a woman easily satisfied.

There was no reason for Marlene to return to Hollywood, even if Hollywood had wanted her. There was no house there, and no one waiting. Maria was in Italy with the USO, following in her mother's footsteps, though hardly (because of her weight) filling her shoes; Rudi and Tamara were in New York coping with aging and America; Josef von Sternberg was preparing to work as an unbilled second-unit director on Selznick's *Duel in the Sun*. Remarque was no longer a force in her life, but was trying to persuade Hollywood she should star in the movie of his novel *Arch of Triumph*, a worldwide publishing success. He failed: Ingrid Bergman played "Dietrich" and critics remarked how much more convincing Marlene would have been.

It wasn't just Hollywood that seemed inhospitable, but all America. Despite all the fan letters from grateful GIs, or their mothers, wives, or sweethearts, she still felt America really "didn't want to be reminded of the existence of the war." It was the universal complaint of the soldier home from the wars: brave hearts deflated by sudden absence of purpose; uplift turned to letdown; and after twenty thousand GIs roaring approval in a single show, the silence from Hollywood was sepulchral.

Worse, she suffered a kind of paralysis of will after the years of being told what to do by Sternberg and Paramount and Pasternak and Feldman, after the security and comfort of a president and an army giving her orders. And the supreme commander—the "the good general"—was now gone. "I was really unable to act without someone telling me what to do," she confessed. Then she thought of someone.

Jean Gabin was in Paris—Jean Gabin *was* Paris. The City of Light was jubilant but weary, and ugly questions of collaboration fluttered like furies (justly or not) around the heads of Chevalier, Danielle Darrieux, and others. Marlene's politics were as unimpeachable as Gabin's, but both were at economic barricades at the end of 1945.

Gabin called it his "gray period," and wrapped himself in Marlene, who swaddled her "little baby who liked best of all," she said, "to curl up in his mother's lap and be loved, cradled, and pampered." Love and lullabies were lovely, but they weren't work. Max Colpet and Margo Lion were recruited to help them find a film to keep them together and solvent.

They read and talked and cuddled and looked for material and didn't find it at Claridge's or at Gabin's bombed-out farm at nearby Sainte-Gemme, where Marlene scrubbed floors. Back in town she scrubbed more floors ("I do like a good clean floor," she said) and prodded Gabin to smart cafés like Fouquet's or to films and the theater where they might find something with film potential. They went with Noël Coward or Colpet or Lion, or newer friends like Jean Cocteau and Jean Marais. She was scrubbing *le tout Paris*, too.

Cocteau considered Marlene "the most exciting and terrifying woman I have ever known" and thought she would be ideal as Death, the poet's muse in his film of *Orphée*, but Marlene found the idea morbid and had had enough of death lately. Besides, Cocteau's Jean Marais was unlikely to step aside for Gabin to play an Orpheus who was forty-one and graying.

One evening's theater expedition brought them together with director Marcel Carné and poet-screenwriter Jacques Prévert. The two had been responsible for the great *Les Enfants du Paradis*, made during the Occupation but released only post-Liberation. Before the war Carné and Prévert had starred Gabin in two other classics, *Quai des Brumes* and *Le Jour Se Lève*, pictures that built on Gabin's culture-hero status after Renoir's *La Grande Illusion*. The four attended a performance of Roland Petit's ballet *Le Rendez-vous*, with music by Joseph Kosma and settings by the photographer Brassaï. Carné and Prévert, who had been sifting through material to find something for Marlene and Gabin to do (neither *Mary Poppins* nor *Candide* seemed quite right, they conceded), instantly decided that Petit's ballet could be a film. Prévert quickly retreated with pen and paper to Saint-Paul-de-Vence to work out a script, and from time to time Gabin and Carné would journey south to discuss his progress. Press announcements about *"Marlène et Jean"* raised Gallic temperatures and expectations, but what sounded like a collaboration *sans pareil* sank like a lead soufflé, becoming one of the odder episodes in film history, with repercussions both personal and professional, and blame would attach to Marlene to the present day.

*　　*　　*

Gabin had for a decade owned the film rights to a novel by Pierre-René Wolf called *Martin Roumagnac*, which he had bought as a vehicle for himself and had promoted in vain to Carné and Prévert ever since 1937, when the three first worked together. *Martin Roumagnac* was hackneyed romance, *crime passionnel* in the provinces, and had been turned down by everyone to whom Gabin had suggested it. *"Madame Bovary manquée,"* they said. Still, it was "the dream of his life," even Carné admitted that, not least because he had invested both judgment and money in it, neither redeemable if no film was ever made.

Work proceeded on the project based on the ballet, now called *Les Portes de la nuit,* for which Prévert wrote a lyric to some music by Joseph Kosma. They tried it out on Gabin in a Paris bar and Gabin asked to hear it over and over and over. It was a haunting song, tailored to Marlene's smoky brand of *Weltschmerz*. They called it "Les Feuilles mortes," and it would become world famous under its English title, "Autumn Leaves." Like "Speak Low" from *One Touch of Venus*, it is one of those songs that seems to have been written for Marlene because it was. That she never sang it, never *could* sing it, resulted from the ensuing recrimination and disaster, at the center of which was Marlene—or "La Grande," as Gabin, then everyone in Paris, started calling her, first in awe, then in outrage.

"What will La Grande say?" Gabin pestered the poet Prévert in the south of France. "What will La Grande do?" "What will La Grande think?" until Prévert erupted with *"Merde!"* and announced his readiness to throw up at the next mention of her name. Prévert was not alone in weariness with Gabin's obsession. Director Carné (who had worked with both Jacques Feyder and René Clair and may have been warned) was annoyed that Gabin refused to make the film without Marlene, but refuse he did. Director and writer fulminated and threatened to throw up, but could never bring themselves to throw out the financing La Grande—not Gabin and not themselves—had attracted from England and America.

Gabin could be sulky and opaque, but he lit up like *son et lumière* with Marlene in Paris and wanted to keep her there. That alone would have assured some deference to her, but the "bull-headed" Gabin (Marlene called him that) had problems with the *Portes de la nuit* script that Prévert and Carné did not care to hear about.

It was set in occupied France against a background of petty racketeering and collaboration that made both stars uneasy. These were unresolved times, and such topics were sensitive to the French. "Autumn Leaves"—no matter how haunting—was not enough to allay anxiety. Marlene finally said—or Gabin said *for* her—that she did not want to make the movie.

Marlene's contract with Pathé, the company financing *Les Portes de la nuit* (with RKO in America and Korda in England) gave her script approval, but Gabin had no such right. Gabin's presence was, in Pathé's and Carné's eyes (and documents) contractually guaranteed, with or without La Grande, and because it was, he had been paid in advance.

If Gabin could not refuse to make the picture because of the script, he did have schedule approval, with which he could define his own availability. He used it to become unavailable for *Les Portes de la nuit* because he was making the project nobody wanted—*Martin Roumagnac*. Gabin had persuaded the uninspired but competent Georges Lacombe to direct it and Marlene, having no more desire to leave Gabin than he had to let her leave, agreed to whatever he wanted.

Gabin's taking the money and running from *Les Portes de la nuit* enraged everybody. Old loyalties made it impolitic for Carné and Prévert to blame him, so they blamed La Grande, and Pathé promptly sued Gabin because they couldn't sue her.

Carné and Prévert angrily barged ahead with *Les Portes de la nuit*, casting Edith Piaf's unknown young lover, Yves Montand, but it still didn't work. The film was yawningly referred to around Paris as *Les Portes de l'ennui* and—incredibly—"Autumn Leaves" became a voice-over for the end credits, and the voice that was over wasn't even Yves Montand's.

"Autumn Leaves" was practically the sole survivor of *Les Portes de la nuit*. The film did nothing for newcomer Montand and was the beginning of decline for Carné. It was his last completed collaboration with Prévert, a historic partnership that ended shortly thereafter in the chaos of a film abandoned in mid-production. All this was viewed as a consequence of Marlene's influence over Gabin or his obsession with her. Carné broadcast his bitterness acidly, noting that he never bothered to see Marlene in *Martin Roumagnac*, even though "the role of a Normandy farm woman [sic] was one she had evidently been put on earth to play."

She didn't play a Normandy farm woman at all and may well have turned down Carné and Prévert because Gabin asked her to. She rarely accepted or rejected projects on the basis of script alone. Co-star or director were always more relevant to her than anything on the page. In any case, Marlene had been, as Gabin endlessly repeated to the deaf ears of Carné and Prévert, his "condition."

Conditions did not improve.

Back at work on *Martin Roumagnac*, La Grande went on being La Grande. She loved being Marlene Dietrich as much as she ever had and posed happily for the press with technicians and crew at the shabby studios in Saint-Maurice where they shot. She had overalls and work clothes shipped in from America to replace the crew's threadbare prewar garb and food to feed them, but reporters were more interested in her relationship with Gabin than her CARE packages. "But there is absolutely nothing between us!" she exclaimed and fed a cherry to a set electrician. "MARLÈNE FLIRTE AVEC L'ÉLECTRICIEN" read the titillating headline. Gabin read it and paused. "*Flirte*"? This movie was the story of a faithless strumpet and her jealous lover. "*Flirte*"?

Martin Roumagnac wasn't that bad as movie material. Marlene may not have read the script carefully, but she could count pages and knew that Gabin's role was dominant and hers a not very sympathetic portrait of an oversexed femme fatale who brings on her own murder. So far, so *noir*. The thing had possibilities, but making Marlene credible as the town whore who is also mistress of the local pet shop was not among them.

Blanche Ferrand (Dietrich) is a recent arrival in Clairval, where she sells birds, lives with her "uncle," and turns tricks in "the room upstairs" (the film's American title). She has arrived via Paris and Australia (to explain her very slight accent when speaking French), and tongues wag in bistros and bars, trilling condemnation of her and her fancy wardrobe. She has finer feelings, however, signaled by the shyly enamored local schoolmaster (Daniel Gélin). He recognizes the virtues beneath the bawd: She sells her lovebirds only in pairs and is passionate about freedom, freedom, freedom, which she will symbolize later by the not entirely fresh device of setting free the canaries.

Everybody in Clairval seems to know about Blanche except Martin Roumagnac (Gabin), the local bridge builder of simple but noble heart, who meets Blanche ringside at a local boxing match. Pulses pound and Fate intrudes disguised as a four-leaf clover. She loses it; he retrieves it. Her wordly ways (she says things like, "In the provinces one needs patience") bring on *amour fou* and a trip to Paris, where Blanche knows her way around headwaiters, to whom (*pourquoi?*) she speaks English.

This sort of thing makes Roumagnac gloomy, as do the many forks on the table; she instructs. He doesn't dance; she does, with an "old friend." They stare at a painted backdrop that represents stars over the Eiffel Tower; they make passionate Parisian love; they go back to dreary Clairval.

The tour of Blanche's Parisian past persuades Roumagnac to build Blanche a simple country house where she might settle down in a straw hat and grow things. *Mais non.* Visitors from long ago and far away turn up to chat about themes more sophisticated than vegetables. Martin has meanwhile had an earful about "the room upstairs" from those ever-wagging tongues. In a fit of rage he beats Blanche unconscious just as she is burning the souvenirs of her tawdry past in her new French provincial fireplace. She's up to her ruffles in ennui with sophistication, but he doesn't know that. He knocks her senseless in her frilly negligée and the house burns down, reducing Blanche, her negligée, and her not-yet-announced love of gardening to cinders.

Martin's spiteful older sister (Margo Lion) provides him with an alibi when he confesses his crime to her. There is a trial. Provincial hypocrisy triumphs, for it is Blanche, not Martin, who stands accused in the dock: all those ruffles. Martin is acquitted: "LIBÉRÉ!" the local headline shouts.

This calls for a fête. All make merry—except the young schoolmaster, whose poetic sense of justice forces him to execute Martin in the garden while everyone else is busy celebrating. Roumagnac takes the bullet as release for his tortured conscience, and a legend explains:

Some deaths are a deliverance.

Then we read again "LIBÉRÉ!" as Roumagnac lies dead, as *libéré* as Blanche's uncaged canaries. FIN.

This is heavy stuff, but Lacombe captured some cutting vignettes of provincial life and there are moments of chemistry between the stars that suggest what was happening offscreen. Memorable touches are few. Marlene is mostly mannered and brittle, usually a sign she has little confidence in her director and is directing herself. As one French critic noted fairly, "She is never false, and never truly convincing."

The film is no worse than other potboilers of the day, but it's a potboiler. Visual interest is confined to Marlene's frilled-up wardrobe, which the fashion-conscious French press snidely called "the envy of every bird sales-lady in France."

What really sinks the picture is that it is Gabin's movie pretending in the billing (she got first) to be Marlene's. The first half is obsessed with her in ruffles, twittering to the birds she will set free or pushing her bicycle (!) across the town square while everybody gossips. Her Norman invasion is sexy enough, but she's always La Grande, and one wonders why no one asks for an autograph as she pushes that bicycle around. When Gabin kills her two thirds of the way through, she and the center of gravity fall out of the picture. There's nothing left and reels to go before he dies.

The main interest of *Martin Roumagnac* was never before the cameras, but behind, where events flirted with parallels to the plot. Gabin was not just Marlene's petted child-man, he was also (she said) "stubborn, ex-tremely possessive, and jealous." It was what made him so right for the movie. He was less likely to woo with *billets-doux* than with a right to the jaw. His romance with a globe-trotting object of desire with admirers of every persuasion on every continent was guaranteed to test his confidence, as he was guaranteed to test *her.* The devil might *be* a woman; Claridge's might *be* Clairval.

Life at Claridge's worsened, and when Marlene turned black and blue she spent nights on the sofa in the Hotel Magellan suite in which she had stowed away Max Colpet. There she nursed her bruises ("He beat her *well*," Colpet remembered) and brushed up on boxing techniques she had observed Hemingway using on Mary Welsh in the Ritz. It was Hemingway and Welsh themselves who witnessed Marlene slugging Gabin, sending him reeling into a Paris snowbank.

This inflamed more than it resolved. If Marlene dressed smartly to go out, Gabin was convinced she was dolled up to entice a lover. If she dressed down, same reason, different lover. If she admired in silence, she was concealing. If she admired openly (as with Gérard Philipe or Edith Piaf), it was some subtle trick to confuse him or drive him crazy.

It wasn't always imaginary, either. Gérard Philipe's neurasthenic beauty and delicate acting style appealed to Marlene's maternal instincts. Piaf was, as her biographer Margaret Crosland noted, "more than a loving friend," but Paris friends who were aware of the women's sexual relationship guarded it carefully from Gabin.

General James Gavin, the dashing paratrooper who had landed virtually at Marlene's feet during the Battle of the Bulge, was less easy to conceal under the heading of mere friendship. He had met Marlene when she felt most vulnerable in war because nearest to her one-time homeland, where she was widely considered a traitor. Now in Paris, Gavin arrived in peacetime, setting Marlene off on an orgy of remembrance, with intrigue brazen enough for Blanche.

Still in his thirties, Gavin was the youngest and most handsome of American generals, and Marlene contrived to meet him at Monseigneur, a Russian-style bar with strolling gypsy violins (it was the model for the bar in *Arch of Triumph* where Joan Madou sang lugubrious Russian songs). Marlene plotted with Max Colpet. He should eavesdrop from a table near the one she would share with Gavin: being Dietrich or La Grande was tastier with an audience.

The general arrived. La Grande arrived. The "audience" arrived. So did gypsy violins, playing Marlene's movie songs to establish mood. Gavin's good looks were set in a slender face which bore a certain resemblance around the eyes to Erich Remarque, which amused Marlene no end. Colpet was sure it was nothing more than "a flirt," though it was, he admitted, "a very long one."

It was long enough that when the then-*Mrs.* General Gavin got wind of it, it looked like grounds for divorce and she promptly filed for one, naming Marlene as cause. Marlene's lawyers got her name dropped from the suit, but the story went around Paris that all that separated Gabin and Gavin was "a French letter," a joke so tasteless it inevitably got repeated everywhere.

Marlene treated it all as a romp, and later told Mitchell Leisen an elaborate, jokey story about "a general" in Paris with whom she moved in for two weeks. "He wants to marry me," she told Leisen, "but I can't be an army wife. What would I say to the other army wives?"

That was less germane than what she would say to Gabin if he got wind of it. If gypsy violinists recognized her across a crowded room, and Mrs. General Gavin did across an ocean, it is hard to imagine Gabin's not hearing about it just across the *arrondisement*, which may have been the idea.

Marlene moved from Claridge's to the Élysées Parc Hôtel. Having her own address was good public relations, anyway, even in sophisticated Paris, and gave her privacy, distance, and relief from all that cradling.

There remained nothing but for life to imitate art, to play out the scenario of *Martin Roumagnac* just short of incineration and execution. Gabin's character in the script tried to force domesticity by installing Blanche in her country cottage, and Gabin did something homey, too, just before his forty-second birthday in May of 1946. When Marlene inquired about a gift, he asked for the mementos he had given her in California before he sailed away to war from Newport News on a tramp tanker: the Vlaminck, the Sisley, the Renoir.

Marlene had thought maybe they were for *her*.

"They belong to you," he hastily agreed, "no question!" He just wanted something to brighten up the apartment at Claridge's in which she no longer cradled and snuggled. "We can hang them on the wall and on my birthday I could look at them. That would be the most beautiful birthday gift you could give me," he said.

Marlene telegraphed and the pictures arrived, moving Gabin to tears. Something else arrived, too: an offer from Mitchell Leisen and (of all places) Paramount. The domestic togetherness of Gabin, Marlene, and Messieurs Vlaminck, Sisley, and Renoir was thoroughly threatened, and Gabin intensified playing house by insisting Marlene marry him.

This was the crunch she had successfully avoided for more than two decades by never divorcing Rudi. Everyone who knew Gabin testified to his fervent desire to marry and father children. Marlene at almost forty-five did not have maternity in mind, not in a world still trying to cope with survival and shortages and no hot water and postwar exhaustion. The relationship with Rudi had shielded her from any permanent alliance for twenty-three years, but this was a new world in which love goddesses everywhere were tying on aprons and coming "down to earth," the title of the new Rita Hayworth movie. It had been the plot of *One Touch of Venus*, and a touch of Venus could keep La Grande grand. Gabin could keep her young and alive and . . . under a jealous thumb.

Her relationship with Gabin had been unique. It combined an outlet for her mothering instincts with the high romantic excitement of a volatile, sexy man ("he had the most beautiful loins in the world," she told friends) who would tell her what to do, whether she actually did it or not. No one doubted she was madly in love with him. She had ignored Hollywood for him, made the film *he* wanted to make, sustained their love affair since 1941 on two continents and all through a war and the scenes and the beatings, no matter how many of her "flirts" came between. It was what she always wanted, she said; but did she want to be married to it?

Yes.

But she did not see any compelling reason her career should take second place to his, which became a *new* Gabin "condition." And flirts with paratrooper generals or doomed young actors or little sparrows or anybody else would sit uncomfortably in the parlor of a middle-aged bride, no matter how many Vlamincks, Sisleys, or Renoirs decorated the walls.

She said "Wait" to Gabin and yes to Paramount and Mitchell Leisen. This time *she* got on the boat, and Gabin did not wave *au revoir* from the pier. He rejected her with a finality short of murder, but nearly as deadly.

Legend (never accurate) had it he never spoke her name again, but he did. La Grande became La Prussienne and what was the most intense love affair of her life since Rudi was over and she didn't quite know it. Marlene was accustomed to intense bonds segueing into friendship, to some continuing affection, perhaps tender feelings to be rekindled while sifting through . . . well, autumn leaves. It might happen that way with Gabin, she thought. It might not, Gabin decided, carving it in stone.

As if to seal the gloomy doom, *Martin Roumagnac's* failure achieved a sort of perfection. "Maybe three people saw it," she later admitted, and all three hated it. Reviews were snide to savage. "Oh lord, oh lord, take it away!" was a not untypical critical comment, and a legend would grow that Gabin tried to buy up all prints of the film, not because it was so bad, but because it was the last souvenir of his life with Marlene.

It was a love affair that could survive absence and a war, Marlene's "flirts" and Gabin's jealousy, but not Career. Years later, when Gabin died after Rudi was already in the grave, Marlene would mourn, "Now I am a widow for a second time." Their friends (or his) argued over whether Marlene left or Gabin threw her out, but it amounted to the same thing. She would not or could not in the end leave her career—or Rudi, the protector she protected, and Gabin refused to continue a relationship in separate apartments or on separate continents with only paintings on a wall to bind them.

"I lost him as you lose all your ideals," she said a bit obscurely, but Maria whispered to friends that her mother's earlier visit to La Quinta sanatorium near Palm Springs in 1942 was evidence of Marlene's coolness to maternity in her forties and Gabin figured it out. His rage was boundless: He didn't know she might be too old to have children now. He didn't know her age—or her friends, or her books, or her poetry, or the depths of her commitment to her career, but he knew he loved her and would have loved her child. *That* he could never forgive.

By August, as *Martin Roumagnac* was being edited, scored, and prepared for a ruinous reception—before she recognized how irretrievably over it was with Gabin—Marlene was back in Hollywood, back at Paramount, back being fêted by Charlie Feldman at the Cabana Beach Club.

There were palm trees there, not autumn leaves. Those *feuilles* were truly *mortes* when she abandoned Paris. But when she left she packed some *souvenirs d'amour* that put the final seal to Gabin's rage: a Vlaminck, a Sisley, and a Renoir.

Before Marlene left Paris, photography had begun on Mitchell Leisen's romantic espionage movie for Paramount. Camera crews invaded craggy mountain locations to capture the hero's flight to the Rhine and his escape from death most wretched at the hands of the Nazis. His derring-do would assure his survival to tell the tale, and an Allied victory, too, for he carried with him a new German recipe for . . . Poison Gas.

The chase was the climax of the picture and had to be shot before the end of 1946 to avoid penalty payments to Leisen under his Paramount contract. The action was photographed in southern California to establish in long shot what would later be intercut with close-ups of adventurous stars. A stunt double for Marlene was costumed and told to cavort in a manner that would make her escape thrilling, poignant, and anonymous. The stunt-woman scrambled over lacerating rocks, negotiated wind-whipped cliffs, crossed perilous torrents, and balanced over chasms profound on logs helpfully left lying about by Mother Nature and the prop crew, both on the side of Paramount and the Allies.

The stuntwoman traversed gaping doom on my-what-a-stroke-of-luck logs, supported every shaky step of the way on *high heels*, and so the unit photographed her. That the character she impersonated was an illiterate Hungarian gypsy who roved the Black Forest in a horse-drawn wagon and scavenged heaven knows where for food when not telling spurious fortunes for handouts did not inhibit the wardrobe department's notions of what a Paramount gypsy should wear in *Golden Earrings*.

When Marlene arrived in Los Angeles in early August to play the ragged, resourceful hellcat, she insisted on playing the role in bare feet. Neither the second unit director nor Leisen himself had foreseen this startling notion and there could be no schedule-breaking retakes to accommodate Miss Dietrich, who (so to speak) dug her heels in. She claimed she had made a thorough study of gypsy encampments around Paris (those gypsy violinists at Monseigneur, perhaps) before reporting for duty, and the gypsy in her soul knew what it was talking about. Such devotion to detail cut no ice with Paramount's production department, which had a relaxed attitude about authenticity. Those spike heels would remain on-again, off-again visible in the finished film as Lydia the Gypsy (or her stunt-double) leaped from log to log, from long shot to close-up, helping her lover escape the Third Reich and win the war, or the poisonous, gaseous part of it anyway.

As it turned out, the high heels were but a minor absurdity in a picture of many thigh slappers. The biggest side-splitter of all, to those who pronounced Marlene finished yet again, was her playing a gypsy in the first place.

This notion did not come from Paramount, to whom Marlene had been anathema ever since *Angel*, when they thought they had paid a quarter of a million dollars to see the last of her. Mitchell (*The Lady Is Willing*) Leisen, however, had weight at Paramount, and when the studio offered him the successful novel *Golden Earrings* by Yolanda Foldes (née Földes Yolán) with freshly anointed Oscar winner Ray Milland to star as the English hero-agent, Leisen's only real concern was casting Lydia, the low-rent Mother Courage with whom the hero falls in love, and for whom Victor Young was already busy plagiarizing a hit song.

Lydia could either make the whole thing credible through some transcendent thespic miracle à la Magnani or play it tongue in cheek for a good time. Star allure might make the melodramatics not matter. Enter Charlie Feldman.

Feldman continued to represent both Leisen and the ex-GI Leisen still thought "the most fascinating woman who ever lived." Both thought Marlene could be the most fascinating *gypsy* who ever lived. In rags, a ratty black wig, and gallons of Max Factor Aztec No. 5, she could *still* project enough sultry glamour to make Ray Milland's stiff upper lip quiver. Together they persuaded Paramount "there's only one woman who can be glamorous under all that and it's Marlene."

Marlene got second billing, but she got out of Paris and back to Hollywood, which suddenly looked like freedom, freedom, freedom. Leisen gave newly divorced Maria a job ("a brilliant actress," he called her) as her mother's dialogue coach. Maria had presumably picked up Hungarian and gypsy dialects at the Reinhardt school. Or on her USO tour in Italy. Or perhaps from her mother's well-known gypsy chum, the tempestuous Tallulah Bankhead, with whom Maria had appeared on Broadway in a small role in Philip Barry's *Foolish Notion*, still calling herself Maria Manton. Working with Marlene might not help mother's accent, but could ease their strained relationship and help pay bills for Maria's move to New York as a graduate drama instructor at Fordham University.

Gypsy Lydia wasn't really a significantly greater departure from dream-of-glamour Marlene than Frenchy had been in *Destry Rides Again*. Comeback lightning might strike twice with an offbeat character role, and at the very least Leisen could dish the dirt with her, as she made clear the moment she got off TWA at Los Angeles airport, gushing "secrets" about Paris and General Gavin through the armfuls of roses Leisen loaded her down with. She also gave Paramount publicity something to sink its hype into, tambourines jangling: *"Dietrich's back! . . .* and wait till you see her bring out the gypsy in Milland!"

Ray Milland had till now successfully masked signs of gypsy temperament. He had been in Hollywood since 1931 when Marlene was Queen of the Lot, and there was always something smug about him on screen, as if he were determined to remember his real name was Reginald Truscott-Jones. He was attractive and smooth enough and had so Americanized himself that few moviegoers remembered he was English, except when his not-very-well-placed voice sounded as if he were choking on a crumpet, which was often. It wasn't until Billy Wilder shrewdly cast him as the alcoholic on a binge in *The Lost Weekend* that his stiffness and some furtive quality about him suddenly worked *for* him: His tightness of manner wasn't forced charm anymore, it was the deviousness of alcoholic desperation.

Milland won his Academy Award against a light field: Bing Crosby in *The Bells of St. Mary's*, Gregory Peck in *The Keys of the Kingdom*, Gene Kelly in *Anchors Aweigh*, and Cornel Wilde in *A Song to Remember*. Such was the Hollywood to which Marlene had returned, where girl stars had next-door names like Betty (Hutton and Grable) or Jane (Wyman, Powell, or Russell). Milland's alcoholic beat out two priests, a sailor, and a composer, confirming the Academy's durable romance with affliction. This inflated Milland's consciousness of his Star at its zenith, just as that of the one-time Queen of the Lot seemed twinkling its last.

Milland didn't like her and she didn't like him, though she had the sense to keep quiet about it. Milland couldn't stop talking, though only after the picture's wow release did he have serious grounds for resentment (he can't have liked those *"Dietrich's back!"* billboards). Perhaps he sensed from the beginning that no actress would so enthusiastically demean herself for a role without a very strong hunch that groveling around in the dirt would pay off. It would have taken a dim actress, indeed, not to know who would reap the publicity as a Hungarian Earth Mother who wore the earth all over her face. Not even veteran screenwriters like Helen Deutsch and Frank Butler (with Abraham Polonsky, before he wrote *Body and Soul* and got in trouble with HUAC) could make it more than a far-fetched hoot, but that was all it needed to be.

* * *

The story is narrated by Major General Ralph Denistoun (Milland) who, as the picture begins, is dozing in his postwar London club when a messenger brings him a small parcel containing . . . golden earrings. Soon he is on an airplane, sitting next to war correspondent Quentin Reynolds (playing himself: there *was* authenticity at Paramount, after all). Reynolds notices Milland's pierced ears and asks. The rest of the picture is a shaggy-dog flashback to explain Major Denistoun's earlobes.

Denistoun was with British intelligence before the war and carelessly got captured by the Gestapo in Germany. This foiled his mission to take delivery of the new poison gas formula invented by good German Professor Krosigk (Reinhold Schünzel). Overpowering the Nazis, Denistoun and an aide dress themselves up in Gestapo uniforms and take separate paths to the professor and the formula.

On his own, Denistoun wanders around the Black Forest until he hears a voice singing the hit song "Golden Earrings." In Hungarian. Convincingly. The singer is stirring up a cauldron of fish heads. This is Lydia, gypsy extraordinaire (Dietrich), a widow woman who travels the forest in covered wagon, filthy petticoats, and bare feet.

Lydia turns out to be a gracious hostess, glad for someone to help her polish off the fish heads. Learning the truth (the Water Spirits had already warned her), she disguises Denistoun as a gypsy, dying his London pallor with walnut juice and piercing his ears for the jewelry of the title. She teaches him that well-known espionage technique, fortune-telling, as well as some things he missed at Eton, like the difference between boys and Earth Mothers.

Eventually they arrive at the gypsy camp (a *place*, not just a sensibility). There Denistoun must challenge and defeat the chieftain, Zoltan (Murvyn Vye, just arrived in the Black Forest via *Oklahoma!*), for the jacket that light-fingered Lydia has lifted from manly Zoltan in the first place. This prop—a boldly checked affair loud enough to drown out the zithers and violins—determines who gets *droit de seigneur*, with which the Code was apparently unfamiliar.

Denistoun proves his manhood, is accepted by the gypsies, and gets to keep the jacket as well as Lydia. Zoltan sings the same hit tune, but *he* has learned it in English.

Denistoun's blood gets paprika-hot; he works on his fortune-telling; he gets to shorten the lifelines of some Nazis by using a Luger. He and Lydia eventually arrive at good Professor Krosigk's house, where a cocktail party is in progress for some Third Reichers. Denistoun signals all over the place (his earrings glinting) that beneath the walnut dye he is None Other than Krosigk's British contact. He and Lydia go into their fortune-telling act, which is full of secret signals but fails to inspire the scientist's confidence.

The Gestapo suddenly arrive to denounce the good professor and toast the outbreak of war. Krosigk, finally Getting It, pays the fortune-tellers with a five-mark note *upon which he has written The Secret Formula*.

Lydia leads Denistoun through much geography to the border and the Rhine, intermittently kicking up her (double's) high heels, and there they part. Denistoun's postwar flight with Quentin Reynolds returns him to the Exact Same Spot in the mountains where he left Lydia, who has spent the war figuring out the name of his London club so she could send off his earrings by parcel post. Lydia's wagon heads them into the sunset, pots and pans clattering. Zithers up.

Such a plot is beyond criticism. In 1939 Hungarian gypsies, like Jews and other non-Aryans, were being rounded up by real-life Nazis, and poison-gas spy plots had gone out with Marlene's *Dishonored* in 1931. In the face of so much improbability, Leisen didn't seem to notice, or had no time to care.

All was not smooth during production. Apart from the stars' hating each other, there was a union dispute that required Leisen, Milland, Marlene, Murvyn Vye (or Marlene *and* Murvyn Vye), and anybody else for whom a cot could be requisitioned to sleep overnight for weeks on end in their dressing rooms to avoid crossing picket lines.

Marlene practiced her zither and drove everybody crazy with a perfectionism that actually showed on screen, where she played a mean zither. She had a brief reunion with Reinhold Schünzel (Professor Krosigk), opposite whom she had played ingenue in the silent *Bogus Baron* twenty years before. Schünzel had fled Berlin after making the original *Viktor/Viktoria* and wound up at MGM directing Joan Crawford as Sonja Henie in *Ice Follies of 1939*, a fiasco that returned him to acting, notably in Hitchcock's *Notorious* and films like this one which required authentic German accents.

There was another old Berliner on the lot, but Billy Wilder was busy putting Bing Crosby through some Viennese paces in *The Emperor Waltz* ("just the cutest thing you ever saw," noted one critic-historian), though Marlene may have been on Wilder's mind, for her old pre-*Blue Angel* theme song, "I Kiss Your Hand, Madame," was in the *Emperor* score to become a hit all over again from Crosby, though no one in America ever associated Madame's kissable hand with Marlene.

Leisen, meanwhile, refereed the interplay of his stars. "[Milland] was a real bastard at first," he remembered. "He calmed down a little by the end, but he and Marlene fought the whole time. When we were shooting the scene where he first meets her as she's eating the stew, over and over, Marlene would stick a fish head into her mouth, suck the eye out, and then pull out the rest of the head. Then, after I yelled cut, she would stick her finger down her throat to make herself throw it up. This whole performance made Ray violently ill."

No such lip-smacking over fish eyes appears in the picture, but Leisen's dish was never drab. "There was a little fire under the [stew] pot, but . . . we put dry ice in the pot to give off the vapors. When we broke for lunch, the prop man stupidly forgot to put the fire out. We came back, and when Marlene saw the water bubbling merrily along, she assumed it was just the dry ice. She stuck her hand in and let out a blood-curdling scream. She had a second degree burn. I suggested we call it quits for the day, but she wouldn't hear of it. . . . We cooled the water off and she kept sticking her burned hand in the pot with the dry ice all afternoon."

Such problems (and the union dispute) caused the picture to lop over into 1947, earning Leisen his penalty payments, but Marlene was finished and on her way back to Europe via New York by then.

Golden Earrings turned out to be universally despised by spoilsports and the humorless. Bosley Crowther in *The New York Times* groaned that "some strange suicidal impulse has apparently inspired [Paramount] to do everything to Miss Dietrich that would submerge her assets . . . and make a greasy ragamuffin of her. . . . It is neither appealing nor artistic to behold La Dietrich, the model of svelte, smeared with some dark and oily ointment and prancing about in dirty duds."

Crowther was fastidious; crowds were fascinated. *Golden Earrings* was hugely popular with audiences. Its mix of comedy and drama wobbles, but today the comedy bubbles along on the surface, inherent in the playing and in Victor Young's over-the-top score. As long as Leisen's touch is light the picture amuses, and so does Marlene's Lydia, full of dark gypsy imprecations and wiles, committing grand larceny in scene after scene. Leisen allowed her to do her own lighting and makeup as on *The Lady Is Willing*, and by controlling the lighting she controlled the camera and strolled away with the picture in her bare feet.

Marlene isn't exactly acting in *Golden Earrings*, or even giving us "Marlene": She's trouping. This is a job, but she has fun with it, letting the audience savor the joke with her, never losing the balance between absurd comedy and glamorously superstitious gypsy lust. Eschewing glamour only reminded everyone how glamorous the "real" Marlene was.

Her identification with the war, with Germany, with antifascism was so complete even in this hokum that when Billy Wilder wandered over from his *Emperor Waltz* set now and then to escape Bing Crosby and the rising tide of Viennese *Schlag*, he reflected not on Marlene's old "I Kiss Your Hand, Madame" (which he had known in Berlin) or even on the ersatz

Hungarian "Golden Earrings" (ubiquitous on every American jukebox), but on something darker, more . . . Kurfürstendamm.

It was just an idea. He would go back to that new little club on Sunset Boulevard—or was it Santa Monica? The Tingeltangel, that place Friedrich Holländer had recently opened that wasn't doing so well, and listen to some of Holländer's new songs and think about it some more.

SEVENTEEN

PRO

1947 - 1950

The *Queen Elizabeth* sailed from New York to Southampton and Le Havre in early January 1947 in four days, eleven hours, twenty-four minutes. "There's no better place to test a man," Marlene teased, "for you have a lot of time on your hands," but this was the fastest crossing in the liner's history. Even a *Queen* could adapt to a quickening era.

Marlene was testing nobody on board but Rudi, who had already passed many tests of discretion in the years he and Tamara (safely left behind in New York) had enjoyed thanks to Marlene's largesse. The husband who never gave an interview about his wife still hoped at fifty to fashion a career as film producer. They were traveling to Paris for the premiere of *Martin Roumagnac*, but Rudi's hope was to make a film about prewar Europe, the world as it had been, using all those German actors who had suffered and survived the gas chambers or the ovens or the Mephistos in their midst. The film's star would be the producer's wife.

It was a dream too late. His future had vanished with the world that was. His identity as Mr. Dietrich or "phantom hubby," as the press dubbed him, was as demeaning as it was true. And maybe the film idea was just a pretext to get an American visa to Berlin for a final visit with his family. The request was relayed from the Paris embassy to the War Department in Washington and was rejected. Neither Marlene's entreaties nor her war record helped. The borders to that prewar world were redrawn; curtains soon would fall.

Marlene used the swift sailing to recover from a New York Christmas, her forty-fifth birthday, and Maria's twenty-second. Maria was divorced now and teaching acting at Fordham. Mother and Father murmured *Gott sei dank* about the young man she met there, a scenic designer called William Riva, who was talented, single, straight, and more interested in Maria than in whose daughter she was. Deciding she would rather be Maria Riva than a one-hundred-and-ninety-pound reproach to her parents, she transformed herself into the beautiful young woman Marlene had wanted for a daughter all along, but did it because that was what Bill Riva wanted for a wife. The two set a significant date: the Fourth of July, Independence Day.

Marlene believed her film future lay in Europe, and she used the press conference when the *Queen Elizabeth* docked to laud local production, dismissing Hollywood technology. *Golden Earrings* was just silly, escapist fantasy dominated by technicians. "You must bear in mind," she said, "the American film public is seventy-five percent children, and you have to meet their standards." When she disembarked at Le Havre, she glowed with praise for Dior's "New Look" and "the atmosphere in the French film studio. . . . Filming in France is technically superb, paradoxical as it may sound, because of the . . . outmoded facilities. The French are inventive enough to overcome and turn these difficulties to advantage. Lighting and sound are far closer to reality than when working with the most up-to-date studio equipment," making it sound as if *Martin Roumagnac* had any more to do with reality than *Golden Earrings*.

The French reporter who recorded Marlene's delight with antiquated Parisian facilities also announced she had just learned she would become a grandmother. A premature but prescient bit of news. No one paid any attention; no one had ever heard of a glamour girl grandmother.

Martin Roumagnac premiered and went belly up. "Oh lord, oh lord, take it away" is just what cinema owners did. The print was shipped to America, where distributor Ilya Lopert would spend almost two years trying to cut it for the Code and the Legion of Decency. Thirty minutes of film fell to the cutting-room floor as it became flashbacks at a tedious trial.

making the American title, *The Room Upstairs*, all but senseless. Decent it became; disaster it remained.

As did the relationship with Gabin. Marlene saw him at the Paris premiere with Rudi at her side; no message so clear. The relationship was dead, but gossip wasn't. It was said she followed Gabin in Paris streets for years and took the apartment in the Avenue Montaigne that she kept for the rest of her life because it was near his. Maybe because it was near Dior. He got married. She rushed to Paris. He wouldn't see her. He bought a gravesite in Normandy near his birthplace. She bought the adjoining plot. He sold. She pined. And saved their love letters and called herself his "widow" when he died.

A reporter thought to ask him in 1949, when the scars were still fresh, what ever happened to their plans for a picture called *Première Mondiale* to follow *Martin Roumagnac*, and he delivered a final verbal blow: "The old woman is too unstable," he said. There was no reply.

Uncertain of her own future, Marlene plunged into other lives. A new look had come to films as well as fashion. Roberto Rossellini's *Open City* opened in Paris and Marlene became an instant convert to neorealism. She dragged friends to it, then to *Paisan*, and when Rossellini and Anna Magnani came to Paris to do Cocteau's one-woman play *La Voix humaine*, Marlene forced everyone she knew into acts of homage: Cocteau himself, Jean Marais, Edith Piaf, Max Colpet. *Open City* and *Paisan* were part of Rossellini's postwar trilogy, the third part of which would be set in Berlin between the known and the unknown: 1945. Marlene knew just the writer.

Max Colpet had been working on French film scripts with little success and was facing the prospect of turning Strindberg's *Dance of Death* into a screenplay for Erich von Stroheim. He was saved from that grim task by Rossellini, who needed a German writer for *Germany—Year Zero*, as part three of his trilogy would be called. Colpet found a secretary who would work for nothing: Marlene. She pecked doggedly away at a portable typewriter, broken fingernails helping her feel neorealistic. When the pages were as perfect as a self-taught typist could get them (never very), she dashed out to buy and brew espresso for the maestro.

Rossellini invited Colpet to Berlin, but Colpet's family had died in German concentration camps (he had been interned by the French) and he had sworn never to return. Marlene persuaded him to go for the sake of the film and his career. Besides, Marlene knew that Colpet's oldest friend and one-time fellow Paris exile was in Berlin: Billy Wilder.

Wilder had been in Berlin after V-E Day as an officer with the U.S. army. It had been his duty then to approve or deny Allied performing licenses, required for every German production. In reviewing the applica-

tion of the revered Oberammergau Passion Play, he noted that almost all
the disciples were portrayed by former Storm Troopers, Jesus himself an
ex-SS man. "Okay," Wilder had said, "on condition the nails are real."

Wilder was not German, but Austrian (or Galician). His screenwriting
career began in Berlin, where he had been a crime reporter and occasional
Eintänzer, a sort of gigolo for ladies with no one else to tango with in
Berlin's syncopated twenties. He read *Mein Kampf* in 1932 and, finding its
humor wanting, left Berlin the day after the Reichstag fire, first for Paris,
then Hollywood.

At the end of the twenties Wilder had made his name as one of the
fathers of a famous semidocumentary about life in Berlin called *People on
Sunday* (Fred Zinnemann worked on it, too). Now he was back in Berlin
with two Oscars (for writing and directing *The Lost Weekend*), finding
found footage: people—or ruins—on the long morning after the Nazi night
before. He encountered strong protest from sensitive Germans who objected to the idea of Hollywood-on-the-Spree. Wilder cut them down to
post-Reich size in his acidic, Austrian-spiced German. He was preparing
something to cure the whipped-cream hangover of *The Emperor Waltz* with
Crosby, and the terrible destruction of Berlin was both sobering and brac-
ing. He left Berlin with miles of footage of rubble as backgrounds for—of
all things—a comedy set in these, the zero years.

The picture would be called *A Foreign Affair* and star Jean Arthur as
Phoebe Frost, a sort of American version of Ninotchka, a strait-laced United
States congresswoman from Iowa on an inspection tour of GI morale (and
morals) in occupied Berlin. There she gets her braids unraveled by falling
in love with a rascally U.S. army officer (John Lund), who is involved with
an ex-Nazi nightclub singer, a "gorgeous boobytrap," who is the former
"strudel à la mode" mistress of a Gestapo bigwig. It was Jean Arthur's return
after a three-year absence brought on by major conflicts with Columbia's
Harry Cohn, for whom she had made Frank Capra's trio *You Can't Take
It With You, Mr. Smith Goes to Washington,* and *Mr. Deeds Goes to
Town*. Arthur had been in films since 1923, had played everything from a
cheesecake Wampas Baby Star to Calamity Jane, and was the smartest,
most appealing of all the girls next door. Wilder's film might have been a
triumph for her if he hadn't chosen as the Nazi nightclub singer the least
likely actress in the world to impersonate a Nazi. On the other hand, he
didn't know any other strudel à la mode with better anti-Nazi credentials
than Marlene.

She had the medal to prove it, and proved it so often when she returned from
Paris to Hollywood to make *A Foreign Affair* that old friends like Lubitsch
made it to a rule to come to parties only if she promised not to wear it.

She had a right to her pride. She was the first woman ever to receive the United States government's Medal of Freedom (Generals Bradley, Patton, and Gavin were men of long memories), which was not then the routine award for show-biz politics that a show-biz president has since made it. It was then the civilian equivalent of the Congressional Medal of Honor, awarded for courage and valor, and was the highest award any civilian could receive. Naturalized-citizen Dietrich received hers in a ceremony at West Point. The medal was pinned on her sober black suit (Dior: no sense looking dowdy) by Major General Maxwell Taylor, and the official scroll cited:

> meritorious service . . . meeting a grueling schedule of performances under battle conditions during adverse weather and despite risk to her life. Although her health was failing, Miss Dietrich continued to bring pleasure and cheer to more than 500,000 American soldiers. With commendable energy and sincerity she contributed immeasurably to the welfare of the troops.

A decorated war hero could play a Nazi in *A Foreign Affair* with as much impunity as, say, a grandmother, and Marlene was working on that, too. Or Maria was. She and William Riva married in New York on the Fourth of July and set up housekeeping in a Third Avenue cold-water flat. Marlene stayed in Paris to avoid competing with the bride at the wedding, but could not resist the call of a kitchen floor. She scrubbed, waxed, and cast *Hausfrau* (or gypsy) spells to make certain the newlyweds were *wed*. It worked, for by the time she wore her Medal of Freedom all over Bel Air and Beverly Hills she was on the way to becoming "the world's most glamorous grandmother," a phrase she relished until journalists set it in permanent type that eventually became exasperating as a constant reminder of age.

A *Foreign Affair* started shooting in December. Marlene moved in with the Billy Wilders, where she and Wilder plotted to elevate the eyebrows of the film colony permanently with Marlene's tales of schooldays seductions in Old Weimar and "women are better." These were merry moments, but there was sadness, too. Ernst Lubitsch died in late November. Wilder revered him as "the master," and despite their differences on *Angel*, Marlene counted Lubitsch a friend whose approval she wanted and mostly got. She wanted it, too, for Gérard Philipe, her Paris discovery, whom she hoped Lubitsch would cast in a film based on *Der Rosenkavalier*. Lubitsch died of a heart attack while showering or in bed with a beautiful woman, depending on the version one believed. Marlene raced from the home of Lubitsch's frequent screenwriter Walter Reisch, where she heard the news, to tell doctors and paramedics what to do. She may not have believed

Lubitsch was truly dead, for she took along recordings of her *Foreign Affair* songs to play for him just in case. He would have liked them.

A *Foreign Affair* shared something with Lubitsch's *To Be or Not to Be* in the furor it aroused about "taste." On release in 1942 *To Be or Not To Be* was denounced as "callous" and "tasteless" for making jokes about Nazis whom Hollywood had, only after years of waffling, decided to take seriously. The uproar focused on a Nazi officer's famous line about Jack Benny's (Polish) ham actor: "What he did to Shakespeare, we are now doing to Poland." Lubitsch (an air raid warden during World War II) refused to cut the line and the outrage the joke inspired is today forgotten and the line remains unkillably quotable.

Taste was sometimes an issue with Lubitsch; it was always an issue with Wilder. To accuse him of cynicism is like accusing the seven dwarfs of being short. He is regularly attacked for vulgarity and cruelty. He effervesces with malicious *mots* about Hollywood and is famous for a "bitter wit." Andrew Sarris pegged him as "too cynical to believe even his own cynicism," and many found A *Foreign Affair* poisonous with it. But it is not the cynicism that disturbs; it is Wilder's feelings about Berlin, which bump into each other so ambivalently that Paramount advertised the picture as "SERIOUSLY! It's the funniest comedy in years."

There is a lot of gloating, a lot of *Schadenfreude* over the fate of the Master Race as we take a guided tour through the ruins of what (in Wilder's tangoing youth) was "the most beautiful" and "the fastest city on earth." This is the city that formed Marlene and the one that drew Wilder there when he might have remained in Vienna—Sammy Wilder, boy law clerk— forever. Beneath the wisecracks ("The Thousand Year Reich . . . that's the one that broke the bookies' hearts") there is a nostalgia for what Berlin *was*, a sense of loss in ruins still smoldering, an ambiguity so resonant it seems, to many, rank.

A *Foreign Affair* is full of references to the Berlin that attracted Wilder, none greater than composer Friedrich Holländer himself, playing piano on screen for Erika von Schlütow (Marlene) at the off-limits Lorelei club, as he had played piano at the Blue Angel in that film. A bass drum advertises the Hotel Eden, one of Unter den Linden's glittering twenties haunts, and The Syncopators, Berlin's most famous 1920s jazz band, who were Holländer's on-screen back-up musicians in *The Blue Angel*.

What offends critics is Wilder's treatment of Capra's Jean Arthur. There is the girl next door to Mr. Smith and Mr. Deeds cavorting in Wilder's ambiguous landscape of nostalgia, cynicism, and ruins. A Viennese prankster seems to be pegging Capra's do-good Americans for rubes. The picture is so Berlin one critical observer wondered where the UFA logo was.

It doesn't need it; it has Friedrich Holländer's songs for Erika/Marlene, the most double-edged songs in any Hollywood picture. Some critics appreciated them and some loathed them. James Agee condemned them as "the perfection" of "rotten taste," but they are the beating, if cankered, heart of the movie. Without those songs, there *is* no movie. Without them it is just an anecdote about a priggish congresswoman who gets her socks knocked off by a playboy in uniform, plus some sharply aimed darts at congressional committees, occupation bad-boys, and American corn (literally: Congresswoman Frost gets drunk and sings "The Iowa Corn Song" to Russians at the off-limits Lorelei, egged on by cunning Erika).

With those songs, the picture has a subtext about survival, a bitter melancholy as close to the sentimental as Wilder ever got. Those songs give *A Foreign Affair* focus and an undercurrent of regret perhaps no one but old Berliners like Wilder and Marlene could feel so keenly, and it cuts deep enough to draw critical blood to the present day.

Holländer wrote them not for the picture, but for the Tingeltangel Club, his failed attempt to create cabaret in Hollywood. They are dark, corrosive, mockingly romantic. Their voice is that of a survivor not sure survival is all it's cracked up to be. "Black Market," the bitterest, reeks with corruption. It sings of "broken-down ideals," now black market coin for Lucky Strikes, nylons, and Spam. Marlene sings it in one of her sequined gowns, her hands uplifted like some ironic Nike strolling through the ruins, a goddess mocking the spoils of victory. "I'm selling out," she sings with the smile of a silky, corrupt used-car salesman:

> *Take all I've got*
> *Ambitions, convictions, the works!*
> *Why not?*
> *Enjoy these goods*
> *For boy, these goods*
> *Are hot!*

And it's a *waltz*! One-two-three through the debris.

Wilder loves the allure of corruption, the glamour of defeat (that's what *Weltschmerz* is all about). "Illusions" personalizes the mood of "Black Market" with Marlene again in sequins, spotlights slicing through the boozy haze of black-market cigarette smoke:

> *Want to buy some illusions?*
> *Hardly used, just like new.*

Erika savors the masochism, which

> *. . . has a touch of paradise,*
> *A spell you can't explain.*

For in this crazy paradise,
You are in love, with pain.

Marlene sings this as a love song to herself and then to the Congress-woman and her army beau, who is also *Marlene's*, though the congress-woman doesn't know that. Phoebe Frost is making her big speech about how it felt to be a little boat adrift on big, gray waves. Until love. Then Marlene and "Illusions" float like specters in the mirror above Phoebe's head. This is masterful stuff, neglected in the justifiable praise Wilder's more familiar (and more obvious) work gets.

The movie is full of wisecracks about moral watchdogs and smart comedy about horny GIs, but it belongs to Erika, the survivor. Charles Brackett, Wilder's producer and co-writer (with Richard Breen), admitted that Erika was a "complete heavy" who needed some "humanization," but there's nothing perfunctory about it. She gets the best speech in the movie, ex-plaining survival to Phoebe Frost:

> This is a beastly thing to do [she says], but you must understand what happened to us here. We've all become animals with exactly one instinct left—self-preservation. Now take me, Miss Frost. Bombed out a dozen times, everything caved in and pulled out from under me. My country, my possessions, my beliefs. Yet somehow I kept going. Months and months in air-raid shelters crammed in with five thousand other people. I kept going. What do you think it was like to be a woman in this town when the Russians first swept in? *I kept going.* It was living hell. And then I found a man, and through that man a roof, and a job, and food and—and I'm not going to lose him.

Congresswoman Frost wonders what this has to do with her. "A little," Erika answers. "You see, you want the same man."

She tells Frost the facts of life with cool pity: "You know this game of love. If you want to take the advice of an old gambler, some people are lucky at it, some people are jinxed; they shouldn't even sit down at the table."

But Phoebe *has* sat down at the table and seems to have lost. She wins in the end; she gets her man and Erika gets carted off to a labor camp. *Maybe.* A five-man military escort goes off with her, and she hikes her skirt to her knees and asks with that smile and that voice: "Is it still raining? If there are any puddles, you'll carry me, won't you boys?"

It's Erika's finest hour, her big exit, her comeuppance in Hollywood terms, but it's a salute to survivorship, too.

For all those unsettled by Jean Arthur's silly congresswoman, hardly anyone failed to find Marlene superb. Bosley Crowther in the *Times* thought the picture "a dandy entertainment which has some shrewd and realistic things to say." He called Jean Arthur "beautifully droll," and John Lund "disarmingly shameless."

"But [he went on] it is really Marlene Dietrich who does the most fascinating job as the German night-club singer and the charmer par excellence. For in Miss Dietrich's restless femininity, in her subtle suggestions of mocking scorn and in her daringly forward singing of 'Illusions' and 'Black Market,' two stinging songs, are centered not only the essence of the picture's romantic allure, but also its vagrant cynicism and its unmistakable point."

Time found Marlene "a past mistress of sardonic comedy and of low-life glamour." *Variety* was appreciative: "Marlene Dietrich personifies the eternal siren as an opportunist German femme who furnishes . . . off-duty diversion. Also, she gives the Dietrich s.a. [sex appeal] treatment to three [Friedrich Holländer] tunes, lyrics of which completely express the cynical undertones of the film." *The New Yorker* savored a "delectable dish" who "looks just as handsome as she did years ago in *The Blue Angel,* and she sings just as well, too, turning a couple of songs . . . into really incandescent chants."

Life put Marlene on its cover and headlined its story "Dietrich steals the show in an uproarious Hollywood view of low life in Berlin." But for many, the cynicism was not vagrant enough, the recent war was still too fresh for comedy. *Cue* wrote of "a messy conglomeration of bumbling humor, pointless vulgarity and occasionally comic caricature. The picture's three central characters are thoroughly repulsive . . . thrown together in a gutter romance."

If critics were mixed, a comedy about American soldiers with blackmarket hearts and ants in their pants outraged the army. The U.S. military banned the picture in postwar Germany, sanctimoniously calling it "crude, superficial, and insensible to certain responsibilities which the world situation, like it or not, has thrust on . . . the movies. Berlin's trials and tribulations are not the stuff of cheap comedy, and rubble makes lousy custard pies."

A Foreign Affair still exercises some of our best critics, who can no longer be reacting to issues of fraternization or black-market corruption. Both Andrew Sarris and Richard Corliss get considerably worked up at Wilder's treatment of Jean Arthur (he "brutalizes" her, they say), but she's dizzy, dreamy, and winning. She just doesn't win the picture.

Marlene's Erika von Schlütow simply stole the show; Phoebe Frost's braids never had a chance. Marlene had those songs and those "nude dresses" (copies whipped up by Edith Head: "You don't design clothes for Dietrich. You design them *with* her"). Marlene had . . . Dietrich.

The corn maiden wins in the end, but it's Marlene's Erika we remember when we leave the theater: She may be the corrupt heart of the movie, but she's wisdom in the rubble, ruing and saluting broken-down ideals with gallows humor. It is a great performance.

Script and photography of A *Foreign Affair* were Academy nominated, but the picture was only a moderate hit and wasn't easy to make. Jean Arthur was unnerved by Marlene's and Wilder's joking in German with Holländer (Arthur was notoriously skittish anyway). She feared Marlene would do to her what she had done to Ray Milland and Ronald Colman: Take the picture and run. Her anxiety about returning to the screen after a three-year absence was not assuaged by Marlene's easy manner and frank fascination with her own glamour. Arthur's "face like a well-scrubbed kitchen floor" retreated to her dressing room while Marlene laughed and told war stories to Lund and the crew. Arthur huddled and cried: Was the floor Marlene was now scrubbing *hers*?

Wilder was torn between admiration for Arthur and impatience with her paranoia, between Marlene's glamour and her own endless appreciation of it. "What a picture," he moaned to John Lund. "One dame who's afraid to look in a mirror, and one who won't stop."

Marlene lived her role, clowning and vamping and flirting all over Paramount. Gerd Oswald, Wilder's assistant (he had met Marlene when a teenager in Berlin, where his father was a famous producer) remembered the atmosphere well. "Marlene was always sitting outside her dressing room watching the parade go by like it was a sidewalk café. Rumor had it she was having an affair with just about everybody who walked past. I remember a couple of muscle men stunt-guys she just *devoured*." John Lund, who calls Marlene a "mixture of siren and homebody, gracious, unfailingly professional and funny," remembered Randolph Churchill visiting the set and making such a pest of himself in pursuit of Marlene that Wilder's wife finally threw a glass of wine at him in disgust. "Forget about Churchill," Lund smiled in remembrance. "There was a sense on that set of a relationship with *every*body."

But they all knew there was a new man in her life.

John Michael Riva's birth on July 19, just before release of A *Foreign Affair* in 1948, focused attention on his grandmother's performance in the picture and outside, too. He took after Maria's—Marlene's—side of the family, and many detected a resemblance to Rudi.

Announcement of his arrival raised a small flag in the still slumbering consciousness of women "of a certain age," for Marlene made it clear that grandmotherhood would change her romantic freedom from convention not at all. No more than marriage, motherhood, and career had done.

Virtually overnight the notion of what a mature female might look and act like altered for millions of women, and not a few men. When Marlene appeared on *Life*'s cover in August, it was in a close-up portrait (by Arnold Newman) of a woman who, with no apparent makeup but lipstick, eyebrow pencil, and a little Vaseline to make her eyelids glisten, challenged the foreground lilies in freshness and clarity. Classic beauty belied the words on the cover: "Grandmother Dietrich."

Marlene went dignified for a while, befitting her new status as matriarch of three generations, but that went with the "New Look" she had been sporting since Paris. She pulled her finely textured hair back into a bun, but fashion decreed it a chignon now, and when she was photographed by Horst or Irving Penn or Richard Avedon or other great fashion photographers she looked more contemporary than ever. There was less of the leg stuff (the New Look fairly precluded that), but there were still the lazy eyelids, the inviting smile, and those symmetrical bones to catch and model light into sculpture. She was both fashion plate and beyond fashion.

She had a man's polo coat made up in white ermine and proved she could still outflash the flashbulbs on opening nights. During the day she wore nurses' uniforms from Bloomingdale's to wheel John Michael Riva through Central Park in nanny anonymity. She bought the baby's parents a brownstone on East 95th Street with her *Foreign Affair* money ($40,000 of it) and moved herself into the Plaza Hotel until she found her own apartment on Park Avenue, close enough for baby-sitting.

The house on 95th Street (worth several million today; some of the Rivas still live there) was within a baby-rattle's earshot of the one belonging to the German-born actress Dolly Haas and her husband, caricaturist Al Hirschfeld, who became close friends of the Dietrich/Riva clan. Dolly Haas had not known Marlene in Berlin, but had sat next to Trude Hesterberg in the Gloria-Palast the night of the *Blue Angel* premiere. It was Hesterberg who had turned to her just before the lights went down and sneered, "Emil Jannings is a *very* great actor and Dietrich, *well . . .*" Emil Jannings was now an unemployable ex-Nazi senator whose reputation rested largely on the film he had made with "Dietrich, *well. . . .*"

Haas's husband had done the drawing of Marlene sitting on top of a piano featured in the ads for *A Foreign Affair*, and he would continue sketching her for decades. A fair-sized album might be published of his affectionate sketches of her, though his famous fluid line is not known to have captured her in nurse drag or changing diapers.

Dolly Haas became a militant Marlene defender, for she knew the affection Marlene lavished on John Michael, then later on John Peter, John Paul, and John David as they arrived in turn, Marlene's quartet of "Jonnys." They called her "Missy" or "*Maus*," and she called them by their second names, sometimes with a German inflection (Paulie became Powlie). Haas recalls Marlene "walking around in nurse's uniform, running like a whirlwind after local scamps who tried to interfere with the baby. She would come back from the park in her uniform and toss aside the latest *Vogue* or *Harper's Bazaar* or whatever with her picture in some glamorous up-to-the-minute something, utterly blasé about all that, but rosy with pride that '*I just beat the bejesus out of some kids*' who were bothering the baby. *That's* the real Marlene," Haas maintains fiercely today. "*That's* the Marlene nobody writes about."

They did write about it. Endlessly. Finally even Marlene got tired of it, but when the role was new she loved it and stayed in New York to cultivate it and cosset the baby. It didn't hurt that John Michael Riva gave his mother a new role too, and common ground on which Maria and Marlene could reconcile some of the past and prepare for some of the future.

Rudi's joy of grandfatherhood was lovingly expressed but distant. He occupied a small New York apartment with the increasingly unstable Tamara, whose psychological condition was not calmed by the repeated abortions Rudi insisted she undergo to keep housekeeping simple. The end of Marlene's love affair with Jean Gabin was the end of Tamara's last hope that Rudi might make her an honest woman. Or let *her* be a mother.

Marlene did not remain unescorted. Her ubiquitous appearance in fashion magazines had a sponsor: I.V.A. Patcevitch, publisher of *Vogue*, an elegant, sophisticated escort and a steadier godfather to John Michael Riva than Rudolf Forster (who went "back to Adolf") had been to the baby's mother.

Grandmother fashion-plate or no, Marlene was still a working woman and needed to be now more than ever. To remain in New York near Maria and the baby and "Pat" Patcevitch, she had "that voice." She had been active in radio off and on from the thirties. She and Clark Gable had inaugurated the *Lux Radio Theater of the Air* from Hollywood in 1936 (hosted by Cecil B. DeMille) with a version of *Morocco* called "The Legionnaire and the Lady." She had done radio versions of her movies and others', and there were dramatic performances on anthology shows and comedy bits with Bing Crosby, Orson Welles, and later Tallulah Bankhead, Perry Como, and others. Radio was an easy way to earn money for herself and the Rivas and Max Colpet, too, now finally in America (Marlene got him a visa and a contract). At the end of 1948 she was heard as Madame Bovary opposite Van Heflin and Claude Rains to launch CBS's *Ford Theater* before an all-star audience. CBS's Frank Stanton escorted her to the all-star supper after. Her Emma Bovary wasn't all that provincial, but she wasn't just a glamour-puss either.

Bovary was directed by Fletcher Markle, husband of Mercedes McCambridge, not yet famous for her Oscar-winning role in *All the King's Men*. Markle wanted to direct films, and Marlene agreed to do a walk-through in (of course) New York's Blue Angel night club in *Jigsaw*, financed mostly by and starring Franchot Tone. *Jigsaw* was a gangster picture with an antifascist, antiracist theme and worth lending one's name and presence to. Marlene, Henry Fonda, John Garfield, Everett Sloane, Marsha Hunt, and Burgess Meredith all did unbilled bits. Their combined star power was too unbilled to help the box office of an underwritten B-picture that *Variety* thought "well-intentioned but lightweight." Not lightweight enough to keep it from sinking like a stone.

Radio money could not support Marlene and her expanding family in the style to which she hoped to accustom them. Some friends thought Pat Patcevitch wanted to marry her. One of them said, "He was deeply in love with her, but she made him feel he was being led around with a ring in his nose."

When in early 1949 she received a few pages of treatment from Alfred Hitchcock, she accepted at once. Hitchcock was in a slump, but had a six-picture deal with Warner Brothers that allowed him to do what he wanted. That turned out to be a novel called *Man Running*, which he retitled *Stage Fright*, a thriller set in the theater: murder and delicious low deeds by dubious high types. Highest (and most dubious) of all was musical comedy diva Charlotte Inwood—Marlene.

The picture starred Jane Wyman, who had just won an Oscar for *Johnny Belinda* and was anxious to get away from Hollywood and a dim ex-husband. Wyman would get first billing (Marlene got second) as Eve Gill, a Royal Academy of Dramatic Arts student whose boyfriend Jonathan (Richard Todd) sets things off at a dangerous clip by announcing he is about to be charged with the murder of glamorous Charlotte Inwood's husband. Jonathan is a chorus boy in Inwood's latest West End hit, and until now it has slipped his mind to tell Eve he is also Charlotte's lover. He explains (in flashback) that the wicked but ravishing Charlotte has come to him in a state—and in a Dior drenched with her husband's blood. She has begged Jonathan to go back to the murder house and get the *other* Dior so she'll have something to wear to the theater, where the show must do what shows must do. Jonathan does, is seen, and police think he, not Charlotte, committed murder most foul. Eve knows a dramatic situation when she hears one (RADA and all that), and hides Jonathan while concocting a plot to trap the Toast of the West End.

Marlene could swank around like nobody's business as a (literal) *femme fatale* of the theater, but there wasn't enough to do. Hitchcock agreed, and the easiest way to expand her role was the way Billy Wilder had: with songs.

338

"La Vie en rose," which Marlene borrowed from her one-time Parisian best girlfriend Edith Piaf, was a natural, but the second song, the big number to be shot in a real theater, was more elusive. Hitchcock suggested Cole Porter's unknown "The Laziest Gal in Town" from 1926, but Marlene didn't want to do it because it was old. The Code people had anyway found all those Porter innuendos "quite offensive." Another Porter song, "Great the First Time," was rejected, as was "Second Hand Rose." Marlene convinced Hitchcock to get a song from London emigré Mischa Spoliansky, who had composed her songs in *It's in the Air* and *Two Bow Ties* all those years ago in Berlin. That didn't work, either, and Marlene rejected an Ogden Nash song proposed by Hitchcock, who was by now referring to her privately as Madame. Something called "Love Is Lyrical" was written and used for an incidental number, but the big show-stopper could not be found. Marlene continued rejecting "The Laziest Gal in Town" until shooting was upon them and there wasn't anything else. The Code insisted on a new verse to replace the risqué original, and Marlene grumpily consented to sing it while lazing around in a marabou-trimmed negligée, slinking from one alluring posture to another on a stage terraced with chaise-longues while showing plenty of leg. The result was classic Dietrich; "The Laziest Gal in Town" would become part of her repertoire for the rest of her life, and one is not surprised to read still that Porter wrote it for her: Her possession of it is so total that he might have, though he didn't.

Marlene demanded and got Dior for *Stage Fright*; Dior demanded and got screen credit; Warners demanded and got a twenty-five percent discount. What Marlene mainly got was one of the best roles of her film career, with which she—once again—effortlessly walked off with the picture. She got a new lover, too.

Michael Wilding had been under contract to British producer Herbert Wilcox, acting in musicals about Mayfair opposite Wilcox's star-wife Anna Neagle, when Hitchcock cast him in *Under Capricorn*, the Ingrid Bergman box-office disaster that preceded *Stage Fright*. Wilding, tall, thin, and elegant as a whip from Asprey's, had charm and a dashing way with the ladies. Hitchcock cast him in *Stage Fright* as the detective on Marlene's trail, with whom Wyman's Eve falls in love as it dawns on her (slowly) that Jonathan isn't very good husband material as he is a psychotic killer. His entire opening flashback about Charlotte turned out to be a lie, which caused no end of grumbling from the critics.

Marlene took one look at Wilding and the laziest gal in town got busy, which bothered Wilding not at all, but made Jane Wyman nervous. Wyman had her Oscar, but Marlene had all those Dior dresses and those songs and the leading man and the glamour to do to *her* what she had just done to Jean Arthur in *A Foreign Affair*.

Wyman's role called for her to impersonate a country cousin of Marlene's dresser as a means of getting inside and trapping Inwood. To do this, she became even mousier than usual, while Marlene went around in marabou and white fox, dripping Dior, diamonds, and the picture's best dialogue.

"I ran into great difficulties with Jane," said Hitchcock. "In her disguise as a lady's maid, she should have been rather unglamorous; after all, she was supposed to be impersonating an unattractive maid. But every time she saw the rushes and how she looked alongside Marlene Dietrich, she would burst into tears. She couldn't accept the idea of her face being in character, while Dietrich looked so great. She kept improving her appearance every day and that's how she failed to maintain the character."

This sounded rather like Marlene herself a dozen years before on *I Loved a Soldier*, but no one remembered that, and word filtered back to Hollywood. Hedda Hopper reported "Jane Wyman's London picture is going through its fourth dozen retakes. Marlene Dietrich looks too good in the close-ups, which is no reflection at all on our little Janie," she announced, jabbing in a hat pin.

Wyman denied all that, claiming with Academy Award graciousness that she had announced, "Well, Marlene, I'll leave the glamour to you." Just so that didn't sound patronizing, she added that Marlene was "the most fascinating person I've ever met. On days when she had no studio call she would come on the set just the same. She'd fix my dress, make suggestions about my hair and makeup, and help me in many ways."

Marlene's punctuality was a lifelong habit, even without Michael Wilding to prepare for. Richard Todd, creepily effective as Jonathan, remembered her being there every morning before the crew arrived, adjusting her tape and wigs in order to be perfect when Wilding arrived. She brought little cakes and things for tea, and was "madly skittish whenever Wilding was around, but she was attentive to us all, helping us through some very difficult scenes which seemed to bore Mr. Hitchcock. He was around, but very cold and diagrammatic in his approach to directing, as if he were not really very interested in the picture. We'd do a scene and he'd pick up a diagram, talk to the cameraman and technicians, ignoring us as if we were a bunch of sheep. We perhaps bleated too little, but it was Marlene who sensed our lack of—*literal*—direction and did something about it. If you asked me who directed *Stage Fright*, I'd have to answer Dietrich, the performances at least. She was the one with the theatricality and know-how and experience and generosity. She was quite girlish around Wilding, but that never diminished her interest in us.

"When we were in the Scala Theater in Charlotte Street for her 'Laziest Gal in Town' number, there was a theater full of extras who watched her

Pen pals: Papa and the Kraut, disembarking in 1937.

Marlene and Fritz Lang in 1935. A telephone—not his monocle—came between them. Later, so did age.

Marlene and Claudette Colbert wore identical eyebrows – and raised a few – at Carole Lombard's amusement park party in June 1935.

Two "traitors." Ernst Lubitsch welcomes Marlene back from the Nazi Embassy in Paris to Paramount, 1937.

Marlene made Technicolor costume tests with John Gilbert, who would have played in *Desire*. He died, instead . . .

. . . while Marlene rediscovered Gary Cooper.

Marlene at Gilbert's funeral, propped up by Dolores del Rio and Cedric Gibbons.

Marlene and Charles Boyer walked off *I Loved a Soldier* at Paramount when Lubitsch got fired . . .

. . . and went right to the Technicolor deserts of David O. Selznick in *The Garden of Allah*.

Maria (*seated at right*) was in *The Garden of Allah*, too. This is the still Marlene couldn't kill. The nun is Helen Jerome Eddy, and Bonita Granville is the girl standing at left, apparently annoyed that "Dietrich's daughter" seems to be the teacher's pet.

Josef von Sternberg and exile Max Reinhardt chat at a
Hollywood party with a former employee, 1936.

On holiday in Salzburg,
Marlene took twelve-year-old
Maria (*left*) shopping. Rudi's
rarely photographed Tamara
is at right.

Berliner
Illuſtrirte Zeitung

Silvester-Heft

Goebbels's anti-Marlene campaign at work:
John D. Rockefeller proposes marriage. "Save up
another billion," she tells him.

Marlene and old employer with new
lover, Erich Maria Remarque.

Bijou Blanche lights up with the U.S. Navy in *Seven Sinners*, 1940.

Herbert Marshall and Melvyn Douglas admire Paramount's idea of "a simple gown" in *Angel*, Diana Vreeland called it "a million grains of golden caviar."

". . . a greater work of art than the Venus de Milo . . ." one editorial called Marlene's Frenchy in *Destry Rides Again*, the greatest comeback in movie history.

Jimmy Stewart mixes with Frenchy.

"Love me!" she wrote to George Raft after they made *Manpower*. He didn't know she was quoting Goethe. 1941.

Marlene and John Wayne got together often. Here he tries on her wardrobe in *The Spoilers* while Randolph Scott wonders what's going on.

Marlene charms Fred MacMurray from the floor in *The Lady Is Willing* to hide her broken ankle. Director Mitchell Leisen approves. 1942.

Marlene as "a gift from Macedonia" in MGM's solid-gold *Kismet*, 1944.

The Flame of New Orleans, remembering when she was "the toast of St. Petersburg."

Lydia the gypsy tries to loosen up Ray Milland in *Golden Earrings,* which was nonsense, but golden for Paramount.

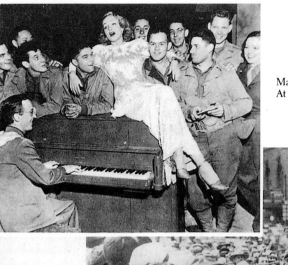

Marlene was "something for the boys."
At the front, 1945.

Marlene winning World War II, 1945.

Marlene and Jean Gabin: soldiers in love.

Marlene and her mother met for the last time in Berlin
at the end of the war. Here they are at Tempelhof
Airfield. Josephine wears a tie, too.

rehearse for, oh, it seemed like two weeks. I was sort of skulking about backstage as the lover she was trying to avoid, and I watched her day after day as she perfected that number. Most stars would have insisted the theater be cleared, but she *wanted* everybody there, she wanted that *audience*. Day after day. Then she did it for the cameras. She knew where every light was, but she was playing to the audience as much as to the camera, and when the number was finished, the extras—who'd been sitting there watching this thing for days—rose as a body and gave her a standing ovation. That wasn't in the film, but it was one of the most moving things I ever saw. This 'mere' movie actress *earned* it. And *loved* it."

Marlene, too, felt a lack of connection with Hitchcock. "I never got to know him," she said, and told John Russell Taylor, "He frightened the daylights out of me. He knew exactly what he wanted, a fact that I adore, but I was never quite sure if I did right. After work he would take us to the Caprice restaurant, and feed us with steaks he had flown in from New York, because he thought they were better than the British meat, and I always thought he did that to show that he was not really disgusted with our work."

He probably was not. His unhappiness with Wyman (who was miscast anyway, as the daughter of the delicious Alistair Sim and dizzy Dame Sybil Thorndyke) was clear. Of Marlene he famously and crisply said, "Miss Dietrich is a professional. A professional actress, a professional cameraman, a professional dress designer." Some find the remark sardonic, but Hitchcock's biographer Taylor regarded it as a sign of the "warm affection" that grew from "a sterling regard for each other's professionalism."

Stage Fright finally is lower-case Hitchcock and upper-case Dietrich. Her performance is seamless but layered, studied but nonchalant, as subtly modulated as if she were playing it on her violin. Her achievement is neglected because of the opening flashback (Jonathan's lie), which causes even sensible critics to call *Stage Fright* a "dishonest whodunit," on which grounds *The Wizard of Oz* must be rejected as Dorothy's "dishonest dream," not to mention *Rashomon*, which is nothing but different versions of one event.

There is no denying the flashback lie created resentment in critics and audiences, though probably no more than the picture's relaxed indulgences. There are too many little set pieces, brilliant in themselves (Miles Matheson's unctuous barfly; Joyce Grenfell's relentlessly cheerful shooting-booth lady; Sim and Thorndyke's crackpot marriage; Kay Walsh, brilliantly nasty as Inwood's dresser), but they derail the narrative. So does Dietrich. Her greatest gift as an actress (this may be a definition of Star) is that when she's on screen the picture is *about* her, but *Stage Fright* shouldn't be. It is supposed to be about Eve, and Jane Wyman couldn't dominate it or Hitchcock wouldn't help her do so.

Critic-commentator Molly Haskell correctly notes that "Marlene Dietrich gives one of the great performances of her career," and points out that the entire film is less about murder and thrills than it is about acting. Charlotte Inwood, Jonathan, Eve are all actors, all acting all of the time. When it turns out Inwood didn't kill her husband, but Jonathan did (for her), Inwood muses, "I suppose I'm what you call 'an accessory,'" already pondering her billing in the papers and the trial.

Charlotte is outrageous and knows it. Haskell sees her as "a woman too magnificent to be contained in a world made to human scale. Her evil is not malicious but an accident of birth, an excess femininity with which only the grandiosity of the theater is commensurate." When seamstresses measure her for the widow's weeds she will wear at the funeral of her murdered husband, she can't resist asking them to lower the neckline "just a little in front, can't you? No? No, I suppose not," she sighs, but we know she'll get the neckline she wants because it's a *costume*. The whole funeral bit, though, is a drag. "Take away these weeds," she sighs, flinging aside her funeral veil. "They make me sad and I don't like to be sad—it's so *depressing*."

Her manipulativeness is as much a part of her as her skin. Now free of her husband (thanks to Jonathan), she's going off with her manager. "Sun. Palms. Lovely. For two weeks," she dreamily tells the stricken Jonathan before the game is up. Then, astonished at his look (what did he expect?): "You didn't think I was going to give up *every*thing, did you?" He answers with the deadliest line in the movie. "*I* did."

However outsize and outrageous, Charlotte is not inhuman. Dressing after a performance, she thanks Eve for her help, gives her a little extra cash and responds to Eve's ambition to be in the theater with: "I can't think why; it's an awful life, really." It's a tiny stab to the heart of what it costs to be and stay the kind of star she is. She doesn't care about Eve, she can't even remember her name. But she's capable of compassion at the very moment Eve is betraying her into a confession of complicity in murder. It *is* an awful life, apparently, but what can she do but fix the white fox to the Dior suit with the diamond clip? She has such elegant authority we want her to get away with it, like Erika von Schlütow.

Hitchcock gives Charlotte a final scene after her arrest. It's so oblique it's obscure, but it swells with star presence. Charlotte may be under arrest, but she's still a star. She asks the guard for a chair, a light for her cigarette, and (playing to the balcony) asks him his name. Melish, he says. She wreathes herself in cigarette smoke, then:

CHARLOTTE: Do you like dogs, Melish?
MELISH: Yes, ma'am, I do.

CHARLOTTE: But not all dogs. If they don't love you, you don't love them. That's right, isn't it?

MELISH: I suppose so.

CHARLOTTE: I had a dog once. He hated me. At last he bit me and I had him shot. When I give all my love and get back treachery and hatred it's—*it's as if my mother had struck me in the face.* . . . Do you understand that, Melish?

MELISH: I've heard that it takes them that way sometimes.

CHARLOTTE: [HUGE CLOSE-UP] Yes. It takes some of them that way.

It's a bad speech. We don't know who or what she's talking about— Jonathan? Her husband? Eve? The theater? But she invests it with such force of personality we can almost feel the treachery, hear that blow of her mother's hand, and we are astonished to realize she *had* a mother and wonder just who wrote those lines. For a split second a whole life opens, then shuts down again in introspection. It's great performing: singer, not song.

Reviews were utterly predictable when the picture opened in early 1950. Marlene got them all. New York's *Sunday Mirror* noted "Miss Dietrich, looking radiant as ever, rather runs away with the honors, as is her custom." The *Journal-American* thought "Grandma Dietrich is so supercharged with sex appeal . . . she makes Jane Wyman look like a Girl Scout leader." *Boxoffice* reported, "Marlene Dietrich, apparently ageless and more sexy than ever, steals the show," and Louella Parsons gushed that "Marlene's imperishable beauty alone is enough to make an audience gasp." The *Los Angeles Times* found her "more gorgeously seductive than at any time since her discovery and development by Josef von Sternberg."

Howard Barnes in the *Herald-Tribune* recognized, "It is Miss Dietrich . . . who dominates *Stage Fright*. She sings sultry songs and charms all her gentlemen callers throughout," but he thought it "only a pity that she and Hitchcock could not have found a more substantial frame for her didoes." *The Hollywood Reporter* thought the picture overlong but "as it stands, the presentation holds attention through nearly two hours principally because of the presence of Marlene Dietrich . . . at her most provocative." *Time* found her "uncannily young and beautiful. . . . If anyone steals the show it is Veteran Dietrich. Dressed to kill and chanting languorous ballads in a husky off-key, she creates an acid-tinged portrait of a glamorous bad lady of the theater."

Miss Dietrich was, as Hitchcock noted, a professional.

Michael Wilding or no Michael Wilding, it was time to go back to Hollywood, and show them *how*.

EIGHTEEN

STAR QUALITY
1950 - 1952

Kenneth Tynan once asked Noël Coward what star quality was, and Coward ("that splendid old Chinese character actress," as he liked to call himself) replied, "I don't know what it is, but I know I've got it." In a less flippant vein, André Malraux tried defining star quality at about the same time and took Dietrich as emblem of the type. "A Star," he wrote, "is in no essential way an actress incorporating a particular role in a film. A Star is a being with the requisite minimum of dramatic talent whose face expresses, symbolizes, and embodies some mass instinct. Marlene Dietrich is not an actress like Sarah Bernhardt; she is a mythical figure, like Phryne."

Whether the Academy of Motion Picture Arts and Sciences was up on its Phryne (another Aphrodite rising from the sea), they knew about star quality. They had never paid much attention to Marlene. They nominated her once—for *Morocco*—and that was that. It wasn't so much that her performances were neglected in favor of more deserving competition as that Academy voters never even thought about her. Not as an actress, anyway. Lola Lola had been *hors de concours* because foreign films weren't then eligible, and Academy voters seemed to regard such disparate characters as, say, Shanghai Lily and Frenchy; or Domini Enfilden and Lydia the Gypsy; or Catherine the Great and Bijou Blanche; or Concha Perez and Lady Maria Barker; or the Queen of the Baghdad Dancers and Charlotte Inwood; or Fay Duval and Erika von Schlütow and X-27 and Helen Faraday and Countess Alexandra and all the rest as the same person, just one effortless and repeated visitation that somehow required nothing but personality and maybe a change of eyelashes and wardrobe.

Marlene was always "Dietrich," they agreed, when anointing Ginger Rogers for *Kitty Foyle*, Joan Crawford for *Mildred Pierce*, Loretta Young for *The Farmer's Daughter*, Joan Fontaine for *Suspicion*, or Marie Dressler for *Min and Bill*, the performance that beat Marlene out the one year she was nominated.

Marlene Dietrich was finally more indelible than the characters she impersonated (though they were paradoxically hard to separate). Because she never made lofty speeches about Art, even those in the audience who should have known better assumed there wasn't any. She didn't seem to mind, though late in life she could get caustic about the Academy, which Josef von Sternberg (also a nonwinner) had told her to ignore and from which he had resigned when they started giving prizes to other people. Marlene never played an alcoholic, a nymphomaniac, an ax-murderess, or victim of any unnamable but nondisfiguring disease. Nor did she try on any of the great literary roles and therefore didn't inspire Academy recognition. On some level this was praise beyond praise: She made being Marlene Dietrich look so easy that no one ever thought to question the effort it took. But if she couldn't bring the Academy to its knees, she could bring it to its feet, and did so in 1950 with her usual irreproachable professionalism.

The Academy Awards were not televised then, and the hullabaloo still took place at the Pantages Theater on Hollywood Boulevard. Marlene was invited to present the then-minor best foreign film award and prepared by asking dressmakers around town what the other presenters would be wearing. Bolts of organdy and younger-than-springtime ball gowns were the order of the day. "So Mama had better be slinky," she decided, "nice, slinky, black." The slinky black should cling to the figure that was better now than it had been in *Morocco*, with a little décolleté. She would look like a sleek, obsidian arrow aimed at the heart of that garden of organdy hollyhocks. She determined which side of the stage she would enter from, so the slit in the skirt to the knee would expose some leg as she floated across the stage in what she called "the Dietrich strut."

She brought the house down. They gave her no award; they gave her a standing ovation for reminding them what star quality was. She was, acclamation suggested, her own Oscar.

A few weeks later Maria made Oscar's surprise hit a grandmother for the second time. Marlene's delight was dimmed only by renewed press buzz about the world's most glamorous grandmother. "Judging by the world press, I am the only grandmother in the world," she was heard to snap, perhaps mindful that Michael Wilding, a dozen years her junior, also read the papers. But not even a new love interest could pull Marlene away from New York and the birth of John Peter Riva.

Maria *needed* a baby-sitter. She was resuming the career she had suspended after her entirely unnoticed Broadway debut with Tallulah Bankhead in *Foolish Notion* (prophetic title) and hoped to combine marriage, motherhood, and work without slighting any of the three, as she was persuaded her mother had done. Once the new baby was delivered (he took after the darker, Riva side of the family), Maria could return to work with her lovely face, a reconditioned figure, and that stage name quite too beautiful to be as real as it was: Maria Riva.

William Riva had begun his own New York career in lighting and scenic design on something short-lived called *Trial by Fire* just after he and Maria married in 1947. Then there was a revival of Eugene O'Neill's *Lazarus Laughed* in 1948, and during Maria's pregnancy with John Peter he worked on Gian Carlo Menotti's short operas *The Medium* and *The Telephone*. He also began making toys and furniture for the little Rivas, an avocation that would later provide a livelihood when the theater did not. He painted the nursery as if it were a set, with clouds and fantasy trees that turned up in full-color pages in *Living for Young Homemakers*, a decorating magazine of the Condé Nast (and godfather "Pat" Patcevitch) empire.

Before Marlene returned to Europe and Michael Wilding she saw to it that the babies were diapered and Central Park'd and Maria's acting career relaunched. Maria would soon be a familiar face to viewers of CBS television's *Studio One*, on which Fletcher Markle (*Jigsaw*) and old Berliner Felix Jackson (*Destry Rides Again*) were both producers. Before that, however, she appeared on a half-hour anthology series called *Sure as Fate* hosted by the bombastically rotund Francis L. Sullivan (whose rotundity and bombast would soon be on display on Broadway in a thriller called *Witness for the Prosecution*). The show debuted on the Rivas' third wedding anniversary (July 4, 1950) and was directed by a sometime-actor, sometime-singer whose exotic charm and wavy black locks failed to divert Marlene from the blues she was feeling about her separation from Wilding. When the television director shaved his head not long after, he got out of television and into big-time fame in a role Marlene's chum Noël Coward had turned down. Had Coward accepted *The King and I*, we might never have heard of Yul Brynner, but Marlene had and would not forget.

While Brynner still had hair, Maria had a job and Marlene returned to Paris to choose the wardrobe for her next picture, which would return her to London and Wilding and Denham Studios, where she had made *Knight Without Armour* fifteen years earlier as the most highly paid woman in the world.

Marlene—"the distilled essence of Movie Actress"—was now to play a glamorous film star on screen, the only time she ever actually played one. To help her look the role, she hied herself to the House of Balmain in Paris to stock up on movie star duds. Balmain's *directrice* Ginette Spanier was taken aback to find Marlene at ten o'clock in the morning "blonde, pale, beautiful beyond words, [and] smileless," gazing at herself in a full-length mirror. Spanier was an aggressive and charming celebrity collector who knew about catering to glamour. She also knew Marlene was one of the rare ones who "see big . . . know how to feed the legend" and was disconcerted as the legend appraised her reflection in the mirror wearing a £4,000 mink cape and coolly pronounced it "rather poor." Spanier snapped haute couture fingers for the longest, costliest mink stole Pierre Balmain had ever trapped and flung it around its cousins in the cape. "I'll take it," said the legend, charging the mink farm to Darryl Zanuck. Spanier wrapped up the pelts and Marlene, too. Marlene became intimate friends with the ebulliently social, English-born Spanier and her French husband, Doctor Paul-Émile Seidmann (they were also pals of Noël Coward). She occasionally slept on their sofa and cleaned their flat until years later a minor row over scrambled eggs escalated to unsheathed fingernails and confirmed Marlene's notion that however wonderful women might be, "you can't *live* with" one.

Adding a mink hat to keep her stole and cape company, Marlene wrapped them around some Dior dresses, scooped up some diamonds from the Dietrich dressing table (she was notorious for leaving gems lying around like used Kleenex) and proceeded to London and Michael Wilding. Also waiting were Jimmy Stewart and *No Highway in the Sky*.

The picture was pre-Arthur Hailey *Airport*, based on a novel by Nevil Shute, an aeronautical engineer who wrote many other books including *On the Beach*. *No Highway* seems today both remarkably prescient and hopelessly dated. It tells of Theodore Honey (Stewart), a scientist with some alarming notions about metal fatigue, which are poo-poo'ed by everyone in the wings business.

Stewart plays not very English but plenty eccentric. Mr. Honey is a forgetful scientist and widower held together by his gravely intelligent eleven-year-old daughter Elspeth (Janette Scott). He is squirrely, shambling, and oblivious to everything but work. "The line between genius and being just plain crackers is so thin," someone remarks in exasperation. Honey realizes with a turn that "it's evidently very difficult to be a person." Marlene's movie star will make him one.

Though he works with aircraft, he's never flown till the picture starts, when he boards a plane with a bag lunch prepared by young Elspeth. After some chat with the stewardess (Glynis Johns), he realizes planes serve food and this one (according to his slide rule) is only heartbeats away from plunging into the Atlantic after losing its tail to metal disintegration.

Across the aisle is Monica Teasdale (Dietrich), who was the favorite movie star de luxe of Mr. Honey's late wife. The Honeys, in fact, spent their last evening at one of her films just before Mrs. Honey died in the Blitz. In a burst of sentiment, Mr. Honey wakes the slumbering, mink-blanketed Miss Teasdale to warn her of imminent disaster. He knows the plane's structural strong points and tells her with some urgency to "go to the men's room, sit on the floor. . . ."

Monica Teasdale has been around, but this is a new one even to her. Still, with nothing to do in the days before in-flight movies, she listens as Mr. Honey gives her a crash course, so to speak, in aeronautics.

Monica might as well listen. She's tired of flinging her minks and eyelashes from Paris to Hollywood. If stage star Charlotte Inwood thought the theater "an awful life, really," Monica Teasdale hasn't found Hollywood much better. She's been through three bad marriages ("I wouldn't be surprised if it was my fault") and "would have stopped working a long time ago if I could have figured out what to do with myself."

She tells Mr. Honey a version of the funeral story Marlene liked to tell the Hemingways (Teasdale adds her agent to the guest list, inconsolable at the loss of his ten percent). She mocks "posterity," wearily summing up her career as "a few cans of celluloid on a junk heap someday."

Marlene's role looks like a fillip to keep metallurgy from sounding drab, but the role was part of Shute's novel and pivotal to the personal story of Honey and his daughter. James Stewart was at the height of his popular stardom then ("It's Jimmy!" the ads hollered, though they also revealed Marlene's leggy durability). Tom Destry got first billing this time, and his shy eccentricity and Marlene's world-weariness complement each other with strangers-on-a-plane intimacy until their airborne coffin fails to disintegrate on schedule. Monica Teasdale removes her mink-swathed head from his shoulder, where it has rested for most of the flight, and notes coolly, "I guess you multiplied someplace where you should have divided."

The plane makes a stop in Gander while the Air Ministry tries to figure out what to do with crackpot Mr. Honey, who disables the plane rather than let it fly on to certain doom. Monica Teasdale knows a dramatic gesture when she sees one and decides "this funny little man is brave and kind and on the level." Back in London she uses diamond-studded celebrity to defend him to British aviation.

She takes an interest in Mr. Honey's daughter, Elspeth, and briefly deludes herself that scrubbing floors and ironing slide rules in a suburban house badly in need of some do-it-yourself (she does some) might be just the antidote to Lotus Land. But publicity about the incident reawakens Hollywood's interest in her career, and she comes to her senses and goes back to "give posterity another break." Mr. Honey is eventually vindicated (he forgot to calculate air temperature) and we are encouraged to believe he and young Elspeth may have a future with stewardess Glynis Johns, who has also been hanging around the ironing-board.

No Highway is a small picture of great charm, unaccountably forgotten today. Henry Koster directed, having earlier guided Stewart in *Harvey*. Koster had known Marlene slightly in Berlin when he was still Hermann Kosterlitz, before Joe Pasternak took him to Universal, where he changed his name and directed all those Deanna Durbin musicals. This was Stewart's picture, but Koster wanted Marlene: "If anybody can play a movie star, it's Marlene," he told Fox's Zanuck. "She without any doubt is a great movie star and a wonderful personality and a most beautiful woman." Zanuck didn't take much convincing. He liked Marlene and had wanted her to play Margo Channing in *All About Eve*. (Joe Mankiewicz talked him out of *that* one.) Koster thought, "Personally, Marlene Dietrich is one of the most charming women I ever met. She cooked once for us. She's a great cook. . . . But on the set she was tense."

She was tense about Michael Wilding off the set and Glynis Johns on. Jimmy Stewart was no longer a romantic issue, as he was now married and expecting twins. Nor was Elizabeth Allan, the English actress who had dressed as (and escorted) Marlene to that Hollywood costume party where Marlene came as Leda and the Swan she most admired. But old romances paved the set with eggshells.

Stewart gave friendly interviews about how Marlene's "beauty has warmth behind it, and heart, and she's got the kind of sex appeal that comes across the screen at you like a ten-ton truck." He nodded to her "adult concept of life," in remembrance of things past, and noted her mastery of screen acting: "Every tiny bit of pantomime she does makes sense."

Wilding, meanwhile, was attentive and adoring. They spent time at Marlene's suite at Claridge's, but Marlene was working and Wilding, then at the height of his matinee-idol charm, was socializing and charming old friends like Margaret Leighton and new ones like the actress scheduled to play Rebecca in MGM's *Ivanhoe*, Mrs. Nicky Hilton, known between marriages as Elizabeth Taylor.

Marlene was forty-nine by the time *No Highway* finished (Taylor was barely nineteen), and she arrived at Denham each morning at dawn to tape, wig, costume, and make herself up before the wardrobe mistress had struck a match for the morning kettle. She kept a supply of freshly cut lemon wedges into which she would bite before each take, not to sweeten her smoker's breath (one cigarette, one holder), but because the citric acid had an astringent effect, tightening her mouth muscles and cheeks, clearing and crisping her diction.

Marlene never conspicuously upstaged Glynis Johns, but her wardrobe took care of that all by itself, and tricks of a long trade were by now second nature. Johns actually had a larger, if less showy role, and was just coming out of her silly starlet phase as "the girl with the upside down eyes." She was wary of Marlene's history and star power and wary of one-time Marlene dress-alike Elizabeth Allan, too. Allan was cast as a neighbor of Mr. Honey who has always hoped to become Elspeth's stepmother. The movie star, the stewardess, and the neighbor-lady all descend on Mr. Honey's suburban cottage (and young Elspeth) while British aviation flaps its wings over Mr. Honey. They descended on the camera, too. The vying for lighting and angles became so pushy and Allan's performance so edgy that the subplot involving her was simply dropped, leaving her with billing (sixth) for what seems to be a guest appearance waving good-bye at the airport. (There are fragments of dialogue in the picture that make no sense as a result.)

Marlene, according to Janette Scott, who played Elspeth, was not the culprit and was far more likely than either Johns or Allan to yield angles to the others and get on with it. Still, in Dietrich and Johns's final scene together, Johns is at the ironing board in Mr. Honey's kitchen as Marlene drinks a cup of what looks to be week-old coffee. All Marlene need do—and she does it—is slouch languidly against the wall and make it impossible for Johns to speak to her without turning her back to the camera.

Marlene was dissatisfied with star billing for a supporting part. She grumbled to Koster, "Oh, my God, aren't we through with this picture yet?" or "I don't even understand this piece of dialogue." In her restlessness, she turned her attention to young Janette Scott. The child was third-generation theatrical (her mother was a prominent music hall personality) and an acting veteran, which didn't mean she knew about cameras. "You'll have to look after yourself," Marlene cautioned her amidst all the competition. "Find the lights. Tilt your head back so the light can hit your cheekbones. . . . Rock back on your heels so the light shines in your eyes and they don't go dead. . . . No, no, rock *forward* on your toes—you've lost the light! No one will see your eyes if you don't find it," and more.

"Miss Dietrich explained to me," remembers Scott, "that a 'basher' was a key light and what a fill-light did [it filled]. She got cameraman Georges Périnal to let me look through the viewfinder and taught me to ask about lenses so I'd know how large I was in the frame and could adjust the size of my gestures to the size of the image. She took me to the editing room and explained cutting to me, roamed with me through the prop room, showed me how the lemon wedges worked, and stressed the importance of dressing well off the screen as well as on. I was positively gleeful. I thought what fun it was to escape the tutors, but I had been around enough to realize I was getting an exceptional tutorial in the technical side of motion picture acting from one of the greatest of screen stars. She didn't teach me glamour; she taught me to be serious about my craft."

It happened that Janette Scott turned eleven during the shooting of *No Highway* and Marlene organized an on-set birthday party. Neither Scott nor anyone realized that December 12 was one day before the birthday of Maria Riva. Learning this forty years later, Scott smiled as she remembered Monica Teasdale's last line in the movie to Mr. Honey about his daughter, just before she takes her minks back to Hollywood: "Keep on telling her she's pretty, will you?"

Every critic welcomed Marlene in *No Highway in the Sky* as if Monica Teasdale weren't in it too. Otis Guernsey in the *Herald-Tribune* noted, "Miss Dietrich appears in the type of throaty glamour role she knows best, and it is good to see her on the screen." *Time and Tide* found "Dietrich's quietly philosophic film star . . . an incredible creature; but does one really care about that when wonderful Marlene, ever so slightly mocking, plays her with probably the only true glamour Hollywood has left these days?"

Campbell Dixon in the *Daily Telegraph* praised the performance which seemed to be the person: "Marlene Dietrich acts extremely well now, but otherwise there is not the faintest sign—not a wrinkle, not a blemish, in those candid, miraculous eyes, not the least thickening or thinning of that beautifully chiselled face—that 22 years have passed since an unknown actress, by no means a child, captivated us in *The Blue Angel*."

If Marlene had star quality, so did Yul Brynner, and was proving it nightly on the stage of the St. James Theater as the king of Siam. He had enough, anyway, to console Marlene for Michael Wilding's inexplicable interest in Elizabeth Taylor. Marlene had lunch in New York with Wilding's former producer Herbert Wilcox and asked, "What's Taylor got that I haven't?"

Wilcox thought Marlene "sensuous and exciting . . . the most feminine woman I have ever met," and was far too gallant to mention the "Y" word in reply.

The "Y" in Yul chased the blues away. He was now a sensation on Broadway, not at all disconcerted to be "making love to a woman whom he had admired since his childhood," recalled his son Rock, who was sometimes present in the dressing room when Marlene wafted in like Venus rising from a sea of Broadway babies. "She was," the younger Brynner reported, "the most determined, passionate, and possessive lover [Yul] had ever known, not in the least concerned about discretion. . . . It was up to Yul to enforce discretion, [so he] rented a studio flat secretly, just for his romantic trysts, and especially for the nights he spent with Marlene."

Marlene had by this time moved into her one-bedroom Park Avenue apartment. She lined the walls with mirrors "to make it look bigger" and to get a better view of Yul. When friends thought this a little "Hollywood," she answered coolly, "What's wrong with Hollywood?" She hung the Vlaminck, the Sisley, the Renoir, and some Cézannes to have something to look at when the king of Siam wasn't around. She also hung the penicillin culture from Sir Alexander Fleming, her Medal of Honor citation, and placed a silver-framed photograph of Hemingway signed "With Love, Papa" on a coffee table stacked with books she was suspected of having read.

The short stories she had written were hidden away, except from Dorothy Parker, who agreed with "trepidation" to look at them and told John O'Hara how relieved she was to find them good. The collection of dressing-room name-plates that followed her for life was hidden, too, perhaps in the bedroom with the indirect lighting from under the bed that was also a little Hollywood, but on dimmers, and flattering at fifty.

The industry's definition of star quality was simply someone who could *cause* a project. This sort of celestial being awakens in writers, directors, producers, and bankers aesthetic impulses hitherto dormant which drive them to fill celluloid with images to fill theaters. Marlene could still cause this kind of creative flurry thirty years after she had first announced, in pinafore and dumb show, "The horses are saddled," and in 1951 she caused what turned out to be her last, true Star vehicle, and it was an error.

There was some confusion between Marlene and old friend and director Fritz Lang over which one of them was really the star of *Rancho Notorious*, though Lang admitted "it was conceived for Marlene Dietrich. I was very fond of her once," he told Peter Bogdanovich.

They had not known each other in Berlin, where Lang was a star director when Marlene was still fiddling in the orchestra pit. They met in Paris in

1933 when Lang was filming *Liliom* with Charles Boyer and had their brief affair after he arrived in Hollywood, which ended when Marlene picked up the bedside phone to make a date with someone else. They remained friends, partly because Lang was the only old Berliner until Billy Wilder with whom she liked to speak German: She enjoyed his untranslatable jokes. After the war she interrupted work on *Golden Earrings* to alert him to libelous fascist rumors about him in the Paris press. He quickly sued Paris and responded to her thoughtfulness with a thank-you telegram signed "All Old Love, Fritz."

It was the "old" part that caused trouble when they began work on *Rancho Notorious* from a script Lang collaborated on with Daniel Taradash. It was a Western about "hate, murder, and revenge," as the folkloric theme song, "The Legend of Chuck-a-Luck," never stopped singing at you (a year before *High Noon* used the same device with a better song). But the movie was mainly about Marlene, a "glory girl" now over the hill, but not so much over that she didn't still look like Marlene and nothing like the fifty years old she was. The murder and revenge part was about solid citizen–cattleman Vern (Arthur Kennedy) tracking down his fiancée's killer, who not only raped and murdered her but stole the fancy brooch Vern gave her. Vern tracks the brooch to Marlene, who is den mother to a gang of outlaws at a hideout she runs—Rancho Notorious—as Howard Hughes, who financed the film, insisted on renaming the picture, once called *Chuck-a-Luck*, which not only implied Fate, but went with the song.

Fritz Lang is everywhere recognized as one of the great directors, mostly for his early German work: his *Nibelungen Saga* and *Metropolis* and the *Dr. Mabuse* films, and his masterful first sound film, *M*, with Peter Lorre as the compulsive child-killer. What Lang never was, was graceful or understated. He tended to use five reaction shots where one would do (always perfectly framed), and was unfailingly precise, exact, and cold. Viennese by birth, he seems the most Prussian of directors, complete with monocle (it later became an eyepatch), and he is today the object of an intense cult, initially chaired by Lotte Eisner, the German-born doyenne of the Cinémathèque Française, who worshipped him and had disliked Marlene since the old Betty Stern days in Berlin.

In America Lang never regained the near godlike culture status of his days in Berlin, but he made genre films as good as they get, like *Scarlet Street* and *The Woman in the Window* (both with Edward G. Robinson, Joan Bennett, and Dan Duryea). His later melodramas, like *The Big Heat* and *Human Desire* (both with Glenn Ford and Gloria Grahame), are tightly controlled and utterly lifeless, though greatly admired by those who admire them. Lang also did some effective, precise, exact, *cold* Westerns and was the closest thing Hollywood had to a true intellectual. He is regarded as the father of the psychological Western and was arrogant, autocratic, and a tyrant.

Marlene's top billing in *Rancho Notorious* suggested the fun of a sequel to *Destry Rides Again*, revealing where Frenchy might have turned up had she survived Bottleneck and a dozen years. The movie started a vogue for Westerns with lady stars who were getting hard to cast: Joan Crawford made *Johnny Guitar*, Barbara Stanwyck made *Cattle Queen of Montana*. Female stars *aged*, while Gables and Coopers *matured*. Dietrich, Crawford, and Stanwyck put on Technicolor and cowboy boots.

Rancho Notorious began with a series of flashbacks about Marlene (named Altar Keane: *alter* means age in German) expressly recalling *Destry*, but Lang's notion was a Frenchy past her prime with a gunslinger lover (played all in black by a miscast Mel Ferrer—*he* is called Frenchy in this version) also past his. The longtime romantic history of this duo gets unhinged by the "hate, murder, and revenge" of young Vern, the good man turned violent by fate.

Marlene was Our Lady of the Outlaws, a sort of blond *Dr. Mabuse* with a syndicate of Western bad guys to lord it over with her legend. She offers protection in exchange for a cut of the outlaws' swag (like the plot-point brooch), which keeps her in business, old Levis, and the occasional chiffon number in which she now and then warbles a tune.

When Vern arrives full of "hate, murder, and revenge," she falls for him, but the "Y" word is all behind her. "I wish you'd go away and come back ten years ago" she sighs. She seemed to think the same about Fritz Lang.

"Marlene resented going gracefully into a little, tiny bit older category," Lang said. "She became younger and younger until finally it was hopeless." Despite old times, Marlene and Lang grew to hate each other and took to speaking to each other in no language at all. It was the clash of old Berliner egos, with Marlene endlessly invoking the triumphs of Josef von Sternberg and Lang countering with those of Lang.

She thought him "a horror!" because of his habit of marking sets with tape for actors' movements, measuring them to his own footsteps, though legs sometimes vary in length. " 'Do it again,' he would scream," Marlene remembered, "with a sadistic exactness of which Hitler would have been proud." His "Teutonic arrogance" looked to her like "pure dilettantism," which sounded odd coming from a graduate of the Sternberg School, but others on the set found him overbearing, too.

Cameraman Hal Mohr, who had shot *Destry*, tried to quit *Rancho Notorious* because Lang was so "abusive." Mohr had "a lot of respect for Marlene," he said, "as a performer, as a professional," and when he wasn't trying to quit, Lang was trying to fire him, so "we never talked to each other . . . we just went ahead and did the work." (Mohr had a sense of humor. When Marlene asked him why she didn't look as good in *Rancho Notorious* as she had in *Destry*, he explained, "I'm ten years older now.")

Arthur Kennedy, as Vern, thought Lang behaved with all the grace of a "depraved aristocrat." The actor had made films before, but came back from Broadway and Arthur Miller's *All My Sons* and *Death of a Salesman* because he wanted to work with the man who had made *M* and *Metropolis*. He found "an aging, jealous man who had the air of a lost lover." Kennedy thought Marlene "a remarkable woman and connoisseur of many good things in life, including sex," which she discussed freely and with great humor. As a trained stage actor, Kennedy observed that "she had technique to burn, but no spontaneity, and it all came to a head one day on the set in what looked to the rest of us like a deliberate attempt to humiliate her.

"Marlene laughed. She was supposed to show her worldly humor or something in this outlaw hideout we're all in, and I'm staring at her cleavage and these two gorgeous boobs she had. Marlene laughed in character and Fritz Lang sat there silent and icy and gave a signal and the camera operator prepared to roll again, and the actors and extras retraced their steps back along these damn dotted lines of industrial tape on the floor—it looked like a goddamn Mondrian, someone said—and Lang called 'Action' again and Marlene laughed. Tried.

"It wasn't hearty or booming or trilling or musical or amused or anything like that. It was tense and sort of clenched. *Fake.* The crew and actors and extras and the great director—maybe even Howard Hughes, listening in on his secret intercom—waited for Marlene to laugh like a laugh.

"So she laughed again. It came out reedy, a kind of honk. Lang just stared at her and the whole thing began all over again. Laughing is hard," Kennedy explained. "It's one of the hardest things an actor can do because it calls on all the involuntary muscle and psychology you *don't* use when you're acting. It calls for spontaneity, and Marlene didn't have that. It needs calm and relaxation and total self-assurance, and Marlene, who was maybe the most self-assured woman I ever met in my life, wasn't relaxed or self-assured around Lang. She was frozen into this thing that looked like a laugh but sounded like a croak, and Lang sat there with that patent-leather hair and that imperial face and those eyebrows arching and—Christ, this was getting embarrassing! Everybody started staring at those tape marks on the floor—*hundreds* of them—and the mike boom swung around again and Hal Mohr at the camera exchanged glances with his operator and avoided looking at Lang *or* Marlene and Marlene went back to her mark and tried to laugh again and Fritz Lang just waited like this could go on all night and day and he didn't care how long it took or how embarrassed anybody was.

I started to think, How can you laugh just because somebody tells you to when all there is to laugh at is your own degradation? And the day wore on and the film ran through the camera and the producer was sweating bone marrow waiting for Marlene to laugh right and I kept looking at those two beautiful boobs she was so proud of, thinking maybe I could help *force* a laugh from her cleavage. But her diaphragm was paralyzed. *She* was paralyzed. And Lang just sat there looking like a snake. What did Marlene have to be paralyzed about, this beautiful, sexy, professional woman? This *star*. Fritz Lang, *that's* what. It was so embarrassing. So embarrassing and deliberately degrading."

The picture doesn't reveal the tension; it reveals the cheapness of the production. Lang had set it up with producer Howard Welsch at 20th Century-Fox, but it fell out at the last minute and went to Hughes's RKO. It was a penny-pinching picture anyway, with Marlene taking only $40,000, the lowest fee she had received for a starring role since *The Blue Angel*. She was to receive a deferment of another $70,000 plus 20 percent of the profits, but the financing was so complicated that no one would receive profits because there wouldn't be any.

The look of the picture hurt it. Reviewers and audiences commented on the back-lot look (exteriors were shot at Universal) or on the painted backdrops that were supposed to be exteriors and obviously weren't. In one of the great stretches of auteurist nonsense, Lotte Eisner rationalized cost-cutting as "serv[ing] to emphasize the moral situation," but all it emphasized was how cheap everything was. Producer Welsch boasted to screenwriter Taradash that in spite of this the picture had been "saved" in the cutting. When Taradash asked what had been cut, the producer serenely answered, "the mood."

Marlene made the covers of *Look* and (again) *Life*, and there were a few good reviews. Eisner, of course, found it "unique among Westerns," full of "imponderables" and "dark undertones"; *Variety* thought "Miss Dietrich is as sultry and alluring as ever, and the whole adds up to pleasant entertainment for good b.o. possibilities." *Time* thought "Marlene sings throatily, lazily crosses her beautiful legs, and looks sultry," but *Newsweek* noted that "the film's personal passions are all accompanied by the distinct sounds of machinery." The *New York World Telegram and Sun* summed up Lang's style as "sending for a piledriver to crush an ant."

There was considerable bitterness following the film's production, and Lang was as uninhibited as Marlene about voicing his displeasure. He would go back to Germany soon anyway, but just before his death, oddly, he backed away from criticism of his star. He had once been deeply attracted to her and perhaps had some sympathy for a once-great beauty unwilling to yield to mid-century notions of age or Time.

When Eisner was finishing her book about Lang (he knew she disliked Marlene), he pleaded, "Please, please, and once again please, drop all the passing shots at Marlene . . . Why? If I couldn't 'handle' her, then I was just a particularly bad director. And leave out all she says about Sternberg, too. It's nothing but silly gossip. Please, please, please!"

Lang's softening of heart was curious and Marlene may never have known of it. She continued for the rest of her life to revile him with vigor. It didn't look at the time as if *Rancho Notorious* was the end of her big movie stardom or the part of it that could *cause* pictures, at any rate. Even after the movie failed at the box office *Life* was putting her on its cover and celebrating "Dietrich and Her Magic Myth," and Hemingway was contributing to it with his much-quoted essay, "A Tribute to Mama from Papa Hemingway." But it would be four more years before anyone asked her to make a picture again, and her antipathy to Lang may have been because he, alone of all the people who worked with her, regarded her as "a tragic figure."

"Marlene once told me," Lang said, "that she wanted always to be a little bit unhappy, a line from one of her songs. She's not a good actress, everybody in the industry knows that. But she's always acting. She hardly knows herself anymore. If she's alone in a room and a cat slinks in, she starts acting. When she takes her grandson walking in Central Park and is unexpectedly seen, she makes a big 'to-do.' Earlier she acted the good mother; now the good grandmother.

"Her whole life is built on a grand illusion. She believes she is the most beautiful and glamorous woman in the world—and she has sold the public on her own picture of herself. That makes her a tragic figure. After so many love-affairs, she is alone. . . . Maybe it's because she was never satisfied with what she had. When she loved a man, she gave herself completely, but still looked around for another. That is the great tragedy of her life. Maybe she has always to prove to herself that because one man loves her, there'll always be another. In her own way I suppose she was always true to her lovers. Sternberg, I believe, was the only man she ever betrayed: Sternberg created her, and the creation destroyed the creator."

The monocle glints with a highly personal gleam here. No other insight, if insight it was, could have been more calculated to earn her enmity, and Lang may not have understood how wrong he was about one thing at least.

She was not alone. Lovers like Brynner and Wilding—like Lang himself once—would come and go, but Rudi and Maria and her grandsons were family, and family was forever. Imperfect, maybe, resentful and neglected and bitter, but forever. Lang couldn't or wouldn't separate Marlene Dietrich from "Marlene Dietrich," and suspected she couldn't either. They had merged; they were the same.

Rancho Notorious had one dramatically positive consequence. When the picture was released in late spring of 1952, Marlene agreed to go on tour to promote it. She made personal appearances with the movie and was paid $5,000 a day for coming onstage in an evening gown or in short shorts and singing "Get Away, Young Man," the song Ken Darby wrote for her for the picture. Mel Ferrer came along as M.C., and Marlene felt the same stage fright she had felt thirty years before in Berlin. "If they don't whistle," she told Ferrer, "I'm lost."

They whistled. And Marlene laughed, comfortable at last. They didn't want to see the picture; they wanted to see *her*. If she could still wake up Chicago, maybe her career wasn't "just a few cans of celluloid on a junk heap someday." Maybe she was nothing like "a tragic figure" at all.

III

LEGEND

NINETEEN

SOLO
1952 - 1954

Hemingway didn't think there was anything tragic about Dietrich; in his *Life* essay he said she knew "more about love than anyone." The claim resonated wide and deep: the daughter of the Weimer Republic, the mother, the grandmother, the loyal companion of giants of literature, of the theater, of cinema dreams, the gallant comrade of generals and GI Joes, and Joe DiMaggio, too. There was the hint of exotic things hidden in her wisdom: forbidden things, maybe, but Papa also wrote that not only was she "brave, beautiful, loyal, kind and generous," but did what she did governed by "her own rules in this life [with] standards of conduct and of decency . . . no less strict than the original ten." He added tribute to "that beautiful body" and "the timeless loveliness of her face," and wrote famously, "if she had nothing more than her voice she could break your heart with it."

The voice that Kenneth Tynan would call her "third dimension" had for more than twenty years now been one of the most provocative and evocative in the world. It was curiously ambiguous, unifying her contradictions: warmly feminine, coolly masculine, its invitation as suitable for a lullaby as a battle cry. It was supple, but never "legitimate," which made it all the more individual; endlessly imitated, always inimitable. It was a voice with a past that seemed to know the future. Marlene finally put it to work by itself.

Jobs were scarce. It wasn't just grandmothers over fifty having trouble with the movies; movies themselves were in trouble. The studios had been forced to separate themselves from their theater chains in the fateful "consent decree" brought about principally by the block-booking practices Paramount had made notorious during Marlene's reign there. They had used her films as the lever for booking lesser product in theaters they did not own. "You want Dietrich? You'll take Sylvia Sidney, too." All the major companies twisted arms and extorted playing time in this way, and the high court separated them from their own theater chains as punishment, removing a key rung from the ladders of vertical integration (production-distribution-exhibition) on which they had climbed to riches and global dominance. At the same time television was making insidious inroads on audience habits and tastes, which were changing in the new postwar rhythms. The studios cut their assets (who went home at night anyway, as the wise wisecrack went), loosing an immense talent pool on the small screen and making possible a new world of independent production no longer ruled by the old moguls and czars, who wandered off to pasture in high dignity (or high dudgeon) to become Popes of Palm Springs while bean counters took over Babylon.

Marlene was not yet ready to succumb to television ("I'll have to defend my title," she said, sounding quite Hemingway). Television was Maria's turf anyway, and radio was inevitable for that voice. It was technically undemanding and mostly in New York, where Marlene could be close to Maria and her grandchildren and Rudi and Yul Brynner.

Radio had been one of the reasons for her nagging Henry Koster about finishing No Highway in England; she wanted to get back to New York and inaugurate her first radio series in January of 1952. It was a half-hour, half-baked thing called Café Istanbul on the ABC network. Every Sunday night Marlene borrowed the name Mademoiselle Madou from Arch of Triumph and wandered through situations borrowed mostly from Casablanca. This was inevitable, as the director of Café Istanbul was Murray Burnett, recycling an unproduced play he had written called Everyone Comes to Rick's, which was the source material for Casablanca.

Marlene usually sang a few bars of "La Vie en rose" or some other

Continental ditty, purred her way through episodes that reeked of all the romance and foreign intrigue thirty minutes a week and sound effects could convey. After less than a year Marlene and ABC decided that *Café Istanbul* needed refurbishing and a new address. Mademoiselle Madou packed her bags (making sure Murray Burnett was tucked inside), changed her name to Diane La Volta, and moved eyelashes and trenchcoat from Istanbul to CBS, where the show got a new title, *Time For Love*, and a theme song for Marlene to record.

Marlene was the dominant force on both shows, rewriting final scripts (mostly Burnett's) with the help of Max Colpet, who kept changing his name on the title pages so the network wouldn't realize that too many scripts were coming from too few writers. All his old names came in handy: his original Kolpenitski, the Berlin Kolpe, the Parisian Colpet, and the Max Colby under which he had become an American citizen because Marlene told him Americans would never know how to pronounce Colpet ("col-pay").

Marlene's voice had deepened slightly with the years, but had come under mature control since the war. Singing had always been part of her screen persona. She made only a handful of pictures without songs and most of those, like *Angel*, *Garden of Allah*, and *Knight Without Armour*, had songs written by the likes of Friedrich Holländer, Max Steiner, or Miklos Rozsa that were cut or never used. She had made recordings since the late twenties; her songs from *The Blue Angel* had been hits in both German and English, and her French recordings from the early thirties had long been collectors' items. There had been American recordings (for Decca) and the new long-playing record encouraged rerelease of all these for the nostalgia market. But nothing did so much to contemporize postwar Marlene and exploit her voice as the American songs she had sung in German for the OSS during the war. Marlene played her old personal masters of the songs for Mitch Miller, Columbia's head of artists and repertoire, suggesting they might be worth releasing for their "historical value." Miller shrewdly heard commercial value in them, but insisted they be rerecorded to then current recording standards in order to release them as an LP.

"Oh, *never*," Marlene told him. "I will never feel that way again," but the recording director insisted, knowing that the voice that had sounded acceptable on shortwave broadcasts during the war would sound even better in a studio with early fifties state-of-the-art equipment and some rehearsal. "I talked to her about breathing," Miller recalled, "and the conscious things she could do with it. We recorded on monaural high-fidelity tape, on which only the most minimal kind of cutting and splicing was possible, and when she concentrated on the artistic, rather than the 'historical' value of what she was doing, her ear took over. It was all spontaneous craft, no tracking, no splicing, *all* performing. She had the craftsmanship, and talent will out if you have craft to carry it. Marlene did."

The ten-inch disk ("Miss Otis Regrets," "The Surrey With the Fringe on Top," "Time on My Hands," and others) became a prestige hit. American songs in German were something new in record stores and more songs were added for a reissue when the twelve-inch format became standard. It may well be the best album she ever made. Her phrasing, tone, and control were never more precisely nuanced, and perhaps because she was singing in her native language, she conveyed emotional depth and humor never achieved again, and none of the effect depended on the listener's understanding a word of German. Pop songs became bulletins direct from the heart, and no need for Berlitz.

The album's reception inspired Miller to team Marlene with young band-singer Rosemary Clooney, who had just become famous with "Come-on-a-My-House." The two made a series of "barrel-house duets," with Marlene as the sophisticate and Clooney the naive, a sort of mother-daughter act Marlene could not fulfill with Maria. They made a Top 40 hit of the female comedy complaint about men who are "Too Old to Cut the Mustard," followed quickly by others. They were released as singles, then as an album, lightening Marlene's image for yet another generation, and preparing the way for more important recordings—and income—to come.

Marlene's high profile on radio and records was sustained by cascades of print. Popular journalism was then entering an invasive mode, with scandal sheets presaging today's supermarket tabloids. Marlene's ambisexual love life was a tantalizing target for the leering pseudomoralists of *Confidential*, but it was the chic, sleek *New Yorker* that aroused her outrage when Lillian Ross profiled Hemingway on a visit to New York. Marlene thought Ross must be some secretary taking notes in the Hemingways' suite at the Sherry Netherland Hotel. Hemingway introduced the two with his much quoted offhand remark, "The Kraut's the best that ever came into the ring."

The Kraut sipped champagne and nibbled at caviar on toast while sighing, "Everything you do, you do for the sake of the children." She pulled out baby snapshots as grandmothers will.

"I'm the baby-sitter," she told Hemingway between sips of champagne. "I go around and look in all the corners and straighten the drawers and clean up. I can't stand a house that isn't neat and clean. I go around in all the corners with towels I bring with me from the Plaza [where she then lived], and I clean up the whole house. Then they come home at one or two in the morning, and I take the dirty towels and some of the baby's things that need washing, and, with my bundle over my shoulder, I go out and get a taxi, and the driver, he thinks I am this old washerwoman from

Third Avenue, and he takes me in the taxi and talks to me with sympathy, so I am afraid to let him take me to the Plaza. I get out a block away from the Plaza and I walk home with my bundle and I wash the baby's things, and then I go to sleep."

Ross's *New Yorker* portrait of Hemingway depicted a man almost constantly under the influence, talking "Indian talk" and applying sports metaphors to his endless competition with Turgenev, Stendhal, and their league. Washerwoman Marlene hit print, too. She was in an "absolute fury," she told Hemingway's friend and biographer, A. E. Hotchner, and not just at Lillian Ross. She believed Hemingway had failed her in not explaining who the "secretary" was, that he had carelessly (or drunkenly) permitted an invasion of her privacy.

Hemingway was bruised but amused and his *Life* essay about Marlene (post-Ross) may have been atonement. He philosophically thought he and Marlene both got off lucky. "Can you imagine," he told Hotchner, "that after having spent the whole night with the Kraut and me, hearing all the things we discussed, all Lillian could write about was that the Kraut sometimes cleaned her daughter's apartment with towels from the Plaza?"

The new press aggressiveness in celebrity coverage inspired Marlene to control her own. Her knowing "more about love than anyone" inspired *The Ladies' Home Journal* to publish "How to Be Loved" under her byline. The *Journal* advertised it as Marlene's views of "creative and bountiful" love, which amounted to *Hausfrau* advice about whipping up scrambled eggs and champignons at the end of a long day to keep husband or lover lively enough to tear away the velvet hostess gown she also recommended and cut some mustard. Marlene's wisdom stimulated copious reader response, most of it tongue-in-cheek or diaper-pins-between-the-teeth, collected under the heading "Listen, Marlene!" A housewife in Paramus, New Jersey, pointed out pragmatically that "Marlene Dietrich is, no doubt, a splendid example of how any woman can look at fifty, if she looked like Marlene Dietrich at twenty-five."

Doubleday contracted with Marlene for an autobiography titled *Beauty Is an Illusion*, which itself proved so illusory that a quarter of a century would go by (accompanied by many publishers and lawyers) before it got set in type.

If Hollywood was not exploiting the Legend, Broadway tried. Marlene turned down *Carnival in Flanders*, fearing her voice was not "strong enough"; then a musical by Frank Loesser for Lawrence Langner and Lee Shubert called *After My Fashion*; a French play by Jacques (*Tovarich*) Deval called *Samarkand*, but Marlene went French only long enough to accept a medal and rosette from the French government, which made her a Chevalier de la Légion d'Honneur in recognition of her war work. She was the first German since the war to receive an honor rarely given to Germans (*or* women), and she noted to the French ambassador as he pinned it to her Dior bodice that the first of her countrymen to receive the honor had been her childhood idol, Johann Wolfgang von Goethe.

There was movie talk that came to nothing. One idea might have re-united her with Billy Wilder in the most startling role of her career if they weren't just joking: a barmaid with a wooden leg. Marlene's old chum Clifton Webb, who had found a new audience with his *Mr. Belvedere* movies, wanted her to co-star with him at Fox in something called *Dream-boat*, which sank without trace when Ginger Rogers took the silent movie–queen role Marlene turned down. Elia Kazan talked to her about playing an itinerant carnival performer (a sort of Lola Lola meets *Mother Courage*) in his and Robert E. Sherwood's behind-the-Iron-Curtain drama, *Man on a Tightrope*, but Gloria Grahame got that job. Marlene turned down a shady aristocrat role in Orson Welles's problem-plagued *Mr. Arkadin* in spite of their friendship. Welles, undaunted, wanted her to play Lady Brett Ashley in Hemingway's *The Sun Also Rises* for a theatrical repertory com-pany he tried to establish during his "gypsy period," but that caravan rolled to a full stop.

With Hollywood inventing wide screens or deep, with stereophonic ev-erything, Marlene found time to make a few recordings of songs by Harold Arlen, on whom she doted and who doted back. She served as den mother and charlady for the cast of Arlen and Truman Capote's musical *House of Flowers* when it was in trouble out of town, advising Pearl Bailey on stage jewelry (big rhinestones, not small diamonds). She rushed to Arlen's bed-side when he was hospitalized in New York, persuading the police depart-ment that her missions of mercy to the man who wrote "Stormy Weather" required an escort complete with screaming sirens. This was fortunate, for the sirens alerted nurses to hustle singer Lisa Kirk out of Arlen's hospital room before Marlene arrived. Marlene knew as little about Lisa Kirk's role in Arlen's life as Mrs. Arlen knew about Marlene's.

Time for Love ran out at CBS, and Marlene's quandary about her future deepened. Her anxiety accelerated sharply in May of 1953 when Rudi required surgery to remove half his stomach, and it was clear that the economic support Marlene provided her husband and Tamara was more crucial and harder to come by than ever. Rudi's career had seldom been much more than an adjunct to Marlene's ever since she left Berlin. He had maintained an admirable silence about his wife and all that her career had cost him (*and* her), but now he could not work at all. Tamara's psyche was frayed beyond repair, held together only by the wedding band she wore which had no legal meaning, whatever its emotional value. Friends located for him an acre and a half of run-down property in the San Fernando

Valley near Sylmar, and a banker-friend called Hans Kohn loaned him $10,000 for the down payment. Rudi and Tamara set down Valley roots to raise chickens—forty thousand of them. Marlene was now fifty-two, and the option of retirement she had talked about so blithely ten years before seemed further away than ever. So did meaningful work. "Chicken-feed" took on new meaning: Marlene paid the bills and the mortgage when the feathered flock didn't.

At almost precisely the same time as Rudi's illness, Maria was invited with some other television and stage personalities to take part in the Cerebral Palsy benefit of the Ringling Brothers, Barnum & Bailey Circus at Madison Square Garden. Maria had been active with Cerebral Palsy causes (so had Yul Brynner) and was to be a clown in the event sponsored by Gloria Vanderbilt Stokowski. "Little Gloria" had already enlisted television stars like Maria, Mary Sinclair, Rita Gam, Buff Cobb, Faye Emerson, and comic Herb Shriner; from the opera she got Patrice Munsel; from Broadway, Mel Ferrer and Audrey Hepburn (then on stage in *Ondine*); and the circus contributed clown Emmett Kelly and Dynamite, the backward-galloping horse.

Most of the guest stars would be clowns or ride around Madison Square Garden on elephants. Marlene agreed to join them if John Ringling North would let her be ringmaster of the whole shebang. North (a Hemingway friend) readily agreed. Marlene outfitted herself in black short shorts and top hat, scarlet tailcoat with diamond (or large rhinestone) buttons, sheer black stockings, gold-banded black boots, and a whip. She walked off with all three rings of the circus as she had with the Oscars, upstaging even the elephants.

Marlene as ringmaster attracted press from the *Daily News* to *Vogue*, and attracted offers, too. Producer Paul Gregory had tried to persuade Marlene to tour with a small orchestra and a ten-man chorus following her *Rancho Notorious* personal appearances the year before. Gregory was piling up prestige with staged readings of Shaw's *Don Juan in Hell* with Charles Boyer and Charles Laughton, and Stephen Vincent Benét's *John Brown's Body* with Tyrone Power, but Marlene turned him down. After the circus, however, Bill Miller of Las Vegas's Sahara Hotel stepped forward with a gaudy offer for an opportunity that would prove pivotal in Marlene's life and career.

Maurice Chevalier begged her not to pivot and Noël Coward pleaded caution. They knew from decades of grueling experience and fickle audiences that what the world now called cabaret was really saloon singing, especially in the newly gold-dusted deserts of Nevada. Doing a solo act in a gambling casino was to beseech attention from the overfed, the overbibulous, and the overextended. Chevalier had matured in that world, Coward had suffered it off and on since the twenties in London, and both of them begged her not to attempt it.

She paid no attention. She went to Las Vegas to watch Eddie Fisher sing "Oh, Mein Papa" and begin an affair with yet another future Mr. Elizabeth Taylor, though her aim may have been nightclub tips more than romance. She took in Tallulah Bankhead's raucous act at the Sands Hotel. If Tallulah could get away with it on no more than bourbon and bravado, there seemed no good reason to deny Las Vegas the magic of Marlene. Within six months she was the most highly paid, most highly publicized nightclub performer in the world.

In retrospect her debut in the Congo Room of the Sahara Hotel on December 15, 1953, was mere rehearsal for what came later. She was required by hotel and casino management only to perform a twenty-minute run-through of a few songs from her movies, lasting just long enough to give customers a glamour break and get them back to the gaming tables. The show was undistinguished. Comedian Dick Shawn warmed up the crowd, then came some ponies and jugglers, and then the audacious, fully unexpected jackpot that made everybody forget why they were in Las Vegas in the first place.

Here came Dietrich. In a gown she had concocted with Jean Louis of Columbia Pictures. "It has to be Folies-Bergère," she had ordered, "but elegant." It was almost skin-tight black net lined with flesh colored silk below the waist and flesh-colored Marlene above. It was a culminating expression of the "nude dresses" she had worn since *Seven Sinners* and all through the war. But this time the transparency was real except for strategically scattered leaf-shaped sequin-and-rhinestone clusters that caressed and riveted attention on her breasts ("those two beautiful boobs she was so proud of," Arthur Kennedy said of them), which were held up and veiled by nothing but black gauze. The transparent garment ended at the neck in a glittery necklace that looked like diamonds (the same rhinestones she loaned Pearl Bailey). Loosely draped around her shoulders was a black chiffon cape trimmed in black fox, which she used as a tease and which swept the floor behind her as she took her position at the microphone, put her hands on her hips, and allowed the cape to fall away, baring all. Photographers' flashbulbs rivaled the lights on the Strip.

When there were no more bulbs to pop Marlene turned "Hello" into the longest two-syllable drawl in nightclub history, and began to sing. Whether anyone heard her over the gasps of the spectators was irrelevant. Show business's first topless grandmother received a five-minute standing ovation. One of those who leaped to her feet was columnist Hedda Hopper, whose moralistic clucking had almost destroyed Marilyn Monroe because of a nude calendar. Hopper now pronounced Dietrich's all-but-exposed breasts a gift from Santa Claus: "Christmas came early to Las Vegas," she wrote.

The orchestra went into a festive drum roll, Marlene disappeared backstage, shed the gown, and reappeared within sixty seconds in the scarlet-coated, silk-stockinged costume she had worn as ringmaster for the circus and cracked her whip. Wire services went into burnout.

There had been no advance warning, and Marlene wasn't finished yet. Her second performance—audience agog with anticipation of black net and nothing—outdid the first. She now appeared in a white duplicate of the black dress, and the flashbulbs and gasps began all over again. The opening night stories and photographs, which had made worldwide headlines, were repeated with *new* photographs of Marlene's duplicate gown (there were actually three: one was flesh-colored with gold sequin-and-rhinestone trim). No one in the media failed to estimate the cost of the dresses (anywhere from $3,000 to $8,000) or report that her fee, at $30,000 a week, was the highest in nightclub history, the highest in the world.

Coward, the Master, had made a rare error in theatrical judgment and started talking about a Las Vegas act of his own. Everybody had something to say. Tallulah Bankhead quipped, "I saw Marlene just before her opening, and she told me she didn't have a thing to wear! And to think—I didn't believe her!" Ed Sullivan pursed his lips and called it "tasteless." Marlene told *Newsweek*, "If you can't wear [this dress] here, you can't wear it anywhere." Jean Louis told *Time* he was "heartbroken," because he had "wanted to make the skirt transparent to show her legs, but she didn't want that." She was saving *that*.

There had almost been no dresses. Not by Jean Louis, anyway, and without them there might have been no show. Louis, a diminutive Frenchman for whom the word *pixie* was minted, was offered to Marlene by his boss, Harry Cohn, at Columbia Pictures. Cohn was being cooperative because he wanted Marlene to play the older woman in *Pal Joey*, which the studio owned. It might have been a great role for her (she could have sung "Bewitched, Bothered, and Bewildered") and she agreed if Joey, the role that made Gene Kelly famous on Broadway, were played by her occasional good friend Frank Sinatra. Cohn suggested a new Columbia contract player named Jack Lemmon, whom Marlene considered "nothing," and she refused to do the picture. Cohn exploded in one of his profane fits and "fired" Jean Louis from working for her.

Louis was "desperate," but found Marlene "marvelous, a very resourceful, bright woman," who assured him, "I'll find a way." She called Cohn's wife, and then the Sahara Hotel, and somebody called Chicago, and somebody in Chicago called Frank Costello, who made Harry Cohn an offer he couldn't refuse by reminding him he had growing children. Cohn capitulated but forbade Marlene to use the front door, forcing her to go through the prop department to Louis's workrooms at Columbia. (Frank Sinatra wound up playing the part in *Pal Joey* anyway, opposite Columbia's old Queen of the Lot, Rita Hayworth, and its *new* Queen of the Lot, Kim Novak. The movie was execrable.)

Marlene commuted from New York every other weekend for fittings at double and triple time for seamstresses, in addition to Louis's own fees and a Columbia "overhead" charge of $7,500, all of which got added to the bills for chicken feed and grandchildren.

"We could work with very sheer material," Louis recalled, "because Dietrich didn't need any foundation. It was all Dietrich in those days, *everything*. She would come directly from the plane through the prop room and stand motionless for eight or nine hours a day in front of mirrors while we made the dresses *on* her. It takes energy and discipline to stand like that, and she's *so* disciplined. She would say, 'I don't like symmetry. Move that sequin,' and we would, but that might make a symmetry with a rhinestone, so we would move *that*, and this went on all day, all weekend. I was terrified these spiderweb fabrics would go up in flames from her cigarettes. Two weeks later she would fly back to go through it all over again, never impatient, because she was a perfectionist who knew exactly what she wanted. She could have been a designer herself—she knew how to sew, how to use a needle and thread, and she repaired her own costumes on the road.

"She was wonderful with the seamstresses, brought them food and cakes and things she baked. Did she bake them on the plane from New York? I don't know. The only tense moment ever was when one of my male cutters told her, 'Oh, Miss Dietrich, I've loved you since I was a *child*!'

"She kept telling me, 'Watch out for these boys, Jean, they will steal your patterns,' and even in the early 1990s, when she saw Cher in a Bob Mackie dress on television she would call me from Paris to say, 'You see! That Mackie boy who worked for you has knocked off our dress again!' And it was true. Those dresses are *all* the Dietrich dresses. Cher owes us royalties!"

Working on weekends was difficult, and Marlene arrived with deadlines because she wanted to visit Rudi in the San Fernando Valley, and did when Tamara was stable enough to endure her presence. When Las Vegas drew near she announced, "We must finish by five so I can make my plane." Five o'clock would come and go and "we would still be sewing sequins and rhinestones by hand," remembered Louis. "Marlene would then announce she had a reservation at six, then another at seven, then another at eight. Finally, we knew the last plane left for the desert at nine and it would be over—she *had* to leave. She studied every sequin, every rhinestone, then just dropped these exquisite, fragile dresses from her shoulders to the floor, *boom!*, wadded them up in tissue paper, threw them in a box like they were her grandchildren's diapers, and got on her broom to Las Vegas. It was a nightmare and a joy because Dietrich knew what she wanted and when you were finished, it *looked* like something!"

Marlene overnight became the most desirable nightclub attraction in the world, though the act had achieved nothing like its final form. She signed a multiyear contract with the Sahara, and one with London's legendary smart nightspot, the Café de Paris. Noël Coward agreed to introduce her there on opening night with a poem he would write for the occasion.

The London performance began a refining process of the show that was to continue for a dozen years (wags called it "the longest out-of-town tryout in history") until she felt, as last, it was perfect and could be "frozen." Peter Matz, her arranger and accompanist in Las Vegas, did not come to London with her, and she was nervous about the musicians there and about the lighting, too. Coward introduced her to the third Joe in her life (after Sternberg and Pasternak), lighting man Joe Davis, who became as much part of her repertoire as the songs. He designed her stage lighting for the rest of his life. Marlene's gown was modified for modesty with sheer silk linings in London (royals would be present), and she began to introduce autobiography (or legend) into the act. She made deliberate points for the local audience, noting she had sung "Laziest Gal in Town" filming in London "for Hitchcock" (not mentioning she had fought the song every measure of the way). She sang *"Frag nicht warum ich gehe"* ("Don't Ask Why I Go") as a tribute to her "great friend," tenor Richard Tauber, a Berlin-to-London exile who was a British public idol until his death. When she introduced "Lili Marlene," she credited its discovery dubiously but graciously to "British soldiers, who made it their own" during the war.

The London press had not been so giddy since the coronation. "It might have been a State visit," wrote one critic. The torrents of publicity began before she got to town, with breathless descriptions of the Dorchester's gold-plated Oliver Messel Suite in which she would rehearse and rest (in the unlikely event she ever did).

The opening night audience exceeded the fire laws by one third and arrived three hours before her midnight appearance. Extra police were assigned to control crowds massed in Piccadilly hoping to get a glimpse of the stars and royals—or possibly even Herself. Coward brought Sir Laurence Olivier and Vivien Leigh and just after midnight recited his introductory poem with characteristic clipped panache:

We know God made trees,
And the birds and the bees,

And seas, for the fishes to swim in.
We are also aware
That he had quite a flare
For creating exceptional *women.* . . .

Now we all might enjoy
Seeing Helen of Troy
As a gay cabaret entertainer,
But I doubt that she could
Be one quarter as good
As our legend'ry, lovely,
Marlene!

"Exceptional was the only word for Miss Dietrich," said the critics. *Variety* reported the show lasted only thirty-five minutes but she "could have held them much longer." No reviewer failed to notice her costume. "She was wearing a dress that could only be described as a masterpiece of illusion. It was transparent enough to make you think you were seeing everything and opaque enough to make you realize you were seeing nothing. Houdini must have designed it." Most, however, restrained themselves to the kind of praise suitable for framing or carving in marble.

"Sheer rapture," the *Evening News* called it, and the *News Chronicle* rolled over for "the purr of the sacred cat [which] is more lovely than the voice of the spheres." Young Kenneth Tynan bound himself in allusions to Sacher-Masoch: "The Venus in furs, with black leather in her voice, over whom applause broke like a cloudburst over the sphinx. She was energy and discipline. Life with its hands on its hips and its chin looking for a right hook. Yet soft withal, as yielding as quicksand and as perilous. London has never suffered at the hands of so compassionate a murderess. May we rest in peace."

Coward as introducer was followed on successive nights by Robert Morley, Alec Guinness, and others, but one thing never varied. She announced "Falling in Love Again" as "the last one and the inevitable one" and when it was over, it was over. She chided the audience when they clamored for encores, "I told you that was the last one." They were to be left wanting more.

They got more when Goddard Lieberson, the shrewdest judge of highroad material ever (he would totally underwrite *My Fair Lady*), released Marlene's London opening night on Columbia Records' prestige Masterwork label. The album, which included Coward's introduction, was packaged in a double slipcase, reproducing Hemingway's essay and the most breathless of the London reviews on the inside cover, and on the outside, just a portrait of Marlene without a word of copy. The face was enough; that and the Arpège with which the first thousand pressings were drenched. The album made permanent a signal moment in her career and led to a series of performance albums over the next decade. Later albums would be better musically and technically and her repertoire would grow more expansive and richer, but the first London album captured a careless and tender freshness, creating as much audience for her new career as memories of her old films did.

Her immense self-assurance was the most unexpected quality for those who had no idea Marlene had stage experience. She seemed effortlessly controlled and at ease. David Craig, the actor-singer and acting and singing teacher, asked her not long after if she had felt stage fright. "She looked at me, puzzled, and asked me why she should. . . . I told her that, having taught actors all my life, most often they were terrified of clubs because the audience was not captive . . . and as I listed other valid reasons, she said, 'I see.' Then, after a moment of thought [while] she stared off into space . . . she said 'Oh, I know why! They are paying to see the most glamorous woman in the world, and I am she!' And she said it completely without ego. No ego at all! *Quod erat demonstrandum.*"

Present on the occasion were Noël Coward, Nancy Walker (Mrs. Craig), Roddy McDowall, and Montgomery Clift, who had gone with Marlene to see Eddie Fisher and Tallulah in Vegas and to whose *Hamlet* Marlene fancied herself as Gertrude on film. After Marlene and Coward left the younger actors alone, Roddy McDowall (who remembered her gold-painted everything at the wartime Hollywood Canteen), explained it all to Craig and the others:

"There she is in her dressing room. There's a rap on the door. The stage manager calls, 'You're on, Miss Dietrich.' She gets up and goes to the mirror for one last fix of what is already perfection and guess who's staring back at her.

"Marlene Dietrich!"

TWENTY

BACK IN
BUSINESS
1954 - 1958

The Café de Paris mounted a gold plaque on a nightclub pillar: "Marlene Dietrich Leaned Here and Helped Save London Night Life." She swept on to the "Night of a Hundred Stars" at the London Palladium with Noël Coward. The glamorous pals faked a cakewalk to "Knocked 'Em in the Old Kent Road," a number neither of them really knew, but nobody minded, for they raised £10,000 for the Actors' Orphanage. The sum was not much more than Marlene's weekly cabaret fee.

In August, she performed for charity again at Monte Carlo's Bal de Mer, a polio benefit, where she was introduced by actor Jean Marais reading an alarming text by Jean Cocteau: "Marlene Dietrich! . . . Your name, at first the sound of a caress, becomes the crack of a whip." Cocteau got a grip on himself for "the secret of your beauty lies in the care of your loving kindness of the heart [which] holds you higher than elegance, fashion or style: higher even than your fame, your courage, your bearing, your films, your songs," but he got hyperbolic again when hailing her as "a frigate, figurehead, a Chinese fish, a lyre-bird, a legend, a wonder . . . !"

Five days later she shrugged off the scales and plumes Cocteau dressed her in for somber trench coat and army cap to march beneath the Arc de Triomphe with former French Resistance workers and American Legion members on the tenth anniversary of the Liberation of Paris. The Medal of Freedom from the United States government and her Légion d'honneur from the French were her only decoration. She looked as beautiful in austerity as in the trappings of show business mythology.

She returned to Las Vegas in October, but stopped off in New York to visit the grandchildren. One of them saw pictures of her in her nightclub costume and piped, "You look just like a Christmas tree!" Marlene consoled Maria on her Broadway failure in *The Burning Glass*, which couldn't be saved even with fellow actors Sir Cedric Hardwicke, Isobel Elsom, and Walter Matthau. Reviewers called Maria "over-anxious," "never relaxed," and her performance "more posturing than portraiture." Maria's career in live television was steady, but the medium was about to be interred and being Dietrich's daughter paid no residuals. Maria's biggest breakthrough, in fact, had been appearing on *Life*'s cover with Marlene in 1952, and though beautiful in her way, it was a self-conscious way, inhibited by her mother's resurgent fame and the comparisons it stimulated.

However much (or little) Maria really wanted a career, she had told her first husband that both Marlene and Rudi expected her, in European fashion, to support them in their old age. Motherhood and the lackluster progress of Maria's career (and her husband's) made that less and less likely. Marlene, who seemed unaware of old age, was footing the major bills, and if her largesse seemed like conscience money to atone for Maria's now-neglected, now-smothered childhood, no one among Marlene's circle detected that. She was simply the bountiful matriarch reveling in (someone noted) "the fabulous illusion that if you earn $100,000, you have $100,000 to spend." By early autumn she was back in California to earn more, working with Jean Louis on new costumes and spending time, money, and herself on Rudi and Tamara.

In the San Fernando Valley she visited Rudi's "ramshackle farmhouse" surrounded by wall, trees, and cacti. She handed down her used wardrobe to the disintegrating Tamara (who would soon be wearing her hand-me-downs in an institution), cooked, played Florence Nightingale to Rudi's ill health, and did the grocery shopping disguised in a babushka and sunglasses. Reporters now and then remembered a "Mr. Dietrich" somewhere in the Valley, living with thousands of chickens and presumably deeply in love with his famous wife. Tamara was unknown to them, and Rudi scrupulously avoided the press about Marlene, allowing that "basically she's a regular guy" on the rare occasions a determined newshound discovered him among his chickens, whom, one said, "he talked to like children." The only hint of bitterness he betrayed was in an offhand remark about his feathered brood: "I prefer animals to people," he said. "They're more grateful."

Marlene began her second season at the Sahara by turning her costuming upside-down. In 1953 she was transparent above; in 1954, below. She was wrapped in white chiffon (or black) which, whipped by a wind machine, billowed off into the Nevada desert, leaving her bare-legged in glamour and little else. She still did the quick change in mid-show, returning in less than sixty seconds, everything covered up by top hat and tails right out of *Morocco*.

When she returned to the Café de Paris in July of 1955, Art Buchwald came up from Paris and informed his readers that "Miss Dietrich comes down the stairway slowly. A draft of air starts blowing on her dress and the material goes hither and yon . . . . You get the feeling that never has a singer owed so much to so few yards of cloth. . . . Miss Dietrich drifts up to the stage. She breathes into the microphone. We all breathe back. Then she starts to sing. Her voice promises almost as much as her gown. . . . She sings to us in French and in German. Some may not understand the lyrics, but the meaning is there—the meaning is there. Several of the pale patrons try to impale themselves on swizzlesticks, but they are stopped in time. . . . Miss Dietrich sings on. . . . The room gets hotter, the panting gets heavier. We dig our nails into the cover charge card. . . . Steam starts pouring from our glass. . . . We [go out and start] nibbling on a palm tree in the lobby."

Local celebrities rushed to introduce her nightly. This year they included Liverpool's Labour M. P. Bessie Braddock, who weighed in at 208 pounds and arrived in a bus. Miss Braddock announced, "I intend as a reciprocal arrangement to invite Miss Dietrich along to the House of Commons." Marlene accepted the invitation, where several alert parliamentarians exclaimed delightedly at the surprise visit of Greta Garbo.

Marlene's new career stimulated her old one. Noël Coward sat down to dash off a musical for the two of them called *Later Than Spring*. Coward said it was "about a fascinating *femme du monde* (Marlene) and an equally fascinating *homme du monde* (me) . . . [with] an articulate pair of companion secretaries (Graham [Payn] and Marti Stevens)." This was old-home-week fantasy, as Payn was Coward's longtime *ami* and Marti Stevens a *nouvelle amie* of Marlene's. Coward called Stevens "the Blonde Beast," less because of her acting or singing than because she was the daughter of

Nick Schenck, Louis B. Mayer's former boss at MGM. None of them did the show, but a few years later Broadway saw it with Elaine Stritch as *Sail Away*.

Hollywood suffered Dietrich's absence in silence in spite of widespread curiosity about what she would actually look like on screen. It took bravado and persuasion to bring her back in her mid-fifties to screens dominated by Mrs. Michael Wilding and Mrs. Arthur Miller, and Avrom Goldenbogen had bravado and persuasion to spare.

Goldenbogen liked to call himself Mike Todd and to think of himself as the greatest showman in the world. He liked to think of Marlene as the greatest show*woman*. The two saw a lot of each other. Before Todd (like Michael Wilding and Eddie Fisher) discovered Elizabeth Taylor, (whom Marlene grew to loathe), he told Marlene they should stop seeing each other because "I'm afraid I'll fall in love with you." Marlene calmed his qualms with, "No man falls in love with me I don't want to have fall in love with me." They made a movie instead.

Todd had tried since the late thirties to get Marlene on stage. In the meantime he had produced some celebrated hits like Maurice Evans's *GI Hamlet* and Gypsy Rose Lee's *Something for the Boys* and some even more celebrated flops, including the disastrous Orson Welles–Cole Porter musical based on Jules Verne's *Around the World in 80 Days*, from which Todd nimbly bowed out before the breaking of the bank.

He still liked the idea and planned to make it as a movie using a wide-screen process he owned with the American Optical Company, modestly dubbed Todd-AO, in which *Oklahoma!* had been filmed. He made *Around the World in 80 Days* in Todd-AO and made it a commercial movie miracle, putting Marlene back on screen and back in the movie business.

It was her first tangible movie offer in almost four years and only a bit part, but in a movie in which bits were played by practically everybody from everywhere, including Charles Boyer, Ronald Colman, Noël Coward, John Gielgud, Fernandel, José Greco, Buster Keaton, Beatrice Lillie, Peter Lorre, and even Edward R. Murrow (as "introducer"). One of the great attractions was "Spot That Star" as David Niven circumnavigated the globe as Phileas Fogg. Todd claimed none of his stars was harder to land than Marlene.

"They told me 'she's the impossible one,'" he revealed to Ezra Goodman. He told her, "I'll shoot the scene and show it to you and forget the cost. I'll burn the negative if you don't like it." Todd claimed the scene cost $150,000, but it gave him "a slogan, 'Stay with the money.' She was the money."

Marlene went along with the story saying, "I just walked in blindly. There was no makeup test, no hairdo test. It couldn't have been better if we worked on it for a month." Marlene never walked blindly into anything and got heaped with sables for her trouble. Her saloon queen of the Barbary Coast opened the postintermission half of the picture with so much glamour she almost brought the globe-trot to a halt. When old friend David Niven as Fogg approaches her trying to find his manservant (Cantinflas), the dialogue gets to the point:

FOGG: I'm looking for a man.
MARLENE: (eyes up, eyes down) So am I.

Marlene appeared as she thought she *should* have in *Rancho Notorious* four years earlier. Here, *Destry*'s Frenchy turns up platinum-wigged, wasp-waisted, and stretching a fifty-foot leg across the wide, wide screen. To keep the Barbary Coast safe for—or *from*—Marlene's saloon queen, old flame George Raft is along as bouncer. Her piano player, revealed as a final sight gag in the sequence, is yet another of the Alumni Association, Frank Sinatra.

Around the World in 80 Days won the Academy Award for Best Picture (and four more), and when Jules Verne's tale was issued as a movie–tie-in paperback, Marlene decorated the cover. The movie's enormous success made Avrom Goldenbogen the legend he always said he was and stilled any doubts about Marlene's looks on screen. United Artists distributed the picture and agreed to her as the star of another, Italian-financed picture they would distribute, *The Monte Carlo Story.*

The Monte Carlo Story is the one about gamblers: the beautiful (but broke) Marquise de Crèvecoeur (Heartbreaker), and the dashing (but broke) Count Dino, each plotting to rake in the other's chips. They glide suavely around Monte Carlo pretending to be rich; they dally; they fall in romance; they discover the threadbare truth. They join forces as "brother and sister," descending on an American father-daughter team who sail into Monte Carlo full of Indiana cash on a yacht called *The Hoosier* (borrowed for the film from King Farouk, complete with pornographic frieze in the main stateroom).

La Marquise charms the father; il Conte charms the daughter. In the end the fortune hunters forgo fleecing their lambs and gamble on love. They putt-putt off on Count Dino's mini-yacht, complete with galley where Marlene can whip up scrambled eggs while a parrot squawks, "*Faites vos jeux!*"

Monte Carlo was much in the news in 1956 (an American girl had married a prince), but the audience for mature fairytales had dwindled, died, or was too feeble to get to the box office. Because first-time director Samuel A. Taylor was a playwright (*The Happy Times, Sabrina Fair, The Pleasure of His Company*), everyone assumed the story was his. It was not.

Because of her first billing, lavish costumes, and publicity during production, everyone assumed it was a Marlene vehicle. It was not.

The whole trouble-in-paradise thing had been concocted from old Lubitsch pictures by producers Marcello Girosi and Dino Risi as a vehicle for Vittorio de Sica. The great director had been acting in films since 1918 and was a romantic screen idol long before he became famous for his neorealistic masterworks *The Bicycle Thief* and *Umberto D.* He was also a compulsive gambler and often acted to raise money for films he directed or to pay debts incurred by unfortunate turns of the wheel.

Asking a gambler to work off gambling debts in Monte Carlo was rather like offering Willie Sutton a work-parole job as a bank guard. Sam Taylor had been hired as screenwriter when it was still assumed de Sica would direct as well as act. In the meantime, de Sica was shocked—*shocked!*—to find gaming going on in Monaco. He also noted that his acting fees vanished at the tables even before production began. De Sica withdrew from directing in order to wreak revenge on croupiers and Taylor took on the assignment. ("The producers didn't want to *pay* anybody experienced," Taylor recalled.) De Sica was there for guidance; Giuseppe Rotunno was behind the camera to keep everybody in soft focus; all they needed was a leading lady now that a picture *by* de Sica had become merely one *with* de Sica.

Marlene was then in America and accepted the role of the Marquise on the strength of the script and friendly reports about Taylor from Billy Wilder, who had filmed Taylor's *Sabrina* with Audrey Hepburn. Marlene arrived in Monte Carlo complete with wardrobe by Jean Louis, knowing no one on the picture but Mischa Auer, from her *Destry* days, who was playing a headwaiter and promptly broke his arm. Perhaps an omen.

"Marlene was exceptionally professional," Taylor said. "Never any trouble, always prepared, always did exactly what you told her. There was some fake publicity about a romance, but she wasn't interested in de Sica at all. They hardly spoke to each other off the set. De Sica was interested in seventeen-year-olds, anyway, and had about three words of English, which didn't help their scenes together."

Equally unhelpful was de Sica's arriving for work unprepared and hung over, recalled another observer. "De Sica would show up looking green from his hangover, with Marlene already on board Farouk's yacht looking greener from seasickness. The only thing they had in common was color."

Taylor remembered, "Marlene was kept busy teasing Arthur O'Connell [as the rich American], who was madly in love with her. She used to leap on him, wrap her legs around him and bite his ears to drive him crazy.

"She asked only one favor during the picture, to go to Paris for a weekend. She told me she had been offered the role of Mrs. Begbick in a recording of *Mahagonny*, and needed to meet with the producers. Could she arrive late on Monday? Well, of course: Brecht, Weill, *Mahagonny!* So we rearranged the schedule. Monday she came back about noon, quite radiant. We finished up, but she didn't say a word about *Mahagonny*. I was eager to hear how it had gone, and finally asked. She looked at me as if I had lost my mind. She laughed and said, 'Sam, you didn't *believe* that story?! *Yul* was in Paris, and I wanted to get laid!'

"She had total candor," Taylor reported. "She had been mad about Brynner, but made no secret that he treated her badly and that all her friends were angry with her for chasing after him. There was a story she told about bumping into him on a plane when he had lied to her about his weekend plans. He was with a young actress who was the new Star *du jour*. Brynner got drunk and morose and tried to climb into Marlene's sleeper-berth in front of God and Pan Am and Little Miss Broadway, adding indiscretion and insult to injury. Marlene didn't tell the story on *him*; she told it as if it were a page out of *Psychopathia Sexualis*.

"Marlene seemed absolutely sex-ridden," remembered Taylor, "but of the *theory* of sex. She understood sex was the ruling physical thing in human life, but I don't think she was personally a very sexy dame. Sex may have been the guiding force in her life, but intellectually. She was fascinated by sex, all kinds, everybody's. She could have written a book to challenge Krafft-Ebing if she had just dictated what she knew. That's what Hemingway meant when he made his famous remark about her knowing everything about love. He meant *sex*."

It seemed sometimes as if the strongest component of a Dietrich affair satisfied the more basic need of simple companionship. She met a now very well known Hollywood socialite-wife in New York in the mid-fifties. The younger woman was then a failed actress with no experience with women, but responded to Marlene's tenderness and what she called her "womanliness." The two embarked on a brief, uncomplicated affair that was "highly sexual," the woman later recalled, but "affection and friendship seemed more the point than the sex, which was expert, and unfailingly considerate."

After a particularly intense love-making weekend, "Marlene suddenly suggested we have dinner with a well-known Hollywood producer. 'I think you'll like him,' " Dietrich told the younger woman. The producer and the young actress met, were obviously attracted to each other, and Dietrich loaned the woman her own jewelry to wear for glamour during the courtship that ensued. "*And* to make certain I didn't seem a gold-digger," the now Hollywood wife recalled. "When we got married, Marlene took me aside at the reception, and I think she decided to handle things with me much as she had with Edith Piaf, becoming Piaf's bridesmaid after *their* affair. She wasn't *my* bridesmaid, but she said to me with great warmth and affection, 'I knew what would be best for you.' She meant it."

Sam Taylor was matinee-idol handsome himself and might have attracted Marlene had she not spent off-camera time with a young Frenchwoman. "With one of those famous old French names," Taylor said. "The girl had been passed on to Marlene by a Hollywood actress friend whose husband was a big agent and part of that [Jack and] Ann Warner crowd, *also* a friend of Marlene's. I had been attracted to this girl myself at the bar of the Hôtel de Paris where we were all living. Suzanne [Mrs. Taylor] was away, and I invited this beautiful girl to have dinner with me the following night. The next morning Marlene called and asked me to visit her rooms to talk about the script. I arrived to find her just out of the shower, wearing a big, white terry-cloth robe and her hair wrapped in a towel like a turban, looking marvelous with no makeup at all—she had no personal vanity whatever, really none—and we went through some perfunctory talk about the script. The whole time we talked this gorgeous French girl was there, sitting on the sofa, not saying a word! Marlene didn't introduce us; the girl might have been invisible. She didn't say anything; I didn't say anything; Marlene didn't say anything. It was a better Lubitsch scene than any I wrote for the picture: Marlene declaring her turf, without a word.

"Marlene was barred from the Casino because of the no slacks dress code, so we used to spend a lot of time at the Sporting Club, where Onassis and Callas were in public heat. There was this famous transsexual who fascinated Marlene. This character was mid-way between injections and surgery and used to press Marlene's face between these brand new breasts. Marlene wanted to know what this person *did*, you know, in bed. She was avid for details, clinical sexological details, and she got them! She had an encyclopedic fund of information and loved to share it. She told us that Garbo was 'awfully big down there,' and had 'dirty underclothes.' She never explained how she knew this, but was graphic enough to be convincing.

"She was fascinated by sex. And by Marlene. Her self-interest was absolutely unique. She walked in her own aura, as if it were a cocoon. She was not selfish—she could be the most generous woman in the world—but she was the quintessence of self-interest, the center of the world to herself, and sometimes that center got lonely.

"Later Marlene and I happened both to be staying at the Beverly Hills Hotel," Taylor remembered, "and she called me at two o'clock in the morning. Woke me up. I answered the phone and she said in that voice of hers, 'Sam . . . Frankie wants me to come up to his house and bring him some cookies. What should I do?' I screamed at her, 'For Christ's sake, Marlene! It's two o'clock in the morning! If you want to take cookies to Frankie, take 'em!' and I slammed down the phone. *Weeks* later it occurred to me she was lonely. Maybe she wanted to bring cookies to *me*, but it was two in the morning and I'm slow to register on things sexual.

"She wanted you to *need* her. My back went out when we were shooting the picture, and I had to direct from a leaning-board the carpenters made for me. Marlene would sidle over every day in her 'Marlene Nightingale' act and coo, 'Is it better, my darling?' before work could begin. She could be wonderfully solicitous."

"And *generous*," added Taylor's wife, Suzanne. "I admired a hat Marlene wore one day during shooting, and the next day a shop delivered three hats to my room, one in each available color. She was lavish with everything, but sometimes I had the feeling she didn't remember my name from one day to the next.

"Later we visited Marlene and Maria and the grandchildren in New York," Suzanne Taylor recalled, "and the sense of family was overwhelming. Marlene was the matriarch, doing a real German Christmas tree with packages beautifully ribboned and wrapped so they could be opened from the bottom and then rewrapped like little props under the tree for the whole holiday season. It was very beautiful and Marlene *adored* her grandsons. Her self-interest ended when they were around."

Sam Taylor finally felt "*The Monte Carlo Story* wasn't important to Marlene or anybody else. I wrote and directed it too slow. *Family*," he stressed. "Family was the steel rod of her life; the thread that stitched it together. She was like a man; she was ambitious and went out to conquer the world and bring it home to her family, like Odysseus."

"Rebecca West once said she was Helen of Troy," someone interjected.

Taylor paused. "Well, she was. *Marlene* was Helen of Troy, but *Dietrich* was Odysseus."

The Monte Carlo Story wasn't *The Odyssey* and nobody thought it was. It pleased no one very much, and United Artists distributed it spottily and not at all in some territories until after Marlene's next picture was in the theaters. *Monte Carlo* looks better today than it did in 1957; distance lends charm to what then seemed merely dated. *Time* noted that "the siren [Marlene] is a bit rusty; yet . . . the belle, even with diminished resonance still rings," while *Newsweek* thought the picture just a "waste of talent."

That Marlene could still walk across the wide screen in "the Dietrich strut" looking no more like her fifty-six years than on the stage was the usual source of wonder. But the total charge she took of her nightclub career (and the paucity of film offers) prompted her to seize control of her movie career as well. For perhaps the first time since Berlin, she aggressively fought for a role.

It was in a courtroom drama United Artists had acquired through old-time B-movie producer Edward Small, based on an Agatha Christie short story that had become a hugely successful play in England and America. Though no one was asking her, Marlene decided she should play the title character in *Witness for the Prosecution*.

Billy Wilder directed the picture, but was not the director of choice; Joshua Logan was. Logan turned it down. Just as well, for his memories of working with Marlene twenty years before on *The Garden of Allah* may have precluded his considering her for Agatha Christie "twash." Wilder maintained he accepted the picture only *because* of Marlene, but this must be taken with a granary of salt. Wilder knew no leading lady could be cast until the leading man had been signed, and whoever that was would share approval over her casting with Edward Small and Small's partner, Arthur Hornblow, Jr. (the actual producer), and with United Artists.

Hornblow wanted Marlene, too, but producer Small, who had paid a record $430,000 for the film rights to the play, wanted a leading man *and* woman who could go directly from the Old Bailey in *Witness* to the Old Testament in *Solomon and Sheba*. First choice actor had been William Holden, who was unavailable, causing Wilder and Hornblow to approach Tyrone Power, who read the script (by Larry Marcus) and said no.

Power would have been dim indeed not to realize his role as accused murderer Leonard Vole was a pawn for his wife and defense attorney, who duel it out in the courtroom while he sits in the dock sweating and clenching his eyebrows.

Power's refusal to play Leonard Vole sent Wilder and Hornblow scurrying for actors acceptable both to United Artists and the Temple of Solomon. If Marlene didn't have Wilder in her pocket (she didn't), she had him in her corner, as his search for an actor focused on one who would accept her as the wife seemingly determined to send her husband to the gallows from sheer perversity. Wilder and Hornblow went to Gene Kelly (then tapped out and trying for a dramatic career), who expressed interest and would accept Marlene, while Small was simultaneously negotiating (a dangerous game) for Ava Gardner *or* Rita Hayworth. Wilder was adamant that Rita Hayworth could not *act* the role, which involved a vital trick in performance, and proposed Kirk Douglas as Leonard Vole. Douglas had worked well for him in *Ace in the Hole*, and Wilder knew Douglas and Marlene had had a brief affair several years before ("affectionate sex," Douglas called it) because he had introduced them.

In his loyalty to Marlene, Wilder went on record that, "If we had to invent someone to be the ideal woman . . . we would have to invent Dietrich." As he and Harry Kurnitz were rewriting the first script, he was in a position to invent her on the page, and more or less did.

Douglas turned down the role or was unavailable. Glenn Ford and Jack

Lemmon were sent scripts. Even then-unknown Roger Moore was considered for the part (at Joshua Logan's suggestion), but finally Tyrone Power reconsidered when Small offered him both *Witness* and *Solomon and Sheba* at fees of $300,000 each. (These high fees proved ironically costly: Power died during production of *Solomon and Sheba* and was replaced by . . . Yul Brynner.)

Power accepted the deal(s) and Marlene, and Wilder set about getting the courtroom drama out of the courtroom while Marlene went back to Las Vegas and got better nightclub reviews than ever. Wilder and Kurnitz decided they and the marquee needed more than Francis L. Sullivan's bombast for defense attorney Sir Wilfred Robarts.

Wilder wanted a "cement block" around whom the plot's tricky construction could revolve. They cast Charles Laughton as wily Sir Wilfred and gave him a heart condition and a relentlessly chipper nurse at whom he could wiggle his wattles: Laughton's wife, Elsa Lanchester. ("If you were a woman, Miss Plimsoll, I would strike you!").

Wilder and Kurnitz concocted a flashback explaining how Leonard Vole and his wife (once Romaine, now Christine) met in postwar Hamburg, in what became a self-homage to *A Foreign Affair*. Christine is another version of Erika von Schlütow, singing in an off-limits dive that was as nearly a replica of the earlier picture's Lorelei Club as art director Alexander Trauner could make it.

Marlene needed a song to sing while playing her accordion and inciting mayhem among the enlisted men she sings to (more *Foreign Affair*), but Friedrich Holländer had gone back to Germany, and Wilder and Marlene went to the archives. They pulled out an old chantey about Hamburg's red-light district called *"Auf der Reeperbahn nachts um halb eins"* ("On the Reeperbahn Half Past Midnight") by Ralph Arthur Roberts, the actor-manager with whom Marlene had worked on stage in Berlin in the twenties. English lyrics turned it into "I May Never Go Home Anymore," and Marlene promptly recorded it and made it part of her nightclub act.

The trick in performance that Wilder had been certain Rita Hayworth couldn't play was the key to the picture's surprise ending. Leonard Vole's wife is bigamously married to him (her never-dissolved first marriage slipped her mind) and is therefore legally permitted to testify against him as witness for the prosecution. Doing so, she destroys his alibi, seemingly condemning him to the gallows. Meanwhile, Sir Wilfred is mysteriously provided incriminating "love letters" by a disreputable Cockney woman eager to destroy Christine's credibility. The letters result in Vole's acquittal. The trick, of course, is that the Cockney woman *is* Christine in disguise, manipulating Wilfred the Fox and justice to save the husband she loves.

Before the picture started shooting, makeup and costume tests were made with Marlene as the Cockney, and both Laughton and Noël Coward coached her with her accent. Coward noted in his diary, "It is not easy to teach Cockney to a German glamour-puss who can't pronounce her Rs but she did astonishingly well." Contact lenses darkened her eyes; wigs, a false nose, and padding did the rest, and the test was a disaster.

Marlene didn't look like a Cockney woman; she looked like George C. Scott in drag. Wilder and Hornblow blanched at what appeared on film. They briefly considered hiring a second actress to impersonate Marlene impersonating Christine impersonating the Cockney woman, but Marlene insisted on trying a second version of her disguise without the proboscis, the linebacker shoulders, or the General Patton posture.

The less violently disfiguring disguise seemed to work, but Wilder was still worried. The point was not so much that the audience not know that Christine and the Cockney woman were the same, but that *Sir Wilfred* not know. The trickery might be revealed to the audience if that minimized any danger of viewers feeling cheated should they see through the disguise (or recognize it *was* one). The choice was surprise or suspense: Reveal the masquerade as a shocker at the end of the picture or let the audience in on it, leaving them to wonder *why* Christine is disguising herself and furnishing self-damning evidence. Reason: her husband is guilty and she *knows* it. But she loves him.

Wilder shot the Cockney woman's telephone scene (in which she offers to meet Sir Wilfred) two ways. In one version we see it is Christine, speaking with a Cockney accent. At the end of the call, she takes from her purse the wig we will later see her wear in disguise. In the other version we see the Cockney woman and think she's just some Cockney woman.

Wilder went for surprise rather than the possibly confusing suspense of knowing Christine was up to something. The decision remains controversial. Marlene's Cockney is widely thought to have gone unappreciated because realized only after the fact. Dietrich supporters claim Wilder's decision cost her an Academy Award nomination, though there are those who insist, even today, that the Cockney isn't Dietrich at all. Others find the impersonation all too bogus, except for the voice, which they allege is dubbed. But it is Dietrich and Dietrich's voice.

Shooting of *Witness* was uneventful, though Elsa Lanchester paid close attention to Marlene and delighted in broadcasting what she called "the dark secrets of her life." Lanchester was actually younger than Marlene and resented her insistence on preserving the illusion of youth and glamour, particularly when it worked so well on Laughton, with whom Marlene formed a giddy mutual admiration society. Marlene had been using her "tape lifts" and wigs for years (they were so standard as theatrical appliances that John Barrymore used them on stage in the twenties). She had never made any professional secret about them, but Lanchester was determined to breach professional etiquette as loudly as possible.

"Marlene would go to bed early," Lanchester tattled, "and get up at 3:00 A.M. and go to Westmore at Paramount to be made up. It took two hours to apply her face lifts. . . . They are pink flesh-colored tabs (rectangular)," she detailed. "One end of the tab has two long black threads hanging from it. The tabs are glued to the side of the head where the skin is to be lifted. After they have dried, the threads are woven into hair at the back of the head, forcing the tabs to pull the skin very taut. A wig then covers the network of threads." The listener most fascinated by this wonder of modern engineering was Laughton himself, who goaded his makeup man into stealing one of the lifts so he might try it out. The picture does not suggest he adopted the strategy, but Lanchester fluted her lofty opinion that "it is ironic that in an effort to be young [Marlene] aged," because "she dared not pull or twist her face for fear of loosening a lift."

This was wicked, but Marlene's performance as Christine Vole *is* tight. She doesn't move her head; she moves her whole body. The impression is of austere control. When twice in the picture Sir Wilfred calls her "a remarkable woman!" it is that look of military rigidity, of steely single-mindedness that prompts his evaluation, first appalled, finally admiring.

Lanchester was correct that in her mid-fifties Marlene was unprepared to yield to age. She tried to vamp Tyrone Power during production, which "embarrassed" the actor, according to his biographer, and even friends sometimes found her reluctance to act her age (or age her act) unseemly. Noël Coward complained that "Marlene, with her intense preoccupation with herself and her love affairs, is also showing signs of wear and tear. How foolish to think that one can ever slam the door in the face of age." But slam it shut she did and made it seem part of the characterization.

Marlene, in fact, looks uncannily young in most of *Witness* (the exception, ironically, is the flashback sequence in which her Erika von Schlütow–like wig cruelly exposes the wear and tear Coward saw privately). Still, it is widely held that her Christine Vole is the best performance of her career. It is, rather, the most obviously *acted* performance of her career, at a time when Marlene needed to reestablish currency on the screen, if only for the reciprocal effect her films would have on her booming nightclub career.

Witness for the Prosecution was an enormous hit and received six Academy Award nominations, including best picture, director, actor (Laughton), supporting actress (Lanchester), sound, and editing. Many complained that Dietrich was not nominated, but mostly for the wrong reasons. Her Cockney is an adequate impersonation, the kind of thing Laughton himself might have succeeded at with all the wigs, false teeth, and contact lenses.

Nor is the real performing Dietrich does in the picture her loss of control when Christine Vole's perfidy is exposed in the courtroom. *"Damn* you! *Damn* you!" she snarls, a moment much admired at the time, though it is painfully forced.

Dietrich's gift was for nuance and tone, not the highs and lows of hysteria and vengeance. She was always at her best at innuendo or implication, when dissembling or playing a subtext. Here, the subtext is that Christine dare not *reveal* her subtext, which is the surprise of the picture: She knows her man is guilty. Wilder and Marlene, to preserve the surprises, go for it straight, and the result is the transformation of Christine Vole from calculating bitch to self-sacrificing wife to desperately wronged woman in a final surprise. When the reversals come there is no way to segue from one to the next, so she lurches. Dietrich could no more easily convey loss of control as an actress than she could as a woman.

Marlene later said Christine Vole was the only role she ever felt emotionally close to. "She's not only brave, but she loves her man unconditionally." This was a variation on all of the roles in which she had been most effective, but *Witness for the Prosecution* recalls something else about the Dietrich persona on screen. From the beginning of her career Dietrich's women were almost always on the other side of convention, often the other side of the law. Her independence as a screen character required an antagonist bigger than "the other woman" or circumstance. She was always an outlaw, threatened by trials, tribunals, judges of one kind or another in that courtroom reserved for the unconventional. It is her brazen freedom from convention that makes *Witness* work, not subtlety of performance. We don't believe what Christine Vole *does*, but what she *is*.

Witness was followed in theaters immediately by another picture with one of her most indelible screen characters and a performance arguably far better than the one she gave Wilder. It was only a bit, a favor for a friend, and she had made it before *Witness* ever started production.

Orson Welles's *Touch of Evil* was released tardily and shabbily by a confused, perhaps angry Universal, who knew no more what to make of it than did critics. The Wilder and Welles pictures were in release at the same time, *Witness* easily overshadowing *Touch of Evil*, though their respective reputations have reversed with time. *Witness* remains a juicy entertainment, while *Touch of Evil* is an infinitely more daring—if feverishly muddled—enterprise. Hardly anyone saw the Welles picture then, and though Marlene played only a guest role, it seems today more emblematic of her career and presence as an actress than the hugely successful but finally insignificant (except as an enduring entertainment) *Witness*.

Touch of Evil was only a melodrama, too, but Welles's intricate visuals repay viewing in a way more satisfying than the carefully expert mechanics of Wilder. Both Dietrich and Welles perpetuated the myth that she worked on *Touch of Evil* for nothing, but it wasn't true. The story enhanced his status as genius and hers for generosity. It also forestalled demands from those who *did* work for nothing (or union scale) like Mercedes McCambridge and Keenan Wynn, but Marlene received mandatory scale plus $7,500 for her one night of work as Tanya, the Mexican madam who animates the bordertown past of Welles's corrupt Sheriff Hank Quinlan.

Marlene's performance was shot in one night between sundown and sunrise, and she arrived at Universal two hours early for her call. It was worth every penny of the $7,500. She lends *Touch of Evil* the kind of specific gravity only star presence can supply, anchoring a movie otherwise close to spinning out of control in its excesses. She doesn't do much as Tanya, yet she does everything to give it and Welles's character a sense of humane, even sentimental past. She focuses the borders between Mexico and the United States, between then and now, between good and evil.

Welles claimed to a biographer that Universal didn't even know Dietrich was in the picture until they saw the dailies, that he had a "brainstorm" and called Marlene the night before, telling her only, "You should be *dark*." Even allowing for hyperbole regarding Universal (not a place where much goes overlooked), it is true the role wasn't written until Dietrich agreed to do it; it does not appear in the shooting script.

Marlene told Welles she thought a Mexican madam "a little out of my line," but she spent an afternoon limo-ing from one Hollywood costume department to another, reassembling Lydia the Gypsy from *Golden Earrings*. But Lydia was camp, and Tanya is Fate to the tune of a honky-tonk player piano. Quinlan wanders into her bordello, needing a fix of nostalgia, a whiff of his youth to shore his waning sense of power. Tanya doesn't even recognize him, but delivers one of those movie lines that get remembered: "You're a mess, honey. . . . You should lay off the candy bars." Whatever Quinlan seeks isn't there anymore, but we sense through her reaction to his wreckage something of the Hank Quinlan who might once have been. Tanya smokes her cheroot and reads her Tarot cards. "Your future's all used up," she tells him. "Why don't you go home?" At the end Quinlan lies bleeding to death in the Rio Grande, and Tanya stands on the bridge in the night wind and speaks the movie's famous last line. Some find it absurd (Pauline Kael calls it "one of the worst lines ever written"), but it lingers. "He was some kind of a man," Tanya says about him. Then, after a long pause, "What does it matter what you say about people?"

The line reverberates back over the entire movie ("I think I never said a line as well," Dietrich admitted). It explicates nothing, but its simplicity suggests Tanya knows there is both villainy and valor and life goes on. She turns, and—in a movie full of delirious camerawork and cutting—the camera holds steady as she walks away from it across the bridge, back across the border to Mexico. She recedes and recedes, turns back to say "Adios," and keeps on going. This is the movie's final shot, and it is impossible to imagine the film without it or without Tanya. She ends the melodrama on a note of the mystery of human needs and motives. The role does not yield to analysis. It is just theatrics because Dietrich was in town and agreed to do it, but it has a kind of weight that validates Welles's genius for effect ("She was superb," he said). She underlined destiny's wayward drift. Welles's too.

Touch of Evil was a doomed picture, thrown away on the bottom half of a double bill with Hedy Lamarr's last picture (directed by Harry Keller, who did some retakes on Welles's film, which had the same producer). It has since attracted a cult and a literature almost as baroque as the film itself. Few admirers fail to credit the powerful grounding Dietrich's performance gives it. Together with Erika von Schlütow in A *Foreign Affair* and Charlotte Inwood in *Stage Fright*, Tanya is one of Dietrich's three great postwar performances and, like them, is marked by simplicity and a sense of the inevitable, which may be the sine qua non of any great performance.

They don't give prizes for guest shots, not in Hollywood, but there were other honors, and other towns. There was, in fact, the world.

TWENTY-ONE

HELEN
OF TROY
1959 - 1960

W*itness for the Prosecution* looked like yet another Dietrich come-back, but was not. The great movie stardom was over. She would not star again on film for another quarter of a century, and then it would be theme and variation on her greatest role: Marlene Dietrich.

She had demonstrated in *Witness* that she could play character, but she had done that before and the Academy gave her not a tumble. She knew parts like Christine Vole were fewer and farther between than ever, the reason she fought for it in the first place. What parts could there be for a woman over fifty-five who persisted in looking and behaving like a legend in public and often in private? Except one.

Her contemporaries were in trouble, too. Garbo had long since become the phantom of the Upper East Side, while Norma Shearer was rich and forgotten in the Beverly hills. Most of the pinup girls of the forties had proved to have short Hollywood shelf lives (with a much longer one on the other sort of shelf). Some, like Merle Oberon and Paulette Goddard, had married money (Goddard married Erich Maria Remarque's) and kept the jewels. A few, like Joan Blondell and Myrna Loy, loosened their girdles and without apparent regret acted their ages. Others watched their younger selves interrupting commercials on *The Late Show*. Or did the interrupting themselves.

The same year Marlene made *Witness for the Prosecution*, Katharine Hepburn did a remake of *Ninotchka* called *The Iron Petticoat* opposite Bob Hope, and *he* got top billing. Dolores Del Rio would return to play Elvis Presley's mother (in *Flaming Star*); Claudette Colbert would be Troy Donahue's (in *Parrish*); Bette Davis and Joan Crawford had yet to discover (or become) the horrors of *What Ever Happened to Baby Jane*. Most of the rest . . . brunched.

Television had tucked in the old folks at home and the new audience wasn't watching movies so much as performing mating rituals, tapping blue suede shoes while waiting for the Fab Four to come along and redefine everything.

Marlene sold records and filled nightclubs and had a hit movie, and purred advice to the lovelorn weekend-in and weekend-out on NBC radio's prestigious *Monitor*, and was being offered $2 million by Revlon to be their television spokeswoman. None of this made her less an anachronism; it just made her an anomaly among the ancients.

She confided to publicist Arthur Jacobs during the making of *Witness* that she had "had only two movie offers in four years" and wanted to counteract "the Legend." She told him "her fabulous build up from the old days ha[d] caught up with her and limited her," and hoped her performance in *Witness* would change all that, but it couldn't and didn't. Marlene wasn't ready to stop being the Legend, and she was businesswoman enough to know it sold tickets and records. In the spring of 1959 as she prepared to tour Latin America, it got institutionalized.

New York's Museum of Modern Art called its spring series of films "Marlene Dietrich: Image and Legend," and the tribute was unprecedented. No such retrospective had ever been presented of any star's work, let alone one only grudgingly considered an actress. It suggested a wholly new, appropriate category: the Star as Auteur.

Dietrich cooperated with the Museum's Richard Griffith (she was always the most assiduous curator of her career), and Griffith wrote a reverential monograph illustrated with photographs from her private collection. Museum staffer Eileen Bowser prepared a filmography that attempted to trace the pre-*Blue Angel* films, getting most of them right, but was finally forced to note diplomatically, "Although [some of] these films have been attributed to Miss Dietrich, she herself does not recall appearing in them."

The "Image and Legend" program spanned *Morocco* through *Witness for the Prosecution* (the print of *The Devil Is a Woman* was her own) in twice-daily screenings from April to early June. Marlene appeared at the opening, a sold-out, black-tie gala on April 7 in benefit of the Museum library. To counter any notion she had become a museum piece, she wore silver lamé overprinted with gold, a costume from *The Monte Carlo Story* she knew few would recognize because few had seen the movie. She had helped prepare a compilation film of scenes everybody had forgotten about over thirty years and added to it the never-seen telephone outtake from *Witness*, loaned by Wilder.

The event was sharpened by irony: 20th Century Fox was even then remaking *The Blue Angel* (intended for Marilyn Monroe but played by Swedish Mai Britt); Brigitte Bardot was remaking *The Devil Is a Woman*; and in just two weeks David Merrick would open *Destry Rides Again* as a Broadway musical in which Frenchy would get her man. Merrick had tried and failed to get Marlene, but she brushed aside latter-day facsimiles of herself and let film clips defend her title for her.

She addressed the opening-night audience in a speech of considerable grace, minimal false modesty, and generous tribute to Josef von Sternberg, who was not present and whose reaction was snide (though the event stimulated a permanent revival of interest in him). She prepared her remarks with the rigor she devoted to everything she did and took umbrage when her friend Leo Lerman referred to it as "a little speech." It was a *performance* piece, she scolded, full of "accents and pauses" and she *performed* it, giving them the legend and distancing herself from it at the same time.

> Thank you [she said], and I don't ask you whom you were applauding— the legend, the performer, or me. I, personally, liked the legend. Not that it was easy to live with . . . but I liked it. Maybe because I felt privileged to witness its creation at such close quarters. I never had any ambition to become or be a film star, but the fascination this creating process held for me gave me the élan to work and work very hard to please Mr. von Sternberg. When I say work very hard I mean it. . . . The legend served me well, and I venture to say it served well all the other directors who took over after he decided that I should go on alone. . . . It has been said that I was Trilby to his Svengali. I would rather say I was Eliza to his Henry Higgins.

This "Evening with Marlene Dietrich" was heady enough for *Variety* to think it proved "no role dreamt up for her has ever been as exciting and glamorous—and, especially, as happy—as the life that Marlene Dietrich has lived." The event was so successful it was rescheduled ten days later as "A Morning with Marlene Dietrich" for students. On hand was young novelist-screenwriter William Goldman, who remembered the impression the compilation film made.

"I don't know how long it went on—an hour, hour and a half maybe—but gradually this thing came over the house: We realized for the first time that this woman was an *actress*. I'd never dreamed that she had such range or skill; I just thought of her always as this broad Hemingway called 'the Kraut,' and that made her A-O.K. [But] these Dietrich scenes just snowed that house full of film nuts, and after it was over, everyone went ape."

Then the reality appeared. "Her hair dazzled, and she was wearing what I remember as a kind of light-beige suit," Goldman said, "and *it* dazzled and *she* dazzled, and the whole house just stood up and gasped. It was incredible. . . . I couldn't believe that any human being could look the way she did. I didn't know people like that existed [and] when she looked at me, what I saw . . . I swear . . . was . . . 'Listen, relax; I only got this way for you.' "

Goldman's prose is leaner than Cocteau's or Tynan's flights of rhetoric, but no less hyperbolic. It captures the breathtaking illusion of intimacy Dietrich had been perfecting since the Stradivarius-like *Kammerspiele* in Berlin almost forty years before. It was the paradox that made her one-woman show work: distance that felt like intimacy, rumor made reality, artifice turned actual. In person, she was, well, a *person* who simultaneously embodied the legend, conveyed it as a performer, enlarged it with the sheer womanliness of her presence. "I didn't know people like that existed," Goldman said, but she said it was just "how people *want* to see me." It was also how she wanted to be seen, how she *made* them see her, and how, increasingly, she saw herself.

Over the half-dozen years since transparency in Las Vegas, she had refined her barroom act into the most polished one-woman show in the world. The gowns were still fabulous, if less revealing (estimates of their cost inflated to $25,000 per frock), and when she went to Rio in July, an estimated twenty-five thousand Cariocas met her at the airport. She recorded a new performance album for Columbia and went on to São Paolo, then to Buenos Aires in August to create the sort of public riot then reserved for Marilyn Monroe and Elvis Presley.

In Buenos Aires she was "a smash, a sellout," *Variety* said, and in faraway Paris she was reported as "the biggest popular success since Peron." In up-to-date Kansas City, the *Star*'s front page carried the wire-service photograph of police lifting and carrying Marlene unconscious through Buenos Aires *avenidas* to the Grand Opera like a fallen warrior or saint. She had fainted (she said) after hiding in an elevator, waiting in vain for the riot to calm down.

The act had become spectacle, sensation, *show*. Gone was the "Hello" that went on as long as the swansdown cape that trailed behind her while audiences got their first good gape. She now took the stage without a pause, just a look of mock surprise that an audience had indeed shown up, and launched into a song called "Look Me Over Closely." It was mediocre as a song, but riveting as a command, and the audience did what she ordered them to do, getting the opera-glass inspections of her and her "diamond-studded gown" over so the show could begin. She wielded her swansdown cape like a matador, or like a lioness switching her tail.

Autobiography had become more remote and more romantic. "I was a student in a theater school," she said when talking about *The Blue Angel*, which audiences accepted without quibbling about arithmetic. They were simply too riveted by the walking, talking, singing, swaying, laughing, teasing, living legend she gave them. The years (closer and closer to sixty) didn't show or matter. She still did the quick change into top hat and tails for the second half of the show. "The woman's part is for men and the man's part is for women," she explained to Art Buchwald. There was a third part that was for everybody, as she joined a chorus line of ersatz Rockettes for high kicks higher than those of the girls, who were maybe a third her age and looked somehow . . . immature. Finally came "Falling in Love Again" to create meltdown, but still no encores. It was over when it was over, a brilliantly calculated evening of theater, and though she was its producer, director, subject, and star, she had help.

His name was Burt Bacharach.

Back when Noël Coward decided he had been wrong about saloon singing and should do his *own* Las Vegas act, Marlene loaned him her first musical director, Peter Matz, and Coward kept him. Matz replaced himself with a friend with composing ambitions who had once had Darius Milhaud as a coach. Burt Bacharach took Marlene's breath and arrangements away, created new ones for her, expanded her repertoire beyond the now too-familiar songbook, and inspired in her the same sort of passionate confidence and will to recreate herself—partly for him—she had felt with Sternberg thirty years before. She called him "my director, my teacher, my maestro," and "the most important man in my life after I decided to dedicate myself completely to the stage." What they did was create a new legend of international theater, something that hadn't happened since Bernhardt or Duse. Marlene called it "the wonderful woman he helped make out of me." Few argued.

Bacharach looked like a leading man at thirty, was well connected in show business (his father was a newspaper columnist), had composed a few unremarkable tunes, but was chiefly known as an arranger who had worked for Mel Tormé, Vic Damone, and Imogene Coca. He had the good luck to meet Marlene at the Beverly Hills Hotel when he was suffering from a cold, inspiring "Marlene Nightingale" to ransack her luggage for Vitamin C and tender remedies.

He listened to Marlene's voice and set it in sound as Sternberg had set her face and body in light and shadow. He knew her voice had a narrow but serviceable one-and-a-half octave range, centered almost precisely as a viola. It needed support, not cover, and a surround that would lend variety and color to what might drone to monotony. He haloed it with strings, boosted it with bass, encouraged her to let go with the surprising power hidden in her slender diaphragm. He added sparkle to her tone, lightened and loosened her rhythm, and forced her to swing.

He let her keep her standards, but added drive and shimmer and Broadway pizazz. "Lola" became more playful, "Lili Marlene" less portentous, "The Boys in the Back Room" flat-out, belt-it-to-the-balcony comedy. The show gained in variety and texture what it lost in familiarity. New songs helped update the image: "You're the Cream in My Coffee" was a teasing prank; "My Blue Heaven" became airborne romance; "One for My Baby" (straddling a chair and smoking a quarter-to-three cigarette) was relaxed, boozy-bluesy; "Making Whoopee" winked and nudged; "I've Grown Accustomed to Her Face" was daring with no gender change in the lyric. Bacharach enlarged "*Frag nicht warum ich gehe*" which, for all its Richard Tauber associations, was just a song from an old Willi Forst movie. Bacharach's arrangement deepened *Weltschmerz* at romantic love's impermanence, his strings and her volume giving it the surprising power of grief. He let her croon, he let her belt, he let her purr and insinuate and suggest and toy, and then there was the inevitable one, and he changed that too. "Falling in Love Again"—her showy anthem—got simple, with just a modest piano escort (his). After a full evening of *acting* songs, he made her throw it away. It became the intimate, scrawled signature at the bottom of a love letter, the one she had been writing with her lights, shadows, costumes, and songs for the whole evening.

The effect was, as Goldman had noted, "I only got this way for you," and she acknowledged the ovations with that enigmatic smile that suggested Tynan's murderess was indeed compassionate. It was a superlative illustration of the collaborationists' art: Bacharach took care of the sound; Dietrich took care of the adoring fury it elicited, wherever it happened.

Paris was a major test, where the legend and the woman had a history. When she arrived in late November to appear at the Théâtre de l'Étoile, the publicity suggested Jeanne d'Arc, not La Grande, had stepped off the plane. "L'ANGE BLEU EST ARRIVÉE" or "LA GRAND-MÈRE CHANTANTE" was on the front page of almost every Paris paper. Jean-Pierre Aumont and Jean Sablon met her at Orly. Every lunch and dinner, drink and telephone call was covered by photographers. The press counted the forty-four pieces of luggage and the one tiny handbag. "Jewels?" they asked. "My costume," she teased.

The press came along when she visited ailing Edith Piaf; they were there when she announced she would not sing "La Vie en rose" until Piaf recovered. (Piaf never did. News of her death caused Jean Cocteau to drop dead when he heard it.) Marlene was on the cover of *Paris-Match* wearing her Légion d'Honneur red ribbon (so discreet). Speculation was rife (this was Paris) about Monsieur Bacharach (whoever *he* might be). Marlene just smiled (so discreet) and stroked his hair (so smooth).

Chevalier would introduce her on her opening night, the papers blazed. Orson Welles would be there, and Jean Cocteau and the Begum, widow of the Aga Khan, and, and, and. . . . And they *were*. *Le tout Paris* was there. Everyone but Jean Gabin.

She opened on what was Thanksgiving Day, 1959, in America. Chevalier spoke discreetly of Paramount. "We were *amoureux*," he said and acknowledged that no courage she had shown in Hollywood or war was as great as that needed to face this, "the least easy public in the world . . . the most perilous." He told them, "I do not ask you to love and admire her as much as I love and admire her. I would become jealous of you, and we would have our difficulties. But if you will accord her just half of my feelings, then this evening, *mesdames et messieurs*, this grand evening, Paris will embrace, Paris will love—[in English] the one and only—Marlène Diétrich."

The audience felt warned. They wrapped their hauteur around their *sang froid* and waited to see. It took more than a minute. The *International Herald-Tribune*'s critic-at-large Thomas Quinn Curtiss was there and felt "unmistakably, a certain hostility . . . especially in the feminine ranks [which] took on the proportions of a morbid mania." She marched up and back in her "diamond-studded gown" as the opera glasses came out to look her over closely; she spoke nearly accentless French; she sang her songs. Finally they forgot how tough and discriminating they were. "Her victory,"

Curtiss wrote, "was one of unconditional surrender. . . . Marlene had taken Paris."

Her reviews were splashed on the front pages and were unanimous: "MARLÈNE TRIOMPHE!" or "UNE AUGUSTE SIMPLICITÉ," or just "MARLÈNE . . . TOUJOURS."

She got only one bad notice, from a surprising source. Noël Coward though she was *too* toujours Marlène. "Marlene is a fabulous success," he told his diary. "She looks ravishing and tears the place up. Privately I didn't like anything she did except 'One for My Baby.' She has developed a hard, brassy assurance and she belts out every song harshly and without finesse. All her aloof, almost lazy glamour has been overlaid by a noisy, 'take-this-and-like-it' method which, to me, is disastrous. However the public loved it."

Another eyewitness, one of a group of students from the Sorbonne who used room and board money for their tickets, remembered it differently. It wasn't "take-this-and-like-it" so much as it was "the gauntlet picked up and thrown back." Her self-assurance had the tone any brave warrior might use with a bully. Helen of Troy, as Rebecca West called her, simply turned the tables: Helen abducted Paris.

She spent offstage time with Margo Lion; with Coward and Cocteau and Jean Marais and Jean-Pierre Aumont and his wife, Marisa Pavan; with Orson Welles; with Italian film star Raf Vallone. "Her new throb!" gloated Coward about Vallone, though he was unaware of her *other* throb, Alberto Giacometti. The artist's biographer, James Lord, tells us Giacometti did not resist "an idol, an objet d'art, a visual creation, and a 'real' person." Both the person and "the goddess . . . went to his studio and sat in the dust while he perched atop his stepladder" sculpting away. Marlene had admired a sculpture of his when she and it were both on display at MoMA in New York, and in Paris her admiration was clear, but her intentions "wonderfully obscure." Marlene started missing dates and sent roses by the dozen. Giacometti finally trudged to her hotel and left at the desk a small plaster sculpture and went off, back to his wife. Marlene took bows at the Théâtre de l'Étoile and flew to Las Vegas. There she did her annual casino show before joining Raf Vallone in Rome after the New Year. Goddess and "throb" told the press, "*Siamo soltanto buoni amici.*"

While they were being "just good friends" for Rome's *paparazzi*, Burt Bacharach made new arrangements for a new concert tour. The triumphs of Las Vegas, London, South America, and Paris led where they had to lead. Home.

She was a German. She always was, she always would be, and if she had accepted and thrown back the gauntlet of the French, she could do no less with her countrymen and the Viennese as well. She would, as it turned out, have to do a good deal more. The announcement of her tour unleashed a firestorm.

The hate mail was extraordinary in volume and venom. It wasn't merely forests of posters reading "Marlene Go Home!," though there were plenty of those; it was the uninhibited outpouring of German resentment at Germany's most famous woman, who had risked her life to rebuke them. Many considered her and did not hesitate to call her "traitor."

"The Jewish snob and the intellectual mob," went one Berliner's letter, "will curl up with rapture over your appearance in Berlin! They and your Jewish backers have succeeded in making the fall of the West, of its morality and culture, an unalterable fact. . . . Traitor!"

The letter was anonymous, misspelled "unalterable" in German, was plainly anti-Semitic, but far from the exception in the bagsful of letters arriving at newspapers, magazines, radio stations, and the Titania-Palast in Berlin. In that theater Marlene had sung for American GIs at war's end, and there she would begin her German tour in May of 1960, after breaking in the German version of her show in Vienna.

The poison pens weren't always anonymous. An electrical firm in Berlin poured printer's ink and acid in a paid open-letter newspaper advertisement: "Honored Madame," it went. "Where actually do you get the nerve to appear in Berlin after your behavior during wartime, which was anything but friendly to the Germans? For our part, we wish you a correspondingly friendly reception readied by the Berlin public." Then, corrosively, "With highest respects . . ."

A *Hausfrau* in the Rhineland asked, "Aren't you ashamed to set foot on German soil as a common, filthy traitor? You should be lynched as the most odious of war criminals." She spoke, she said, "for all my German brothers and sisters."

The huge-circulation tabloid *Bild* ran pages of letters from readers. "An outrage! We will receive her appropriately!" threatened Herr Werner from Hamburg, while Herr Ruhland from Rüsselsheim noted, "Germans hate her, but she loves the hard German mark. Marlene, stay away!" From Hildesheim Herr Reitz wrote, "If Marlene Dietrich is thinking of singing German folk songs, I recommend she do so wearing the French uniform [sic] in which she marched into Paris at the head of the Allied troops [sic] in 1944 [sic]; and on which she should pin her Légion d'honneur."

Dietrich supporters demanded and got equal *Bild* space. A Hamburg priest called Father Beyer wrote, "Beginning with 1933 we drove out our spiritual greatness and robbed Marlene of her most precious friends. Who showed more character: Marlene, who resisted all the lures of an admiring Hitler and went into battle without compromise against criminal Nazi

Germany, or we, who bowed before the Nazi cross?" Herr Kaynig of Düsseldorf wrote, "Artists like Marlene Dietrich and Thomas Mann knew that their homeland had fallen into the hands of a band of criminals. Should they have remained silent, just because they were Germans? Was Marlene perhaps not a better German for demonstrating that there were *other* Germans?" And Franz Petzak of Bremen reminded readers that she wore her American uniform "in a defensive war against the Nazi regime; she never took up arms against the German people."

Editorial writers took up arms. The news magazine *Der Spiegel* asked Germany to welcome her; an editor in Baden-Baden thought perhaps "it would be better for Marlene and for us if she stayed where she is. It would save her a lot of trouble and make it easier for us to forget the ardent enemy of the Germans, and to keep in memory only the great actress."

Marlene was bloodied but unbowed by the public outcry. She told Art Buchwald, "I'm going no matter what happens," noting that she had *never* worn a French uniform, but marched in Paris in 1954, not 1944, wearing a trench coat and an American Legion cap. "I don't understand it," she said. "Before the war I was attacked by Göring for becoming an American citizen. After the war I was attacked by the German press because I wouldn't come to Germany, and *now* they're attacking me because I am going. The logic . . . escapes me."

So did ticket sales. Marlene had entrusted her tour to American promoter Norman Granz and his German partner, Kurt Collien, in spite of pleas from the Sol Hurok organization that their concert experience equipped them better to handle the "realistic and practical" problems of a return to Germany. Marlene admitted to Coward she had "mismanaged the arrangements for her German tour and it is all in a state of chaos." It was not too late to cancel in the face of furor, but this was never a woman to flinch from challenge. She bristled with Prussian resolve to confront Prussian provocation.

Vienna cancelled. Then Essen. Then the five days in Berlin became three; seventeen cities dwindled to twelve. The Titania-Palast was forced to give out "paper," free tickets to fill the house. Marlene stiffened her image of unflappability, telling *Newsweek* and *Time* that all she worried about was the threats of rotten tomatoes and eggs. Eggs "leave such awful gooey streaks in the clothing," she said, smiling. "I have a swansdown coat, and if an egg ever hits it, I don't know what I'll do. You couldn't clean it in a million years."

Her blitheness wasn't very convincing, but the non-German press accepted her equanimity as a sign of courage in the face of calumny. It is important to recall that the German notion of Dietrich was very different from that of the rest of the world. Press attacks against her had begun early in the Third Reich and continued unabated from 1933 to 1945. During that time not one word that appeared in German print about her got there without approval from Dr. Goebbels and his Ministry of Enlightenment and Propaganda. Most of her films had been banned in Germany, starting with *Song of Songs* in 1934, and even after the war, films like *The Garden of Allah, Angel,* and *Destry Rides Again* were unknown to her one-time countrymen. *Destry Rides Again,* in fact, was just then released in Berlin to coincide with and publicize her return.

Germans in 1960 knew little more than what Nazi papers had written, and they had been too busy digging themselves out of their own rubble and building their economic miracle with the help of the Marshall Plan to admit to curiosity about "a traitor."

But they *were* curious. She was German, the most famous German woman of the century, their one true world star, a culture symbol whether she wanted to be or not. She was an emblem of the Weimar Republic and embodied ideals of duty and discipline bred in the bone of empire. She was part of the history of their times. And not just theirs. At the Brussels World's Fair in 1958, visitors to the U.S. Pavilion were invited to name "the greatest immigrant to the United States": Einstein came in first; Dietrich came in fourth.

The Blue Angel was still one of the two or three most famous German films ever made, and when her postwar pictures were finally released in Germany, *Stage Fright* was called *Die rote Lola* (*The Red Lola*) and *Rancho Notorious* was *Engel der Gejagten* (*Angel of the Hunted*), as if memories of her first great film—made in Germany—were ineradicable, which they were.

They might have forgiven her had she been Jewish (Germans are good about forgiving their victims), but they might have been worse, too. Had they known she had financed "her war" against them by selling almost everything they imagined she had left them to acquire, they might have hated her more.

Not all of her countrymen joined in the chorus of hate by any means. Willi Fritsch, a hugely popular idol during the Third Reich who had acted with her forty years before for Reinhardt, spoke out against anti-Dietrich propaganda: "The reason can only be that the hue and cry of the Third Reich Film Commission's witch-hunt against Dietrich was so effective that it still slumbers in the [German] subconscious."

The German press, now free to say what democratic freedom of the press would allow, continued to crank out stories that she refused to speak German or had forgotten how, that she hated Germans and Germany, and the word traitor is even today attached to Dietrich as if it were part of her name. As late as 1990, she successfully brought suit against a German parliamentarian who marched in the streets with a placard attributing anti-German sentiments to her.

Counteracting the ugliness in 1960 required and was met with courage and the goodwill of, among others, Mayor Willi Brandt, who headed a delegation meeting her plane when she arrived in Berlin. She was taken by Brandt to the Rathaus in Schöneberg, only blocks from the apartment house in the Sedanstrasse where she was born, to sign the Golden Book of honored visitors. John F. Kennedy would proclaim himself *"ein Berliner"* from the balcony of the same building not long after, to be greeted by tears, not jeers.

Also meeting Marlene's plane was German actress Hildegard Knef, whose career was faltering after Hollywood and Broadway, where she had starred as Hildegarde *Neff* in *Silk Stockings*, Cole Porter's musical of *Ninotchka*. Neff's American career never quite worked (though her footprints are in the forecourt of Hollywood's Chinese Theater: Dietrich's are not), and Marlene had insisted on Knef's presence at the airport reception because friends told her Knef needed the press coverage.

Marlene toured the UFA studios (then in East Berlin) where she had made *The Blue Angel*, greeting everyone from the studio head to the chimney sweep. She was embraced by two German-born American citizens who had returned to work in Berlin, Curtis (Kurt) Bernhardt, her *The Woman One Longs For* director, and William (Wilhelm) Dieterle, director of *Man by the Wayside* and *Kismet*.

Willi Brandt and press coverage did not divert from "Marlene Go Home!" posters at the Titania-Palast when she opened on May 3. Nor did they help fill the house. The Titania-Palast has 1800 seats, and fully 400 of them were empty, with hundreds of others papered. Scalpers had been hawking tickets priced twice as high as those for Maria Callas, but were forced to reduce the fare to one-quarter of the box office price. The second night Dietrich played to a lonely-looking audience of only five hundred, and the final night's house was filled by giving out free tickets and ignoring the exchange rate for East Berliners, who were permitted to buy tickets with their all but worthless Eastern currency at a 1:1 ratio, an exchange rate not available between East and West Berlin until the Wall came down thirty years later. By anybody's reckoning the Berlin engagement was a financial disaster. It was also an artistic and critical—and perhaps even ideological—triumph.

Bacharach had provided new arrangements for nearly a dozen German songs she had never sung in concert before (all of them recorded in Munich and Cologne). She turned the concert upside down, beginning with "Falling in Love Again" (in German), playing her major German trump at the very outset like a preemptive attack. She followed immediately with "Lola," also from *The Blue Angel,* and followed that with the German song she had actually sung in her screen test for Josef von Sternberg ("*Wer wird denn weinen*") instead of "You're the Cream in My Coffee," which she usually sang. The program was rich with Friedrich Holländer songs from Weimar Berlin, and when she sang the great "*Allein in einer grossen Stadt*" she announced it was written by Franz Wachsmann and Max Kolpe. They had remained pseudonymous in Germany until the very moment she spoke their names out loud on stage because of Nazi racial laws that had never quite been revised to give credit where it was due. She braved all hazards by singing "Lili Marlene" in German, placing her war years front and center, and perhaps reminding them too that Goebbels had banned the song—their very own—when the countdown for the Thousand Year Reich grew short.

If she had picked up the gauntlet in Paris, she parried with it in Berlin. It was mailed fist or velvet glove, stretched across barbed-wire years; they could take their choice. She displayed a dignity that rose above the fray without ever denying it. Her performance was romantic, full of show-biz savvy, but utterly unyielding. She asked no quarter and gave none until the end of the show. Then she pulled from her song book a small gesture of genius and sang Holländer's haunting "*Ich weiss nicht, zu wem ich gehöre*" ("I don't know to whom I belong"), which ends on the lyric, "the sun, the moon, they belong to all—Perhaps *I* belong, all alone, to just *me.*" She followed immediately with a graceful closing number, "*Ich hab' noch einen Koffer in Berlin,*" ("I still have a suitcase in Berlin"), a nostalgic song that allowed—just perhaps—a hint of homesickness for what used to be.

Willi Brandt leaped to his feet on opening night. He was joined by the 1400 others, cheering. For the first time in her concert career, she gave encores, rewarded by eighteen curtain calls. Truce, if not yet absolution.

That came by the end of the tour in Munich, Hitler's "capital of the movement," and it came through her artistry. Standing room was sold out. She entered to what the press called "a hurricane of applause," and at the end did encores until there were no more, and then bowed in that deep, head-to-the-floor bow for an incredible sixty-two curtain calls.

Every important German review was a love letter. "MAJESTY IN SWANS-DOWN," they headlined. "She is a legend . . . fascinating as a woman of the world, of the intelligence, of the spirit," they wrote. One thought her voice "the sound of an epoch," while others saw her as "half portrait of Dorian Gray, half American in Paris, [and while] others may have more voice, even more artistry, she has more character."

Munich's most important newspaper, the *Süddeutsche-Zeitung,* informed the skeptical, "Yes, it is true. [She is] ravishing, devastating—but the miracle of the image takes second place before the miracle of the performance—and that is preceded by the miracle of the personality. Altogether this adds up to the miracle of Dietrich. . . . She remains for encores and encores which the audience demands with iron enthusiasm. Victorious and helpless at once, she stands in the tumult of the cheers. Dozens and dozens of times the curtain rises and falls and still the audience remains like a wall; the youngsters desert the balconies to storm the stage screaming, 'Come back, come back.' A memory was born." The headline at the end of her tour was apt summation: "MARLENE DIETRICH'S LOVELY ART."

It had been uphill all the way, and for all the reviews and curtain calls and courage, it ended in the ugliness with which it had begun. It happened in Düsseldorf, when Marlene left the Park Hotel to go to the theater. Two thousand fans jostled each other outside the hotel, hoping for a glimpse of her. As she crossed the lobby, a girl of eighteen dashed from the crowd, reached to caress the sleeve of the Dietrich mink. Marlene turned to her, and the girl began to tear at the coat, trying to pull it from her, then cried out "Traitor!" and spat in her face.

Onlookers were shocked, of course. The police arrested the girl, who turned out to have been born in 1942 when Marlene was already forty, already an American, already at war. Marlene went on to the theater, performed, and received ovations, but when it was over, she said to a friend, *"Das Lied ist aus"*—"The song is ended." It was the alternative title to *"Frag nicht warum ich gehe"*—"Don't ask me why I go."

"It was terrible," said Bernard Hall, the friend and factotum Marlene said it to. He had seen the girl spit in Marlene's face and could shudder three decades later. "I personally think Marlene had gone to Germany in the first place to see if she might one day go back to retire there, live out her days in her birthplace. We were drinking late in the hotel one night, and she said, 'Just maybe . . .' Perhaps she was drunk, but I don't think so. Not bloody likely after that spit in the face! That made it clear she could never go home again, because they didn't want her."

She played out the German tour without further incident, except in Wiesbaden, where she grew unsteady and fell off the stage. She scrambled back up in her tail coat, brushed off her trousers, and waved to the crowd, laughing at herself and her inelegant pratfall.

A doctor was called to examine her, but when she heard him say it was a "typical paratrooper jump injury," she recalled her days with paratrooper General Gavin and tried to ignore it with old-soldier indifference. She tied her upper arm to her body with the belt of her raincoat and finished the tour with a broken shoulder no audience was allowed to guess.

It was a warning. Her habit of sipping scotch and champagne backstage between numbers to face the crowds, to get through the arduous work as she entered her sixties, eased the pain, but did not add to steadiness on unfamiliar stages.

When all was said and done Germany could have been worse. Her beloved Rilke once wrote, "Wounds take time and do not heal by having flags stuck in them." Neither do they mend by being ignored. Her German audience didn't know she had signed for another movie role, the last important one she would ever play, and it would be colored by the experience of her homecoming. She would play a German aristocrat, a member of the elite, cultured, obedient class that had failed in spite of everything to prevent her nation's embrace of catastrophe. She intended it as reconciliation; it would read to the unrepentant like reprisal. It would be a movie to rake up that most painful, that ugliest of all German coals: Nuremberg.

TWENTY-TWO

ODYSSEY
1960 - 1967

"We were such wonderfully good friends, my body and I," Rilke wrote late in life. "I do not know how it is that we have separated and become strangers to one another."

Dietrich may have thought something similar as she climbed back on that stage in Wiesbaden. Her spill would have felled a paratrooper, but she forced herself to laugh, wave, and go on displaying artistry without revealing pain. Only her intimates knew the damage of the fall and even they were not certain why it happened. Bernard Hall, her secretary, choreographer, companion, and general factotum since he saw her looking "green" in Monte Carlo in 1956, thought she had had "too much courage" before going on. He, like Maria and one or two others, knew that the showy

Dietrich strut on stage—even without a broken shoulder—was kept floaty on a wave of pills and alcohol.

As she approached sixty, a neck-to-ankle foundation garment had become necessary to preserve the illusion of perfection, and that and four decades of smoking slowed circulation of blood to the famous legs. They cramped and swelled; the elegant hand-made shoes bit into swollen ankles; the tailor-made Levis and high-topped boots she wore offstage were not fashion statements: They hid swelling while she hid pain.

She had Buerger's Disease, a circulatory ailment common to smokers, which often vanishes when nicotine does. Blood vessels contract, blood flow slows, numbness, sudden cramps, and other ills are progressive. Pain can be crippling, not greatly eased by the shot of scotch with a champagne chaser, or the Darvon, or the cortisone, or the prescribed or over-the-counter drugs she took to relax nerves or her throat (Las Vegas's dry air bothers everyone who sings there). She soaked her feet after performances and blamed it on the shoes she wore to give an extra bit of height on stage—for "the line," she said—but it was to increase blood flow into limbs that could turn gangrenous without it. Amputation was the price paid by England's King George VI; it could happen to her.

The irony was cruel. No other star ever used cigarettes with greater style in stills, on screen, even on stage (as when she sang "One for My Baby"). She made a famous bet with Noël Coward that she could quit smoking and he could not. They treated it as comedy, and in a demonstration of the Dietrich discipline, she won. But the damage to her circulatory system was not fully reversible. Pain, swelling, and the treachery of her legs' turning against her were secret burdens hidden under spangles as she continued to appear uncannily young and beautiful and healthy all over the world. The cost in discipline and pain was enormous.

She would not, could not allow anything to defeat illusion. It was how she made her living—she was illusion's mistress; it was hers. The temporary lifts Elsa Lanchester gossiped about became sterile surgical needles to which her hair was braided. They were then embedded painfully into her scalp to pull her face taut, daubed with an antibiotic to prevent infection from the stage wigs that hid them. Giving up smoking (and taking uppers for performing) caused insomnia, eased by sleeping pills and increasing her scotch and champagne intake. Drink was courage: It enabled her to fight the war of age as apple brandy had once helped her fight another war.

After the German tour, Marlene took her broken shoulder to Copenhagen and told jubilant audiences she and the Germans "no longer speak the same language." She proved her remark was metaphorical in Tel Aviv, where she shattered the Israeli prohibition against the German language by singing it on stage. She asked who in Israel's largest (sold-out) auditorium would object to "Lili Marlene" in the original language. Not a hand was raised— for many it was *their* original language too—and they gave her a thirty-five-minute standing ovation. "It's bad enough to lose your Fatherland," she said. "I couldn't give up the language, too."

She asked to stay an extra day after Jerusalem and Haifa to sing for Israeli orphans. Management obliged and sold out the benefit concert by eleven o'clock in the morning on nothing but word of mouth. "Only in Israel," said Dietrich, and told her audience, "I have suffered with you through the years. But for tonight, it has been worth it."

Dietrich's identification with the "good Germany" was so complete she could bring the aura whole to Stanley Kramer's war-crimes movie, *Judgment at Nuremberg*, as Madame Bertholt, a German general's widow. "Who else would you *get?*" Kramer asked in astonishment. That there was a Dietrich to play it inspired the role.

Abby Mann had written his drama for television, where it was a 1959 *Playhouse 90* directed by George Roy Hill. The only actor retained for the film was Austrian-born (now Swiss) Maximilian Schell as the defense attorney for German judges on trial for complicity in Third Reich crimes. The trial was a fictional amalgam of many and asked, in effect, "Who judges the judges?" and answered, in effect, Spencer Tracy.

"There was so much distribution objection at United Artists to this downbeat, uncommercial subject," Kramer said later, "that the only way to get it made was with an all-star cast." The casting got the movie made but inspired wisecracks. Most quoted was Gavin Lambert's: "An All-Star Concentration Camp Drama, with Special Guest Victim Appearances." Tracy played an American judge modeled on Supreme Court Justice Robert Jackson, who had sat on the bench at the original Nuremberg trials; Burt Lancaster played a German judge on trial (Olivier was unavailable); Richard Widmark was an American officer for the prosecution; Judy Garland and Montgomery Clift played pawn and victim of Nazi crimes committed through the courts.

Dietrich's was the only role not in the original teleplay and enlarged the cultural context of a film confined to courtrooms without her. This seemed opportunistic to some, an excuse for glamour on the marquee. Her performance was brief and critics found it "glassy" or noted that "Miss Dietrich is very carefully photographed in a very wooden performance."

The criticisms are not unjust (she is so tightly taped it is surprising she can speak), but miss the point. The role was overshadowed by her own "star narrative" (as Richard Schickel would call it). Kramer was concerned that "the fictional trial put a denominator on the whole German nation that wasn't totally fair, and the Dietrich character was there to embody the 'other' Germany that either hadn't known of the horrors, or had actually opposed Hitler. As a public figure Dietrich was way beyond reproach and represented an aristocratic, pre-Hitler Germany. Still, [Madame Bertholt] tried to deny knowing, but *must* have been aware of *something*."

Madame Bertholt opened the courtroom to glimpses of the cultural life of Germany, the landscape of Bach, Beethoven, and Brahms, but also of obedience and discipline easy to confuse with honor. She added a hint of mature romance with Spencer Tracy's judge (a widower in the movie; his wife is with him in the teleplay). Madame Bertholt knows parts of America better than the judge does. Her former house and servants are requisitioned for his use during the eight months of the trial; *she* lives in a bombed-out room with a hot plate and a portrait of her dead husband, hanged as a war criminal after an earlier trial. Madame Bertholt and the judge attend a concert by a Jewish pianist driven out by the Nazis' Nuremberg Laws; they sip Moselle to tea-dance music as in old days; she pours ersatz coffee and sympathy; she makes do. "I am a daughter of the military," she explains, domestic Spartan and cultural Athenian. They stroll through the ruins and (in an early version of the script) visit Hitler's aerie at Berchtesgaden.

Dietrich accepted the role after a single reading of the first draft. Playing opposite Spencer Tracy was a powerful inducement to take the supporting role (she received fourth star billing). She admired Tracy ("wonderful, wonderful man," she called him) and he liked her. Witnessing their duet in the picture stirs curiosity as to how they might have played together in younger days, how his New England grain might have roughed up her European polish (though the notion of them as George Sand and Chopin for Capra still startles). "You're really not my type," he would kid her on the set with a leer. "You're Continental; I'm just an old fart." Marlene brought him strudel and cookies he ate while telling everyone, "Kate [Hepburn] says they come from a factory she owns in the Valley!"

Kramer rehearsed the actors for two weeks before shooting in early 1961, mainly on the back lot of Revue Studios in Hollywood. Actor contributions to the roles were often incorporated by Kramer or Abby Mann.

"I leaned very heavily on Dietrich," recalled Kramer, "and her contributions were important. She was a standard-bearer for us. She knew Germany. She understood the implications of the script, the ramifications of German behavior better than anybody. Certainly better than Schell, who wasn't really German, as he reminded everybody, every day, every hour on the hour. The speech about Madame Bertholt being 'a daughter of the military' and learning discipline as a child was right out of Dietrich's past, and you feel that."

You feel Dietrich invoking autobiography throughout, though Madame

Bertholt is an imperial monument whose bronzed perfection conceals a hollow core. Her "mission," she tells the judge, is "to convince you that we're not all monsters." She describes aristocrats' attitudes toward Hitler, sounding very like Dietrich herself (or her mother, who lived in a room like Madame Bertholt's at war's end). "We hated Hitler. I want you to know that," she says. "And he hated us. He hated my husband because he was a real war hero and the little corporal couldn't tolerate that. And he hated him because he married into the nobility, which was my family. Hitler was in awe of the nobility, but he hated it."

Dietrich wasn't nobility (and sister Elisabeth—still living a good-*Hausfrau* life near Belsen—was now a nonperson to Marlene), but the speech rides on the *idea* of Dietrich, even though Madame Bertholt misses the point of the trials and Germany's tragedy by a country mile. "We have to forget if we are to go on living," she says, but what she remembers is unworthy, meretricious. She quotes Lancaster's judge putting Hitler in his place: "Chancellor, I do not object so much that you are ill-mannered. I do not object to that so much. I do object that you are such a *bourgeois*." As if social class were on trial.

Madame Bertholt grieves that her husband was executed by hanging and not allowed the dignity of a firing squad. She plays with such elegant sincerity it is hard not to sympathize with the subtleties of execution etiquette. This woman represents the culture and breeding whose pride in discipline (Hitler counted on it) made possible the obedient horrors of the Third Reich. The picture is quite clear about this and Tracy's rock-of-New England face shows it in every rill and crevice. Madame Bertholt withdraws at the end, unable to comprehend that the virtues of discipline and class do not transcend the sanctity of (this is Tracy), "Justice, Truth, and the value of a single human being." We see her at the end in shadow, a bottle at her elbow, rigid before the dead General's portrait and unable to pick up the telephone ringing with Tracy's farewell call. She is lost.

So is the audience thinking about this role. Dietrich's presence may, in fact, undermine it. The film score by Ernest Gold quotes from "Lili Marlene," even allows Dietrich to hum a few bars as she and Tracy walk through the ruins of Nuremberg. The evocative power of the song is so great, so fused to Dietrich's wartime image that it sends a false romantic message about Madame Bertholt, one Dietrich's composed, patrician performance reinforces. "Lili Marlene" was a whore, faithful to the heart; Madame Bertholt is noble, faithful to form.

Dietrich knew what she was playing and researched it, giving the lie to decades of "I just show up and say my lines." Rumors flew that Billy Wilder was secretly rewriting her dialogue, rumors Abby Mann believed and Kramer didn't. Wilder may well have worked on the role with her, but she based her characterization on the widow of Field Marshall Wilhelm Keitel, hanged at the end of the first Nuremberg trials. The choice was acute. Keitel had been marked for execution by the Nazis themselves as the Reich collapsed, and at his trial he asked to be shot rather than hanged: "I believed, but I was wrong," he said. "I did not see that there is a limit set even for a soldier's performance of his duty." Even so, his last words as the noose tightened around his neck were, "*Alles für Deutschland! Deutschland über alles!*"

Kramer never knew, Mann never knew that Dietrich built her performance from this history. Taped up, glassy, or wooden, her Madame Bertholt complicates the cultural texture of the drama. Without that extra layer of ambiguity, Tracy's summation speech as judge would be poorer: "The real complaining party at the bar in this courtroom is civilization," he says, but civilization is also *in* the dock. The guilty verdicts are read as we cut to Madame Bertholt's face in the courtroom. She listens, stricken, unable to accept her place in a larger community of guilt. This was Dietrich's last important film role and she may well have known it; it was also a final message to her homeland.

The message went unheard. *Judgment at Nuremberg* was premiered in Berlin (a major error) in the presence of Willi Brandt, who made a very careful speech. Spencer Tracy was there (with Katharine Hepburn), as were Stanley Kramer and Montgomery Clift, who made a tragic, drunken spectacle of himself before audiences already appalled by the very idea of the picture. Kramer recalled a headline that read "THE JEW KRAMER RETURNS TO REMIND US" and noted the absolute silence of the audience as they read the legend on screen at the end:

> . . . of the 99 men sentenced to prison by the time the Nuremberg trials ended on July 14, 1949, not one of the guilty is still serving a sentence.

The New York Times reported from Berlin that "many sat spellbound," but the spell was horror or outrage. "There was a party afterward at the Congress-Halle, a modern, shell-like place Berliners nicknamed 'the pregnant oyster,'" Kramer remembered. "We set up for a thousand people. Maybe a hundred showed up and they *had* to, or were connected with the movie. Marlene and I had discussed her coming to Berlin for the premiere, and she was willing but afraid her presence would hurt the picture more than help it because of German attitudes about her. *Nothing* could have hurt it more than what it was, which proved the point of the movie. They were like Madame Bertholt; they wanted to forget. They didn't want to be reminded or understand, then or ever. The picture opened and closed that night and was not released in Germany until twenty years later after *Holocaust* was a hit on German television, and even then it was a disaster."

Elsewhere the picture was received with more respect than jubilation. It opened in New York on December 19, 1961, at a gala Marlene attended with Adlai E. Stevenson, then American ambassador to the United Nations. Bosley Crowther in *The New York Times* found it "a fine dramatic statement of moral probity [with] a stirring, sobering message to the world," only "sometimes glib."

Hollywood responded reverently. The Academy nominated it in eleven categories, including Best Picture, Best Director, and Best Screenplay. Both Tracy and Schell were nominated as Best Actor, and Garland and Clift for their supporting roles. Schell won. So did Abby Mann, who accepted his Oscar not only for himself but for "all intellectuals," a remark used ever since to ridicule him and the picture.

Judgment at Nuremberg is the kind of picture easy to smirk at but very, very hard to get financed. It was one of the last of its sort before the movie industry's capitulation to television made such subject matter impossible *except* on television, as drama-bites to space commercials. Kramer was neither a great director nor pretentious enough to style himself one, but there was courage in confronting a project even he, at the peak of his considerable Hollywood prestige, had trouble mounting. In spite of the accolades of the Academy, it barely broke even. The triumph was not aesthetic or commercial; it was that it got made at all.

Marlene turned sixty the week after *Judgment at Nuremberg* opened in New York. A young man she had once danced with on the Riviera was in the White House; another, for whom she had run barefoot across a desert in *Morocco*, died. Ernest Hemingway put a shotgun to his head. An ugly Wall went up overnight, dividing Berlin for what looked like forever.

Maria and her family had moved from New York to London. Maria gave up her career after a tour in stock with *Tea and Sympathy* in 1957 and the birth of a third son, John Paul. They called him "Powlie," in the German manner, and accepted with equanimity his Thalidomide-caused birth defects. John David would arrive in three years to complete the Riva quartet of sons.

Marlene was changing, too. In 1962 she checked herself into the Niehans Clinic in Switzerland for injections of fresh cells of unborn lamb and recuperated by spending Christmas, her sixty-first birthday, and New Year's with Noël Coward and "the Blonde Beast," Marti Stevens, at Coward's Swiss chalet.

The big movie money was over, though she was without challenge as a solo attraction in the theater, which made it easier to do movie work for nothing at all when she believed in the job. She narrated a $50,000 documentary called *The Black Fox*, based on a version of an old fable called *Reineke-Fuchs* (*Reynard the Fox*) by Marlene's own Goethe. It treated Hitler's rise allegorically, using archival footage juxtaposed with the nineteenth-century artwork for Goethe's tale by Wilhelm von Kaulbach and works by Doré, Picasso ("Guernica"), and Grosz. There was even a still photograph of a young woman with beautiful legs in silk stockings and a top hat, sitting on a barrel in a cabaret from a famous film made in pre-Hitler Berlin.

The Black Fox won the Academy Award as Best Feature-Length Documentary. Bosley Crowther noted that "Miss Dietrich's narration, strongly and exquisitely phrased and packing the authority of her German background . . . lends to this film a distinction—a personal sincerity—that rivets the auditor's attention and carries tremendous weight."

It carried no weight in Germany, where it was never distributed, and surprisingly little in England, where every major distributor rejected it even after it won the Academy Award. Finally Marlene appeared at an invitational screening in the West End, during which she stood at attention during the entire hour and a half presentation and told the audience the film "kept alive what Hitler did to the world." A small British company accepted the film, moved by the catch in her voice as she narrated, "They didn't even spare the children." The *Guardian* commented, "Our clammy climate cannot breed such incomparable, ageless stars. The Beatles are nowhere."

They were somewhere. On stage with Marlene at a Royal Command Performance in London in November 1963. "She was electrified by them, *electrified!*" said Bernard Hall. The Four were not yet fully Fab, but newcomers (so *Variety* called them) invited to appear with headliner Marlene, along with Erroll Garner, Harry Secombe and his *Pickwick* cast, and Tommy Steele and his *Half a Sixpence* cast. The Command Performance took place at the Prince of Wales Theatre in the presence of the Queen Mother to benefit vaudeville performers. The Queen missed Marlene and the Beatles due to the birth of Prince Edward, though she could catch them on BBC television a few days later and perhaps did.

Before that Marlene performed at the Albert Hall in a reunion concert for veterans of El Alamein and shortly after would be seen by hardly anybody in a mistake from Paramount called *Paris When It Sizzles* starring Audrey Hepburn and William Holden. The picture had two distinctions: Marlene as Marlene, alighting from a Rolls-Royce (as in *Desire*), and Hubert de Givenchy, who got screen credit for Audrey Hepburn's perfume. The screen credit for the normally deft and witty George Axelrod as writer and producer was perhaps a joke, too, wryer or more ironic than anything in the picture.

Marlene, in flesh freshened up by Dr. Niehans's cells, became ubiquitous. She appeared to triumphs in San Francisco, Dallas, Colorado Springs, Toronto, back to Las Vegas at the Riviera, where she performed "C'est Si Bon" with Louis Armstrong. Back to Paris, on to Amsterdam and Rotterdam and John F. Kennedy's Washington, D.C., having already bowed low to President De Gaulle at the Palais de Chaillot.

The Dietrich shows were received everywhere with such tumult that Goddard Lieberson of Columbia made a private recording for her of nothing but her ovations: sixty-two in Munich, thirty in San Francisco, and so on. Dietrich carried the record around with her to thrill her friends as they listened stupefied to endless applause. "That was Rio," she would note. "That was Cologne." "That was Chicago."

The ovation record became famous when Judy Garland gasped about it on NBC's *Tonight Show*, then hosted by Jack Paar. "We sat there listening for *hours*," Garland said, "and I turned to Noël and whispered, 'I hope there isn't another side,' and Noël just looked at me. There *was*!!"

The world longed to give ovations, even parts of it that already had. Legendary impresario Binkie Beaumont tried to entice her back to London, perhaps with his own interpretation of "Falling in Love Again" complete with top hat atop a piano. His performance was greatly admired in certain private circles and one may have been terminally successful: he died.

London would not be denied another opportunity to worship at the shrine, but first Marlene had engagements off the beaten track: Warsaw and Moscow. She went to give three concerts at Warsaw's Palace of Culture in late January of 1964 and stayed to give six, all of them sold out. She laid flowers at the Memorial of the Warsaw Uprising, the monument to ghetto heroes, and felt German and guilty when she walked through the ruins of the city. Her 1931 recording of "Jonny" was rereleased and became a Top 10 hit in Warsaw. Critics wrote of "an inseparable integration of all the elements which can be utilized by a singer and actor. Every song she interprets is a poem for eye and ear alike."

The Polish wanted encores and got them. She pleaded there *were* no more songs, so they settled for five more renditions of "Falling in Love Again" and "Lili Marlene." The Association of Polish Theater and Film Artists gave her a reception and she appeared before the Polish University Students' Debating Society to talk about the war.

After her final concert she was taken at midnight to the Café Oczki, a Warsaw coffee house, to meet members of the Polish Medical Students' Film Club. She answered questions about Berlin and Hollywood in French,

German, and English, shifting languages to accommodate her translator, who had met her when his father was Polish military attaché to Weimar Berlin and he was a boy. The Café Oczki boasted only an out-of-tune upright but a student knew her records and could play her arrangements and she sang all night long to a tiny audience easily as rewarding as the twenty thousand who had filled the Palace of Culture. Polish coffee and vodka flowed.

A decade later she would do the same while accompanying her friend Marti Stevens, then in the road company of Stephen Sondheim's *Company*, to San Francisco. Larry Kert, star of the show, had introduced Dietrich to the audience following the last performance as "our wardrobe lady," which astonished an audience with no idea Dietrich was *in* the city, let alone ironing costumes for Stevens and other cast members backstage during their run. Following the ovation the "wardrobe lady" received, she ambled with the cast to a nearby actors' bar, where the proprietor begged her to sing after hours for habitués. She resisted until she was offered "*any*thing you want," according to Lee Goodman, part of the cast. "Dietrich looked up, smiled and said, 'Oh, all wight. I'll do it fow a beew!' She got the beer and sang away the night for us old gypsies. So much," noted Goodman perceptively, "for doing it only for the money. She did it because she was a performer, and loved performing."

Tears flowed in Moscow at the Variety Theater near the Kremlin. Then in Leningrad. Then *again* in Moscow. Her antifascist reputation preceded her and she answered reporters who asked how she had fought fascism, "By myself."

Because most Russians thought of her as German, she performed in English and refused a Russian translator, allowing her songs to communicate for her. She and Bacharach were astonished to find the Moscow musicians hired to accompany her had obtained copies of her arrangements and had memorized every note.

Eleven thousand seats sold out at once. Soviet Minister for Culture Yekaterina Furtseva and poet Yevgeny Yevtushenko paid their respects. She bowed again and again in the swansdown coat and after eleven curtain calls retreated to her dressing room. The Russians took up the rhythmic clapping that is their greatest accolade, and she reappeared for a twelfth curtain call in her wrap-around blue cotton dressing gown.

Barefoot, she made a curtain speech in English: "I have loved you for a long time. I have loved your writers, your composers, and your soul. . . . I think I have a Russian soul myself." She disappeared on the night train back to Leningrad where, in the midst of another ovation, she knelt dramatically on stage at the feet of Russian writer Konstantin Paustovsky, the Scarlet Empress humbling herself to a poet.

Neither Warsaw, Moscow, nor Leningrad had been immune to the Dietrich glamour, the "diamond-studded" gown, the swansdown cape, or the shimmer of Bacharach's orchestrations, but there was a new dimension added in the perpetual drive for freshness that kept illusion so contemporary. It was a new song, and Marlene fought it at first as she had once fought "The Laziest Gal in Town." Maria found it, had perhaps heard it with one of her sons: Pete Seeger's "Where Have All the Flowers Gone," folk anthem of the then-burgeoning antiwar movement. Marlene thought it all wrong for her. She was a warrior, not an antiwarrior. Maria and Bacharach pushed her to try it. When she discovered it translated easily and with equal power into French and German she tried it first in Paris, then in Germany, then in Israel, then made it a passionate part of her repertoire and added to it Bob Dylan's "Blowin' in the Wind." She recorded both, and her versions became pop hits on Continental juke boxes. They hymned the latest Dietrich persona: Mother Courage.

She returned to London at the Queen's Theatre in Shaftesbury Avenue in December of 1964. The cabaret act that had filled Piccadilly to overflowing was now a theatrical experience of far greater range and appeal. Gone was the quick change into top hat and tails, and gone with it were the chorus girls and their Rockettes number. Gone too were the opening vaudeville acts that cheapened the aura of Theater. Dietrich the international theater star didn't need such props, and the quick change in the wings was too tiresome and tricky at sixty-three.

The work was harder now and champagne and pills helped less, but no one knew that. No one knew she was ill, either, and she feared to acknowledge it even to herself. Certainly the critics couldn't tell. Not Kenneth Tynan, back again ten years after he had reviewed her "compassionate murderess":

> She stands as if astonished to be there, like a statue unveiled every night to its own inexhaustible amazement. She shows herself to the audience like the Host to the congregation. And delivers the sacred goods. She *knows* where all the flowers went—buried in the mud of Passchendaele, blasted to ash at Hiroshima, napalmed to a crisp in Vietnam—and she carries the knowledge in her voice. She once assured me that she could play Bertolt Brecht's *Mother Courage*, and I expect she was right. I can picture her pulling a wagon across the battlefields, chanting those dark and stoical Brechtian songs, and setting up shop wherever the action erupts, as she did in France during the Ardennes offensive—this queen of camp followers, the Empress Lili Marlene.

Sex was almost beside the point now. Love was the theme and she its incarnation. That London show was the model for all future concerts, and

it was not Tynan, but Harold Hobson in the *Times* who noted the vulnerability that underlined her performances, replacing the "take-it-or-leave-it"
Coward had criticized five years before. Hobson thought what she did on
stage "genius," but he noted "words utterly fail me" when he came to speak
of "Where Have All the Flowers Gone?" He found some. "Not all the
sirens in Homer could sing it as Miss Dietrich sings it. [She] is grave and
thoughtful, and beneath the dusky tones of her low and quiet voice there is
a mastered passion, a controlled tempest of emotion. Her pale beauty is
quite extraordinary; what makes it unique is that she looks as if she has
brought it back from the gates of hell. It is an appalled and a significant
beauty. . . . It is the face of someone who has seen unmentionable things,
the massacre of children. . . . This of course is only an appearance; it tells
us nothing of the real experiences of Miss Dietrich. But on the stage it is a
tremendous, an unforgettable thing. . . . It exalts, it strengthens, and we
leave the theatre with hearts uplifted. . . . The world seems a better and
braver place, and a happier one."

It wasn't a happier one for Marlene. That sense of vulnerability behind the
perfection was real, though she tried to ignore it and shared it with no one,
not even Bernard Hall, who discovered the truth only later.

She had cancer of the cervix. The diagnosis was confirmed by a Swiss
gynecologist in January 1965 just after her London triumph ended. Her
friend Gertrude Lawrence had died of the same disease during the Broadway run of *The King and I* (not liver cancer as was announced). Marlene
may have know this, and her general mistrust of doctors was put aside as she
underwent radium implants in Switzerland. The brush with mortality did
nothing to reduce her alcohol and pill consumption or improve her humor.

She had another fear for her future, one with emotional and practical
impact. At the Edinburgh Festival, where her ovations were as tumultuous
as everywhere else, she learned that the man on whom she depended for
"*amitié amoureuse*," as she liked to call it while stroking his hair for photographers, was leaving her.

Burt Bacharach had always wanted to be a composer. She had known
that, but in their whirl around the globe she had discounted how much he
wanted a settled life with marriage and children. He had found the woman
with whom to settle, film actress Angie Dickinson.

Marlene had known the day would come, which did not lessen the shock
or rage when it did. Dickinson had gone to London to meet Bacharach and
travel on to Edinburgh. A healthy sense of dread sent her to Clive Donner,
director of *What's New Pussycat?* for which Bacharach had provided a hit
song. She asked him to come along for company while Bacharach conducted, "but really for moral support," intuited Donner.

"Marlene went into a fury," he said, "more in sorrow than in anger, perhaps, but it looked and sounded a good deal like anger." Another observer shuddered and closed his eyes, remembering what he said "was not a pretty sight." Donner was struck by Dietrich's voicing "a certain helplessness without Bacharach that was completely contradicted by the imperiousness of her rage. She told him he was ruining *his* career. Not by leaving her to compose and conduct for films, but by marrying someone who wasn't a *star*. It was as if she were thinking in the third person like an advisor or agent, and he had chosen a nobody over Marlene Dietrich! I wondered what her reaction would have been if he had said, 'Marlene, I'm leaving you to marry Garbo.' She might not have been so outraged."

Nothing—not concealed illness, onstage pain, imperious rage, or the prospect of helplessness without her musical mentor—could stay a star performance. Donner remembered they "got through the evening somehow. We left the theater and piled into a limousine at the stage door, where hundreds of fans were waiting. Dietrich had a clutch of signed postcards with her photograph in the famous gown and slipped them one by one through the partially open window of the car. She kept telling the driver, 'Slower, slower,' and then, just as we reached the corner where the car had to turn, she shouted, '*Fast!*' and as the car turned the corner, she released a great arc of hundreds of these postcards. They fluttered through the air like ticker-tape at a parade. The fans dove after them as Dietrich sat back and smiled. It was a brilliant display of theater. Angie Dickinson couldn't do *that*."

Bacharach left behind two estimable musical conductors, the American Stan Freeman and the English composer-conductor William Blezard, but no one could replace Bacharach in Marlene's affections. His departure meant a "fix" of her show. There would be changes to the repertoire, occasional new arrangements, but for the most part the rest of her concert career was as Bacharach had shaped and polished it. She had been a good pupil all her life and knew how to use what she had learned from him, as she had done with an earlier mentor.

She continued to speak of him with affection that surpassed any professional debt. His marriage didn't last, and he would keep his counsel about the years with Dietrich, saying only that it was a friendship both "treasured and loving." He might equally well have echoed Sternberg, saying, "Everything I have to say about Miss Dietrich, I have said with the music," captured on albums that remain shimmering testimony to their collaboration, their *amitié amoureuse*.

Years later a reporter spoke to Bacharach trying to elicit anecdotes he preferred not to share and intuited he had not read Dietrich's memoirs with their effusive love and praise. The reporter read them to him. Bacharach wept.

Rudi wept. For Tamara. She died on March 26, 1965, murdered by another patient at Camarillo, the California state mental institution. Marlene paid her burial bills as she had paid bills for most of her life.

Tamara was buried in the Russian Orthodox section of Hollywood Memorial Park Cemetery under a stone bearing her real name, Tamara Nikolaevna. Rudi had the words "My Beloved" carved into it and Tamara's date of birth was chiseled "1930." It *was* a kind of birthdate; the year Marlene went to Hollywood and left Rudi and Tamara to go to Paramount, which (no one could invent the irony) backs onto the cemetery, its giant sound stages looming over the headstones and trees.

Marlene and man-of-all-work Bernard Hall flew to spend two weeks with Rudi among the chickens and cacti in the San Fernando Valley. Marlene—Granny, as Hall called her—washed and ironed and cooked and scrubbed floors while recovering from her own ordeal with cancer. Hall fed chickens and goats and cleared strawberry beds and warmed to the man Marlene had married. "He was the sweetest, loveliest man I ever met," Hall remembered. "He wasn't well and napped every afternoon. One day Marlene urged me to get in bed with him, to 'see what would happen.' I didn't need much coaxing; even in his sixties Rudi was attractive and he was a *man* and there wasn't much to do on that farm. I got under the covers and he just *slept*. He wasn't bent anyway, not the slightest, and I don't know what Marlene had in mind. Maybe she thought *I* could get a rise out of him when she couldn't.

"When we left she wept all the way to the airport. 'He doesn't love me,' she cried. 'Of course he does,' I said, but she kept weeping these great bloody tears. 'How could he love me and say the bitter things he does?' she asked. I told her 'He's *mourning*!' Then I added, trying to be funny, 'Anyway, he's a flop in bed.' She just exploded, went off like a roman candle. '*You're* the flop!' she said. 'Rudi's *divine*! Rudi's *divine*!' She still loved him, you see. Then she pulled herself together and said, 'He always was the world's best sleeper.' "

The tours resumed. Someone finally threw the dreaded eggs at her on stage in a return to Warsaw. It turned out to be a disgruntled photographer trying to get a reaction. He got one from a judge: three months in jail. She sang for all-white audiences in South Africa, and to atone for the Johannesburg Civic Theater's racism personally carried dinner out to her black driver, not allowed to enter a restaurant with her.

When she went to Australia in October the fans were so uncontrolled they broke two of her ribs in a crush. They made up for the injury with an ovation that was, *Variety* reported, "as great, perhaps greater, than that accorded Joan Sutherland in her recent Melbourne season." As usual now "the applause was no longer for a legend—it was for one of the world's great artists."

In Sydney she appeared as the last great star at the now razed Theater Royal where Sarah Bernhardt had been the first. Her final ovation lasted for fifty minutes, until finally she begged them, "Please go home, I'm *tired!*"

She was not too tired to spend an entire night walking up and down Sydney beaches to be photographed for a Sunday newspaper's photographic supplement, captions to be written by a persistent journalist. He had written her begging for an interview on which, he said, food for his children depended. He got his interview.

His name was Hugh Curnow and a co-worker described him as "twenty-five, broad-shouldered, pink-cheeked, tweed-jacketed, a young Hemingway . . . in his rugged sexual assurance [and] apparently uncomplicated masculinity." Curnow was married with children (three), but well known as a frequent flyer through Sydney's ambisexual bar scene.

"Curnow was a dreadful opportunist. I didn't like him at all," declared William Blezard, her conductor in Australia then and later. "All Marlene was to him was a *scoop.*"

He scooped up more than he bargained for, and Marlene something less. "It was her feelings," explained Blezard. "She's a whole-hogger, very intelligent, very perceptive, but she would throw caution to the winds to follow her feelings, even to her own detriment. In some ways she's had a raw deal in life, because she feels things so deeply. Nobody guesses that—or when they do, they take advantage."

Curnow did. She did feel deeply enough about him to get him official leave from his newspaper to ghost-write her memoirs, still unwritten and shifted from Doubleday to Macmillan. Curnow would guide her pen in Paris, in the Avenue Montaigne.

A future Dietrich biographer may have played inadvertent cupid in the Dietrich-Curnow romance. Charles Higham had himself contemplated having an affair with Marlene when she was in Australia (research, perhaps), but believed she knew him to be too independent for her. When fellow journalist Curnow played that part in Paris, it was Higham who received the bulletins of complaint.

"She's made of finest steel," Curnow confided, but "totally without shame in her vanity." He wrote that she was bound by "bandages" to keep her figure trim and had to be "*unwound*—like a mummy!" by her maid. Then she would pull out the scrapbooks from under the bed for nightly review.

"Home life? No. No. It was never that. . . . I wanted to go out, make love," Curnow wrote. "She made love the French way . . . hated to have me on top of her. . . . She simply wouldn't let me fuck. I like to fuck. . . . Man, woman, anything."

The journalist did not know of her recent illness and seemed not to care that he was there to help write her life, that turning private scrapbook pages with her guidance might provide insight into the private workings of a legend. He was forty years younger than she, and he complained.

"It didn't pay to complain with Marlene," says Blezard. Marlene shoved the scrapbooks back under the bed and sent Curnow packing back to his wife and children. Perhaps Curnow was playing out scenes from *Sunset Boulevard* with himself as Joe Gillis trying to turn Marlene into Norma Desmond. If so, he underestimated the ability of "finest steel" to retain tensile strength and cut losses, whatever feelings lingered. He (and Higham, who deposited these letters with a university for researchers to wonder at) also forgot that in the movie Joe Gillis finally had the decency to feel shame.

Some time later Marlene returned to Australia for an appearance at the Adelaide Festival. She saw Curnow in Sydney, but declined to rearrange her schedule for him. That same day he was killed in a freak accident while covering a story on an oil rig. He was decapitated by a helicopter blade.

When Marlene heard the news she was stricken and said to Blezard, "If I hadn't come to Adelaide, it wouldn't have happened." Blezard saw how shaken she was. She had to go on that night and sing a song about irretrievable things called "Everyone's Gone to the Moon" a song she had first heard there. Blezard thought she had never felt it so deeply or stoically.

She kept going. Scandinavia, South Africa, Australia, Japan; Las Vegas again; Israel again (a boozy evening with Jerusalem's mayor, Teddy Kollek). Denmark, England, Scotland, Wales. Sellout crowds wherever she went. In Liverpool there was a backstage reunion with her cousin Hasso. He and Marlene had not seen each other since Berlin, had not crossed paths since Marlene confirmed his identity for the U.S. army in Salzburg in 1945 when he was a Russian prisoner of war. Hasso Felsing now had a British passport and a British wife of great charm and warmth. Shirley Felsing knew her mother-in-law Jolly, now remarried and living in Switzerland, and recognized Jolly in Marlene. "The long fingernails, the way she wore her jewels, the way she moved, the aura, the glamour, were all the same. They could have been sisters." She was not surprised to hear Marlene tell her that Hasso's mother was "the most beautiful woman I ever saw in my life."

*   *   *

Birmingham, Bristol, Brighton, Glasgow, Oxford, London again. Warsaw, Danzig, Breslau. Ottawa and Montreal. The collection of brass and gold dressing-room doorplates grew; the scrapbooks full of accolades fattened. Only show-business Olympus was missing, and in 1967 she consented to collect that dressing room plaque too.

She had resisted New York and its critics and producers for almost fifteen years, knowing her value to Broadway could only increase as her international successes accumulated. All that suddenly changed because of what happened in Sylmar.

Rudi suffered a near fatal heart attack in May 1967, followed by a stroke. Marlene flew to his bedside from Paris, cancelling vacation plans in Switzerland. He was in a coma when she arrived, his condition critical. Marlene took a room in the hospital to be with him twenty-four hours a day and stayed there until he was out of danger, a severely weakened man, now seventy, with half a stomach and a damaged heart, living alone with a housekeeper, some chickens, and a photograph of Tamara never out of his sight.

Rudi would never work again. Maria and her family were living in London, where William Riva was not getting rich designing children's games. With four boys in school in England or at La Rosay in Switzerland, the need for income was more vital than ever, and she was franker than ever about it.

"Do you think this is glamorous?" she asked a reporter. "That this is a great life and that I do it for my health? Well, it isn't. It's hard work. And who would work if they didn't have to?" All the costs of mounting her solo act—costumes, orchestra, publicity, lighting crew, wind machine, everything—were paid out of her own pocket, and she claimed she paid eighty-eight cents of every dollar she earned to American taxes. "So," she said, "I work. And as long as people want me, and I have them eating out of my hands, I shall continue."

They might not do that forever, she knew; nor with her own circulatory ailments and the slow, secret recovery from cervical cancer, might she be able forever to satisfy them. At sixty-five, it was time to take the Legend to Broadway and bring home the bacon.

TWENTY-THREE

"QUEEN OF
THE WORLD"
1967-1975

Marlene yielded to Broadway and the persuasions of Alexander H. Cohen, who produced plays, musicals, and the annual telecast of the Tony Awards show, Broadway's more tasteful equivalent to the Oscar hoopla. Cohen's style itself was tony. He had hits and flops like everyone else (his London imports, like Richard Burton's *Hamlet*, were prestigious), and he had a sense of style rapidly vanishing as the Great White Way turned into a motley slum. He once decreed no one would be admitted to an Alexander H. Cohen opening night who was not in evening dress and he made it stick. Black tie did not add greatly to the art of anything, but showed respect for the event of theatergoing in the age of nudity on stage and heaven-knew-what in Broadway precincts offstage.

Cohen knew how to treat stars (he presented Chevalier's one-man show on Broadway), and Marlene agreed to dine with him on her way from Paris to concert dates at Montreal's Expo 67 in June, shortly after Rudi's health stabilized. Cohen sent assistant Davina Crawford to meet Marlene at the airport and bring her to the city so she might stay in her own Park Avenue apartment before flying to Montreal in the morning. Crawford, a show business–savvy and stylish young Englishwoman, remembered, "It was terribly important that we clinch her, and my accent was supposed to add that 'touch of class.' " Crawford was appalled as dozens of pieces of luggage rolled directly onto the tarmac without the scrutiny of U.S. Customs. She suggested Marlene leave them with airport security rather than "schlep them" to the city and back. Marlene didn't trust JFK security and thought it more prudent to take a room in an airport hotel, storing the luggage there. Crawford could pick everything up and check it on Marlene's flight the next morning while Marlene arrived by limousine.

That evening at dinner Dietrich got clinched for six weeks on Broadway, but only on what she called "the absolutely crucial condition" that Cohen pay for Bacharach as conductor. Cohen agreed. He also agreed to Joe Davis for lighting and to secure the Lunt-Fontanne Theatre.

"*Everybody* wanted Dietrich," said Davina Crawford. "It was an enormous *coup*. Elated that we had her, I left for the airport the next morning to get the luggage and confronted the nightmare of my life." The hotel room was "a shambles, ransacked—open suitcases looking like a rather up-scale jumble sale." She was terrified to call Dietrich, still in the city. "I thought she'd have a heart attack and drop dead and there would go Alex's overhead for the year! But Dietrich was terrific. She only said, 'Now, Davina. Calm down. Look around for a small, thin, brown cardboard box held together by rubber bands. It's a little scuffed.' " It was there. "Good," Dietrich said. "That's *all* that matters. The *dress!*"

Thieves had taken junk jewelry and furs and thrown wigs around, but overlooked a Jean Louis concert dress in a cardboard box that looked as if it contained laundry. "I was so relieved I almost wept," said Crawford. "I repacked everything, and after all the rumors I expected to find masks and trusses and maybe wooden legs! Nothing like that; just a few show wigs—*and* Dietrich's secret! Six economy-size jars of Boots' cold cream! Must have cost all of two quid!"

Marlene Dietrich opened as a Nine O'Clock Theater Production at the Lunt-Fontanne Theatre on Broadway on October 9, 1967, with Burt Bacharach conducting from his onstage piano, Joe Davis working the lightboard, and Marlene performing magic, two months shy of sixty-six. The engagement was a virtual sellout from the time it was announced, and extra police were stationed to handle crowds mobbing 46th Street.

Her opening was more recorded for posterity than reviewed, as if she were simply beyond criticism. Vincent Canby in *The New York Times* wrote of "a combination of nostalgia, iron will, technique, and perhaps even a little hypnosis" as the elements "with which Miss Dietrich spellbinds her listeners." Canby noted, "Miss Dietrich is not so much a performer as a one-woman environment, assaulting the senses in all manner of means. She looks unreal, as one lady in the audience observed, like a life-size Marlene Dietrich doll. But she is so completely in control of herself, and the audience, we are helpless to be anything but cheerfully amazed. . . . This star is a cool, self-possessed cookie, and anyone who wants a lesson in thought control had better get over to the Lunt-Fontanne sometime in the next six weeks."

Time ungallantly called her "Old Gal in Town" and spoke of "the illusion of youth" and "the illusion of sex," but admitted that illusion still worked. Jack Kroll in *Newsweek* found her dazzle "an incandescent apparition, a dream returned to haunt its veteran dreamers . . . a kind of Mother Courage of the gone glamour world . . . the perfect face of a past that only happens in dreams."

Canby's *Times* review appeared next to a news story about the party at the Rainbow Room after the premiere. Guests gathered skyscraper high while Marlene sat backstage at the theater soaking her swollen feet in a tub of salt water. Mr. and Mrs. Goddard Lieberson (Vera Zorina) came backstage, and Zorina asked why on earth she wore high heels if they made her feet swell so badly. Marlene answered as always, "I'm too short. Heels preserve the *line*."

When she could get back into shoes, police on 46th Street hoisted her above the mob to the top of a limousine, where she signed autographs and posed for photographers. Meanwhile, the Rainbow Room milled with celebrity friends like singer Dionne Warwick, Greek film director Michael Cacoyannis with actress Irene Pappas, the irrepressible Tallulah Bankhead, the trendy Sybil Burton and Jordan Christopher, the classic Liebersons, the photogenic Burt Bacharach and Angie Dickinson. When Marlene arrived at midnight, the band broke into "See What the Boys in the Back Room Will Have," and she dove under a table to evade photographers, knowing nothing could attract them more.

As they fought for photos, celebrities fought for views of each other. Few but Davina Crawford noticed what she described as "a frail leprechaun" from California. "Dietrich was this triumphant, fabulous *thing* pretending to hide under tables, and there was Rudi Sieber, shrunken and small and old, but very sweet, and you could envisage him in his heyday as amusing and appealing—but only a little."

Rudi's stay in New York was brief, and after he left Marlene was lonely.

Crawford recalled that "during the run she used to call Alex's secretary or me and invite us to dinner. Nothing fancy, just someone to eat with. She *owned* New York, she was the biggest thing on Broadway since electricity, and had no one to eat dinner with. I had the impression she was bored by it and only did it for Maria and the grandsons. And Rudi, I guess, but after the opening we never saw him again. It was always, 'Maria and the kids,' 'Maria and the kids.' "

Rex Reed portrayed the worker in a long *New York Times* Sunday piece called "Dietrich: 'I'm Queen of Ajax,' " a reference to her scrubbing down backstage with household cleanser while he interviewed her. Reed's piece was irreverent and many may have thought he was joking, but not about the Ajax. Dietrich had shortly before sent Crawford a hand-delivered, self-typed letter reeking with it. She had personally inspected and swabbed down every dressing room in the theater undeterred by guards because, as she pointed out, there weren't any. She checked every phone connection, light bulb, air conditioner filter (mostly dirty), the condition of the stage (to stand on or to view from the balcony), the carpeting in public and private areas (filthy), wallpaper (peeling), and pronounced the theater no better than a provincial playhouse in Romania.

"She was demanding, but not unreasonable," Crawford said. "Of course, that 'Queen of Ajax' line was too true, but it may have given Alex the idea for the billing when he brought her back to Broadway in 1968."

"Queen of the World."

Remaining Queen of the World was no easier than becoming Queen of the World had been. *The New York Times* thought the soubriquet sounded "on the right track," but not everyone did. Not long before Marlene's "coronation," one who had done as much as anyone to make her worthy of the title published a book. Josef von Sternberg called his autobiography *Fun in a Chinese Laundry* (the title came from an early Edison film), and it remains the most artful of all Hollywood memoirs. It is erudite, scathing, and as elusive and multilayered as his films. When his view from ivory-tower isolation was published, no reviewer failed to note a paucity of generosity to the woman who had called him "the man I wanted to please most."

He had more to say, it turned out, than what he had already said with a camera. Much of it was grudging, none of it was gracious. He painted her as a more than usually obedient prop and brushed aside any possible reaction with "should she be angry once more, when she reads this, she might recall that she was often angry with me, and for no good reason."

It was at once self-aggrandizing, powerful, and petty. Every literate reporter tried to get Marlene's response. She never gave one. Nor did she mention the years of financial support, the sacrifice that had delivered to him the ill-fated *I, Claudius,* or mention that he had asked to be hired for her concert tours as her introducer. When she revealed the request to friends, all she could say was, "Imagine!"

Shortly after Sternberg's book was published, Marlene received another award in recognition of her war work, the Medallion of Valor from the Israeli government. It was presented in Los Angeles, and one of Sternberg's students was with him in his garage-turned-den in Westwood when the news came over the radio. "Do you ever hear from her?" the student asked. "Only when she *needs* something," came the bitter reply. The student looked up at the giant photographs she had inscribed to him lining the walls—"*You God, you!*" or "*Without you I am nothing!*" they said—and wondered what on earth she could *need* from him that she hadn't long since received.

When he died in December 1969 it was minor news from the land of the dinosaurs. The funeral was small and no reporter noted the woman in the babushka standing in the shadows, a discreet mourner, a silent puppet. Screenwriter and old friend Walter Reisch spotted Marlene, but she motioned him to silence. This was *Jo's* curtain call, not hers. What she *needed* from him—the creator's approval of his creation—would forever be withheld.

In 1968 there was another Broadway theater to prowl and scour (the Mark Hellinger), a slightly varied program to perfect, and hundreds of letters to type with two fingers and have hand-delivered to Alexander Cohen. "She sits there at her typewriter and bangs away at it," he groused. "If she has nothing to complain about, she invents things to keep me on the alert." But that was better than when she was in Paris. Then "she sends me cables six or seven pages long. She uses the international telephone like I call the Stage Deli."

Cohen called her Queen of the World on the marquee. In private he called her "certifiable" or "The Singing Hun." This may have been because he was paying her a huge forty percent of the box-office gross (minimum guarantee: $25,000), and he was making, well, *nothing,* what with the high cost of air conditioner filters and sprucing up Romania.

Cohen had plans for recoupment. Marlene received a special Tony Award for her one-woman show and accepted it on the television pageant he produced. It was the first time the general public ever had a glimpse that her health or sobriety might be wobbly. She almost stumbled on stage but laughed charmingly and made it seem evidence of excitement: The Tony was the only professional award she had ever received.

Cohen knew what he was doing getting her before cameras. "Don't *ever* ask me to do TV," she had told him, to which he had reacted with flawless show-business logic: "I knew it was the beginning of her campaign to do TV."

Marlene had avoided television as long as Maria worked there, but as soon as Maria retired Marlene seriously entertained Revlon's two-million-dollar offer to be their hostess for a series of specials. That and other schemes (notably Orson Welles directing her in a special based on her 1959 Paris show) had come to nothing because of taxes. "They've offered me the moon," she told Rex Reed, "but I'm still a virgin in that area. Who needs it?" Especially if the government took eighty-eight cents on the dollar.

Which did not dissuade Cohen. When he inquired on the phone about television, she hung up on him. Clearly, she was in the bag! He went searching for a network and a sponsor. CBS would do nicely. Kraft Cheese would do nicely. And England . . . weren't tax laws different in England?

Meanwhile, Marlene struggled to remain Queen of the World without Bacharach. After her first concert with her new American conductor, Stan Freeman, she dialed Bacharach (from a bar) in Freeman's presence to announce, "He's tewwible! He's tewwible! Come back!" Freeman then felt no pressing need to finish his drink or anything else, but Bacharach persuaded the two to try again, and Marlene eventually pronounced Freeman, "My wock of Gibwaltaw!" as he recalls with grim laughter today.

Becoming a "wock" required stamina to equal her own. "You couldn't let her shove you around," Freeman said. One evening he thought an especially lengthy ovation had resulted in an especially lengthy scotch in the wings and was furious to find himself summoned to her presence following the concert.

"That orchestwa sounded like a dance band tonight!" she accused.

"The way you sang, the New York Philharmonic would sound like a dance band!" he retorted.

"Get out!" she ordered.

"I will!" he agreed. "Good-bye and good luck!"

"Oh, Schweetheart," she said, as she saw him calling her bluff. "Did you see that *dweadful* show on television last night? *Hear* that *dweadful* music?"

He stayed.

"She could be a tyrant, but I think she liked me. She was either impossible to be with or incredibly generous. When we did Expo I came down with diarrhea and she sent to *Paris* for pills. She'd invite me for dinner. She invited a whole *ship* for dinner on the way to Sweden. Barrels of Dom Perignon. Vats of shrimp. Fifty thousand waiters. She fixed up my dressing room in New York, put up curtains she made herself, and a bedspread. But she had to be in control. Complete control.

"That's what she did onstage. She had control and command and she *was* Queen of the World. What she willed her audience to do, they did.

That first sweep out on stage at the beginning of every show was one of the most thrilling moments in show business. I got a chill every single time she did it. She was in total professional control—until *I Wish You Love*, the television show. *That* was a laugh and a half."

I Wish You Love was taped in London in the fall of 1972 for broadcast New Year's Day, 1973, on the BBC and January 13 on CBS. Marlene was edgy, for her few earlier encounters with television had seemed messy, amateurish. She had walked out on a talk show in Canada when the host wanted her to discuss German politics instead of the concert she was there to publicize; her Tony Awards near-stumble embarrassed her; she had sung "Where Have All the Flowers Gone" for UNICEF on German television, which was followed by a fist fight between managers when another singer receiving scale discovered Marlene was getting scale plus $6,000. There had been a few clips for television in Stockholm and Paris and some news footage, but the only trouble-free television she had ever done was the Royal Command Performance almost ten years before with the Beatles, and that was back in the BBC's Stone Age, a photocopy of an event.

I Wish You Love had two goals: first, to make a permanent document of Dietrich in concert, and second, to provide Maria with a nest egg. Marlene was to receive $250,000 (then the highest one-shot television fee ever paid), and rights to the show would revert to Maria.

The plan was fine; the show was not. Television is a technician's medium, not a performer's, and Marlene was denied the control that made her concerts models of professionalism—witty, majestic, moving. She and Alexander Cohen decided to tape in the New London Theater in Drury Lane, the most up-to-date facility in which a concert might be filmed. The New London Theater was so new it wasn't even finished. Construction continued with workers still swarming when taping was scheduled, and schedules are everything in television: They may be what television *is*.

The set by Rouben Ter-Arutunian looked like "red sails in the sunset," said Marlene, when it didn't look orange. "Am I supposed to sing 'La Vie en orange'?" she demanded. The set was replaced with a pink scrim bearing the René Bouché sketch of the Dietrich face that was now her advertising logo. Television lighting cancelled Joe Davis's subtlest effects; bulky cameras cruised up and down theater aisles like cattle on rubber wheels. "Why don't you two get married?" she shouted at a pair of electronic bovines winking their red eyes at each other instead of her.

Marlene and Alexander Cohen had never been warm, and Stan Freeman watched them get cooler. "Alex wanted to see her about something and she didn't want to see him, maybe *ever*. He waited backstage six hours.

It was a duel; who could outwait whom, and Alex forgot that Marlene had outwaited Hitler.

"She could treat stagehands like menials, and I guess she thought Alex was just a high-priced stagehand. *He* wasn't down on his hands and knees scrubbing the stage—*she* was; I saw her do it. Or climbing over cement mixers while they tried to finish the theater. She knew what it should be—lighting, sound, everything—and she knew how to get it. Except on television. She was doing Theater, everybody else was working electronics or videotape, and Alex kept pressuring her to meet the sponsors in the middle of all the chaos."

"*Kwaft Cheese?!*" she would explode. "He wants me to meet *Kwaft Cheese* when I have a show to do?!" She wouldn't meet her sponsors even as a courtesy. Kraft was paying her the highest fee in history, but they were just hucksters. Cohen was to handle the sponsors and provide financing and facilities. "But," remembers Freeman, " the show was being line-produced by this London-based Hungarian who idolized Marlene, just worshipped her. She couldn't take her frustrations out on Alex or the Kraft Cheese people, so she took them out on him. By the time it was over he was backstage sobbing like a baby.

"Nothing went right. Seats weren't yet bolted down for a black-tie, non-paying audience invited by Alex. They were there to be on television, not to see her. She needed that audience and who was she going to play to? *Me?* I was hidden by this scrim thing that looked *very* pink on television. I couldn't pick up the rhythmic cues she used to give us, and our sound reached her a fraction of a beat late over speakers she couldn't *hear*. There's an interplay between orchestra and singer, but not when you're doing it by remote.

"This was a woman who would rehearse everybody—*and* herself—into the grave to get it right, but 'Kwaft' didn't know from rehearsals, and the only grave was the *show*."

Taping was all mechanical, but there were retakes that eliminated what little flow of concert mood Marlene was able to sustain for an audience she resented anyway. She retired to the Hotel Savoy with video machines to edit the final product, which seemed more and more absurd to her as she thought about it because it was free for viewers, with none of the excitement of event. It cost them nothing to turn her on—or off. "I never got nothing for nothing in my life," she growled.

The unspeakable truth—which she must have realized as she watched the tape hour after hour—was that the television special came too late. For years she had brushed aside questions about her age by telling reporters she was seventy-one, but now she really *was* seventy-one. She didn't look it, but on the small screen with the big stare she didn't look the distant goddess of dreams wishing them love, either. She was a curio in a box selling cheese. She looked insecure and angry. One hears she is off rhythm, because of the speakers' musical delay. You can see her listening for the beat. The cameras crudely expose artifice meant to be viewed from seventh row center. Her mouth doesn't quite work, it drags down on the right side; the wig is obviously inorganic to any human scalp. She seems out of it, lost in an affront to the perfectionism she tries with will and star power to dignify.

And almost does. She sings her usual songs, and once in a while her immense authority cancels the harshness of the cameras. She sings "La Vie en rose" with tender nostalgia, and "Where Have All the Flowers Gone" (at the height of the Vietnam War) attains a sorrowing grandeur. Her look on television suggests wisdom of the ages, a mixed blessing for a show that also tries to be flip and hip with a disastrously forced "I Get a Kick Out of You." She seems assailed by technology happening to her, not for her. She had not looked so uncomfortable since *The Little Napoleon* almost exactly fifty years earlier. At seventy-one, she was a beginner all over again.

She thought it a disaster and said so. "It's a disaster," she told journalist Rex Reed, who was not likely to keep it to himself. "They are all robots, these people in TV," she added, seeming to include Alexander Cohen and "Kwaft" Cheese. "But I have only myself to blame," she allowed with no great sense of self-incrimination. "So you always get back to the question of why did I do it. Ask me why I did it," she ordered.

"Why did you do it?" Reed obeyed.

"For the money, honey."

Blunt, but true. And she had endangered much more. She still had concert dates all over the world, including New York's Carnegie Hall, and ticket buyers were likely to think her stage performances were as stiff and lifeless as this television thing she wanted to bury. CBS and the cheese people were not about to allow her uninhibited *Schrei* of catastrophe to continue. They flew 150 television reporters to New York for a press conference at the Waldorf-Astoria. Marlene showed up to tell them all how terrible it was. She was not publicizing CBS's or Alexander Cohen's television show; she was defending the rest of her professional life. Even *The New York Times* recoiled from her "barely-controlled rage."

"Jesus, where did they get those idiots?" she asked *Time* magazine, and Alexander H. Cohen asked a judge to shut her up. Cohen refused to pay the final $100,000 payment due on broadcast because she was wildly damaging the show. He filed a libel suit, claiming her interview with Rex Reed had defamed him as "unprofessional" and a "robot." He had already filed a similar suit in London (where Reed's article and the show ran two weeks earlier) and in London he won.

It is highly unlikely that Marlene was manipulating publicity (as some thought) to attract attention to the show. She had never before warned audiences to stay away, and those who had never seen her on stage and had nothing to compare the television performance with were baffled by her denunciations of it. Even some who had witnessed her at her zenith found little to criticize on the small screen.

Cecil Beaton didn't. He said, "I sat enraptured and not a bit critical as I had imagined I might be. The old trooper [sic] never changes her tricks because she knows they work, and because she invented them. . . . Somehow she has evolved an agelessness. Even for a hardened expert like myself, it was impossible to find the chink in her armour. . . . Marlene has created another career for herself and is certainly a great star . . . with a genius for believing in her self-fabricated beauty. . . . She magnetizes her audience and mesmerizes them (and herself) into believing in her."

Ratings were depressed by the brouhaha and reviews were mostly kind, but *I Wish You Love* sadly remains the chief visual document of the Dietrich concerts. She was right when she said, "It ain't as good." It wasn't even close, and one headline posed the fatal question. It came from an admiring critic in Germany who gently asked: *"Sind Götter doch sterblich?"* "Can the gods be mortal, after all?"

Marlene ought not to have talked to Rex Reed at all. Reed was a popular journalist highly paid to get the Famous to say things he could tattle to the non-Famous. In the "Queen of Ajax" interview of 1967, she had remarked about Vietnam, "What are we going to do . . . kill Johnson?" The right-wing French novelist Roger Peyrefitte picked that up, put it in a novel, and triggered a lawsuit. She wasn't so angry at Peyrefitte's suggestion that she might have proposed the assassination of the president of the United States as she was that he referred to her as "an ex-co-citizen of Hitler." Completely forgetting that she *had* been until 1939, she exploded, "Like hell I was." She won that round in a French court, but the court of public opinion remained angry with her for another remark she made to Reed: "All my friends are dead."

Among the living were a few who took personal umbrage, but her back-to-back Broadway triumphs made them forget they were angry in 1967 and 1968. Her 1972 "robot" interview resulted in the Cohen lawsuit (which would drag on in America for another four years), and Reed let her rattle on long enough to make two more casual remarks that suggested there was less Ajax in the dressing room than champagne.

His interview on the eve of *I Wish You Love* was also on the eves of Christmas and her birthday. When asked how she planned to spend her holidays, she replied, "Oh, I am always alone. My daughter, Maria, went to Switzerland to ski with my money, and left me alone." That sounded churlish to those who never guessed the extent to which Marlene footed bills.

"Why didn't you go [to Switzerland], too?" Reed asked. "You could visit Noël Coward."

"Oh, he could be dead before I get there," she said. "All of my friends are dead already, Hemingway, Jean Cocteau, Erich Maria Remarque, Edith Piaf," not to mention (though she did) Judy Garland, who "wanted to die, so I was glad for her. If you want to die, go die. But don't be a bore about it."

Many (including Reed) thought Marlene was being the bore, and only Noël Coward, for whom friends were outraged by Marlene's remarks, found it all high old camp. He knew Marlene was referring to an old joke of his about the high probability of his "dying before lunch." "Why lunch, sweetheart?" Marlene had asked in mock innocence. But now *Sir* Noël (as he had belatedly become) was in New York, truly ailing, and Marlene's ricocheting from one cranky comment to the next seemed indiscriminate and tactless.

"The Master" was in New York for a black-tie, invitation-only gala of *Oh! Coward*, a revue of his lifework in song the night after *I Wish You Love* was aired on CBS. Coward's shrewd inspiration was to arrive at his gala on the arm of none other than loose-tongued Marlene. It was high-profile forgiveness for her remarks to Reed and a sign of the affection that had held them together through many small spats since the thirties. Coward mischievously warned Marlene that Rex Reed might be in the audience. "If I see him," she snarled, "I shall kick him in the balls. If he has any balls."

Marlene and Coward had them. Coward was bent and frail, and Marlene (dressed in a chic pantsuit) helped him into the theater looking none too steady herself. Myrna Loy thought it unclear who was propping up whom as they made their way past photographers and the elect of New York show business.

It was gallant and touching. Coward was gamely witty ("I came out humming the tunes!" he told the press), and Marlene clung to and love-patted his hand and he allowed it to prove that friendship could forgive anything. It was, as it turned out, Coward's last public appearance; he died two months later. It was fitting that he made it with Marlene. Together they represented a century of purest Star Quality: They also personified the rarest of virtues anywhere—loyalty.

"She always loved you more *after* you were dead," said Bernard Hall. Her circle of friendship was drawing tighter, faster, and her public toughness about death was, to Hall, her method of denial. She complained endlessly about having to work for money, without the slightest signal she was prepared to quit or surrender the guard she kept over the legend. Or *legends*. She had now spent twenty years building a new one and increasingly denigrated the old. "I hated being a film star," she said, adding she was sick of "pansy" film fans who only wanted to talk about *Shanghai Express*. She was no museum piece or relic of retrospectives, but a living presence who could still "*Do* something!" as her mother had drilled into her almost three quarters of a century before. Duty—to herself, to her family's livelihood— was bred in the bone and would not fail until the bone did, and even then it wouldn't.

But anxiety grew. Pills and alcohol and pain talked more than they should. Tolerance diminished for anything or anyone that threatened perfection. She had never been undemanding, but in her seventies her behavior seemed imperious even for majesty. Touring is a special form of show-business torture, and comfort is vital to sustaining the energy to endure it. When Marlene refused accommodations near Brussels because there was no lift in the hotel (she feared for her legs), she panicked proprietors who had lovingly converted a seventeenth-century convent into a luxury inn. "This place may be seventeenth century," she bellowed. "I am not!" When she found her room was on the ground floor in what had once been the chapel, she agreed to stay but insisted the steps to the bed, on what had been the altar, might cause her to trip in the middle of the night. Carpenters installed an entirely new floor in the chapel suite while Marlene told them how to do it.

In Japan she checked into the Imperial Hotel and immediately delivered her order to room service:

1. twelve wastepaper baskets
2. thirty-seven luggage stands
3. one ironing board
4. one electric typewriter (American keyboard)
5. twenty-four telephone pads and pencils
6. one electric hot plate
7. one saucepan
8. double-strength light bulb replacements
9. bottled spring water to fill the kitchen refrigerator
10. the name of a good Japanese restaurant

This last was because someone told her the Imperial kitchen staff could prepare only American food, and she could do that on the hot plate she ordered.

Hotel staff were allowed in her rooms only in her presence, and *never* in the room where her costumes or foundation garments were laid out. Special lighting was installed in bathrooms so she might never be without full stage makeup. Suspicious-looking bottles of "cleaning fluid," "astringent," and "liniment" were strategically stashed away for the occasional dash of courage, in addition to the Dom Perignon promoters were expected to provide by the case.

Before performance, fully braided, stretched, surgically knifed to her scalp, daubed with antibiotic ointment, taped, wigged, made up, and dressed in bugle beads and rhinestones, she cleaned the apartment herself, disinfecting the bathroom only she used, setting all twelve wastepaper baskets in the hall, and either supervising maids as they changed towels and bed linens or doing it herself.

Rearranging hotel furniture was routine, if only to make room for all the luggage stands. If hotel staff in Tokyo, Brussels, or Stockholm were off duty when she arrived, she moved it herself with the help of the local promoter, the executive manager of the hotel, or reporters. Suites with two bathrooms with tubs were de rigueur: one tub for bathing, the other for the mountains of cut flowers she received, hated, and dumped in the second tub without reading the cards.

She grew increasingly bored by meeting local nabobs. She had avoided "Kwaft Cheese" and didn't see why "Suntowy Liquors" or anybody else should have claim on her privacy. On her final night in Tokyo a huge reception was organized at the Imperial Hotel. She was to be presented with two rare, antique kimonos. "I have *enough* dresses!" she boomed. Her wardrobe lady (Jean, married to Chick, the guitar player) gently pointed out that tickets for her Tokyo concert had cost $350, had been completely sold out, that the entire audience including the ushers had rushed the stage at the end of the show, and that the only thing missing from the ballroom where the ancient kimonos awaited was the ancient emperor. She made her appearance in slacks, had a tall scotch, and made a quick getaway with the kimonos. In Framingham, Massachusetts, her promoter waited two hours after the show before discovering she had climbed out her dressing room window and gone to bed.

When she returned to Paris in June 1973 to appear in L'Espace Pierre Cardin, the chic theater opened by the chic couturier, Cardin had new velvet curtains installed in the auditorium, redecorated two dressing rooms and an adjoining bath, covered the walls in fabric, and installed new plumbing fixtures, carpets, refrigerator, and antique mirrors from his own Paris flat. Dietrich inspected her surroundings and advised Cardin, "Stick to pressing pants; you obviously know nothing about the theater."

On opening night she fled the stage when photographers invaded the performance. She announced over a backstage microphone, "I will continue singing only if the photographers leave the theater." Thinking they had, she resumed the concert. A camera clicked, a fist fight broke out in the black-tie audience (leaving a photographer bloodied), while Cardin fainted into the waiting arms of Ginette Spanier's husband, who happened to be his doctor. Marlene announced she would never appear in France again, at least not until Cardin had the stage floor re-covered. He did the next day. She did the Dietrich strut back and forth, and said, "It still cweaks."

Her energies in Paris were distracted by Vogue. They asked her to edit the year-end issue, which would have a chic, black cover bearing only the words (in gold)

VOGUE
par
Marlène Diétrich.

Marlene sought the help of Karl Lagerfeld, who decided he was busy elsewhere. She turned in eighty-three pages of Dietrich photographs and tributes by Hemingway, Cocteau, Coward, Tynan, Malraux, and all the rest. She divided them into sections: "*Moi, vue par les grands photographes,*" "*Moi, vue par les grands poètes,*" and "*Moi, vue par moi-même.*"

This was more *moi* than Vogue had counted on. The magazine asked where the contemporary fashion pages were, and Marlene explained that haute couture today was "repulsive" and the models "impossible." Vogue said *merci*, reduced *moi* to thirty pages, and turned the issue over to art director Jocelyn Kargère, who had wanted Charlie Chaplin in the first place and told the press, "She is incapable of doing anything not about her." Vogue sold out anyway.

Some of this behavior was forgivable, some not, but Bernard Hall thought almost all of it was caused by her health, her drinking, and her having given up smoking ten years before. "The dramas ever after were definitely above average," Hall remembered. "She became Dr. Jekyll and Madame Hyde. I really think she went mad for a while, dreaming about cigarettes and having terrible depressions and temper tantrums. Without her cigarettes, she was odious. She had practically been a *symbol* of the tobacco industry in all those millions of photographs with cigarettes. But realizing how much strength it cost her to stop overnight—and it was ghastly, whatever she said—she never touched another. She *loved* being around smokers for the second-hand smoke and encouraged everybody else to puff themselves to death. She would say smoking didn't cause anything more dire than drinking did, and she knew about *that*, because Granny could knock it back, and I know, because what she *didn't* knock back, I *did*.

"She was always breaking something. The shoulder in Germany. Then she stubbed her foot on a piano and broke her toes. Next she broke her thumb taking a suitcase from a shelf. Ribs in Australia. She'd go out on stage in agony and I'd ask, 'How can you breathe onstage when everything is broken?' and she'd say, 'I breathe through the shoulder I didn't break yet.'

"She was accident-prone. Every time she stumbled or tripped she'd laugh and say, 'Drunk again!' even if she wasn't. It's dark backstage and she didn't see well and wouldn't wear glasses in public. The Jim Beam and champagne between numbers didn't make her vision any clearer, but the famous nightmare time, I don't think she had a drop to drink. That was the one we called 'The Night Stan Freeman tried to Kill Marlene.' "

It was at Shady Grove Music Fair in suburban Washington, D.C., in late 1973. Stan Freeman still cannot discuss it without winces of sympathetic pain: "It was our second night in this place, which had a deep orchestra pit, with the stage quite high above us. At the end of every performance Marlene would acknowledge the orchestra and shake my hand or kiss me on the cheek if we were all onstage, but here it was difficult for her to bend over to reach me in the pit. The second night I decided to make it easier for her by standing on the piano bench. She grabbed my hand and suddenly I could feel the piano bench giving way and I shouted, 'Marlene, let *go!*' but she couldn't hear me over the applause and music. I went over backwards with Marlene still clutching my hand and over she came, scraping against loose nails and instruments and I don't know what. There she was on the floor of the orchestra pit, a bloody mess, and the orchestra is still sawing away at [he sings], "Falling in Love Again," and the audience is applauding and shouting, "Beautiful show!" and she's screaming, "Go *home! Go home!*" but they didn't know what had happened and just kept on applauding. Finally she says, 'What do they *want?* I should do it *again?!*' "

She was badly hurt, having fallen on a protruding nail that ripped open not only her gown, but an entire flap of skin half the length of her left thigh. She was bleeding profusely, and when carried backstage insisted on calling Edward Kennedy, chairman of the Senate Subcommittee on Health, demanding that his doctor be sent to her hotel room to sew her up. Kennedy's doctor was then busy amputating the leg of the senator's son and Dietrich, according to Hall and Freeman, refused to see anyone else. She wrapped hotel towels around her thigh to staunch the bleeding, but by morning, when the leg was much worse, she allowed the hotel doctor to examine her. He sent her by ambulance to George Washington University Hospital for emergency repairs. She shoved aside doctors and nurses, announcing she had no intention of remaining in bed. "I survived two world wars," she told them. "It'll take more than falling off stage to make me cancel a performance."

Stitched and bandaged, she fulfilled her dates and, defying medical advice, flew the next week to Toronto and the Royal York Hotel. By now her wound was even worse, her leg was turning black, and the pain was so

Marlene as the ex-Nazi nightclub singer in Billy Wilder's
A Foreign Affair. Friedrich Holländer, who wrote the great songs,
is at the piano. 1948.

Marlene, John Lund, and Jean Arthur
in *A Foreign Affair,* as seen by the great
Al Hirschfeld.

"The world's most glamorous grandmother" and
John Michael Riva, who made her that.

Hitchcock got "the laziest gal in town" in
Stage Fright, and she got Christian Dior,
Cole Porter, and Michael Wilding, too. 1950.

Only Marlene and young Janette Scott
would show their profiles in *No Highway in
the Sky.* Glynis Johns and Elizabeth Allan
get a lesson in professionalism, though
Allan may be trying to forget old times in
Hollywood when she was Marlene's
"escort."

Two working mothers: the
Ringmaster and the Clown.
Marlene and her daughter at the
circus, 1953.

Marlene singing to a wind machine in Las Vegas, 1954. The dress also came in white.

Marlene's transparent Las Vegas dress made her the world's most highly paid nightclub performer.

Even legends need love. Marlene and Judy at Garland's Palace Theater "comeback," 1951.

Marlene and Noël Coward rehearsing in London, 1953. It was true loyalty, true love.

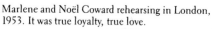

Marlene was "electrified" by the Beatles, November 1963. She was the headliner, they the newcomers.

Marlene as the cockney woman in *Witness for the Prosecution*, evolved from . . .

. . . the earlier disguise, which made her look like George C. Scott in drag. This failed costume test has never been published, and almost scotched the whole idea of Marlene's double role.

Backstage in Las Vegas, the "wardrobe woman" inspects the legend's costumes.

Outrage in Berlin. "Marlene Go Home," they shouted on her return in 1960.

Left: After her first stage fall in Wiesbaden in 1960. She doesn't know it (and neither does the audience), but her left shoulder is broken. Note the dust marks on her pant leg.

Marlene and Spencer Tracy almost played George Sand and Chopin for Frank Capra twenty years before, but settled for the General's widow and the American judge in *Judgment at Nuremberg*, 1961.

Marlene's voice "could break your heart," Hemingway said. Here at a recording session in the fifties, she contemplates a future breaking the hearts of the world. The spectacular diamond and ruby bracelet would be the last of the jewels, her legacy to Maria – sold at auction in 1992.

Tumult in London . . . 1964.

Tumult in Warsaw . . . 1964.

Tumult in Stockholm . . . 1963.

Tumult in Amsterdam . . . 1963.

intense she needed a wheelchair to get from her suite to her dressing room. Somehow she managed to step smartly out on stage before sellout crowds, performing for seventy-five minutes, four nights in a row. There was not the slightest sign of her excruciating pain except that the Dietrich strut was a little more careful.

Marlene had performed with broken bones ever since Berlin's *Broadway* in 1928, but at almost seventy-two she could not heal by force of will alone. She took her last curtain call in Toronto and flew to Houston to be treated by heart-transplant pioneer Dr. Michael De Bakey, who told her only skin grafts could close the wound, and only bypass surgery to her legs could provide blood-flow for the grafts to heal. She had quit smoking a decade before, but the damage that could lead to amputation had been done.

It was terrifying and bitter medicine. Bypass and skin-graft surgery forced her to cancel Carnegie Hall in early January of 1974. She spent Christmas and her birthday in traction in a hospital bed in Houston, insisting she would appear in Dallas as scheduled on January 10. She did not. Nor was she well enough to return to Los Angeles in February.

Adding insult to injury, an indiscreet clerk in East Berlin discovered the birth registration Marlene's father had signed when she was born, establishing that she was not—as most of the world thought—in ill health at the age of sixty-nine, but at seventy-two. The crueler wags did imitations of Marlene singing "Falling Off Stage Again." A famous film director aroused malicious laughter with "attending a Dietrich concert is an act of necrophilia."

Reentering the ring was for her an act of necessity, and she would do so back in London at the Grosvenor House for impresario Robin Courage. He announced in July that she would do six September concerts. Richard Burton agreed to introduce her on opening night; expensive posters of the René Bouché sketch printed on silver paper were run off and posted; and as curiosity and expectation rose, she fell in her Paris apartment in August, breaking her right hip.

She was flown to New York on a Pan Am 747, occupying eight flattened, curtained-off first-class seats, and checked into Columbia-Presbyterian Medical Center for more surgery. A steel pin was inserted to mend the break. News leaked in media-alert New York, and London's *Private Eye* magazine ran what appeared to be an ad for her Grosvenor House engagement. It was identical in every respect to the gleaming silver posters Robin Courage had printed: dates, telephone numbers for tickets, typeface, billing, everything, except that instead of the chic René Bouché drawing of her face beneath the sketched sweep of hair, there was a skull. Which appeared to be wearing a wig. It wasn't satire; it was scurrility.

With such advance "publicity," a leg on which bypass surgery and skin grafts had not perfectly healed, and a hip pinned together with steel only weeks before, no one would have blamed her for cancelling or retiring altogether. But no one knew. Nor would they be allowed to glimpse any hint of compromise to the illusion of indestructible glamour. She opened on September 11, introduced "uneasily" by Richard Burton, according to Sheridan Morley, who reviewed the perilous evening for the London *Times*.

Marlene had remained hidden away in her rooms at the hotel until just before her performance, when she was rolled in a wheelchair through service hallways and the kitchen to just off stage. She rose unsteadily, then, with will unknown to science, compelled herself to walk on stage and make magic for an audience that included Princess Margaret.

She was "an old and defiant German lady with a slight limp," Morley recorded, who "seems to have survived a century." This was an ambiguous beginning for a review, but Morley summoned simple eloquence to leave no doubt about the art Dietrich and discipline could still create on stage.

"At the end, the audience gave her a standing ovation and somehow it didn't seem quite enough; the first of her kind and almost certainly the last of it," he concluded, she is "a living statue of liberty [and] offers the greatest solo turn I have ever witnessed."

Morley was not being kind. It is unlikely anyone who saw Dietrich on stage ever forgot it—or ever will—because she unfailingly confounded expectation. She always delivered the legend, but always more. "Oh, she got *better!*" said William Blezard, who conducted for her in Australia, Japan, and much of England. Even Noël Coward marveled at her artistry when he last saw her perform. "She has learned so much, so much," the Master had said in final benediction.

She had no competition. She was unique, a troubadour-actress, acting her songs as Bernhardt and Duse had acted their roles. She liked to say she knew her limitations, but that was never the same as accepting them. She made what she did look effortless, belying the almost superhuman discipline it took. The steel kept sentiment from becoming sentimental, and the beautiful mask was her vehicle for conveying wisdom of the heart. She was generous *and* stern with her wisdom; she respected *and* instructed her audience. Only a soldier could have sung antiwar songs and made them sound so sorrowful and true; only a lover could have told us the sad truths from that front, too. Only a great beauty could throw away love songs as lullabies, and only a survivor would have dared be there at all, sparing herself nothing and offering herself unflinchingly for our inspection at sixty, seventy, and beyond.

Survival itself was her last great theme. Her kind of long-term endurance acquired a moral dimension for its stamina, grace (under pressure no one knew), and courage—what Remarque had called "the fleeing forward." Some of it was manifest in her songs; some in her history; most of it in sheer presence, in the dignity she displayed and granted her audience. She endured, and burdened us with no compromise, with no confessional pleas for sympathy or indulgence. She never embarrassed us by embarrassing herself. She never asked for our approval; she won it.

There was pride, necessity, and heroism in her performing at the Grosvenor House. Almost seventy-three, ill, racked by wounds that would never fully heal, insulted cruelly by a contemptible brat-press, her mere appearance would have earned the standing ovation that award dinners for dead careers invariably do in Hollywood. But it was more than that; the Art was there, purer than ever. Sheridan Morley was not alone in admiration. *Variety* was there and reported "a superb display of showmanship, stamina and—you name it." She was still "one of the most polished and charismatic solo turns in the business," doing all of it "with style and unfaltering assurance." Those who never saw her on stage cannot know what she did there, but Harold Hobson, we remember, tried to describe it for us. "She becomes," he wrote, "quite suddenly, immensely and shudderingly beautiful, and incomparably touching [and] the world seems a better and a braver place, and a happier one."

There was a press flap as usual. Princess Margaret had organized a party of swells for after the show, including Richard Burton, Franco Zeffirelli, and Kenneth and Kathleen Tynan. Miss Dietrich declined to attend, announcing, "I haven't got anything to wear." She muttered to Stan Freeman, "I'm a *queen*; I should stay up late for a *princess*?" But she needed to restore the energy the London engagement cost her. She was accompanied, anyway, by a "camp follower," a wealthy Canadian in her twenties called Ginette Vachon, now trailing after Marlene from city to city with the doggedness that once won her a place on an Olympic tennis team.

Marlene left London for Miami, Atlanta, Dallas, back to London at Wimbledon, and on to Los Angeles for the second time. There she played the immense Dorothy Chandler Pavilion, where Oscars are awarded to Hollywood's elect. Dan Sullivan, who reviewed her on Broadway, rereviewed her six years later for the *Los Angeles Times* and saw the humanity behind the sequins. "Miss Dietrich stepped out from behind the icon and made contact. . . . [She] hadn't come to pose this time. She had come to perform." Intimations of mortality were shading her performances now, and Sullivan (known in Los Angeles as a demanding critic) must have felt that when he wrote, "Late Dietrich at its best . . . is like late Yeats, the heart wilder and more willful than ever. A much more interesting lady than a plasticized love goddess. . . . One begins to see what Hemingway meant."

Film critic Kevin Thomas saw her there, too, and thought "she regarded her talent as a rare and precious wine that she would pour out drop by drop, and until it was gone it would be the most perfect, most refined of all." Thomas met Rudi, whom Marlene brought out of his San Fernando Valley seclusion. The film critic remembered him as "a natty little man with a toupée, beaming away at this vision of heart-stopping beauty he was married to. He was a little thick-set, an old man [he was now seventy-seven], but Marlene displayed him like a jewel she had saved for her old age, and introduced him with the greatest pride—as if he were the Oscar she didn't need to win, because she had him."

The club dates kept coming, but after twenty years the pickings were leaner and expenses were not. She was still paying for everything: orchestra, conductor, advertising, insurance, travel, housing, food. She began making economies that before her multiple surgeries would have been unthinkable. In Los Angeles she stayed at the swank Beverly Wilshire Hotel, but now she took a standard double room and insisted that Bernard Hall share it with her to save money.

She appeared in theaters in the round that seemed to confuse her. Film historian Charles Silver had seen her on Broadway and maintains today, "I have never experienced anything comparable." In 1974 he saw her again in the Nanuet Star Theater in upstate New York. A reviewer called her "magic," but Silver thought her "unfocused, uncontrolled. She was slurring her words, confused. The circular theater was full of polyester and beer-drinkers and blue-haired ladies younger than she was. Not a Dietrich audience; not a Dietrich performance. A Dietrich mistake."

She announced the unthinkable, a return to Germany, and tried the inadvisable, a return to Australia. It was her third tour there in ten years, and Bernard Hall and William Blezard went with her. Ticket sales were slow and Hall thought her unusually tired. He attributed her fatigue not to the long flight or even the pain that was her constant companion, but to the disappointing ticket sales and the immense effort required each night to do it one more time.

Melbourne had been enthusiastic but not sold out, and when she opened in Sydney at Her Majesty's Theater on September 22 the house was heavily papered and still not full. Her Australian promoter, Cyril Smith, told the press he expected to lose a quarter of a million dollars on the tour.

One week into her Sydney engagement, playing to a half-empty house, William Blezard took his position before the onstage orchestra, his back to the audience as always, and raised his baton. "Falling in Love Again" soared up and out in Bacharach's overture, that grandiose carpet of music on which she made her entrance. Blezard watched his musicians for nods indicating she had come onstage. "I heard a kind of dissonant suspended blues chord," he said later, "and I thought 'God, that's a funny chord, it shouldn't sound like that!' and then the chord started to disintegrate and I realized later it was at that moment they saw her fall."

She had been favoring her right hip with the pin in it for over a year, and that evening, just as she stepped onto the stage with a little too much "courage" to get her through it one more time, the additional stress she placed on the opposite leg, already torn, bypassed, and grafted, caused it simply to snap under her.

She grasped for the curtain as the femur in her thigh broke and tore through the skin. She fell backward to the floor. Perhaps she heard the sarcastic applause from the audience as the orchestra lost control in their alarm, not quite sure what had happened. Blezard turned to see her struggling on the floor, and she cried out to him, "Get the curtain down! Get it *down!*"

"The curtain came down *boom!*" Blezard said. "The drummer and I got her into the wings from the stage. He had a better grip than I and she wasn't very happy that she was being carried unevenly with that compound break, right through the skin. The promoter, a great tough guy with a beard, came running up, hoisted her on his shoulders, and carried her all the way down the corridor to her dressing room. All we could think of was her leg and all we could hear was the audience making mysterious sounds behind the curtain. Outrage? Shock? Sympathy? I don't know. All I know is it was one of the most horrible nights of my life."

She was rushed to St. Vincent's Hospital and swathed in sheepskin to cushion her against jostling until she could be encased in plaster from waist to ankle. Lady-in-waiting Ginette Vachon cradled her in her arms in the ambulance.

There was news: good, bad, and worse. The good was that Lloyd's of London discovered an insurance policy on the Dietrich legs was still in force—by four days. The bad was that all future bookings had to be cancelled, and doctors told her unequivocally that her stage career was over. The worse was that Rudi had suffered another stroke.

She was forklifted in plaster onto a plane bound for New York, but insisted on being forklifted off again in Los Angeles to check into UCLA Medical Center in a room adjoining Rudi's. Maria then insisted her mother be removed to New York's Columbia-Presbyterian Medical Center for treatment, where she was checked in as "Mrs. Rudolf Sieber."

Marlene did not see Rudi at UCLA. The whole notion had been impulsive and reckless; one patient immobilized in plaster, the other drifting in and out of coma after a stroke. But, as William Blezard reminds us, her *feelings* were always ascendant, even when absurd. Whatever she felt, she couldn't see Rudi then; she would never see him again.

TWENTY-FOUR

MONSTRE SACRÉ
1976 - 1982

She was broken, but there was breath in that body. Her removal from UCLA to New York without seeing Rudi one last time she later called "the greatest mistake of my life." But the decision was Maria's and made medical sense. Columbia-Presbyterian had repaired her broken hip only the year before. Doctors and nurses this time found their Hippocratic Oath sorely tested by the commotion of a long-term Dietrich recovery. Trapped in plaster from waist to ankle, she was utterly disabled and found the helplessness and indignity intolerable. The hospital found *her* intolerable.

Old friends like Katharine Hepburn and Joshua Logan tried to bring cheer but were turned away by the sign on the door: "No Visitors! No Information!" She rejected flowers and gifts as they arrived; threw things at nurses she didn't like and demanded their suspensions; refused meals she judged inedible at a glance; demanded (in vain) dinners delivered from favorite restaurants. To the press the hospital staff called her (mildly enough) "the impatient patient."

In May she was released from plaster and traction and flown to Paris for more bed rest and recovery. Worldwide obituaries of her career continued. Then came the dreaded, literal one only weeks after her hospital discharge.

Rudi was seventy-nine when he died on June 24, 1976. He died at home in the Valley house he had shared with Tamara. Marlene was forbidden by doctors to attend the funeral but, as always, she received the bills.

She had him buried in a plot in Hollywood Memorial Park Cemetery a hundred yards or so from Tamara's grave, but still within the shadows of Paramount just over the wall. His stone was carved simply "RUDI" with the dates "1897–1976." The big celebrity in that part of the cemetery is Mel Blanc, the voice of Bugs Bunny: "That's All, Folks!" his tombstone jokes. There is no clue to indicate that "RUDI" was "Mr. Dietrich" for fifty-three years, or even "Mr. Sieber" ever. The inscription is anonymous, like the man.

"Marlene's career died with Rudi," Bernard Hall said. "Everyone assumed her broken bones were the end, but not *her!* She thought she could behave badly in that hospital in New York and then go back to Paris to recover and hit the road again. It wasn't her health that stopped her; it was Rudi."

Her two conductors had the same impression. She had telephoned Stan Freeman and William Blezard to talk about going back to work. Encased in plaster, she buzzed Freeman cheerily, "Let's do it again!" as if it had all been fun. In traction she asked Blezard, "Where shall we begin?" as if they could. These men had heard her bones break or seen her bleeding at the bottom of an orchestra pit, but both knew better than to underestimate her will. When Rudi died, their relief mingled with regret. There would be no more one-night-stand concerts, no more tantrums, no more self-punishing discipline; no more ovations either, no more magic.

"She was shattered when Rudi died," said Blezard. "She always claimed she worked for Maria and the children and would go on until she dropped, but after Rudi's death she said, 'I can't go on,' and I knew that was the end."

"Rudi was the love of her life," Hall maintains, "the only man she ever really loved." Blezard says, "I wouldn't know about that, but she deeply respected him. He joined us once for dinner in Los Angeles. Marlene's friend Marti Stevens was there, but Marlene deferred to Rudi like an old-fashioned wife to an old-fashioned husband. He was the man; he was in control. She accepted that; she wanted that. At *dinner.*"

She mourned Rudi privately and contemplated ways to "*do* something!"

She still needed money for her family. Maria was over fifty now, with sons in their teens to twenties. She had not given up the house her mother still paid for on East 95th Street, though she had moved to London in the fifties and to Spain in 1970. The grandsons used the New York brownstone now, and Maria and her husband (soon to be gravely ill himself) would settle in Switzerland.

The insurance money from Lloyd's of London was not remotely what her income had been or needed to be, but there were assets, courtesy the Legend. Recordings still sold. She had made two albums of German songs in the early sixties and some in French, as well as the concert albums. There were a few jewels left, mostly rubies, but they were in a safety-deposit box in Geneva. For Maria. For Marlene there was very little left: scrapbooks, spangles, and swansdown. Souvenirs. She had earned millions, but had always lived up to her income, sharing it with others without hope or expectation of repayment. She resented taxes more than ever as an "un-American activity," and physically immobilized or not, was determined to continue providing. She had no choice.

Rudi's death freed her to write her life, and few had lived one publishers were so eager to market. Doubleday in 1960 had cobbled together the incomplete *Beauty Is an Illusion* manuscript into *Marlene Dietrich's ABC*, opinions about life, aphorisms about love, and recipes for *pot-au-feu* and leftovers set down with a sense of knowing practicality. The book Marlene had hoped Hugh Curnow would help her write was long dead, the money returned to Macmillan. Now she was offered $300,000 by Simon & Schuster, who announced they had a deal. A month later G. P. Putnam's announced *they* had a deal, for $100,000 *less*. Putnam's had agreed to waive book-tour provisions, deftly capturing a book contract from a rival unaware that negotiations by Marlene were continuing elsewhere. Neither publisher knew she could no longer tour at all.

Marlene typed in Paris while Simon & Schuster filed suit for $3.5 million. Her agent, Robert Lantz, concluded deals with Putnam's and Collins in England. Her London editor was biographer Philip (*Mountbatten*) Ziegler, who found Marlene's independence on the page quite as daunting as impresarios had found it on the stage. He received the first installment of the "Bloody Book" (as she called it) and noted what he called a "certain poetic sensibility" and a curious absence of facts or dates. Miss Dietrich responded from Paris that she was writing memoirs, not a *diary*, and who cared about dates?

Ghost writers were proposed and rejected. Marlene gave her typing to Irwin Shaw and Kenneth Tynan. Shaw, she said, liked it. Tynan offered down-to-earth market advice:

"Dear Marlene," he wrote her, "You tell me: 'Nobody of any stature ever related with whom they slept.' Well Stendhal did; and so did Boswell and Samuel Pepys and Jean-Jacques Rousseau. . . . You will help us to understand you if we know the kind of men who attracted you physically as well as intellectually. You will also help us to *like* you."

This was, for all Tynan's insights into Marlene, a vain tack. She had never in her life or career begged for an audience to *like* her and wasn't about to start now. She wrote what she considered literary criticism of Hemingway and Remarque instead of more intimate observations her publishers hoped for. Of *course* she had letters, but the Marlene who learned to contrive discreet versions of her past while still a young woman was not about to spill the beans as an old lady.

All those rumors, she decided, were quite mysterious anyway. She began asking friends on the telephone how on earth they got started and took pains to deny romances that newspapers and magazines had reported on for decades. One reader of her first draft found it a chaste revelation: "According to Marlene, she has never been touched by man, woman, or beast. On the evidence, Maria Riva would seem to be the world's second recorded case of Immaculate Conception!"

Marlene grew impatient with editorial niggling and—suddenly—the giant German publisher Bertelsmann announced *they* were publishing the book in German (she wrote it in English). German newsmagazine *Stern* would serialize up to sixty percent of the contents and German *Esquire* would publish a childhood chapter with Marlene on its cover.

This was news to everybody (everybody said) and placed the original publishers in the expensive position of having advanced monies on a manuscript they found unpublishable which was now going to appear in translation by somebody altogether new to the difficult process of getting the manuscript in the first place. In addition, the translation (by Max Colpet) would be uncredited, making it appear to German book-buyers that she had written it in her native tongue.

Her English-language publishers could sue a bedridden woman of advanced age on whom public sympathy would surely descend; ask her to return the advances already paid (and spent) and cancel the contracts; or forget the whole thing. This was no win in a big way. No one could look good except Marlene, who had after all written *something*. The publishers dealt with it by not dealing with it. They didn't forget about it, but they didn't sue either. Their contracts simply sat there, tangling publication rights on a manuscript they refused to publish for anyone who might care to do so. When the tangle unraveled ten years later, the memoirs were published (by others) in a version based on a German translation of a French translation of the original English, translated *back* into something resembling the language in which it had been written. Much got lost.

"Autumn Leaves," the great song written for her in her Jean Gabin days, was called "Dead Leaves," after the literal French "*Les Feuilles mortes.*" Well-known Hemingway and Coward quotations went through the English to French to German and back into English translation mill and came out ground to a garble. The cavalier disingenuousness of the tell-almost-nothing text so angered English critic Gilbert Adair that he titled his review "Witness for the Prosecution." Marlene's two fathers became one very shadowy figure, her sister Elisabeth does not exist, and the imagery of near-aristocratic urban gentry utterly ignored the shifting residences and fortunes of her childhood. The long and fiercely ambitious climb from the orchestra pit to the sound stages of UFA and Josef von Sternberg was dismissed in the familiar, "I was a student . . ." whopper.

The Museum of Modern Art's Stephen Harvey reviewed it for *The New York Times*, noting "her humility has its limits." Dietrich wrote Harvey to say she had no *idea* it was being published in English until she read his review, she had written it in German, and his reservations about it were all wrong anyway.

Movie-star autobiographies are not invariably profound, but critics had hoped for more from the pal of Hemingway and inamorata of Remarque, with or without letters. Her original manuscript, in fact, contained graceful passages about childhood and powerful ones about war, but that version was never published. The book sold poorly but there were two notable after-effects. One was that Simon & Schuster, having (perhaps gratefully) long since dropped its lawsuit, signed another writer who might tell the same story from a different viewpoint. Contracts specified the book could not be published until after Marlene's death. The writer: Maria Riva.

The second consequence was more immediate, though no less startling: Marlene, defying every professional and medical prediction, was returning to the screen.

She had actually had a film offer after her hospitalization, from Billy Wilder. He sent her a script based on Tom Tryon's *Fedora*, the story of a legendary and "ageless" star whose agelessness turns out to belong to her daughter, trapped into a life of impersonating her wheelchair-ridden, heavily veiled mother. Wilder wanted Marlene to play mother to Faye Dunaway as daughter, with William Holden along to make the picture a sort of companion piece to *Sunset Boulevard*. Marlene sent the script back to Wilder in outrage, scrawling on the cover, "How could you possibly think . . . !"

Wilder guessed that Marlene had read the script as an oblique and unintended comment on her relationship with Maria, but it is unlikely she fancied herself acting a heavily veiled wheelchair legend who was, in fact, a fraud. At least Marlene respected Wilder, and *Fedora* might have allowed her to segue into Ethel Barrymore–like roles, not mobile, but noble. Instead, she chose the Legend she had spent a lifetime constructing and took a role in a film memorable only for the distressing fact she was in it.

Just a Gigolo was one of several vain attempts to make a film star of David Bowie. The English rocker had been living in Berlin (where he hankered to act the life of painter Egon Schiele). Bowie's delicate, decadent look seemed suited to Berlin of the twenties in a screenplay that simultaneously deplored and adored the depravities not yet plucked from the carcass of the Weimar Republic by *Cabaret*.

Gigolo's financing included subsidy money from the Berlin Senate, and distributor investment was predicated on an "international" cast. Apart from English Bowie, it came from yesterday's Atlas: Sydne Rome (American, but popular in Italy), Kim Novak (American), Maria Schell (Swiss), Curd Jürgens (Bavarian), and as a pimp operating a gigolo service out of Berlin's fabled Hotel Eden, Trevor Howard (English).

Howard was so typecast for the role of a debauchee that he couldn't play it anymore and screenwriter Joshua Sinclair had the brainstorm to offer the role to Dietrich. Director David Hemmings and German producer Rolf Thiele agreed, knowing the pimp could easily become a madam and add authenticity to a picture about Berlin, shot in Berlin, financed partly *by* Berlin, which had not one Berliner in it. She could sing the title song, too, better than Trevor Howard.

Maria handled the deal. Her mother would shoot for no more than two days, would not leave Paris, would not climb stairs or sing "Just a Gigolo," which she called "that terrible song" and had loathed since it was a hit in Berlin when she was still the girl from the Kurfürstendamm.

It was announced that Marlene would be paid $250,000 for two days' work. She got one tenth that, according to Hemmings, though adding the fee Maria negotiated for *herself*, plus the cost of building an exact duplicate of the Berlin set in Paris and flying in German cast and crew, may well have amounted to the larger figure. Dietrich's brief scenes would be intercut with those of David Bowie, who had long since finished and was on a concert tour in America.

David Hemmings, as an actor himself (*Blow-Up*), was left to persuade Marlene to sing the title song, but that could wait. More important was that no one had *seen* Marlene but scriptwriter Sinclair, who had concocted this threnody to decadence in the first place. He had handled negotiations with Maria, then met with Marlene in Paris and secured her trust by telling her how much he liked her autobiography.

"The tension was enormous," recalled Hemmings as the crew waited for Marlene to arrive. "There had been so many rumors about her health and we didn't know *what* to expect, *what* she'd look like. Finally, a car arrived at the studio, and out came a lumpish looking middle-aged German lady and somebody gasped, 'Oh, my God' before we realized that was *Maria*. Dietrich got out of the car very slowly and came up the ramp to the studio very slowly, supported by a cane on one side and Maria on the other. She didn't look remotely like 'Marlene Dietrich.' She looked like my Granny, like your Granny, like everybody's Granny if Granny wore a jeans pant-suit, a Dutch-boy wig and cap, and huge dark glasses. She was frail and obviously infirm and shuffled unsteadily into the immense silence that had fallen over the sound stage. Then I saw it. She had made herself up at home. She had painted on a mask of what Dietrich looked like to her forty or fifty years before, an image and age-fix from which she either didn't know how to retreat or just couldn't *see*.

"It was all very polite and hushed and we ushered her into a dressing room we had built for her on the stage, a curtained-off place where our makeup man, Anthony Clavet, saved her *and* us. He adored her and was able to give her the confidence that she was beautiful now—as she was—and that he could bring out that beauty rather than relying on the caricature she had painted on. There were later all sorts of fictions about 'silk face masks' and such, but it was Anthony's skill with Dietrich's face as it then was—those *bones*—and the confidence he gave her. And the veil.

"She took her time being made up and costumed as the baroness-madam in high boots and the skirt with the slit to the thigh and the big hat. Then the curtains parted. The woman who came out was *not* the feeble Granny who had come in on her cane. This was Nuclear Dietrich, a Star back in her element. It was a breathtaking transformation and the first thing she did was check the lights. She had forgotten *nothing*.

"She was quaking with nerves. She hadn't faced a camera since *Judgment at Nuremberg* sixteen years before. I don't know what intuition drove me, but I suddenly said to my assistant (this was in the morning, mind you), 'You know what I'd really like? A *large* scotch and water!' Suddenly I was being pulled by the hand like a small boy into her dressing room.

"Everyone was aware Maria watered down anything she *knew* her mother had, but there was this innocuous-looking airline bag. Dietrich zipped it open to reveal dozens of little airline bottles, all scotch, I believe. Out they came and Dietrich and I sat there having our little nips. It was—I don't know—*camaraderie* that eased everything immeasurably. It was the kind of thing two actors would do, covering nerves no audience ever suspects. It was 'I know you better now,' and she relaxed and so did I and we did our work.

"She even agreed to sing 'Just a Gigolo'; it was a statement of the film and the *title* and she realized we needed it even if she loathed it. I made it much harder for her because I wanted her to come through the arched doorway, walk to the piano without a cane, and stand there singing the song in one long take. I knew she was in pain, but I wanted people to *see* she could walk and so did she. She had her own pianist, a man called Raymond, and we made two takes in English, then two in German to make sure we had it. All perfect. She walked to the piano without a wince, sang a song she hated quite perfectly and with a majestic sort of nostalgia. The crew and writer and producer were all there, and when she finished I was supposed to say 'Cut!' and I couldn't. The moment was so charged and the spell she cast so total that the beats went by, one-two-three-four, until finally I came to my senses and said 'Cut!' and there was—literally—not a dry eye in the house. We had been admitted to a moment of great professional privilege.

"She was incredibly *self*-fulfilling as an actress," Hemmings said later. "That may have been her secret. She was acutely sensitive and infinitely more giving than her peers might suggest—or *be*. She shared her professionalism, gave it and expected it from you. She was a working actress who couldn't *help* being a star.

"People hear her sing 'Just a Gigolo' today and find it self-referential, self-allusive, especially that last line that 'life goes on without me.' But she gave no sign of that at all. If she reacted to anything in the song, it was the German lyric which ends '. . . *people pay, you keep on dancing.*' That's was what she was doing. Still dancing, after all those years. But with *majesty!*"

After shooting, crew members wanted photographs, and only then, after singing in German, did she speak it. A group photograph was made of "the baroness and her boys," and without warning Marlene launched into a speech.

"There are many people," she said in German, "who imagine I betrayed Germany during the war. . . . They forget. I was never—*never*—against Germany; I was against the Nazis. Even the press seems not to comprehend that. You can't know how it feels. You're all going home [to Germany] tomorrow, but I can't. I lost my country and I lost my language. No one who hasn't gone through that can know what I feel."

"This came out of nowhere," Hemmings said. "She was in costume and makeup and the moment was somewhat acted, but her words were nakedly sincere. Everyone there was aware this might be her last moment on a sound stage. That's why she was cast, in truth, and here she was saying something she desperately needed to say, ending this great, great film career in an artificial Berlin in an artificial movie. She shamed us without meaning to; she was the real thing the movie never turned out to be."

Just a Gigolo was the most expensive German-made film since World War II, was recut by its producer, and was so unspeakable in its swoony decadence that critics preferred to speak of the few minutes that featured the emblem of Weimar Germany. They were under the impression that Dietrich's fee (a tenth of what was announced) had been almost as great as the total subsidy of the Berlin Senate, and hostility to the film focused on Germany's greatest star.

Der Spiegel was brutal: "[Dietrich] plays the mistress of a gigolo service in a mummified appearance that suggests nothing more than the limitless possibilities of makeup. Of her performance of the title song, we had best remain silent. But no matter what, after seventeen years' absence from the screen, she does not deserve to appear in such a botch." *Die Welt* was kinder, but not much. Finding the picture "silk-Sodom and glitter-Gomorrah," it went on to "the old face still beautiful in the merciful shadows of a hat . . . her voice . . . pains us as a parody of herself."

She was less parody than ghost, whisper-quiet, a shadow hinting at what used to be. The soundtrack included "I Kiss Your Hand, Madame," and "Jonny" to stir old Dietrich memories, but her very presence recalled so many things of which the film was not worthy that the few who saw it felt betrayed—by her. The light of eternal youth and beauty had at last observably failed, and failed those she had made believe in it. But it was not they who were betrayed—it was she. *Gigolo* was the parody, using her callously to authenticate a specious facsimile of something derivative in the first place.

"When you prostitute yourself, you have to get paid for it," she said, sounding like her character in the film and putting things in perspective. The pay had been smaller than anyone knew and the cost to the legend more painful than she had imagined. She drew the veil closer around her and would never knowingly or willingly allow herself to be photographed again for the rest of her life.

Not that people with cameras didn't try. As her reclusiveness grew following the release of *Just a Gigolo* and the publication of her memoirs, creative cameramen tried bribing her concierge in Paris or hiring cherry-picker cranes for glimpses into the fourth floor of the building on the Avenue Montaigne. The fame she had sought and cultivated all her life now hounded her, had become a kind of "hell," she said. She wanted peace and privacy, but needed money, and only the Legend—that thing with a life of its own—could bring it in. That legend built with such unwavering diligence needed equal diligence to bear. It was livelihood and legacy and burden.

In 1977 and 1978 the Berlin Film Festival mounted a two-part, two-year retrospective of her film career, retrieving prints from dusty vaults in Prague and Moscow and dusting off negatives in Berlin and Vienna to make new prints of films she still claimed never to have made. A two-volume scholarly work was published to go with the retrospective, which put her—in films spanning half a century—back on the Kurfürstendamm. The city of Berlin offered its highest decoration, honorary citizenship, if she would come to her birthplace to accept it. She stayed in bed on the Avenue Montaigne.

A German filmmaker tried to release something called *Adolf and Marlene*, in which a fictional Marlene is the love object of a not-very-fictional Führer and pays him a visit at Berchtesgaden in order to reject his romantic advances. "I needed a contrast for the horror figure of Hitler," the filmmaker said, "a beauty for the beast." Marlene made sure through the courts it would not be *her*.

Rumor spread that Marlene herself might be fictional. No one saw her. Billy and Audrey Wilder, Douglas Fairbanks, Jr., other friends and acquaintances reported calling her when in Paris only to be told by the maid who sounded oddly Marlene-like, "Miss Dietrich is lunching at Versailles," or "Miss Dietrich is driving to Zurich," or "Miss Dietrich is on a plane to Tokyo."

There was a Portuguese cleaning lady who came in once a day and left simple meals outside the bedroom door, and a secretary once or twice a week to help with the immense volumes of mail still stimulated by the legend. Marlene sent off books of poetry from her own collection to mere acquaintances who might enjoy them and was besieged by requests for money from total strangers. "Naturally I throw such letters away," she told someone, "unless they're really in *trouble*." Mostly she sat in bed, reading, watching television, talking on the telephone, sipping at her scotch.

News emerged in late 1979 that she had fallen again and rebroken her left thigh the previous January. This time the bone would not mend, and her body's fragility was never to be acknowledged. Horror of pity prevented it as much as her need to preserve the legend, for the legend still had duties.

"Duties are what make life most worth the living," she had said all her life. "Lacking them, *you are not necessary to anyone*. And this would be like living in empty space. Or not being alive at all."

She *was* necessary. To herself and to a family that had grown. John Michael Riva, her oldest grandson, had married and adopted his wife's child; the marriage didn't work but the adoption did. Her second grandson, John Peter, was the father of Sean, born in London in 1979. She was two times a great-grandmother, which gave her more people to be necessary *to*.

She read more (her poets sustained her) and watched more television. She didn't much care for old movies, but was passionate about news and tennis tournaments; she liked watching the legs of young tennis stars she fancied.

Even that became a problem. Her vision worsened. As she could not go out to doctors, they had to come to her. Optometrists' examination equipment was not easily portable, so she took to sending her old glasses to friends in faraway places like Tarzana, California, for off-the-rack lenses so she could read and see the television screen.

Television.

The medium she hated working in, on which the legend seemed ubiquitous, spinning money for Paramount or Universal or United Artists or MGM or Warner Brothers or Columbia, while she received nothing. And movies were *cannibalizing* her. "The Man's in the Navy" from *Seven Sinners* was cut into a horror called *Myra Breckinridge*. The "Hot Voodoo" number from *Blonde Venus* was the title sequence for a compilation film called *The Love Goddesses*. *Destry*'s Frenchy turned up as a lampoon called Lily von Schtupp in *Blazing Saddles*. She was all over the place making money for everybody but her.

Which gave her the idea. *Marlene: A Television Show*. The Legend stepping from old reels of film onto the little home box, young and beautiful as ever, with Marlene's voice—"her third dimension"—underlining and mining the legend that was her final capital.

It took two years to organize. Orson Welles was her first choice as director but was unavailable. Peter Bogdanovich had peaked and fallen on hard times, and she didn't need a director with heavy-duty credits anyway. She knew the film clips she wanted and the hundreds of thousands of feet of newsreels that existed, from her arrival in America in 1930 to war footage to her descents on capitals of the world, here, there, or anywhere. She only required someone to put it together to her instructions and a promoter to raise money to pay her for narrating her career, to finance the cutting and pasting, and to make network deals in America and around the world.

Maximilian Schell, whom she knew only slightly from *Judgment at Nuremberg*, seemed an acceptable, even inspired final choice for her to have made. In addition to acting, he had produced and directed and had an enormous plus neither Welles nor Bogdanovich could offer. He spoke both English and German so that a dialogue might develop between subject and director that could serve as narration in two languages, without the necessity of dubbing or making a duplicate sound track for Germany.

Marlene never intended that her television documentary would become the peak event of her late career; or that it would make her seem obstreperous, imperious, and cranky; or that she would loathe it and try to block and disavow it; or that it would win major awards and be nominated for an Oscar for Best Feature-Length Documentary. Least of all did she suspect that—once she saw it—she would come grudgingly to accept it.

*   *   *

It was an unseasonably warm autumn day in 1982 when Maximilian Schell entered the luxurious apartment building on the Avenue Montaigne, stepped into the lift, and pressed the button for the fourth floor. With him was a jet-lagged man named Terry Miller. The two exchanged pleasantries about the heat, and Schell joked about the taping he had come to do. "This time it's *really* by ear," he said, then added somberly, "How she behaves will depend on her confidence."

Confidence was, indeed, the name of this game, for Schell and Miller shared a secret to which Marlene was not privy. Her television documentary—ninety minutes about the career, small screen, nothing fancy—for which she and Schell were about to record sound-track small talk, was not for television at all.

"They don't need *me* for television," Schell muttered as elevator cables whirred.

"This is *not* for television," Miller agreed firmly.

Terry Miller sounded more confident than he was. Miller was Marlene's mostly retired booking agent from her earliest Las Vegas appearances, the kind of business associate who prefers to remain largely invisible to the general public. He had flown from Florida to Paris to protect her interests, even if that meant protecting them from *her*. Schell, the gifted and handsome Oscar-winning actor, was equally intent on protecting Marlene from Marlene, from any tunnel vision focused only on the Legend everybody already knew. He felt the same thrill of historic opportunity that David Hemmings had felt directing Marlene's final footfall on a sound stage. Some of the same apprehensiveness, too. Schell was going to make *Marlene: A Feature*—"A Film by Maximilian Schell"—and with it enter the ranks of Sternberg, Lubitsch, Wilder, Lang, Hitchcock, Clair, Welles, and all the rest who had made Beauty movie-immortal. Only a fool or a charlatan would have failed to thrill to the opportunity awaiting him on the fourth floor, and Schell was neither. Nor was he unaware of the perils of bearding the lioness in her lair with a hidden agenda.

There was a problem: Though Marlene had approved Schell and agreed to tape conversations—six daily sessions of two hours each, half in English, half in German—she had not yet signed any kind of contract. Until she signed a piece of paper she could *un*agree to anything. But Schell hadn't signed *his* contract, either, because he had no real idea what *Marlene: A Feature* was going to be except *his*. He had come armed to *dis*arm. He had with him a secret weapon—a jar of marmalade.

The elevator stopped at four. Schell rang a bell labeled "Do Not Ring." It rang. The door to the flat was opened (with a raised eyebrow at the offending bell) by Bernard Hall, retrieved from retirement in London. Marlene had flown him to Paris for the taping sessions as host, factotum, and gofer, all the things he had been for her since Monte Carlo, through all the great concert years until, after Sydney, there was nothing more to pay him with or for.

Hall told "S&M" (as he later dubbed Schell and Miller) that "Granny" would be out presently. She had broken a toe the day before, he explained carefully, by ramming it into a piano leg while dashing to answer the telephone. This minor injury, he said, would account for her using a wheelchair. Schell and Miller murmured concern that sounded as if they believed it.

All was readied in the living room dominated by the two Blüthner grand pianos she had been given in lieu of royalties that East Germans could not pay in hard currency for records they pirated behind the Wall. Both pianos were highly polished and out of tune. On one rested photographs of two little girls—sisters—taken around the turn of the century. Windows to the bright south terrace were shaded; those giving directly onto the avenue and the Hôtel Plaza-Athénée opposite were open to the warm breeze, curtained in white muslin.

Marlene did not dally. As Hall wheeled her in, she called out cheerily, "Hello, stranger!" and explained away her wheelchair by telling them she had broken her toe by tripping over the piano bench on her way to the photocopy machine. Hall winced. Marlene swept away his frown in protests that she was not in pain, that she had already broken every bone in her body and displayed with pride the injured toe's arresting shade of blue. She behaved nothing like a legend.

Hall set the brakes on her wheelchair. "So you don't *roll away*," he said darkly. He pointed out the table and the bell she could ring should she need him. He withdrew.

"No '*fraternizing*,' Bernard," she called after him in high spirits and laughed an old comrade's knowing laugh.

Technicians scurried in and out as cables were laid and sound levels checked. Schell decided equipment and sound recordists should remain around the corner in the entry, so he and Marlene would not feel they were being watched and where (he did not add) tapes could roll unobserved. Anytime.

Later rumors about those warm days on the Avenue Montaigne, and the impression created by artful editing of those unseen rolling tapes, would suggest Marlene was so reclusive that no one but Schell was allowed into her presence. In some versions even *he* was not there, banished instead to a sound table in the hallway next to the lift. The reality was more hospitable. Marlene was accessible to everyone, blue toe and all. Her guests included production manager Peter Genee, producer Karel Dirka, and technicians and staff who wandered freely in and out of the living room, like Norbert Lill, the sound man who had learned his English in South Carolina and was thus dubbed Carolina by his hostess. Marlene respected and liked such people: They were workers, *professionals*.

Schell passed on greetings from "Maria." Marlene at first thought he meant *her* Maria, then realized he meant his sister, actress Maria Schell, by whom Marlene was underwhelmed. Schell paused, then continued with a greeting from Elisabeth Bergner in London. This prompted reproach from Marlene that Bergner had left wartime exile in England for safer exile in America. "The English never forgave her," she said, old-soldier stern. Schell paused again, then produced his pièce de résistance: the jar of marmalade he had not only cooked himself, but for which he had personally plucked the berries.

Pause.

Marlene was speechless, perhaps with gratitude. She suggested they get to work. Schell began with memories that might evoke some of her own. He spoke of his birth in Vienna, childhood in Switzerland, work and residence in Germany and America. She listened politely until he rambled to a point. Did she, like he, suffer from a sense of homelessness?

"*Quatsch!*" she boomed, using a Berlin term meaning rubbish or baloney. Homelessness was a romantic sentiment from a bad nineteenth-century novel, pure *Kitsch*, utter *Quatsch*. "I have feelings for *people*, not for cities. Mostly I live in suitcases," she said from her wheelchair. Besides, what did this *Quatsch* have to do with her documentary?

Pause.

Perhaps Schell was nervous. She softened; she got gracious; she invited him to remove his coat in all this heat. She offered Evian and delicacies "I prepared myself." (Bernard Hall, eavesdropping around the corner and fatigued from shopping, rolled his eyes.) Marlene called out to "Carolina," wondering if her voice came clearly through the small lapel mike she did not entirely trust because it seemed such "amateur sort of stuff." Assured that every decibel was coming through, she turned back to Schell. "What are we going to see on the screen? . . . You can't have a black screen, dear. . . . I just want to know what's on the screen—what do we *see*?! It has to keep *mooovin'*, dear!"

She knew what *she* wanted to see, every scene down to the second. She had been doing her homework for two years. She had submitted to Schell and her producer many months before a list of film clips they should acquire from Hollywood. She had also (she now casually revealed) personally contacted owners of that footage and discovered that no one had yet purchased a single frame of film or even made inquiry about doing so. Until they did, she pointed out, they were taping a radio show. To Schell (and anyone wearing earphones—an old Paramount trick, muttering at the end of a film take) she whispered that the producer was "not my favorite person," might even be, "how do we say that in Jewish? A . . . *Goniff* [crook]!"

Schell, who had planned a very different kind of footage in his secret heart, explained that Hollywood companies sell footage at breathtaking prices per foot or per second, and there was no point in buying anything until he, the director, knew what he wanted to use in the finished film but he had brought along videocassettes of her movies. This was "amateur sort of stuff," she said. Videocassettes were *Quatsch*. Amateur stuff was *Quatsch*. This room was, her voice hinted, hip-deep in *Quatsch*.

Pause.

Schell began again, his tone inviting an exchange of confidences. Dismissing questions she had already answered (or not) thousands of times, she explained, "It's in my book." When he asked her to repeat something from her book for the tapes, she answered, "It's copyrighted!" as if copyright law prevented her quoting herself. Copyright was not *Quatsch*. And had nothing to do with her television documentary.

Schell carefully mentioned the word *feature*.

"*Feature!?*" she asked in astonishment. "For what? This is for a television documentary, ninety minutes long, and that's all. Nothing else! . . . It's only for the career. That's what the contract calls for. The career. . . . It is to tell the life story of an *actress*, not as a person, not as a private person, no. . . . That is why we must always think what are we showing on the television box."

Schell said he thought he was there to make a feature.

"Then they told you wrong," she clarified.

Pause.

A shift to biography, to those two little turn-of-the-century girls framed in silver on one of the pianos.

"You had no brothers or sisters?" he asked.

"No," she said, slamming that chapter shut.

And anyway, this was not filling up the black screen. "We are making a te-le-vi-si-on doc-u-men-ta-ry, dear." Anything else was in her book, copyrighted, or had nothing to do with what a television audience might want to see on the screen.

Schell mentioned Proust and madeleines.

"Nothing so boring!" she boomed. "You'll never sell that in America!"

Pause.

Schell forged ahead. He knew that to make more than a television "and-then-I-made" scrapbook he needed character, reminiscence and rumination, confidences and candor, and for all that he needed to be more than an interviewer. He *was* more. He was a director: a Sternberg or Lubitsch or Wilder. He said so. He was now, he said, "like Josef von Sternberg."

"You're not a film director *now*, dear!" she told him. (And thanks for the marmalade! thought Bernard Hall.)

The second day of taping got no further than the first. With self-reference that seemed never to fail him, Schell told her of pondering his life and those odd moments in which one does not know which way to go, or why, or What It All Means. She stared at him in silence before muttering, "You're much too clever for me." She repeated it several times, sending Schell back into solipsistic angst trying to find a way into her view of life. Finally he gave up, nettled by, "You're much too clever for me," which seemed something she would not have said to Josef von Sternberg.

The third day he brought it up again. What had she meant?

She had meant what she had said. "I wish I knew what you were after," she said with solicitude. "I wish I *knew*." She didn't know because no one, including the ever-present and mostly silent Terry Miller, bothered to broach the real objective, to bare the hidden agenda. She didn't get it because no one had the courage or daring to throw it. Wouldn't or couldn't, and she kept saying *"Quatsch"* when Schell drifted with no discernible creative rudder. His playing one of the out-of-tune Blüthner grand pianos for her didn't demonstrate auteur decisiveness any more than the marmalade had.

"What are we going to see on the *box?*" she demanded. "We've got to keep them from going to the kitchen and preparing dinner."

What Schell wanted to show on the box was, well, *Marlene:* the last close-up. Here was one of the century's great camera subjects after four years of total seclusion, and Schell was *right there in the room with her* and she kept saying, "So ask me something."

He asked her something: to photograph her.

"I have been photographed enough," she said firmly and flatly. Besides, Marlene today had nothing to do with her documentary about her career. "I have been photographed to death, and I don't want it anymore!"

Schell paused. He knew this was dangerous territory, forbidden by the still unsigned contract; he also knew this was what he wanted, that Marlene today was *part* of the career. He went for another Oscar: "In front of me you are sitting, Marlene, in my opinion more beautiful than ever. . . . I found often when I watched the films that there was a certain image of Marlene. I have the great privilege to see not that image but to see yourself. You are sitting in your apartment in Paris. You are sitting by a table which is very beautifully prepared by Bernard, your help—"

"He's a *friend*," she boomed, spelling out categories of relationship with ominous clarity.

This *was* dangerous. Her tone left no doubt. And there, Schell realized, was his film: Max meets the Monstre Sacré; Protagonist vs. Antagonist; conflict, drama! If she wouldn't cooperate with a design she had barely heard the first word about, he'd help her *un*cooperate and *that* would be the film. The lioness growling at sticks poked through the self-erected bars of her lair. It was better than nothing, and nothing had been captured on tape for three of the six allotted days that could possibly be used in any cele- bration, any final close-up of Marlene Dietrich the woman. In truth he could not even make *her* version of the documentary with nothing more than, "It's in my book" or "It's copyrighted" on a sound track.

There was material, however. At the end of each day, when she thought that work was at an end and that the tapes had been turned off and she relaxed with tea (laced with "courage" by Bernard), she stopped being guardian of her legend. She became a garrulous hostess on a warm, leafy Paris avenue, and who knew the tapes were rolling? She thought she was speaking privately to Terry Miller, to Schell, to Bernard Hall; confidentially regaling the sound crew with amusing anecdotes about the old days. Then, when she thought she was the private Marlene chatting to pros who un- derstood and respected professional confidences, she would lighten up, sip a little more "tea," get a little chatty, and a lot more indiscreet. When she became *too* indiscreet Terry Miller rushed to turn off tape machines *he* knew were still running. She had said nothing libelous, but she had a wicked sense of humor and opinions that could peel paint, that could embarrass friends should anyone happen to make duplicate copies of the tapes, and duplicate copies would be needed in any event. For safety purposes.

This was the Marlene Schell wanted to make a film about: fast, funny, irreverent, spicing her survivor wisdom with a little salty wickedness, blue- toed, wheelchaired, wigged, and spectacled. The fiery spirit that could look so cool was still alive and well within that cage of broken bones. But she wasn't knowingly giving him that Marlene. Nor was she about to, and Terry Miller, sympathetic as he was to Schell's ambitions, wasn't helping by leaping up to turn off the unseen tapes every time Marlene said something too far out of school to preserve for posterity—or for Maximilian Schell, director.

The director was not without craft. He was intimidated, frustrated, and dedicated to getting more than she was willing to give. He had what sounded like obstreperous crankiness on tape, and if *she* wouldn't be photographed, *he* would. He could photograph himself back in Munich in a studio, the creative director in trauma over not being able to photograph *her*. If he couldn't photograph her apartment ("We are not going to talk about what's hanging on any wall or anything because you won't have anything on the screen there. This is a *documentary* and it says 'then she did' or whatever and 'the next film she did'—one, two, three—so we can't talk about pianos!"), then he could construct a set that looked like the apartment on a sound stage and photograph *that*. His very failure to make the film would *be* the film, and he could still call it *Marlene: A Feature*!

He and Miller talked it over man to man. Miller's professional duty to protect Marlene's interests did not protect anything without a film. Nor, without it, would she be paid fee or royalties—or he an agent's commission. Nor would her reputation be enhanced by a project that didn't get made because she was intractable.

The co-conspirators decided to play good-cop (Miller) bad-cop (Schell), hoping to shock Marlene into cooperating with a purpose she still had not heard one word about beyond Schell's tentative "feature" remark, which had never been raised again. Miller would be the good cop just by being there. Schell would be the bad cop by reminding her *he* hadn't signed *his* contract, either, and might not do the film at all if she didn't stop talking about her book and copyright, in which case she would not be paid money she needed to pay bills, including the rent on the very apartment in which they sat day after day getting nowhere.

By the fifth day, Schell had adopted a pose of petulant, long-suffering silence. "*If* I do the film" became a refrain as he insisted on looking at videotapes of her old films. "You don't *have* to show me anything!" she protested. "I *know* it all! I've DONE it! And you're wasting time, you're wasting tape, you're wasting. . . . You have to be *brief* for a documentary!" she bawled. "We are doing a documentary, a te-le-vi-si-on do-cu-men-ta-ry, dear!"

Finally, Schell looked up out of his nowhere and said, "I can't work this way." And walked out. The unseen tapes kept rolling. Marlene, contrary to everyone's fervent expectation, went mute. Terry Miller sat there; Bernard Hall did not "fraternize"; Carolina listened to silence on his headphones. Maximilian Schell had picked up his ego and taken a hike.

Marlene's speechlessness proved short-lived. After Schell did not return and no one knew what to say or do, the sound people were told to go home and Marlene and her agent flew into what Miller later said was "a terrible row." Marlene pronounced the waste of time the most unprofessional *Quatsch!* she had ever seen in her life and Terry Miller countered with home truths about unsigned contracts and withheld fees and unpaid rent and her refusal to humor Schell with his videotapes and what she kept denouncing as "amateur sort of stuff."

Marlene wheeled herself off as if jet-propelled. Miller sat down and wrote a letter saying that unless she signed her contract at once he would no longer be responsible. After he slammed the door behind him, she read the letter, scrawled her signature across the contract, and left it on the table for him to find the next morning—if there *was* a next morning.

There was. Maximilian Schell was punctual. He and Terry Miller waited for an ominously unpunctual Marlene. Miller described the fallout of the previous day. Both agreed that good-cop/bad-cop had failed dismally. Marlene had thrown a tantrum, but not on tape. She had even behaved with gracious dignity when inviting the sound crew to go home. That she had signed her contract was small victory. Schell could now use the tapes, but had very little on them and only a grudging agreement to look at some old movies on videotape. It occurred to him "it would be quite nice to have a succession of scenes where she says 'No, that scene speaks for itself, ' " but admitted to Miller that what he expected was that Marlene would wheel herself into the room like a fury and slap him jobless.

That might have been good for the tapes, but she did nothing of the kind. She made a wheeled entrance oiled with milk and honey. Her "Hello" had a sweetness to it, suggesting the curl of conduct was right in the middle of her forehead to prove how very, very good she could be in the face of other people's conduct, however horrid.

Video equipment had been moved in so Schell could at last run his videotapes. There was polite conversation about her Mexican madam in Orson Welles's *Touch of Evil*, with which he wanted to begin. Marlene allowed cryptically that she found it typical he would want to begin at the end of her career instead of the beginning, but never mind. Schell suggested her Tanya was "a key figure in [Welles's] film." She demurred. "Oh, I don't think so. No, no, no, no, no." Schell knew the role had not been in the screenplay and asked if she had improvised. As improvisation seemed the essence of Schell's meandering method, she spoke with that calm that presages all manner of thunder and lightning.

"Well, dear," she said as if explaining right from left to a backward rube, "you don't seem to know the business! We get a script. Don't they do that in your country?"

Schell muttered about the joys of improvisation. Marlene countered with Welles as exemplar of the Compleat Director: "He is a professional man and all professional people know that every actor has to have a script and has to know what to do. You don't leave anything around. . . . That's *amateur* kind of stuff!"

A cuckoo clock could not have missed her point.

Schell started his videotapes.

Marlene grumbled, "No one wants to see this stuff, it's so ridiculous!"

But they watched. She watched. She harrumphed as the images went by, and when they were over she thundered that the process was a "waste of effort, waste of time, waste, *waste*. If I ever hated *anything* it's waste!"

SCHELL: Would you like to comment on this scene?

DIETRICH: *No!*

It was sharp and short and warm as Mont Blanc. But the hoped-for theme was emerging: Diva vs. Director; Director in the Lion's Den. Then:

DIETRICH: What can I comment? I told you Orson Welles is a genius, that we all worked for him for nothing because the studio wouldn't give him enough money. What can I comment? I'm not an 'actory' actress. I'm not a prima donna like you are!

SCHELL: [taken aback] I'm not a prima donna.

DIETRICH: Yes, you are. We do our work!

SCHELL: I do my work, too.

DIETRICH: No. Not yesterday. No, no!

SCHELL: I tell you, Marlene, I'm not here as an interviewer. I'm here as a partner for talk. If you don't get that, then I don't know what to do anymore. Then I am at a loss. It's not my job to prepare questions like an interviewer. We said very clearly that we would talk together and try to develop *your* documentary together. That's what I'm trying to do all the time [sic]. If you don't get that I'm very, very sorry, but you have to cooperate, you have to help me. If I show these scenes it's a way to make you talk, to say something about Orson Welles. Not just that he's a genius—that we *know*. Something very—what you *feel* about him, or otherwise I can just quote from your book. But this is a documentary that will be shown in America and in—

DIETRICH: Oh, are you that *sure*?! That they will buy it? The way you talk they won't *ever* buy it!

SCHELL: Well, that I don't know. I can only say that I'm trying my best to get some opinion from you, not just "yes" or "no" or "you can read that in my book."

DIETRICH: I did not say "yes" or "no."

SCHELL: You say it constantly, Marlene. You say it constantly. You say constantly, "This is all written in my book." You always say, "No, I don't want to comment"—

DIETRICH: Because my book is copyrighted!

SCHELL: Well, then say it in different words!

DIETRICH: I *said* what I feel about him! What more do you *want*?! I told you, you should cross yourself before you mention his name!

SCHELL: I *do*. I admire him very much.

DIETRICH: You *should*!

SCHELL: I know what I should! You don't have to tell me what I should and what I should not!

DIETRICH: Oh, I could tell you! You don't get up and leave a lady! You should go back to Mama Schell and learn some manners! You don't get up and walk out on a lady and Mr. Miller here and young men. We all didn't know what to do! You walked out like a *prima donna*! Terrible, terrible manners! Terrible manners!

SCHELL: I don't think so. I think either I'm very patient or—

DIETRICH: That's good manners, to walk out on somebody?!

SCHELL: Well, it depends what that somebody did.

DIETRICH: Nobody *ever* walked out on me. *Ever*. You are the first one—

SCHELL: It's a good thing!

DIETRICH: —and the *last*, that I can tell you! And I have sat at the table with the greatest politicians and the greatest artists and nobody ever behaved like that! *Never*! You just walked out and we all sat here and we didn't know what! We didn't *know*! We thought you might go to the toilet. You didn't say a word!

SCHELL: Marlene, if somebody says to me you didn't do your work, *while* I'm doing my work. . . . If you accuse me that I don't do my work and I didn't prepare my questions . . . I don't *have* to prepare questions!

DIETRICH: [disbelief] You *don't*?!

SCHELL: No!!

DIETRICH: Then how can you do an interview . . . ?!

SCHELL: I don't *do* an interview! You said you would comment—and that's also in the contract—that you would comment on scenes. We took your list and on that list we prepared for you to see—

DIETRICH: [triumphantly] A *year ago*!

SCHELL: —I came into this picture much later, and the documentary I would like to make—*if* I make it—[is] a different kind of documentary.

DIETRICH: [calmly] Then you should have let us in on that secret before.

For all her anger she was still in control. She rejected his impertinent claim to partnership, his invocation of Sternberg, Wilder, and other names as if he were part of that pantheon. But director's pride was working, and once again he invoked Orson Welles. *Her* friend! It was (at last!) too much!

DIETRICH: *You KNOW him? You DO?! Oh, how WONDERFUL!!*

The wild energy of her response shocked Schell into regaining focus. With painful calm he embarked on a tale of discussing with Welles a film based on *Crime and Punishment*. Marlene, too angry to follow clearly, flashed on Sternberg's version of the Dostoyevski novel and brushed Schell's anecdote aside with, "Mr. von Sternberg made the film. That's all old stuff. That's *all* down the river, honey, *all* down the river!"

"Well," replied Schell calmly, seizing on the nonsequitur, "a documentary is *about* old stuff."

"*Big deal!*" she exploded.

Tapes rolled on. Schell had the makings of a film. *His*.

Marlene: A Feature may well be the most eccentrically fascinating star documentary ever made. Most critics thought so. It won best-documentary prizes from the New York Film Critics, the National Society of Film Critics, the National Board of Review, and was nominated for (it did not win) the Academy Award.

What Schell found in the process of editing was that clips from her great film triumphs, from television appearances, rare outtakes, and still photographs could form a visual collage about Legend, against which the Legend's resistance to X ray could play as dramatic counterpoint. He put himself in it (he is the subtext: This film is a duel, not a duet). We see him heaping his head with film, torturing himself with his failure to root out the reality of Marlene. He photographed the set-built "apartment," the cutting rooms, even got Anni Albers on camera (she was the widow of Bauhaus artist Josef Albers and Schell is an Albers collector) to pose his own bewildered question for him: "What is actually *real* here?" the thread tying together all the clips and out-of-context sound bites.

For Schell it was a mixed triumph. Most critics agreed with Jack Mathews in the *Los Angeles Times* that "whether by intuition or design, Dietrich forced Schell to make a better film than he would have had she agreed to be on camera." Schell agreed that "it was clearly the virtue of the film. She gave herself greater presence by not being seen."

For Marlene it was a last portrait of defiance and control, but it got that way only by artful juxtapositions that seldom, if ever, conveyed the lack of candor in the recording process. "All that counts is what is on the screen!" she had told Schell over and over and was professional enough in the end to accept that he had made a portrait that was not the one she intended, nor perhaps a true one, but one that was memorable and salable.

Vincent Canby in *The New York Times*, who had once called her "a one-woman environment," found it "a portrait of a remarkable strong-willed woman, stage-managing her career right up to the bitter end. It's also an examination of the very particular, possibly bitter legacy of movie stardom."

If bitter, then because that legacy haunts and mocks. Those beautiful images don't go away, don't age, don't hurt or have unpaid bills. They go on forever like reproaches to human frailty. The film Dietrich wanted to make would not have been so interesting. It would have been no more telling than her memoirs or the fantasy autobiography with which she had introduced songs in her concert performances. Certainly Schell's film manipulates and distorts, but it is finally the work of an admirer, a reluctant and unrequited lover. He sought and found (whatever the means) glimpses into those feelings William Blezard believed dominated her. Feelings for *people*, as she had told him at the beginning, for the cast of characters who played supporting roles to the Legend's star turn: Rudi, Maria, her grandsons—above all, her mother.

At the end of his film Schell cut in some after-hours tape from the end of the fourth day. He had urged her to read from her autobiography the poem that the Dragon had used in teaching her to read. She thought the tapes were turned off and had had a little "courage." One hears it and forgives it: She was tired, she was almost eighty-two years old, she was broke. She began to recite for him:

> O, love, while still 'tis yours to love!
> O, love, while love you still may keep!
> The hour will come, the hour will come,
> When you will stand by graves and weep . . .

and then she did. Tears broke on the lines:

> So quickly came the hateful word,
> O God, 'twas never meant to hurt . . .

She sobbed out words that were not part of the poem: "*I never meant to hurt.*"

IV

EXIT
MUSIC

CODA

"ALLEIN IN EINER GROSSEN STADT" 1983 - 1992

I t took almost four years for *Marlene: A Feature* to cross the sea. It was the sold-out, unqualified hit of the New York Film Festival in September 1986 and opened in November in cinemas across America and around the world. The attention, nominations, and awards poured in to embellish Dietrich's eighty-fifth birthday in December.

She hated the film, but Maria liked it (and asked Schell not to say she did). Bernard Hall liked it too. He let Schell cut into the film a brief interview in which the old comrade said he believed Marlene was lonely. "Can't laugh alone!" she had written him in his own London seclusion. His appearance in her film elicited rage, not chuckles: "You're a disgrace to the gay community!" she thundered, as if Hall had betrayed her to that large part of her audience and acquaintance she called "kinder, nicer than 'normal' men." Neither Noël Coward, Jean Cocteau, Hubsie von Meyerinck, nor Clifton Webb would have said any such thing about her—not out loud.

Hall knew his belief that she was lonely might be projection. He had spent almost thirty years working, traveling, and living with her in a relationship seldom free of friction. "I cannot bear the loneliness of living without her loyalty and her love," he admitted now and longed each year for Christmas to arrive with its annual plane ticket to Paris. He would deal with holiday and birthday mail, rerouting gifts and flowers to hospitals Marlene had listed in green ink and block letters before the parade of delivery men even arrived. He and she would drink and laugh and make fun of television together; they would gossip and fight and make up, and promise each other to go through the same ritual next year, one more time.

Marlene forgave Hall and forgave *Marlene: A Feature*, too. She even offered to dub her German into English or French if that would help television sales. As for the assertion she might be lonely . . . *Quatsch!*

The rent problem in the Avenue Montaigne had been severe even as taping began in 1982, and it got worse as she waited in vain for income from the movie ("Not one cent!" she raved). Finally, in June 1984, her Belgian-born landlords (Emmanuel, Eric, and Daniel Janssen) stopped sending dunning letters and served her with eviction papers, taking her to court. Marc van Beneden, speaking for Frères Janssen, told the court, "Madame Diétrich thinks she is above the law." Marlene's lawyer, the formidable Maître Jacques Kam, said Madame thought herself only above outrageous costs for concierge photocopiers and new uniforms for the doorman, not the rent. The eviction order was vacated by the court, but the press carried stories Madame might be exiled to the streets. From a building that also housed the brother of the former Shah of Iran, who knew about exile and the high cost of uniforms.

There was in any case a little-known humanitarian law in Paris that prevented eviction of the bedridden. The City of Light had special affection for resident members of the Légion d'Honneur and they promoted Marlene from Chevalier to Commandeur, and quietly picked up the rent. The French, as is well known, have a feeling for public monuments.

She hung France's third-highest honor on what she called her "Awards wall." This gallery of citations, medals, and ribbons (including an autographed photo of Henry Kissinger) complemented the "Dead wall," graced with photographs of the departed. Books overflowed shelves to heap on every available surface except the tabletop covered with engraved dressing-room door-plates, little brass and gold signposts to stopovers on a global career.

Mostly Marlene stayed near her telephone, where that maid who sounded so Marlene-like told callers Miss Dietrich wasn't lonely or broke; she was "lunching" or "driving" or "on a plane" to wherever. The traveler confided her busy schedule to an acquaintance one day when she was bored. "I keep my car in the garage of this building," she said, forgetting that she did not drive. "The elevator takes me directly to the garage and I get in my car and drive to the airport in sunglasses with a scarf around my head. That's why photographers who hang around the building never see me. Do they think I go in and out the *front door*? When I know they're *waiting*? I'm not *meshuga!*"

She got more bored, had a little "courage," and fell again, inflicting another leg wound in October 1986. The doctor who rushed to her was so appalled by her bleeding he insisted she go at once to a clinic. She refused. She preferred gushing blood to gushing printers' ink of the kind that flowed from Columbia-Presbyterian in New York in 1976. No word had leaked of her radium treatments for cervical cancer in Geneva or bypass surgery to her legs in Houston, but she may have feared that once in a clinic, never out. The doctor sewed her up himself and allowed her to stay home.

There were assets, though she would not call on them, as if she no longer regarded them as hers except for the mortgages and taxes. The house on East 95th Street was home to John Paul ("Powlie") and his young French wife, as well as John David, the unmarried youngest grandson. Powlie was studying to be a doctor and David worked briefly for Marlene's former agent, Robert Lantz, whose father, Adolf, had written the screenplay for *Tragedy of Love*, the movie on which Marlene had met Rudi. The apartment on upper Park Avenue was mostly occupied by (John) Peter, now a press agent in New York. Maria and her husband had moved to Switzerland, where he survived surgery that removed cancer from his brain. Marlene paid the bills for that, too.

John Michael Riva, the oldest, most cherished grandson, was fortyish now and building a career in Hollywood as an art director on important films like *Brubaker, Ordinary People*, and *The Color Purple*. Marlene was intensely proud of his success and independence: Few in Hollywood knew he was her grandson. She decided her favorite movie star was Robert Redford, director of *Ordinary People*, and her new favorite director was Steven Spielberg, director of *The Color Purple*. Spielberg sent her an *E.T.* poster autographed, "With all my love and admiration." Marlene thought it "sweet" and sent it at once to Maria to be packed away for auction after her death.

She wanted to save everything until after she was gone. "I'm worth more dead than alive," she would say, adding unsentimentally, "Don't cry for me after I'm gone; cry for me *now*." She had followed the auction of the late Duchess of Windsor's jewels (prizes of a marriage Marlene had once tried to prevent) with frank envy and in November 1987 allowed Christie's to open the bank vault in Geneva and auction off some baubles to finance current expenses: a set of diamond and sapphire cuff-links; gold cigarette cases encrusted with diamonds; a necklace of seventy graduated diamonds from Van Cleef & Arpels; a gold, diamond-studded compact inscribed "To Marlene, Vittorio." Each buyer received a signed letter from her as guarantee of provenance.

The stage costumes (with repairs by the Diva's own needle and thread) were still unique items of great beauty. Drag artists in Paris begged to buy them (for pittances) in order to impersonate Dietrich in Dietrich's own costumes. Someone with a clearer sense of their value undertook to sell them for her in 1987 and found a buyer for the "diamond-studded" gown and the famous swansdown coat—in Berlin. The German Film Foundation paid very near the original cost of what were genuine museum pieces now. The money went into a New York City bank account in the names of "M. Sieber and M. Riva."

Incredibly enough, as eighty crept toward ninety, there was work. She discovered that the interviews she had dodged for years could now produce income. Germany's respected *Die Welt* paid her for a long-distance chat in 1987, promising her a fifty-fifty split for foreign rights and astonishing her by living up to the agreement when the interview was published in bits and pieces around the world. *Der Spiegel* came along later and reportedly paid her $20,000 for responding by mail to a written list of one hundred questions. She answered the ones she wanted to, often just "yes," often just "no," and ignored those that were *Quatsch*.

She recorded again. She spoke the verse to "Illusions," the great Friedrich Holländer song from A *Foreign Affair*, and to Holländer's haunting *"Wenn ich mir was wünschen dürfte"* ("If I could wish for something"), which she had recorded half a century earlier in Berlin. Her spoken words were fillips to a nostalgia album by German pop-singer Udo Lindenberg. The "third dimension" was papery and thin now, but irrepressibly jaunty, love's old warrior at it again.

She liked recording because she could speak into a microphone without moving from her bed. Katharine Hepburn had told her of something called talking books and she badly wanted to record some. She had two pet projects. One was to recite Rilke, Goethe, and other German poets she still knew by heart. The scheme she saw as the *real* moneymaker, though, was "Marlene Dietrich Reads Jewish Jokes."

"I have the Jewish inflection," she told an acquaintance one day while trying to track down *Joys of Yiddish* author Leo Rosten for new material. She launched into a volley of jokes in what she fondly believed "the Jewish inflection" to be. She still couldn't say her r's, but her sense of humor was sharp as ever, especially when she could impersonate a Jewish mother who came out sounding oddly like Marlene Dietrich. Or perhaps Marlene Dietrich's "maid." There were many jokes. "I have a gweat one about a Jewish gynecologist!" she said, and she did. She acted jokes the way she had acted songs: expertly, relishing performance and having an audience to play to again, even if only on the telephone.

Berlin's major radio station, *Sender Freies Berlin*, was more eager to have her read German poetry than Jewish jokes, and a deal was constructed in which she would recite Rilke, rights to the tapes reverting to her after two public broadcasts. She was offered a reading fee of $10,000 but found the deal stingy or felt unwell or simply lost interest, and the tapes were never made.

She broadcast on transatlantic telephone instead, especially when outraged by some political development. The French trial of Nazi war criminal Klaus Barbie, "the butcher of Lyon," particularly incensed her because the French seemed not to care. She was furious that her secretary, a Jewish woman from Chicago called Norma, didn't seem interested. She railed at the same time she wished she could forget. "I shouldn't let it eat me up like this," she sighed, but forgetting was hard. "I went through Belsen," she remembered aloud (omitting, of course, the meeting with her sister there), "and I saw it all. The smoke was still rising from the chimneys. The French don't give a good goddamn," she complained. "All they want to do is eat, sleep, sit around the Deux Magots pretending to be writers. I don't want to deny them their pleasures, but how can they forget Auschwitz?"

She called Nazi-hunter Beate Klarsfeld to discuss the Barbie case and brooded that Jewish Norma-from-Chicago sensed no irony in Rudolf Hess, the Führer's deputy and co-criminal, being then seemingly fit as a fiddle as the sole prisoner in Spandau. "I met him once," she said. "He was the least—how do we say that?—*coupable*, because he was the most crazy." She abruptly decided "they must have the best food and medical care in the *world* at Spandau!" and asked Klarsfeld facetiously what you had to do to get a room there. "Kill a Jew," said Klarsfeld. "Oh, *Norma!*" Dietrich called out.

Gallows humor was preferable to sentimentality as her circle of friends grew smaller, suggesting her famous candle-lit funeral at Notre Dame might be a sparsely attended affair. She had not spoken to one-time fashion *directrice* Ginette Spanier for years, but when Spanier died in London Marlene was on the phone to everyone who needed to know. Then Margo Lion, her old "best girlfriend" from *It's in the Air*, died, one of her last links to the Berlin theater. She called another, Curt Bois, with whom she had been on stage in *From Mouth to Mouth* in 1926. "Curt, it's Marlene," she said. "Marlene *who?*" he growled, thinking sixty years a long time between telephone calls. Bois cultivated a reputation for wickedness, anyway, but was not so wicked he could forget how beautiful Marlene had been when they were both twenty-five. Nor could he forgive Margo Lion's not taking Marlene's phone calls before her death for fear she might be asked for a loan. Soon Curt Bois was gone too. Marlene even outlasted Garbo, who was four years younger and *rich*. Dietrich the survivor promptly announced her decision to live to one hundred.

An American jack-of-all-arts in Paris called Jim Haynes was inspired by the notion of compiling all Marlene's movie musical numbers in one film and calling it simply *The Dietrich Songs*. From "Falling in Love Again" to "Just a Gigolo" Marlene sang half-a-century of womanliness in everything from top hat and silk stockings to veil and high boots. It was as much a revelation of her musical showmanship as her compilation film at the Museum of Modern Art had been on her dramatic range some thirty years before. There seemed no allure, worldly wisdom, or irony she had not perfected, maybe even invented. If ever the complicated rights to songs and footages could be cleared, Marlene promised to record an introduction to *The Dietrich Songs*.

The "Dead wall" filled and so did the one for awards. She received a European Film Award for Lifetime Achievement in 1989 and recorded a little acceptance speech. She received another Lifetime Award from the Council of Fashion Designers of America. Katharine Hepburn wrote a prose poem for the occasion and designer Calvin Klein accepted on Marlene's behalf. *Vogue's* Leo Lerman added his own loving tribute to the program after fifty years of friendship. Hollywood's Motion Picture Academy was silent or forgetful or annoyed by her having ridiculed what she called "the deathbed Oscar" in her book and in Schell's film. An Oscar would have been hard to hang on the "Awards wall," anyway.

When she turned ninety in December of 1991, the big Wall, the one in Berlin, had come down and her homeland was reunited. She was—for the first time really—celebrated by the country with which she had had such a long and contentious relationship. Almost every newspaper, magazine, television and radio station in Germany paid her tribute, broadcasting the films (including *Marlene: A Feature*) and the recordings for days on end, outdoing each other in salutation and accolade. Germany's minister of the interior, Rudolf Seiters, sent an official birthday telegram and the director of the Frankfurt Film Museum, Walter Schobert, thought it "high time to understand" that her war work was "her form of loyalty and love for her old homeland." Besides, he pointed out, she was "the only world star Germany produced."

A sound stage at legendary and newly resurgent UFA was to be named *Metropolis*-Halle after Fritz Lang's masterpiece, but it was discovered at the last minute that the space had been built a few weeks *after* Lang finished his film. The records showed, however, that on that same cavernous stage

Marlene had first sung "Falling in Love Again." They christened the sound stage Marlene-Dietrich-Halle.

Through all the celebrations of her longevity and art she never admitted she was ninety or in anything but perfect health. There was no blemish on the festivities until two weeks later, when London's *Sunday Times* announced in a front-page headline, "DIETRICH'S DAUGHTER BETRAYS STAR'S SECRETS."

Simon & Schuster in America, which had long ago lost the deal for Marlene's autobiography, had in the meantime declined to publish the book they had contracted in its place for reasons that remained unspoken. Maria Riva's story of life with Mother went instead to Alfred A. Knopf. Two weeks after Mother turned ninety, the book that was not to appear until after Marlene's death could not, Knopf or somebody judged, wait around for that event. Or Maria's bill collectors couldn't. Worldwide rights were gaudily auctioned by Knopf as Marlene's friends reeled in protest and dismay at promises of dirty laundry and what columnists called *Marlene, Dearest*. Knopf had already sold the rights to Germany rather quietly, and the publicity was said to have been spread not by Maria or Knopf at all, but by a disgruntled and lordly English publisher who had hoped for an "exclusive" he didn't get.

Marlene threatened to sue her own daughter to prevent publication during her lifetime, but the rights commanded big money in the storm of ugly hype, and then it turned out Maria and the bill collectors—on generous advances against royalties—could wait for the funeral after all.

Two weeks later Germany's huge *Bild* newspaper published a banner headline: MARLENE DIETRICH: *DAS FOTO*. The headline accompanied a front-page photograph of a very old lady in a wheelchair on some street in Paris. She was wearing a mink coat, a turban, and bedroom slippers. One of the grandsons denied it was Marlene. Rightly so. Even if it was.

The photograph may well have been the old woman who lived in seclusion on the Avenue Montaigne, surrounded by books and photographs and memories (that turban in the photograph looked very Jolly Felsing), but it made no difference. That old lady, as she insisted to Maximilian Schell, was a "private person," and had nothing to do with "Dietrich," who was a legend, a myth, maybe even a figment of the imagination of Marie Magdalene Dietrich, a strong-willed girl from Schöneberg who turned a figment into a phenomenon.

"I, personally, liked the legend" she told her audience at the Museum of Modern Art, and it showed in every performance she ever gave. One is constantly amazed at how many otherwise sensible observers of contemporary phenomena accept her protestations that she never cared about her career. The denial is part of the strategy of the legend; it made her seem as inevitable as a season or a tide ("I just got this way for *you*," her image seemed to say to young William Goldman). Believing that she never cared is tribute to how effortless she made the diligence look. Her life is testimony to how fiercely—even ruthlessly—she cared.

From the first time the girl felt that craving for "public fame on the podium" or intuited in herself what feminist professor Carolyn Heilbrun calls those "great possibilities, great desires," she was unsparing in attempting to fulfill them, both as a woman and as a *working* woman. She imagined who Marlene Dietrich might become and became it and then became more. She had help and luck and the love of men and women who helped her identify how much there was to realize and fulfill, and until her body betrayed her, she never for one moment gave less than the best she had to give.

It was never, of course, just for us; she would have sold the jewels and property and given it up long before if it had been. John Lahr has noted that "the performing self is the perfected self." The need for that may be what makes performers performers, what makes them different from the rest of us, and from poets and painters, too. The performer's raw material and instrument *is* the self—the pen and palette—and from that self the art is fashioned. The artifact is not the person, but the perfected person, "surrounded by light and glory," as Lahr puts it, "self-empowered and invulnerable." We the audience confuse that light and glory with its source, but the rare ones who shine with it know its daily cost. But even they cannot explain the ultimate mystery. Max Beerbohm voiced it: "In every art," he wrote, "personality is the paramount thing, and without it artistry goes for little."

"*Ich bin ein praktischer Mensch*," she liked to say, and so she withdrew when she had to, forbidding any image or rumor that might betray the legend she had created and delivered all those years. What that was, Noël Coward said, was "the substance of dreams," fantasy made palpable, a fantasized self made perfect. It was most perfect in her greatest achievement, that two decades and more of concert appearances that are, ironically, the least retrievable of her incarnations by any technology but memory. The magic—that "poem for eye and ear alike," as the Warsaw critic called it—left the stage with her. Echoes remain. The lights and shadows and sounds of the earlier career are undiminished. As long as there are projectors and people to sit in the dark, the beauty will continue to stop hearts, and the voice will break and then mend them.

She told Maximilian Schell in a much-quoted remark in the talks they had together that "one should be afraid of life, not of death," and even her critics would concede she faced life with uncommon courage and grace.

Facing death, she wondered aloud to this chronicler if she were not, per-haps, "just jealous that I can't believe in an afterlife. I lost my faith during the war and can't believe they are all up there, flying around or sitting at tables, all those I've lost. All, all, all," she sighed. "I suppose I'm jealous I can't believe, but I can't. If it were true," she added with steely certainty, "Rudi would be there, and would give me a message."

The services took place not at a candle-lit Notre Dame, after all, but at the Église de la Madeleine, in the center of the City of Light. The French tricolor draped her coffin, and on it rested medals from grateful nations for a warrior's courage.

She had fallen asleep on the afternoon of May 6, 1992, surrounded by her books and memories and photographs of friends. Crowds milled in the Avenue Montaigne below, where posters marched beneath leafy, spring-time trees announcing the 1992 Cannes Film Festival to begin the next day, dedicated this year to her. Every placard bore her image as Shanghai Lily: *all that beauty*—indestructible and timeless.

The crowds had somehow heard that she had stopped eating several days before. Time to go; time to rest. Muscle atrophy and a near century brought closure to what turned out to be—surprisingly to many—a circle. For there was another service after the one at the Madeleine.

Her coffin was draped in an American flag and flown to Berlin. There the flag of reunified Germany—red, gold, black—covered the box that was lowered into perhaps the only earth in which she could truly rest, in the cemetery next to her mother, that other good general.

Love's old warrior was home at last. But still the injunction to "Do something!" would be obeyed. Those images, those lights and shadows and sounds would do it for her—*will* do it for her—allowing her in the end to cheat death. And time. That's what artists do. That's what they do it *for*.

APPENDIX A
THEATER
CHRONOLOGY

The following theatrical history has been compiled from theater programs, advertisements, reviews, production photographs, interviews, letters, and memoirs of other actors with whom Marlene Dietrich worked in Berlin and Vienna during the 1920s. All productions are documented, though the list is very likely incomplete. The odd cabaret appearance, the stand-in job for a friend, the spontaneous Sunday afternoon *musicale* at this or that theater which was too fleeting to find its way into print or memory happened simultaneously with other aspects of Dietrich's career and are indicative of Berlin's rich theatrical life during the Weimar Republic and of the varied professional training that shaped this performer.

1. DER GROSSE BARITON / THE GREAT LOVER, BERLIN, 1922

American romantic comedy in three acts by Leo Ditrichstein and Fred and Fanny Hatton [no translator credited]; directed by Eugen Robert; stage design: Leo Impekoven. Premiere January 20, 1922, Theater am Kurfürstendamm, Berlin; moved to Schloßparktheater, Berlin, October 7, 1922.

Cast: Albert Bassermann (Jean Paurel), Adolphe Engers (Maestro Cereale, conductor), Jaro Fürth (Dr. Müller, German director), Hermann Vallentin (Mr. Stapleton, Opera Impresario), Felix Norfolk (Farnald, his secretary), R. H. Marxs (Ward, publicity chief), Erich Hofmann (Kartzag, Paurel's understudy), Richard Franz (Carl Losseck), Ernst Winar (van Stratten), Fritz Jessner (Carlo Sonino), Wladimir Agajeff (Posansky), Margarethe Rühmkorff (Mlle. Treiler Beinbrich), Else Bassermann (Giulia Sabitini), Margarethe Schlegel (Ethel Warren), Margarethe Ebinger (Biana Sonino), Martha M. Newes (Mrs. Peter Van Ness, Mrs. Fred Schuyler), Jaro Fürth (Dr. Stetson), John Gottowt (Potter, Paurel's dresser).

Marlene Dietrich, still a Reinhardt apprentice, appeared as a replacement for Anni Mewes as a young fan of the Albert Bassermann opera star character after the play moved from the Kurfürstendamm to the Schloßparktheater, which had newly come under the direction of Eugen Robert.

2. DIE BÜCHSE DER PANDORA / PANDORA'S BOX, BERLIN, 1922

By Frank Wedekind; directed by Carl Heine; settings and decorations by Ernst Stern. Premiere December 20, 1918, in the Kleines Schauspielhaus. Moved in 1919 to the Kammerspiele at the Deutsches Theater.

Cast: Friedel Harms (Lulu), Ludwig Körner (Alwa Schön), Max Nemetz (Rodrigo Quast), Paul Günther (Schigolch), Hans Schweikart (Alfred Hugenbert), Helene Körner (Countess von Geschwitz), Fritz Rasp (Marqui Casti-Piani), Herwarth Retslag (Baker Puntschu), Werner Pledath (Journalist Heilmann), Margarethe Kupfer (Magdelone), Grete Mosheim (Kadéga di Santa Croce), Ilse Baerwald (Bianette Gazil), *Marlene Dietrich* (Ludmilla Steinherz), Gertrud Borck (Bob, a groom), Georg Hilbert (Mr. Hunidei), Rudolf Amendt (Kungu Botu, Imperial Prince of Uahubee), Marcel Mermino (Dr. Hilti, university lecturer), Max Remez (Jack).

Marlene Dietrich first appeared in this production on September 7, 1922 and played a total of nine performances through March of 1923.

3. TAMING OF THE SHREW, BERLIN, 1922

By William Shakespeare; directed by Iwan Schmith, based on the production by Max Reinhardt; sets and costumes by T. C. Pilartz; music by Klaus Pringsheim. Premiere October 2, 1922, in the Großes Schauspielhaus in Berlin.

Cast: Prologue—Ludwig Körner (a Lord), Wilhelm Diegelmann (Christopher Sly, a tinker), Margarethe Albrecht (Hostess), Gerhard Bienert (a hunter), Willi Gernhard (a page); Play—Robert Garrison (Baptista), Fritz Daghofer (Vincentio), Hans Brockmann (Lucentio), Eugen Klöpfer (Petruchio), Siegmund Nunberg (Gremio), Ludwig Jubelsky (Hortensio), Ernst Pröckl (Tranio), Fritz Rasp (Biondello), Paul

Graetz (Grumio), Herwart Retslag (Curtis), Karl Zander (a Pedant), Elisabeth Bergner (Katharina), Erika von Thellman (Bianca), *Marlene Dietrich* (Widow), Hanns Deppe (Tailor), Werner Pledath (Haberdasher), with Gerhard Bienert, Erich Fiebler, Günther Urbenk, and Maximilian Gross (servants).

Marlene Dietrich played "Widow" through November 18, 1923 for a total of forty-two performances.

4. TIMOTHEUS IN FLAGRANTI, BERLIN, 1923

Comedy in three acts by Charles-Maurice Hennequin and Pierre Véber (translated from the French by Bruno Frank); directed by Iwan Schmith; women's costumes by Max Beder (Vienna); hats by Agnes Gallewski. Premiere October 27, 1922, Deutsches Theater, Berlin.

Cast: Max Gülstorff (Timotheus Ploumanach), Erich Pabst (André Courvalin), Otto Treptow (Lambusque), Johanna Terwin (Aurelie), Rudolf Amendt (Auguste), Anni Mewes (Suzanne), Hermine Sterler (Baroness Lepinois), *Marlene Dietrich* (Anne-Marie), Dorothea Thies (Martha), Grete Mosheim (Francine), Friedel Harms (Miss Simpson), Kurt Lucas (Commissar), Kurt Noak (writer), Konrad Lehmann (first policeman), Arthur Laubert (second policeman), Walter Bluhm (messenger).

Marlene Dietrich entered the cast on January 11, 1923, and alternated as Suzanne, Anne-Marie, and Miss Simpson for a total of nine performances.

5. THE CIRCLE, BERLIN, 1923

Comedy in three acts by W. Somerset Maugham; directed by Bernhard Reich; sets by T. C. Pilartz. Premiere January 24, 1923, Kammerspiele, Berlin.

Cast: Erich Pabst (Clive Champion-Cheney), Ferdinand von Alten (Arnold Champion-Cheney, M.P., his son), Max Gülstorff (Lord Porteus), Hans Brausewetter (Edward Luton), Johanna Terwin (Lady Catherine Champion-Cheney), Elisabeth Bergner (Elizabeth), *Marlene Dietrich* (Mrs. Shenstone), Rudolf Amendt (George, the butler).

Marlene Dietrich played twenty-three performances as Mrs. Shenstone.

6. PENTHESILEA, BERLIN, 1923

Tragedy by Heinrich von Kleist; directed by Richard Révy; sets by Edward Suhr; music by Klaus Pringsheim. Premiere February 6, 1923, Deutsches Theater, Berlin.

Cast: Agnes Straub (Penthesilea), Charlotte Hagenbruch (Prothoe), Renée Stobrawa (Meroe), Lotte Fließ (Asteria), Leonie Duval (High Priestess), Paul Hartmann (Achilles), Ferdinand Hart (Odysseus), Curt Lucas (Diomedes), Aribert Wäscher (Antilochus), Max Nemetz (Captain), Ferdinand Faber (a Myrmidon),

Hans Rodenberg (an Aetolian), Carl Hannemann (a Doloprian), Friedel Harms (Amazon Colonel), *Marlene Dietrich* (Amazon Captain), Helene Körner, Margarethe Placzek (Amazons), Grete Mosheim, Grete Scheer, Vera John (flower girl), Gerhard Bienert (Greek prisoner).

Marlene Dietrich remained in this production at least through the end of April 1923. Willi Fritsch went in as a Herold on April 23, 1923.

7. ZWISCHEN NEUN UND NEUN / BETWEEN NINE AND NINE, BERLIN, 1923

Tragicomedy by Hans Sturm, based on the novel by Leo Perutz. Premiere [before July 1923], Theater in der Königgrätzerstraße.

Cast: (Stanislas Demba), (Alice Leitner), (Eisner), (a park-chair renter lady), (pretzel saleslady), (Steffi), (Sonja), (Miksch), (bond delivery man), (ambulance lady), (Elly, daughter), (Fritz, son), (policeman), (gentleman), (Georg Weiner), (Dr. Fuhrmann), (Herma), (Trude), (waiter), (renter).

[Note: no program is known to exist. Details are taken from annotated playscript with letter dated July 5, 1923, referring to Marlene Dietrich in the cast. Notes on the playscript suggest she played the daughter and doubled for the mother.]

8. MEIN VETTER, EDUARD / MY COUSIN, EDWARD, BERLIN, 1923

Comedy by Fred Robs [Fritz Friedmann-Friedrich and Ralph Arthur Roberts]; directed by Roberts. Premiere September 12, 1923, Komödienhaus, Berlin.

Cast: Ralph Arthur Roberts (Eduard), Georg Baselt (Adolf), Hilde Hildebrandt (Marianne, his wife), Olga Engl (Anita, her aunt), Arthur Retzbach-Erasimy (Hannibal, her divorced husband), *Marlene Dietrich* (Lilian Berley, their daughter), Annemarie Möricke (Josefine, Adolf's secretary), Robert Klupp (orderly), Erich Nadler (consular official), Paul Lipinski (servant).

9. A MIDSUMMER NIGHT'S DREAM, 1924

By William Shakespeare (translated by August Wilhelm von Schlegel); directed by Reinhard Bruck; music by Mendelssohn; choreography by Katta Sterna. Premiere February 9, 1924, Theater in der Königgrätzer Straße, Berlin.

Cast: Kurt Lucas (Theseus, Duke of Athens), Adolf Kurth (Egeus, father to Hermia), Werner Schott (Lysander), Heinz Stieda (Demetrius), Hans Hermes (Philostrate, Master of the Revels to Theseus), Adolphe Engers (Peter Quince, a carpenter/prologue in the play), Ernst Behmer (Snug, a joiner / lion in the play), Harald Paulsen (Nick Bottom, a weaver / Pyramus in the play), Hermann Picha (Francis Flute, a bellows mender / Thisby in the play), Hugo Bauer (Robin Starveling, a tailor / Moonshine in the play), Paul Lipinski (Tom Snout, a tinker / Wall in the play), *Marlene Dietrich* (Hippolyta, Queen of the Amazons, betrothed to Theseus), Erika Meingast (Hermia), Maly Delschaft (Helena), Sybille Binder

(Oberon, King of the Fairies), Hilde Hildebrand (Titania, Queen of the Fairies), Hans Hermann (Puck, or Robin Goodfellow), Charlotte Bosien (Peaseblossom), Gertrud Heschek (Cobweb), Wally Bosien (Moth), Gertrud Richard (Mustardseed), Lotte Schinck (voice of Mustardseed).

10. FRÜHLINGS ERWACHEN / SPRING AWAKENING, BERLIN, 1924

By Frank Wedekind. Premiere February 23, 1924, Theater in der Königgrätzer Straße.

Cast: (Wendla), (Martha), (Thea), *Marlene Dietrich* (Ilse), Willi Fritsch (Melchior), (Moritz), (Hans), (Ernst), (Lammermeier), (Georg), (Diethelm), (Ruprecht), (Helmuth), (Reinhold), (Frau Bergmann), (Frau Gabor), (Judge Gabor), (Professor Corona Radiata), (Professor Tonguetwister), (Professor Total Loss), (Professor Strychnine), (Pastor Hirsute), (Schnell), (Procrustes), (Locksmith), (Man in the Mask).

[Programs are apparently lost. Willi Fritsch in his autobiography refers to appearing with Marlene in this production.]

11. WENN DER NEUE WEIN WIEDER BLÜHT / WHEN THE NEW VINE BLOOMS, BERLIN, 1924

By Björnstjerne Björnson; directed by Dr. Reinhardt Bruck. Premiere March 8, 1924, Theater in der Königgrätzer Straße, Berlin.

Cast: Lucie Höflich (Frau Arvik), Hermann Vallentin (Herr Arvik), Paul Bildt (Propst Hall), Erika Meingast (Helene), with Maly Delschaft, Hilde Hildebrand, *Marlene Dietrich*, Annemarie Möricke, Heinz Stiede, and Gertrud Richard.

12. THE IMAGINARY INVALID, BERLIN, 1924

Comedy by Molière. Premiere April 1924, Theater in der Königgrätzer Straße, Berlin.

Cast: Prologue—(Shepherdess); Play—(Argan), (Béline, his second wife), (Angélique, his daughter), (Louison, his younger daughter), (Béralde, his brother), (Cléante), (Mr. Diafoirus, a doctor), (Thomas Diafoirus, his son), (Mr. Pugon, Argan's doctor), (Mr. Fleurant, an apothecary), (Mr. Bonnefoy, a notary), *Marlene Dietrich* (Toinette, a servant), Hilde Hildebrand.

13. BACK TO METHUSALEH (EVENING TWO: PARTS THREE TO FIVE), BERLIN, 1925

Comedy by George Bernard Shaw; directed by Viktor Barnowsky; stage design by Cesar Klein; music by Klaus Pringsheim; dance direction by Claire Bauroff. Premiere November 26, 1925, Theater in der Königgrätzer Straße, Berlin.

Cast: (Part Three): Curt Götz (Burge Lubin), Ferdinand von Alten (Barnabas), Fritz Kortner (Confucius), Hester Harvey (Negress), Theodor Loos (Archbishop),

Tilla Durieux (Mrs. Lutestring); (Part Four): Rudolf Forster (the Ancient), Curt Götz (Gesandter), Ilka Grüning (his wife), Fritz Kortner (Napoleon), Anne Kersten (Zoo), Wilhelm Dieterle (Zozim), Tilla Durieux (Delphic Oracle); (Part 5): Hans Heinrich von Twardowski (Strephon), Roma Bahn (the newborn), Ferdinand von Alten (Pygmalion), Fritta Brod (Eve), Wilhelm Dieterle (Cain), Anne Kersten (the serpent), Tilla Durieux (Lilith), and *Marlene Dietrich* (Eve).

14. BACK TO METHUSALEH (EVENING ONE: PARTS ONE AND TWO), BERLIN, 1926

Comedy by George Bernard Shaw; directed by Martin Kerb; stage design by R. G. Neher. [Note: This production opened on September 21, 1925. Dietrich was added to the cast when it moved to the Tribüne on January 24, 1926.]

Cast: (Part One): Josef von Fielitz (Adam), *Marlene Dietrich* (Eve), Anne Kersten (the serpent), Wilhelm Dieterle (Cain); (Part Two): Joseph von Fielitz (Franklin Barnabas), Margit Barnay (Wildy, his daughter), Ferdinand von Alten (Konrad, his brother), Karl Urich (Haslam, pastor), Julius E. Herrmann (Joyce-Burge), Max Kaufmann (Lubin), Erna Reigbert (barmaid).

15. DUELL AM LIDO / DUEL ON THE LIDO, BERLIN, 1926

Comedy in three acts by Hans J. Rehfisch; directed by Leopold Jessner; settings by Emil Pirchan; ladies costumes by Modellhaus Becker. Premiere February 20, 1926, Staats-Theater (Schauspielhaus), Berlin.

Cast: Fritz Kortner (Limal), Lucie Mannheim (Ellen), Rudolf Forster (Cederstroem), Albert Patry (Roberti), Albert Florath (Achille Carrère, leather dealer from Grenoble), *Marlene Dietrich* (Lou Carrère, his daughter), Heinrich Schnitzler (Gil Carrère, his son), Anton Pointner (John Hippolyte Reinstadler, journalist from Vienna), Paula Knüpffer (his wife), Veit Harlan (Ferruccio, plumber), Eugen Burg (Saxoni, Privy councillor from Vienna), Elsa Wagner (Nina), Willi Brose (Lord), Otto Laubinger (hotel manager), Erich Dunskus, (porter), and Manfred Frömmchen.

16. DER RUBICON / THE RUBICON, BERLIN, 1926

Comedy by Eugène Bourdet; directed by Ralph Arthur Roberts. Premiere April 4, 1926, Tribüne, Berlin.

Cast: Ralph Arthur Roberts, Toni Tetzlaff, Carola Toelle, Arthur Schröder, and *Marlene Dietrich*.

17. VON MUND ZU MUND / FROM MOUTH TO MOUTH, BERLIN, 1926

Revue in eighteen scenes by Erik Charell; directed and choreographed by Erik Charell; music by Hermann Darewski, interpolations by Jerome Kern ("Who?"), Irving Caesar ("I'm a Little Bit Fonder of You"), Richard Myers ("Go South"),

Friedrich Holländer ("Raus mit den Männern aus dem Reichstag"), and Rudolf Friml ("Dear love, my love"); musical direction by Bernard Ette; sets and costumes by Ernst Stern and Walter Trier. Premiere September 1, 1926, Großes Schauspielhaus, Berlin.

Cast: Marlene Dietrich (Erika, "Mistress of Ceremonies," as replacement for Erika Gläßner), Claire Waldoff (Claire), Wilhelm Bendow (Willi), Curt Bois (Curt), Hans Wassmann (Hans), Karl Elzer (a painter), Evan Held (first girl), Bert Bloem (poet), Walter Groß (composer), Erich Nürnberger (tailor), Raul Lange (magician), Alexa von Porembski (magician's daughter), Alma Barnes (Maja).

18. WENN MAN ZU DRITT / THREE'S COMPANY, VIENNA, 1927

Comedy revue by and directed by Max Brod. Premiere Summer 1927, Kammerspiele, Vienna.

Cast: Max Brod, *Marlene Dietrich*.

19. BROADWAY, VIENNA, 1927

Contemporary comedy in three acts by George Abbott and Philip Dunning; translation by Otto Klement; directed and choreographed by Franz Wenzler; costumes and sets by Alfred Kunz; musical direction by Oskar Jerochnig. Premiere September 20, 1927, Kammerspiele, Vienna.

Cast: Arthur Peiser (Nick Verdis, owner of the Paradise Nightclub), Harald Paulsen (Roy Lane), Emmy Schleinitz (Lil Rice), Käte Manig (Katie), Peter Lorre (Joe the bartender), Lena Amsel (Mazie), *Marlene Dietrich* (Rubie), Elisaweta Alexandrowa (Pearl), Loni Lentholf (Grace), Tilla König (Ann), Friedel Haerlin (Billie), Ewald Schindler (Steve Crandall), Kurt Wentzel (Dolph), Wilhelm Voelcker ("Porky" Thompson), Theodor Grieg (Scar Edwards), Edwin Jürgensen (Detective Dan McCorn), Fritz Falkner (Larry), Oskar Kleiner (Mike).

20. DIE SCHULE VON UZNACH ODER NEUE SACHLICHKEIT / UZNACH'S SCHOOL OR THE NEW OBJECTIVITY, VIENNA, 1927

Comedy in four acts by Carl Sternheim; directed by Emil Geyer; sets and costumes by Thea Sternheim; music by Walter Goehr. Premiere November 28, 1927, Theater in der Josefstadt, Vienna.

Cast: Hermann Romberg (Dr. Siebenstern), Herbert Dirmoser (Klaus Siebenstern, his son), Hans Herrmann-Schaufuß (Heinrich Andresen), Hans Finohr (Franz von Klett), Maria Holsten (Mary Vigdor), *Marlene Dietrich* (Thylla Vandenbergh), Eva Geyer (Vane von Peschel), Ruth Landshoff (Maud Panhorst), Maria Bard (Sonja Ramm), Liselott Medelsky (Mathilde Enterlein).

21. BROADWAY, BERLIN, 1928

Contemporary comedy in three acts by George Abbott and Philip Dunning; translation by Otto Klement [dramaturg Felix Joachimssohn]; directed by Eugen Robert;

sets and decorations by Ludwig Kainer; musical director Walter Goehr, featuring the Broadway-Band jazz orchestra; choreography by Koloman Latabar; costumes by Hermann J. Kaufmann Costume House; shoes by Hermann Trattner. Premiere March 9, 1928, Komödienhaus, Berlin.

Cast: Arthur Peiser (Nick), Harald Paulsen (Roy Lane), Rosa Valetti (Lil Rice), Ruth Albu (Mazie), *Marlene Dietrich* (Rubie), Elisabeth Lennartz (Pearl), Cara Guyl (Grace), Marianne Kupfer (Ann), Charlotte Ander (Billie), Heinrich George (Steve Crandall), Franz Schafheitlin (Dolph), Harry Lambertz-Paulsen ("Porky" Thompson), Erich Kaiser-Titz (Scar Edwards), Hans Leibelt (Detective Dan McCorn), Inge Carlson (Katie), Victor Bell (Joe the Bartender), Herbert Brunar (Benny), Hugo Bauer (Larry), Alfred Kühne (Mike).

22. NACHTKABARETT / NIGHT CABARET, BERLIN, 1928

Third part of the Theater Festival to honor the fiftieth anniversary in theater of Guido Thielscher. One night only: March 27, 1928, Lustspielhaus, Berlin.

Directed by Dr. Martin Zickel; piano, Victor Holländer and choral director Hühn; choreography by Heinz Lingen; Master of Ceremonies, Willi Schaeffers.

Cast: Paul Graetz, Willy Prager, Otto Reutter. As the Thielscher-Girls in Thielschers-Girl-Kabarett: Charlotte Ander, *Marlene Dietrich*, Alice Hechy, Trude Hesterberg, Elli Hoffmann, Hella Kürty, Trude Lieske, Renate Müller, Ilse Muth, Friedel Nowack, Lea Seidl, Molly Wessely. Unser Guido (Our Guido): Paul Morgan, (*Quodliebet*), with Max Adalbert, Siegfried Arno, Wilhelm Bendow, Curt Bois, Wilhelm Diegelmann, Adolphe Engers, Max Ehrlich, Paul Graetz, Max Gülstorff, Max Hansen, Paul Heidemann, Martin Kettner, Leopold von Ledebur, Gustav Matzner, Paul Morgan, Max Pallenberg, Harald Paulsen, Ralph Arthur Roberts, Willi Schaeffers, Ferry Sikla, Ludwig Stössel, Szöke Szakall [C. Z. "Cuddles" Sakall], Jacob Tiedtke, Otto Wallburg, Hans Wassmann, Paul Westermeier.

23. ES LIEGT IN DER LUFT / IT'S IN THE AIR, BERLIN, 1928

Revue in twenty-four scenes; book and lyrics by Marcellus Schiffer; music by Mischa Spoliansky; directed by [Robert] Forster Larrinaga; music conducted by Mischa Spoliansky; settings, Walter Trier and Emil Pirchan; dummies, Dodo Wolff; dance solos, Geza von Erdelyi; girls' dances, Phyllis Page; costumes, Hermann Gerson; phonograph recordings of Whisperin' Jack Smith and Oskar Karlweis on Electrola Records. Premiere May 15, 1928, Komödie, Berlin.

ACT I

SCENE 1: Elevator: Hans Carl Müller, Hubert von Meyerinck.

SCENE 2: Clearance: *Marlene Dietrich*, Otto Wallburg, Ida Wüst and girls.

SCENE 3: Lost and Found: Leni Sponholz, Renate Rosner.

SCENE 4: Dogsitter: Margo Lion.

SCENE 5: Toy Department: Hans Carl Müller, Renate Rosner, Oskar Karlweis, Käte Lenz.

SCENE 6: "Jokes and Gags" Department: Otto Wallburg, Leni Sponholz, Willi Prager, Ida Wüst, Hans Carl Müller, Oskar Karlweis, Käte Lenz, *Marlene Dietrich*, eight girls.

SCENE 7: Perfume Department: Margo Lion.

SCENE 8: Kleptomaniacs: Hubert von Meyerinck, *Marlene Dietrich*.

SCENE 9: Political Department: Otto Wallburg.

SCENE 10: Order Department: Käte Lenz, Oskar Karlweis.

SCENE 11: Bridal Wear: Margo Lion, Leni Sponholz, Oskar Karlweis, Käte Lenz, Renate Rosner, Hans Carl Müller, bridesmaids, including *Marlene Dietrich*.

SCENE 12: Revolving Door: Willi Prager.

SCENE 13: "It's in the Air": Margo Lion, Oskar Karlweis and the ensemble.

ACT II

SCENE 14: Knick-knacks: Otto Wallburg, *Marlene Dietrich*, Hans Carl Müller, Margo Lion, Käte Lenz.

SCENE 15: "Somehow": Willi Prager.

SCENE 16: Music Department: Ida Wüst, Otto Wallburg, Käte Lenz, *Marlene Dietrich*, Oskar Karlweis. "The Four Admirals": Jack Keyes, Norman Bartlett, Henry Duvrett, Joe Leigh.

SCENE 17: Theater Ticket Counter: Willi Prager, Renate Rosner.

SCENE 18: Marriage Night: Käte Lenz, Ida Wüst, Otto Wallburg.

SCENE 19: Sisters: Margo Lion, *Marlene Dietrich*, Oskar Karlweis. [Song: "My Best Girlfriend."]

SCENE 20: Passport Photos: Margo Lion, Hans Carl Müller, Oskar Karlweis, Leni Sponholz.

SCENE 21: Information Counter: Otto Wallburg, Willi Prager.

SCENE 22: Athletic Equipment: Margo Lion, Käte Lenz, *Marlene Dietrich*, Otto Wallburg, Hans Carl Müller, Oskar Karlweis.

SCENE 23: Stockroom Boy: Louis Douglas.

SCENE 24: Exchange Desk: Entire ensemble.

Girl dancers: Tala Birell, Fritzi Dannemann, Dolly Hagen, Hildegard Seidler-Winkler, Lily Jung, Mary Grosse, Trudy Burg, Sonja Lewand, Ninon Lloyd, and Tamara Matul.

Instrumentalists: Max Heuserer, Charles Herstoff, Harald Kirchstein, Arno Olewsky, Fritz Freed, Kurt Arlt, and Mischa Spolianski on piano.

[The Berlin production closed September 11, 1928, in Berlin to go on tour (without Marlene Dietrich) in Vienna. It played 140 continuous performances in Berlin, at that time a phenomenal run.]

24. MISALLIANCE / (ELTERN UND KINDER), BERLIN, 1928

Comedy by George Bernard Shaw (translated by Siegfried Trebitsch); directed by Heinz Hilpert; settings by Erich E. Stern. Premiere September 12, 1928, Komödie, Berlin.

Cast: Otto Wallburg (John Tarleton), Else Heims (Mrs. Tarleton), Oskar Simi (Johnny, their son), *Marlene Dietrich* (Hypatia, their daughter), Paul Otto (Lord Summerhays), Heinz Rühmann (Bentley Summerhays, his son), Fritz Odemar (Joey Percival), Lili Darvas (Lina Szczepanowska), Paul Hörbiger (the young man "Mr. Gunner").

[Note: Else Heims was the first wife of Max Reinhardt; Lili Darvas the then wife of Ferenc Molnàr]

25. DER MARQUIS VON KEITH / THE MARQUIS OF KEITH, BERLIN, 1928

Drama in five acts by Frank Wedekind. Special one-night memorial for actor Albert Steinrück; eulogy by Heinrich Mann; directed by Leopold Jessner; assistant, Karlheinz Martin; settings, Emil Pirchan; stage music, Weintraubs Syncopators; stage inspector, Karl Rupprecht; prompter, Marg. Krüger; stage manager, Franz Kaiser. March 28, 1929, Schauspielhaus am Gendarmenmarkt, Berlin.

Cast: Werner Krauss (Consul Casimir), Carola Neher (Hermann, his son), Heinrich George (the Marquis von Keith), Lothar Müthel (Ernst Scholz), Eleonore von Mendelssohn (Molly Griesinger), Tilla Durieux (Anna, Countess Werdenfels), Jacob Tiedtke (Saranieff, painter), Conrad Veidt (Zamrjaki, composer), Max Pallenberg (Sommersberg, literary man), Max Hansen (Raspe, Criminal commissar), Hermann Vallentin (Osterneier, brewer), Otto Wallburg (Krenzl, builder), Albert Florath (Grandauer, restaurateur), Gisela Werbezirk (Frau Ostermeier), Rosa Valetti (Frau Krenzl), Mady Christians (Freifrau von Rosenkron), Maria Bard (Freifrau von Totleben), Elisabeth Bergner (Sascha), Fritzi Massary (a serving girl), Käthe Dorsch (Simba), Alexander Granach, Fritz Kortner, Victor Schwanaecke, Paul Wegener (butcher boys), Rodolf Forster, Kurt Gerron, Veit Harlan (porters), Paul Bildt, Hans Brausewetter, Walter Janssen, Eduard von Winterstein (valets), Trude Hesterberg, Tilly Wedekind (bakers' wives), Hans Albers, Ernst Deutsch, Kurt Goetz (waiters). *With:* Roma Bahn, Sybille Binder, *Marlene Dietrich*, Gertrud Eysoldt, Käthe

Haack, Else Heim, Leopoldine Konstantin, Maria Koppenhöfer, Hilde Körber, Till Klokow, Lina Lossen, Lucie Mannheim, Renate Müller, Martha Maria Newes, Asta Nielsen, Maria Paudler, Henny Porten, Hannah Ralph, Frida Richard, Dagny Servaes, Agnes Straub, Erika von Thellman, Irene Triesch, Elsa Wagner, Ida Wüst (female guests of the Marquis)
and: Alfred Abel, Ferdinand von Alten, Alfred Braun, Julius Falkenstein, Walter Franck, Max Gülstorff, Paul Graetz, Fritz Kampers, Arthur Kraußneck, Otto Laubinger, Hans Leibelt, Theodor Loos, H. C. Müller, Paul Otto, Johannes Riemann, Albert Patry, Dr. Max Pohl, Emil Rameau, Heinrich Schnitzler, Heinrich Schroth, Ernst Stahl-Nachbaur, Hermann Thimig, Hans Wassman, Mathias Wiemann, Wolfgang Zilzer (male guests of the Marquis).

Weintraubs Syncopators:
Friedrich Holländer: piano
Horst Graff: saxophone, trumpet, clarinet, flute
Ansko Bruinier: trumpet, cello, woodwinds
Kurt Kaiser: tenor saxophone, cornet, clarinet
Paul Aronowici: banjo, violin
Stefan Weintraub: drums and celeste

26. ZWEI KRAWATTEN / TWO BOW TIES, BERLIN, 1929

Revue in nine scenes by Georg Kaiser, with music by Mischa Spoliansky; produced by Robert Klein; directed by [Robert] Forster Larrinaga; musical direction Hans Schindler; sets and dummies, Erich E. Stern; choreography, Sammy Lewis; concert master, Paul Godwin; technical direction, Hans Sondheimerd; costumes, Hermann J. Kaufmann; wardrobe for Marlene Dietrich, Margarete Koeppke and Rosa Valetti by Modellhaus Becker; shoes, Siegmund Reiß. Premiere September 5, 1929, Berliner Theater, Berlin.

Cast: Hans Albers (Jean), *Marlene Dietrich* (Mabel), Richard Tomaselli (Charles, first gentleman), Hanna Waag (lady), Hugo Flink (ball guest), Walter Bluhm (waiter, first reporter, fourth gentleman), Margarete Koeppke (Trude), Hans Wassmann (barman, senator), Erich Walter (bar guest, railroad engineer), Erwin Bootz (piano player), Jakob Tiedtke (Bannermann), Camillo Kossuth (deck officer), De Haven (lawyer), Nice (writer), Rosa Valetti (Mrs. Robinson), Marcel Mermino (second reporter), Berti Hirschlaff (lady reporter), Harriet Adams (lady reporter), Oskar Graß (first controller, man), Franz Feschemacher (second controller), Karl Neisser (a passenger), Otto Matthies (second gentleman), Willi Norman (third gentleman), Eduard Wiemuth (waiter), R. Ciesso, P. Comosin, W. Normann, F. Rittermann, E. Schäfer, E. Wiemuth, H. H. Adams, M. Cerconi, F. Dannemann, E. Eras, E. Helmke, B. Hirschlaff, R. Jacobsen, S. Lindblatt, S. Spira, H. Voss (guests at the ball), V. Hackenberger, M. Menzel (passengers and sailors, plus Moore and Lewis, De Haven and Nice, St. Leger and The Comedian Harmonists: Robert Biberti, Erich Collin, Erwin Bootz, Roman Cycowski, Ari Leschnikoff, Harry Frommermann).

APPENDIX B
FILMOGRAPHY

The following film titles and credits are compiled from contemporary records, production reports, call sheets, and other documentation which supplement credits found on the films themselves.

Certain film titles have been advanced elsewhere that are purely speculative. There is no known evidence, for instance, for Dietrich's having worked in films like *Im Schatten des Glücks / In Fortune's Shadow* (1919), *Der Mönch von Santarem / The Monk from Santarem* (1924), two films she is rumored to have made and of which no copies are known to exist.

G. W. Pabst's *Die Freudlose Gasse / Joyless Street* is discussed in the text in Chapter Four. Dietrich was giving birth when the picture was shot and the actress misidentified as her is Hertha von Walther, who died in Munich in 1988.

Previous filmographies have included a short film made privately by Rudolf Sieber featuring domestic scenes of Marlene and her daughter. The film (referred to as *Die glückliche Mutter / The Happy Mother*) is said to have been theatrically released in Germany during the 1920s, but no such film appears in any official documentation. German law then required official cataloguing of every film of whatever length or nature (including the pornographic) publicly exhibited anywhere in Germany. Such a film—or home movies like it—may well have been made (Dietrich herself made home movies during the thirties), but no evidence exists to warrant its inclusion in the film record. Someone may yet turn up the odd "bit" in a forgotten film in some warehouse or private collection. Until then, the following is a comprehensive listing of Dietrich's total film work, excluding compilation films, newsreels, and so on. The exception is the final item, whose unique interest warrants its inclusion here.

SO SIND DIE MÄNNER / THAT'S HOW MEN ARE (also known as DER KLEINE NAPOLEON / THE LITTLE NAPOLEON and /or NAPOLEONS KLEINER BRUDER / NAPOLEON'S LITTLE BROTHER, GERMANY, 1922

[Production dates June to November 1922 at Schloß Wilhelmshöhe bei Kassel and in the Efa studios in Berlin. Premiere November 29, 1923, Marmorhaus, Berlin.

Production company: Europäische Film-Allianz (Efa); director, Georg Jacoby; screenplay by Robert Liebmann and Jacoby; camera, Max Schneider (or Snyder), Emil Schünemann; art director, Martin Jacoby-Boy.

Cast: Egon von Hagen (Napoleon Bonaparte), Paul Heidemann (Jérome Bonaparte), Harry Liedtke (Georg von Melsungen), Jacob Tiedtke (Jermias von Katzenellenbogen), Antonia Dietrich (Charlotte), Loni Nest (Lieselotte), Alice Hechy (Annemarie), Kurt Vespermann (Florian Wunderlich), Paul Biensfeldt (Field Marshall), Kurt Fuss (Director of the Royal Ballet), Marquisette Bosky (prima ballerina), *Marlene Dietrich* (Kathrin, Charlotte's chambermaid), Wilhelm Bendow (servant), and Loni Pyrmont.

TRAGÖDIE DER LIEBE / TRAGEDY OF LOVE (US release title *The Apache's Revenge*, GERMANY, 1922-1923

[Production dates 1922 in May Film Ateleier, Berlin-Weißensee, south of France. Premiere Parts 1 and 2 on October 8, 1923, UFA-Palast am Zoo in Berlin; Parts 3 and 4 on November 7, 1923, in the same theater.]

Production: May-Film, Berlin; producer/director, Joe May; seceenplay by Leon Birinski and Adolf Lantz; camera, Sophus Wangoe and Karl Puth; art direction, Paul Leni; costumes, Ali Hubert; music, Wilhelm Lövitt; production manager, Rudolf Sieber; assistant director, Robert Wüllner; still photographer, Hans Lechner.

Cast: Mia May (Manon de Moreau), Rudolf Forster (Comte François Moreau), Hedwig Pauly-Winterstein (Adrienne, his mother), Emil Jannings (Ombrade), Erika Gläßner (Musette), Guido Herzfeld (Marcel Géraud), Wladimir Gaidarow (André Rabatin), Ida Wüst (Madame de la Roquère), Irmgard Bern (Yvonne), Kurt Götz (district attorney), Kurt Vespermann (deputy district attorney), *Marlene Die-*

trich (Lucie), Arnold Korff (Henry Beaufort, detective), Hermann Vallentin (police commissioner), Eugen Rex (Jean, servant of the Comte de Moreau), and, Lena Amsel, Charlotte Ander, Paul Biensfeldt, Paul Graetz, Karl Gerhardt, Ernst Gronau, Albert Patry, Hans Kuhnert, Fritz Richard, Rudolf Lettinger, Ferry Sikla, Hans Waßmann, and Loni Nest.

DER MENSCH AM WEGE / MAN BY THE WAYSIDE, GERMANY, 1923

[Production dates end of April to the middle of May 1923 in Schleswig (locations) and in the Mutoscop-Ateleier in Lankwitz (interiors). Press premiere June 6, 1923, Alhambra, Berlin.]

Production company: Osmania-Film, Berlin; director, Wilhelm Dieterle; screenplay, Dieterle, based on short stories by Tolstoy ("Wodurch die Menschen leben," and "Das Patenkind" in *Tolstoy: Volkserzählungen and Legenden*); camera, Willy Hameister; art director, Herbert Richter-Luckian; production manager, Willy Habantz.

Cast: Alexander Granach (cobbler), Emilie Unda (his wife), Wilhelm Dieterle (Michael, the "human" angel), Heinrich George (squire), Wilhelm Völcker (coachman), Sophie Pagay (shopkeeper's wife), *Marlene Dietrich* (shopkeeper's daughter), Wilhelm Diegelmann (innkeeper), Fritz Rasp (farmhand), Werner Pledath (farmhand), Liselotte Rolle (cobbler's daughter), Dr. Max Pohl (civil servant), Ludwig Rex (watchman), Ernst Gronau (doctor), Dolly Lorenz and Seeberg (maids), and Gerhard Bienert, Georg Hilbert, Fritz Kampers, Max Nemetz, Hermine Körner, Lotte Stein, Bäk, Gerlach-Jacobi, Hagewald, Härting, Herbst, Matt, Rausch, Zeiselmaier, Brockmann.

DER SPRUNG INS LEBEN / LEAP INTO LIFE, GERMANY, 1923

[Production dates late July to early August 1923, locations on the North Sea, interiors filmed at Jofa-Atelier post-August, 1923. Premiere February 4, 1924, Tauentzienpalast, Berlin.]

Production company, Messter-Film (UFA); producer, Erich Pommer; director, Dr. Johannes Guter; screenplay, Franz Schulz; cameraman, Fritz Arno Wagner; art director, Rudi Feld.

Cast: Xenia Desni (Idea, a circus acrobat), Walter Rilla (Frank), Paul Heidemann (Dr. Rudolf Borris), Frida Richard (his aunt), Käte Haack (Dr. Borris's secretary), Hans Brausewetter (Borris's friend), Leonhard Haskel (the ringmaster), Lydia Potechina (ringmaster's wife), Dr. Gebbing (trainer), *Marlene Dietrich* (girl on the beach), Hans Heinrich von Twardowski (violinist), with Max Gülstorff, Erling Hanson, Max Valentin, Ernst Pröckl, and Hermann Thimig.

MANON LESCAUT, GERMANY, 1926

[Production dates June to September 1925 at UFA studios at Tempelhof, Berlin; September/October 1925 at Neubabelsberg. Premiere February 15, 1926, UFA-Palast am Zoo, Berlin.]

Production company, UFA; director, Arthur Robison; screenplay, Robison and Hans Kyser from the novel by Antoine François Prévost d'Exiles; cameraman, Theodor Sparkuhl; art direction and costumes, Paul Leni.

Cast: Lya de Putti (Manon Lescaut), Wladimir Gaidarow (Des Grieux), Eduard Rothauser (his father), Fritz Greiner (Marquis de Bli), Hubert von Meyerinck (the younger de Bli), Theodor Loos (Tiberge), Trude Hesterberg (Claire), *Marlene Dietrich* (Micheline), Frida Richard and Emilie Kurz (Manon's aunts), Lydia Potechina (Susanne), Siegfried Arno (Lescaut), and Olga Engl, Karl Harbacher, Hans Junkermann, Hermann Picha.

EINE DUBARRY VON HEUTE / A MODERN DUBARRY, GERMANY, 1926

[Production dates April to August 1926 in the UFA studios at Tempelhof and Neubabelsberg. Locations in Spain and on the French Riviera. Premiere January 24, 1927, UFA-Palast am Zoo, Berlin.]

Production company, Felson-Film-UFA; director, Alexander Korda; screenplay, Robert Liebmann, Alexander Korda, and Paul Reboux from the novel by Ludwig (Lajos) Biro; cameraman, Fritz Arno Wagner; art director, Otto Friedrich Werndorff; music, Werner R. Heymann.

Cast: Maria Corda (Toinette), Alfred Abel (Sillon), Friedrich Kayßler (Cornelius Corbett), Julius von Szöreghi (General Padilla), Jean Bradin (Sandro, King of Astorra), Hans Albers (Darius Kerbelian), Alfred Gerasch (Count Rabbatz), Albert Paulig (Clairet), Hans Waßmann (theater director), Karl Platen (servant), Eugen Burg (Levasseur), *Marlene [Marlaine] Dietrich* (coquette), Hilda Radney (Juliette), Julie Serda (Aunt Julie), Hedwig Wangel (Rosalie), Lotte Lorring (model), and Hidigeiga the cat.

DER TÄNZER MEINER FRAU / MY WIFE'S DANCING PARTNER (English release title DANCE MAD), GERMANY, 1926

[Production period late 1926. Premiere November 6, 1926, UFA Theater Kurfürstendamm.]

Production company, Felsom-Film-UFA; director, Alexander Korda; screenplay, Adolf Lantz and Korda (based on a comedy by Armont and Bousquet); cameraman, Nikolaus Farkas; art direction, Paul Leni; production assistant, Rudolf Sieber.

Cast: Maria Corda, Willy Fritsch, Victor Varkonyi, Livio Pavanelli, Lea Seidl, Hans Junkermann, Olga Limburg, Hermann Thimig, with *Marlene Dietrich* and Alexander Choura as dance extras.

MADAME WÜNSCHT KEINE KINDER / MADAME DOESN'T WANT CHILDREN, GERMANY, 1926

[Production dates October/November 1926 at the UFA studios at Tempelhof. Premiere December 14, 1926, Capitol, Berlin.]

Production company, Deutsche Vereins-Film AG (Deutsche Fox-Defa/Fox Europa Production); producer, Karl Freund; director, Alexander Korda; screenplay Adolf Lantz and Béla Balázs, based on the play *Madame ne veut pas d'enfants* by Clément Vautel [1924]; cameraman, Theodor Sparkuhl and Robert Baberske; art direction, Otto Friedrich Werndorff; costumes, Maison Deuillet; production associate, Karl Hartl; production manager, Rudolf Sieber; still photographer, Lichtenstein.

Cast: Maria Corda (Elyane), Harry Liedtke (Paul), Maria Paudler (Louise), Trude Hesterberg (Elyane's mother), Dina Gralla (Lulu, Elyane's sister), Hermann Vallentin (Paul's uncle), Camilla von Hollay (Louise's maid), Olga Mannel (Louise's cook), Ellen Müller (Elyane's maid), with *Marlene Dietrich*, Camilla Horn, and John Loder as dance extras.

KOPF HOCH, CHARLY / CHIN UP, CHARLY, GERMANY, 1926

[Production dates September 1926 at the EFA studios, location footage shot in Paris, Hamburg and New York. Premiere March 18, 1927, UFA-Theater Kurfürstendamm, Berlin.]

Production company, Ellen Richter; director, Dr. Willi Wolff; screenplay, Robert Liebmann and Wolff, from a novel by Ludwig Wolff (1926); cameramen, Axel Graatkjaer, Georg Krause; art direction, Ernst Stern.

Cast: Anton Pointner (Frank Ditmar), Ellen Richter (Charlotte "Charly" Ditmar), Michael Bohnen (John Jacob Bunjes), Max Gülstorff (Harry Moshenheim), Margerie Quimby (Margie Quinn), George de Carlton (Rufus Quinn), Angelo Ferrari (Marquis d'Ormesson), Robert Scholz (Duke of Sanzedilla), Nikolai Malikoff (Prince Platonoff), Toni Tetzlaff (Frau Zangenberg), *Marlene Dietrich* (Edmée Marchand), Blandine Ebinger (seamstress), Albert Paulig (Bunje's servant).

DER JUXBARON / THE BOGUS BARON, GERMANY, 1926

[Production dates October/November 1926 at the UFA studios at Tempelhof. Premiere March 4, 1927, Mozartsaal, Berlin.]

Production company, Ellen Richter-Film, released through UFA; director, Dr. Willi Wolff; screenplay, Robert Liebmann, Wolff, based on the operetta by Pordes-Milo, Hermann Haller, and Walter Kollo (music); cameraman, Axel Graatkjaer; art director, Ernst Stern.

Cast: Reinhold Schünzel (the title character, called "Robin Blue-Breast"), *Marlene Dietrich* (Sophie Windisch), Henry Bender (Hugo Windisch, her father), Julie Serda (Zerline Windisch, her mother), Teddy Bill (Hans von Grabow), Colette Brettl (Hilde von Grabow), Albert Paulig (Baron von Kimmel), Trude Hesterberg (Fränze), Karl Harbacher ("Stuttering William"), Hermann Picha (tramp), Fritz Kampers (policeman), Heinrich Gotto (houseguest), Karl Beckmann (innkeeper).

SEIN GRÖSSTER BLUFF / HIS BIGGEST BLUFF, GERMANY, 1927

[Production dates January 24 through the end of February 1927 in the Berlin-Grunewald studios. Premiere May 12, 1927, Alhambra-Palast, Berlin.]

Production company, Nero Film: director, Harry Piel; assistant Rudolf Sieber; screenplay, Henrik Galeen; camera, George Muschner, Gotthardt Wolf; art director, W. A. Herrmann; production manager, Walter Zeiske; assistant director, Edmund Heuberger; titles, Dr. Herbert Nossen.

Cast: Harry Piel (Henry and Harry Devall, twin brothers), Toni Tetzlaff (Madame Andersson), Lotte Lorring (Tilly, her daughter), Albert Paulig (Mimikry), Fritz Greiner (Hennessy), Charly Berger ("Count" Koks [note: "Koks" was Berlin slang for cocaine]); Boris Michailow (Sherry), *Marlene Dietrich* (Yvette), Paul Walker (Goliath, a dwarf), Kurt Gerron (Maharajah of Johore), Eugen Burg (police prefect), Ossip Darmatow ("Count" Apollinaris), Vicky Werckmeister (Suzanne), Paul Moleska, Oswald Scheffel, Curt Bullerjahn, Charles François, Wolfgang von Schwind (gangsters), with Hans Breitensträter.

CAFÉ ELECTRIC (Austrian title), WENN EIN WEIB DEN WEG VERLIERT / WHEN A WOMAN LOSES THE WAY (German Title), AUSTRIA, 1927

[Production dates Summer 1927, Vienna. Premiere November 25, 1927, as *Café Electric* in Vienna; March 22, 1928 at the Emelka-Palast, Berlin, as *Wenn ein Weib den Weg verliert.*]

Production company, Sascha Film, Vienna; director, Gustav Ucicky; screenplay, Jacques Bachrach, based on the play *Die Liebesbörse / The Love Exchange* by Felix Fischer; cameraman, Hans Androschin; art director, Artur Berger; assistant director, Karl Hartl.

Cast: Willi Forst (Ferdl), *Marlene Dietrich* (Erni Göttlinger), Fritz Alberti (her father), Anny Coty (his mistress), Igo Sym (Max Stöger), Vera Salvotti (Paula), Nina Vanna (Hansi), Wilhelm Völcker (Dr. Lehner), Albert Kersten (Herr Zerner), Felix Fischer [author of the source play] (newspaper editor), and Dolly Davis.

PRINZESSIN OLALA / PRINCESS O-LA-LA / (English release title ART OF LOVE, 1929), GERMANY, 1928

[Production dates Summer 1928 at UFA-Tempelhof. Premiere September 5, 1928, UFA-Theater Kurfürstendamm, Berlin.]

Production company, Super Film; production, Julius Haimann; director, Robert Land; screenplay, Franz Schulz, based on the operetta by Jean Gilbert (music), Rudolf Bernauer and Rudolf Schanzer (book); cameraman, Willi Goldberger; art director, Robert Neppach; production manager, Fritz Brunn.

Cast: Hermann Böttcher (the Prince); Walter Rilla (Prince Boris, his son); Georg Alexander (the Chamberlain); Carmen Boni (Princess Xenia); Ila Meery (Hedy, her friend); *Marlene Dietrich* (Chichotte de Gastoné), Hans Albers (René, Chichotte's friend), Karl Götz [Carl Goetz] (an old cavalier), Julius von Szöreghy (a strong man), Lya Christy (Lady Jackson), Aribert Wäscher (police superintendent), and Alfred Abel.

ICH KÜSSE IHRE HAND, MADAME / I KISS YOUR HAND, MADAME, GERMANY, 1928

[Production dates 1928, Efa studios, Berlin, with location work in Paris. Premiere January 17, 1929, Tauentzien-Palast, Berlin. (Released in America as *I Kiss Your Hand, Madame*, 1932.)]

Production company, Super-Film; director, Robert Land; screenplay, Land, from an original story by Land and Rolf E. Vanloo; cameraman, Carl Drews, Gotthardt Wolf; camera assistant, Fred Zinnemann; music, title song by Ralph Erwin, lyrics by Fritz Rotter, sung on soundtrack by Richard Tauber; art director, Robert Neppach; assistant director, Friedel Buckow; production manager, Fritz Brunn.

Cast: Harry Liedtke (Jacques, the headwaiter), *Marlene Dietrich* (Laurence Gérard), Pierre de Guignand (Adolphe Gérard, her ex-husband), Karl Huszar-Puffy (Talandier, her attorney).

DIE FRAU, NACH DER MAN SICH SEHNT/ THE WOMAN ONE LONGS FOR (U.S. and English release title, THREE LOVES), GERMANY, 1929

[Production dates, early 1929 at the Terra-Glashaus. Premiere, April 29, 1929, Mozartsaal, Berlin. (American premiere, August 1929, The Playhouse, New York.)]

Production company, Terra-Berlin; producer, Hermann Grund; director, Kurt Bernhardt; screenplay, Ladislaus Vajda, from the novel by Max Brod (1927); camera, Kurt Courant, Hans Scheib; art direction, Robert Neppach; production manager, Otto Lehmann; Original score, Dr. Giuseppe Becce; songs: "Stascha" and "Are You the Happiness I Longed For?" (*"Bist du das Glück, nach dem ich mich gesehnt?"*). Additional score for 1931 synchronized version, Edward Kilenya and Walther Bransen.

Cast: Marlene Dietrich (Stascha), Fritz Kortner (Dr. Karoff), Uno Henning (Henri Leblanc), Frida Richard (Frau Leblanc), Oskar Sima (Charles Leblanc), Edith Edwards (Angèle), Karl Ettlinger (her father), Bruno Ziener (servant of Leblanc family).

DAS SCHIFF DER VERLORENEN MENCHEN / THE SHIP OF LOST SOULS (English release title THE SHIP OF LOST MEN, 1930), GERMANY, 1929

[Production dates, early 1929 in Staaken and on the North Sea. Premiere, September 17, 1929, UFA-Pavillon am Nollendorfplatz, Berlin.]

Production company, Max Glaß Productions; director, Maurice Tourneur; screenplay, Maurice Tourneur, based on a novel by Franzos Keremen; camera, Nikolaus Farkas; art direction, Franz Schroedter [and Fritz Maurischat]; production manager, Rudolf Strobl; assistant director, Jack (Jacques) Tourneur.

Cast: Fritz Kortner (Captain Fernando Vela), *Marlene Dietrich* (Ethel Marley), Robin Irvine (T. W. Cheyne), Wladimir Sokoloff (Grischa, ship's cook), Gaston Modot (Morain, escaped convict), Boris de Fas (tattooed man), Feodor Chaliapin, Jr. (Nick), Max Maximilian (Tom Butley), with Fritz Alberti, Robert Garrison, Heinrich Gotho, Harry Grunwald, Emil Heyse, Fred Immler, Alfred Loretto, Gerhard Ritterband, Aruth Wartan, Heinz Wemper.

GEFAHREN DER BRAUTZEIT / DANGERS OF THE ENGAGEMENT PERIOD, GERMANY, 1930

[Production dates, summer 1929 in Staaken. Premiere, February 21, 1930, Roxy-Palast, Berlin.]

Production company, Strauß-Film; director, Fred Sauer; screenplay, Walter Wassermann, Walter Schlee; camera, Laszlo Schäffer; art direction, Max Heilbronner; production manager, Robert Leistenschneider.

Cast: Willi Forst (Baron von Geldern), *Marlene Dietrich* (Evelyne), Lotte Lorring (Yvette), Elza Temary (Florence), Ernst Stahl-Nachbaur (McClure), Bruno Ziener (Miller), with Albert Hörrmann, Otto Kronburg, Hans Wallner.

DER BLAUE ENGEL / THE BLUE ANGEL, GERMANY, 1930

[Production dates, November 4, 1929, to January 28, 1930, UFA Studios, Neubabelsberg, in German and English versions. Premiere, German version, April 4, 1930, Gloria-Palast, Berlin. American premiere, English version, December 5, 1930.]

Production company, UFA; producer, Erich Pommer; director, Josef von Sternberg; screenplay, Robert Liebmann, based on the novel *Professor Unrat* by Heinrich Mann, adapted by Dr. Karl Vollmöller and Carl Zuckmayer; English dialogue, Josef von Sternberg and Carl Winston; cameraman, Gunther Rittau, Hans Schneeberger; art direction, Otto Hunte, Emil Hasler; editor, Sam Winston; sound, Fritz Thiery and Herbert Kiehl; songs: music by Friedrich Holländer and Robert Liebmann, *"Nimm dich in Acht vor blonden Frauen," "Ich bin die fesche Lola," "Kinder, heut' abend such' ich mir was aus," "Ich bin von Kopf bis Fuß auf Liebe eingestellt"*; English lyrics by Sam Lerner and Carl Winston; costumes, Tihamer Varady and Karl-Ludwig Holub; makeup, Waldemar Jabs.

Cast: Emil Jannings (Professor Immanuel Rath), *Marlene Dietrich* (Lola Lola), Kurt Gerron (Kiepert, magician and compère), Rosa Valetti (Guste, his wife), Hans Albers (Mazeppa), Reinhold Bernt (clown), Eduard von Winterstein (school director), Hans Roth (Pedell), Rolf Müller (Angst), Roland Varno (Lohmann), Carl Balhaus (Erztum), Robert Klein-Lörk (Goldstaub), Karl Huszar-Puffy (owner of "The Blue Angel" nightclub), Wilhelm Diegelmann (ship's captain), Gerhard Bienert (policeman), Ilse Fürstenberg (Rath's landlady), Friedrich Holländer (piano player), Weintraubs-Syncopators (musicians).

PARAMOUNT'S NEW STAR: MARLENE DIETRICH (trailer), USA, 1930

[Production date, May 1930, Paramount Studios. Exhibition, Summer 1930, Paramount sales department distribution.]

Director, Josef von Sternberg, [Producer, Albert Kaufman]

Cast: Marlene Dietrich .

MOROCCO, USA, 1930

[Production dates, July/August 1930, Paramount Studios and Universal back lot, Hollywood, exteriors Palmdale, Guadaloupe. Premiere, November 14, 1930, Rivoli Theater, New York; November 25, 1930, Graumann's Chinese, Hollywood.]

Production company, Paramount; producer, Hector Turnbull; director, Josef von Sternberg; screenplay, Jules Furthman from *Amy Jolly, die Frau aus Marrakesch* by Benno Vigny (1927); camera, Lee Garmes, Lucien Ballard; art direction, Hans Dreier; costumes, Travis Banton; songs: "Give Me the Man Who Does Things" (unused), "What Am I Bid for My Apple?" by Leo Robin and Karl Hajós; "Quand l'amour meurt" by Octave Crémieux and G. Millandy; editor, Sam Winston; sound, Harry D. Mills.

Cast: Gary Cooper (Tom Brown), *Marlene Dietrich* (Amy Jolly), Adolphe Menjou (La Bessière), Ullrich Haupt (Adjutant Caesar), Juliette Compton (Anna Dolores), Francis McDonald (Corporal Tatoche), Albert Conti (Colonel Quinnovieres), Eve Southern (Madame Caesar), Michael Visaroff (Barratire), Paul Porcasi (Lo Tinto), Émile Chautard (French General).

Awards: Academy Award nominations for director (Sternberg), actress (Dietrich), photography (Lee Garmes), sound recording (Harry Mills). *Morocco* won the award for sound, shared with *Dishonored*.

DISHONORED, USA, 1931

[Production dates, October to November 29, 1930, Paramount, Hollywood. Premiere, March 5, 1931, Rialto Theater, New York.

Production company, Paramount; producer/director, Josef von Sternberg; screenplay, Daniel H. Rubin, from a story by Sternberg; camera, Lee Garmes; art direction, Hans Dreier; musical score, Karl Hajós, with quotations from Ivanovici ("Danube Waves") and Beethoven ("Moonlight Sonata"), with miscellaneous "themes" by Josef von Sternberg; costumes, Travis Banton; sound, Harry D. Mills.

Cast: Marlene Dietrich (X-27), Victor McLaglen (Lieutenant Kranau), Lew Cody (Colonel Kovrin), Gustav von Seyffertitz (Chief of the Austrian Secret Service), Warner Oland (General von Hindau), Barry Norton (young lieutenant), Davison Clark (court official), Wilfred Lucas (General Dymov), Bill Powell (manager), and George Irving.

SHANGHAI EXPRESS, USA, 1932

[Production dates, late 1931, Paramount, Hollywood, Bakersfield, and Chatsworth. Premiere, February 2, 1932, Rialto Theater, New York.]

Production company, Paramount; producer/director, Josef von Sternberg; screenplay by Jules Furthman, based on a story by Harry Hervey; cameraman, Lee Garmes, [uncredited exteriors, James Wong Howe]; art direction, Hans Dreier; music, W. Franke Harling; costumes, Travis Banton.

Cast: Marlene Dietrich (Madeleine/Shanghai Lily), Clive Brook (Captain Donald Harvey), Anna May Wong (Hui Fei), Warner Oland (Henry Chang), Eugene Pallette (Sam Salt), Lawrence Grant (Mr. Carmichael), Louise Closser Hale (Mrs. Haggerty), Gustav von Seyffertitz (Eric Baum), Émile Chautard (Major Lenard), Claude King (Albright), Neshedo Nimoru (Chinese Spy), Willie Fung.

Awards: Academy Award nominations for Best Picture, Best Director, Best Photography. The Paramount sound department won the award for overall achievement and Garmes won for Best Photography.

BLONDE VENUS, USA, 1932

[Production dates, May/June 1932. Premier, September 22, 1932.] Production company, Paramount; producer/director, Josef von Sternberg; screenplay by Jules Furthman and S. K. Lauren (from a story by Josef von Sternberg and Marlene Dietrich, uncredited); camerman, Bert Glennon (with Paul Ivano, uncredited); art direction, Wiard Ihnen; music, Oskar Potoker; songs: "Hot Voodoo" and "You Little So-and-so," music by Ralph Rainger, lyrics by Sam Coslow; "I Couldn't Be Annoyed," music by Richard Whiting, English lyrics by Leo Robin [French lyrics by Marlene Dietrich]; costumes, Travis Banton.

Cast: Marlene Dietrich (Helen Faraday), Herbert Marshall (Edward Faraday), Cary Grant (Nick Townsend), Dickie Moore (Johnny Faraday), Gene Morgan (Ben Smith), Rita La Toy ("Taxi Belle" Hooper), Robert Emmett O'Connor (Dan O'Connor), Sidney Toler (Detective Wilson), Francis Sayles (Charlie Blaine), Morgan Wallace (Dr. Pierce), Evelyn Preer (Iola), Robert Graves (La Farge), Lloyd Whitlock (Baltimore manager), Cecile Cunningham (Norfolk manageress), Émile Chautard (Paris nightclub patron), James Kilgannon (janitor), Sterling Holloway (Joe), Charles Morton (Bob), Ferdinand Schuman-Heink (Henry), Jerry Tucker (Otto), Harold Berquist (fat fellow), Dewey Robinson (Greek restaurant owner), Clifford Dempsey (judge), Bessie Lyle (Grace), Gertrude Short (receptionist), Hattie McDaniel (maid), Brady Kline (New Orleans cop).

SONG OF SONGS, USA, 1933

[Production dates, February–May 1933, Paramount, Hollywood. Premiere, July 19, 1933, Criterion Theater, New York.]

Production company, Paramount; producer/director, Rouben Mamoulian; screenplay, Leo Birinski, Samuel Hoffenstein [and Mamoulian], based on Hermann

Sudermann's novel (*Das Hohelied*, 1908) and the play *Song of Songs* by Edward Sheldon; camerman, Victor Milner; art direction, Hans Dreier; music, Karl Hajos and Milan Roder; songs: "*Heideröslein*," music by Franz Schubert, text by Johann Wolfgang von Goethe, "Jonny," music by Friedrich Holländer, English lyrics by Edward Heyman, ("You Are My Song of Songs," music by Ralph Rainger, lyrics by Leo Robin, not used); musical direction, Nathaniel W. Finston; costumes, Travis Banton; sculptures, S. C. Scarpitta.

Cast: Marlene Dietrich (Lily Czepanek), Brian Aherne (Richard Waldow), Lionel Atwill (Baron von Merzbach), Alison Skipworth (Frau Rasmussen), Hardie Albright (Walter von Prell), Helen Freeman (Fräulein von Schwartzfegger), with James Marcus, Richard Bennett, Morgan Wallace, Wilson Benge, and Hans Schumm.

THE SCARLET EMPRESS, USA, 1934

[Production dates, spring 1934; Premiere, May 19, 1934, Carlton, London.]

Production company, Paramount; producer/director, Josef von Sternberg; screenplay, Manuel Komroff "based on a diary of Catherine the Great"; cameraman, Bert Glennon; art direction, Hans Dreier, Peter Ballbusch (sculpture), and Richard Kollorsz (icons); music, W. Franke Harling, John M. Leipold, Milan Roder, based on themes from Tchaikowsky, Mendelssohn, and Richard Wagner; costumes, Travis Banton; special effects, Gordon Jennings; uncredited footage from *The Patriot* (1928), by Ernst Lubitsch.

Cast: Marlene Dietrich (Sophia Frederica, later Catherine the Great), John Lodge (Count Alexei), Sam Jaffe (Grand Duke Peter), Louise Dresser (Czarina Elisabeth), Maria Sieber (Sophia Frederica as a child), C. Aubrey Smith (Prince August), Ruthelma Stevens (Countess Elizabeth), Olive Tell (Princess Johanna), Gavin Gordon (Gregory Orloff), Jameson Thomas (Lieutenant Ovtsyn), Hans Heinrich von Twardowski (Ivan Shuvolov), Davison Clark (Archbishop Simeon Tevedovsky), Erville Alderson (Chancellor Bestuchef), Marie Wells (Marie), Jane Darwell (Mlle. Cardell), Harry Woods (the doctor), Edward Van Sloan (Herr Wagner), Philip G. Sleeman (Count Lestocq), John B. Davidson (Marquis de la Chetardie), Gerald Fielding (Lt. Dmitri), James Burke (guard), Belle Stoddard Johnstone (first aunt), Nadine Beresford (second aunt), Eunice Moore (third aunt), Petra McAllister (fourth aunt), Blanche Rose (fifth aunt), James Marcus (innkeeper), Thomas C. Blythe (first Narcissus), Clyde David (second Narcissus), Richard Alexander (Count von Breummer), Hal Boyer (lackey), Bruce Warren (lackey), George Davis (jester), Eric Alden (lackey), Agnes Steele, Barbara Sabichi, May Foster and Minnie Steele (Elizabeth's ladies-in-waiting), Katherine Sabichi, Julanne Johnston, Elinor Fair, Dina Smirnova, Anna Duncan, Patricia Patrick, and Elaine St. Maur (Catherine's ladies-in-waiting).

THE DEVIL IS A WOMAN, USA, 1935

[Production dates, Ocober 1934 to mid-January 1935. Premier, May 3, 1935, Paramount Theater, New York.]

Production company, Paramount; producer/director, Josef von Sternberg; screenplay, John Dos Passos, Sam Winston, and Sternberg, based on "The Woman and the Puppet" by Pierre Louys (1898) [theatrical version by Louys and Pierre Frondaire, 1910]; cameraman, Joseph von Sternberg, assisted by Lucien Ballard [uncredited]; art direction, Hans Dreier; music, "Caprice Espagnol" by Rimsky-Korsakov, arranged by Ralph Rainger and Andrea Setaro; songs: "Three Sweethearts Have I" and "If It Isn't Pain, It Isn't Love" (cut before release), music by Ralph Rainger, lyrics by Leo Robin; editor, Sam Winston; costumes, Travis Banton.

Cast: Marlene Dietrich (Concha Perez); Lionel Atwill (Don Pasqual), Cesar Romero [replacing Joel McCrea] (Antonio Galvan), Edward Everett Horton (Don Paquito), Alison Skipworth (Concha's mother), Don Alvarado (Morenito), Morgan Wallace (Dr. Mendez), Tempe Pigott (Tuerta), Jill Dennett (Maria), Lawrence Grant (conductor), Charles Sellon (letter writer), Luisa Espinal (gypsy dancer on train), Hank Mann (railroad man), Edwin Maxwell (tobacco factory superintendent), with Donald Reed, Eddie Borden.

THE FASHION SIDE OF HOLLYWOOD, USA, 1935

[Production dates, February 1935. Release, spring 1935.]

Production company, Paramount; producer, William H. Pine; [director for Dietrich, Josef von Sternberg].

Cast: Kathleen Howard and Travis Banton; *Marlene Dietrich,* Joan Bennett, Carole Lombard, George Raft, Claudette Colbert, Mae West.

The Fashion Side of Hollywood is a one-reel short subject about costume and fashion, designed to play commercial theaters as a trailer for upcoming Paramount product. The Dietrich footage is extensive, and opens and closes the picture. It is called a "costume test" by Banton in the narration, but was specially photographed and is not a test.

The Dietrich clips from this film are featured in Mikail Romm's full-length Russian documentary, *Ordinary Fascism.*

DESIRE, USA, 1936

[Production dates, September 16, 1935, to December 21, 1935. American premiere: April 11, 1936, Paramount Theater, New York. *Desire* opened as *Sehnsucht* ten days earlier in Berlin.]

Production company, Paramount; producer, Ernst Lubitsch; director, Frank Borzage (retakes by Lubitsch); screenplay, Edwin Justus Mayer, Waldemar Young, and Samuel Hoffenstein, based on *Die schönen Tage von Aranjuez,* by Hans Szekely and R. A. Stemmle, a German film of 1933 directed by Johannes Meyer, starring Brigitte Helm and Gustaf Gründgens (French version with Helm and Jean Gabin); camera, Charles Lang, Victor Milner; art direction, Hans Dreier, Robert Usher; sets, A. E. Freudeman; music, Friedrich Holländer; songs: "Awake in a

Dream," "Whispers in the Dark," and "Desire" (the latter two unused), music by Holländer, lyrics by Leo Robin; editor, William Shea; costumes, Travis Banton; sound, Harry D. Mills and Don Johnson; special effects, Farciot Edouart, Harry Perry; assistant director, Lew Borzage; additional photography [European locations], Eric Locke.

Cast: Marlene Dietrich (Madeleine de Beaupré), Gary Cooper (Tom Bradley), John Halliday (Carlos Margoli), William Frawley (Mr. Gibson), Ernest Cossart (Aristide Duval), Akim Tamiroff (policeman), Alan Mowbray (Dr. Pauquet), Zeffi Tilbury (Aunt Olga), Harry Dep (clerk), Marc Lawrence (valet), Henry Antrim (chauffeur), Gaston Glass, Armand Kalia (jewelry shop employees), Albert Pollet (French policeman), George Davis (garageman), Constant Franke (border official), Robert O'Connor (customs official), Stanley Andrews (customs inspector), Rafael Blanco (hay wagon driver), Alden Chase (hotel employee), Tony Merlo (waiter), Anna Delinsky (chambermaid), Alice Feliz (Pepi), Enrique Acosta (Pedro), George MacQuarrie (clerk with gun), Isabel La Mal (nurse), Oliver Eckhardt (husband), Blanche Craig (wife), Rollo Lloyd (clerk in mayor's office), Alfonso Pedrosa (oxcart driver).

Awards: "Whispers in the Dark" was written for *Desire* but not used until 1937 in *Artists and Models,* for which it and the score by Holländer received an Academy nomination.

I LOVED A SOLDIER (or INVITATION TO HAPPINESS or HOTEL IMPERIAL), USA, [1936]

[Production dates: January 3 to February 11, 1936; never completed.]

Production company, Paramount; producer, Benjamin Glazer [and Ernst Lubitsch]; director, Henry Hathaway; screenplay, John van Druten, with rewrites by Hathaway, Grover Jones, and Lubitsch; based on the play *Hotel Stadt Lemberg* by Lajos Biro (1917) and the silent film version, *Hotel Imperial* (1927), directed by Mauritz Stiller from a screenplay by Jules Furthman and titles by Edwin Justus Mayer; sound, Harry D. Mills; assistant director, Ray Lissner.

Cast: Marlene Dietrich, Charles Boyer, Akim Tamiroff, Walter Catlett, Paul Lukas, Victor Killian, Samuel S. Hinds, Ted Oliver, Nester Aber, Siegfried ("Sig") Rumann, Lionel Stander, John Miljan, Harry Cording, Brandon Evans, Bob Kortman, Robert Middlemass, Fred Kohler, Sam Jaffe, Michael Mark.

[Never completed, *Hotel Imperial* was eventually made with Isa Miranda and Ray Milland in 1939, and remade as *Five Graves to Cairo* by Billy Wilder with Anne Baxter and Erich von Stroheim.]

THE GARDEN OF ALLAH, USA, 1936

[Production dates, April 15 to July 8, 1936; locations, California desert near Yuma, Arizona, Chatsworth; Selznick Studio interiors. Premier, November 19, 1936, Radio City Music Hall, New York.]

Production company, Selznick-International, released by United Artists; producer, David O. Selznick; director, Richard Boleslawski (uncredited retakes: William Wellman); screenplay, W. P. Lipscomb, Lynn Riggs (from an uncredited adaptation by Willis Goldbeck), based on the novel by Robert Smythe Hichins (1904); assistant to the producer, Willis Goldbeck; camera, W. Howard Green, Virgil Miller, Wilfred Cline, Robert Carney, John Waters; "photographic advisor," Harold Rosson; color production designer, Lansing C. Holden; special effects, Jack Cosgrove; makeup, Sam Kaufman; art directors: Sturges Carne, Lyle Wheeler, Edward Boyle; music, Max Steiner; editor, Hal C. Kern, Anson Stevenson; sound, Earl A. Wolcott; special effects, Jack Cosgrove; color consultant, Natalie Kalmus (Technicolor); color advisors, Denny Holden, John Sturges; costumes, Ernst Dryden, Janette Couget; production manager, Phil Ryan; unit manager, Bob Ross; assistant directors, Eric Stacey, Arthur Fellows, Bob Stillman, Jack Roberts, Chauncey Pyle; dialogue director, Joshua Logan; technical advisor, Jamiel Hasson; script clerk, Corynn Kiehl; makeup, Sam Kaufman, Jim Collins; Miss Dietrich's hairdresser, Nellie Manley.

Cast: Marlene Dietrich (Domini Enfilden), Charles Boyer (Boris Androvsky), Basil Rathbone (Count Anteoni), C. Aubrey Smith (Father Roubier), Tilly Losch (Irene, the dancer), Joseph Schildkraut (Batouch), John Carradine (sand diviner), Alan Marshall (De Trevignac), Lucile Watson (Mother Superior), Henry Brandon (Hadj), Helen Jerome Eddy (nun), Charles Waldron (the Abbé), John Bryan (Brother Gregory), Nigel de Brulier (the Lector), Pedro de Cordoba (gardener), Ferdinand Gottschalk (hotel clerk), Adrian Rosely (Mustapha), "Corky" (Bous-Bous), Robert Frazer (Smain), David Scott (Larby), Andrew McKenna (Mueddin), Bonita Granville, Marcia Mae Jones, Betty Jane Graham, Ann Gillis, (convent girls), Marian Sayers, Betty Van Auken, Edna Harris and Frances Turnham (oasis girls), Leonid Kinsky (voluble Arab), Louis Aldez (blind singer), Barry Downing (little Boris), Jane Kerr (Ouled Nails's madam), Russell Powell (Ouled Nails's proprietor), Eric Alden (Anteoni's lieutenant), Michael Mark (coachman), Harlan Briggs (American tourist), Irene Franklin (wife), Louis Mercier, Marcel de la Brosse and Robert Stevenson (De Trevignac's patrol), and [uncredited] *Maria Sieber* as a convent girl.

Awards: Academy Award, Best Color Photography; nominated for Best Musical Score.

KNIGHT WITHOUT ARMOUR, ENGLAND, 1937

[Production dates, late July to November 1936, Denham Studios, England. Premiere, September 2, 1937, Cinéma Avenue, Paris; September 20, 1937, London Pavillon, London.]

Production company, London Films, released in America by United Artists; Alexander Korda; director, Jacques Feyder; screenplay, adaptation by Frances Marion; script by Lajos Biro with "dialogue and scenario" by Arthur Wimperis, based on the novel of the same title [*Without Armour*, US title] by James Hilton (1933); camera, Harry Stradling; camera assistant, Bernard Browne; camera operator, Jack Cardiff;

settings, Lazare Meerson; assistant art director, Halfdan Waller; costumes, George Benda; editors, William Hornbeck and Francis Lyon; special effects, Ned Mann; sound, A. W. Watkins; music, Miklos Rozsa; musical director, Muir Mathieson; assistant director, Imlay Watts; dialogue director, Maxwell Wray; technical advisor, Roman Goul.

Cast: Marlene Dietrich (Alexandra), Robert Donat (Fothergill), Irene Vanburgh (Duchess), Herbert Lomas (Vladinoff, Alexandra's father), Austin Trevor (Colonel Adraxine, Alexandra's husband), Basil Gill (Axelstein), David Tree (Maronin), John Clements (Poushkoff), Frederick Culley (Stanfield), Lawrence Hanray (Forrester), Dorice Fordred (maid), Franklin Kelsey (Tomsky), Lawrence Baskomb (commissar), Hay Petrie (station master), Miles Malleson (drunken Red commissar), Alan Jeayes (White General), Lyn Harding (bargeman), Raymond Huntley (White officer), Peter Evan Thomas (General Andreyevitch), Torin Thatcher (clerk), Peter Bull (belligerent Red soldier), and Miklos Rozsa (piano player).

ANGEL, USA, 1937

[Production dates, April to June 14, 1937; Paramount studios with second-unit European locations. Premiere, November 3, 1937, Paramount Theater, New York.]

Production company, Paramount; producer/director, Ernst Lubitsch; screenplay, Samson Raphaelson [Frederick Lonsdale, uncredited], based on the play *Angyal* by Melchior Lengyel [*Engel*, Vienna, Berlin, pub. 1934], English adaptation [*Angel*, New York, 1932] by Guy Bolton and Russell Medcraft, adaptation by Worthington Minor; camera, Charles Lang; musical score, Fredrich Holländer; song, "Angel," music by Holländer, lyrics (not used) Leo Robin; musical director, Boris Morros; art direction, Hans Dreier, Robert Usher; sets, A. E. Freudeman; editor, William Shea; sound, Harry D. Mills, Louis Mesenkop; special effects, Farciot Edouart; costumes, Travis Banton; assistant director, Joseph Lefert; additional photography [Europe], Harry Perry and Eric Locke; production supervisor, John Hammell.

Cast: Marlene Dietrich (Maria Barker), Herbert Marshall (Sir Frederick Barker), Melvyn Douglas (Anthony Halton), Edward Everett Horton (Graham), Ernest Cossart (Walton), Laura Hope Crews (Grand Duchess Anna Dmitrievna), Herbert Mundin (Greenwood), Ivan Lebedeff (Prince Vladimir Gregorovitch), Dennie Moore (Emma), Lionel Page (Lord Davington), Phillis Coghlan (maid), Leonard Carey, Gerald Hamer (footmen), Eric Wilton (English chauffeur), Herbert Evans (butler), Michael S. Visaroff (Russian butler), Olaf Hytten (photographer), Gwendolyn Logan (Maria's companion), James Finlayson (second butler), George Davis, Arthur Hurni (taxi drivers), Joseph Romantini (headwaiter), Duci Kerekjarto (violinist), Suzanne Kaaren (woman at gaming table), Louise Carter (flower lady), Gine Corrado (assistant hotel manager), Major Sam Harris (man at club).

DESTRY RIDES AGAIN, USA, 1939

[Production dates, September 7, 1939, to November 2, 1939; Universal Studios and locations in Kernville, California. Premiere, November 29, 1939, Rivoli Theater, New York.]

Production company, Universal; producer, Joe Pasternak; director, George Marshall; screenplay, Felix Jackson, Henry Myers and Gertrude Purcell, based on the novel by Max Brand [Frederick Faust, 1930]; cameraman, Hal Mohr; art director, Jack Otterson, Martin Obzina; set decoration, R. A. Gausman; musical director, Charles Previn; musical score, Frank Skinner, editor; Milton Carruth; sound, Bernard B. Brown; assistant director, Vernon Keays; second unit director, Ford Beebe; sound, Bernard B. Brown, Robert Pritchard; associate producer, Islin Auster; Miss Dietrich's costumes, Vera West; songs: "Little Joe the Wrangler," "You've Got That Look," "See What the Boys in the Back Room Will Have" and "Frenchy" (sung by Lillian Yarbo), music by Friedrich Holländer, lyrics by Frank Loesser.

Cast: Marlene Dietrich (Frenchy), James Stewart (Tom Destry), Charles Winninger (Wash Dimsdale), Mischa Auer (Boris Callahan), Brian Donlevy (Kent), Irene Hervey (Janice Tyndall), Una Merkel (Lily Belle Callahan), Allen Jenkins (Bugs Watson), Warren Hymer (Gyp Watson), Billy Gilbert (Loupgerou), Samuel S. Hinds (Hiram J. Slade), Tom Fadden (Lem Claggett), Jack Carson (Jack Tyndall), Lillian Yarbo (Clara), Edmund MacDonald (Rockwell), Dickie Jones (Eli Whitney Claggett), Virginia Brissac (Sophia "Ma" Claggett), Ann Todd (Sister Claggett), Joe King (Sheriff Keogh).

SEVEN SINNERS, USA, 1940

[Production dates, August 1940. Released, November 1940.]

Production company, Universal; producer, Joe Pasternak; director, Tay Garnett; screenplay, John Meehan and Harry Tugend, based on an original story by Ladislas Fodor and Laszlo Vadnai; camera, Rudolf Maté; art direction, Jack Otterson, Martin Obzina; editor, Ted Kent; assistant director, Phillip Karlstein; Miss Dietrich's gowns, Irene; set decoration, R. A. Gausman; musical director, Charles Previn; musical score, Frank Skinner and H. J. Salter; songs: "I've Been in Love Before," "I Fall Overboard" (not used), "The Man's in the Navy," music by Fredrich Holländer, lyrics by Frank Loesser, ["I Can't Give You Anything but Love, Baby," music by Jimmy McHugh, lyrics by Dorothy Field]; sound, Bernard B. Brown, Robert Pritchard.

Cast: Marlene Dietrich (Bijou), John Wayne (Lt. Bruce Whitney), Albert Dekker (Dr. Martin), Broderick Crawford (Little Ned), Anna Lee (Dorothy Henderson), Mischa Auer (Sasha), Billy Gilbert (Tony), Richard Carle (court official), Samuel S. Hinds (Governor Henderson), Oscar Homolka (Antro), Reginald Denny (Captain Church), Vince Barnett (bartender), Herbert Rawlinson (first mate), James Craig and William Bakewell (ensigns), Antonio Moreno (Rubio), Russell Hicks (first governor), William Davidson (police chief), Willie Fung (shopkeeper).

THE FLAME OF NEW ORLEANS, USA, 1941

[Production dates, January–February, 1941, retakes in March. Premiere, April 24, 1941, Orpheum Theater, New Orleans.]

Production company, Universal; producer, Joe Pasternak; director, René Clair; screenplay, Norman Krasna [and Clair]; camera, Rudolph Maté; art direction, Jack Otterson, Martin Obzina, Russell A. Gausman; music, Frank Skinner; musical direction, Charles Previn; songs: "Sweet as the Blush of May," "Salt of the Sea," "Oh, Joyous Day" by Charles Previn and Sam Lerner; editor, Frank Gross; sound, Bernard B. Brown: costumes, René Hubert.

Cast: Marlene Dietrich (Claire Ledoux, or Ledeux), Bruce Cabot (Robert Latour), Roland Young (Charles Giraud), Mischa Auer (Zolotov), Andy Devine, Frank Jenks, Eddie Quillan (sailors), Laura Hope Crews (Auntie), Franklin Pangborn (Bellows), Theresa Harris (Clementine), Clarence Muse (Samuel), Melville Cooper (brother-in-law), Anne Revere (Giraud's sister), Bob Evans (William), Emily Fitzroy, Virginia Sale, Dorothy Adams (Giraud's cousins), Anthony Marlowe and Gitta Alpar (opera singers), with Gus Schilling, Bess Flowers, and Reed Hadley.

MANPOWER, USA, 1941

[Production dates, March 24 to May 12, 1941, retakes in June. Premiere, July 1941, Strand Theater, New York.]

Production company, Warner Bros.–First National; executive producer, Hal B. Wallis; associate producer, Mark Hellinger (replaced by Jerry Wald); director, Raoul Walsh; screenplay by Richard Macauley and Jerry Wald, based on film *Tiger Shark* directed by Howard Hawks, 1932; cameraman, Ernest Haller, Will Shurr, V. Larsen, Charles Alexander; music, Adolph Deutsch; musical director, Leo F. Forbstein; art director, Max Parker; costumes, Milo Anderson; editor, Ralph Dawson; sound, Dolph Thomas; special effects, Bryon Haskin, H. F. Koenekamp; dialogue director, Hugh Cummings; assistant directors, Russell Saunders, Alma Dwight; technical advisor, Verne Elliott; songs: "I'm in No Mood for Music Tonight" (unused) and "He Lied and I Listened," music by Fredrich Holländer, lyrics by Frank Loesser. (Uncredited songs: "Chinatown," "Limehouse Blues.")

Cast: Edward G. Robinson (Hank McHenry), *Marlene Dietrich* (Fay Duval), George Raft (Johnny Marshall), Alan Hale (Jumbo Wells), Frank McHugh (Omaha), Eve Arden (Dolly), Barton MacLane (Smiley Quinn), Ward Bond (Eddie Adams), Walter Catlett (Sidney Whipple), Joyce Compton (Scarlett), Lucia Carroll (Flo), Egon Brecher (Pop Duval, Fay's father), Cliff Clark (Cully), Joseph Crehan (Sweeney), Ben Welden (Al Hurst), Barbara Pepper (Polly), Dorothy Appleby (Wilma), Carl Harbaugh (Noisy Nash), Barbara Land (Marilyn), Isabel Withers (nurse), Faye Emerson (nurse), James Flavin (orderly), Chester Clute (clerk), Nella Walker (floor lady), Harry Holman (justice of the peace), Beal Wong (Chinese singer), Murray Alper (lineman), Dick Wessel (lineman), Jane Randolph (hat check girl), Lynn Baggett (model).

THE LADY IS WILLING, USA, 1942

[Production dates, August–October 1941. Premiere, February 17, 1942.]

Production company, Columbia/A Charles K. Feldman Group Production; producer/director, Mitchell Leisen; screenplay, James Edward Grant, Albert McCleery, based on a story by Grant; camera, Ted Tetzlaff; art direction, Lionel Banks, Rudolph Sternad; music, W. Frank Harling and M. W. Stoloff; song, "Strange Thing (And I Find Love)" by Jack King and Gordon Clifford; sound, Lodge Cunningham; editor, Eda Warren; choreography, Douglas Deane; musical conductor, Morris W. Stoloff; costumes for Miss Dietrich, Irene; hats for Miss Dietrich, John-Frederics; jewels for Miss Dietrich, Paul Flato.

Cast: Marlene Dietrich (Elizabeth Madden), Fred MacMurray (Dr. Corey McBain), Aline MacMahon (Buddy), Stanley Ridges (Kenneth Hanline), Arline Judge (Frances), Roger Clark (Victor), Marietta Canty (Mary Lou), twins David and James "X" (Baby Corey), Ruth Ford (Myrtle), Sterling Holloway (Arthur Miggle), Harvey Stephens (Dr. Golding), Harry Shannon (Detective Barnes), Elisabeth Risdon (Mrs. Cummings), Charles Lane (K. K. Miller), Murray Alper (Joey Quig), Kitty Kelly (Nellie Quig), Chester Clute (tax advisor), Robert Emmett Keane (hotel manager), Eddie Acuff (Murphy), Lorna Dunn (maid), Eugene Borden (steward), Judith Lindon (stewardess), Neil Hamilton (Charlie), Helen Ainsworth (decorator), Lou Fulton (mop man), Billy Newell (counter man), Jimmy Conlin (panhandler), Charles Halton (Dr. Jones), Romaine Callender (bald man), Ray Walker (reporter), Roy Crane (doorman), Georgia Backus and Frances Morris (nurses), Myrtle Anderson (maid), Ernie Adams (doorman), Paul Oman (violinist), Edward McWade (Boston doorman).

THE SPOILERS, USA, 1942

[Production dates, mid-January through February 1942; filmed at Lake Arrowhead and Universal Studios. Released May 8, 1942.]

Production company, Universal/Charles K. Feldman Group; producer, Frank Lloyd; associate producers, Lee Marcus, Jack Skirball; director, Ray Enright; screenplay, Lawrence Hazard, Tom Reed, based on the novel by Rex Beach (1905, theatrical version 1906); camera, Milton Krasner; art direction, Jack Otterson, John B. Goodman, R[ussell] A. Gausman, Edward R. Robinson; editor, Clarence Kolster; gowns, Vera West; assistant director, Vernon Keays; special photographic effects, John P. Fulton; dialogue director, Gene Lewis; musical director, Charles Previn; musical score, H. J. Salter; sound, Bernard B. Brown, Robert Pritchard.

Cast: Marlene Dietrich (Cherry Malotte), Randolph Scott (Alexander Mac-Namara), John Wayne (Roy Glennister), Margaret Lindsay (Helen Chester), Harry Carey (Dextry), Richard Bathelmess (Bronco Kid Farrell), George Cleveland (Banty), Samuel S. Hinds (Judge Stillman), Russell Simpson (Flapjack), William Farnum (Wheaton), Marietta Canty (Idabelle), Jack Norton (Mr. Skinner), Ray Bennett (Clark), Forrest Taylor (Bennett), Art Miles, Charles McMurphy (deputies), Charles Halton (Jonathan Struve), Bud Osborne (Marshall), Drew Demorest (Galloway), Robert W. Service (poet/himself), Irving Bacon (hotel owner), Robert McKenzie (restaurant owner), Chester Clute (Montrose), Harry Woods (mine owner), Robert Homans (ship captain), William Gould (Marshall Thompson), William Haade (deputy), Willie Fung (Chinaman), Lloyd Ingraham (Kelly), and Ray Bennett (Mark).

Awards: Academy nominated for Best Art Direction, Best Set Decoration.

PITTSBURGH, USA, 1942

[Production dates, September/October 1942. Premiere, December 11, 1942, Criterion Theatre, New York.]

Production company, Universal; producer, Charles K. Feldman; associate producer, Robert Fellows; director, Lewis Seiler; screenplay, Kenneth Gamet, Tom Reed, based on an original story by George Owen and Reed; additional dialogue, John Twist; camera, Robert de Grasse; special effects, John P. Fulton; art direction, John B. Goodman, Russell A. Gausman, Ira S. Webb; musical score, Frank Skinner, H. J. Salter; musical direction, Charles Previn; editor, Paul Landres; costumes, Vera West; assistant director, Charles Gould.

Cast: Marlene Dietrich (Josie "Hunky" Winters), Randolph Scott (Cash Evans), John Wayne (Pittsburgh Markham), Frank Craven (Doc Powers), Louise Allbritton (Shannon Prentiss), Shemp Howard (Shorty), Thomas Gomez (Joe Malneck), Ludwig Stössel (Dr. Grazlich), Samuel S. Hinds (Morgan Prentiss), Sammy Stein (Killer Kane), Paul Fix (Burnside), John Dilson (Wilson), William Haade (Johnny), Charles Coleman (butler, Mike), Nestor Paiva (Barney), Harry Cording (miner), Douglas Fowley (Frawley), Ray Walker (silent reporter), Charles Arnt (construction worker), William Gould (Burns), Harry Seymour (theater manager), Virginia Sale (Mrs. Bercovici), Wade Boteler (mine overseer), Mira McKinney (Tilda), Alphonse Martell (Carlos), Charles Sherlock (chauffeur), Bess Flowers (woman), Hobart Cavanaugh (derelict).

FOLLOW THE BOYS, USA, 1944

[Production date, 1943. Released April 1944.]

Production company, Universal; producer, Charles K. Feldman; associate producer, Albert L. Rockett; director, Eddie Sutherland; screenplay, Lou Breslow and Gertrude Purcell; camera, John P. Fulton, David Abel; choreographer and dance director, George Hale, Joe Schoenfeld; art direction, John B. Goodman, Harold H. MacArthur, Russell A. Gausman, Ira S. Webb; musical director, Leigh Harline; editor, Fred R. Reitshaus, Jr.; gowns, Vera West; sound, Bernard B. Brown, Robert Pritchard; assistant director, Howard Christie; songs: "The Bigger the Army and Navy," "I'll Get By," "Mad About Him Blues," "I'll Walk Alone," "I'll See You in My Dreams," "Beyond the Blue Horizon," "Good Night," "Furlough Fling," "Shoo Shoo, Baby," "Swing Low, Sweet Chariot," "Merriment," "Besame Mucho," "Sweet Georgia Brown," "Is You Is, or Is You Ain't My Baby?" "Tonight," "I Feel a Song Coming On," "The House I Live In," "A Better Day Is Comin'," "Andrews Sisters' Medley," "Kittens with Their Mittens Laced," "Some of These Days," Sammy Cahn and Jule Styne, Kermit Goell and Walter Donaldson, Billy Austin and Louis Jordan, Dorothy Fields and Jimmy McHugh, Sheldon Brooks, Inez James and Buddy Pepper, Phil Moore, Leo Robin with W. Franke Harling and Richard Whiting, Roy Turk and Fred Ahlert, Dick Charles and Larry Markes.

Cast: George Raft (Tony West), Vera Zorina (Gloria Vance), Charley Grapewin (Nick West), Grace McDonald (Kitty West), Charles Butterworth (Louie Fairweather), George Macready (Walter Bruce), Elizabeth Patterson (Annie), Theodore von Eltz (William Barrett), Regis Roomey (Dr. Jim Henderson), Ramsey Ames (Laura), Spooks (Junior). As themselves: Jeanette Macdonald, Orson Welles, *Marlene Dietrich*, Dinah Shore, Donald O'Connor, Peggy Ryan, W. C. Fields, The Andrews Sisters, Artur Rubinstein, Carmen Amaya and Company, Sophie Tucker, Delta Rhythm Boys, Leonard Gautier's dog act "The Bricklayers," Agustin Castellon Sabicas, Ted Lewis's Band, Freddie Slack and His Orchestra, Charles Spivak and His Orchestra, Louis Jordon and His Orchestra, Louise Beavers, Clarence Muse, Maxie Rosenbloom, Maria Montez, Susanna Foster, Louise Allbritton, Robert Paige, Alan Curtis, Lon Cheny, Jr., Gloria Jean, Andy Devine, Turhan Bey, Evelyn Ankers, Noah Beery, Jr., Gale Sondergaard, Peter Coe, Nigel Bruce, Thomas Gomez, Lois Collier, Samuel S. Hinds, Randolph Scott, Martha O'Driscoll, Elyse Knox, Philo McCullough (Hollywood Victory Committee member). Also, Mack Gray (Lt. Reynolds), Molly Lamont (secretary to Miss Hartford), John Meredith (blind soldier in Miss MacDonald's number), Ralph Gardner (patient in Miss MacDonald's number), John Estes (patient), Doris Lloyd (nurse), Charles D. Brown (Colonel Starrett), Cyril Ring (*Life* photographer), Emmett Vogan (Harkness), Addison Richards (McDermott), Frank LaRue (mailman), Tony Marsh (first officer), Stanley Andrews (Australian officer), Lane Chandler (ship's helper), Leslie Denison (reporter), Leyland Hodgson (Australian reporter), Bill Healy (ship's officer), Frank Jenks (Chick Doyle), Ralph Dunn (Loomis), Billy Benedict (Soldier Joe), Gandon Rhodes (George Grayson), Howard Hickman (Dr. Wood), Edwin Stanley (Taylor), Ray Darmour (Taylor's assistant, Eddie), Carl Vernell (choreographer Terry Dennis), Wallis Clark (Victory Committee man), Richard Crane (Marine officer), Frank Wilcox (Cpl. Williams), Jimmy Carpenter, Bernard Thomas, John Whitney, Walter Tetley, Joel Allen, Carlyle Blackwell, Charles Kind, Mel Schubert, Stephen Wayne (soldiers), Dennis Moore (HVC officer), Billy Wayne (columnist), Jack Wegman (Major), Odessa Lauren, Nancy Brinckman, Janet Shaw, Jan Wiley (telephone operators), Duke York (M.P.), George Eldredge (submarine officer), Nicodemus Stewart (Lt. Reynolds), George "Shorty" Chirello (assistant in Orson Welles's magic act), Nelson Leigh, Tony Hughes, Edwin Stanley, Janice Gay, Jane Smith, Marjorie Fectean, Doris Brenn, Rosemary Battle, Lolita Leighter, Mary Rowland, Eleanor Counts, Linda Brent, Bill Wolfe, Bobby Barber, Carey Harrison, William Forrest, Steve Brodie, Clyde

Cooke, Tom Hanlon, Bob Ashley, Lennie Smith, Don Kramer, Allan Cooke, Luis Torres, Nicholai, John Duane, Ed Browne, Clair Freeman, Bill Meader, Eddie Kover, Daisy Lee Bennett, and Baby Marie Osborne.

KISMET, USA, 1944

[Production dates, October 23 to December 31, 1943. Premiere, August 22, 1944, Astor Theatre, New York.]

Production company, Metro-Goldwyn-Mayer; producer, Everett Riskin; director, William Dieterle; screenplay, John Meehan, based on the play by Edward Knoblock [Eduard Knoblauch, 1911]; camera, Charles Rosher; art direction, Cedric Gibbons, Daniel B. Cathcart, Edwin B. Willis, Richard Pfefferle; music, Herbert Stothart; songs: "Willow in the Wind," "Tell Me, Tell Me, Evening Star," music by Harold Arlen, lyrics by E. Y. Harburg; editor, Ben Lewis; sound, Douglas Shearer; costume supervision, Irene; costume execution, Karinska; hair, Sydney Guilaroff; choreography, Jack Cole; special effects, A. Arnold Gillespie, Warren Newcombe; assistant director, Marvin Steward.

Cast: Ronald Colman (Hafiz), *Marlene Dietrich* (Jarmilla), James Craig (Caliph), Edward Arnold (Grand Vizier), F. Hugh Herbet (Feisal), Joy Ann Page (Marsinah), Florence Bates (Karsha), Harry Davenport (Agha), Hobart Cavanaugh (Moolah), Robert Warwick (Alfife), Beatrice and Evelyne Kraft (court dancers), Barry Macollum (Amu), Victor Kilian (Jehan), Charles Middleton (the miser), Harry Humphrey (gardener), Nestor Paiva (police chief), Roque Ybarra (miser's son), Eve Whitney (café maiden), Minerva Urecal (retainer), Joe Yule (attendant), Morgan Wallace (seller), John Maxwell (guard), Walter de Palma (detective), Jimmy Ames (Captain Domo), Charles La Torre (Alwah), Noble Blake (Nubian slave), Anna Demetrio (café owner), Dan Seymour (fat Turk), Carmen D'Antonion (dancer), Jessie Tai Sing, Zedra Conde, Barbara Glenz, Frances Ramsden (café girls), Charles Judels (rich salesman), Dale Van Sickel (assassin), Harry Cording, Joseph Granby (policemen), Frank Penny, Peter Cusanelli (salesmen), Zack Williams (executioner), John Merton, Eddie Abdo, Dick Botiller, Jack "Tiny" Lipson (Mansur's henchmen), Lynne Arlen, Leslie Anthony, Rosalyn Lee, Sonia Carr, Carla Boehm, Yvonne de Carlo, Eileen Herric, Shelby Payne (queen's court), Paul Singh (Caliph's servant), Eddie Abdo (Arab emissary), Pedro de Cordoba (Muezzin), Paul Bradley (magician), Louis Manley (fire-eater), Sammy Stein (policeman), John Schaller, Ramiro Rivas, William Rivas (acrobats), Cy Kendall (herald), Mitchell Lewis (Sheik), Phiroz Nair Asit Ghosh and Gabriel Gonzales.

Awards: Academy nominated, Best Color Photography, Best Art Direction, Set Decorations, Sound Recording.

MARTIN ROUMAGNAC (US release title THE ROOM UPSTAIRS, 1948), FRANCE, 1946.

[Production dates, Summer 1946, Saint-Maurice Studios, Paris. Premiere, December 1946, Paris.]

Production company, Alcina, released in the US by Lopert Films; producer, Marc Le Pelletier; director, Georges Lacombe; screenplay, Pierre Véry, from the novel by Pierre-René Wolf (1935); adaptation and dialogue; Georges Lacombe; camera, Roger Hubert; art direction, Georges Wakhevitch; music, Marcel Mirouze; sound, Le Breton.

Cast: Marlene Dietrich (Blanche Ferand), Jean Gabin (Martin Rougmagnac), Margo Lion (Jeanne, Martin's sister), Marcel Herrand (consul), Jean D'Yd (uncle), Daniel Gélin (young lover), Jean Darcante (attorney), Henry Poupon (Gargame), Marcel André (judge), Marcel Pérèz (Paulot), Camille Guerini (postman), Charles Lemontier (Bonnemain), Lucien Nat (poorhouse superintendent), with Michel Ardan, Paul Faivre, Marcelle Geniat, Rivers Cadet, and O. Barencey.

GOLDEN EARRINGS, USA, 1947

[Production dates, August 6 to October 17, 1946. Premiere, August 27, 1947.]

Production company, Paramount; producer, Harry Tugend; director, Mitchell Leisen; screenplay, Abraham Polonsky, Frank Butler, Helen Deutsch, from the novel by Yolanda Foldes [Földes Yolan] (1945); camera, Daniel L. Fapp; process, Farciot Edouart; special photographic effects, Gordon Jennings; art direction, Hans Dreier, John Meehan; set direction, Sam Comer, Grace Gregory; music, Victor Young; song: "Golden Earrings," music by Victor Young, lyrics by Jay Livingston and Ray Evans; music consultant, Phil Boutelje; orchestrations, Leo Shuken, Sidney Cutner; choreography, Billy Daniels; sound, Don McKay, Walter Oberst; editor, Alma Macrorie; costumes, Mary Kay Dodson; makeup, Wally Westmore; assistant director, Johnny Coonan; Marlene Dietrich's dialogue coach, *"Maria Manton* [Maria Sieber Goodman]."

Cast: Ray Milland (Col. Ralph Denistoun), *Marlene Dietrich* (Lydia), Murvyn Vye (Zoltan), Bruce Lester (Byrd), Dennis Hoey (Hoff), Quentin Reynolds (himself), Reinhold Schünzel (Professor Krosigk), Ivan Triesault (Major Reiman), Hermine Sterler (Greta Kosigk), Eric Feldary (Zweig), Fred Nurney (first agent), Otto Reichow (second agent), Gisela Werbiseck (dowager), Larry Simms (page boy), Haldor de Becker (telegraph boy), Gordon Richards and Vernon Downing (club members), Leslie Denison (Miggs), Tony Ellis (dispatch rider), Gwen Davies (stewardess), Robert Cory (doorman), Hans von Morhart (SS man), Henry Rowland (Pfeiffer), William Yetter, Sr., and Henry Guttman (peasants), William Yetter, Jr., and Leo Schlesinger (soldiers), Ellen Baer (girl), Louise Colombet (flower woman), Carmen Beretta (tourist), Frank Johnson (waiter), Maynard Holmes (private), Fred Giermann (sergeant), James W. Horne (soldier), Roberta Jonay (farm girl), Harry Anderson (German farmer), Caryl Lincoln (his wife), Robert Val, Gordon Arnold, Pepito Perez (gypsies), George Sorel, Hans Schumm (policemen), Martha Bamattre (fortune teller), Antonia Morales (gypsy dancer), Jack Wilson (Hitler Youth leader), Charles Bates (small boy), John Dehner (SS man), Howard Mitchell (naval officer), Arno Frey (major), John Good (SS lieutenant), Jack Worth, Walter Rode (Nazi officers), Peter Seal (police chief), John Peters (officer), Al Winters (Colonel), Great Ullmann, Catherine Savitzky (German wives).

A FOREIGN AFFAIR, USA, 1948

[Production dates, December 1947 to February 1948, studio work at Paramount in Hollywood, exteriors in Berlin. Premiere, August 20, 1948.]

Production company, Paramount; producer, Charles Brackett; director, Billy Wilder; screenplay, Charles Brackett, Billy Wilder and Richard L. Breen from a story by David Shaw, adaptation by Robert Harari; camera, Charles B. Lang, Jr.; process, Farciot Edouart, Dewey Wrigley; special effects, Gordon Jennings; art direction, Hans Drier, Walter Tyler, Sam Comer, Ross Dowd; music and musical direction, Friedrich Holländer; songs, "Black Market," "Illusions," "The Ruins of Berlin," music and lyrics by Friedrich Holländer ["Isn't It Romantic," score interpolation, music by Richard Rodgers, lyrics Lorenz Hart]; sound, Hugo Grenzback, Walter Oberst; costumes, Edith Head; editor, Doane Harrison; production manager, Hugh Brown; script supervisor, Harry Hogan; assistant cameraman, Guy Bennett; assistant directors, C. C. Coleman, Jr., and Gerd Oswald.

Cast: Jean Arthur (Congresswoman Phoebe Frost), *Marlene Dietrich* (Erika von Schlütow), John Lund (Captain John Pringle), Millard Mitchell (Col. Rufus J. Plummer), Peter von Zerneck (Hans Otto Birgel), Stanley Prager (Mike), Bill Murphy (Joe), Gordon Jones (first M.P.), Freddie Steele (second M.P.), Raymond Bond (Pennecott), Boyd Davis (Griffin), Robert Malcolm (Kraus), Bobby Watson (Hitler), Charles Meredith (Yandell), Michael Raffeto (Salvatore), James Larmore (Lt. Hornby), Damiel O'Flynn (lt. colonel), Harland Tucker (General McAndrew), George Carlton (General Finney), James Fenton (major), William Neff (Lt. Lee Thompson), Fredrich Holländer (Erika's piano player).

Awards: Academy nominations, Best Screenplay (Brackett, Wilder, Breen), Best Black and White Photography (Lang).

JIGSAW, USA, 1949

[Production dates, late 1948. Premiere, March 1949, Mayfair, New York.]

Production company, Tower Pictures (released through United Artists); producer, Edward J. Danziger, Harry Lee Danziger; director, Fletcher Markle; screenplay, Fletcher Markle, Vincent McConnor, from a story by John Roeburt; camera, Don Malkames; music, Robert W. Stringer; editor, Robert Matthews; special effects, William L. Nemeth; sound, David M. Polak; makeup, Fred Ryle; assistant director, Sal J. Scoppa, Jr.

Cast: Franchot Tone (Howard Malloy), Jean Wallace (Barbara Whitfield), Myron McCormick (Charles Riggs), Marc Lawrence (Angelo Agostini), Winnifrid Lenihan (Mrs. Hartley), Betty Harper (Caroline Riggs), Hedley Rainnie (Sigmund Kosterich), Walter Vaughn (district attorney Walker), George Breen (Knuckles),

Robert Gist (Tommy Quigley), Hester Sondergaard (Mrs. Borg), Luella Gear (pet shop owner), Alexander Campbell (Pemberton), Robert Noe (Waldron), Alexander Lockwood (Nichols), Ken Smith (Wylie), Alan Macateer (museum guard), Manuel Aparicio (department store guard), Brainard Duffield (butler), *Marlene Dietrich*, Fletcher Markle (night club guests), Henry Fonda (night club waiter), John Garfield (vagrant), Marsha Hunt (secretary), Leonard Lyons (columnist), Burgess Meredith (bartender), and Everett Sloane.

STAGE FRIGHT, ENGLAND, 1950

[Production dates, 1950, Elstree Studios, London; June 10, 1949 to September 21, 1949. Premiere, February 23, 1950, Radio City Music Hall, New York.]

Production company, Warner Bros./First National; producer, Alfred Hitchcock; director, Alfred Hitchcock; production manager, Fred Ahern; screenplay, Whitfield Cook, with additional dialogue by James Bridie; adaptation, Alma Reville, based on the novel *Man Running* [US title, *Outrun the Constable*] by Selwyn Jepson (1948); camera; Wilkie Cooper; art direction, Terence Verity; music, Leighton Lucas; musical direction, Louis Levy; songs: "La Vie en rose," music by Marguerite Monnot and "Louiguy" (Louis Guglielmi), lyrics by Edith Piaf (English lyrics by Mack David); "The Laziest Gal in Town," words and music by Cole Porter; and "Love Is Lyrical" (uncredited); editor, Edward Jarvis; sound, Harold King; costumes for Jane Wyman, Milo Anderson; costumes for Marlene Dietrich, Christian Dior; makeup, Colin Guarde.

Cast: Jane Wyman (Eve Gill), *Marlene Dietrich* (Charlotte Inwood), Michael Wilding (Inspector Wilfred Smith), Richard Todd (Jonathan Cooper), Alastair Sim (Commodore Gill), Kay Walsh (Nellie), Sybil Thorndike (Mrs. Gill), Miles Malleson (drunk), Hector MacGregor (Freddie), Joyce Grenfell (shooting gallery lady), Andre Morell (Inspector Byard), Patricia Hitchcock (Chubby), Irene Handel, Arthur Howard, Everley Gregg, Helen Goss, Cyril Chamberlain, and Alfred Hitchcock (man on street).

NO HIGHWAY (US release title, NO HIGHWAY IN THE SKY),
ENGLAND, 1951

[Production dates, December 1950 to January 1951. Premiere, August 2, 1951, Odeon, London.]

Production company, 20th Century-Fox; producer, Louis D. Lighton; director, Henry Koster; screenplay, R. C. Sherriff, Oscar Millard, and Alec Coppel from the novel by Nevil Shute (1948); camera, Georges Perinal; editor, Manuel del Campo; art director, C. P. Norman; sound, Buster Ambler; production supervisor, Robert E. Dearling; dialogue coach, George Morre O'Farrell; assistant director, Bluey Hill; Miss Dietrich's wardrobe, Christian Dior; costume advisor, Margaret Furse; casting director, Ben Lyon.

Cast: James Stewart (Mr. Honey), *Marlene Dietrich* (Monica Teasdale), Glynis Johns (Marjorie Corder), Jack Hawkins (Dennis Scott), Ronald Squire (Sir John),

Janette Scott (Elspeth Honey), Niall McGinnis (Captain Samuelson), Elizabeth Allan (Shirley Scott), Kenneth More (Dobson), David Hutcheson (Penworthy), Ben Williams (guard), Maurice Denham (Major Pease), Wilfrid Hyde-White (Fischer), Hector MacGregor (first engineer), Basil Appleby (second engineer), Michael Kingsley (navigator), Peter Murray (radio operator), Dora Bryan (Rosie).

RANCHO NOTORIOUS, USA, 1952

[Production dates, October to end of December, 1951. Premiere, May 15, 1952, Paramount Theater, New York.]

Production company, Fidelity Pictures (released through RKO); producer, Howard Welsch; director, Fritz Lang; screenplay, Daniel Taradash from a story by Sylvia Richards; camera, Hal Mohr; production manager, Ben Hersh; production designer, Wiard Ihnen; set decorator, Robert Priestley; music, Emil Newman; songs: "Gypsy Davey," "Get Away, Young Man" (sung by Marlene Dietrich), "The Legend of Chuck-a-Luck" (sung by William Lee), by Ken Darby; editor, Otto Ludwig; sound, Hugh McDowell, Mac Dalgleish; Marlene Dietrich's costumes, Don Loper; costumes, Joe King; makeup, Frank Westmore; Marlene Dietrich's hair stylist, Nellie Manley; color consultant, Richard Mueller; assistant director, Emmett Emerson.

Cast: Marlene Dietrich (Altar Keane), Arthur Kennedy (Vern Haskell), Mel Ferrer (Frenchy Fairmont), Gloria Henry (Beth), William Frawley (Baldy Gunder), Lloyd Gough (Kinch), Lisa Ferraday (Maxine), John Raven (Dealer), Jack Elam (Geary), Dan Seymour (Paul), George Reeves (Wilson), Rodric Redwing (Rio), Frank Ferguson (Preacher), Charles Gonzales (Hevia), Francis MacDonald (Harbin), John Kellogg (Factor), Stuart Randall (Starr), Roger Anderson (Red), Felipe Turich (Sanchez), José Dominguez (Gonzales), Stan Jolley (Warren), John Doucette (Whitey), Charlita (Mexican girl), Ralph Sanford (politician), Lane Chandler (Hardy), Fuzzy Knight (barber), Fred Graham (Ace Maguire), Dick Eliot (narrator), William Haade (Bullock), Russell Johnson (dealer) Dick Wessel.

AROUND THE WORLD IN 80 DAYS, USA, 1956

[Production dates, 1956. Premiere, October 17, 1956, Rivoli Theater, New York.]

Production company, Michael Todd Company (released by United Artists); producer, Michael Todd; associate producer, William Cameron Menzies; director, Michael Anderson; screenplay: S. J. Perelman, James Poe, and John Farrow, based on the novel by Jules Verne (1872); camera, Lionel London; music, Victor Young; song, "Around the World," music by Victor Young, lyrics by Harold Adamson (sung by Eddie Fisher); art direction, James Sullivan, Ken Adam; settings, Ross Dowd; costumes, Miles White; choreography, Paul Godkin; sound, Joseph Kane; editor, Paul Weatherwax, Gene Ruggiero; assistant directors, Ivan Volkman, Lew Borzage, Dennis Bertera, Farley James; second unit director, Kevin McClory; special effects, Lee Zavitz; titles, Saul Bass.

Cast: David Niven (Phileas Fogg), Cantinflas (Passepartout), Shirley MacLaine (Princess Aouda), Robert Newton (Inspector Fix), Charles Boyer (Monsieur Casse),

Joe E. Brown (stationmaster), Martine Carol (tourist), John Carradine (Colonel Proctor Stamp), Charles Coburn (writer), Ronald Colman (railroad manager), Melville Cooper (steward), Noël Coward (Roland Hesketh Baggott), Finlay Currie (whist player), Reginald Denny (police chief), Andy Devine (first officer), *Marlene Dietrich* (Barbary coast saloon owner), Luis Miguel Dominguin (bullfighter), Fernandel (coachman), Sir John Gielgud (Foster), Hermione Gingold (sporting lady), José Greco (Spanish dancer), Sir Cedric Hardwicke (General Sir Francis Gromarty), Trevor Howard (Fallentin), Glynis Johns (drinking companion of Gingold), Buster Keaton (train conductor), Evelyn Keyes (Parisian flirt), Beatrice Lillie (Salvation Army lady), Peter Lorre (steward), Edmund Lowe (ship's engineer), Victor McLaglen (helmsman), Col. Tim McCoy (cavalry commander), A. E. Mathews (Reform Club member), Mike Mazurski (man in Hong Kong), John Mills (coachman), Alan Mowbray (British consul), Robert Morley (Ralph), Edward R. Murrow (narrator, prologue), Jack Oakie (ship's captain), George Raft (bouncer), Gilbert Roland (Achmed Abdullah), Cesar Romero (waiter), Frank Sinatra (piano player), Red Skelton (drunk), Ronald Squire, Basil Sidney (Reform Club members), Harcourt Williams (servant), Ava Gardner (lady spectator).

Awards: Academy Awards, Best Picture, Best Screenplay (adapted), Best Color Photography, Editing, Musical Score. Additional Academy nominations: Director, Costumes, Art Direction.

THE MONTE CARLO STORY, USA/ITALY, 1957

[Production dates, Summer/Fall, 1956, Titanus-Studios, Rome and Monte Carlo. Premiere, June 1957.]

Production company, Titanus (released by United Artists); producer, Marcello Girosi; director, Samuel A. Taylor [Italian-language dubbing director, Guilio Macci]; screenplay, Samuel A. Taylor from a story by Girosi and Dino Risi; camera, Giuseppe Rotunno; art direction, Ferdinando Ruffo; settings, Gastone Medin; music, Renzo Rossellini; songs: "Les Jeux Sont Fait (Rien ne Va Plus)" by Michael Emer, "Back Home Again in Indiana," "*Vogliamoci tanto bene amore mio*" by Renato Rascel (not used); sound, Kurt Doubrawsky; editor, Georges White; production manager, Nino Misiano, Silvio Clementelli; Miss Dietrich's costumes, Jean Louis; wardrobe, Elio Costanzi; assistant directors, Luisa Alessandri, Roberto Montemurro, Maria Russo.

Cast: Marlene Dietrich (Maria, Marquise de Crevecoeur), Vittorio De Sica (Count Dino della Fiaba), Arthur O'Connell (Mr. Hinkley), Natalie Trundy (his daughter), Jane Rose (Mrs. Freeman), Clelia Matania (Sophia), Alberto Rabagliati (Albert), Mischa Auer (Hector), Renato Rascel (Duval), Carlo Rizzo (Henri), Truman Smith (Mr. Freeman), Mimmo Billi (Roland), Marco Tulli (François), Guido Martufi (Paul), Jean Combal (hotel manager), Vera Garretto (Caroline), Yannick Geffroy (Gabriel), Betty Philippsen (Zizi), Frank Colson (Walter), Serge Fliegers (Harry), Frank Elliott (Mr. Ewing), Gerlaine Fournier (German woman), Simone-

Marie Rose (lady in magenta), Clara Beck (American oil heiress), Betty Carter (Mrs. Ewing), and Mario Carotenuto.

TOUCH OF EVIL, USA, 1958

[Production dates, February–March 1957, Universal Studios and Venice, California. Premiere, February 1958.]

Production company, Universal; producer, Albert Zugsmith; director, Orson Welles; screenplay, Orson Welles, based on the novel *Badge of Evil* by Whit Masterson (1956) and an earlier script by Paul Monash; camera, Russell Metty; art direction, Alexander Golitzen, Robert Clatworthy; settings, Russell A. Gausman, John P. Austin; music, Henry Mancini; musical direction, Joseph Gershenson; sound, Leslie I. Carey, Frank Wilkinson; editor, Virgil W. Vogel, Aaron Stell, Edward Curtiss; costumes, Bill Thomas; assistant directors, Phil Bowles, Terry Nelson; camera assistant, John Russell; production manager, F. D. Thompson; direction of additional scenes, Harry Keller.

Cast: Orson Welles (Hank Quinlan), Charlton Heston (Ramon Miguel "Mike" Vargas), Janet Leigh (Susan Vargas), Joseph Calleia (Pete Menzies), Akim Tamiroff ("Uncle Joe" Grande), Valentin De Vargas (Pancho), Ray Collins (Adair), Dennis Weaver (motel clerk), Joanna Moore (Marcia Linnekar), Mort Mills (Schwartz), *Marlene Dietrich* (Tanya), Victor Millan (Manuelo Sanchez), Lalo Rios (Risto), Michael Sargent ("Pretty Boy"), Mercedes McCambridge (motorcycle gang leader), Joseph Cotten (coroner), Zsa Zsa Gabor (strip-club owner), Phil Harvey (Blaine), Joi Lansing (blonde), Harry Shannon (Gould), Rusty Wescoatt (Casey), Wayne Taylor, Ken Miller, Raymond Rodriguez (gang members), Arlene McQuade (Ginnie), Dominick Delgarde (Lackey), Joe Basulto (delinquent), Jennie Dias (Jackie), Yolanda Bojorquez (Bobbie), Eleanor Dorado (Lia), John Dierkes (plainclothes cop), Keenan Wynn (crowd extra).

WITNESS FOR THE PROSECUTION, USA, 1958

[Production dates, June through August 1957, Goldwyn Studios, Hollywood. Premiere, January 30, 1958, Leicester Square Theatre, London; February 1958 in USA.]

Production company, An Edward Small–Arthur Hornblow Production released by United Artists; producer, Arthur Hornblow; director, Billy Wilder; screenplay, Billy Wilder, Harry Kurnitz; adaptation, Larry Marcus, based on the play (1954) and the short story (1948) by Agatha Christie; camera, Russell Harlan; art direction, Howard Bristol; settings, Alexander Trauner; music, Matty Malneck; musical arranger, Leonid Raab; musical director, Ernest Gold; song, *"Auf der Reeperbahn,"* retitled "I May Never Go Home Anymore" by Ralph Arthur Roberts, English lyrics by Jack Brooks; editor, Daniel Mandell; sound, Fred Lau; costumes, Joseph King; Marlene Dietrich's costumes, Edith Head; makeup, Ray Sebastian, Harry Ray, and Gustaf Norin; assistant director, Emmett Emerson.

Cast: Tyrone Power (Leonard Vole), *Marlene Dietrich* (Christine Vole), Charles Laughton (Sir Wilfrid Robarts), Elsa Lanchester (Miss Plimsoll), John Williams (Brogan-Moore), Henry Daniell (Mayhew), Ian Wolfe (Carter), Una O'Connor (Janet MacKenzie), Torin Thatcher (Mr. Meyers), Francis Compton (judge), Norma Varden (Mrs. French), Philip Tonge (Inspector Herne), Ruta Lee (Diana), Molly Roden (Miss McHugh), Ottola Nesmith (Miss Johnson), Marjorie Eaton (Miss O'Brien).

Academy nominations: Best Picture, Best Director, Best Actor (Laughton), Best Supporting Actress (Lanchester); Best sound.

JUDGMENT AT NUREMBERG, USA, 1961

[Production dates, January 22 to May 1961 in Revue Studios, Universal City, with location shooting in Berlin and Nuremberg in April. Premiere, December 14, 1961, Kongreβhalle, Berlin.]

Production company, Roxlom Films; producer/director, Stanley Kramer; screenplay, Abby Mann based on his teleplay (directed by George Roy Hill, produced by Herbert Brodkin for CBS, April 16, 1959); camera, Ernest Laszlo; art direction, George Milo; music, Ernest Gold; songs: "Lili Marlene" by Norbert Schultze, Hans Leip, Thomas Connor, "Liebeslied" by Ernest Gold, Alfredy Perry; sound, James Speak; editor, Frederic Knudtson; sound editor, Walter Elliott; music editor, Art Dunham; costumes, Joe King; Miss Dietrich's costumes, Jean Louis; production designer, Rudolph Sternad; production manager, Clem Beauchamp; assistant director, Ivan Volkman; first camera assistant, Charles Wheeler; script supervisor, Marshall Schlom; makeup, Robert J. Schiffer; props, Art Cole; lighting, Don Carstensen; titles, Pacific Title; German staff, Richard Richtsfeld, L. Ostermeier, Lyn Hannes, Pia Arnold, Albrecht Hennings, Laci von Ronay, Hubert Karl, Egon Haedler, Frank Winterstein, Richard Eglseder, Hannelore Winterfeld.

Cast: Spencer Tracy (Judge Dan Haywood), Burt Lancaster (Ernst Janning), Richard Widmark (Colonel Tad Lawson), *Marlene Dietrich* (Madame Bertholt), Maximilian Schell (Hans Rolfe), Judy Garland (Irene Hoffmann), Montgomery Clift (Rudolf Petersen), William Shatner (Captain Byers), Edward Binns (Senator Burkette), Kenneth MacKenna (Judge Kenneth Norris), Werner Klemperer (Emil Hahn), Alan Baxter (General Merrin), Torben Meyer (Werner Lammpe), Ray Teal (Judge Curtis Ives), Martin Brandt (Friedrich Hofstetter), Virginia Christine (Frau Halbestadt), Ben Wright (Halbestadt), Joseph Bernard (Major Abe Radnitz), John Wengraf (Dr. Wieck), Karl Swenson (Dr. Geuter), Howard Caine (Wallner), Otto Waldis (Pohl), Olga Fabian (Mrs. Lindnow), Sheila Bromley (Mrs. Ives), Bernard Kates (Perkins), Jana Taylor (Elsa Scheffler), Paul Busch (Schmidt).

Awards: Academy Award, Maximilian Schell, Best Actor; Abby Mann, Best Screenplay. Nominations: Picture, Director, Actor (Tracy), Supporting Actor (Clift), Supporting Actress (Garland), Photography, Editing, Costumes, and Art Direction.

THE BLACK FOX, USA, 1962

[Production dates, 1962. Premiere, September 6, 1962, Venice Film Festival, Venice, Italy; official US release, December 1962.]

Production company: Arthur Steloff–Image Productions, distributed by Metro-Goldwyn-Mayer; executive producer, Jack Le Vien; producer, Louis Clyde Stoumen; director and screenplay, Louis Clyde Stoumen; production supervisor, Richard Kaplan; animation supervisor, Al Stahl; music, Ezra Laderman; editor, Kenn Collins, Mark Wortreich; narrator, *Marlene Dietrich*.

Awards: Academy Award, Best Feature-Length Documentary, 1962.

PARIS WHEN IT SIZZLES, USA, 1964

[Production dates, fall 1963. Premiere, April 1964, Trans-Lux Theater, New York.]

Production company, Paramount; producers, Richard Quine, George Axelrod; associate producers, Carter de Haven, John R. Coonan; director, Richard Quine; screenplay, George Axelrod, based on *La Fête à Henriette* by Julien Duvivier and Henri Jeanson; camera, Charles Lang, Jr.; art direction, Gabriel Bechir; settings, Jean D'Eaubonne; music, Nelson Riddle; orchestrations, Arthur Morton; sound, Jo De Bretagne, Charles Grenzbach; editor, Archie Marshek; Miss Hepburn's wardrobe, perfume, Hubert de Givenchy; Miss Dietrich's wardrobe, Christian Dior; makeup, Frank McCoy; assistant director, Paul Feyder; special camera effects, Paul K. Lerpae.

Cast: William Holden (Richard Benson), Audrey Hepburn (Gabrielle Simpson), Gregoire Aslan (police inspector), Noël Coward (Alexander Meyerheim), Raymond Bussieres (gangster), Christian Duvallex (maître d'), *Marlene Dietrich* (herself), Tony Curtis, Mel Ferrer, Fred Astaire (voice), Frank Sinatra (voice).

I WISH YOU LOVE, ENGLAND / USA, 1972 [TELEVISION]

[Production dates, late 1972, London; initial air dates BBC-England and CBS-America, January 1973.]

Produced by Alexander H. Cohen; directed by Clark Jones; orchestra conducted by Stan Freeman; lighting by Joe Davis; setting by Rouben Ter-Arutunian; costumes by Jean Louis; Dietrich sketch by René Bouché.

Cast: Marlene Dietrich

SCHÖNER GIGOLO, ARMER GIGOLO / JUST A GIGOLO, WEST GERMANY, 1978

[Production dates, 1977–78, West Berlin, Paris; Premiere: November 16, 1978, Gloria-Palast, West Berlin.]

Production company, Leguan, Berlin; producer, Rolf Thiele; director, David Hemmings [retakes by Charlotte Läufer]; screenplay, Joshua Sinclair [and Ennio de

Concini]; camera, Charly Steinberger; camera assistant, Gernot Köhler; production designer, Lutz Winter; art director, Peter Rothe; music, Günther Fischer; songs: "Just a Gigolo," music by Leonello Casucci, lyrics Julius Brammer, English lyrics Irving Caesar (1929); "I Kiss Your Hand, Madame (*Ich küsse ihre Hand, Madame*)," music by Ralph Erwin, lyrics by Fritz Rotter (English lyrics William Blackman, Sam Lewis, 1928–1929); "Jonny," music and lyrics by Friedrich Holländer [1920]; "Don't Let It Be Too Long," music by Günther Fischer, lyrics by David Hemmings (1978); "Revolutionary Song" by David Bowie and Jack Fishman (1978); sound, Günter Kortwich; editor, Alfred Sirp; choreography, Herbert F. Schubert; costumes, Ingrid Zore, Max Mago; makeup, Anthony Clavet, Ingrid Thier, Alfred Rasche, Karin Bauer; production manager, Axel Bär; props, Mario Stock, Wolfgang Kallnischkies; head electrician, Rudi Hartl; special effects, Erwin Lange; assistant director, Eva-Maria Schönecker; producer's assistant, Ingrid Windisch.

Cast: David Bowie (Paul), Sydne Rome (Cilly), Kim Novak (Helga), David Hemmings (Hermann), Maria Schell (Paul's mother), Curd Jürgens (Prince), *Marlene Dietrich* (Baroness von Semering), Erika Pluhar (Eva), Rudolf Schündler (Gustav), Hilde Weissner (Aunt Hilda), Werner Pochath (Otto), Bela Erny (von Lipzig), Friedhelm Lehmann (von Müller), Rainer Hunold (Lothar), Evelyn Künneke (Frau Aeckerle), Karin Hardt (Frau Üxkull), Gudrun Genest (Frau von Putzdorf), Ursule Heyer (Greta), Christiane Maybach (Gilda), Martin Hirthe (director), Reinhard Kolldehoff (agent), Günter Meisner (drunken worker), Peter Schlesinger (man in bath), Raymond Bernhard (the Baroness's pianist).

MARLENE: A FEATURE, WEST GERMANY, 1984

[Production dates, 1982–1983, Paris interviews (MD/MS), September 1982. Premiere, Feburary 26, 1984, West Berlin; USA, New York Film Festival, September 1986.]

Production company, Oko-Film, West Germany (USA, Alive Films); producer, Karel Dirka (America, Zev Braun); director, Maximilian Schell; screenplay, Meir Dohnal, Maximilian Schell; camera, Ivan Slapeta; editors, Heidi Genee, Dagmar Hirtz; costumes, Heinz Eickmeier; sound, Norbert Lill; makeup, Regine Kusterer; production manager, Peter Genee.

Cast: **Marlene Dietrich**, Maximilian Schell, Karel Dirka, Bernard Hall, Anni Albers, Heidi Genee, Dagmar Hirtz.

Awards: New York Film Critics, National Society of Film Critics, National Board of Review. Nominated for Academy Award.

THE DIETRICH SONGS: A SCRAPBOOK FILM, FRANCE, 1990

Producer, Jim Haynes; director, Jack Henry Moore; music director, Michael Hoenig; script by Jack Henry Moore and Roxy Holman. [At this writing commercially unreleased, the film is available only for noncommercial distribution.]

APPENDIX C
DISCOGRAPHY

T he following list of Marlene Dietrich's recordings is comprehensive without attempting to include pirated recordings made from sound tracks, radio programs, or those "stolen" during live performance. For the curious or truly avid a few such recordings are listed as "miscellany" at the end of the appendix.

The listings are by date of recording rather than release. Mostly, though not all, of the recordings Dietrich made are currently available to satisfy the needs of the lively nostalgia market. A number of titles are available that were never before released, their current availability the triumph of market judgment over aesthetics. Some items are now available that were never meant for the commercial market and have only curio value, mostly for the die-hard collector.

No attempt has been made to catalogue every currently available recording, as the proliferation of compilation albums in different countries (not all of them legal) makes such a listing temporary at best and more confusing than useful. Record or label numbers are those of the original recordings in country of origin.

A caveat: in almost all cases original vinyl recordings (if they can still be found) are of superior sound quality to the compact-disk reissues, which are often over-mastered or, conversely, not remastered at all in spite of what is advertised. Dietrich's "Café de Paris" recording of 1954, for instance, is vastly superior to the currently available compact disk. This is generally true of the CD reissues, whatever their value might be as documents.

1,2. Two-sided potpourri from *Es Liegt in der Luft* (*It's in the Air*), (Mischa Spoliansky, Marcellus Schiffer). June 1928. Two sides: Electrola EH-146. With Marlene Dietrich, Käte Lenz, Margo Lion, Ida Wüst, Oskar Karlweis, Otto Wallburg, Hubert von Meyerinck. A medley of songs from the hit revue, featuring the composer at the piano and the theater orchestra. Dietrich can be heard in several songs, most distinctively in her duet "Kleptomanen" ("Kleptomaniacs") which she sings with Meyerinck.

3. "*Wenn die beste Freundin*" ("My Best Girl Friend") (Spoliansky, Schiffer). June 1928. Electrola EG-892. Duet by Marlene Dietrich and Margo Lion, joined by Oskar Karlweis; Mischa Spoliansky on piano.

4. "Falling in Love Again" (Holländer, Connelly, Sam Winston) from *The Blue Angel*. January 1930. His Master's Voice B 3524 (Victor 22592). Dietrich's first recording of her most famous song was in English and was released in America before the film.

5. "*Nimm dich in archt vor blonden Frau'n*" (Holländer, Rillo) from *The Blue Angel*. January 1930. Electrola EG-1170.

6. "Blonde Women" (Holländer, Connelly), (English version of no. 5). January 1930. HMV B 3524.

7. "*Ich bin die fesche Lola*" (Holländer, Liebmann). February 1930. Electrola EG 1802.

8. "*Kinder, heut' abend such' ich mir was aus*" (Holländer, Liebmann). February 1930 [See no. 7].

8a. "This Evening Children," English language version of no. 8 was recorded as 7 EG 8275, and not released until 1958.

9. "*Ich bin von Kopf bis Fuβ* auf Liebe eingestellt" (Holländer). February 1930. Electrola EG 1770.

10. "*Wenn ich mir was wünschen dürfte*" (Holländer). February 1930. Electrola 2265.

11. "Peter" (Rudolf Nelson, Holländer). March 1931. Polydor 522751.

12. "Jonny" (Holländer). March 1931. Polydor 522751.

12a. Same as no. 12, but with bridge sung instead of instrumental. Clearly a discarded take, this cut was released on CD in 1990 on Pro Arte Digital CDD 517.

13. "*Leben ohne Liebe kannst du nicht*" (Spoliansky, Robert Gilbert). March 1931. Electrola EG 2285.

14. "*Quand l'amour meurt*" (Crémieux, Millandy; English lyric by Leo Robin). March 1931. Electrola EG 2775.

15. "'Give Me the Man" (Karl Hajos, Leo Robin). March 1931. See no. 14. [Written for *Morocco*, not used in full form.]

16. *"Assez"* (Wall-Berg, Stern, Jean Tranchant), accompanied by Peter Kreuder and the Wall-Berg Orchestra. Paris. July 1933. Polydor 530000, Decca M. 452.

17. *"Moi, je m'ennuie"* (Wall-Berg, Stern, Franqis). See no. 16.

18. *"Ja, so bin ich"* (Robert Stolz, Walter Reisch). Paris, July 1933. Polydor 524182.

19. *"Allein in einer großen Stadt"* (Wachsmann, Kolpe [Colpet]). Paris, July 1933. Polydor 530001.

20. *"Mein blondes Baby"* (Peter Kreuder, Rotter). See no. 19.

21. *"Wo ist der Mann?"* (Kreuder, Kolpe). Paris, July 1933. Polydor 47199.

[NOTE: No. 12 and nos. 16–21 were reissued as long-play album *Marlene Dietrich Sings* by VOX PL 3040, 1950.]

22. "'(If It Isn't Pain) Then It Isn't Love" (Ralph Rainger, Leo Robin). Los Angeles, 1934. Decca B-1972-A. Special *Devil Is a Woman* issue, though the song was cut from the picture.

23. "Three Sweethearts Have I" (Rainger, Robin). See no. 22.

24. "I've Been in Love Before" (Holländer, Frank Loesser), accompanied by Victor Young and his Orchestra. Los Angeles, 1939. Decca 23139.

25. "You Do Something to Me" (Cole Porter). See no. 24.

26. "You've Got That Look" (Holländer, Loesser). See no. 24. Decca 23140.

27. "You Go to My Head" (Coots, Gillespie). See no. 26.

28. "Falling in Love Again" (Holländer, Winston). See no. 24. Decca 23141.

29. "The Boys in the Back Room" (Holländer, Loesser). See no. 28

30. "The Boys in the Back Room" (Holländer, Loesser, additional lyrics unknown). Los Angeles, October 1941. Issued in 1990 on Pro Arte CDD 517. Parody version private recording made as a salute to director Mitchell Leisen for the end of shooting party on *The Lady Is Willing*. Not meant for commercial release.

31. "Lili Marlene" (Schultze, Leip, Dietrich). New York, September 1945. Decca 23456. Sung in English.

32. "Symphonie" (Alstone, Tabet, Bernstein). See no. 31. Sung in French.

[NOTE: Nos. 24–29 and 31–32 were issued as long-play album *Marlene Dietrich Souvenir Album* by Decca DL 5100, 1949.]

33. "Illusions" (Holländer). New York, January 1949. Decca 24582.

34. "Black Market" (Holländer). See no. 33.

[NOTE: Nos. 35–42 below were issued as Columbia album *Marlene Dietrich Overseas* LP CL 105 in the original 10-inch version. Columbia added numbers 43–46 to the 12-inch reissue called *Lili Marlene* CL 1275.]

35. "The Surrey with the Fringe on Top" (Richard Rodgers, Oscar Hammerstein II). New York, November 1951. Columbia 47215. Sung in German.

36. "Annie Doesn't Live Here Any More" (Victor Young, Johnny Burke, Jack Spina). See no. 35. Columbia 47216.

37. "Lili Marlene" (Schultze, Leip) See no. 35. Columbia 47217.

38. "Taking a Chance on Love" (Vernon Duke, John Latouche, Ted Fetter). See no. 35. Columbia 47218.

39. "I Couldn't Sleep a Wink Last Night" (Adamson and McHugh). See no. 35. Columbia 47219.

40. "Mean to Me" (Turk, Ahlert). See no. 35. Columbia 47220.

41. "Time on My Hands" (Vincent Youmans, Harold Adamson, Mack Gordon). See no. 35. Columbia 47221.

42. "Miss Otis Regrets" (Cole Porter). See no. 35. Columbia 47222.

43. "*Muß i' denn*" (traditional). New York, December 1951. Columbia 1275.

44. "*Du hast die Seele mein*" (traditional). See no. 43.

45. "*Das Hobellied*" (Ferdinand Raimund, Kreutzer). See no. 43.

46. "*Du, du liegst mir im Herzen*" (traditional). See no. 43.

47. "*La Vie en rose*" (Marguerite Monot, Louiguy [Louis Gulielmi], Edith Piaf). New York, February 1952. Never released.

48. "No Love, No Nothin' " (Harry Warren, Leo Robin). See no. 47.

49. "Something I Dreamed Last Night." See no. 47.

50. "Let's Call It a Day" (De Sylva, Brown, Henderson). See no. 47.

51. "Too Old to Cut the Mustard" (Max Showalter, Ross Bagdasarian). Duet with Rosemary Clooney. New York, April 1952. Columbia 39812.

52. "Good for Nothin' " (William Engevick, Alec Wilder). See no. 51. Columbia 47455.

53. "Love Me" with Jimmy Carroll Orchestra. New York, May 1952. Columbia 39797.

54. "Come Rain or Come Shine" (Harold Arlen, Johnny Mercer). See no. 53. Columbia 47449.

55. "A Guy Who Takes His Time" (Ralph Rainger). See no. 53. Not issued until 1991 on Sony MDK 47254.

56. "Time for Love" (Alec Wilder, William Engvick). With the Jimmy Carroll Orchestra. New York, January 1953. Columbia 39959.

57. "Look Me Over Closely" (Terry Gilkyson, Mitch Miller). See no. 56. Columbia 48841.

58. "Dot's Nice—Donna Fight" (Showalter, Bagdasarian). Duet with Rosemary Clooney, Jimmy Carroll Orchestra. February 1953. Columbia 39980.

59. "It's the Same" (Robert Wright, George Forrest). See no. 58. Columbia 48867.

[NOTE: Nos. 51, 52, 58, 59 above were later issued by Columbia as a 45 RPM "extended play" album called *Rosie and Marlene*.]

60. "Besides—He's a Man." Duet with Rosemary Clooney. See no. 58. England: Philips. PB 314. Never released in America.

61. "By Land, Sea, and Air." See no. 60.

62. "Baubles, Bangles, and Beads" (Borodin, Wright & Forrest). June 10, 1954. See no. 55. Unreleased until 1991.

63. "Falling in Love Again" (Holländer), see no. 62. Not released.

64. "Lili Marlene." See no. 62. Not released.

65. "*Ich hab' noch einen Koffer in Berlin*" (Siegel, Pinelli). See no. 62. Columbia 40497. From the film *I Am a Camera*.

66. "Peter" (Nelson). See no. 65.

[NOTE: Nos. 67 through 78 below were issued by Columbia as a 12-inch LP in a double-jacketed edition, initial copies of which were scented with Arpège, called *Marlene Dietrich at the Café de Paris*. Columbia ML 4975.

In England a 10-inch Philips version omitted no. 70 ("Lazy Afternoon") and no. 74 ("No Love, No Nothin' "), but included no. 79 ("Go 'Way from My Window"), omitted from the American album.

The currently available CD on Sony MDK 47254 is slightly different from the original LP, omitting no. 73 (*"Frag nicht warum ich gehe"*), and is of lamentably inferior sound quality to the original vinyl version. This CD reissue seems to have been made from the original tapes, in which spoken song introductions (especially to "Lili Marlene") are variants.]

67. "Introduction by Noël Coward" (Coward). London, June 21, 1954. Columbia ML 4975.

68. *"La Vie en rose."* See no. 67.

69. "The Boys in the Back Room." See no. 67.

70. "Lazy Afternoon" (Jerome Moross, John Latouche). See no. 67.

71. "Lola" (English). See no. 67.

72. "Look Me Over Closely." See no. 67.

73. *"Das Lied ist aus"* (*"Frag nicht warum ich gehe"*) (Robert Stolz, Walter Reisch). See no. 67.

74. "No Love, No Nothin' " (Harry Warren, Leo Robin). See no. 6.

75. "The Laziest Gal in Town" (Cole Porter). See no. 67.

76. "Jonny." See no. 67.

77. "Lili Marlene." See no. 67.

78. "Falling in Love Again." See no. 67.

79. "Go 'Way from My Window" (John Jacob Niles). See no. 67, issued on Philips LP BO 7684R.

80. "I Am a Camera" with the Wally Stoot Orchestra. London, July 1954. Philips PB472.

81. *"Das zerbrochene Ringlein"* with the Jimmy Carroll Orchestra. New York, July 1954. Never issued.

82. "True Love" (Cole Porter). See no. 81.

83. *"Du, du liegst mir im Herzen."* See no. 81.

84. *"Aus der Jugendzeit."* See no. 81.

85. *"Alle Tage ist kein Sonntag."* See no. 81.

86. "Near You" (Craig, Goehl). Burt Bacharach, conductor and arranger. New York, 1957. Dot 15645.

87. "Another Spring, Another Love" (Shayne, Paris). See no. 86.

88. "I May Never Go Home Anymore" (Roberts, Brooks). See no. 86, Dot 15723.

89. "Kisses Sweeter Than Wine" (Newman, Campbell). See no. 88.

[NOTE: Nos. 90–100 make up Columbia WS 316 *Dietrich in Rio.*]

90. "Look Me Over Closely." Arranger and conductor, Burt Bacharach. Rio de Janeiro, July 1959. Columbia WS 316.

91. "You're the Cream in My Coffee" (De Sylva, Brown, Henderson). See no. 90.

92. "The Boys in the Back Room." See no. 90.

93. *"Das Lied ist aus."* See no. 90.

94. *"Je tire ma révérence"* (P. Bastia). See no. 90.

95. "Well, All Right!" (Calhoun, McCoy, Singleton, Wexler, Ertegun). See no. 90.

96. "Makin' Whoopee" (Kahn, Donaldson). See no. 90.

97. "One for My Baby" (Harold Arlen, Johnny Mercer). See no. 90.

98. "I've Grown Accustomed to Her Face" (Frederick Loewe, Alan Jay Lerner). See no. 90.

99. "I Will Come Back" (G. Giltnan, K. Vannah). See no. 90.

100. *"Luar de Sertao"* (Catullo de Paixao Cearense). See no. 90.

[NOTE: Nos 101–112 comprise the album *Wiedersehen mit Marlene*, recorded during Dietrich's concert tour in Germany in 1960. Most of the songs were recorded in Cologne and Munich. The American album on Capitol T10282 and the English album on Electrola E 83 220 are concert albums. The American album omits no. 111 (*"Sag mir wo die Blumen sind"*) and no. 114 (*"Kinder . . ."*). An East German pressing on Amiga 8-40-030 omits the applause between numbers, destroying any sense of concert. It, like the American album, omits no. 111.

101. *"Ich bin von Kopf bis Fuß . . ."* Arranged and conducted by Burt Bacharach. Germany, May 1960. See NOTE following no. 100.

102. *"Ich bin die Fesche Lola."* See NOTE following no. 100.

103. *"Wer wird denn weinen?"* (Hugo Hirsch, Arthur Rebner). See NOTE following no. 100.

104. *"Mein blondes Baby."* See NOTE following no. 100.

105. *"Peter."* See NOTE following no. 100.

106. *"Allein in einer großen Stadt."* See NOTE following no. 100.

107. *"Wenn ich mir was wünschen dürfte."* See NOTE following no. 100.

108. *"Jonny."* See NOTE following no. 100.

109. *"Marie-Marie"* (Gilbert Bécaud, Delanoe; German by Max Colpet). See NOTE following no. 100.

110. *"Lili Marlene."* See NOTE following no. 100.

111. *"Sag mir wo die Blumen sing"* (Pete Seeger's "Where Have All the Flowers Gone," German by Max Colpet and Marlene Dietrich). See NOTE following no. 100.

112. *"Ich weiß nicht, zum wem ich gehöre"* (Holländer, Liebmann). See NOTE following no. 100.

113. *"Ich hab' noch einen Koffer in Berlin."* See NOTE following no. 100.

114. *"Kinder heut' abend . . ."* See NOTE following no. 100.

115. "Marie-Marie (Bécaud, Delanoe). Burt Bacharach and orchestra. Paris, May 1962. Pathé EGF597.

116. *"Déjeuner du Matin"* (Joseph Kosma, Jacques Prévert). See no. 115.

117. *"Qui peut dire ou vont les fleurs?"* (Seeger; French by Lemarque, Rouzaud). See no. 115, Columbia C83469.

118. *"Cherchez la rose"* (Salvador). See no. 115.

119. *"Die Welt war jung"* (Philippe Gérard, Vannier, German by Max Colpet). Electrola E 22180.

120. *"Sag mir wo die Blumen sind."* See no. 119.

[NOTE: Nos. 121–132 were released as *Die neue Marlene: Marlene Dietrich Sings in German* on Electrola 83788 and by Capitol in America. Arrangements by various arrangers, recorded 1964.]

121. *"Wenn die Soldaten"* (traditional; arr. Pronk). See NOTE following no. 120.

122. *"Die Antwort weiß ganz allein der Wind"* ("Blowin' in the Wind," Bob Dylan; German by Hans Bradtke; arr. Bacharach). See NOTE following no. 120.

123. *"In den Kasernen"* (Gérard, Koch). See NOTE following No. 120.

124. *"Und wenn er wiederkommt"* (Gérard, Maurice Maeterlinck, Max Colpet). See NOTE following no. 120.

125. *"Sag mir wo die Blumen sind"* (Seeger; Germany by Max Colpet, Marlene Dietrich). See NOTE following no. 120.

126. *"Auf der Mundharmonika"* (Mischa Spoliansky, Robert Gilbert; arr. Stott).

127. *"Der Trommelmann"* ("The Little Drummer Boy") (Simeone, Onorati, Davis, Buschor). See NOTE following no. 120.

128. *"Wenn der Sommer wieder einzieht"* ("A Little on the Lonely Side") (Cavanaugh, Weldon, Robertson, Metzl). See NOTE following no. 120.

129. *"Ich werde Dich lieben"* ("Theme for Young Lovers") (Welch, Dietrich). See no. 126.

130. *"Paff, der Zauberdrachen"* ("Puff the Magic Dragon") (Peter Yarrow, Leonard Lipton; German by Oldörp). See no. 123.

131. *"Sch-, kleines Baby . . ."* ("Hush Little Baby") (Siegel, Costa, Dietrich). See no. 126.

132. *"Mutter, hast du mir vergeben?"* (Niemen, Grau, Dietrich). See no. 126.

133. *"Kleine, treue Nachtigall"* ("Message to Michael") (Bacharach, Colpet). Paris, 1964. Barclay 60394.

134. *"Bitte geh nicht fort"* (Jacques Brel; German by Colpet). See no. 133.

[NOTE: Nos. 135–147 were issued by Columbia as *Marlene Dietrich in London Live at the Queen's Theatre* as album OS 2830, excluding no. 143, which was never released.]

135. "I Can't Give You Anything But Love, Baby" (Jimmy McHugh, Dorothy Fields). Arranged and conducted by Burt Bacharach. November 1964. Columbia OS 2830.

136. "The Laziest Gal in Town." See no. 135.

137. *"Shir Hatan"* (Hebrew) (Sahar). See no. 135.

138. *"La Vie en rose."* See no. 135.

139. "Jonny." See no. 135.

140. "Go 'Way from my Window." See no. 135.

141. *"Allein in einer großen Stadt."* See no. 135.

142. "Lili Marlene." See no. 135.

143. "Mona Lisa" (Evans, Livingston, and Young). See no. 135. Never released.

144. "Lola." See no. 135.

145. "I Wish You Love" ("*Que reste-t-il de nos amours?*") (Charles Trenet). See no. 135.

146. "Honeysuckle Rose" (Fats Waller, Andy Razaf). See no. 135.

147. "Falling in Love Again." See no. 135.

[NOTE: Nos. 148–164 comprise *Marlene singt Berlin, Berlin* (*Marlene Dietrich's Berlin* in America and England), recorded in Berlin in 1965. Orchestrations and accompaniment by Bert Grund, record produced by Max Colpet. Polydor 238 102. Dietrich told Maximilian Schell this was her favorite and best album.]

148. "*Solang noch Untern Linden*" (Walter Kollo). Conducted by Bert Grund, January 1965. Polydor 238 102.

149. "*Du hast ja keine Ahnung, wie schön du bist, Berlin*" (Jean Gilbert). See no. 148.

150. "*Durch Berlin fließt immer noch die Spree*" (Jean Gilbert, Robert Gilbert). See no. 148.

151. "*Mit dir, mit dir, da möcht ich sonntags angeln geh'n*" (Kollo, Hermann Haller, Willi Wolff, Rideamus). See no. 148.

152. "*Nach meine Beene ist ja ganz Berlin verrückt*" (Walter Kollo, F. W. Hardt). See no. 148.

153. "*Ja, das haben die Mädchen so gerne*" (Jean Gilbert). See no. 148.

154. "*Wenn ein Mädel einen Herrn hat*" (Walter Kollo). See no. 148.

155. "*Lieber Leierkastenmann*" (Willi Kollo). See no. 148.

156. "*Das war in Schöneberg*" (Walter Kollo, Rudolf Bernauer, Rudolph Schanzer). See no. 148.

157. "*Untern Linden, untern Linden*" (Kollo Bernauer, Schanzer). See no. 148.

158. "*Das Zillelied*" (Willi Kollo). See no. 148.

159. "*Wenn du einmal eine Braut hast*" (Hugo Hirsch, Max Heye, E. Urban). See no. 148.

160. "*Es gibt im Leben manches Mal Momente*" (Walter Bromme, Will Steinberg, Robert Gilbert). See no. 148.

161. "*Wo hast du nur die schönen blauen Augen her?*" (Ralph Erwin, Robert Katscher). See no. 148.

162. "Berlin, Berlin" (Willi Kollo). See no. 148.

163. "*Solang noch Untern Linden*" (Walter Kollo). See no. 148.

164. "*Berlin bleibt doch Berlin.*" See no. 148.

165. "*Ich hab' noch einen Koffer in Berlin.*" See no. 148. Not released.

166. "*Für alles kommt die Zeit*" ("Turn, Turn, Turn"; arr. Bacharach). Paris. Barclay 45 10278 AU.

167. "*Bitte geh nicht fort*" (Jacques Brel, German by Max Colpet). See no. 166.

168. "If He Swing by the String" (John Addison, Moore). London, 1965. Kapp HLR 9883.

169. "Such Trying Times" (Addison, Moore). See no. 168.

170. "Where Have All the Flowers Gone?" (Seeger; arr. Bacharach). London, 1965. Capitol 72474.

171. "Blowin' in the Wind" (Dylan). See no. 170.

172. "Candles Glowing" (Bader, Harrison). Decca 45 32076.

173. "This World of Ours" (Debout, Colpet). See no. 171.

174. "*Glocken läuten.*" 1966. Philips 45 346024 BF.

175. "*Still war die Nacht*" ("*Cette nuit là*") (J. J. Debout, Max Colpet). See no. 174.

176. "Just a Gigolo" (Casucci, Julius Brammer, English by Irving Caesar). 1978. Columbia DB 9050.

177. "Illusions" (Holländer), verse spoken in English, on *Hermine: Udo Lindenberg singt Lieder von 1929 bis 1988.* 1988. Polydor.

178. "*Wenn ich mir was wünschen dürfte*" (Holländer), verse spoken in German: See no. 176.

MISCELLANY

For Dietrich's Broadway one-woman show at the Lunt-Fontanne Theater in New York, a special disk was pressed and printed for sale as part of the souvenir booklet. It included:

a) "Where Have All the Flowers Gone?"
b) "Go 'Way from My Window"
Both bore the label Columbia 45 4-44326.

Two compilations records that seem to be taken off the air or from soundtracks have material not available through conventional commercial outlets. They are:

1) *M.D. Live* from Wildebeest-Maclon Records, LP #5290, Kazze Junction, Kentucky. This album includes all three songs from *Blonde Venus* ("Hot Voodoo," "You Little So-and-so," and "I Couldn't Be Annoyed") as well as "Awake in a Dream" from *Desire* and several other songs not available elsewhere;

2) *Ann Sheridan and Marlene Dietrich* from Marsher Records in Canada, LP no. 201. This very poor quality recording includes "Sweet as the Blush of May" from *Flame of New Orleans* as well as the Holländer songs from A *Foreign Affair* and the two songs from *Morocco.*

Dietrich performances on radio are sometimes available in out-of-the-way record shops, including her performance with Clark Gable in "The Legionaire and the Lady," the radio adaptation of *Morocco* which initiated the Lux Radio Theatre in Hollywood in 1936. Also available on an off-label is a curiosity: Dietrich playing the Garbo role in *Grand Hotel* opposite Warren Williams. Various other radio shows have found their way onto disk or cassette, including the entire ABC radio series *Café Istanbul,* but these are of dubious copyright. It may well be, however, that collectors provide as much—or more—preservation service of such performances than any official agencies.

ACKNOWLEDGMENTS

The author is deeply grateful to the many people who have contributed to this work. It could not have been written without the time, wisdom, and welcome extended with such friendly patience. A personal sadness is that many whose insights and kindness were so valuable did not live to read the pages they helped inform. I have avoided the awkward "the late" when naming them, because they do not feel anything but present to me and because I hope some of their personal and professional grace lingers in or between the lines. I have also respected the wishes for anonymity of those who requested it; my debt to them is often as great as to those who are named.

Several I can no longer thank cast a sustaining light on every moment of the research and writing of this book: Josef von Sternberg, Arthur Knight, and Arthur and Lilli Mayer. The first was a great artist, more generous than he knew. Arthur Knight was mentor, friend, and exemplar in ways no words can fully repay. It was he who led me to my subject when I was his graduate assistant at the University of Southern California Film School. There, too, I met Arthur and Lilli Mayer, who allowed me to think of myself as their "adoptive grandson." I did and do, and not a day goes by that is not richer for my having known them. All four share my gratitude with those named on the dedication page, as do my father and mother, who so admired the subject of this book and did not live to see its completion.

I am very grateful to be able to thank:

Mischa Allen, Peter Baxter, Olive Behrendt, Davina Crawford (Belling), William Blezard, Curt Bois, Kevin Brownlow, Scott Busby, James Card, Milton Chwasky, Max Colpet, David Craig, Raymond Daum, Homer Dickens, Clive Donner, William K. Everson, Douglas Fairbanks, Jr., Mr. And Mrs. Rudi Fehr, Dr. and Mrs. Hans Feld, Hasso and Shirley Felsing, Leatrice Gilbert Joy Fountain, Stan Freeman, Otto Friedrich, Sarah Giles, Dean Goodman, Lee Goodman, Dolly Haas, Bernard Hall, Donald Hall, John Hargreaves, Kitty Carlisle Hart, Stephen Harvey, Jim Haynes, Berndt Heller, David Hemmings, Jan-Christopher Horak, Camilla Horn, Dr. and Mrs. Arnold Horwell, and Jean Howard.

Thanks also to Edward Jablonsky, Felix Jackson, Manuela Kasper, Steve Kenis, William Kenly, Arthur Kennedy, James Kirkwood, John Kobal, Stanley Kramer, Frau Gertrud Kröger, Gavin Lambert, Robert Lantz, Brigitta Lieberson, Jean Louis, John Lund, Christa Maerker, Robert Macmillan, Rouben Mamoulian, Roddy McDowall, Mitch Miller, Manuel Moses, Eva and Herbert Nelson, Gerd Oswald, Barry Paris, Robert Paterson, Kai-Stefan Pieck, Rudi Polt, Mr. and Mrs. John Pommer, George Pratt, Robert Raymond, Gottfried and Sylvia Reinhardt, Mrs. Walter Reisch, Betsy Blair (Reisz), Wolfgang E. von Richthofen, Jocelyn Rickerts, Hans Sahl, Maximilian Schell, Volker Schlöndorff, Dr. Cornelius Schnauber, Janette Scott, Irene Mayer Selznick, Hans-Jürgen Sembach, Charles Silver, Ginette Spanier, Nicholas von Sternberg, Samuel A. and Suzanne Taylor, Kevin Thomas, David Thomson, Richard Todd, John Willett, and Fred Zinnemann.

Thanks, too, to Burt Bacharach and Carolyn G. Heilbrun for correspondence that came at critical points in my research. The friendly encouragement of Leo Lerman was as valuable as his advice was wise and graceful. Alexander Walker was a generous and witty counselor. These pages could not have been written without the friendship and generosity of Werner Sudendorf.

The following organizations provided invaluable help with research and I gratefully acknowledge my debt to them and to the individuals there who were so patient and helpful:

Austrian Theater Collection, National Library (Herr Greisenegger), Austrian Film Archive (Herr Pflugl), Austrian Film Museum (Herr Kronwecker), all in Vienna; the Bauhaus-Archiv, Museum für Gestaltung (Frau Bremer), Berlin; Berlin (West) *Polizei Präsidium* and officers; the staff of the British Film Institute Library and Projection Services, London; Christie's (International) S.A., Geneva; Columbia University, Oral History Collection, Butler Library: Rare Books and Manuscripts Room, New York; Council of Fashion Designers of America (Robert Raymond), New York; Czechoslovakian Film Institute and Archive, Prague (especially Eva Kačerova); Det Danske Filmmuseum (Ib Monty and Uffe Lomholt Madsen), Copenhagen; Deutsches Institut für Filmkunde, (Frau Micky Glässge, Eberhard Spiess), Frankfurt-am-Main; Deutsches Institut für Filmkunde (Frau Dorothea Gebauer), Wiesbaden; George Eastman House (Jan-Christopher Horak and Kay MacRae), Rochester; Imperial War Museum (Caroline Marsden), London.

I am also pleased to thank the librarians of the Institute for Contemporary History, Munich; Library of Congress (Cooper C. Graham), Washington, D.C.; the staff of the Margaret Herrick Library, Academy of Motion Picture Arts and Sciences, Beverly Hills; Munich Film Museum (Enno Patalas, Gerhardt Ullman, and Petra Meyer-Schön), Munich; Museum of Modern Art, Film Study Center (Charles Silver), New York; the staff of the Theater Collection of the New York Public Library of the Performing Arts (especially David Bartholomew); Royal Film Archive, Brussels; Royal Film Museum, Amsterdam; Schöneberg Heimat Museum, Schöneberg/Berlin; Southern Methodist University Oral History Collection (Dr. Ronald L. Davis and Thomas Culpepper), Dallas; Stiftung Deutsche Kinemathek (especially Werner Sudendorf, but also Wolfgang Jacobsen and Gero Gandert); Süddeutsche-Verlag (Frau Steinmayr), Munich; Universität zu Köln, Theatermuseum (Dr. Roswitha Flatz), Schloss Wahn-Cologne; University of Texas at Austin, Harry Ransom Humanities Research Collection, which houses the David O. Selznick Collection (thanks to Dr. Charles Bell and especially Daniel Selznick and Jeffrey Selznick for access, guidance, and permissions); University of Southern California Cinema Library (Leith Adams and the extraordinarily helpful Ned Comstock for guiding me to and through the Warner Brothers Archives and the Joe Pasternak, Constance McCormick, and related collections).

Robert Lescher is not only my agent, but friend and guide. Among the many things I owe him is my editor at William Morrow, Maria Guarnaschelli, who possesses a clear eye, sensitive ear, relentless intelligence, and a patient heart.

Kathleen Morahan has been a meticulous copy editor of impeccable taste, skill, and a kind of modesty out of all proportion to the improvements she brought to this work. Bob Aulicino has provided both eye and wit.

In England the enthusiasm and faith of Simon King and Carol O'Brien, who commissioned this book there, sustained me throughout the research and writing. Michael Thomas of A. M. Heath has been helpful, friendly, and judicious in his dealings on my behalf and on behalf of the book. Stuart Proffitt and Robert Lacey shepherded the manuscript and book through a change of management with conscientious, professional support I gratefully acknowledge. Philip Lewis's design skills are evident in the photographic sections of the book.

For sustenance and preservation of spirit I wish to thank: Annabel Davis-Goff, Robert Doggett, Stephen Hollywood, James Kellerhals, Maurice Pacini, Richard and Carol Schickel, Elisabeth and Nicola Waltz, and Robert and Judy Wunsch, all of whom made things easier in ways they may not suspect.

SOURCE NOTES

Complete citations for published sources can be found in the Bibliography. A list of abbreviations found in the Source Notes and Bibliography follows.

ABBREVIATIONS

AMPAS—Academy of Motion Picture Arts and Sciences
BFI—British Film Institute
COHC—Columbia University Oral History Collection, Butler Library, New York
DAZ—Deutsche Allgemeine Zeitung
DDR—East Germany
DIF—(see also Wiesbaden) German Film Institute (Deutsches Institut für Filmkunde, Wiesbaden/Frankfurt-am-Main)
DM—Deutsche Morgenpost

DOS-Texas—David O. Selznick Archive, University of Texas at Austin
HR—Hollywood Reporter
HT—Herald-Tribune (see also IHT and NYHT)
IHT—International Herald-Tribune
int.—interview
"KUR"—Film-Kurier, Berlin
LAE—Los Angeles Examiner
LAH—Los Angeles Herald
LAHE—Los Angeles Herald-Examiner
LAT—Los Angeles Times
Marbach—Schiller National Museum, Marbach, Germany
MoMA—Museum of Modern Art, New York
MPAA—Motion Picture Association of America
n.d.—undated
n.p.—unpaginated
NFP—Neue Film Post, Vienna
NYHT—New York Herald-Tribune
NYPLPA—New York Public Library of the Performing Arts
NYS—New York Sun
NYT—New York Times
NYWT—New York World Telegram
NYWTS—New York World Telegram and Sun
SAG—Screen Actors Guild
SDK—German Film Foundation (Stiftung Deutsche Kinemathek)
SMU—Southern Methodist University Oral History Collection, Dallas, Texas
USC—University of Southern California, Los Angeles
Wiesbaden—(see also DIF-Wiesbaden) German Film Institute (Deutsche Institut
für Filmkunde)

A NOTE FROM THE AUTHOR

Page
x   Re Tynan: Frewin, p. 10.
x   Father and mother: Dietrich family dates recorded by Willibald Conrad
         Felsing, Marlene's uncle (her mother's brother), in 1928 for family use. Plus
         int. SB/Hasso Felsing, April 22, 1989.
x   Walker quote: Walker, p. 9.
xi   Mother, grandmother: Dietrich, *Marlene*, pp. 14, 17.
xii   The editor was Philip Ziegler: letter, MD to PZ, December 11, 1977.

OVERTURE : A VISIT TO THE THEATER: 1929

This account is based primarily on conversations with Josef von Sternberg, 1966–
1967 and on interviews with (November 23, 1988) and letters from (July 26 and
August 20, 1990) John Pommer. For Vollmoeller's orgies and Josephine Baker:
Kessler, pp. 479ff. For Dr. Klein: unpublished letter, Klein to *Life* magazine,

September 3, 1952, NYPLPA. Hotel Esplanade and Ette's Jazz-Symphonie-Orchester: promotional material of the period. For "Not that whore!": Everett, p. 106. For Ruth Landshoff: Landshoff-Yorck, also Kessler as above. Dialogue from *Two Bow Ties:* Kaiser, p. 116; program details from original program. Additional sources cited in notes for Chapter Six on the making of *The Blue Angel.*

CHAPTER ONE : BEGINNINGS: 1901–1918

Page
13   Birth of Marie Magdalene Dietrich: *Standesamt des Magistrats von Berlin, DDR; Standesamt Schöneberg, West Berlin.* Sedanstrasse 53 is today Leberstrasse 65. Due to the holidays, her birth was not registered by her father until January 2, 1902. Mari̲e Magdalen̲e is the correct spelling on all official documents. Additional family data, here and later, courtesy Hasso Felsing.

14   Berlin statistics: "*Berlin für Kenner,*" in Schutte and Sprengel, pp. 95–99.
14   "the one true Emperor": Craig, "The Kaiser and the Kritik," p. 17.
14   "Satan": Tuchman, p. 14.
14ff.   Schöneberg: Schöneberg details, *Adreßbuch für Berlin und seine Vororte,* August Scherl Verlag, Berlin, 1901. Also Winz: Grimms brothers, p. 77; 1898 as independent suburb [p. 5]; Sedanstrasse building, p. 100ff.; other details and incorporation into Berlin, pp. 117ff.

15   Lieutenant Dietrich: Dietrich's military and police career here and later (and his father's) from documents and interviews at the Berlin *Polizei Präsidium,* March/April 1986. Departmental records compiled by Paul Schmidt, 1898ff. For military decorations: int. SB/Hermann's Historica, Munich, July 15, 1989. General: Craig, *Germany,* p. 244.

16   Felsings re "Dietrich": int. SB/Hasso Felsing, April 22, 1989.
16   "Stable" as allusion to breeding: Dietrich, *Marlene,* p. 17.
17ff.   Völtzing/Felsing family genealogy here and later from documents prepared by Willibald Albert Conrad Felsing (c.1925), and other unpublished family papers. Also int. SB/Hasso Conrad Felsing (March 8, April 22, 1989). Felsing firm: *1850 Altmeister der Berliner Uhrenmacher Innung,* Berlin, 1850, (n.p.); misc. advertising (c.1900).

Felsing family, for the record: Albert Karl Julius Felsing (the second "Conrad") was Marlene's grandfather, born November 10, 1827. He died January 9, 1901. From his second marriage he had a son (called Conrad, born on July 17, 1872) who did not survive. His third wife, Elisabeth Hering, Marlene's grandmother, was born June 14, 1856, in Dresden and died on January 29, 1919. She bore Marlene's mother on November 11, 1876, and her uncle, Willibald Albert Conrad Felsing, on July 5, 1878. Courtesy Hasso Felsing.

18   "Berlin's first . . . movie theater": Stiege. This odd coincidence has gone unnoticed. Oskar Messter was a key pioneer of German film, an optical instrument maker turned producer and exhibitor. He produced films from

the beginning and dominated European distribution until World War I, with Pathé and Gaumont in France. His company was a key component of what became UFA. See Holba, pp. 261ff.; Rhode, p. 170. His memoirs are cited in the Bibliography.

18   "thin and pale": Dietrich, *Ich . . . Berlinerin*, p. 11; *Marlene*, p. ix.

18   Family lore: int. SB/Hasso Felsing, April 22, 1989.

19   "photographed to death": Dietrich/Schell, *Marlene*.

19   Examination results December 18, 1901, and May 23, 1903: *Polizei Präsidium*, Berlin.

19   For the record: The family moved from Sedanstrasse 53 to the Kolonnenstrasse 48/49 (still standing) in 1904; in 1906 to the Potsdamer Strasse 45 II; in 1907 to the Akazienallee 48. In 1908 Marlene's mother moved to Tauentzienstrasse 13 II in downtown Berlin, listing herself as *Witwe*, widow, in the telephone directory published in 1909. *Adreßbücher für Berlin und seine Vororte*: August Scherl, Berlin (1901–1909).

19   Father's death: Kolarz, *Stern*. The exact date of his death is not known, but it was presumably 1907.

19   "shadowy silhouette": Dietrich, ms., p. 31; (in *Marlene*, p. 22, the phrase is translated as "blurred portrait").

19   "Paul": Dietrich, *Marlene*, p. 14; on Liesel: int. SB/Hasso Felsing. "my father's place": *Marlene*, p. 37.

20   "a good General": Dietrich ms., pp. 17–19; (*Marlene*, p. 15). Hemingway: Hemingway based a character on Dietrich in *Islands in the Stream*: "She was a delightful and charming woman who had never altered a plan that she had made in her life. Her plans were always made in secret, *like those of a good general*, and they were as rigidly enforced" (emphasis added), *Islands*, p. 4.

20   "The Dragon": int. SB/Hasso Felsing, April 22, 1989.

20   "My mother": Dietrich, ms., p. 20 (The quotation appears in the manuscript only). "The rules": ms., p. 19 (*Marlene*, p. 15).

20   The poem is by Ferdinand Freiligrath, the translation is Dietrich's, ms., p. 16. A translation considerably less good appears in *Marlene*, p. 13. For its ability to reduce her to tears, see Dietrich/Schell, *Marlene*.

21   "glorified housekeeper": the classmate was Elli Marcus, the well-known photographer, quoted in Higham, p. 39.

21   "joy": Dietrich, *ABC*, p. 99.

21   First violin and cost: letter, MD to Julius Levin, July 2, 1921. Schiller Nationalmuseum: Marbach am Neckar, hereafter "Marbach." "Bach" quote: *Marlene*, p. 36.

22   "Public fame": *Marlene*, pp. 25–29.

22   "little gray mouse": Elli Marcus is again Higham's source.

22   Mademoiselle Breguand: Dietrich, ms., pp. 3–4; (*Marlene*, pp. 5–6).

22   Henny Porten's eyebrows and Marlene: mostly from Marlene's classmate Gertrud Seiler (today Kröger), letter GSK to SB, July 1, 1989. Also Porten's autobiography and Bemmann, pp. 17–18.

23ff. Marlene's school subjects and the war: Marlene Dietrich to SB, July 3 and August 17, 1987.

23 "cards afresh" quote: Fest, p. 65.

23 "Cast party" quote: Eksteins, p. 61.

23ff. Brooke: quoted in Fussell, pp. 129–130. Hitler: Shirer, p. 52, and Fest, pp. 65–68. Hitler letter: *Süddeutsche-Zeitung*, May 3, 1990, p. 4.

24 "the first bereaved": Dietrich, ms., p. 6; (*Marlene*, p. 7).

24 "Barbarians" quote: Dietrich, ms., p. 6; (*Marlene*, pp. 6–7).

24 "God . . .": Dietrich, ms., p. 10; (*Marlene*, p. 10). Confirmation and the cook: Higham, p. 40. "the fact": Dietrich, ms., p. 30; (*Marlene*, p. 21).

24ff. On the war here and later: Schrader/Schebera, pp. 7–10. Marlene's school details: Gertrud (Seiler) Kröger: GSK to SB, July 1, 1989.

24 "Gott strafe England!": Hardly a memoir of the period fails to mention this daily war cry. Fritz Gilbert, Walter Slezak, Dietrich herself, countless others remember it as a constant refrain of World War I childhood.

25 Potato Office: Craig, *Germany*, p. 357. Turnips: *Marlene*, p. 20; letter, GSK to SB, as above.

25 "Sawdust" in bread: Gilbert, p. 32.

25 "Girls": GSK to SB, as above. "Boys": Gilbert, p. 31.

25 "woman's world": *Ibid.*, p. 31; (*Ibid.*, p. 22.). "a world without men": Dietrich, German *Esquire*, 1975.

25ff. "This war": Dietrich, ms., p. 34; (*Marlene*, p. 24).

26 Josephine's marriage, von Losch's death, and Felsing family reaction: int. SB/Hasso Felsing, April 22, 1989. Marlene was registered in Dessau as "Magdalene von Losch," apparently a name of convenience. She was not adopted by von Losch and the name was never legally hers: Antonetten Lyzeum, Dessau, school records 1916–1917; int. SB/Hasso Felsing; Wiechers.

26ff. Diploma: school records, Viktoria-Luisen-Schule, today the Goethe Gymnasium. Marlene had the equivalent of a tenth-grade American education and received an *Abschlußzeugnis*, or "certificate of completion." The graduation *Abitur* was granted only after final examinations and an additional three years' study.

26 "Bedroom eyes" and "scandal": GSK to SB, July 1, 1989. Other details of Marlene's final year of school confirmed by Frau Hertha Saade, a classmate, courtesy Werner Sudendorf, Stiftung Deutsche Kinemathek, Berlin, hereafter "SDK."

27 Hildegard Sperling, other school details, including courses, grades, attitudes, photograph, etc.: GSK to SB, as above.

27 For the record the girls in the photograph are:
(*First row, left to right*): Wally Leibrich, Christiane Lachmann, Erna Frischmann, Marlene Dietrich, Hildegard Sperling; (*second row, seated, l. to r.*): Charlotte Knuth, Edith Benn, Hertha Saade, Mary Bayczinsky (the American girl), Edith Förster, Gertrud Seiler, Käthe Bethke, and, full figure at the end of the row, Else Püttmann; (*standing row, l. to r.*): Hildegard Lilie,

Eva Guradze, Erika Daunehl, Ilse Smierz, Annemarie Bracht, Lilly Holz, Gertrud Wenzel, Charlotte Seliger, Charlotte Spanier, Elisabeth Preiß; (*top row, l. to r.*): Dora Seeck, Lotte Köhler, Irma Achsel. Identifications by Gertrud Seiler Kröger to SB, and Hertha Saade to Werner Sudendorf, SDK.

CHAPTER TWO : WEIMAR AND BACK: 1919–1921

29   Stefan Zweig: quoted in Schrader/Schebera, p. 11.

30   Ludendorff quote: *Ibid.*, p. 12.

30   Kaiser quote: Friedrich, p. 23.

31   Kessler quote: *Ibid.*, pp. 34–37; Kessler, pp. 9–88 for full accounts. Translation here mostly Friedrich.

32   Gay quote: Gay, pp. 1–2.

32   The roommate, Gerde Noack, is quoted here and later from: Kochanowski.

33   Poem: Bemmann, p. 20. The original (author unknown) is:
Aus Berlin kam die Marlen'
Und wir gerne sie hier seh'n.
Lustig sein ist ihr Plaisier,
Und das ist die Hauptsach' hier.

33   "*geradezu obszön*," and "cooperative": Noack again in Kochanowski. She made these remarks in 1977 (emphasis added).

34ff.   Marlene and Alma Mahler-Gropius: Schreyer, pp. 211–224. (emphasis added).

35   Heilbrun quotes: Heilbrun, pp. 96–98, letter to SB from Professor Heilbrun, September 17, 1989.

35   "*What did she say*": Schreyer, p. 224 (emphasis in original).

35ff.   Wolfgang Rosé: quoted in Higham, p. 44.

36   Marlene's memory: *Marlene*, p. 35.
"I could play": *Ibid.*

36   Gropius: quoted in Gay, p. 101.

37ff.   The correspondence from Marlene to Dr. Levin consists of twelve letters or cards, dating from July 2, 1921, to January 19, 1925, most written July/ August 1921. The collection is housed at Marbach.

38   Billy Wilder: Billy Wilder/Volker Schlöndorff interview transcripts, June 1988 (courtesy Schlöndorff). The Weimar stories later circulated widely in Berlin. See Riess, vol. 2, p. 92; there "the violin teacher" is a "tenor"; see also Jameson, *Kalenderjahre zählen nicht*, p. 274. For Moss Hart and Kitty Carlisle's recollections: int. SB/Kitty Carlisle Hart, June 6, 1991.

38   The letter from MD to Dr. Levin about Professor Reitz's later peccadillos is undated. It seems to date c. 1923–1924.

39   *Hochschule für Musik*: It is usually reported that the records omit her or were destroyed during World War II. Neither is correct: The records have never been catalogued and therefore remain closed.

39   "Broken dream": Dietrich, *ABC*, p. 168.

39   Fairbanks and Hollywood movies by 1919: Brownlow, p. 34.

41   *Passion:* Kracauer, p. 3.

42   Eugene Ormandy: *New York Times*, October 2, 1989, p. 16.

42   Giuseppe Becce quote: taped interview, GB/Gerhardt Lamprecht, 1953, SDK. Becce was a highly accomplished film composer. His most famous "silent" score (extant) was for F. W. Murnau's *The Last Laugh:* von Zglinicki, pp. 70ff.

42   Dr. Flesch: Bemmann, p. 21. Flesch was Jewish and escaped via Hungary to Switzerland in the thirties.

43   Dr. Daniel: int. SB/Dr. Hans Feld, May 25, 1990.

43   Georg Will: Wiechers, [n.p.], courtesy *Deutsche Institut für Filmkunde,* hereafter "Wiesbaden."

43   Elisabeth's marriage, the Felsings: int. SB/Hasso Felsing.

44   *Girl-Kabarett:* Seydel, p. 26.

44   Nelson revues: int. SB/Herbert and Eva Nelson, October 1987. Letter, Camilla Horn to SB: March 29, 1990.

44   "The girl from the Kurfürstendamm": the phrase is ubiquitously applied to her in memoirs of the period. See, for instance, Rühmann, *Das war's,* p. 114.

45   Rilke and "memory": Dietrich recited and translated countless Rilke poems to SB as these pages were being written.

45   "A dangerous profession": *Marlene,* p. 38.

CHAPTER THREE : THE SORCERER'S APPRENTICE: 1921–1923

46ff.   Reinhardt: mostly from Huesmann, Sayler, Styan, and Gottfried Reinhardt; plus ints. SB/Gottfried Reinhardt, 1988–1990.

47   "Barnum": quoted in Styan, p. 101.

48   Reinhardt quote: Max Reinhardt, "The Actor," reprinted in Cole and Chinoy, pp. 295–299.

48   "[Reinhardt's] eyebrows": *Fun,* p. 236.

49   *Faust* translation: Philip Wayne, Penguin Classics, 1949.

49   The audition cushion story is in Dietrich, *Nehmt . . . ,* pp. 46–47. A slightly different version is in *Marlene,* p. 37, and a wholly different version is in Dietrich, *ABC,* pp. 149–150.

49   Reinhardt and tears: see *ABC* as above. In her memoirs, Dietrich admits never having seen him at the school.

49   Reinhardt quote: *op.cit.,* p. 297.

50   Reinhardt and Vollmoeller seeing Marlene: int. SB/Gottfried Reinhardt, June 2, 1988.

50   Valetti: Jameson, *Kalenderjahre,* p. 277.

51   "Rather a fool": Mosheim quoted by Higham, p. 50.

51   "It is to the actor": Reinhardt, *op. cit.,* p. 295.

52   Reinhardt on Shakespeare: Willett, p. 36.

52   Marlene's lines in *Shrew: Marlene,* p. 40.

52   Re *The Circle: Ibid.*, pp. 41–42. The character appears (with many expository lines) in the first two acts. She disappears in the third.

52   Agnes Straub incident: Dietrich/Schell, tapes.

53   Anni Mewes and Rilke: see Rilke, *Selected Letters*, pp. 295–297.

53ff.   Uncle Willi and Jolly Felsing: int. SB/Hasso Felsing, April 22, 1989.

55   Greta Keller: taped interview, SDK. Grete Mosheim: quoted in Higham, p. 51.

55   "The most beautiful woman": MD to Shirley (Mrs. Hasso) Felsing, int. SB/Shirley Felsing, April 22, 1989.

56ff.   The screen test and Uncle Willi: for Uncle Willi's involvement, Kurt Milte. The test: Lorant, "When Marlene Dietrich Failed a Screen Test"; also Silver, p. 12; and letter, Lorant to Richard Griffith, July 20, 1959, Museum of Modern Art, hereafter MoMA. Decla was an important firm that shortly became part of UFA.

57   "Halo" quote: *Collier's*, p. 26.

57   Efa: Horak, "Rin Tin Tin," ms. pp. 11–12.

57   Uncle Willi and Georg Jacoby: Milte.

58   Berlin review: *Der Film*, December 2, 1923, p. 15.

58   Madame Dubarry/Efa quote: Horak.

58   "flirtation" quote: Higham, p. 51.

59   Dieterle quotes: Flinn.

59   Her first paid ad was in *Der Film*, June 5, 1923 [n.p.]; production detail, same source, April 29, 1923, p. 30. *SDK.*

59   "Sympathetic": *Reichsfilmblatt*, no. 24, 1923, p. 19. "Superficial": *Berliner Tageblatt*, June 17, 1923. Also *Neue Illustrierte Filmwoche*, no. 12, 1925 [n.p.] SDK.

60   Sieber as actor: he so identified himself on his marriage license.

60   Eva May: Dietrich, *Nehmt . . .* , p. 51. Other versions of the Dietrich memoirs misidentify May, apparently through translation error. For Eva May, see: Riess, vol. 1, pp. 204ff.

61   "too innocent": *Marlene*, pp. 43–44.

61   Maurischat: quoted in Higham, pp. 51–52.

61   Mia May quotes: *Ibid.*, p. 52.

62   "The man I want": *Marlene*, p. 44.

62   In Marlene's scenes in the courtroom balcony the film is stop-printed (each frame duplicate-printed) and the image enlarged, so that we see a sort of slow motion extension of her actual, much briefer footage. This print is in the collection of George Eastman House, Rochester, New York.

62   Marlene and Rudi's courtship: *Marlene*, pp. 44–45.

63   Eva May: After Rudi, May got involved with the Austrian munitions magnate Fritz Mandl, who later married Hedy Lamarr. See Riess, *op. cit.* The specific cause of her suicide, of course, is unknown.

CHAPTER FOUR : THE PERFECT COUPLE: 1923–1927

65   Kerr quote: *Berliner Tageblatt*, February 10, 1924.

65   Exchange rate: Friedrich, p. 141.

65   Baby: Dietrich, *ABC*, p. 19.

65   The Siebers first lived in the Nassauische Strasse. The new address was Kaiserallee 54. Josephine lived at no. 135: *Reichskino Adressbuch*, 4th ed., *Verlag der L.L.B.*, Berlin, 1925 [n.p.].

65   Children quote: MD to SB, telephone, March 24, 1987.

66   *Joyless Street:* Virtually every Dietrich filmography includes this title in her credits. The actress with whom she is confused was Hertha von Walther, who died in Munich in 1988 and understandably resented the misidentification. According to *Joyless Street* production dates, Marlene was having her baby when the film was shot.

66   Rudi and Marlene's marriage: the openness of the Sieber marriage was so well known in Berlin that some (incorrectly) questioned Rudi's paternity. Comments here based on int. SB/Herbert Nelson, November 2, 1987, and confidential sources.

66   "It was a splendid time": Aufricht, p. 43.

66ff.   Barzini quotes: Barzini, p. 75.

67   Loos and Zweig: quoted in Friedrich, pp. 128–129.

67   Dupont and *Varieté*: Skutesky, who was the assistant.

67   Max Wolf was editor of the *BZ*: Jameson, *Wenn ich . . .* , pp. 242–244. The pseudonym he used was Bruno Wohl. Liebermann quote: Cziffra, *. . . Ballnacht*, p. 16.

68   Barnowsky and Bergner: Sudendorf, vol. 2, pp. 73–74.

68   *Manon* reviews: *BZ*, February 16, 1926, SDK; second, unsourced clip, SDK.

68   *Variety* review: December 15, 1926. In America *Manon Lescaut* was issued with two different endings, one happy, one not, but still had to compete with John Barrymore's *When a Man Loves*, in which Manon (Dolores Costello) played support to Barrymore as Des Grieux.

69   Frankfurt offer: letter MD to Dr. Levin, undated (c. 1923–1924); Marbach.

69   Barnowsky, Meinhard, and Bernauer: Willett, p. 220. Eckart von Naso, a novelist who was also Barnowsky's dramaturg, said Marlene prevailed upon Forster to force her to Barnowsky's attention: von Naso, p. 516. "Chill": Lorant.

70   Veit Harlan: *Institut für Zeitgeschichte, München*. Four of a projected ten volumes of Goebbels's diaries, detailing Harlan's zeal for his work, have to date been published.

70   Rehfisch, Jessner in American exile: Willett, p. 196. For Harlan, see Hull. This valuable book is replete with Harlan's attempts to whitewash and rehabilitate himself for posterity. He may not have known about the Goebbels diaries.

70   "Enough Already!": *Berliner Illustrirte Zeitung*, March 1925.

70   *Duel on the Lido* review quotes: Seydel, p. 43. *Rubicon* and Uncle Willi: Tolischus, p. 130.

71   *Dubarry* review: *Der Film*, February 1, 1927, p. 14.

71   Stefan Lorant article: *Berliner Zeitung*, June 15, 1926; also letter Lorant to Richard Griffith, July 20, 1959, Museum of Modern Art, New York, hereafter MoMA.

71   Korda to Marlene: Tabori.

71   Tamara and *Dance Mad:* Choura, p. 26. Tamara Matul (sometimes spelled Matull in programs) danced in Berlin revues and musicals of the twenties.

72   *Chin Up, Charly: Kopf hoch, Charly* in German. "Kopf hoch" means "chin up" in English, not "heads up" as it is usually translated. Ellen Richter's heirs agreed to withhold this film (and the next Marlene made for Richter) from exhibition during Dietrich's lifetime. The next, *The Bogus Baron*, is in museum collections. SDK. Reviews: "mediocre" *Reichsfilmblatt*, March 26, 1927, p. 40. "not for": *Der Film*, April 1, 1927, p. 10.

73   Erik Charell: mostly Jansen, p. 128ff. *Girlkultur:* Willett, p. 99.

73ff.   *From Mouth to Mouth*: int. SB/Curt Bois, April 27, 1990; Jansen, pp. 155–156; Willett, p. 99.

74   "A yellow dress": Meyerinck, p. 147.

74   Waldoff as victim: She died in relative obscurity in 1957; the movie about her life was made for East German television in 1987. Additional information: Int. SB/Curt Bois, April 27, 1990.

74   Janet Flanner: Flanner, p. 400. "How bee-oo-tee-ful": Riess, vol. 2, p. 94. Flanner was writing in 1935 one of the earliest and best analyses of the appeal of Adolf Hitler. *The New Yorker* published the piece in 1936 and it was out in book form in 1940 as cited in the Bibliography.

74   "Marlene's style": int. SB/Curt Bois, April 27, 1990. Billy Wilder: Wilder/Schlöndorff interviews, 1988.

Wilder: "She [Marlene] said, 'I guess I better tell you in between [men] there was the first [time?] with a woman.' There was a woman, an actress, called Claire Waldoff; that was fifty years ago. Claire Waldoff. And the people stared, and then she [Marlene] said just one sentence to them: 'Are we boring you?' " Courtesy Volker Schlöndorff.

74   Tynan: What he wrote was, "She has sex, but no particular gender." *Playbill*, October 1967, reprinted in *Profiles*, p. 216. He said the same thing about Hepburn and Garbo.

Dietrich's androgyny was something she discussed freely. "She could have written a book to rival Krafft-Ebing," according to Sam Taylor. Int. SB/Sam and Suzanne Taylor, June 6–7, 1987.

75   *Bluff* reviews: *Reichsfilmblatt*, June 14, 1927, p. 27; *Film-Kurier*, June 13, 1927 [n.p.].

75ff.   Betty Stern: Robert Lantz directed my attention to Betty Stern. She is the character Betty Stein in Erich Maria Remarque's novel *Shadows in Paradise*.

75   Bergner dress: Marcus, p. 178.

76   Herbert Nelson: int. SB/Herbert and Eva Nelson, November 2, 1987. See also Marcus, p. 178.

76   Cocaine: Drug use is abundantly documented during the period. Fritzi Massary commented on it in a reminiscence about Marlene (Seydel, p. 85); also Schrader and Schebera, p. 45; Friedrich, pp. 341–342.

76   Eisner: *Ich hatte:* p. 200. For "legs": p. 61. Eisner and Betty Stern both ended up in Paris exile, the one a film historian, the other an agent. Eisner was a culture snob who looked down on Stern because of her poor French accent and thought her "vulgar."

76   " 'Marlene' ": Hildenbrandt, p. 91.

76ff.   Willi Forst: mostly from Dachs.

76   Count Kolowrat: Dachs, pp. 9–14; Lachmann, p. 13.

77   Screen test: Hartl quoted in Dachs, pp. 15–16. Higham (pp. 67–68) misidentifies Hartl as producer. He was then a printshop apprentice breaking into films.

77   *Café* reviews: *Mein Film,* no. 100, p. 14; *Reichsfilmblatt,* no. 12, 1928, p. 28; *Film im Bild,* April 5, 1928, p. 14.

77   Igo Sym: Higham, pp. 18, 69–70. Higham quotes Walter Reisch that Sym was a "whole heart and soul" love of Marlene's life. Reisch's widow (int. SB/Mrs. Walter Reisch, August 18, 1989) thought her husband was being facetious.

77   Kolowrat and Marlene: Dachs, p. 14. Higham quoting Hartl is the source of the hospital visit, p. 69.

78   The program for *Broadway* in Vienna reversed the authors' names to George Dunning and Philip Abbott, a mistake that persists in European theater histories to the present day.

79   Felix Salten review: *NFP,* November 30, 1927 (Institut für Theaterwissenschaft, Vienna).

79   Otto Preminger: Preminger, p. 34; Frischauer, p. 50.

79   Al Jolson: The New York premiere of *The Jazz Singer* was earlier.

CHAPTER FIVE : BREAKTHROUGH: 1928–1929

80   Parrot/Vitaphone joke: Brownlow, p. 571. On early sound see: Knight, pp. 146–150; Brownlow, pp. 566–577; Rhode, p. 260; Kracauer, p. 16. Sound had been around from the beginning, but this was The Moment.

81   Weill's opera: *The Czar Has His Picture Taken,* libretto by Georg Kaiser. *Der Lindberghflug* was later de-Americanized by Brecht (against Weill's wishes), becoming *Der Ozeanflug.*

81   Letter to Forster: MD to RF, Vienna to Berlin [undated: c. November 1927]; Marbach. Marlene also wrote director Eugen Robert, who would direct the production. She had known Robert since 1922, when she did stand-in work in his *The Great Baritone* production for Albert Bassermann.

82   "indecisive": int. SB/Felix Jackson, November 20, 1987.

82   Baum quote: Baum, p. 376. "Sally Mayer": Marcus, pp. 189–192.

82   Lennartz quote: int. Christa Maerker/EL, June 7, 1976, courtesy Christa Maerker.

82   Masseuse quote: Marcus, p. 192.

82   Käthe Haack quote: int. Christa Maerker/KH, June 19, 1976, courtesy CM.

82   Lennartz quote re arm: int. CM/EL, as above.

82   Coworkers and "panties . . . bra": Lennartz, as before. Lennartz found Marlene "daring," but added, "She was altogether very trustworthy, always on time for rehearsals, always punctual. . . . She was nice, friendly, and great—a very unique person."

83   Joachimsohn (later Jackson): int. SB/Felix Jackson, November 20, 1987.

83   Robert Klein: from correspondence, Klein to Harry Ham, London, September 12, 1935 (office of Myron Selznick); to *Life* magazine (undated, late August, 1952; acknowledged September 3, 1952). Both NYPLPA, Klein File. On Klein: Willett, pp. 114, 135, 140, 217ff.

84   Schiffer: int. SB/Felix Jackson, as above.

84   Dietrich on duet: Dietrich, *Marlene*, pp. 47–51. She claims she was still a student at the Reinhardt school, where her teachers failed to comment on the sensation she was causing all over Berlin.

84   Klein quote: letter to *Life*, NYPLPA.

85   Lyric freely translated by SB.

85   Ihering review: *Berliner Börsen-Courier*, June 16, 1928. Reprinted in Ihering, pp. 320–321.

85   Nelson quote: int. SB/HN, as above.

85   Legs: "artificial silk" from Seldes, p. 166. Insurance story: *Die Woche*, August 14, 1926, pp. 810–811 and Barthel, p. 31; American photo, unsourced clip, date stamped August 15, 1928, NYPLPA.

86   Review: *Film-Kurier*, September 6, 1928.

86   "Garbo eyes, Swanson nose": Axel Eggebrecht in *Der Montag Morgen*, September 10, 1928. "the glance": Werner Bonwitt, September 6, 1928. Garbo/Dietrich cover: *Berliner Illustrirte Zeitung*, no. 43, December 22, 1929.

86   Brooks and Pabst: Paris, p. 280. Brooks is the only source for this story, though it is usually presented as a quote from Pabst. Marlene is supposed to have said, "Imagine Pabst choosing Louise Brooks for Lulu when he could have had me!" (Paris, p. 279), but Brooks may have "improved" events.

87   Shaw: *Misalliance*, pp. 144, 119.

87   Hypatia speech: Shaw, p. 129.

87   Reviews: Kerr, Ludwig Sternaux, and "H.W.F." [Hans Feld in *Film-Kurier*]: quoted in Seydel, p. 64.

87   Darvas quote: Seydel, p. 84.

88   Brooks: quoted in Brownlow, p. 363, and Paris, p. 280.

88   "Banal": *Der Abend*, January 18, 1929.

88   Reviews: *Kreuz-Zeitung*, January 20, 1929; Georg Herzberg, *Film-*

Kurier, January 18, 1929. "Why must they": Hanns G. Lustig, *"Filmlärm und das stumme Gesicht einer Frau,"* *Tempo*, January 18, 1929.

89ff.   Zinnemann quote: int. SB/Fred Zinnemann, July 23, 1987.

89   "Hubsie" story: Hans Feld, int. SB/HF, as above. Tauber recital story: Felix Jackson, int. SB/FJ, as above.

89   Klein quote: Klein letter to *Life*, as above.

90   Film historian James Card maintains Marlene was cast as compensation for losing *Pandora's Box*. Card says Pabst felt guilty about his treatment of her and convinced director Kurt Bernhardt to cast Marlene as consolation prize for losing out to Louise Brooks. Int. SB/James Card, November 7, 1987. Brod's novel was popular enough that the role of Stascha was a prize and difficult to cast, but Bernhardt was not the original director, and Ladislaus Vajda, who wrote both *Pandora's Box* and *Three Loves*, may have suggested Marlene. Gennaro Righelli was the announced director: 1928–1929 Berlin trade advertisements. Bernhardt was to have filmed Wedekind's *Spring's Awakening*, made instead by Richard Oswald.

91   Bernhardt quotes: Kiersch, pp. 37–40.

91   Sternberg to Bernhardt: Kiersch, p. 39 (emphasis added). It was not typical of Sternberg, and surely personal, as he was apolitical. He was the only major Hollywood figure to sign a petition protesting U.S. immigration policy barring Sergei Eisenstein from reentry after the debacle of *Que Viva Mexico*.

92   Fred Zinnemann: int. SB/FZ, July 23, 1987.

92ff.   Photo booth story: Dietrich told this to many people, though never in print; here from int. SB/John Lund, June 2, 1988. "She never moved": Bernhardt in Kiersch, p. 38 (emphasis added).

93   Brod and Bernhardt: Brod, *Berliner Tageblatt*, May 17, 1929; Bernhardt, *Film-Kurier*, May 22, 1929.

93   "Lips" review: *Deutsche Allgemeine Zeitung*, May 4, 1929.

93   Becce: Film scores for the period received their own separate reviews. Becce's for this film was in *Film und Ton*, September 21, 1929. Sheet music was published from the score and sold briskly.

93   Reviews: "overrated," Hans Sahl in *Der Montag Morgen*, May 6, 1929; "lifeless" by "J.R." (unsourced clip, SDK).

93   Lobby comments and Garbo comparison: Frank Maraun, *DAZ*, May 4, 1929.

94   Rand: quoted in Schickel, *The Stars*, p. 129.

94   Depression over reviews: Sternberg, *Fun . . .* , p. 225.

95   "Hollywood principles" and production detail: *Film-Kurier*, July 24, 1929.

95   Marlene's costume, ship, etc.: *Die Filmwoche*, nos. 21 and 22, pp. 493–494.

95   Everson: New School Program Notes, Film Series 35, Program no. 3, October 12, 1979.

96   Eisner: *Film-Kurier*, July 22, 1930.
96   "booed off the stage": *Tempo*, "*Pfeif konzert im Ufa-Pavillon*," September 19, 1929. Review: *Berliner Volks-Zeitung*, September 25, 1929.
96   Barnowsky: quoted in *Heyne*, p. 38.
96   Lines in *Two Bow Ties*: Dietrich, *Marlene*, p. 51; von Sternberg, *Fun*, p. 231.

CHAPTER SIX : THE BLUE ANGEL: 1929

98   Reviews: *Berliner Börsen-Courier*; "veiled voice": *BZ am Mittag*, both September 6, 1929.
98ff.   Josef von Sternberg here and later:
Much material on Sternberg is based on his autobiography *Fun in a Chinese Laundry* (hereafter: *Fun*), a book to be relished warily. Sternberg was as much self-fabulist as artist. The man who wrote the book in 1963 was not the man who made the films he wrote about.

I met Sternberg in Paris in 1960 and spent time with him from 1966 through 1967 while a Ph.D. candicate at the University of Southern California writing about the director's work. Sternberg was then lecturing at UCLA, and allowed me to audit his lectures and visit his home and sit with him through screenings of every extant Sternberg film: *The Salvation Hunters* through *The Saga of Anatahan*. Those months provided invaluable foundation for this text.

There are many works on Sternberg, cited below and in the Bibliography. They need to be approached carefully. His "followers" or "disciples"—as he liked to call them—are often cultists rather than reporters or critics. The films alone should alert one that Sternberg had little interest in realism and was master of shadow and the uses of silence.
98   "howled like a dog": *Fun*, p. 5.
99   "I can reproduce": *Ibid.*, p. 16.
100   Vienna, 1921, book: Dörfler, in Peter Baxter, pp. 10–12. Dörfler suggests Adolph may have been Sternberg's teacher.
101   UA payment: John Baxter, p. 31.
101   "Oh Hollywood": B. G. Braver-Mann, quoted in Peter Baxter, p. 28.
101   "outrage": int. SB/Nicholas von Sternberg, June 2, 1988.
101   "horrible" and quote: Brownlow, p. 190. The actor was Clive Brooks, later star of *Shanghai Express*.
101   "When a director dies" and "the least human": both John Grierson. Grierson wrote in the *New York Sun*, November 18, 1926. Quoted in *Fun*, pp. 163, 316.
102   Chaplin quote: Griffith and Mayer, p. 216. Also, David Robinson, p. 451. Robinson notes the uncommerciality of the film and its in 1933 destruction for "tax purposes."
102   "normal": *Fun*, p. 207.
102   Winchell quote: *Ibid.*, p. 211.

102   B. P. Schulberg's wife took credit for bringing Sternberg to her husband's attention and Paramount. Brownlow, p. 192.

103   Hecht wire: *Fun*, p. 215.

103   Hollywood extra story: Brownlow, p. 196.

103   "last remaining actor": *Fun*, p. 133.

103   Riza Royce on set: Wray, p. 105.

103   Mexican divorce and remarriage: John Baxter, p. 52.

104   UFA and Parufamet: Berg-Ganschow/Jacobsen; Esser; Bezirksamt Tempelhof. Also Rhode, pp. 170–171; Horak, "Rin Tin Tin" ms.

104   Gay on Hugenberg: *Weimar Culture*, p. 133–134.

104ff.   *Rasputin*: Jannings had discussed *Rasputin* with Paramount in 1927 and Vollmoeller began writing character sketches then (which survive). Sudendorf, vol. 1, p. 66. Werner Sudendorf of the *Stiftung Deutsche Kinemathek* (SDK) guided me through the day-by-day UFA corporate minutes and other UFA documents. Their permanent home is the Bundesarchiv in Coblenz.

105   Sternberg statement: *Film-Kurier*, August 16, 1929.

105   Sternberg quotes and "Sonny Boy": *Film-Kurier*, August 17, 1929.

105   Sternberg and *Rasputin*: see *Fun*, pp. 135–136; *Blue Angel* introduction, p. 10. Pommer's papers were destroyed by fire in the late thirties, but the UFA minutes leave no doubt that the subject was *Rasputin*.

106   *Rasputin* lawsuit: Napley. Napley's entire book is about the lawsuit, which he claims cost MGM the modern equivalent of ten million dollars, p. 202.

106   Jannings and Murnau, 1924: Sudendorf, vol. 1, p. 67.

106   Hugenberg/Thomas Mann: Nigel Hamilton, p. 235.

106   Hugenberg: UFA minutes, August 28, 1929. When the book was reissued in 1916, it had inspired attacks from the right, who viewed it (correctly) as an indictment of just what Hugenberg feared it might be an indictment of.

107   Model for Mann's cabaret singer: Mann based the novel on an incident he read about in a newspaper in Florence twenty years earlier.

107   "Without the electricity": *Fun*, p. 232.

107   Title: all participants agree that the title was Sternberg's. The original title was a play on the name "Raat" (not "Rath" as is usually reported). The German word *Unrat* means "excrement" or "offal." Raat equals the German *Rat*, meaning counsel or advisor, as in *Rathaus*—City Hall, or literally, "House of Advisors."

107ff.   Riefenstahl: int. SB/Hans Feld, May 25, 1990. Also, Riefenstahl, pp. 118–125. Riefenstahl must be approached carefully. Hans Feld, *Film-Kurier* editor, says Riefenstahl (then a close friend) boasted of having the part.

      Riefenstahl story: Riefenstahl, p. 120. The point Riefenstahl is making here is her friendship with Sternberg. *Der Spiegel* called Sternberg one of her "show Jews" when she published her memoirs. She had it in for Dietrich then and later (they were neighbors), which is not reflected in the anecdote she says she told Sternberg.

108   *"Der Popo"*: *Fun*, p. 231.

108   Pushing Marlene: letters and int. SB/John Pommer cited above. Voll-moeller and Landshoff: see Landshoff, pp. 41–48, who claimed she pushed Marlene with Vollmoeller's assent. Actress Alexandra von Porembsky re-membered Vollmoeller as "very persistent: he wanted Marlene." Int. Christa Maerker/Alexa von Porembsky, June [10?], 1976, courtesy CM.

108   NYT review: September 9, 1929, p. 30. *Three Loves* opened in New York in August.

108   "Toulouse-Lautrec": *Fun*, p. 232.

108   Albers pissing on Sternberg: Riess, vol. 2, p. 114.

109   "study in apathy": *Fun*, p. 233.

109   "nature of a woman": *Ibid.*, p. 120.

109   "theater . . . energy": *Ibid.*, p. 225. "Never before": *Ibid.*, p. 226.

109ff.   "She was": *Ibid.*, p. 235. "promised everything": int. to *Blue Angel*, p. 12.

110   Mannheim audition: Holländer, pp. 235–240; Sternberg, *Fun*, p. 236.

110   Paramount and the Dietrich test: Lasky, pp. 221–222. Pommer: the producer was already persuaded. John Pommer (letter to SB, July 26, 1990) wrote: "My father insisted on Dietrich and Jo accepted her."

110   Test: Jobst von Reith-Zanthier, quoted in Sudendorf, vol. 1, pp. 95–96. Also, MD to Maximilian Schell, tapes.

110   "She came to life": Sudendorf, vol. 1, p. 237.

110   "rue the day": *Ibid.* for Jannings's claim, see Jannings, p. 198.

110   Pommer quote: letter John Pommer to SB, July 26, 1990.

110   Riefenstahl: int. SB/Hans Feld, May 25, 1990. Feld said "Leni's jaw dropped to the floor when she heard the news."

111   Silhouette and Holländer: Holländer, pp. 240–243.

111   "No comprehensive scenario": Sternberg in introduction to *The Blue Angel*, p. 15. A copy of the shooting script is in the *Stiftung Deutsche Kinemathek* signed by Marlene Dietrich.

111   On Mann as model for Professor: Sudendorf, vol. 1, pp. 89–91.

111   Sternberg's notorious assumption of *The Blue Angel* writing credit was part of a lawsuit occasioned by the 1959 remake: "Court Records, Superior Court of the State of California in and for the County of Los Angeles. Complaint for Damages #736126 (For Unfair Competition and Misappro-priation)."

        The case deserves further study. It challenged 20th Century-Fox for producing a remake not of Mann's novel, but of the film itself, with partic-ular regard to story changes, though not limited to them. It was, in essence, an attempt to assert the auteur principle legally and was settled out of court. To make his case coherent, Sternberg simply claimed credits that were not his, though he did so out of the courtroom as well, often to this author, and not just on *The Blue Angel*.

        UFA files record the following screenplay payments: Vollmoeller, 26,780 marks, including overages during shooting; Zuckmayer, 15,776.20

marks; Liebmann (on contract to Pommer), 10,000 marks, plus 1,500 for song lyrics. The mark was near four to the dollar: final accounting letter Alfred Feldes, July 14, 1949. UFA files, SDK.

112   Jannings and microphone: Jannings, p. 198.

112   "new incarnation": Kracauer, p. 217.

113   Fanck and Riefenstahl: Arnold Fanck, *Filmhefte*, no. 2, Summer 1946, p. 10; Riefenstahl, pp. 121–122. In book form, Riefenstahl quotes Sternberg: "Marlene, behave yourself!" ["*Marlene, benimm dich!*]; in an earlier publication the line was, "Marlene, don't behave like a swine!" ["*Marlene, benimm dich nicht wie ein Schwein!*"], *Bunte*, p. 122.

113   Pommer on Sternberg and Marlene: letter, John Pommer to SB, July 26, 1990.

114   Jannings's "strangling": Holländer, pp. 247–248.

114   Press Ball suicide threat: Riefenstahl, p. 124. They were photographed by Alfred Eisenstaedt, reproduced here. Riefenstahl misnames Eisenstaedt as "Eisenstein." Wong was filming something from a script by Vollmoeller, as it happens. Her casting in *Shanghai Express* may have begun that night.

115   Kent cable: Lasky, p. 221.

115   Pasternak: Pasternak, pp. 123–124.

116   The picture was later recut so that final shots are of Lola Lola singing her song on stage. This ending is more effective than admitted by purists, but not the sequence of shots as made by Sternberg.

117   Paramount contract: *Licht-Bild-Bühne* of February 14, 1930, announced the deal on its front page. *Film-Kurier* on the same date announced a "five-year" contract, which was incorrect.

117   Bavarian newspaper: *Münchner Neueste Nachrichten*, February 25, 1930.

117   Klein, Vollmoeller, Paramount: two undated letters MD to KV, *Bundesarchiv*, Coblenz; letter RK to *Life* (see Chap. 5, n. 12), and RK to Harry Ham, September 12, 1935, NYPLPA, Klein file. To Ham, who worked for Myron Selznick in London, he wrote, "It [the settlement] was much to [sic] cheap!!"

118   Heinrich Mann: Peter Baxter uses this well-known quotation for his article "On the Naked Thighs of Miss Dietrich," *Wide Angle*, Spring 1978, pp. 18–25.

118   Haas: int. SB/Dolly Haas, October 4, 1989. Hesterberg quote: Sudendorf, vol. 1, p. 78.

119ff.   Sternberg quotes: *Fun*, p. 239, 237, 113.

120   "I, the well brought-up": *Marlene*, p. 65.

120   Felsing party and chauffeur: Int. SB/Hasso Felsing, as above. Hasso Felsing was the boy who lost his ice cream cone to Marlene's driver. "Tickets": Dietrich, *"Ueberfahrt," Film-Kurier*, May 17, 1930, SDK.

CHAPTER SEVEN : FAME: 1930–1931

126ff.   Reviews: "first work of art," *Berliner Zeitung*, April 2, 1930; "the Experience" and "Extraordinary," Ihering, *Börsen-Courier*, same date. Others: Hans Wollenberg, *Licht-Bild-Bühne*; Ernst Jäger, *Film-Kurier*; Hanns G. Lustig, *Tempo*, all same date. "one artist poorer," Hans Sahl: *Der Montag Morgen*, April 7, 1930.

127 Marlene and Bianca Brooks: Schulberg, p. 278. "Jimmy Walker": *New Yorker*, December 20, 1930; Dietrich, *"Ueberfahrt."*

128 Chidnoff photographs: Sembach, pp. 20–21.

128 Wanger: Dietrich, *Marlene*, pp. 73–74. She misstates the hotel as the Ambassador. The author worked for Wanger in the sixties, and this account draws on Wanger's version of events.

129 Script: the first script of *Morocco* was dated April 8, 1930. MPAA files, Margaret Herrick Library, Academy of Motion Picture Arts and Sciences, hereafter AMPAS.

129 *Paramount on Parade: Berliner Tageblatt*, no. 351, p. 5. All Berlin trade papers reported Dietrich in the picture and Paramount circulated stills, too.

129 Dietrich trailer: *Fun*, p. 247.

129ff. Irene Selznick anecdote: int. SB/Irene Selznick, October 1, 1989.

130 "Why don't you" and "I'd as soon . . . cobra": Higham, p. 102. Higham interviewed Riza Royce before her death.

130 Sternbergs and divorce: undated clips, AMPAS. Peter Baxter and Robert Macmillan clarified details of the Sternberg divorce action for me.

130 "most beautiful thing": quoted in Aronson, p. 69.

131 "of extreme": *Fun*, p. 225.

132 Cooper and Selznick: Swindell, p. 114. "harmless": *Fun*, p. 247. "by proxy": *Ibid.*, p. 73.

133 Code and "Apple" and key: letters MPAA files, AMPAS, Jason S. Joy to B. P. Schulberg, April 15, 1930; September 25, 1930. The September letter refers to the finished film with an additional song, "Give Me the Man (Who Does Things)" in the picture. Though cut from the film, it was later recorded by Marlene.

134 Modern critic: Capsule review of *Morocco* [Kael?], *The New Yorker*, December 30, 1991, p. 20.

134 Paramount and *The Blue Angel*: Paramount had no connection with *The Blue Angel* other than granting Sternberg the sabbatical in which to make it.

135 Cooper quote: Sternberg, *Fun*, p. 255.

135 Furthman anecdote: Swindell, pp. 122–123.

135 Fainting anecdote: *Fun*, p. 254.

135 "Help": *Ibid.*, pp. 248–251. Dietrich retells the same story in *Marlene*, pp. 77–78.

135 "Turn your": *Ibid.*, p. 253. "She was": *Ibid.*, p. 246. "Symphony of ego": confidential source.

135 "The man": Dietrich, *ABC*, p. 151.

136 "Overnight": *New York Times*, [undated], NYPLPA.

136   *Photoplay*: Albert, p. 60.

136   *Los Angeles Times*: " 'Morocco' Sets Mark in Showing at New York," LAT, November 23, 1930, pt. 3, p.1.

136   Chinese premiere: *Los Angeles Times*, November 30, 1930, pt. 3, p. 19.

137   Parsons: *Los Angeles Herald-Examiner*, November 26, 1930.

137   Board of Review: Wilton A. Barrett, *National Board of Review Magazine*, November 1930.

137   "cruel" interview: Boland.

137   Selznick on cakes: int. SB/Irene Selznick, as above.

137ff.   Contract: the first contract for $1,750 per week was for fifty weeks a year, or $87,500. Under the new contract, her guaranteed earnings were $250,000 per year, almost three times as much.

140   "It came too late": Hildenbrandt, p. 94.

CHAPTER EIGHT : EMPRESS OF DESIRE: 1931–1932

141   Heidede as German, school: *Licht-Bild-Bühne*, *"Marlene ist wieder da!"* December 18, 1930.

142   Nazis and *Blue Angel*: *Reichsfilmblatt*, December 8, 1930.

142   Holländer show: Ebinger, pp. 138–139. Blandine Ebinger wrote of her anger at this episode and of Marlene. Holländer had written "Jonny" for his ex-wife, which Marlene famously appropriated, another source of permanent resentment.

142   Jolly Felsing and Ernst Udet, Uncle Willi, Hasso: int. SB/Hasso Felsing, April 22, 1988.

143   Statue: *New York Times*, February 1, 1930. Press Ball: misc. news reports; the Eisenstaedt photograph remains a famous Berlin image. Chaplin: *Licht-Bild-Bühne*, "Chaplin erobert Berlin," "Attacke auf Charlie," *Film-Kurier*, both March 10, 1931.

143   *Tragedy*: The script was by Samuel Hoffenstein, but Sternberg claimed he wrote it himself and was blamed for it by Dreiser and critics: Weinberg, p. 59.

144   *Farewell to Arms*: Swindell, pp. 149–151.

144   *Dishonored* reviews: Parsons, *Los Angeles Examiner*, March 14, 1931; NYT, March 6, 1931, p. 16; *Variety* undated clip, AMPAS.

145   "mother complex": Biery, p. 113. American women's groups: *Licht-Bild-Bühne*, July 30, 1930; *Hamburger-Abendzeitung*, July 26, 1930.

145   Jewelry, cocktails: Barrett.

145   Heidede to America: *Reichsfilmblatt*, April 18, 1931. Peter Kreuder's memoirs (see Bibliography) are often quoted. He cites this departure as the night of *The Blue Angel* premiere. He was not there and is an unreliable source.

146ff.   Marlene's projects: *Nana* was a pet project of Schulberg's; Marlene brought from Berlin a Stefan Zweig novella that later became Max Ophüls's *Letter From an Unknown Woman*. There was a play called *Cobra*, which had been a Judith Anderson vehicle on Broadway: Curt Kaiser, p. 154. A Dashiell Hammett original for her regrettably never saw the light of day: Johnson, p. 100.

146ff.   Cohen to Schulberg: Paramount interoffice cables, August 7, 1931.

147   *Shanghai Express:* The original treatment is at the Museum of Modern Art in New York. Charles Silver, who heads Film Studies there, brought this to my attention.

147   Legs: Leonard Hall, "Perils . . ."

148   Riza Royce suit: *Film-Kurier,* August 10, 1931; quotes from Slater. Headline: *Los Angeles Herald,* August 8, 1931. Fan magazine title and Dietrich statement: Slater.

150   Sarris: p. 35.

151   "Empress of Desire": Sarris, *Ibid.*

151   *Variety:* February 23, 1932.

151   Reviews: London and *New York Times:* quoted in Dickens, p. 103. Grierson, *Grierson on Documentary.*

152   *Vanity Fair:* Harry Alan Potamkin, VF, March 1932, p. 52.

152   Nazi ban of *Dishonored: Licht-Bild-Bühne,* January 8, 1932, p. 1. *All Quiet* premiere: Riefenstahl, p. 102.

152ff.   Chevalier: Harding, pp. 107–108; Chevalier, pp. 196–197, 201–202, 207. Whitley and London: *Licht-Bild-Bühne,* November 23, 1931, front page.

153   Lubitsch, Tiomkin: *New York Herald-Tribune,* April 3, 1932. Cecil Beaton photographed Marlene as the Merry Widow in froufrou and feathers, a famous portrait.

153   Cable: E. Cohen to B. P. Schulberg, August 7, 1931.

153ff.   Writer contracts for what became *Blonde Venus* include a waiver of credit by Marlene for her story. Paramount memos reflect studio outrage at the payment she received. Paramount internal documents: confidential source.

154   "The urge" and "Germany": unsourced clip, February 7, 1932, AMPAS.

154   Riza Royce suits: *Ibid.,* March 23, March 24, 1932, AMPAS.

154   Paramount and "sex stuff": letter, Lamar Trotti to Will H. Hays, April 22, 1932, AMPAS.

156   Maria's claim: Peter Baxter, "The Birth of Venus," p. 4. Maria made the claim before an audience at a *Blonde Venus* screening in London in 1974.

    Baxter's forthcoming book about *Blonde Venus* examines the film in light of social conditions during its making. The author is grateful for the manuscript Baxter shared.

157   Trap in Beverly Hills: Dietrich, *Marlene,* p. 85.

157   Kidnap note: *Los Angeles Times,* June 3, 1932.

157   Rudi to Paris: NYT, June 4, 1932. Maria observing Dickie Moore: Peter Baxter, *op.cit.;* Dietrich, *Marlene,* p. 85. Royce settlement: Higham reports the $100,000 figure in an account that misstates other details; *Marlene,* p.

113. The Beverly Hills Police Department has no records of any kind of the kidnap or extortion threat.

158   Cary Grant: Wansell, p. 71; Schickel, *Cary Grant*, pp. 39–41. Marlene's private comments about Grant were caustic: confidential source.

158   Moore: *Süddeutsche-Zeitung*, December 24–26, 1988, p. 30.

158   Sam Jaffe: Higham, p. 126.

160   Reviews: Mordaunt Hall, *NYT*, September 24, 1932; *NYHT* [undated], NYPLPA; Dwight Macdonald, "Notes on Hollywood Directors," *Symposium*, April and July, 1933; Pare Lorentz, *VF*, November 1932, p. 58.

CHAPTER NINE : APOTHEOSIS: 1933–1934

163   "I will never": Biery, "Is Dietrich Through?" p. 29.

163   Dorothy Parker: quoted in Reinhardt, p. 99.

163   "This is not": Biery, p. 110.

163   Rudi in America: *NYT*, December 20, 1932. Script from Zuckmayer: "*Der Unfall Marlene Dietrichs*," *Mein Film*, no. 380, 1933, p. 6. The *Love Story* project had already been announced for Gustav Ucicky, who directed Marlene in *Café Electric*.

164ff.   *Song of Songs* and Hays office: letters from Hays office (Fred W. Beetson) to Schulberg, October 20 and 22, 1931, AMPAS files.

166   Paramount suit: *NYT*, January 3, 1933; *NYHT*, same date.

166   Sternberg to Germany and Hugenberg: *Fun*, p. 229. Marlene back to work: *NYT*, January 5, 1933.

166   The nude statue: it was made by an Italian sculptor named Scarpitta, who had sculpted Mussolini, a leader much admired in Hollywood executive circles then.

167   Overalls: *New York Sun*, October 26, 1933.

167   Mamoulian letter: June 5, 1933, AMPAS files.

168   Vera Zorina, "Jo, Jo" and advances: int. SB/Zorina, August 1986, May–June 1988. See also Zorina, pp. 114–115. Marlene posed with Amelia Earhart on the set.

168   MD and Mamoulian as lovers: confidential source, though Mamoulian confirmed their brief affair to John Kobal, who confirmed it to the author.

168   Brian Aherne: Aherne, pp. 198–204. Long Beach earthquake: "How the Earthquake Affected the Stars," (unsourced clip), AMPAS.

168ff.   Marlene, Stokowski, and the Ballet Russe: Zorina, pp. 113–114, plus ints. SB/Vera Zorina, as above.

169   Sternberg and the Reichstag: *Fun*, p. 229.

170   Mann quote: Taylor, p. 43.

170   Hauptmann: Marlene disliked Nobel prize–winner Hauptmann and noted his political accommodation in her *ABC*, pp. 74–75.

171   Reviews: *Hollywood Reporter*, June 12, 1933; Los Angeles *Examiner*, August 4, 1933; London *Times*, *NYT*, *Newsweek*, quoted in Dickens, p. 111.

171   Alfred Kerr: "*Marlene—an der Seine*," *Das Neue Tagebuch*, September 9, 1933.

171 Ban: *"Dietrich-Film Verboten," Licht-Bild-Bühne*, March 16, 1934.

171 Dollar quote: *Licht-Bild-Bühne*, May 13, 1933.

171ff. Marlene and Mercedes de Acosta: de Acosta, pp. 241–244. Douglas Fairbanks, Jr., stressed this relationship; int. SB/DF, June 2, 1987. See Gronowicz for Garbo's relationship with de Acosta, pp. 312–321. Alice B. Toklas story: confidential source.

173 Martin Kosleck: one of his paintings of her is in the SDK, Berlin.

173 Sternberg and MGM: Sternberg to SB, 1966. There was talk of a picture with Clark Gable, who was suspicious of a man he considered a "woman's director." Sternberg later worked at MGM without billing on *I Take This Woman* with Hedy Lamarr and as billed director on *Sergeant Madden* with Wallace Beery.

174 Writing de Acosta: de Acosta, p. 250.

174 "Jeered": *New York Sun*, May 19, 1933.

174 Police: "Miss Dietrich Watched," *New York World-Telegram*, May 22, 1933.

174 *New Yorker* quote: Flanner, *Paris*, p. 97.

174ff. Weill songs: one was set to a text by one of Marlene's favorite poets, Erich Kästner, called *"Der Abschiedsbrief"* ("The Farewell Letter"), the other from a German text sketched in German by Jean Cocteau, called *"Es regnet"* ("It's Raining").

175 Colpet, Wilder, Wachsmann, Lorre, et al.: Colpet, pp. 75–86. Also, int. SB/Max Kolpe [Colpet], October 22, 1987.

175 Aherne in London: Stuart Jackson.

176 Vienna, Prater, Willi Forst: *"Rund um Marlene," Mein Film*, no. 390, p. 8.

176 Forst film and Marlene's financing: letter, MD to Werner G. Plack, May 3, 1977, SDK.

176 Vienna, autographs: *Mein Film*, as above. For Hans Jaray, *Die Bühne*, no. 354, June 1933, pp. 6–7; no. 382, August 1934, p. 21.

176 MD to Forster: letter mailed from Paris August 16, 1933. It is one of a series written to Forster that summer, all expressing frustration and nostalgia. Marbach.

177 "Hell on earth": *Der Spiegel*, December 1991.

177 French ship, Pola Negri: NYT, September 11, 1933; *New York Sun*, September 26, 1933. Negri shortly thereafter returned to Germany and made *Mazurka*, directed by Willi Forst, possibly at the suggestion of Marlene. It was a stunning film, but there was no place in the Third Reich for Negri, though Goebbels personally signed papers making her "Aryan" despite her Jewish antecedents.

177 Queens: Rankin, Ruth. "They're All Queening It," *Photoplay*, December 1933.

177 "If this film": Dietrich, *Marlene*, p. 94.

177 Sternberg quote: *Fun*, pp. 264–265.

178 Music: Mackenzie, quoted in Peter Baxter, BFI, p. 45.

178   Maria to Shirley Temple: Black, pp. 64–65.

181   "Miss Dietrich is me": Bogdanovich, "Encounters with . . ." p. 24.

181   London *Times:* May 10, 1934.

181   "assassinate": *Fun,* pp. 264–265. "Comedy": John Baxter advances this curious notion, p. 115. Robin Wood in Lyon, vol. 2, p. 414, suggests audience's reluctance to be amused.

181   Watts: *New York Herald-Tribune,* December 15, 1934.

181   Sarris: Sarris, p. 40.

182   *Variety:* September 18, 1934.

182   Dietrich quotes: Dietrich, *Marlene,* pp. 92, 95.

182   Sam Jaffe: The author interviewed Jaffe in 1966. Other quotes here come from his SMU Oral History interview, courtesy Ronald L. Davis.

183   Horse fall: de Acosta, pp. 249–250.

183   When the author was writing about Sternberg for his Ph.D. thesis, Sternberg correctly emphasized again and again his economy as a director. He was not profligate with money, but was a master at making it look that way. To *be* lavish was abhorrent to him; to be *thought* lavish (in Hollywood) satisfied his professional ego.

184   "final tribute": *Fun,* p. 266.

CHAPTER TEN : TRIBUTE AND FAREWELL: 1934–1935

185   Dietrich quote and German edict: Calhoun, p. 32.

186   Marlene's gift: anon., "Marlene Dietrich Makes Nazi Gift; Held Reconciled," *New York Evening Post,* March 14, 1934, AP report datelined Berlin. Ban on *Song of Songs* and quote: *Licht-Bild-Bühne,* March 16, 1934. It is quite possible that Marlene's "contribution" was made by Paramount to avoid this ban, which was made under Nazi propaganda law Paragraph 7 of February 16, 1934.

186   Marlene as Russian: *"Marlene Dietrich Russin?" Badische Presse* (Karlsruhe), November 10, 1934.

186ff.   Hemingway story: Hotchner, quoted in *Hemingway and . . . ,* p. 122.

187   Hemingway and Marlene: Dietrich quote, MD to SB, July 31, 1987. She told Maximilian Schell, tapes: "Never, never, never." For Hemingway and "your girls," see Mary Hemingway, pp. 128–129.

187   Hemingway writing re Marlene: Meyers, p. 484, identifies Marlene as the model for the actress-wife of Thomas Hudson in *Islands.* Hemingway describes her: "She was a delightful and charming woman who had never altered a plan that she had made in her life. Her plans were always made in secret, like those of a good general, and they were as rigidly enforced." *Islands,* p. 4. *Garden of Eden* deals with androgyny as a central theme.

187   Coward quotes: Lesley, pp. 175–176.

187   Garbo and Dietrich quotes: Gladys Hall, p. 34. Paramount publicist quote: Lang, p. 96.

188   Marlene and Ethel Merman: Schallert, p. 68.

188   Marlene/Rockefeller cover: *Berliner Illustrirte Zeitung*, December 27, 1935.

188   Sternberg statement: quoted in John Baxter, p. 130.

189   Herman Mankiewicz: quoted in Schulberg, pp. 486–487.

189   Cohen and conflict of interest: *Ibid.*

189   *Red Pawn*: announced in Lang, p. 96.

191   Schickel quote: *The Stars*, p. 129. "most vicious": John Baxter, p. 123.

191   Rosen: *Popcorn Venus*, p. 164.

192   MD courting Frances Dee: Kobal, *People*, p. 301.

193   Sternberg to Bogdanovich: Bogdanovich, "Encounters," p. 25.

194   Hays office: letters, Hays to Zukor, April 25, 1935; critique, memo to Joe Breen, April 18, 1935, AMPAS.

194   Code suggestions: Breen to Hays, April 17, 1935; Breen to John Hammell (Paramount), April 19, 1935.

194   "extra-code question": Breen to Hays, April 17, 1935.

195   Reviews: All quoted in *Hollywood Reporter*, May 10, 1935. *Variety* review, February 23, 1935.

195ff. Spain: Spanish protest cabled to Will Hays from Mr. Deane of Paramount, October 24, 1935.

196   Zukor quote: NYT, October 24, 1935.

196   November 27 letter: Joe Breen to recipients noted, AMPAS.

197   "Best film . . . the least successful": Bogdanovich, "Encounters," p. 25.

197   "Crowning masterpiece": David Stewart Hull, *Film Society Review*, November 1964, p. 12.

197   Dietrich on Sternberg's leaving: *Pour Vous*, Vienna, April 14, 1935.

197   Dietrich quote: Griffith, pp. 9–10.

198   Thomson quote: *Dictionary*, p. 138.

198   *"folie à deux"*: Taylor, p. 31.

198   French critic: Michael Aubriant, *France-Soir*, January 20, 1966.

198   American critic: Lewis Jacobs, p. 468.

199   Thomson: *Movie Man*, p. 47.

199   "I failed him": Chet Green, p. 42.

199   "The man": Dietrich, *ABC*, p. 151.

CHAPTER ELEVEN : SAVING DIETRICH: 1935–1936

201   Empress Josephine: *Licht-Bild-Bühne*, March 18, 1935. This report also named Lubitsch as director and was announced by Zukor. Casino de Paris: *Licht-Bild-Bühne*, July 31, 1934.

203ff. Gilbert and Mayer: Fountain, p. 131. John Gilbert sources include: Ints. SB/Leatrice Joy Gilbert Fountain, April 1, 1989; letters LJGF to SB, May 27, 1989. Mrs. Fountain also provided me with copies of her correspondence with MD from the period immediately following her father's death.

206   Lubitsch reshoots: *Variety*, February 4, 1936.

206   Color tests: These tests exist in a private collection in New York. Collectors are subject to criminal laws, but are very often, in the face of movie companies' disdain for their own history, unheralded film preservationists.

206   "Romantic fabrication": Leatrice Fountain says the Garbo-Gilbert reunion story was invented by Garson Kanin: int. SB/LJGF, April 1, 1989.

206   Cooper's wife and *Morocco*: Schickel, *Schickel on Film*, p. 186. Cooper's biographer cites active rumors: Swindell, pp. 181ff.

206   Parsons: quoted in Fountain, p. 251.

207   Irene Selznick: int. SB/IMZ, October 3, 1989. Selznick to Leatrice Fountain: int. SB/LJGF, April 1, 1989.

207   Leatrice re Maria: letter, LJGF to SB, May 27, 1989.

208   Schickel on Cooper: *Schickel on Film*, p. 181.

208   *Time*: March 9, 1936.

208   Kael: quoted in Kael's capsule review of *Desire*, *The New Yorker*.

208ff.   Reviews: Parsons, *Los Angeles Herald-Examiner*, March 13, 1936; *NYT*, April 13, 1936; *Variety* dated April 15, 1936 (NY and *Daily Variety*); *Film Daily*, February 4, 1936; *Time* and *Newsweek*, undated clips, NYPLPA.

209   Hathaway later told John Kobal that "when [Sternberg] left the business, he'd forgotten more about movies than most directors knew": Kobal, *People*, p. 618.

210   Glazer: quoted in Dickens, p. 125.

210   Hathaway memories: Higham, *Marlene*, pp. 169–170.

211   *I Loved a Soldier*: It was a doomed project. Paramount got a script finally and cast Margaret Sullavan, who promptly broke her arm. In 1939 the chambermaid became Italian import Isa Miranda (opposite Ray Milland), and then in 1943 she was Anne Baxter in *Five Graves to Cairo*, which director Billy Wilder threw to director-turned-actor Erich von Stroheim, who easily upstaged the maid. A Pola Negri vehicle had become a showcase for "the man you love to hate."

    "Facts" re *I Loved a Soldier*: "Dietrich Picture Halted, Awaiting Complete Script," *Hollywood Reporter*, February 12, 1936, p. 1ff. Additional information: Selznick-International memos, Bob Ross to [Phil] Ryan, January 31–February 12, 1936, detailing Ray Lissner's reports (Lissner was assistant director on *I Loved a Soldier*). David O. Selznick Collection, Harry Ransom Humanities Research Center, University of Texas at Austin, hereafter DOS-Texas.

211   Crawford: Memo, Selznick to J. J. Cohn, MGM production manager, March 5, 1935, DOS-Texas. That version would have been directed by George Cukor.

211   *Variety*, even then: *Variety*, September 7, 1927.

212   Kay Brown: Cable, KB to DOS, December 27, 1935, DOS-Texas.

212   Selznick on Marlene: Behlmer, p. 136. In spite of Selznick's coolness toward Sternberg, Thomas Schatz suggests the director's team concept on the Dietrich pictures at Paramount inspired Selznick's similar operation: Schatz, pp. 75–76.

212   Marlene's inquiry: Gregory Ratoff, a mutual friend, had made the inquiry on her behalf. Selznick notebook: Ray Daum, DOS-Texas, letter to SB, January 26, 1988.

212   To Marlene's inquiry: Behlmer, p. 135.

212   Re "a superb actor": Memo, DOS to Kay Brown, March 17, 1936, DOS-Texas.

212   Gabin: Memo, KB to DOS, March 27, 1936, DOS-Texas.

212   Rathbone as Boris: letter, BR to DOS, March 21, 1936. Niven et al.: casting memos, Charles Richards to DOS, March 30 and April 20, 1936, DOS-Texas.

213   Oberon payoff: Cable, George Schaefer (UA) to UA branch offices, March 27, 1936. The cable announced Oberon and *Dark Victory* (DOS-Texas).

213   Mercedes de Acosta: Cable, Harry Edington to DOS, March 18, 1936, DOS-Texas.

213   Goldbeck: Memo, Val Lewton to DOS, March 5, 1936, refers to "the Goldbeck script" (DOS-Texas). Goldbeck also had a credit on Tod Brownings's *Freaks*.

214ff.   Logan and "twash": Logan, *My Up etc.*, pp. 87–88. Also Logan, *Movie Stars etc.*, pp. 145–146.

215   Logan, MD, and Sternberg: The Reminiscences of Joshua Logan in the Oral History Collection of Columbia University, hereafter Logan COHC. Quotes here from part 5, pp. 189, 192, 199.

215   "Candles": Logan, *My Up etc.*, p. 100.

215   "Think over": *Ibid.*, p. 101.

215   Goldbeck and Marlene: int. SB/Irene Selznick, October 3, 1989.

215   Logan and Tilly Losch: Logan COHC, part 8, pp. 328–330.

215ff.   Selznick "pep talk": Memo, DOS to Boleslawski, April 14, 1936, DOS-Texas.

216   Hal Rosson: Logan COHC, part 5, p. 196.

216   Boleslawski on Boyer: letter, RB to DOS, April 15, 1936, DOS-Texas.

216   Boyer's toupee: Memo, JL to DOS, April 16, 1936, DOS-Texas.

216   Boley on script: Cable, RB to DOS, April 14, 1936, DOS-Texas.

217   "A poker game": Dietrich, *Marlene*, p. 176.

217   "Miss Dietrich's Hair": DOS to RB, June 17, 1936, DOS-Texas.

217   Riggs and "the bitch": Braunlich, p. 141. Marlene and Rathbone: Cable, RB to DOS, April 27, 1936, DOS-Texas.

217ff.   Cable: DOS to RB, April 28, 1936, DOS-Texas.

218   Marlene on scripts: RB to DOS, April 30, 1936, DOS-Texas.

218   Marlene and Goldbeck: Cable, RB to DOS, May 1, 1936, DOS-Texas.

218   Selznick emissary: this was Ray Klune, Haver, p. 188.

219   MD and "repulsive": MD's term in discussing Selznick with Gavin Lambert. Int. SB/GL, November 28, 1988.

221   Marlene on *Normandie*: *Vogue*, September 1936.

221   Maria and "purgatory": int. SB/Bernard Hall, December 5–6, 1986. Bonita Granville: SMU Oral History Collection; courtesy Ron L. Davis.

221   Maria's photographs: Cable, Russell Birdwell to DOS, November 15, 1936, DOS-Texas. Birdwell was the publicity man, and his cable cites "censoring," which he claimed "Dietrich suggested." Maria's small scene is intact in presently available versions of the film. She is unlisted in the credits.

222   Arrival in England and quotes: Dixon, Campbell, "Marlene Comes to London," *Daily Telegraph*, July 31, 1936.

223ff. Fairbanks quotes: int. SB/DF, Jr., June 2, 1987; Fairbanks, pp. 373–374.

223   Paley in Scotland: Smith, p. 107. Other Paley details and Fairbanks quotes from int. SB/DF, Jr., as above.

224   Fairbanks's statue of Marlene: Fairbanks, p. 481. The artist showed SB a copy of the statue, which is executed with grace.

224   "a wonderfully": Fairbanks, p. 377. "rather naughty": int. SB/DF, Jr.

225   MD on Mrs. Simpson: MD to SB, April 5, 1987.

225   Abdication: Fairbanks, pp. 384–385; int. SB/DF, Jr.

226   Selznick cable: [undated], DOS-Texas.

226   Luce was furious: *Time* had exclusive production photos for its Marlene cover. Whitney and *Newsweek* got around this by using for their cover the color photograph of Marlene (with Boyer) that decorated the walls of Whitney's office. That photo was "private," they claimed, which did not markedly improve Luce's humor. Files: DOS-Texas.

226   *Allah* reviews: Winsten, November 20, 1936; *Variety*, November 25, 1936; *World-Telegram*, November 30, 1936; *NYT* quoted in Dickens, p. 131; *Newsweek*, November 21, 1936.

226   *Time: Time*, November 30, 1936, p. 40. Niven Busch is noted in the Selznick files, DOS-Texas.

226   London opening: Cable, Lowell Calvert to DOS, DOS-Texas.

226ff. Graham Greene: Greene, p. 126.

227   Sternberg quote: *Fun*, p. 173. Sternberg claims Korda turned the picture over to him because Korda couldn't handle Laughton, but Korda never intended to direct the picture.

227   Fairbanks on MD and Sternberg: int. SB/DF, Jr., as above.

228ff. *I, Claudius*: Simon Callow, in his biography *Charles Laughton, A Difficult Actor*, quotes Philip Jenkinson on Herbert Wilcox's visit to Oberon following the accident. Oberon, according to this account, said shooting had to be abandoned because of "poor Jo," confined to Charing Cross Psychiatric.

        Sternberg's memoirs are very hard on Laughton in discussing *Claudius*, and his enduring resentment of the actor provides the best clues as to what went wrong on the picture.

        Sternberg never disclosed what he knew about the Oberon "accident." Terence Young, later a film director, was an assistant on the picture, responsible for daily call sheets, and told the author Korda had forewarned him Oberon would not be shooting because she was "going to have an accident."

CHAPTER TWELVE : EXILE: 1937–1939

230   Hitler and Marlene: Riefenstahl, p. 289.

231   Ossietzky was awarded the Nobel Prize while in Papenburg concentration camp, where he died in 1938. His Nobel Prize so outraged Hitler that Germans were forbidden to accept the prize from that time until the end of the Third Reich.

231   Maedy Soyka and others: Soyka is cited as Goebbels's messenger by Pem in the *Allgemeine Wochenzeitung der Juden in Deutschland*, April 5, 1963. As payment from the Nazis for her trouble, she is said to have received a coffee house on the Champs-Élysées, where she was murdered by French Resistance workers during the war. Her husband, Jonny Soyka, once represented Marlene in Berlin. The story that Friedrich Holländer's song "Jonny" was written for him is apocryphal: Holländer wrote it for his then-wife, cabaret singer Blandine Ebinger, still living in Berlin in 1992. The Goebbels and Ribbentrop rumors are ubiquitous, but no personal visits by them are recorded.

231   Hess as "Black Bertha": *New York Times*, June 9, 1991, p. 1ff.

231   Marlene and Hess: MD to SB, July 31, 1987. Dietrich said: "When Hess came to London I was there. It was Christmas. I let him wait for a day. Maria said you can't do this, ask him up. He came up and said, 'The *Führer* wants you to come home,' and I said 'No, *never*.' "

231   Marlene's citizenship application and "I live here": *Los Angeles Times*, March 6, 1937. "America has been": *Time*, October 17, 1938.

231   "Deserts": *Los Angeles Herald-Examiner*, March 6, 1937. Constance McCormick Collection, USC.

232   *Der Stuermer*: German denunciation of Marlene was reported widely in America. This quotation is from the *Los Angeles Herald-Examiner*, [n.d., circa July 1937], McCormick Collection, USC.

232   Marlene's nude swims and Lang: Fairbanks, pp. 394–395; int. SB/DF, Jr., as above.

232   Marlene and Lang: int. SB/Kevin Thomas, August 30, 1990. Lang's companion Lily Latté is the source for Lang's brief affair with Marlene.

233   Sarris quote: Sarris, *American*, p. 67.

234   Vreeland quote: McConathy and Vreeland, p. 23.

235   MD on *Angel*: Dietrich/Schell, tapes.

235   Langner: Langner, pp. 431–432.

235   Fairbanks and letters: Fairbanks, p. 396. Fairbanks was troubled by Rudi's relationship with Tamara: int. SB/DF, Jr., as above.

235   *Angel* and the Code: Universal had tried to buy *Angel* for director John Stahl in early 1934 and encountered immediate problems because of its theme of a "double standard for women." As early as March 9, 1934, elimination of "most if not all of the adultery" and in October of the "Parisian brothel" caused Universal to drop the project.

        Paramount bought it for Lubitsch and Dietrich, and the subject aroused "grave concern . . . great objections" in late December of 1936. Hence, Lubitsch's wanting to shoot two versions: memo to files, Geoffrey Sherlock, March 16, 1937. Seal granted: memo to files, Joseph I. Breen, June 22, 1937. Revocation of seal: telegram to Breen from Sherlock, October 4, 1937. "Staggering": letter to Breen from Sherlock quoting Paramount, October 5, 1937.

236   *Angel* reviews: *HR*, September 14, 1937; *Variety* and *Weekly Variety*, September 15, 1937; "eyelashes" review is Basil Wright in *The Spectator*, November 26, 1937; C. A. Lejeune reprinted in *Humour in Criticism*; *NYT* quoted in Dickens, p. 139; *Literary Digest*, November 1937, p. 34.

237   Paramount settled Marlene's contract and fired her on December 22, 1937. *French Without Tears* was later made with Ray Milland and Ellen Drew. The infamous "box-office poison" ad was placed by Harry Brand on behalf of fellow exhibitors and ran on May 3, 1938, though *Angel* was the direct cause of Marlene's inclusion in it.

238ff.   Remarque: details mostly from Barker and Last. Ekstein is also a Re-marque source. The powerful Ullstein firm, which published *All Quiet*, claims it is still the century's bestseller. As far as one can tell, the only language in which it was ever out of print was German, under the Nazis.

239   MD and Remarque and Rilke: MD to SB, July 31, 1987.

239   Marlene and "dwarf Goebbels": MD to SB, July 31, 1987.

240   Goebbels's diary entry: November 12, 1937. "*Gegen Gerüchte um Marlene Dietrich*," *Film-Kurier*, November 19, 1937. The Goebbels dia-ries are published by the Institute for Contemporary History, Munich. Four of a projected ten volumes have appeared. Heinz Hilpert's diaries record his meetings with Marlene in Paris at Goebbels's request: Dillman, p. 138.

240   "Marlene's Sewing Circle": this was a fairly ubiquitous gag line in Hollywood: "Four Queens at the Races," [undated clip], McCormick Col-lection, USC. Marlene and Ann Warner were captured together in a famous photograph by their mutual friend Jean Howard. Warner's first husband, Don Alvarado, had been in *The Devil is a Woman* as Concha's bullfighter "cousin."

241   Thalberg quote: Gabler, p. 338.

241   *Arch of Triumph*: "steel orchid," p. 257; "face" citations pp. 5 and 95. "Madonna" and "Madeleine" word play, Barker and Last, p. 93.

242   "To M.D.": The novel was published with this dedication, later re-moved by Paulette Goddard when she married Remarque.

242   Georg Will and reunion: Wiechers. Will told Wiechers that Goebbels said to him, "If we succeed in bringing Marlene back to German film, then not only the export of German films is assured, but their reputation abroad as well, which has markedly suffered. The prominence of your sister-in-law can polish all that up."

242   Goebbels and UFA: UFA Protokol #1348, January 1, 1939.

243   Chevalier incident: Flanner, *Paris Was*, p. 188.

243   De Acosta in Paris: De Acosta, p. 281.

243   Hemingway on Remarque: Hotchner, *Papa*, p. 27. Hemingway refers to Remarque as "the worthless R." Remarque on Hemingway: Barker and Last, p. 23.

244   Marlene's citizenship: Judge Hollzer quoted in *Los Angeles Examiner* [n.d., June 1939], McCormick Collection, USC.

244   Marlene and the I.R.S.: undated clips, *Herald-Tribune* and *Daily News*, both p. 1 (NYPLPA); *Daily Mirror* (London), June 15, 1939, p. 1.

245   Remarque in Cannes: Colpet, pp. 103–105.

245ff.   Marlene's stories re Carstairs et al.: Billy Wilder to Volker Schlöndorff, tapes; int. SB/Kitty Carlisle Hart, June 6, 1991. Marlene's ribald reminiscences for Wilder's guests were so well known they came to be known as "the Billy and Marlene Show" and ended with Wilder (according to Hart) or Marlene (according to Wilder) asking the audience, "Are we boring you?"

246   Pasternak and "shimmering": Pasternak, p. 124. Further Pasternak quotes, pp. 199–210.

246   Feldman, Paulette Goddard: int. SB/Jean Howard, June 4, 1991. (Howard was Mrs. Charles Feldman).

246   Sternberg quote: Griffith, p. 11.

CHAPTER THIRTEEN : PHOENIX: 1939–1941

249   Marlene's salary: Pasternak Collection, USC.

251   Marshall quote: *Action*, int. by Bob Thomas and T. J. Flicker with James Stewart, James Meade, Hal Mohr, Felix Jackson, and George Marshall, October 25, 1972, MoMA. Mohr quote: Maltin, p. 128.

251   Jackson on Remarque and Marlene: int. SB/FJ, November 20, 1987.

251ff.   *Destry* figures and dates: Production reports September 8 to December 23, when final costs were entered. Universal Studios Collection, USC. Also, Pasternak Collection, USC.

252   Venus de Milo quote: J. M. Patterson, *New York Post*, [n.d.], NYPLPA.

253   Stewart on *Destry*: McDowall, p. 67.

253   "Never fall in love with an actress": Odets, pp. 275–279.

253   Maria Sieber on Marlene and Stewart: int. SB/confidential source, June 14, 1990.

254ff.   Reviews: Erskine Johnson, *Los Angeles Examiner*, November 29, 1939; Sara Hamilton, same paper, January 13, 1940; New York *Daily News*, November 30, 1939; *New York Times*, November 30, 1939 and undated follow-up, NYPLPA. *Variety*, December 6, 1939.

255   Baseball: the game was August 8, 1940, at Los Angeles's Wrigley Field. Program: Lucien Littlefield Collection, USC.

255   I.R.S. settlement: [unsourced press clip, datelined Hollywood, May 10, 1941, NYPLPA.

256   Violla Rubber: ints. SB/Dean Goodman, March 2, 1989; June 9, 1990.

257   "There's an octoroon": The picture, cited by Sarris, *American*, p. 130, was *Her Man* with James Gleason and Helen Twelvetrees.

257ff.   Garnett on Marlene and Wayne: Garnett, pp. 244–245.

258   Wayne and Marlene: Shepherd, Slatzer, and Grayson, p. 179.

258   MD on Wayne: Dietrich, *Marlene*, pp. 183–184.

258ff.   Zolotow quote: Zolotow, *Shooting Star*, p. 168.

259ff.   Reviews: *NYT*, November 10, 1940; Boehnel, [n.d.]; *Daily News*, November 17, 1940; *H-T*, [n.d.]: all NYPLPA.

260   Marlene and France: For "my arch" see *Colliers*, p. 28; for the Comédie Française: *New York Herald-Tribune*, April 3, 1940. The picture was to have been called *The Lady of the West*, to be shot in Rome.

261   Clair quote: Samuels, p. 80.

261   Krasna quotes here and below: McGilligan, p. 223. The other four writers were Norman Reilly Raine, Joseph Moncure March, John B. Sanford, and Lillie Hayward. "Notice of Tentative Credits," dated March 11, 1941, Universal, to those listed, Pasternak Collection, USC.

261   Dietrich on Clair: Dietrich, *Marlene*, p. 135, 184.

262   Raft quotes: Yablonsky, pp. 146–147.

263   Salaries on *Manpower*: Warner Brothers budget memo, March 18, 1941, USC, Warner Brothers Collection.

263   Robinson quotes: Robinson with Spiegelgass, pp. 243–244.

263   Warners complaint against Raft: letter, WB to SAG, April 30, 1941, USC, Edward G. Robinson Collection.

264   Walsh quote: Walsh, p. 317.

264   Reviews: *New Yorker*, July 12, 1941; *Variety*, July 9, 1941; *Life*, [n.d.]; *NYT* and *H-T*, July 5, 1941.

265   Leisen to Marlene: Chierichetti, p. 177.

266   Silver quote: Silver, p. 107.

266   Leisen on Marlene: Chierichetti, p. 175.

266ff.   Reviews, "lively": Boehnel, [n.d.], NYPLPA; *HR* and *Variety*, both January 23, 1942; *NYT*, April 24, 1942, p. 21.

CHAPTER FOURTEEN : HOME FRONT: 1942–1943

268   Hasso Felsing and Jolly's son: int. SB/Hasso Felsing, April 22, 1989.

269ff.   HUAC: Both John Russell Taylor in *Strangers* and Ian Hamilton discuss pre-WW II HUAC in Hollywood. Shirley Temple tells of being investigated in Black, pp. 252–253, and refers to Davis and Hopkins and the "League of Women Shoppers."

270   Heinrich Mann at Warners: Friedrich, *Nets*, p. 57. European Film Fund and further on Mann: Taylor, *Strangers*, pp. 146–151.

270   Rudolf Forster: Preminger, p. 61; Dietrich, *Marlene*, p. 187; int. SB/Mrs. Walter Reisch, August 18, 1989.

271   Elfriede Remarque [Remark]: Barker and Last, p. 22. Her trial was colored by the fame of her brother. She was executed for her involvement

with the Scholls and the "White Rose" resistance group at the University of Munich.

271   Bond sales and Governor: *Los Angeles Times* [undated clip], USC, McCormick Collection.

271   Roosevelt: quoted from Dietrich, *Nehmt*, pp. 144–145. See also Dietrich, *Marlene*, p. 189.

271ff.   MD re Charles Feldman: MD to SB, August 17, 1987.

272   Reviews: *Daily News*, May 22, 1942; *NYT*, May 22, 1942, p. 27; *Time*, [n.d.], NYPLPA.

273   *Pittsburgh* reviews: *NYT*, February 25, 1943, p. 27; *New Yorker* (David Lardner), February 27, 1943; *H-T* quoted in Dickens, p. 167.

273   Marlene on retirement: quoted in Parrish, p. 199.

273   Berlin, Todd, Shuberts: *New York World-Telegram*, January 7, 1938; *New York Daily News*, November 9, 1939, NYPLPA. Porter had made several attempts to interest Marlene, partly through her friend Clifton Webb. He wrote *You Never Know* for her, which was the show in which Lupe Velez did her Dietrich parody.

274   Marlene and Wilde: *NYT*, July 18, 1942; *New York Journal-American*, February 6, 1942. Re musical version of *Rain*: clips, [n.d.], *NYT*, NYPLPA. The Sadie Thompson musical finally got June Havoc and closed out of town.

275   Welles, Marlene, and Del Rio: Leaming, p. 208.

275   Welles re Marlene: *Ibid.*, p. 268.

275   Raft and Wayne after Marlene: Raft's photo, Yablonsky, p. 228; Wayne and Goddard, Shepherd *et al.*, p. 179. The two co-starred in Cecil B. DeMille's *Reap the Wild Wind*.

275   Odets quoting Remarque on Marlene: Odets, p. 279.

276   Remarque: *Arch*, quotes pp. 414, 252, 196.

276   Marlene on Gabin: "an ideal being" Dietrich, *Marlene*, p. 142; "helpless," p. 135; "his mother," p. 136.

277   Marlene in Palm Springs: *New York Times*, "Marlene Dietrich Ill," March 9, 1942 [n.p.], NYPLPA.

277   House in Brentwood and Garbo: Brunelin, pp. 347–348.

277   Welles on Gabin: Leaming, p. 268.

277   Marlene in Welles's act: *Ibid.*, pp. 268–269.

277   Gabin's jealousy: Brunelin, p. 382; int. SB/Sam and Suzanne Taylor, June 6/7, 1987. Both confirm Dietrich's frank, "He used to beat me." Gabin's wanting to marry Marlene and have a child was a theme of his life in the forties. See Brunelin; int. SB/Max Colpet, as above.

278   Maria and Haydn: the engagement was reported in *Time*, June 25, 1943. Gabin left for the war in late April.

279   Cheryl Crawford: Crawford, p. 118. See also Drew, p. 64, for Weill, who thought Marlene's contribution to the songs was "considerable." Marlene's signed contracts for *Venus* are in the Crawford Collection, NYPLPA.

279   Marlene and *Venus*: Crawford, p. 124; Sanders, pp. 323–324; Herr-

mann, pp. 147–149. Marlene's contract [NYPLPA] gave her first refusal and control over the movie deal, which was made with Universal. Ava Gardner played the role in the film.

279ff.   Dean Goodman and Maria: quotes here and later from ints. SB/Dean Goodman, March 2, 1989, June 9, 1990; also letter, DG to SB, April 19, 1989.

280   Marlene to press: *Los Angeles Times*, August 24, 1943. USC, McCormick Collection.

281   Dieterle: *Colliers*, p. 26.

281   Legs quote: *Ibid*.

281   Dieterle's first version of *Kismet* was one of several German-language versions of American films he made, which led to his prolific American career. As a Reinhardt star, Dieterle knew Lubitsch's oriental fantasy *Sumurûn*, which starred Pola Negri in 1919, to which the MGM *Kismet* owes a debt.

282   Marlene on astrology: Dietrich, *ABC*, p. 15.

282   *Life* on "Gilded Dietrich": *Life*, November 29, 1943, pp. 119–123.

283   "The—well": Ethan Mordden, *The New Yorker*, July 3, 1989, p. 88.

284   Reviews: *NYT*, August 23, 1944, p. 16; *Variety, Film Daily*, "age" remark *Harrison Reports*, August 28, 1944. *Time, Newsweek*: undated [August 1944], NYPLPA. Barnes in *H-T*: August 28, 1944.

284   Marlene and *Kismet* screenings: She particularly wanted Maximilian Schell to see it when he made his documentary feature of her life. He missed it. Schell/Dietrich: tapes.

284   Marlene's MGM money: Walker, p. 163.

284ff.   Selznick writing desk: letter, Selznick files, MD to DOS, January 12, 1938, Courtesy David Thomson.

285   Colman anecdote: Colman, p. 214.

285   Mike Nichols: MN to SB, in conversation, August 1985.

286   McDowall quote: int. SB/Roddy McDowall, November 20, 1986.

286   Remarque and letters: Barker and Last, p. 81.

286   "one was": Dietrich, *Marlene*, p. 192.

286   Public auction: auction advertisement, *Los Angeles Times*, April 2, 1944.

287   "The only important thing": Sergeant, p. 93.

CHAPTER FIFTEEN : LILI MARLENE: 1944–1945

288   "I will not": Lerman, "Welcome, Marlene," p. 191.

289   "I sometimes wonder": Sargeant, p. 97.

289   Danny Thomas: Dietrich, *Marlene*, p. 209.

289   Marlene's act: Lerman, *op. cit.*, p. 154.

290   Fort Meade: *Baltimore Sun*, March 21, 1944.

290   New York to Algiers: Dietrich, *Marlene*, p. 204ff.

290   Danny Thomas quotes: Higham, *Marlene*, p. 210.

291   Algiers bombing raid, Gabin: UP dispatch, April 12, 1944, "Marlene Sees Night Air Flight," NYPLPA; Gabin: *Picture Post*, June 10, 1944, p. 17; Brunelin, pp. 359–362.

291ff. Logan: Logan COHC, part 8, 328–329.

292   "Lili Marlene," history and Steinbeck quote: Bemman, pp. 113–116.

292ff. Dietrich to Lerman: Lerman, *op. cit.*, pp. 154, 188. Spurious versions of this interview are often quoted. Citations here are from the original, courtesy Mr. Lerman. Also, Lerman Collection, NYPLPA, ms.

293   Dietrich quote on Rome: Lerman, p. 190.

294   Goebbels's jazz broadcasts: A number of these recordings have survived. They continued until the final days of the war and, ironically, made many jazz converts among their listeners. Florian Steinbiss and David Eisermann, *Propaganda Swing: Dr. Goebbels' Jazz-Orchester*, 1989 (television documentary).

295   "There's something about a soldier": Dietrich quoted by Lerman, p. 188. "We were happier then": Dietrich, *Marlene*, p. 207.

295   "Of all": Dietrich, *Marlene*, p. 207. "Lonely men": Dietrich, ABC, p. 6.

295   Woman in every sense: MD to Arthur Kennedy, int. SB/Arthur Kennedy, October 2–3, 1989.

296   "stiff, formal": Dietrich, *Marlene*, p. 149.

296   Mary Welsh Hemingway on MD: Hemingway, *How It Was*, p. 127.

296   Hemingway as "pope": Dietrich, *Marlene*, p. 146. "Impossible to explain": *Ibid.*, p. 149.

296   "You coward": Hemingway, *How*, p. 131ff.

296   "I didn't" and marriage proposal: Dietrich, p. 149–150. Mary Hemingway described events differently in *How*, pp. 131–134. She said Hemingway proposed himself.

296   Remarque: quoted by Dietrich, ABC, p. 41.

296   "Fear": Dietrich, *Marlene*, p. 201.

296   Calvados: *Ibid.*, p. 217. This was, of course, Remarque's leitmotif in *Arch of Triumph*.

297   Funeral story: Hemingway, *How*, pp. 128–129. Also, Joseph Laitin in *Colliers*, p. 26. Many versions of the story exist, updated from time to time to reflect the expanding ranks.

297   "useful": Hemingway, *How*, p. 144.

297   "scabies": Hemingway, *Ibid.*, pp. 144–145.

298   Crabs, Eisenhower, etc.: The stories were recounted to the author by Arthur Kennedy, who heard them from Marlene. Int. SB/Arthur Kennedy, October 2–3, 1989. See also *Marlene*, pp. 212–215; for Eisenhower, p. 126.

298   "It's not difficult": Sergeant, p. 93.

298   "I'm not afraid": Dietrich, *Marlene*, p. 198.

298   "They'll shave": *Ibid.*, p. 198.

298   Himmler order: Shirer, *Rise and Fall*, p. 1413.

299   "Germany deserves": *Los Angeles Examiner*, February 3, 1945. This remark has been the subject of considerable debate. Here it is cited from

Conniff, "Marlene Dietrich Quits as Film Actress," International News Service, datelined "With American Forces at Stolberg, Germany, Feb. 2 [1945]."

299 "If they had": Sergeant, p. 93.

299ff. Grace Moore and Coward: Coward, *Diaries*, p. 57; Lesley, p. 293; Coward, *Autobiography*, p. 494.

300 Paris Stage Door Canteen: *Life*, April 9, 1945, pp. 126–129.

300 Gabin tank incident: Brunelin, pp. 368–371. Gabin's biographer here quotes from *Flash-back*, the memoirs of Gilles Grangier, who witnessed the incident. Dating based on correspondence noted below as well as army reports.

300 "Jesus Christ": Curtis Mitchell, quoted in Abzug, p. 86. Other Bergen-Belsen details from Abzug, p. 83ff and Gill, pp. 28, 71, 392ff, 429–435, plus author interview cited below.

300ff. MD at Bergen-Belsen: int. SB/Arnold Horwell, September 21–22, 1991. Plus correspondence: Arnold Horwell to Mrs. Horwell, May 9, 1945; MD to AH, May 31, 1945; MD to AH from Berlin [undated: c. August 1945]; AH to Commanding Officer, 618 Military Governor's Detachment, Belsen, September 20, 1945, in response to a letter AH received from Elisabeth Will's son, Hans-Georg, which complained of Allied treatment. Thanks to Carolyn Marsden of the Imperial War Museum, London, for putting me in touch with Dr. and Mrs. Arnold Horwell.

302ff. Georg Will: Will discussed Belsen with Wiechers. For Dietrich's denial of her sister see: Schell, *Marlene*, in which she claims she was an only child. Dietrich's biography nowhere alludes to the existence of her sister, and Elisabeth has been cropped from family photographs. Dietrich wrote her cousin Hasso on the occasion of Georg Will's death, expressing her relief that he was dead, her bitterness over pain he had caused Elisabeth, and calling him "a Nazi."

304 Marlene's revolver and customs: *Los Angeles Examiner*, July 13, 1945.

304 Return to New York, St. Regis, and quote: Dietrich, *Marlene*, pp. 219–221.

304 War quote: Dietrich, *ABC*, p. 171.

304 *Life*: August 6, 1945.

305 *Yank* and quotes: Sgt. Al Hine, "DP Dietrich," *Yank*, August 26, 1945.

305 Marlene waiting at Chatou: Dietrich, *Marlene*, p. 219.

306 At Frau von Losch's: von Meyerinck, pp. 151–152; also, int. Christa Maerker/Alexandra von Porembsky, courtesy Maerker.

307 Marlene and Berlin's Titania-Palast: Press clippings, "*Auf Wiedersehen, Marlene Dietrich: Zum Berliner Aufenthalt der Künstlerin*," October 10, 1945; "*Marlene Dietrich und Amateure: Amerikaner zogen eigene Bühne auf*," September 27, 1945; untitled clip, October 6, 1945. All courtesy *Deutsches Institut für Filmkunde*, Wiesbaden.

307 Frau von Losch and the family firm: int. SB/Hasso Felsing, April 22, 1989. The Russian demand for repairs to bombed out structures was prelude

to East German seizure of property. Property rights are still being sorted out following the unification of Germany.

307ff.   Mother's funeral: Dietrich, *Marlene*, p. viii; von Meyerinck, p. 152.

CHAPTER SIXTEEN : SURVIVOR: 1946–1947

309   "I am through": Conniff.

310   Remarque and *Arch* movie: Barker and Last, p. 24; *Los Angeles Times*, June 12, 1948.

Remarque also tried to get United Artists to cast Marlene in *The Other Love*, based on one of his stories. Barbara Stanwyck got that part. *Arch of Triumph* was a famous disaster with Bergman and Charles Boyer, since remade for television with Lesley-Anne Down as "Dietrich" opposite Anthony Hopkins.

There are traces of Dietrich in "Natascha," the Russian model in Remarque's exile novel set in New York, *Shadows in Paradise*. Marlene's and Remarque's old Berlin friend Betty Stern is an important character there as Betty Stein.

310   Dietrich war quote: Dietrich, *Marlene*, p. 222.
310   "I was unable": *Ibid.*, p. 220.
311   Gabin's "gray period": Brunelin, p. 372ff.
311   "a little baby": Dietrich, *Marlene*, p. 137.
311   Cocteau: quoted in *Collier's*, p. 26.
311ff.   Carné, Prévert, and *Les Portes de la nuit*: mostly Carné [n.p.]; Brunelin, pp. 372–385; Colpet, pp. 197–198.
312   "bullheaded": Schell, *Marlene*.
313   "the role": Carné.
313   Marlene as "condition": Brunelin, p. 373.
313   "overalls": Sergeant, pp. 92–93.
314   Headline and quote: Michel Sergines in *l'Écran français*, June 5, 1946, p. 9.
315   "She is never": Jean Vidal, *L'Écran français*, December 21, 1946, pp. 5–6.
315   Dietrich's wardrobe: Henriette Pierrot in *L'Écran français*, February 10, 1947.
315   Gabin as "stubborn": Dietrich, *Marlene*, p. 137.
316   "Boxing lessons" and the snowbank: Hemingway, *How it Was*, p. 134; int. SB/Max Colpet, October 22, 1987; int. SB/Sam and Suzanne Taylor, June 6–7, 1987.
316   MD and Piaf: Crosland, p. 89; confidential source, June 14, 1990.
316   Gavin "flirt": Colpet, p. 195–197; int. SB/MC, October 22, 1987.
316   "French letter" joke: Higham, p. 219.
317   Marlene to Leisen: Chierichetti, p. 260.
317   Gabin and the paintings: Brunelin, pp. 386–387.
318   "beautiful loins": She told Sam and Suzanne Taylor this. Int. SB/Taylors, June 6–7, 1987.

318   Careers: Kathleen Tynan, p. 369. Dietrich told Kenneth Tynan this was the crux of the break-up with Gabin.

318   "never spoke her name": *L'album souvenir du dernier Monstre Sacré de notre cinéma: Jean Gabin," Paris-Match*, November 26, 1976.

318   "Maybe three people": Dietrich to Schell, tapes.

318   "Oh lord": William Whitebait in *The New Statesman*, December 10, 1949.

318   "Now I am a widow": quoted in Higham, *Marlene*, p. 303.

318   "I lost him": Dietrich, *Marlene*, p. 142.

318ff.   Maria and Marlene's pregnancy: int. SB/confidential source, June 14, 1990.

319   Cabana Beach Club: Invitation from Feldman to Selznick. Courtesy David Thomson: Letter, DT to SB, August 31, 1989.

319   Marlene and paintings: Brunelin, p. 386. Gabin's biographer is clear that Gabin had given her the paintings, in spite of Gabin's later refusal to admit it.

320   Hit song: "Golden Earrings" was credited to Victor Young but he based it on a Hungarian melody in the public domain.

320   "There's only one woman": Chierichetti, p. 260.

320   Leisen on Maria: *Ibid.*, p. 262.

323   Picket lines: *Ibid.*, p. 262.

323   "just the cutest": Eames, p. 186.

323ff.   Leisen quote: Chierichetti, pp. 260–261.

324   Burn story: *Ibid.*, pp. 261–262.

324   Crowther: *NYT*, December 4, 1947, p. 41.

CHAPTER SEVENTEEN : PRO: 1947–1950

326   Ship quote: Holland, p. 72.

326ff.   Rudi, his film, his father: "Dietrich Legs Fail to Faze U.S. Embassy," *Los Angeles Times*, February 18, 1947.

327   Dietrich quotes: "You must bear in mind," January 10, 1947, "OAB." "The atmosphere": *"Hollywood oder Paris?"* January 18, 1947, "KUR." (Both courtesy Wiesbaden)

327   Grandmother: *"Hollywood oder Paris?"*

328   "widow": MD to Marcel Dalio, quoted Higham, p. 303.

328   The end of Gabin/Dietrich: Brunelin, pp. 388–391, 411. Grave story: int. SB/Gavin Lambert, November 28, 1988. Lambert was told the story by Toni Scotti and Sylvie Vartan. "Old woman": *Deutsche Film Illustrierte*, December 20, 1949, p. 49. (*"Die Alte ist zu unbeständig"* was the quote.)

328   Rossellini, Dietrich, Colpet: Colpet, pp. 201–208.

329   Wilder and Oberammergau: int. SB/Max Colpet, October 22, 1987.

329   Wilder in Berlin: int. SB/Gerd Oswald, June 2, 1988.

329   Marlene's medal: int. SB/Mrs. Walter Reisch, October 19, 1989.

330   Lubitsch: Herta-Elisabeth Renk, *"Ernst Lubitsch privat," Süddeutsche-*

Zeitung, January 28, 1992, p. 11; Marlene and phonograph records at Lubitsch's, int. SB/Mrs. Walter Reisch, as before.

331   *To Be or Not to Be:* Taylor, *Strangers*, pp. 178–179.

331   Sarris quote: Sarris, *American Cinema*, p. 165.

331   UFA logo: Stuart Schulberg, p. 435.

332   Agee: review in *The Nation*, July 13, 1948, reprinted in *Agee on Film*, vol. 1, p. 311.

333   "humanization": Brackett, p. 68.

333ff.   Crowther: *NYT*, July 1, 1948.

334   Reviews: *Time*, July 26, 1948; *Variety*, June 16, 1948; *The New Yorker*, July 14, 1948; *Life*, August 9, 1948.

334   *Cue*, July 3, 1948.

334   US Military: the quote is from Stuart Schulberg, p. 436. Schulberg served with *Blue Angel* producer Erich Pommer in vetting American films for postwar German distribution. *A Foreign Affair* was forbidden and it is only in recent years that it has been released in Germany, where it is greatly admired and viewed as "nonpolitical."

334   Edith Head: *Colliers*, p. 28.

335   Wilder to Lund: int. SB/John Lund, June 2, 1988.

335   Marlene on set: int. SB/Gerd Oswald, June 2, 1988.

335   Randolph Churchill: int. SB/John Lund, as above.

336   Haas here and later: int. SB/Dolly Haas, October 4, 1989.

337   Tamara and abortions: int. SB/confidential source, June 14, 1990.

338   *Jigsaw: Variety*, March 9, 1949.

338   Re Patchevitch: int. SB/Mitch Miller, June 18, 1992.

339   "Madame": Hitchcock, cable to Steve Trilling at Warner Brothers, April 29, 1949, USC, Jack L. Warner Collection.

339   "The Laziest Gal in Town" and song problems: Letters and memos, MPAA to Jack Warner: April 8, 1949; April 26, 1949; July 15, 1949; November 16, 1949; telegram, Hitchcock to Steve Trilling, April 29, 1949; interoffice WB memo from Steve Trilling, February 9, 1950; MPAA to WB, February 13, 1950. All Warner Brothers Archive, courtesy USC.
   The Code seal was not granted until February 13, 1949, as "Laziest Gal" was still problematic for the Code. The picture opened only ten days later in New York.

340   Hitchcock quote: Parish et al., pp. 398–400.

340   Hedda Hopper: *Los Angeles Times*, August 19, 1949.

340   Wyman quotes: Parish, op. cit.

340ff.   Todd quotes: int. SB/Richard Todd, November 26, 1986; letter RT to SB, December 30, 1986.

341   Dietrich on Hitchcock: Schell, *Marlene*, tapes; Taylor, *Hitchcock*, pp. 211–212.

341   Hitchcock: quoted in Griffith, p. 6.

341   "warm affection"; Taylor, op. cit.

341   "dishonest whodunit": Alexander Walker, p. 171. Walker is not alone in his assessment.

342   Haskell quotes: Haskell, "Molly Haskell on *Stage Fright*," pp. 49–50.

343   Reviews: *Sunday Mirror*, March 12, 1950; *Journal-American*, [n.d.]; *Boxoffice*, March 4, 1950; Parsons, *Cosmopolitan*, May 1950; *Los Angeles Times*, April 1, 1950; Barnes, *H-T*, [n.d.]; *HR*, February 23, 1950; *Time*, March 13, 1950.

CHAPTER EIGHTEEN : STAR QUALITY: 1950–1952

344   Coward quote: Tynan, *Profiles*, pp. 33, 35.

344   Malraux: "Film und Mythos," *Film Forum*, November 1952.

345   "So Mama": Sergeant, *Life*, p. 87.

346   Grandmother quote: Dietrich, *ABC*, pp. 69–70.

347   Spanier: Spanier, pp. 14, 223.

347ff.   Spanier: int. SB/Ginette Spanier, July 23, 1987. The final row: int. SB/Bernard Hall, December 6, 1986. Marlene and Spanier declared themselves bitter un-friends, but when Spanier died in 1988 (in London), English papers took no notice. Paris papers *did* and it was Marlene who made sure Spanier's friends knew of her passing by calling worldwide.

349   Marlene and *All About Eve*: Gussow, p. 145. Mankiewicz had wanted Claudette Colbert, who was ill. Bette Davis thus got the role of her life almost by default.

349   Koster quotes: Koster/Atkins, p. 103.

349   Stewart quotes: "Life with Grandma Dietrich," *Screen Guide* [n.d.], USC, McCormick Collection.

350   Marlene at Denham: here and later, int. SB/Janette Scott, September 21, 1989.

350   Marlene to Koster: Koster/Atkins, p. 103.

350ff.   Scott: int. as above

351   Reviews: *H-T*, September 22, 1951; *Time and Tide*, August 11, 1951; Campbell Dixon in *Daily Telegraph*, August 6, 1951.

351ff.   Marlene and Wilcox: Wilcox, p. 148.

352   Brynner: Rock Brynner, p. 57. Brynner's son claimed "he was crazy about her, too" and seems never to have realized that Marlene was married.

352   Mirrors: *Colliers*, p. 28. Also, int. SB/Mitch Miller.

352   Dorothy Parker: quoted by John O'Hara, "Appointment with O'Hara," *Collier's*, March 19, 1954.

352   Bogdanovich, *Lang*, p. 77.

352ff.   Lang on Marlene: He told Lily Latté, with whom he spent his last years. Latté, who had been a schoolmate of Marlene's in Berlin, often repeated the story. Int. SB/Kevin Thomas, August 30, 1990.

353   Marlene and Lang's "fascism": Letter, MD to FL, September 11, 1946; telegram, FL to MD, September 27, 1946. Courtesy Dr. Cornelius Schnauber, USC.

354 "Marlene resented": Bogdanovich, p. 77.

354 "a horror!": Schell, *Marlene*.

354 " 'Do it again' ": Dietrich, *Marlene*, p. 185–186.

354ff. Mohr on Lang: Maltin, pp. 129–130.

355ff. Kennedy on Lang and Marlene here and following: int. SB/Arthur Kennedy, October 1/2, 1989.

356 Deals on *Rancho Notorious*: *Variety*, October 17, 1951, pp. 1, 11. The deal was complicated by loan agreements and RKO overhead, which amounted to $207,000 on a budget of roughly $750,000.

356 Eisner: Eisner, p. 302.

356 Taradash and Welsch: Taradash, *American Film*, August 1990, p. 25. There is evidence that more than "mood" was cut. Early prerelease trade reviews cite action scenes that are not in the finished picture. One actor, Lloyd Gough, who played the chief villain of the piece, received no billing at all because of his troubles with HUAC, a McCarthy-era footnote of note.

356 Reviews: Eisner, *op. cit.*; *Variety*, February 6, 1952; *Time*, March 10, 1952; *Newsweek*, March 24, 1952; *NYWTS*, May 15, 1952.

357 Eisner and Marlene: Eisner, *Ich hatte. . .* , p. 200.

357 Lang quote: Letter, to Eisner, June 21, 1970. Courtesy Dr. Cornelius Schnauber, USC.

357 Lang on Marlene: Wolff and Laitin, *Die Weltwoche*. Parts of this same speech were quoted in *Collier's*, attributed to "a movie director" and "a movie executive," but they are both Lang, and the German and the English are combined here. The song Lang refers to is Holländer's "*Wenn ich mir was wünschen dürfte*," which speaks of "homesickness for the lonely times."

358 Marlene on stage in Chicago: "Dietrich Makes Her Stage Bow," *Look*, May 6, 1951, pp. 96–97.

CHAPTER NINETEEN : SOLO: 1952–1954

361 Hemingway: *Life*, August 18, 1952, pp. 91–92. For Joe DiMaggio, same source.

362 Tynan: Tynan, Beaton, *Persona Grata*, p. 37.

362 "I'll have to": *Time*, January 21, 1952, p. 42.

362 Re *Café Istanbul*: Dunning, p. 107; "Marlene's Joint," *The New Yorker*, November 29, 1952; *Time*, as above.

363 Max Colpet as Marlene's writer: int. SB/Colpet, October 22, 1987.

363 Mitch Miller and recording: int. SB/Mitch Miller, June 18, 1992. Also, Mitch Miller: SMU Oral History, March 25, 1986, courtesy Ronald L. Davis.

364 *Confidential*: the magazine was finally undone by lawsuits. "The Untold Story of Marlene Dietrich" by Kenneth G. McLain [n.d.] is part of the McCormick Collection at USC.

364 Hemingway and Lillian Ross: Ross's Profile was called "How Do You Like It Now, Gentlemen?" *The New Yorker*, May 13, 1950. Quotes here from pp. 44–45. For Hotchner see *Papa Hemingway*, p. 107.

365   *Ladies' Home Journal:* "How to Be Loved" was contracted with Marlene and Leo Lerman, letter, Elizabeth McKee (LHJ) to LL, May 6, 1952. The final article bore Marlene's byline and copyright. *LHJ,* January 1954, pp. 36–87, Lerman Collection, NYPLPA. "Listen, Marlene": *LHJ,* April 1954, pp. 4–6.

365   Doubleday: Contract dated March 20, 1953. The profits were to be divided equally between Dietrich and Lerman, who was to "ghost" the book. Quoted from contract, Lerman Collection, NYPLPA.

365   *Légion d'Honneur:* Interpress, Hamburg, May 14, 1952. Courtesy Wiesbaden.

366   *Carnival in Flanders:* NYHT, October 3, 1952. Loesser, Langner, Schubert: undated clip, NYPLPA; *Samarkand, Theatre Arts,* September 1951. The French play was abandoned in 1953. For *Man on a Tightrope,* memo in *Garden of Allah* files, DOS-Texas. Dietrich was unavailable for dubbing *Allah* into German after the war because of her tentative commitment to Kazan for *Man on a Tightrope.*

366   Welles and *Mr. Arkadin:* Brady, p. 467. Brady thinks Marlene turned Welles down because she was making *The Monte Carlo Story,* but that was two years later. On *The Sun Also Rises:* Leaming, p. 396.

366   Marlene and Harold Arlen: ints. SB/Edward Jablonsky, March 30, 1989; September 30, 1989. On *House of Flowers:* Castle, p. 179, plus Jablonsky.

366   Tamara's wedding band: Rolph Th. Branner, "*Mister Marlenes merkwürdige Memoiren,*" *Esslinger Zeitung,* June 27, 1958, courtesy SDK.

367   Hans Kohn: Higham, *Marlene,* p. 244.

367   Gregory: Parrish, p. 205.

367   Chevalier later admitted his error in judgment to John Gale in *The Observer,* November 22, 1964.

368   Eddie Fisher: Fisher, pp. 92ff.

369ff. Jean Louis here and later: int. SB/Jean Louis, November 22, 1988.

369   Hedda Hopper: *Los Angeles Times,* December 18, 1953, USC, McCormick Collection.

369   Las Vegas opening: unsourced clips, NYPLPA. Press accounts of the opening are voluminous.

369   Sinatra: Kitty Kelley quotes an undated Sammy Cahn interview for Dietrich's private relationship with Sinatra, with whom she was photographed on numerous public occasions. Kelley, pp. 112, 524.

371   Tauber: Tauber recorded the song, but it was written for a film starring Marlene's former lover Willi Forst. The Austrian film was called *Das Lied ist aus,* which is the alternate title for the song.

371   "State visit": Cecil Wilson, *Daily Mail,* June 22, 1954.

371   Coward: Payn and Morley, p. 237. The introduction, edited here, is preserved on disk. See Discography.

372   "Exceptional": Wilson, *Daily Mail,* June 22, 1953.

372   *Variety:* "Rege," datelined June 23, 1954.

372   Reviews: quoted from liner notes, "Café de Paris," Columbia ML 4975.

373   Hamlet: *Newsweek*, "Periscope" item, [n.d.], NYPLPA.

373   Craig, McDowall quotes: letter, David Craig to SB, January 16, 1990.

CHAPTER TWENTY : BACK IN BUSINESS: 1954–1958

374   Coward and Marlene: *Diaries*, Payn and Morley, p. 238.

374ff.   Cocteau: the text here is translated by Christopher Fry. It was delivered August 17, 1954, in Monaco.

375   Marlene in Paris: *Daily Mirror*, August 23, 1954, [n.p.], BFI.

375   "You look": *Collier's*, p. 29.

375   Maria's reviews: *NYT*, March 5, 1954, p. 15; *NYT*, March 14, 1954, II, p. 1ff.

375   Maria and "old age": ints. SB/Dean Goodman, March 2, 1989; June 9, 1990.

375   "Fabulous illusion": Sergeant, p. 96.

375ff.   Rudi and the press: "grateful" quote, *Woman's Sunday Mirror*, April 13, 1958, others: *Sunday Mirror*, November 29, 1964; "ramshackle farmhouse," *Sunday Express*, September 1, 1974.

376   Buchwald: "A Cat in a Hot London Cellar," originally in the *NYH-T*, here from London *Sunday Chronicle*, July 19, 1954.

376   Bessie Braddock: *Time*, July 18, 1955. "Garbo": Higham, *Marlene*, p. 252.

376   Coward: *Diaries*, p. 309; Marti Stevens, *Ibid.*, p. 457.

377   Dietrich and Todd: Cohn, *Nine Lives . . .* , pp. 285–286.

377   Todd and Marlene: Ezra Goodman, "Todd Cajoled Big Names to do Bits," *Life*, [n.d.], NYPLPA, and Goodman, pp. 191–193.

378   Marlene and Niven: Niven, p. 199. As a young actor in Hollywood, Niven experienced Dietrich's Florence Nightingale ministrations.

378   Sinatra and Dietrich: Kelley, p. 112, already cited.

379   De Sica's and "green": Bernard Hall, ms. IV, 1.

379ff.   Re MD and *Monte Carlo Story*: ints. SB/Sam and Suzanne Taylor, June 6–7, 1987.

380   MD and "Hollywood wife": int. SB/confidential source, July 29, 1988.

382   Rebecca West: Glendinning, p. 228. West made the remark after attending Marlene's Café de Paris opening with Leo Lerman.

382   Reviews: *Time*, March 17, 1958; *Newsweek*, July 29, 1957.

383   Joshua Logan: letter JL to Arthur Hornblow, Jr. [AH hereafter], May 29, 1956, declining the job because of his commitments on *Sayonara* and *Fanny*. Edward Small Collection [hereafter, ES Collection], USC.

383   Wilder and Marlene: Dietrich claimed she had been offered the part by producer Arthur Hornblow in New York, Dietrich, *Marlene*, p. 127. Wilder's version was: "Marlene came to me and said, 'Listen . . . Hornblow is making it with United Artists, and I tell you that I will play it only if you . . . [direct

it].' Then I read it and told her, 'Good.' " Wilder/Schlöndorff, tapes, June 1988, courtesy Volker Schlöndorff.

383   Marlene's casting not set: Cables, Arthur Hornblow to Edward Small, October 2, 1956; ES to AH, October 3, 1956. The correspondence clearly indicates that no actress would be cast until the leading man had been set. ES Collection, USC.

383   Small, purchase price of *Witness*, and *Solomon and Sheba*: production files, "Misc. Correspondence," ES Collection, USC.

383   Gardner and Hayworth: Small mentions awaiting word from both actresses in his cable to Hornblow of October 3, 1956, ES Collection, USC.

383   Douglas and Dietrich: Douglas, p. 192.

383ff.   Power and casting: William Holden, ES to AH, April 23, 1956; Power's turndown in cable ES to AH, September 27, 1956; Glenn Ford and Jack Lemmon, letter AH to ES, June 8, 1956. Wilder on Rita Hayworth: quoted by AH in letter AH to ES, September 30, 1956; Gene Kelly, cable AH to ES, October 4, 1956. Wilder on Marlene and Kirk Douglas: in letter AH to ES, September 30, 1956. Power's casting was settled in November, 1956. ES Collection, USC.

384   "cement block": Wilder to Schlöndorff, tapes. Francis L. Sullivan was an early choice: Memo to Roger Lewis from Arthur Jacobs (publicity), April 10, 1956, ES Collection, USC.

385   Coward: *Diaries*, p. 361.

385   Cockney scene: the Museum of Modern Art own the out-take with Dietrich making the telephone call as Christine and then looking pensively at the wig. Makeup and costume stills reveal the evolution of the makeup and its successful conclusion.

385   Not Dietrich: see Homer Dickens, p. 207, where this story is repeated. Critic-biographer Alexander Walker, p. 182, thinks it is so obviously Dietrich it couldn't have fooled anybody. Dubbing: see Griffith, p. 12, who makes this claim. If so, then the MoMA out-take of the unused scene is also dubbed, which is unlikely. It is perfectly played and synchronized and at the end Wilder's own voice can be heard complaining off camera that the take is "too long."

386   Lanchester on Marlene: courtesy Donald Hall.

386   Dietrich and Power: Arce, p. 270.

387   "She's not only brave": Griffith, p. 13.

388   Dietrich's fee: Universal Collection, USC. Dietrich's contract and work sheets are on file. Her fee was to be kept "confidential."

388   Welles claims: Leaming, pp. 422–423.

388   Shooting script: Universal Collection, USC. The shooting script contains a bordello and an old crone who is sleeping or drugged and has no dialogue. This is the earlier version of Quinlan's past that Welles revised into Tanya.

388   "A little out of my line": Schell/Dietrich, tapes.

388   Kael quote: Kael, *Kiss Kiss, Bang Bang*, p. 361.
388   "I never": Brady, p. 500.

CHAPTER TWENTY-ONE : HELEN OF TROY: 1959–1960

391   Dietrich did ninety-six sound clips of three to four minutes' advice about "love" on *Monitor* beginning October 4, 1958. TV: Revlon offered her a three-year, $2 million deal to hostess a series of specials (*Variety*, July 22, 1959). The deal could never be made for tax reasons: Marie Torre, *New York Herald-Tribune*, August 25, 1959, p. 6.

391   Dietrich to Jacobs: Confidential memo to publicity staff on *Witness* from Arthur P. Jacobs, May 29, 1957, NYPLPA.

391ff.   "Although": Griffith, p. 28. Bowser's filmography: Arthur Knight had tried to compile a record of early Dietrich films (making similar errors) for *Films in Review*, December 1954. Knight interviewed Dietrich, who denied having made any films at all before *The Blue Angel*. When he insisted he had seen some of them, she showed him the door. Int. SB/Arthur Knight, August 30, 1990.

392   Screenings: the films included all the American-made Josef von Sternberg films except for *The Scarlet Empress*, plus *Desire, Destry Rides Again, A Foreign Affair*, and *Witness for the Prosecution*.

392   Marilyn Monroe: Louella Parsons *Los Angeles Examiner*, June 17, 1957. Monroe posed as Marlene in her *Blue Angel* role for Richard Avedon and *Life*. The Brigitte Bardot film was *La Femme et le pantin; Destry* opened on Broadway with Dolores Gray (who also played Marlene's role in the film version of the musical *Kismet*) on April 23, 1959.

Parsons reported (same date) that Leland Hayward had tried to interest Dietrich in a Broadway version of *The Blue Angel*. It was done as a Duke Ellington musical called *Pousse-Café* starring French actress Lilo. It failed.

Heinrich Mann's story has seen many forms, including a ballet by Roland Petit, a German musical version (not the first) with Ute Lemper in spring 1992. Recently Madonna hoped to remake the movie and asked to meet with Dietrich, who refused. "I *played* vulgar; she *is* vulgar." Dietrich's candidate for the role in a film remake was, surprisingly, Tina Turner. "I love Tina Turner," she said. MD to SB, August 17, 1987.

392   *Destry*: David Merrick tried to talk Dietrich into Frenchy on stage. She used his interest to force him to keep John Osborne's *Epitaph for George Dillon* open on Broadway, instead. Coward, *Diaries*, p. 389; Gaskill, p. 30.

392   Sternberg: see *Fun*, pp. 224, 261–262. The screening of *The Devil Is a Woman* was repeated at the Venice Film Festival that Fall. The Sternberg revival was under way.

392   Dietrich's "little speech": MD to LL, [n.d.], in a long communique handwritten on both sides of eighteen 3x5 cards. Leo Lerman Collection, (cage file) NYPLPA. The Museum of Modern Art does not retain a copy of

her remarks, but they were quoted in Paris's *France-Soir*. They are quoted here as MD transcribed them for Lerman.

392ff.   *Variety*: Leonard Levinson, "Marlene Dietrich as N.Y. Museum's Image-Legend," April 14, 1959.

393   Goldman quote: Goldman, pp. 105–106. The compilation film featured scenes from *The Blue Angel, Morocco, Dishonored, Shanghai Express, Blonde Venus, The Devil Is a Woman, Destry Rides Again, A Foreign Affair,* and *Witness for the Prosecution*, including the out-take telephone scene, as well as scenes from *Touch of Evil*. MoMA program, "Students Repeat Performance," April 18, 1959.

393   MD to Lerman: as above.

393   Buenos Aires: *Variety*, August 26, 1959. Paris: *Paris Match*, August 29, 1959. Dietrich's picture was on the front page of the *Kansas City Star* on August 14, 1959.

394   Buchwald: "La Dietrich Great Anywhere She Goes," *New York Herald-Tribune*, December 13, 1959.

394   Bacharach, here and below: with Milhaud, Robert Wahls, "The Bacharach Beat," *New York Daily News*, October 29, 1967. Dietrich quotes: *Marlene*, pp. 231, 241.

395   Viola range: int. SB/William Blezard, October 15, 1987. Blezard was Dietrich's English conductor.

396   Paris headlines: *Le Parisien libéré, Paris-presse l'intransigeant*, both November 21, 1959.

396   Piaf, front-page news: *Paris-presse l'intransigeant*, November 22/23, 1959. *Paris Match* cover, November 29, 1959.

396   Chevalier: his opening-night speech was printed on the front page of *Paris-Jour*, "Voici Marlene," November 28–29, 1959.

396   "unmistakably": Curtiss, "Surrender to Marlene Dietrich," *New York Herald-Tribune*, November 30, 1959.

397   Paris reviews: miscellaneous, unsourced clippings (SB).

397   Coward: *Diaries*, p. 422. Payn and Morley in the diaries mistake the theater as the Olympia. It was the Étoile.

397   The other eyewitness was the author.

397   Coward on Vallone: *Diaries*, p. 421.

397   Giacometti: Lord, *Giacometti*, pp. 405–409. With Vallone in Rome: "Vacanze Romane di Marlene Dietrich e Raf Vallone," cover story, *Visto* (Milan), February 20, 1960.

398   "The Jewish snob": quoted in Sudendorf, pp. 22–24. Original letters from this source are in the collection of the SDK, Berlin.

398   "Dear Madame" and "Aren't you ashamed": *Ibid.*

398   *Bild* letters: *Bild-Zeitung* (Hamburg), anti-Dietrich, March 12, 1960; pro-Dietrich, March 25, 1960.

399   *Der Spiegel*: no. 19, 1960; *Badisches Tagblatt*, Baden-Baden, March 24, 1960, courtesy DIF, Wiesbaden.

399 Buchwald: Buchwald, "D-Day for Marlene," *NYHT*, April 9, 1960. In the original, Dietrich misstates 1954 as 1955.

399 Hurok: letter, Walter Prude of Hurok Organization to MD, December 14, 1960, Lerman Collection, NYPLPA.

399 Coward: *Diaries*, p. 433.

399 Tomatoes, eggs: "gooey": *Newsweek*, May 2, 1960. "I have": *Time*, April 18, 1960.

400 Brussels: *Newsweek*, May 5, 1958.

400 "The reason": Fritsch, p. 40. Fritsch and Marlene were both in *The Taming of the Shrew* for Reinhardt, Fritsch as a replacement with Marlene playing "widow."

400ff. Political suit: *International H-T*, June 15, 1990, p. 24. The posters carried her picture and the words "Germany? Never again!" *"Deutschland: nie wieder!"* The politician was a woman, Jutta Ditfurth, of the environmentalist "Greens" party, who said the poster's intent was misconstrued.

The author encountered "traitor Dietrich" attitude often among ordinary Germans while researching this book. Officially she is regarded as a culture hero.

401 Knef and the publicity: this is from Max Colpet, int. SB/MC, October 22, 1987. Colpet claims that by the late eighties Dietrich could not get Knef on the telephone.

Knef, though twenty years younger, was also born in Schöneberg's Sedanstrasse. The two women were friendly in America and Knef's memoir, *A Gift Horse*, is rich in praise of Dietrich's generosity to her there.

401 Box office: *Variety*, May 10, 1960, p. 2. Scalper prices: *Die Welt*, May 5, 1960.

402 Munich "hurricane": *Abendzeitung*, quoted from Dietrich program.

402ff. Reviews, "Majesty" and "Lovely Art": *Frankfurter Allgemeine-Zeitung*, May 5 and May 30, 1960. "She is a legend": *Handlesblatt* (Düsseldorf), May 20/21, 1960. "sound of an epoch": *Berliner Zeitung*, May 5, 1960. "half Dorian Gray": Karena Niehoff, *Tagesspiegel*, May 5, 1960. "Yes, it is true": *Suddeutsche-Zeitung*, quoted from Dietrich program.

403 "*Das Lied ist aus*": int. SB/Bernard Hall, December 5/6, 1986.

403 Wiesbaden, shoulder injury: *New York Times*, May 23, 1960; Dietrich, *Marlene*, pp. 234–237; int. SB/Bernard Hall, as above. Hall cites Dietrich's drinking and her upset at public attacks on her as the reason for the Wiesbaden fall.

404 Rilke: *Selected Letters*, p. 296.

CHAPTER TWENTY-TWO : ODYSSEY: 1960–1967

405 Rilke: *Selected Letters*, p. 438.

406 Dietrich's health: smoking and circulation, surgical pins for "lifting," sleeping pills, etc.: ints. SB/Bernard Hall, November-December 1986. Hub-

sie von Meyerinck was one of the few who knew Marlene had broken her shoulder and saw the pain when he visited her in Munich, where she continued to perform. Meyerinck, p. 226.

406   She and the Germans: *Variety*, June 7, 1960. German in Israel: NYT, June 29, 1960. "It's bad enough": in Eugene Archer, "Light From an Undiminishing Star," NYT, September 9, 1960.

407   Stayover in Israel: Josef Sryck, "*Ein Mensch ist angekommen*," *Aufbau*, September 1960. "I have" Paul Kohn in Tel Aviv, quoted in Dietrich program.

407   Kramer quotes: here and later, int. SB/Stanley Kramer, November 30, 1988.

407   Lambert: quoted in Kael, *Kiss Kiss*, p. 208.

407   "Glassy": David Thomson to SB, letter September 1991. "wooden": Kauffmann, p. 12.

408   "earlier version": The *Playhouse 90* teleplay and first draft of the screenplay are in the Abby Mann Collection, USC. The final screenplay was published (see Bibliography). Quotations here are from the film.

408   "Wonderful": Dietrich/Schell, tapes.

408   Tracy quote: int. SB/Stanley Kramer, as above.

408   Baked-goods factory: int. SB/Irene Selznick, October 3, 1990. Mrs. Selznick made the same remark to the author.

409   Billy Wilder rewriting: Davidson, p. 188. Davidson's source was Abby Mann. Kramer (int. SB/SK, as above) dismissed the notion.

410   Dietrich and Keitel: MD to SB, July 31, 1987. Dietrich told the author she still received indignant letters from Germans asking how she could dare play Keitel's widow.

410   Keitel: Martin Bormann called for his execution in the final days of the war, according to William Shirer, p. 1469. Keitel's last words and request to be shot instead of hung: Conot, pp. 501–506.

410   NYT: December 15, 1961.

411   Crowther: NYT, December 20, 1961, p. 36.

411   Academy: for ridicule, see Pauline Kael, *Kiss Kiss*, p. 209. Also nominated were Ernest Laszlo for photography, Fred Knutson for editing, Jean Louis for costumes, and Rudolph Sternad and George Milo for art direction.

411   Thalidomide: John Paul Riva's birth defects were first reported by Radie Harris in *The Hollywood Reporter*, November 2, 1981. Harris announced a book on the subject written by Maria Riva called *Mother and Son*, which remains unpublished. Dietrich discussed Thalidomide and her grandson's birth defects with the author: MD to SB, March 24, 1987.

411   Niehans and Marti Stevens: Coward, *Diaries*, p. 521.

412   No fee: Barry Norman, London *Daily Mail*, November 1, 1963.

412   Crowther: NYT, April 30, 1963.

412   England: The distribution company was Contemporary Films. The film had been presented at the Venice Film Festival and was praised by Penelope Gilliat, among others. The Dietrich quote and *Guardian* comment: Novem-

ber 11, 1963. Dietrich refusing to sit: int. SB/Bernard Hall, December 5–6, 1986.

412   Marlene and the Beatles: *Variety*, "Marlene Dietrich, Erroll Garner Among Royal Command Vaude Gala's 19 Acts," dateline October 22, 1963. "Electrified": int. SB/Bernard Hall, as above.

412   Albert Hall: Chicago *Sun-Times*, October 26, 1963.

413   De Gaulle: June 1, 1960, at the Nuit de la Chancellerie. Dietrich was presented to De Gaulle along with Maria Schell, Danielle Darrieux, Sacha Distel, and Giulietta Massina.

413   Beaumont: Coward, *Diaries*, p. 506; Huggett, p. 29. Beaumont's Dietrich impersonation is thought to have been his last act the night he died.

413   German guilt in Warsaw: Dietrich, *Marlene*, p. 241. Three concerts becoming six and "Jonny": *Die Welt*, January 18, 1964.

413   Warsaw reviews: quoted in "Marlene Dietrich Sings in Warsaw" by "J.K.," in *Théàtre en Pologne*, no. 2, 1964, Polish Center of the International Theatre Institute, p. 26.

413ff.   Medical students: This account is from the unpublished memoir "La Dietrich in Polen," by Leon Bukowiecki, April 28, 1977. Courtesy SDK. Bukowiecki himself was the translator.

414   MD in San Francisco: int. SB/Lee Goodman, June 2, 1987.

414   Moscow: "By myself," *NYT*, May 20, 1964. Other accounts: curtain speech: *NYT*, May 22, 1964; *New York Journal American*, May 22, 1964; *Variety*, "Moscow's Marlene Madness," June 17, 1964. audience in tears: *Süddeutsche-Zeitung*, May 23–24, 1964.

414   Moscow musicians: Dietrich, *Marlene*, p. 240. She had finally taken Sol Hurok's advice and put herself under his management for this tour.

414   Paustovsky: *Ibid.*, pp. 154–155.

415   Tynan: written for *Playbill*, 1967; reprinted in Tynan, *Profiles*, p. 217.

416   Hobson: "The Perfections of Dictrich", London *Times*, November 29, 1964; "Some Glory in Virtue," London *Sunday Times*, December 5, 1964. Hobson's two pieces are combined here.

416   Dietrich's cancer: int. SB/Bernard Hall, November-December 1986; int. SB/confidential source, June 14, 1990. Re Gertrude Lawrence: confidential int. with Lawrence's attending physician. Liver cancer was the "public" explanation for a disease not then mentionable.

416ff.   Dickinson, Edinburgh: int. SB/Clive Donner, August 15, 1986.

417   The other observer was William Blezard, one of the two conductors who took over when Bacharach left. Int. SB/William Blezard, October 15, 1987.

417   Bacharach: letter, Burt Bacharach to SB, March 1, 1989.

417   "Amitié": Dietrich, *ABC*, p. 20.

417   The reporter was Sarah Giles of *Vanity Fair*: int. SB/Sarah Giles, October 3, 1989.

418   Tamara's burial: billing records, Hollywood Memorial Park Cemetery. Maintenance charges for the plot are today billed to Maria Riva, c/o Marlene's one-time New York address.

418   Bernard Hall on Rudi: int. SB/Bernard Hall, December 5–7, 1986.

418   Eggs in Warsaw: *Frankfurter-Allgemeine-Zeitung*, March 2 and April 12, 1966.

419   Ribs in Australia: *Weltwoche* (Zurich), November 19, 1965; *Variety*, October 13, 1965.

419   Curnow: the Sydney colleague was Charles Higham, whose diary is in the Higham Collection at USC. Higham published some of the material in his Dietrich biography.

419   Curnow, bars: int. SB/confidential source, July 29, 1988. Other details from Higham, *Marlene*, pp. 286–289, plus notes in Higham Collection, USC; int. SB/William Blezard, October 15, 1987.

419   Blezard on Curnow: int. SB/WB, as above.

419   The memoirs: The first attempt was assembled as a book of aphorisms and miscellany called *Marlene Dietrich's ABC*, which was very successful.

419ff.   Curnow to Higham: Higham Collection, USC.

420   Liverpool reunion: int. SB/Hasso and Shirley Felsing, April 22, 1989.

420   Work and money: Clive Hirschhorn, "It's the money I work for, says Marlene," *Sunday Express*, August 15, 1965.

CHAPTER TWENTY-THREE : "QUEEN OF THE WORLD": 1967–1975

423ff.   Crawford: int. SB/Davina Crawford Belling, September 26, 1986.

424   Canby review: *NYT*, October 10, 1967, p. 52.

424   *Time*: unsigned, October 20, 1967; Kroll: *Newsweek*, October 23, 1967.

424   Salt water: int. SB/Vera Zorina, June 3, 1987.

424   Party: Donal Henahan, "Celebrities Hunt for Celebrities at Party for Marlene Dietrich," *NYT*, October 10, 1967.

424   Rudi: int. SB/Davina Crawford Belling, as above.

425   "Romania": letter MD to DC, October 1, 1965. The author is grateful for copies of this correspondence dating from July 28, 1965, to August 18, 1970.

425   "on the right track": Dan Sullivan, *New York Times*, October 4, 1968.

425   "the man": Dietrich, *ABC*, p. 151.

425   "Should she be": Sternberg, *Fun*, p. 269.

426   Sternberg as introducer: Dietrich told the story to Sam Jaffe, SMU Oral History, August 14, 1978. Courtesy Ronald L. Davis, SMU, Dallas.

426   "Only when she *needs*": The student was the author, the date December 3, 1965. Re MD's presence at Sternberg's funeral: int. SB/Dr. Cornelius Schnauber, August 14, 1989.

426   Cohen quotes: Earl Wilson, *New York Post*, December 30, 1972.

426   "The Singing Hun": int. SB/Stan Freeman, November 30, 1988. "Certifiable": Cohen to SB, September 27, 1989.

426   "Nothing": Goldman, *The Season*, p. 107. Cohen told Goldman and *Variety* that he made no profit on the Dietrich shows.

426   Dietrich's TV stumble: Bernard Hall said she was drunk, but it may

equally have been her difficulty with walking. Int. SB/BH, December 6, 1986.

427   Reed quote: *NYT*, October 2, 1967.

427ff.   Freeman quotes: int. SB/Stan Freeman, as above.

428   Canadian TV: *Variety*, October 25, 1961.

428   Fist fight: *Variety*, datelined July 2, 1964. The occasion was the Baden Record Festival, 1964.

428   Television quotes: Jim Sirmans, "Marlene Spectacular," *Vogue*, February 1973.

429   "I never": *Vogue*, February 1973.

430   Reed: Rex Reed, "If Bored, Marlene Lisps a Lot," *Sunday Daily News*, January 7, 1973.

430   "Barely": Angela Taylor, *NYT*, December 16, 1972.

430   *Time*: "Marlene Rides Again," January 15, 1973.

430   Cohen suits: the London suit (against the *Daily Mail*) was settled in Cohen's favor. The New York suit was eventually dropped when Cohen agreed in 1977 to pay Dietrich the final monies owed her for the show. *Evening Standard*, January 13, 1973.

431   Cecil Beaton: *Self-Portrait*, pp. 417–418.

431   "It ain't": *Time*, January 15, 1973.

431   Reed: "Ajax": *NYT*, October 22, 1967. Peyrefitte's book was *Les Américains*. Dietrich's lawsuit and quote are in *Newsweek*, September 16, 1968. When Peyrefitte lost the suit, he told the press, "I kiss, my angel, the gold of your hair, the blue of your wings." *Münchner Merkur*, October 12, 1968.

431ff.   Reed quotes: *Sunday Daily News*, January 7, 1973.

432   Coward joke: Lesley, p. 465.

432   "If I see him": *Ibid.*, pp. 525–526.

432   Myrna Loy: Loy, Kotsilibas-Davis, p. 308.

433   "I hated": Derek Prouse, *Sunday Times* (London), November 22, 1964. "pansy": Reed, "Queen of Ajax."

433   Brussels, Tokyo: int. SB/Bernard Hall, December 12, 1986. Also, Hall, *Memoirs* [n.p.]

433   Imperial hotel list: courtesy Bernard Hall.

434   Tokyo and Framingham, Mass: int. SB/Stan Freeman, November 30, 1988.

434ff.   Cardin: Hall, *Memoirs*, [n.p.]; *Münchner Merkur*, June 22, 1973; *Süddeutsche-Zeitung*, June 25, 1973. In spite of conflicts, Dietrich returned to perform for Cardin in September/October of 1973.

435   *Vogue*: *Stern*, December 27, 1973, p. 106.

435   Smoking, drinking, bone-breaks: Hall, *Memoirs*, [n.p.]

436   Fall off stage: int. SB/Stan Freeman, Bernard Hall, as above; *Time*, November 19, 1973.

436   "I survived": *Süddeutsche-Zeitung*, November 10, 1973.

436   Toronto: *Variety*, December 5, 1973, p. 2.

437   De Bakey: ints. SB/Bernard Hall and SB/Stan Freeman, both as above.

De Bakey also consulted on neurological treatments for Marlene's grandson: MD to SB, March 14, 1987.

437   Skin grafts, cancellations: *Variety*, January 2, 1974; *NYT*, January 25, 1974, p. 29. Bypass: Bernard Hall, ints. cited.

437   "famous film director": who asked not to be identified, in conversation with SB, 1972.

437   *Private Eye*: the issue date was August 23, 1974, and the reproduction of the poster, which was exact except for the skull, bore a corner signature, "Scarfe."

438   Morley: London *Times*, September 13, 1974.

438   Coward: *Diaries*, pp. 581–582.

439   *Variety*: September 18, 1974. Hobson quotes: an amalgam of November 29, 1964 and December 5, 1964, both London *Times*.

439   Princess Margaret: Roderick Gilchrist, "Superstar Marlene snubs royal party," unsourced clip, SDK; ints. SB/Freeman, Hall, as above. Ginette Vachon: same sources, plus int. SB/William Blezard, October 15, 1987. Vachon was called "a camp follower" by all three interview sources.

439   Sullivan: *Los Angeles Times*, April 17, 1974.

440   Thomas: int. SB/Kevin Thomas, August 30, 1990. Thomas was introduced to Rudi in Las Vegas.

440   Hotel sharing: int. SB/BH, December 15, 1986.

440   Nanuet: review, Harry Haun, *Daily News*, May 13, 1975; int. SB/Charles Silver, November 2, 1987.

441   Leg break: int. SB/William Blezard, as above.

441   Ginette Vachon in ambulance: wire service photos reveal the scene.

441ff.   UCLA and Columbia-Presbyterian: *NYT*, undated clip, NYPLPA. Lloyd's of London: *Daily News*, October 1, 1975. Plaster and flight: *Newsweek*, October 13, 1975. Dietrich on Rudi's UCLA hospital confinement: int. SB/Rudi Polt, November 13, 1989.

CHAPTER TWENTY-FOUR : MONSTRE SACRÉ: 1976–1982

443   "The greatest": according to Bernard Hall; int. SB/BH, December 15, 1986.

444   Hospital: *Midnight*, April 19, 1976; *Berliner Morgenpost*, January 14, 1976.

444   Rudi's death: obituaries did not give a cause of death, but Germany's Burda publishing concern stated it was due to intestinal cancer. Burda-*Hausmitteilung*, June 28, 1976.

444   Hall on end of career: int. SB/BH, as above.

444   Freeman and Blezard: ints. SB/SF and WB, November 30, 1988 and October 15, 1987.

444   Blezard quote: int. SB/WB, as above.

445   Rivas to Spain: letter, MD to Davina Crawford, August 18, 1970.

445   Lloyd's insurance was "many thousands of dollars": New York *Daily*

News, October 1, 1975. Dietrich complained of the bills on the New York brownstone to the author, March 24, 1987.

445 Safety-deposit and rubies for Maria: MD to SB, April 10, 1987.

445 Taxes: Dietrich, *ABC*, p. 53.

445 S&S and Putnam's: There were other factors. Dietrich claimed publicity was the major one in a letter to her agent, Robert Lantz, March 16, 1979. Confidential source.

445 Lawsuit: *NYT*, December 1, 1976, reported the Putnam's deal at $200,000. *New York Post*, January 6, 1977, reported the S&S lawsuit against Robert Lantz, claiming he had induced breach of a $300,000 deal. The suit was withdrawn in 1978: *Variety*, August 23, 1978.

445 "Bloody book": Kathleen Tynan, p. 368.

445ff. Tynan: *Ibid.*, p. 369.

446 Dietrich said of Hemingway's letters that she would "do everything possible to prevent" anyone from "earn[ing] a penny from them": Dietrich, *Marlene*, p. 145. Hemingway himself left a letter prohibiting publication of his letters after his death: Mary Hemingway, *How It Was*, p. 504. Remarque had always feared Marlene would publish his letters to her: Barker and Last, p. 23.

446 Rumors: Roddy McDowall was grilled by Dietrich about her reputation, as was the author. Int. SB/RMcD, November 1986.

446 "According to Marlene": confidential source, June 3, 1987.

446 *Esquire*: issue no. 3, 1976. Max Colpet was the go-between with the magazine and did the translation without credit, as he did for the first version of the book.

446 "Unpublishable": confidential source. Correspondence on the autobiography between Dietrich and her publishers and agents is voluminous and contentious. It dates from January 1977 to February 1986. The uncredited translation: int. SB/Max Colpet, October 22, 1987. Dietrich never liked that translation, and a subsequent German version was published with a translation credit to Nicola Volland, who translated into German from the French translation of the original English.

446 Salvator Attanasio was the translator; he told the author he was unaware there *was* an original English version.

447 "Witness": Gilbert Adair in *The Spectator*, May 13, 1989; Stephen Harvey wrote in the *NYT Book Review*, May 28, 1989. Dietrich to him: int. SB/Stephen Harvey, October 1, 1989. The author saw portions of Dietrich's original manuscript; it is better than any of its translations. The English language version (see Bibliography) was published with the help of friends Leo Lerman and Alexander Lieberman. MD to SB, March 24, 1987.

447 The original manuscript: the author received portions of it from a confidential source.

447 Wilder and *Fedora*: int. Volker Schlöndorff and Billy Wilder, June 1988, courtesy VS. The picture was made with Dietrich's friend Hildegard Knef as Fedora and Marthe Keller as the daughter. It was a failure.

448ff.   *Gigolo* quotes: here and later, int. SB/David Hemmings, October 22, 1989.

450   Dietrich's speech: composed from Hemmings and from undated article from *Stern* [c. 1978], courtesy SDK.

451   Reviews: *Der Spiegel*, November 20, 1978; *Die Welt*, November 18, 1978.

451   "When you": MD to SB, July 31, 1987.

451   "hell": int. SB/Max Colpet, October 22, 1987.

452   The Dietrich retrospective was in two parts, shown at the Festivals of 1977 and 1978 in the Astor Theater on the Kurfürstendamm. The Astor was the old Rudolf Nelson Revue Theater, where she had danced as a chorus girl in the twenties. The two-volume work was Werner Sudendorf's, who shared the story of "Honorary Citizenship."

452   *Adolf and Marlene: NYT*, March 18, 1977; London *Sunday Times*, March 27, 1977.

452   Dietrich on the telephone: the author heard this tactic from Dietrich himself on several occasions.

452   Book and money to strangers: Dietrich sent the author a volume of Rilke after reciting most of its contents to him on the telephone. "Unless they're really in *trouble*": MD to SB, July 31, 1987.

452   Thigh break: *Münchner Merkur* and *TZ*, both August 2, 1979. Also int. SB/Bernard Hall, December 5–6, 1986.

452   "Duties": quoted in Hall, "Marlene the Magnificent," p. 90. The emphasis in the quote is in the original.

453   Legs: int. SB/Bernard Hall, as above. Tennis: Schell/Dietrich, tapes.

453   Glasses to Tarzana: MD to SB, August 17, 1987.

453ff.   Quotations regarding the Schell film and its making are, except where otherwise noted, from Dietrich/Schell, *Marlene: A Feature*. Additional material from ints. SB/Bernard Hall, December 6–8 and 15, 1986; Dietrich/Schell, *Die Zeit*; Dietrich/Schell, *The Manipulator*. The author is grateful to the confidential source who allowed him to hear tape copies on which this chapter relies.

454   "Marmalade" is from the Dietrich/Schell tapes. Schell's frame of mind he expressed to the Lincoln Center New York Film Festival audience in an on-stage interview with David Denby following the festival screening of *Marlene: A Feature*, September 1986. The author was present.

456   German delicacies: int. SB/BH, December 5–6, 1986.

459   "tea" and "courage": int. *Ibid.*

464   Mathews and Schell quote: Mathews, "Schell vs. Dietrich: It's a Draw," *Los Angeles Times*, February 2, 1987.

464ff.   Canby: *NYT*, September 21, 1986.

CODA: "ALLEIN IN EINER GROSSEN STADT": 1983–1992

469   Homosexuals quote: MD to SB, July 31, 1987.

469   Hall quote: Hall ms.

469ff.   Maria Riva, Bernard Hall on *Marlene: A Feature*: Maximilian Schell to David Denby, New York Film Festival, September 1986, as cited. Hall was annoyed with Schell for quoting MD's remark to him, but admitted it was true. int. SB/BH, as cited. "Can't laugh alone!" letter [n.d.] MD to BH, courtesy BH.

470   Income from *Marlene*: MD to SB, August 28, 1987. She was, in fact, paid a fee for her participation.

470   Eviction proceedings: *Newsday*, July 15, 1984; *Süddeutsche-Zeitung*, June 27, 1984.

470   *Commandeur*: IHT, January 4, 1990, *Süddeutsche-Zeitung*, January 3, 1990. "Walls": int. SB/Bernard Hall, December 5–6, 1986.

471   Garage story: MD to SB, April 5, 1987.

471   Leg wound: "*Die Dietrich wollte nicht in die Klinik*," Abend-Zeitung (Munich), October 14, 1986.

471   Maria's husband's surgery: MD to SB, March 24, 1987. Dietrich called it a brain tumor; Bernard Hall said it was cancer of the eyeball.

471   Spielberg poster to Maria: MD to SB, August 17, 1987.

471   "Worth more dead": MD to SB, August 17, 1987.

472   Christie's auction: Quoted from Christie's catalogue of sale, Geneva, November 12, 1987.

472   Costume sale: Werner Sudendorf, SDK. No commissions or expenses were charged back to Dietrich by the middleman.

472   *Die Welt*: April 21, 1987. Surprise at payments: MD to SB, July 3, 1987. The *Der Spiegel* interview ran June 17, 1991. The amount was reported to Werner Sudendorf of the SDK by Max Colpet.

472ff.   The listener was the author: MD to SB, April 5, 1987.

473   MD and SB Berlin: the deal was made partly through the SDK in Berlin. Telegram MD to SB, March 23, 1988, letter MD to SB, April 13, 1988.

473   Re Barbie trial and the French: MD to SB, July 31, 1987; "I shouldn't let it eat me up": MD to SB, April 5, 1987.

473   Re Norma: Norma Kaplan is married to the writer and editor Alain Bosquet (né Anatol Bisk), then with Gallimard. MD to SB, July 31, 1987.

473   MD calling Curt Bois: int. SB/Curt Bois, April 27, 1990. Bois told SB the story about Margo Lion, as did Max Colpet, int. SB/MC, October 22, 1987.

474   Jim Haynes: Haynes generously shared *The Dietrich Songs* with the author. It is an extraordinary document, needing only to clear away the "*Quatsch*" of tangled copyright. See Appendix II, Filmography.

474   European Film Award: Paris, November 25, 1989, program; Council of the Fashion Designers of America Awards program, 1986 (presented 1987); other details courtesy Robert Raymond.

474ff.   Birthday honors and quotes: *IHT*, December 28–29, 1991. Re *Metropolis*-Halle, Werner Sudendorf.

475   London *Sunday Times*: January 12, 1992, by James Dalrymple.

475   "lordly English publisher": confidential source, April 27, 1992.

475   *"Das Foto"*: February 3, 1992. The photograph was taken by freelance photographer Peter Sylent and published around the world. Color shots were published in Germany's *Die Aktuelle,* same date.

476   Lahr quote: Lahr, p. 30.

476   Beerbohm quote: Behrman, p. 130.

477   MD to SB on afterlife and Rudi: August 17, 1987.

BIBLIOGRAPHY

BOOKS

The following bibliography is selective rather than exhaustive, and includes all works cited in short form (usually by author's last name) in the endnotes. Other works named were consulted during the author's research. Most were helpful or valuable, though previous Dietrich biographies and works on Hollywood must be approached with care. Reliability is not a hallmark of either genre.

A. DIETRICH: By or concerning Marlene Dietrich.

"Aros" [Alfred Rosenthal]. *Marlene Dietrich: ein interessantes Künstlerschicksal.* Berlin: Verlag Scherl, 1932.
Baxter, John. *The Cinema of Josef von Sternberg.* London: A. Zwemmer, 1971.
Baxter, Peter, ed. *Sternberg.* London: British Film Institute, 1980.
Bemmann, Helga. *Marlene Dietrich: ihr Weg zum Chanson.* Berlin, GDR: VEB Lied der Zeit, 1987.

Carr, Larry. *Four Fabulous Faces*. New York: Penguin, 1978.

de Navacelle, Thierry, trans. Carey L. Smith. *Sublime Marlene*. London: Sidgwick & Jackson, 1984.

Dickens, Homer. *The Films of Marlene Dietrich*. Secaucus, N.J.: Citadel, 1968.

Dietrich, Marlene. *Marlene Dietrich's ABC*, rev. ed. New York: Frederick Ungar, 1984.

———. *Ich bin, Gott sei Dank, Berlinerin*, translated from the French by Nicola Volland. Frankfurt: Ullstein, 1987.

———. *Marlene*, translated from the German by Salvator Attanasio. New York: Grove Press, 1989.

———. *My Life*, translated from the German by Salvator Attanasio. London: Weidenfeld & Nicolson, 1989.

———. *Nehmt nur mein Leben . . .* , translated from the English, uncredited, by Max Colpet. Munich: Bertelsmann, 1979.

———. *Marlène D.*, translated from the English by Boris Matthews and Françoise Ducout. Paris. 1984.

———. *Vogue par Marlène Diétrich*. Paris: Condé Nast, December 1973.

Droz, René. *Marlene Dietrich und die Psychologie des Vamps*, translated by Ursula von Wiese. Zurich: Sanssouci, 1961.

Editions Cinémania. *Marlene Dietrich: Films/Portraits*, No. 8. Paris, June–July 1979.

Erman, Hans. *Eine Große Dame*. Unpublished manuscript. Erfurt, GDR: [1955].

Frewin, Leslie, *Blonde Venus: A Life of Marlene Dietrich*. New York: Roy, 1955.

———. *Dietrich: The Story of a Star*. New York: Avon, 1967. (rev. ed. of *Blonde Venus*, new intro.)

———. translated by Keto von Waberer, with Christa Bandmann. *Marlene Dietrich: Ihre Filme—ihr Leben*. Munich: Heyne, 1984. (NB: Though published as a translation, this is a reworked, substantially different text, endnoted as "Frewin-Heyen."]

Georg, Manfred. *Marlene Dietrich: Eine Eroberung der Welt in sechs Monaten*. Berlin: Künstler und Filme, 1931.

Griffith, Richard. *Marlene Dietrich: Image and Legend*. Garden City, N.Y.: Museum of Modern Art/Doubleday, 1959.

Hessel, Franz. *Marlene Dietrich*. Berlin: Kindt & Bucher, 1931.

Higham, Charles. *Marlene: The Life of Marlene Dietrich*. New York: Norton, 1977.

Kobal, John. *Marlene Dietrich*. London: Studio Vista, 1968.

Mollica, Vincenzo, ed. *Marlene Dietrich & Betty Boop*. Montepulciano, Italy: Editori Del Grifo, 1985.

Morley, Sheridan. *Marlene Dietrich*. New York: McGraw-Hill, 1977.

Noa, Wolfgang. *Marlene Dietrich*. Berlin: Henschelverlag, 1975.

Parrish, Robert. *The Paramount Pretties*. New York: Castle, 1972.

Polt, Rudi. *The Marlene Dietrich Songbook with Discography*. Honolulu: Film Archives, [n.d.].

Salmon, André. *Marlène Dietrich*. Paris: La Nouvelle Librairie Française, 1932.

Sarris, Andrew. *The Films of Josef von Sternberg*. New York: Museum of Modern Art, 1966.

Sembach, Klaus-Jürgen (intro.). *Marlene Dietrich: Portraits 1926–1960*. Munich: Schirmer/Mosel, 1984.

Seydel, Renata. *Marlene Dietrich: Chronik ihres Lebens in Bildern und Dokumenten*. Henschelverlag. GDR: Berlin, 1984.

Silver, Charles. *Marlene Dietrich*. New York: Pyramid, 1974.

Sternberg, Josef von. *Fun in a Chinese Laundry*. New York: Macmillan, 1965.

[Sternberg, Josef von]. *Morocco and Shanghai Express: Two Films by Josef von Sternberg*. New York: Simon and Schuster, 1973.

Studlar, Gaylyn. *In the Realm of Pleasure: Von Sternberg, Dietrich, and the Masochistic Aesthetic*. Urbana and Chicago: University of Illinois, 1988.

Sudendorf, Werner, ed. *Marlene Dietrich: Dokumente, Essays, Filme*, 2 vols. Munich: Hanser, 1977.

Walker, Alexander. *Dietrich*. New York: Harper & Row, 1984.

Weinberg, Herman. *Josef von Sternberg: A Critical Study of the Great Film Director*. New York: Dutton, 1967.

Worm, Hardy. *Marlene Dietrich: die Geschichte einer Karriere. Mein Film Sonderpublikation*. Vienna: *Mein Film*, 1947.

Zucker, Carole. *The Idea of the Image: Josef von Sternberg's Dietrich Films*. London and Toronto: Associated University Presses, 1988

B. GENERAL WORKS

Abzug, Robert H. *Inside the Vicious Heart: Americans and the Liberation of Nazi Concentration Camps*. New York: Oxford, 1985.

Aherne, Brian. *A Proper Job*. Boston: Houghton Mifflin, 1969.

Appignanesi, Lisa. *Cabaret: The First Hundred Years*. New York: Grove, 1984.

Arce, Hector. *The Secret Life of Tyrone Power*. New York: William Morrow, 1979.

Aronson, Steven M. L. *Hype*. New York: Morrow, 1983.

Aufricht, Ernst Josef. *Erzähle, damit Du dein Recht erweist*. Berlin: Propyläen, 1966.

Bab, Julius. *Albert Bassermann; Weg und Werk*. Leipzig: Erich Weibezahl Verlag, 1929.

Ball, Gregor. *Heinz Rühmann: Seine Filme—sein Leben*. Munich: Heyne, 1981.

Barker, Christine R. and R. W. Last. *Erich Maria Remarque*. London: Oswald Wolff, 1979.

Barzini, Luigi. *The Europeans*. New York: Penguin, 1984.

Baum, Peter. *Eines Menschen Zeit*. Munich: Droemer-Knaur, 1972.

Baum, Vicki. *Es war alles ganz anders*. Berlin: Ullstein, 1962.

Beaton, Cecil. *The Face of the World*. London: Weidenfeld & Nicolson, 1957.

———. *Self Portrait with Friends: Selected Diaries 1926–1974*, Richard Buckle, ed. New York: Times Books, 1979.

——— and Kenneth Tynan. *Persona Grata*. London: Allan Wingate, 1953.

BIBLIOGRAPHY

Behlmer, Rudy, ed. *Inside Warner Brothers: 1935–1951*. New York: Viking, 1985.

Behrman, S. N. *Portrait of Max: An Intimate Memoir of Sir Max Beerbohm*. New York: Random House, 1960.

———, ed. *Memo From: David O. Selznick*. (int. by S.N. Behrman). New York: Avon, 1973.

Benjamin, Walter. *Berliner Kindheit um neunzehnhundert*. Frankfurt: Suhrkamp, 1987.

Benson, Renate. *German Expressionist Drama: Ernst Toller and Georg Kaiser*. London: Macmillan, 1984.

Berg-Ganschow, Uta, and Wolfgang Jacobsen, eds. *. . . Film . . . Stadt . . . Kino . . . Berlin*. Berlin: Argon, 1987.

Bergner, Elisabeth. *Bewundert viel und viel gescholten . . . Unordentliche Erinnerungen*. Wilhelm Goldmann, 1981.

Bernauer, Rudolf. *Das Theater meines Lebens: Errinerungen*. Berlin: Blauvalet Verlag, 1955.

[Bernhardt, Curtis.] *Curtis Bernhardt: A Director's Guild of America Oral History*, interview by Mary Kiersch. Metuchen, N.J.: DGA and The Scarecrow Press, 1986.

Berstl, Julius, ed. *25 Jahre Berliner Theater und Victor Barnovsky*. Berlin: Berstl Verlag, 1930.

———. *Odysee eines Theatermannes*. Berlin: Arani, 1963.

Berteaut, Simone. *Ich hab' gelebt Mylord: Das unglaubliche Leben der Edith Piaf*, translated by Margaret Carroux. Munich: Scherz, 1969.

Bezirksamt Tempelhof von Berlin, ed. *Die Ufa: aud den Spuren einer großen Filmfabrik*. Berlin: Elefanten Press, 1987.

Bier, Marcus (introduction by Klaus Völker, portraits by Klaus Richter). *Schauspielerportraits: 24 Schauspieler um Max Reinhardt*. Berlin: Edition Hentrich, 1989.

Björnson, Björnstjerne. *"Wenn der neue Wein blüht"* in *Gesammelte Werke*, vol. 5. Berlin: S. Fischer, 1911.

Black, Shirley Temple. *Child Star: An Autobiography*. New York: Warner, 1989.

Bogdanovich, Peter. *Fritz Lang in America*. New York: Praeger, 1969.

Bois, Curt. *So schlecht war mir noch nie*. Konigstein: Athenäum, 1984.

———. *Zu wahr, um schön zu sein*. Berlin: Henschel, 1982.

Bollé, Michael and Bothe, Rolf, eds. *Eldorado: Homosexuelle Frauen und Männer in Berlin 1850–1950*. Berlin: Frölich & Kaufmann/Berlin Museum, 1984.

Bourdet, Eugène. *Der Rubicon*. [unbound ms.] [Münchner Theatermuseum.] [1926.]

Brady, Frank. *Citizen Welles: A Biography of Orson Welles*. New York: Scribner's, 1989.

Brasillach, Robert, and Maurice Bardèche. *The History of Motion Pictures*. New York: W. W. Norton and the Museum of Modern Art, 1938.

Brian, Denis. *The True Gen*. New York: Grove, 1988.

Briers, Richard. *Coward & Company*. London: Futura, 1989.

Brinnin, John Malcolm. *Truman Capote: A Memoir*. London: Sidgwick & Jackson, 1987.

Brod, Max. *Die Frau nach der man sich sehnt*. Hamburg: Rowohlt, 1960. (reprint)

Brooks, Louise. *Lulu in Hollywood*. London: Arena, 1987.

Brownlow, Kevin. *The Parade's Gone By*. New York: Knopf, 1968.

Brunelin, André. *Jean Gabin: Leben-Filme-Frauen*. Munich: Herbig, 1989.

Bruno, Michael. *Venus in Hollywood*. New York: Lyle Stuart, 1970.

Brynner, Rock. *Yul: The Man Who Would Be King*. London: Collins, 1989.

Bucher, Edmund, and Albrecht Kindt, eds. *Film Photos wie noch nie*. Giessen: Kindt & Bucher Verlag, 1929.

Busch, Ernst. *Schauspieler Werden in Berlin: Von Max Reinhardts Schauspielschule zur Hochschule für Schauspielkunst*. Berlin: Gerhard Ebert, 1987.

Buxton, Frank, and Bill Owen. *The Big Broadcast: 1920–1950*. New York: Avon/Flare, 1973.

Cadenbach, Joachim. *Hans Albers*. Munich: Universitas, 1982.

Callow, Simon. *Charles Laughton: A Difficult Actor*. London: Methuen, 1987.

Carné, Marcel. *La Vie à belles dents*. Paris: Jean-Pierre Ollivier. 1975.

Castle, Charles. *Oliver Messel: A Biography*. London: Thames and Hudson, 1986.

Chevalier, Maurice, as told to Eileen and Robert Mason Pollock. *With Love: The Autobiography of Maurice Chevalier*. London: Cassell, 1960.

Chierichetti, David. *Hollywood Director: The Career of Mitchell Leisen*. New York: Curtis, 1973.

Clarke, Gerald. *Capote: A Biography*. New York: Simon and Schuster, 1988.

Cohn, Art. *The Nine Lives of Mike Todd*. New York: Random House, 1958.

———, ed. *Michael Todd's Around the World in 80 Days Almanac*. New York: Random House, 1956.

Colman, Juliet Benita. *Ronald Colman*. New York: Morrow, 1975.

Colpet, Max. *Sag mir wo die Jahre sind*. Munich: Langen Müller, 1976.

Conot, Robert E. *Justice at Nuremberg*. New York: Harper & Row, 1983.

Corliss, Richard. *Talking Pictures: Screenwriters in the American Cinema*. Woodstock, N.Y.: Overlook Press, 1974.

Coward, Noël. *Autobiography* (introduced and edited by Sheridan Morley.) London: Methuen, 1986.

———. The Noël Coward Diaries, ed. by Graham Payn and Sheridan Morley. London: Macmillan, 1982.

Craig, Gordon. *The Germans*. New York: G. P. Putnam's Sons, 1982.

———. *Germany: 1866–1945*. Oxford: Oxford, 1981.

Crawford, Cheryl. *One Naked Individual: My Fifty Years in the Theatre*. New York: Bobbs-Merrill, 1977.

Crosland, Margaret. *Piaf*. London: Hodder and Stoughton, 1985.

Czech, Stan. *Schön ist die Welt*. Berlin: Argon, 1957.

Dachs, Robert. *Sag beim Abschied* . . . Vienna: Museen der Stadt Wien, 1992.

———. *Willi Forst: Eine Biographie*. Vienna: Kremayr & Scheriau, 1986.

Dahlke, Günther, and Karl Günter, eds. *Deutsche Spielfilme von den Anfängen bis 1933*. Berlin, GDR: Henschelverlag, 1988.

Davidson, Bill. *Spencer Tracy: Tragic Idol*. London: Sidgwick & Jackson, 1987.

de Acosta, Mercedes. *Here Lies the Heart*. New York: Reynal & Co., 1960.

Dillman, Michael. *Heinz Hilpert: Leben und Werk*. Akademie der Künste, Berlin: Edition Hentrich, 1990.

Douglas, Kirk. *The Ragman's Son*. New York: Simon and Schuster, 1988.

Dreifuss, Alfred. *Deutsches Theater Berlin: Schumannstraße 13a*. Berlin (East): Henschelverlag, 1987.

Drew, David. *Kurt Weill : A Handbook*. London: Faber & Faber, 1987. [Galleys].

Dümling, Albrecht, and Peter Girth, eds. *Entartete Musik: Eine Kommentierte Rekonstruktion zur Düsseldorfer Ausstellung von 1938*. Düsseldorf: Exhibition catalogue, 1988.

Dunning, John. *Tune in Yesterday: The Ultimate Encyclopedia of Old Time Radio 1925–1976*. Englewood Cliffs, N.J.: Prentice-Hall, 1976.

Durgnat, Raymond. *The Crazy Mirror: Hollywood Comedy and the American Image*. New York: Horizon Press, 1970.

Dyer, Richard. *Stars*. London: British Film Institute, 1979.

Eames, John Douglas. *The Paramount Story*. London: Octopus, 1985.

Ebermayer, Erich, Werner R. Heymann (music) and Robert Gilbert (lyrics). *Professor Unrat* (play in eight scenes adapted from the novel by Heinrich Mann). Berlin-Charlottenburg: Felix Bloch Erben, [n.d.].

Ebinger, Blandine. *"Blandine . . ."* Zurich: Arche Verlag, 1985.

Edwards, Anne. *Judy Garland: A Biography*. New York: Simon and Schuster, 1975.

Eisner, Lotte H. *Fritz Lang*. London: Secker & Warburg, 1976.

————. *The Haunted Screen: Expressionism in the German Cinema and the Influence of Max Reinhardt*, translated by Roger Greaves. Berkeley: University of California Press, 1977.

————. *Ich hatte einst ein schönes Vaterland: Memoiren*. Heidelberg: Wunderhorn, 1984.

Eksteins, Modris. *Rites of Spring: The Great War and the Birth of the Modern Age*. Boston: Houghton Mifflin, 1989.

Esser, Michael, ed. *Berlin und das Kino*. Berlin: Stiftung Deutsche Kinemathek, 1987

Everett, Susanne. *Lost Berlin*. New York: Gallery Books, 1979.

Fairbanks, Douglas, Jr. *The Salad Days*. London: Collins, 1988.

Fechner, Eberhard. *Die Comedian Harmonists: Sechs Lebensläufe*. Weinheim and Berlin: Quadriga, 1988.

Fischer, Lothar. *Anita Berber: 1918–1928 in Berlin*. Berlin: Haude & Spener, 1988.

Flanner, Janet. *An American in Paris: Profile of an Interlude Between Two Wars*. London: Hamish Hamilton, 1940.

————, Irving Drutman, ed. *Paris Was Yesterday: 1925–1939*. New York: Viking, 1972.

Forster, Rudolf. *Das Spiel mein Leben.* Berlin: Propyläen, 1967.

Fountain, Leatrice Gilbert, with John R. Maxim. *Dark Star: The Untold Story of the Meteoric Rise and Fall of the Legendary John Gilbert.* New York: St. Martin's Press, 1985.

Frank, Gerold. *Judy.* New York: Harper & Row, 1975.

Friedmann-Friederich, Fritz, and Ralph Arthur Roberts. *Mein Vetter Eduard.* Berlin: Drei Masken Verlag, 1924.

Friedrich, Otto. *Before the Deluge: A Portrait of Berlin in the 1920's.* New York: Fromm, 1986.

———. *City of Nets: A Portrait of Hollywood in the 1940's.* New York: Harper & Row, 1986.

Frischauer, Willy. *Behind the Scenes of Otto Preminger.* London: Michael Joseph, 1973.

Fritsch, Willy. *. . . das kommt nicht wieder: Erinnerungen eines Filmschauspielers.* Zürich: Werner Classen Verlag, 1963.

Fussell, Paul. *Wartime: Understanding and Behavior in the Second World War.* New York: Oxford, 1989.

Gabler, Neal. *An Empire of Their Own: How the Jews Invented Hollywood.* New York: Crown, 1988.

Garnett, Tay, with Fredda Dudley Balling, *Light Your Torches and Pull Up Your Tights.* New Rochelle, N.Y.: Arlington House, 1973.

Gaskill, William. *A Sense of Direction: Life at the Royal Court.* London: Faber, 1988.

Gay, Peter. *Weimar Culture: The Outsider as Insider.* New York: Harper & Row: 1968.

Geduld, Harry M., ed. *Film Makers on Film Making.* Bloomington: Indiana University Press, 1967.

Gersh, Wolfgang. *Chaplin in Berlin: Illustrierte Miniatur nach Berliner Zeitungen von 1931.* Berlin: Argon Verlag, 1989.

Giannetti, Louis. *Masters of the American Cinema.* Englewood Cliffs, N.J.: Prentice-Hall, 1981.

Gilbert, Felix. *A European Past: Memoirs 1905–1945.* New York: Norton, 1988.

Gilbert, Jean. *Jean Gilbert—Album,* Alfred Schönfeld, ed. Berlin: Globus Verlag, [1913].

Gill, Anton. *The Journey Back from Hell: Conversations with Concentration Camp Survivors.* London: Grafton, 1989.

Giraudoux, Jean, and Chas-Laborde. *Berlin 1930: Straßen und Gesichter.* Nördlingen: Greno, 1987.

Goldman, William. *The Season: A Candid Look at Broadway.* New York: Bantam, 1970.

Gonzalez-Crussi, Frank. *On the Nature of Things Erotic.* New York: Vintage, 1988.

Gottlieb, Polly Rose. *The Nine Lives of Billy Rose.* New York: Crown, 1968.

Granach, Alexander, *Da geht ein Mensch.* Munich: Piper, 1990.

Greene, Graham. *The Pleasure Dome*, John Russell Taylor, ed. Oxford: Oxford University Press, 1980.

Griffith, Richard and Arthur Mayer. *The Movies*. New York: Simon & Schuster, 1957.

Grosz, George. *George Grosz: An Autobiography*, translated by Nora Hodges. New York: Macmillan, 1983.

Hall, Bernard. *Memoirs*. Unpublished manuscript. [© Outpost Productions. New York. 1987.]

Hamilton, Ian. *Writers in Hollywood: 1915–1951*. London: Heinemann, 1990.

Hamilton, Nigel. *The Brothers Mann*. New Haven: Yale, 1979.

Harding, James. *Maurice Chevalier: His Life 1882–1972*. London: Secker & Warburg, 1982.

Harris, Warren G. *Gable and Lombard*. London: Cassel, 1976.

Hart, Kitty Carlisle. *Kitty: An Autobiography*. New York: Doubleday, 1988.

Haskell, Molly. *From Reverence to Rape: The Treatment of Women in the Movies*. New York: Holt, Rinehart and Winston, 1974.

Hausner, Hans Erik, ed. *Zeit Bild: Die "goldenen" zwanziger Jahre*. Wien-Heidelberg: Ueberreuter, 1982.

Haver, Ronald. *David O. Selznick's Hollywood*. New York: Knopf, 1980.

Hecht, Ben. *A Child of the Century*. New York: Simon & Schuster, 1954.

Heilbrun, Carolyn G. *Writing a Woman's Life*. New York: W. W. Norton, 1988.

Heilbut, Anthony. *Exiled in Paradise: German Refugee Artists and Intellectuals in America from the 1930s to the Present*. Boston: Beacon Press, 1983.

Heinzlmeier, Adolf; Berndt Schulz; Karsten Witte. *Die Unsterblichen des Kinos*. Frankfurt: Fischer, 1982.

Hemingway, Ernest. *The Garden of Eden*. London: Grafton, 1987.

———. *Island in the Stream*. London: Collins, 1970.

———. *Selected Letters: 1917–1961*, ed. by Carlos Baker. New York: Scribner's, 1981.

Hemingway, Mary Welsh. *How It Was*. New York: Knopf, 1976.

Hermann, Dorothy. *S. J. Perelman: A Life*. New York: Simon & Schuster (Fireside), 1987.

Hessel, Franz. *Spazieren in Berlin*. Munich: Rogner & Bernhard, 1968.

Heymann, C. David. *Poor Little Rich Girl: The Life and Legend of Barbara Hutton*. London: Hutchinson, 1985.

Hickethier, Knut, ed. *Grenzgänger zwischen Theater und Kino: Schauspielerporträts aus dem Berlin der Zwanziger Jahre*. Berlin: Edition Mythos, 1986.

Higham, Charles. *Hollywood Cameramen: Sources of Light*. Bloomington: Indiana University Press, 1970.

———. *Orson Welles: The Rise and Fall of an American Genius*. New York: St. Martin's Press, 1985.

Hildenbrandt, Fred. *. . . ich soll dich grüßen von Berlin: 1922–1932*. Frankfurt: Ullstein, 1986.

Hippen, Reinhard. *Das Kabarett-Chanson: Typen-Themen-Temperamente*. Zurich: Pendo Verlag, 1986.

Lasky, Jesse L., with Don Weldon. *I Blow My Own Horn*. Garden City, N.Y.: Doubleday, 1957.

Leaming, Barbara. *If This Was Happiness: A Biography of Rita Hayworth*. London: Weidenfeld Nicolson, 1989.

———. *Orson Welles: A Biography*. New York: Viking Penguin, 1985.

Leff, Leonard J. *Hitchcock and Selznick*. New York: Weidenfeld & Nicolson, 1987.

Lesley, Cole. *The Life of Noël Coward*. London: Penguin, 1978.

Liebe, Ulrich. *Verehrt, Verfolgt, Vergessen: Schauspieler als Naziopfer*. Berlin: Beltz/Quadriga, 1992.

Lipmann, Anthony. *Divinely Elegant: The World of Ernst Dryden*. London: Pavilion, 1989.

Loos, Anita. *A Girl Like I*. New York: Viking, 1966.

Lorant, Stefan. *Wir vom Film*. Berlin: Böhm, 1968 (reprint of 1928 edition).

Lord, James, *Giacometti*. New York: Farrar, Straus, Giroux, 1985.

Lyon, Christopher, ed. *The International Dictionary of Films and Filmmakers*. Vol. 1: *Films*. Vol. 2: *Directors*. London: Papermac, 1984.

Ludwig, Emil. *Wilhelm Hohenzollern: The Last of the Kaisers*, translated by Ethel Colburn Mayne. New York: G. P. Putnam's Sons, 1927.

Luft, Friedrich, and Alexander von Baeyer, eds. *Facsimile Querschnitt durch die Berliner Illustrirte*. Bern and Munich: Scherz, [n.d.]

Lynes, Russell. *The Lively Audience: A Social History of the Visual and Performing Arts in America 1890–1950*. New York: Harper & Row, 1985.

Lynn, Kenneth S. *Hemingway*. London: Simon and Schuster, 1987.

McBride, Joseph, ed. *Filmmakers on Filmmaking: The American Film Institute Seminars on Motion Pictures and Television*, 2 vols. Los Angeles: J. P. Tarcher, 1983.

McConathy, Dale, and Diana Vreeland. *Hollywood Costume*. New York: Harry Abrams, with the Metropolitan Museum of Art, 1976.

McDowall, Roddy. *Double Exposure: Take Two*. New York: Morrow, 1989.

McGilligan, Pat. *Backstory: Interviews with Screenwriters of Hollywood's Golden Age*. Berkeley: University of California Press, 1986.

MacQueen-Pope, W. *Ivor: A Biography of Ivor Novello*. London: W. H. Allen, 1952.

Madsen, Axel. *Billy Wilder*. London: Secker & Warburg, 1968.

Maltin, Leonard. *The Cinematographer's Art*. New York: New American Library, 1971.

Manchester, William. *The Arms of Krupp: 1587–1968*. Boston: Little, Brown, 1968.

Mann, Abby. *Judgment at Nuremberg*. Unpublished telescript. [USC Archives.]

———. *Judgment at Nuremberg: The Script of the Film*. London: Cassell, 1961.

Mann, Henrich. *Professor Unrat*. Hamburg: Rowohlt, 1951 (reprint of 1905 edition).

———. *The Blue Angel* (English translation of *Professor Unrat* by "Professor Unrat" [sic]). (reprint, London, 1932), pub. with *The Blue Angel* film script (no tr., intro. by Stanley Hochman). New York: Frederick Ungar, 1979.

Mann, Thomas. *Reflections of a Nonpolitical Man* (1918, translated by Walter D. Morris). New York: Ungar, 1987.

Manvell, Roger. *Love Goddesses of the Screen*. London: Hamlyn, 1975.

Marcus, Paul Erich. *Heimweh nach dem Kurfürstendamm*. Frankfurt: Ullstein, 1986.

Marion, Frances. *Off with Their Heads: A Serio-Comic Tale of Hollywood*. New York: Macmillan, 1972.

Mast, Gerald, ed. *The Movies in Our Midst: Documents in the Cultural History of Film in America*. Chicago: University of Chicago Press, 1982.

Maugham, W. Somerset. *The Circle*, in *W. Somerset Maugham Selected Plays*. London: Pan in association with Wm. Heinemann, 1976.

McClelland, Doug. *The Unkindest Cuts*. New Jersey: A. S. Barnes, 1972.

Messters, Oskar. *Mein Weg mit dem Kino*. Berlin: [private pub.], 1936.

Meyer, Alfred Richard ["Munkepunke"] *1000% Jannings*. Hamburg-Berlin: Prismen-Verlag, 1930.

Meyers, Jeffrey. *Hemingway: A Biography*. New York: Harper & Row, 1985.

Mordden, Ethan. *The Hollywood Studios: House Style in the Golden Age of the Movies*. New York: Knopf, 1988.

Morgan, Ted. *Maugham: A Biography*. New York: Simon & Schuster, 1980.

Morley, Sheridan. *A Talent to Amuse: A Biography of Noël Coward*. London: Penguin, 1974.

Nabokov, Vladimir. *Stadtführer Berlin*. Stuttgart: Reclam, 1985.

Nacache, Jacqueline *Lubitsch*. Paris: Edilig, 1987.

Napley, Sir David. *Rasputin in Hollywood*. London: Weidenfeld & Nicolson, 1990.

Naso, Eckart von. *Ich liebe das Leben*. Hamburg: Krüger, 1953.

Niehoff, Karena. *Stimmt es—Stimmt es nicht?* [n.p.]: Horst Erdmann Verlag, 1962.

Niven, David. *The Moon's a Balloon*. London: Hamish Hamilton, 1971.

Odets, Clifford. *The Time Is Ripe: The 1940 Journal of Clifford Odets*, introduction by William Gibson. New York: Grove, 1988.

Paris, Barry. *Louise Brooks*. New York: Knopf, 1989.

Parish, James Robert. *Actors' Television Credits: 1950–1972*. Metuchen, N.J.: Scarecrow Press, 1973.

———— and Don E. Stanke with Roger Greene and Thomas Nocerino. *The Forties Gals*. Westport, CT: Arlington House, 1980.

Pasternak, Joe, as told to David Chandler. *Easy the Hard Way*. New York: G. P. Putnam's Sons, 1956.

Paul, William. *Ernst Lubitsch's American Comedy*. New York: Columbia University Press, 1983.

Pitts, Michael R. *Radio Soundtracks: A Reference Guide*, 2nd edition. Metuchen, N.J.: Scarecrow Press, 1986.

Pfeiffer, Herbert. *Berlin Zwanziger Jahre*. Berlin: Rembrandt, 1961.

Preminger, Otto. *Preminger: An Autobiography*. New York: Doubleday, 1977.

Prinzler, Hans Helmut, and Enno Patalas, eds. *Lubitsch*. Munich and Lucerne: C. J. Bucher Verlag (Internationale Filmfestspiele Berlin), 1984.

Rathbone, Basil. *In and Out of Character* (reprint). New York: Limelight, 1989.

Rehfisch, Hans J. *Duell am Lido*. Munich: Theaterverlag Kurt Desch [acting copy, no date].

Reinhardt, Gottfried. *The Genius: A Memoir of Max Reinhardt by His Son*. New York: Knopf, 1979.

Reinhardt, Max. "The Enchanted Sense of Play" (also known as "The Actor") in *Actors on Acting*, edited by Cole, Toby, and Helen Krich Chinoy. New York: Crown, 1970.

Reitz, Jürgen. *Jean Gabin*. Berlin: Henschelverlag, 1970.

Remarque, Erich Maria. *Arch of Triumph*, translated by Walter Sorell and Denver Lindley. New York: NAL, 1950.

———. *Schatten im Paradies*. Munich: Droemer Knaur, 1974.

Renoir, Jean. *Mein Leben und Meine Filme*. Munich: Piper, 1975.

Rhode, Eric. *A History of the Cinema from Its Origins to 1970*. London: Allen Lane, 1976.

Riefenstahl, Leni. *Memoiren*. Munich: Albrecht Knaus, 1987.

Riess, Curt. *Das gab's nur einmal*, 3 vols. Frankfurt: Ullstein, 1985.

Rilke, Rainer Maria. *Selected Letters 1902–1926*, translated by R.F.C. Hull, introduction by John Bayley. London: Quartet, 1988.

Robinson, David. *Chaplin: His Life and Art*. London: Collins, 1985.

Robinson, Edward G., with Leonard Spiegelgass. *All My Yesterdays: An Autobiography*. New York: Hawthorn, 1973.

Röhl, John C. G. *Kaiser, Hof und Staat: Wilhelm II. und die deutsche Politik*. Munich: Beck, 1987.

Rose, Phyllis. *Jazz Cleopatra: Josephine Baker in Her Time*. New York: Doubleday, 1989.

Rosen, Marjorie. *Popcorn Venus*. New York: Coward, McCann & Geoghegan, 1973.

Rotha, Paul, and Richard Griffith. *The Film Till Now: A Survey of World Cinema*, rev. ed. Feltham, GB: Spring Books, 1960.

Rozsa, Miklos. *Double Life: The Autobiography of Miklos Rozsa*. Tunbridge Wells: Baton Press, 1982.

Rühmann, Heinz. *Das war's*. Berlin: Ullstein, 1982.

Samuels, Charles Thomas. *Encountering Directors*. New York: Da Capo Press, 1987.

Sanders, Ronald. *The Days Grow Short: The Life and Music of Kurt Weill*. New York: Holt, Rinehart and Winston, 1980.

Sarris, Andrew. *The American Cinema: Directors and Directions, 1929–1968*. New York: Dutton, 1968.

Sayler, Oliver M., ed. *Max Reinhardt and His Theatre*. New York: Brentano's, 1924.

Schatz, Thomas. *The Genius of the System*. New York: Pantheon, 1988.

Schebera, Jürgen. *Damals im Romanischen Café*. Braunschweig: Westermann, 1988.

———. *Kurt Weill: Leben und Werk*. Königstein, GDR: Athenäum, 1983.

Schickel, Richard. *Cary Grant: A Celebration*. London: Pavilion, 1983.

———. *The Men Who Made the Movies: Interviews with Frank Capra, George Cukor, Howard Hawks, Alfred Hitchcock, Vincente Minnelli, King Vidor, Raoul Walsh, and William A. Wellman*, New York: Atheneum, 1975.

———. *The Stars*. New York: Bonanza, 1962.

Schmidt, Paul. *Die ersten 50 Jahre der Königlichen Schutzmannschaft in Berlin*. Berlin: Mittler & Sohn, 1898.

Schrader, Bärbel, and Schebera, Jürgen. *Kunst Metropole Berlin 1918–1933*. Berlin: Aufbau-Verlag, 1987.

———. *The "Golden" Twenties: Art and Life in the Weimar Republic*, translated by Katherine Vanovitch. Leipzig, GDR:, Leipzig Edition, 1987.

Schreyer, Lothar. *Erinnerungen an Sturm und Bauhaus: Was ist das Menschen Bild?* Hamburg/Berlin: Deutsche Hausbücherei, 1956.

Schulberg, Budd. *Moving Pictures: Memories of a Hollywood Prince*. New York: Stein and Day, 1981.

Schutte, Jürgen, and Peter Sprengel, eds. *Die Berliner Moderne: 1885–1914*. Stuttgart: Reclam, 1987.

Schwartz, Charles. *Cole Porter: A Biography*. New York: Dial, 1977.

Seldes, George. *Witness to a Century*. New York: Ballantine, 1987.

Selznick, Irene Mayer. *A Private View*. New York: Knopf, 1983.

Sennet, Ted. *Hollywood's Golden Year, 1939*. New York: St. Martin's, 1989.

Shakespeare, William. *A Midsummer Night's Dream*, ed. by Wolfgang Clemen. New York: NAL, 1986.

———. *The Taming of the Shrew*, by G. R. Hibbard, ed. London: Penguin, 1968.

Shaw, George Bernard. *Back to Methuselah*, adaptation by Arnold Moss. New York: Samuel French, 1957.

———. *Misalliance and the Fascinating Foundling*. London: Penguin, 1984.

Shepherd, Donald, and Robert Slatzser with Dave Grayson. *Duke: The Life and Times of John Wayne*. London: Weidenfeld & Nicolson, 1986.

Siclier, Jacques. *Le mythe de la femme dans le cinéma Américaine*. Paris: Éditions du Cerf, 1956.

Sinclair, Andrew. *Spiegel: The Man Behind the Pictures*. London: Weidenfeld & Nicolson, 1987.

Slezak, Walter. *Wann geht der nächste Schwan?* Munich: Piper, 1964.

Smith, Sally Bedell. *In All His Glory: The Life of William S. Paley*. New York: Simon & Schuster, 1990.

Sontag, Susan. *Against Interpretation, and Other Essays*. New York: Farrar, Straus & Giroux, 1966.

Spanier, Ginette. *It Isn't All Mink*, introduction by Noël Coward. London: Collins, 1959.

Stern, Fritz. *Dreams and Delusions: National Socialism in the Drama of the German Past*. New York: Vintage, 1989.

Sternheim, Carl. *Die Schule von Uznach* in *Dramen III*. Neuwied. 1964.

Stiftung Deutsche Kinemathek, ed. *Aufruhr der Gefühle: Die Kinowelt des Curtis Bernhardt*. Munich: C. J. Bucher Verlag, 1982.

Sturm, Hans. *Zwischen Neun und Neun* (play from the novel by Leo Perutz). (acting copy) Berlin, 1923.

Styan, J. L. *Max Reinhardt*. New York: Cambridge University Press, 1982.

Sudermann, Hermann. *The Song of Songs*, translated by Thomas Seltzer. New York: Viking, 1909.

Swindell, Larry. *The Last Hero: A Biography of Gary Cooper*. London: Robson, 1981.

Szepansky, Gerda. *"Blitzmädel" "Heldenmutter" "Kriegerwitwe": Frauenleben im Zweiten Weltkrieg*. Frankfrut: Fischer Taschenbuch, 1989.

Taylor, John Russell. *Hitch: The Life and Times of Alfred Hitchcock*. New York: Pantheon, 1978.

———. *Strangers in Paradise: The Hollywood Emigres, 1933–1950*. London: Faber & Faber, 1983.

Terrace, Vincent. *Encyclopedia of Television Series, Pilots and Specials: 1937–1973*, vol. 1. New York: New York Zoetrope, 1986.

Thielscher, Guido. *Erinnerungen*. Berlin: Landsmann, 1938.

Thomson, David. *A Biographical Dictionary of Film*. New York: Morrow, 1976.

———. *Movie Man*. New York: Stein and Day, 1967.

Todd, Richard. *Caught in the Act: The Story of My Life*. London: Hutchinson, 1986.

Toller, Ernst. *Look Through the Bars*, translated by R. Ellis Roberts. New York: Farrar & Rinehart, 1937.

Tötter, Otto, ed. *Hans Albers: Hoppla, jetzt komm ich*. Hamburg: Rasch und Röhring, 1986.

Tuchman, Barbara. *August 1914*. London: Constable, 1962.

Tyler, Parker. *The Hollywood Hallucination*, introduction by Richard Schickel. New York: Simon and Schuster, 1970.

———. *Magic and Myth of the Movies*. New York: Henry Holt, 1947.

Tynan, Kathleen. *The Life of Kenneth Tynan*. London: Weidenfeld and Nicolson, 1987.

Tynan, Kenneth. *Curtains*. London: Longmans, 1961.

———. *Profiles*, preface by Simon Callow, introduction by Kathleen Tynan. London: Nick Hern Books/Walker, 1989.

———. *Show People: Profiles in Entertainment*. London: Weidenfeld and Nicolson, 1980.

——— and Cecil Beaton. *Persona Grata*. London: Allan Wingate, 1953.

Vickers, Hugo. *Cecil Beaton: The Authorized Biography*. London: Weidenfeld and Nicolson, 1985.

Viertel, Salka. *The Kindness of Strangers*. New York: Holt, Rinehart and Winston, 1969.

———. *Das unbelehrbare Herz*, German translation of above by Viertel and Helmut Degner, with introduction by Carl Zuckmayer. Hamburg: Rowohlt, 1987.

Vigny, Benno. *Marokko: Amy Jolly, Die Frau aus Marrakesch* (reprint of *Amy Jolly*, 1927). Leipzig: Kittler, 1931.

Vinson, James. *International Dictionary of Films and Filmmakers. Vol. III: Actors and Actresses.* London: Papermac, 1988.

von Cziffra, Géza. *Es war eine rauschende Ballnacht.* Frankfurt: Ullstein, 1987.

———. *Kauf dir einen bunten Luftballon.* Munich: Herbig, 1975.

von Hofmannsthal, Hugo. *Der Tor und der Tod.* Frankfurt: Insel Verlag, 1987.

von Kleist, Heinrich. *Penthesilea.* Stuttgart: Reclam, 1983.

von Meyerinck, Hubert. *Meine berühmten Freundinnen: Erinnerungen.* Munich: DTV, 1969.

von Zglinicki, Friedrich. *Die Wiege der Traumfabrik.* Berlin: Transit, 1986.

Waldoff, Claire, *Weeste Noch . . . !: Aus meinen Erinnerungen.* Düsseldorf-München: Progress-Verlag, 1953.

Walsh, Raoul. *Each Man in His Time.* New York: Farrar, Straus & Giroux, 1974.

Wansell, Geoffrey. *Haunted Idol: The Story of the Real Cary Grant.* New York: Ballantine, 1983.

Webb, Michael, ed. *Hollywood: Legend and Reality.* Boston: Little, Brown/Smithsonian Institution, 1986.

Wedekind, Frank. *The Lulu Play and Other Sex Tragedies*, translated by Stephen Spender, edited by J. M. Ritchie. New York: Riverrun Press, 1989.

———. *Spring Awakening*, translated by Tom Osborn. London: Calder, 1981.

Weinberg, Herman G. *The Lubitsch Touch: A Critical Study.* New York: Dutton, 1968.

———. *A Manhattan Odysssey: A Memoir.* New York: Anthology Film Archives, 1982.

Welles, Orson. *Mr. Arkadin.* London: Star, 1988.

———. *Touch of Evil.* Unpublished shooting script. [USC Cinema Archives.]

———. *Touch of Evil*, edited by Terry Comito. New Brunswick, NJ: Rutgers University Press, 1985.

West, Rebecca. *1990.* London: Weidenfeld & Nicolson, 1982.

Wilcox, Herbert. *Twenty-Five Thousand Sunsets.* London: The Bodley Head, 1967.

Wilder, Billy, and Volker Schlöndorff. (unedited, unpublished interview transcripts, June 1988)

Willett, John. *The Theatre of the Weimar Republic.* London: Holmes and Meier, 1988.

———. *The Weimar Years: A Culture Cut Short.* London: Thames and Hudson, 1984.

Winz, Helmut. *Es war in Schöneberg: aus 700 Jahren Schöneberger Gechichte.* Berlin: Bezirksamt Schöneberg von Berlin, Haupt & Puttkammer, 1964.

Wolf, Sylvia, and Ulrich Kurowksi. *Das Münchner Film und Kino Buch*, edited by Eberhard Hauff. Ebersberg, West Germany: Edition Achteinhalb, 1988.

Wray, Fay. *On the Other Hand.* New York: St. Martin's, 1989.

Yablonsky, Lewis. *George Raft*. New York: McGraw-Hill, 1974.

Zolotow, Maurice. *Billy Wilder in Hollywood*. New York: Putnam, 1977.

———. *Shooting Star: A Biography of John Wayne*. New York: Putnam, 1974.

Zorina, Vera. *Zorina*. New York: Farrar, Straus & Giroux, 1986.

Zuckmayer, Carl. *Als wär's ein Stück von mir*. Stuttgart: Deutscher Bücherbund, 1966.

———. *Das unbelehrbare Herz*, German translation of above by Viertel and Helmut Degner, with introduction by Carl Zuckmayer. Hamburg: Rowohlt, 1987.

Zukor, Adolph, with Dale Kramer. *The Public Is Never Wrong: The Autobiography of Adolph Zukor*. New York: Putnam's, 1953.

ARTICLES

For abbreviations of sources (e.g., Wiesbaden, NYPLPA), see p. 533 at beginning of notes section.

A. BY OR CONCERNING MARLENE DIETRICH

Albert, Katherine. "She Threatens Garbo's Throne." *Photoplay*, December 1930, pp. 60ff.

Archer, Eugene. "Light from an Undiminishing Star." *New York Times*, September 4, 1960.

Baker, Kenneth. "War Clouds in the West?" *Photoplay*, December 1933.

Bandow, Marga. "*Marlenes Vater und Großvater*." *Abend-Zeitung* (Munich), n.d. (Wiesbaden)

Barrett, Olive. "The 'Blue Angel' Girl." *Picturegoer* (London), May 1931.

Baxter, Peter. "The Birth of *Venus*," *Wide Angel*, v. 10, no. 1, n.d.

———. "Just Watch!" *Iris*, (Paris) No. 8, 2e Semestre, 1988.

Bazil, O. E. "*Das ist meine Welt . . .*" *Film und Frau*, nos. 27–30, 1950.

Benayoun, Robert. "*L'Ascension de Galatée*." *Positif*, no. 75, May 1966.

Berg, Louis. "Dietrich Rides Again." *This Week*, August 13, 1944.

Biery, Ruth. "Is Dietrich Through?" *Photoplay*, January 1933.

———. "Marlene Is Free at Last." *Photoplay*, July 1933.

———. "She's Not a Parrot." *Photoplay*, October 1931.

Bogdanovich, Peter. "Encounters with Josef von Sternberg." *Movie*, no. 13, Summer 1965.

Boland, Elena. "Garbo Likeness Deplored." *Los Angeles Times*, November 23, 1930.

Brooks, Louise. "Marlene." ms., GEH. [originally published in French in *Positif*, no. 75, May 1966]

Buchwald, Art. "A Cat in a Hot London Cellar." *New York Herald-Tribune*, 1955 n.d. (NYPLPA).

———. "La Dietrich Great Anywhere She Goes." *New York Herald-Tribune*, December 13, 1959.

Calendo, John. "Dietrich and the Devil." *Interview*, nos. 26, 27, October, November 1972.

Calhoun, Dorothy. "Hitler Demands Return of German Stars!" *Motion Picture*, January 1934.

Canby, Vincent. "Theater: Dietrich Debut." *New York Times*, October 10, 1967.

Choura, Alexander. "*So zerbrach die Ehe der Dietrich.*" *Schweizer*, December 24, 1973, pp. 24–26.

Collier's references: See "Dietrich: The Body and the Soul."

Conniff, Frank. "Marlene Dietrich Quits as Film Actress." International News Service, February 2, 1945.

Cruikshank. " 'I'm No Trilby,' says Marlene Dietrich." *Motion Picture*, June 1935.

Cummings, Jean. "Why Dietrich Wears Trousers." *Modern Screen*, April 1933.

Davidson, Bill. "The Dietrich Legend." *McCall's*, March 1960.

Dietrich, Marlene. "*Eine Jugendzeit–Welt ohne Männer.*" *Esquire* (*Deutschland*), no. 3, pp. 59–66.

———. "How to Be Loved" *Ladies' Home Journal*, January 1954, pp. 36ff.

———. "*Man darf nie 'nein' sagen!*" *Mein Film* (Vienna), no. 100, 1927, p. 19.

———. "*Marlene Dietrich an eine Unbekannte.*" *Illustrierter Film-Kurier.* (Berlin), 1930. (*The Blue Angel* premiere program.)

———. "*Meine erste Rolle.*" *Film Welt*, no. 16, April 4, 1935.

———. "The Most Fascinating Man I Know." *This Week*, February 13, 1955.

———. "My ABC's." *Look*, October 24, 1961.

———. "*Ueberfahrt.*" *Film-Kurier*, May 17, 1930.

——— and Maximilian Schell, edited by David Colby. "The Dietrich Tapes." *The Manipulator*, no. 2, 1984.

———. "I Have Been Photographed to Death." *Die Zeit*, no. 13, March 25, 1983.

"Dietrich: The Body and the Soul." *Collier's*, May 14, 1954, pp. 25–29 plus cover. (compiled by Victoria Wolff and Joseph Laitin)

Dixon, Campbell. "Marlene Comes to London." *Daily Telegraph* (London), July 31, 1936.

Evans, Kay. "Will Marlene Break the Spell?" *Photoplay*, February 1932.

Fanck, Arnold. Interview. *Filmhefte*, no. 2, Summer 1946.

Felsing, Hasso Conrad. "*Gedächtnisschwäche einer schönen alten Frau.*" *Die Zeit*, no. 17, 1983.

Field, Edward. "Dietrich" (poem). *The New Republic*, December 17, 1990, p. 33.

Frischauer, Willi. "The Marlene Dietrich Story." *Reynolds News* (London), June 6–20, 1954.

Grant, Jack. "Marlene Dietrich Answers Her Critics." *Screen Book*, 1933.

Green, Chet. "For the First and Last Time—Dietrich Talks." *Photoplay*, December 1935.

Green, O. O. "Six Films of Josef von Sternberg." *Movie*, no. 13, Summer 1965, pp. 26–31.

Hall, Gladys. "Why Garbo and Dietrich Lead Solitary Lives." *Motion Picture*, June 1934.

————. "Marlene the Magnificent." *TV Radio Mirror*, February 1959.

Hall, Leonard. "The Extra-Private Life of Marlene Dietrich." *Photoplay*, November 1931.

————. "Garbo vs. Dietrich." *Photoplay*, February 1931.

————. "The Perils of Marlene." *Photoplay*, May 1931.

Heimer, Mel. "Dietrich 'Home' Again." *King Features Syndicate*, 1944.

Hepburn, Katharine. "Marlene." *The 1986 Council of Fashion Designers of America Awards* (edited by Robert Raymond). CFDA, New York 1986.

Hine, Sgt. Al. "DP Dietrich." *Yank*, August 26, 1945.

Hirschhorn, Clive. "It's the Money I Work for, Says Marlene." *Sunday Express* (London), August 15, 1965.

Hobson, Harold. "The Perfections of Dietrich." *Times* (London), November 29, 1964.

————. "Some Glory in Virtue." *Sunday Times* (London), December 5, 1964.

————. "Timeless Star." *Christian Science Monitor* (n.d., n.p.) (NYPLPA).

Hyams, Joe. "Miss Dietrich Explains Her Magic." *New York Herald-Tribune*, September 13, 1960 (NYPLPA).

Jackson, Stuart. " 'Marlene' by Her Latest Leading Man [Brian Aherne]," *Film Pictorial*, June 3, 1933.

Jay, James A. "Making Marlene Popular," *Picturegoer*, December 26, 1931.

Kaiser, Eric. "The Real Life Romance of Marlene Dietrich." *Picturegoer*, Vol. 1, nos. 24–26; Nov. 7, 14, 21, 1931. (Also published in book form, n.a.).

Karasek, Hellmuth. *"Heiß oder kalt, aber nie lauwarm"* (interview) *Der Spiegel*, June 17, 1991.

Keene, Dave. "The Secret of Marlene Dietrich." *Picturegoer*, April 25, 1936.

Kochanowski, Bodo. *"Die Berlinerin, die mit Marlene Dietrich ins Mädchen-Pensionat ging." Berliner Zeitung*, March 10, 1977.

Kolarz, Henry. *"Der blaue Engel kehrt zurück," Stern*, no. 18, 1960.

Knight, Arthur. "Marlene Dietrich. Notes on a Living Legend." *Films in Review*, December 1954.

Kyrou, Ado. *"Sternberg avant, pendant, après Marlene." Positif*, no. 75, May 1966.

Labsenski, Jurgen. *"Die Freudlosse Gasse."* (Hertha von Walther) *ZDF-Journal*, no. 22, October 28, 1974.

Lang, Julie. "The Revolt Against Dietrich," *Photoplay*, September 1934.

Lee, Sonia. "Marlene Dietrich in Love for the Second Time?" *Motion Picture*, June 1933.

Lerman, Leo. ". . . On Meeting Marlene." *The 1986 Council of Fashion Designers of America Awards* (edited by Robert Raymond). CFDA, New York 1986.

————. "Welcome, Marlene." *Vogue*, August 15, 1944, pp. 154ff.

Littlejohn, Josephine. "Directing Dietrich." *Motion Picture Classic*, May 1931.

Lorant, Stefan. *"Bummel durch die Ateliers bei Heinrich IV und der Dubarry von heute." B.Z.-Mittag*, June 15, 1926.

————. "When Marlene Dietrich Failed in a Film Test." *New Chronicle* (London), October 1, 1935.

Malraux, André. *"Film und Mythos."* *Film Forum*, November 1952.

Manners, Dorothy. "Not Another Garbo." *Motion Picture*, January 1931.

————. "Will Dietrich Stay in America?" *Motion Picture*, September 1931.

Manners, Mary Jane. "Dietrich Is Different." (unsourced clip, c. 1943, NYPLPA.)

"Marlène Dietrich, l'ange rose." *Ciné-Miroir*, July 10, 1931.

"Marlene Dietrich Makes Her Own Troubles!" *Screen Guide*, May 1941.

"Marlene Dietrich menacerait-elle la suprématie de Greta Garbo?" *Ciné-Miroir*, January 9, 1931.

"Marlene Dietrichs Alter ist kein Geheimnis mehr." *Die neue Post* (Frankfurt), April 7, 1964.

"Marlene's Joint." *The New Yorker*, November 11, 1952.

Maugé, André R. *"Ach! die Marlene."* *Revue du Cinéma*, no. 27, October 1, 1931.

Milte, Kurt. *"Marlene Dietrich filmte in Wilhelmshöhe."* *Braunschweiger Zeitung*, March 21, 1964.

"The Most Famous Legs in History Lose Their Job." *Life*, January 3, 1938.

Plack, Werner G. "Questions and Answers to Marlene Dietrich." (unpublished, 1978. Stiftung Deutsche Kinemathek.)

Powers, James. "Still What the Boys in the Front Row Will Have." *Hollywood Reporter*, April 29, 1968.

Rankin, Ruth. "They're All Queening It." *Photoplay*, December 1933.

Reed, Rex. "Dietrich: 'I'm Queen of Ajax.'" *New York Times*, October 22, 1967, pp. D1, D11.

Reeve, Warren. "What Is Dietrich's Destiny?" *Photoplay*, July 1935.

"Reunion." *Newsweek*, August 29, 1960.

Schallert, Elza. "Is Dietrich Indifferent to Her Public?" *Motion Picture*, September 1933.

Shabad, Theodore. "Dietrich Sings, Moscow Smiles." *New York Times*, May 22, 1964.

Shawell, Julia. "Garbo or Dietrich?" *Pictorial Review*, July 1933.

Shippey, Kim. "Dietrich's Radio Artistry." *Christian Science Monitor*, July 1, 1966.

Skutesky, Victor. *"Drei Begegnungen."* (Unpublished memoir, courtesy SDK.)

Slater, Weldon. "Is Marlene a Love Pirate?" *Screen Book Magazine*, October 1931.

Starr, Helen. "Marlene Changes Her Mind." *Liberty*, 1933.

Sternberg, Josef von. "Acting in Film and Theatre." *Film Culture*, I, nos. 5–6, winter 1955, pp. 1–4, 27–29. Reprinted in Geduld, *Film Makers on Film Making*.

Sternberger, Dolf. *"Marlene Dietrichs schöne Kunst."* *Frankfurter Allgemeine Zeitung*, May 30, 1950.

"Still Champion." *Time*, January 21, 1952.

Thoms, Ewald. *"Berliner Venus mit Kopf und Herz."* *B.Z. am Abend*, Jan. 20–Feb. 10, 1966.

Tolischus, Otto. "Dietrich—How She Happened." *Photoplay*, April 1931.

Watts, Richard, Jr. "Miss Dietrich Takes Over London." *New York Post*, July 29, 1954.

"What Dietrich Will Do." *Newsweek*, September 1, 1958.

White, Kenneth. "Garbo and Dietrich." *Hound & Horn*, Jan.–March, 1932.

Wiechers, Hanns J. "*Marlene Dietrich hieß nie von Losch . . .*" *Westdeutschland-Rundshau.* (Bonn), April 21, 1960.

Wolff, Victoria, and Joe Laitin. "*Plus und Minus eines Stars.*" *Die Weltwoche* (Zurich), no. 1670, November 12, 1965.

Wolff, Dr. Willi. "*Warum ich 'Kopf Hoch, Charly' gedreht habe!*" *Deutsche Film-woche*, no. 12, 1926.

B. GENERAL ARTICLES

Brackett, Charles, and Herbert Luft. "Two Views of a Director—Billy Wilder. A Matter of Decadence/A Matter of Humor." *The Quarterly of Radio, Film and TV*, Vol. VII, 1952–1953. (See also Schulberg, Stuart below)

Brod, Fritta. "*Der Himmel kam herunter. Bilder aus der Kindheit: 1901.*" *Suddeutsche-Zeitung* (Munich), November 14/15, 1987, [n.p.].

Craig, Gordon A. "The Kaiser and the Kritik." *New York Review of Books*, February 18, 1988.

"Film Stars for the Invasion." *Picture Post*, June 10, 1944.

Flinn, Tom. "Dieterle." *The Velvet Light Trap* (Wisconsin), no. 15, fall 1975.

Haskell, Molly. "Molly Haskell on *Stage Fright.*" *Film Comment*, vol. 6, no. 3, fall 1970.

Holland, Jack. "Gentlemen Prefer—Marlene!" (clip file, NYPLPA, c. 1947), pp. 40, 72.

Horak, Jan-Christopher. "Good Morning, Babylon: Maurice Tourneur's Battle Against the Studio System." *Image* (Rochester, New York), vol. 31, no. 2, September 1988.

———. "*Rin Tin Tin erobert Berlin oder Amerikanische Filminteressen in Weimar.*" (unpub. ms.), September 1989.

Joll, James. "Goodbye to All That." *New York Review of Books*, April 14, 1988, pp. 3–4.

Lachmann, Götz. "*Als Wien noch Hollywood Konkurrenz machte.*" *Süddeutsche-Zeitung*, October 13, 1987.

Prossnitz, Gisela, and Edda Fuhrich. "*Max Reinhardt und der Film: eine unglückliche Liebe.*" *Parnass*, no. 4, July/August 1986.

Rockwell, John. "When Berlin Was an Artistic Cauldron." *New York Times*, June 21, 1987.

Schulberg, Stuart. "A Communication: A Letter About Billy Wilder." *Quarterly of Film, Radio and TV*, vol. VII, 1952/53. (Reply to Brackett/Luft above.)

Spiess-Hohnholz, Mareike. "*Verlorener Kampf um die Erinnerung.*" *Der Spiegel*, August 10, 1987.

Stiege, Rudolf (and Dieter Strunz). *"Kinoknüller kommen am laufenden Meter in die filmverrückte Stadt."* Part 50, *"Berlin bleibt doch Berlin,"* Berliner Morgenpost (Berlin), March 31, 1987.

Stock, Wolfgang Jean. *"Die schnellste Stadt der Welt."* Süddeutsche-Zeitung (Munich), September 3, 1987, p. 42.

Stone, Shepard. "Looking Back on the Place Where Everything Happened." *International Herald-Tribune*, December 16, 1986.

Wolff, Victoria. *"Erinnerungen an Remarque."* Madame, July 1971.

INDEX

Steven Bach (1938–2009) was educated in Chicago, Paris, and Los Angeles; he studied with Josef von Sternberg, Marlene Dietrich's "discoverer" and the director of some of her most famous films. He taught American literature before becoming a film producer and head of production for United Artists, where he was involved in the making of dozens of films, including *Sleuth*, Woody Allen's *Manhattan*, Martin Scorcese's *Raging Bull*, and the Karel Reisz/Harold Pinter film of John Fowles's *The French Lieutenant's Woman*. He wrote the critically acclaimed best seller *Final Cut: Dreams and Disaster in the Making of "Heaven's Gate."*